Mother
The Oak Woods
Hwy 165
Mer Rouge, La
71261

The Best of
New York

REVISED EDITION

Written by
Christian Millau

Editor
Deborah Patton

Assistant Editor
Colleen Dunn Bates

Contributing Editors
**Suzy Davidson, Jean-Pierre de Lucovich,
Michael Demarest, Robert Egan, Andrew
Fabricant, Jillian Lieder, Robert Low, John
Mariani, Nancy Naglin, Grace D. Polk,
Charles Rice, Alexander & Joan Shihwarg,
Wendy Smolen, Joseph Stamps, Judi Whyte**

Crown Publishers, Inc.
New York

Gault Millau's Best of the World Collection
The Best of France
The Best of Italy
The Best of London
The Best of New York
The Best of Paris

The *Best of New York* went to press in May 1984,
and is completely up-to-date as of then.

Original design by Jack Bordnick and Associates
Illustrations by Sue Truesdell and
Suzanne Dunaway

Published in the United States of America in 1984
Crown Publishers, Inc.
Copyright © 1984 by Crown Publishers, Inc.
One Park Avenue, New York, New York 10016

Printed in the United States of America

Library of Congress Cataloging in Publication Data
Millau, Christian.
The best of New York.
Rev. ed. of: The best of New York/written by Henri Gault
& Christian Millau, 1982.
Includes index.
1. New York (N.Y.)—Description—1981–　　—Guidebooks.
I. Gault, Henri, 1929–　　. Best of New York.
II. Patton, Deborah. III. Title.
F128.18.G3313 1984　917.47'10443　84-7075
ISBN 0-517-55328-7

10　9　8　7　6　5　4　3　2　1

First Edition

CONTENTS

New York

The City Evolves

I wouldn't wish on any Americans the fate of publishing a guide to Paris in French. As soon as they did, my dear compatriots would load them with abuse and accuse them of getting tangled up in something that is of absolutely no concern to them. We French are like this: we accept criticism only under the condition that it is we who are the critics. Yet in the United States, however, I was both touched and impressed by the reception of our first English-language guide to New York two years ago. It was not only a great success with the public, but not one reviewer or critic from the press, even when he or she didn't like what we wrote, played on the fact that we are foreigners—pretentious Frenchmen who would be better off minding our own business.

Now I understand why millions of people across the world dream of America; for them, New York is its most brilliant symbol. Your city is hard, often without pity, but there is always a place for people who come from elsewhere with their good faith, their enthusiasm and their wildly divergent opinions. In short, you are good sports, and this is why we have returned once again.

A first guide of this sort can never be perfect. Nor can the second. But there is a chance we can make it better. You will be the judge. In any case, we have had the opportunity to correct our errors and, above all, to go into more depth—even though at the last minute before we go to press, we discover, to our horror, that life goes too fast, especially in New York City, where the present has a troublesome tendency to immediately get lost. Someday someone must write a study on the frustrations of being a guidebook author. Yet the permanent upheaval that opens and closes restaurants, nightclubs, hotels or boutiques leaves me terribly euphoric. Scarcely has our guide come out, and I'm already thinking of the next one.

Christian Millau
Gault Millau America—311 West 75th Street—New York—
New York—10023

TheRESTAURANTS

THE WALTZ OF
THE CHEFS

If Johann Strauss were still of this world and living in New York City, he would be able to compose a marvelous piece of music entitled, "The Waltz of the New York Chefs." It's true that in Paris we also have restaurants that open and others that close, but this is nothing compared with what goes on in New York. As soon as you turn your back, one restaurant opens its doors, another closes its own, a third that you have adored loses its chef, and a fourth gives him a new home. In New York, where nothing is ever done halfway, this is a veritable nightmare for a gastronomy critic who honestly tries to stay au courant. His only hope when he publishes a book such as this, which requires months and months of preparation, is that the reader doesn't punish him too severely for the inevitable mistakes that are impossible to avoid in this town.

The situation is very frustrating, but it could be worse. For example, if I were a gastronomy critic in Moscow, I wouldn't have to go to a new restaurant more than once every 25 years. The whirlwind that has swept New York over the past few years is rather fatiguing. And the rapidity with which new fashions surge and disappear is more than a little irritating. But, in any case, with all this great excitement, I never have any time to get bored.

All of this translates into a cultural phenomenon that is extremely important: the revolution that has taken place in American taste. We are proud to have been the first in Europe to encourage this profound mutation. It developed under the astonished gaze of old Europe, which believed it could withhold its worldwide monopoly of gastronomy and the culinary arts for eternity. Fifteen years ago, it was almost impossible not to make fun of American tourists who asked for Coca Cola with their poulet au vinaigre. Today, in the same restaurants, we get exhausted from praising the finesse of their palates and the extensiveness of their culinary knowledge. And, it's not unusual to hear French people, who upon their return from New York, exclaim in a slightly anguished tone, "But they eat just as well as we do!" But this is to be expected with all the French chefs who crisscross the Atlantic. The French willingly admit that God created Earth, but as for cuisine, why they invented it themselves. It's going to take them some time to get used to the idea that they aren't the only people in the universe who know how to prepare a boeuf bourguignon or a salmon with sorrel. Moreover, at the rate things are going, soon Americans will be convinced *they* invented cuisine.

It has become all too frequent to hear New Yorkers tell you that they eat much better in their own town than in Paris or Lyon. But if they are really so convinced, they create a big problem for New York restaurants; if they are as remarkable as New Yorkers believe, there is no need for progress or growth. And having visited and compared some several hundred places, we have an opinion that is slightly less ecstatic. It is incontestable that there are establishments that rival those in Paris, Brussels, Lausanne or Munich. But New York still doesn't have its own Paul Bocuse (Lyon), Michel Guérard (Eugenie-les-Bains), Alain Senderens (l'Archestrate in Paris), Fredy Girardet (Crissier near Lausanne), Pierre Wynants (Comme Chez Soi in Brussels) or Ekkart Witzigmann (l'Aubergine in Munich). In New York, you can find very good professionals, but not, at least for the moment, true creators. To earn this title, it takes more than a chef spending each summer in France and putting the best dishes he has discovered on his own menu. Sadly, this is too often the case.

Actually, I think it is the West Coast or Southwest that will produce the really creative and original talents in the years to come. Perhaps the European influence in New York is still too strong to allow the development of an authentic and sincere American cuisine as it is developing in the rest of the country. Or perhaps it is as experience proves, that a return to its original sources and recovery of its roots is how a cuisine can truly find its own identity and will inspire a new wave of chefs with fresh and inventive models.

It might seem paradoxical that we enthusiastically encourage American chefs to fulfill the culinary destiny of their own country by trying to differentiate themselves from our traditions and history. It would be so much simpler to restate what so many others have said in the past: the French have the best cuisine and there's no choice but to imitate it. We love cuisine too much to be so arrogant, and as in all other countries throughout the world, we continue to say the same thing: "You're in your own home; show us what you can do."

Gastronomy in the western world has been colonized for too long, and the best way for America to prove that it has its own, authentic cuisine, is to put it to the test with American talents. We are on the precipice of something revolutionary: American chefs have the rare opportunity to create a change in cuisine as significant as what happened in France in the '70s when our chefs opened the floodgates of *nouvelle cuisine*. One of the most important conditions to allow this sort of change is to be able to exercise natural talent freely. Paul Bocuse said one of the most elementary and important things in recent culinary history, "Cuisine belongs to the chefs." Although it may sound rather basic, it is significant because chefs *must* be able to run their own places and not be financially dependent on people whose only concern is to make quick, easy money.

Bocuse's prophecy has come true in France and most of Western Europe. In the past, many of the big restaurants were owned by financiers or businessmen; chefs were merely employees. Today, the most prestigious places are owned and run by chefs who are masters of their own decisions on food products, recipes and style. In New York, the inverse of this rule still exists. True there are a few places where the chef is also the owner. But in most restaurants, the chefs have to bend to the rules of profit in contradiction to the true nature of good cuisine. It is generally agreed that it is extremely difficult to cook to perfection for more than 60 or 85 covers, but many chefs are required to serve three or four times as many meals at the same seating. With this in mind, it's not surprising to witness such unsettling irregularity, even in the most famous places. The desire to make money is apparently more important than maintaining true quality. In the long term, this can have the same effect as mortal poison. One can become a millionaire by wanting to create good cuisine. But, one can rarely create good cuisine by wanting to become a millionaire.

The other weakness in the New York restaurant scene is its elitism. To eat well here, you literally have to spend a fortune. There is no middle ground between the deluxe and bargain places, as opposed to Europe where, in spite of the current economic difficulties, little inns and family bistros capable of serving good food for extremely reasonable prices continue to proliferate. This sort of social structure and tradition is hard to find in America, particularly in the big cities. The only exceptions are the ethnic restaurants that have managed to hold onto their traditions and values from their developing countries. The abundance and quality of these "exotic" places makes New York a treasure trove for adventurous people who have the palate to appreciate them. There are, for example, infinitely more good Asian restaurants in New York than you can find in all of the major European cities. But, there is no guarantee this situation will last forever; with the overall rise in standard of living in New York and owners' developing good business sense, these little places will no doubt become more luxurious, their staffs will be enlarged, and consequently the prices will rise.

Having read all this, you might accuse us of being exaggerated pessimists. But, this is a false impression. We are only reacting to the excesses of self-satisfaction that surfaces in the restaurant community and in the media. Gastronomy can't progress by choking itself on superlatives and hyperbolic praises. Chefs and restaurants are going to do themselves in if they continue to be so incensed by even the least amount of criticism. Their pretensions could make them unbearable, and it's good that from time to time guides like this put them in their places and remind them they aren't necessarily the geniuses they think they are.

This said, we are more comfortable in saying all the *good* things we feel about many New York restaurants. Severity doesn't dampen our enthusiasm. To the contrary, we don't know how to be coldly critical. (If gastronomic criticism starts to resemble an analysis of how the Stock Exchange runs, we have no choice but to change professions.) We have no interest in withholding the truth. In this incomplete review of New York restaurants, we have simply given *our* truth, and the moment it is given, it's understood that nothing is more versatile and changing than a restaurant—especially in New York.

Symbol Systems

Restaurants are ranked in the same manner that French students are graded, on a scale of one to twenty. The rankings reflect only the quality of the cooking; decor, service, welcome and atmosphere are explicitly commented on within the reviews. Restaurants that are ranked thirteen and above are distinguished with toques (chef's hats), according to the following table:

Exceptional	🎩🎩🎩🎩	4 toques, for 19/20
Excellent	🎩🎩🎩	3 toques, for 17/20 or 18/20
Very good	🎩🎩	2 toques, for 15/20 or 16/20
Good	🎩	1 toque, for 13/20 or 14/20

These ranks are *relative*. One toque for 13/20 is not a very good ranking for a highly reputed restaurant, but it is quite complimentary for a small restaurant without much culinary pretension.

Unless otherwise noted, the prices given are for a complete meal, including an appetizer, main course, dessert, a half-bottle of wine per person, and service. The prices are naturally approximations, and, unfortunately, many will have risen by the time you read these lines.

As we have stated above, New York's chefs have a tendency to move about frequently, and the cuisine can go from good to bad overnight. Menus are also subject to the winds of change, and the dishes we've described may no longer be available when you visit. We confirmed everything pre-publication, and ask your forgiveness if the restaurant has changed when you visit—we've done all we can!

Lower Manhattan— TriBeCa

10/20
Acute Café
**110 W. Broadway
(Duane St.)
349-5566**
*Lunch Mon. to Fri. 1:30 P.M. to 3:00 P.M.; dinner Mon. to Fri. 6:00 P.M. to 11:00 P.M.; Sat. 6:30 P.M. to 12:30 A.M.
AE, MC, V*
French
(classical/nouvelle)

Things seem to be going downhill here at a sharp 30 degree slant. We remember several good meals in this slickly designed restaurant, with its white tiled walls and floors, TriBeCa-lofty ceilings, random potted palms and attractive seating. But, as is so often the case, the chefs have changed, the menu has changed, and we have been disappointed by overcooked scallops on a bed of radicchio and a so-called sausage en croûte that is nested in a slice of white bread, all chosen from a menu that is, at best, uninspired. Veal with chanterelles is nothing special, particularly since the quality of the meat is less than stellar; sole stuffed with spinach is passable; and the pepper steak, rack of lamb, lobster and duck hold no surprises. The Acute Café has such promise, since it is one of the most attractively decorated places of this ilk, the service is sincere and friendly and the music keeps clients cheerful. The kitchen needs to be overhauled to bring the cuisine back to its original potential, or perhaps it should offer just a simple burger fare menu to draw a more decorative and enthusiastic crowd. The wine list is limited and expensive. Dinner for two with wine will run about $100—too much for this type of cooking.

13 📖
Bridge Café
**279 Water St.
227-3344**
*Lunch daily noon to 3:00 P.M.; dinner nightly 6:00 P.M. to midnight
No credit cards (personal checks accepted)*
American

You're wrong. That is not Frank Perdue sitting over there, picking at a salad; it is His Honor Mayor Koch with some of his cronies from City Hall. The mayor never seems to have trouble getting a table, even though the restaurant does not take reservations. This is the mayor's kind of place: an old bar and grill (the floor seems to be sliding into the East River), a tin ceiling, a few posters and prints and—surprise—quite good food. Leslie Revsin has finally "found herself" in this kitchen. We thought she was too ambitious in concocting nouvelle-type dishes when she had her own place on Cornelia

Street, and she couldn't cope with the volume when she was at 24 Fifth Avenue. Here, with a shorter and somewhat simplified menu, Ms. Revsin's real talent can be seen. Her poached oysters with spinach and a white wine reduction are delicious; her marinated fresh tuna with leeks and fresh basil is her own creation and is wonderfully refreshing. Ms. Revsin also knows how to prepare duck so it arrives at the table as if it had been cooked to order, and how to cook fish so it is flaky and not overdone. Her ventures into the cuisines of the world come off equally well: chicken breasts with goat's cheese, prosciutto and sage would bring credit to an experienced chef trained in Milan, and smoked pork with red cabbage has a lightness that eludes all but the best of Germany's new breed of cooks. There is an honesty about all of these dishes that is truly disarming. In these informal and unpretentious surroundings, a block from the South Street Seaport, you have a right to expect overcooked hamburgers and watery quiches. So you will be surprised and happy here—particularly when you receive the check, which will not run higher than $30 per person, with wine.

12/20
Capsuoto Frères
451 Washington St. (Watts St.) 966-4900
Lunch and dinner Tues. to Sat. noon to 2:00 A.M.; dinner nightly 6:00 P.M. to 2:00 A.M.
AE
French (provincial/classical)

We can't imagine a more attractive place to meet friends for a Saturday lunch. This lofty space with wood beams, Belle Epoque lights, classical music and pretty wood floors reminds us of the old cafés on the Left Bank, where the atmosphere is charming. Specials are presented on blackboard menus; they vary from good grilled swordfish, chicken sautéed with fine herbs, tasty cold roast leg of veal and an underrealized cassoulet (the meats and sauce are excellent, but the beans appear to have been added to the dish at the last minute, denying the dish its traditional appealing thickness). The bistro menu is filled with the classics, which are quite good: you'll enjoy the calf's liver, steak with frites, sole meunière, smoked trout and escargots. Desserts are acceptable, the wines are compatible with the menu, and the service is friendly. All in all, it's a delightful spot. About $20 per person, without wine.

10/20
Delphi
109 W. Broadway (Duane St.) 227-6322
Lunch and dinner daily noon to 11:30 P.M.
No credit cards
Greek/Mediterranean

This is a neighborhood restaurant in TriBeCa with a Mediterranean cafeteria feeling. Tables are close together, families come on weekends with squirming children, and both levels of the restaurant tend to be crowded. The large portions and the low prices, however, provide an alternative to the influx of expensive, fashionable restaurants in the area. Don't come for good Greek food; the menu includes vine leaves, hummos, souvlaki and shish kebab (presumably all made Greek with the consistent addition of "Greek herbs"), but it suffers from the effects of cafeteria-style cooking. On the other hand, the restaurant is clean, the staff is friendly, and the food could be a lot worse (it could be expensive). Dinner for two, with wine, will be about $30.

9/20
Fraunces Tavern Restaurant
54 Pearl St. (Broad St.)
269-0144
Lunch and dinner daily 11:45 A.M. to 9:30 P.M.
All major credit cards
American

Although on December 4, 1783, General Washington hosted a farewell dinner in the tavern of Samuel Fraunces, he was happy enough just to toast his officers with a glass of wine after his return from Mount Vernon. If the food today is the same as it was then, he wasn't wrong to stick to wine. All the same, you don't come here for a gastronomic celebration, but rather more simply to admire, before a salad, broiled fish or prime roast beef that is so-what, the decor of this pretty restored colonial house, whose top two floors have been transformed into a museum. About $30 to $35 per person, with a glass of wine.

14
The Odeon
145 W. Broadway (Spring St.)
233-0507
Lunch Mon. to Fri. noon to 2:30 P.M.; dinner nightly 7:30 P.M. to midnight (late supper to 2:30 A.M.); brunch Sun. noon to 3:00 P.M.
AE, MC, V
American

After several disappointing experiences at Odeon for lunch, we unequivocally suggest that you come here in the dark of night. The evenings are much more entertaining, in any case. One of our favorite sights was a distinctive young lady who either just walked off the stage of *Cats* or whom her priest escort had recently exhumed from the grave. Of course, there are so many other fascinating people to watch: young SoHo saleswomen dressed in up-to-the-minute androgynous chic, New Wave changelings, patrons of the wearable decorative arts, all of whom are overrun by young Wall Street lawyer types: pinstriped men with attachés and suited women who are always ready for another subway strike in their Adidas running shoes. The crowd gets better the later it gets, and by supper time at 1:00 A.M. it's a veritable movable feast for the eyes.

This unusual collection of people is served some very good food, dished up by Patrick Clark, who has a light touch when it comes to nouvelle interpretations. You couldn't ask for anything more refined than his poached oysters gently napped with a Champagne beurre blanc, his chilled artichoke soup that mercifully tastes like artichokes and his delightful steamed mussels with an herbed butter sauce and finely slivered vegetables. The entrees have also maintained their quality over the years. The loin of lamb is perfectly rare and tender, flavored with a garlic cream sauce; the calf's liver is, happily, not massacred as in other American restaurants and is brightened with honey vinegar and celery root; the filet mignon is a tasty piece of meat, accompanied with a golden raisin–brandy sauce; the fettuccine with pesto is as marvelous as is the sautéed lotte with leeks and coriander; and the fresh seafood salad is refreshing on a hot summer night. Desserts are weak here; the so-called "very special" apple tart is incredibly sweet and not special at all, and the lemon tart is lifeless—but the crème brûlée saves the day, with an exquisitely smooth and delicious cream that melts in your mouth. The wine list is perfunctory, but you can find a good, reasonably priced Chablis Premier Cru to make your dinner even more enjoyable. About $40 per person, with wine.

13

Saint Jean des Prés
**112 Duane St.
(Broadway)
608-2332**
*Lunch and dinner Mon. to Fri.
11:00 A.M. to 1:00 A.M.; dinner
Sat. 5:30 P.M. to 1:00 A.M.
All major credit cards*
Belgian

The French have a favorite game: making fun of the Belgians with stories that are as successful as Polish jokes are in America. To our great regret, however, we can't find anything mean to say about this elegant brasserie that opened two steps from Odéon. You are not even assailed by the fragrance of frites and mussels (so typical in Belgium) when you step into this immense room with New Yorkish high ceilings, red lacquered walls, a brass chandelier, an interminable bar and quite the "in" crowd (at lunch as well as dinner). Only Hercule Poirot in person could divine that this superb place is the American adventure of the Belgian chain of Saint Jean des Prés. In spite of this, there are several clues, such as the light accent of the seductive owner and one or two waitresses and the discreet presence of several Belgian specialties on the menu—for example, tomato with shrimp, sole with asparagus, or waterzoi. The tomato and shrimp, for which the Belgian people would go to war if it were denied to them, is a delicious dish when you get rid of the tomato and eat only the shrimp in their mayonnaise. Saint Jean des Prés imports these particularly flavorful little gray shrimp directly from the North Sea, along with the fat, admirably tender sole from Ostende; the endives and asparagus are from inland Malines. The chef, also imported from Belgium, knows how to cook fish, which is to say not too much, not too little; and he is also responsible for remarkable sauces. You will be convinced after tasting his exquisite waterzoi of lobster (a soup of lobster with baby vegetables, supplemented with cream that is unorthodox but very good), his pavé de boeuf Sambre et Meuse (a bit overcooked) accompanied by a sauce of white wine and shallots, as well as his sole with asparagus. The thin, beautifully golden frites are better even than McDonald's, which is one of the rare places in America that doesn't massacre french fries. The dessert cart, filled with treasures from Wittamer, the Belgian Lenôtre, will make you faint away. There is only one discordant note: the rabbit and prune pâté is so undercooked that it must be from an ancient recipe of Genghis Khan's for his Tatar knights. Thanks to a remarkable choice of excellent regional French wines that are almost unknown in New York (Fitou, Gaillac, Fronsac, Herault), priced from $5 to $15 a bottle, you will spend about $35 per person, noise included—when this beautiful place is full, it resonates like war drums. There is a prix fixe menu at $15 for an excellent salad of sweetbreads, scallops with lime, exquisite passion fruit cake and superb coffee.

12/20
Sammy's Roumanian Jewish Restaurant
157 Chrystie St.
(Delancey St.)
673-0330
Dinner nightly 4:00 P.M. to 11:00 P.M. (Sat. to midnight)
All major credit cards
Central European

If you're moved to speak with sentimental emotion about the cuisine of Sammy's Jewish momma, you'd best open the kitchen door and take a look inside. This Jewish mother is a tall, laughing black man who is doubtless still chuckling over having received three stars from the most powerful paper in New York. Moreover, everything here resembles a big practical joke; Sammy no longer cooks Roumanian in this room, which looks about a hundred years old, with its low ceilings, filthy walls covered with postcards and souvenirs and tables covered with questionably white tablecloths, but has really existed less than ten years. Stan Zimmerman, the young owner, came from Brooklyn, like everyone else, and the least we can say is that he was born under a good star. He must have a formidable business sense to have made such a success out of a shabby restaurant in a shabby neighborhood. Stan greets you as though you are his long-lost childhood friend, and who cares if his good mood is good for business or is superficial—it is so explosive that it communicates itself to a whole staff of charming young people, who seem to be part of the family but who are actually unrelated, as well as to the clientele who, just as in Montmartre, sings in chorus to a piano player and violinist. This openness may be a fabrication, but it is impossible not to succumb to it, making dinner at Sammy's, particularly on Sunday nights, the best cure for melancholy.

As for the food, don't expect any miracles. Although Roumanian cuisine is refined and interesting, what you'll find here has no special distinction. It is strictly Central European cooking that fills the stomach honestly. The quality is uneven; fried onions are bad, chopped chicken livers mediocre and little pieces of fried chicken inedible. On the other hand, baked green peppers are flavorful if you don't fear garlic, stuffed cabbage is excellent, kishka (fried stuffed beef intestines) are of superior quality, and the grilled meats, served in enormous portions and covered with chopped garlic, are particularly tender and juicy. Less juicy is the veal, but even though it is not aged according to tradition in Jewish cuisine, it is of exceptional tenderness. But you have to have the appetite of a wolf to order the Roumanian skirt steak tenderloin, rib steak, veal rib chops or veal sausages, which are excellent. The potato pancakes served with applesauce are also good; the little pieces of strudel with jam are as heavy as lead but full of flavor. Escape at all costs the abominable red wine served by the glass; if you really want to get into the spirit of the place, have an egg cream, so named, no doubt, because it contains neither cream nor egg. This concoction is totally disturbing to French wine drinkers, but it pleases momma so. About $30 per person, without wine.

8/20

Sloppy Louie's

92 South St. (Fulton St.) 952-9657

Lunch and dinner daily 11:30 A.M. to 10:00 P.M.
MC, V

American (seafood)

Neither Wall Streeters nor tourists visiting the South Street Seaport around the corner could be aware of everything we are going to tell you about this place, because they continue to stand in line to get in. True, Sloppy Louie has cleaned up his act (new paint and fixtures, and the flies are gone), but he hasn't yet done anything noticeable to improve the kitchen. So we find the same old chowders (clams are tough—when you can find them), grilled fish (not quite as flaky as you have a right to expect, since this place is across the street from the Fulton Fish Market), some Italian-style seafood combinations (seemingly reheated just before serving). We recommend instead starting with fresh oysters (the kitchen can do little to spoil them), following those with a grilled fish (specify that you are not fond of flour or paprika) and finishing with a baked apple for dessert. Order a beer to make sure everything goes down nicely. The waiters can offer you only a chablis (which is not a Chablis) or a rhine wine (which is not a Rhine wine). About $20 per person, without wine.

7/20

Sweet's

South Street Seaport 2 Fulton St. (Water St.) 825-9786

Lunch and dinner Mon. to Fri. 11:30 A.M. to 8:30 P.M.
AE

American (seafood)

Sweet's boasts of being the oldest seafood restaurant in New York, and it prides itself on serving fresh fish daily. Both claims are true, and with its new facelift (presumably to fit into the newness of the South Street Seaport) Sweet's is looking better than ever. The Belle Epoque surroundings provide a cheerful environment, particularly at lunch, when sunlight streams in through the windows and brightens up the pinstripe-suited crowd, which gives Sweet's a Wall Street men's club look by day. Loyal clients return regularly and expect unchallenging food at premium prices.

Sweet's is basically a meat and potatoes kind of place, but seafood is substituted for beef. The portions are quite generous, but unfortunately what is served here is nearly inedible. It's a shame that such a pretty place is such a culinary waste. Fried oysters are tasteless, broiled scallops swimming in butter are overcooked, haddock is broiled to oblivion (it seems to have been steamed first, to ensure that there is little or no taste at all), seafood chowder tastes like chicken vegetable soup, hash brown potatoes are a crisped mass of mashed potatoes, the crabmeat sauté needs more than a dash of sherry to liven it up, and the apple pie, prepared elsewhere, is a gelatinous concoction that defies description. In a word, Sweet's isn't sweet at all. With beer it's about $27 per person, which is far too much for such mediocre food.

12/20

Tenbrooks
**62 Reade St.
(Broadway–Church
sts.)
349-5900**
*Lunch and dinner Mon. to Fri. noon
to 10:30 P.M.*
All major credit cards
American

It's hard to tell if the City Hall and downtown office worker crowd takes much notice of owner-chef Peter Klein's nouvelle menu. But we think they might want to pay attention, because some interesting things are happening in this pastel-colored dining room that also doubles as an art gallery (frequently featuring the paintings of Chef Kip Incheck). Although there is a barlike feeling to the place, the cuisine is refined and imaginative. Fennel sausage and an oyster stew gratin are good as creative starters, as is the unlikely sounding combination of a duck, fig and pistachio pâté. The agnolotti filled with mushrooms or pesto and served in a rich basil cream sauce is as delectable as the light escabeche of whitefish. You will also enjoy sampling the steamed red tuna accompanied by vegetables; the mildly spicy lamb Louisiana prepared with chili, fennel and garlic; duck with quince, rum and lime; and acorn squash filled with scallops—all partnered with wine from the primarily Californian wine list. Desserts are from Mother Klein, and some are quite good, such as the chocolate whiskey torte and triple layer cheesecake, though the walnut spice cake is less memorable. Plan on about $50 for two, with wine.

11/20

Le Zinc
**139 Duane St.
(W. Broadway)
732-1226**
*Lunch Mon. to Fri. noon to 3:00
P.M.; dinner Mon. to Sat. 7:00 P.M.
to 12:30 A.M.*
AE
French (provincial)

Gerard Blanès and Georges Guenancia, the French owners of Café Un Deux Trois, have joined Philippe Bernard and opened this bistro-brasserie near Odéon and Saint Jean des Prés that is bubbling, loud and full of life—it's where Paris and New York sit side by side. The cuisine, served rapidly by a smiling staff, is unpretentious, and for $25 to $30 you can have a salade folle (haricots verts, foie gras, lobster, and radicchio), a good black boudin with fries, pavé de boeuf à la bordelaise or a leg of lamb with flageolets; chocolate cake; and a carafe of house wine. It's all simple, honest and congenial.

WORLD TRADE CENTER

13

American Harvest Restaurant

Vista International Hotel
3 World Trade Center
Plaza Level
938-9100

Lunch Mon. to Fri. noon to 2:30 P.M.; dinner Mon. to Sat. 6:00 P.M. to 10:00 P.M.
All major credit cards

American (regional)

The Hilton organization, which, as everyone knows, has ensured the preservation of America's cultural heritage since the beginning of the eighteenth century, had the excellent idea to revive traditional American cuisine—the true cuisine of dear grandmothers and their venerable ancestors, not that of Japanese chefs who believe they are creating American cuisine by adding shiitake mushrooms to Michel Guérard's recipes. Each month the American Harvest presents a new dinner menu; the place of honor is reserved for fresh products found in regional markets, and these are used in dishes that recall America before the disembarkment of Breton cooks. This simple, even a little naive, cuisine has the charm (if not always the flavor) of an old engraving. The meal starts, for example, with a delicious Martha's Vineyard corn pudding, a delectable Gwaltney Smithfield ham or a good grilled eggplant stuffed with tomatoes and herb butter. This is followed by a delicious chilled melon soup or squash and apple soup, then by a delicate, charcoal-broiled salmon Potlatch style with juniper berries and lemon mayonnaise, a good crisp duckling with plum sauce or a Maryland-fried chicken (with spoon bread that is not of an airy lightness) or an agreeable flounder poached with crabmeat, Chesapeake Bay style. But perhaps the most interesting are the seasonal vegetables (freshly picked corn on the cob, corn oysters, new beets), which are exquisitely fresh and cooked to perfection. The desserts are created by the hand of a master—particularly the chocolate fudge layer cake, apple pie with cheddar cheese, praline-peach shortcake and blueberry summer pudding.

The list of American wines is less impressive than that of its neighbor, Windows on the World, but you won't regret sampling the Ste. Michelle Cabernet Sauvignon from Washington State, with its admirable finesse. A complete dinner (minus wine) costs between $28 and $32, only if the chosen main course is reasonable. The tables are well spaced, the comfort perfect and the service excellent, but it's a shame that this somewhat impersonal and poorly lit room isn't more reminiscent of a Federalist townhouse. But the good ideas are on your plate, not around you.

17

Cellar in the Sky

Windows on the World
One World Trade Center
107th floor
938-1111

Dinner seatings Mon. to Sat.
7:30 P.M.
All major credit cards

American/French
(nouvelle)

Madrid
3 star

Each time we return to a great New York restaurant we are in anguish. The main question is whether the chef is still there. With these moving luminaries, the work of a food critic seems more like that of an astronomer observing the trajectory of the sky's shooting stars. But at Cellar in the Sky, we have good reason to feel more secure; the cuisine has, like elsewhere, its good and its less good days, but the eventual departure of a chef is never an irreparable catastrophe. Cellar in the Sky is, in fact, a very special restaurant inside of another, Windows on the World, which serves hundreds of meals a day in the dining room and private meeting rooms. All is overseen by Toni Aigner and Alan Lewis, who run this giant operation with not one but three chefs. There is French Chef Arnaned Briand, formerly with Michel Guérard and Gaston Lenôtre; German Chef Eberhardt Mueller, who worked with Alain Senderens; and Chef Herman Reiner, an Austrian who came from the Vienna Hilton. One of these three chefs is responsible for the 36 meals in Cellar in the Sky for each two-week period, and he creates a special menu that changes when the next chef takes over. This system ensures a continuity in quality, and we continue to be enchanted whenever we visit this intimate mini restaurant. Each meal is composed of an appetizer, three courses, a cheese selection and dessert, all served on the simple pine tables in an elegant cellar that is warm in spite of its somberness, perched on the rooftop of the World Trade Center. You may be so fortunate (we have been) as to be served a dinner of a delicious salad of shrimp cut into thin slices and napped with a noisette sauce; a fine tomato soup with basil; a remarkable striped bass poached in a cabbage leaf; a fillet of veal, tender and cooked to perfection, served with a parsley mousse and pieces of apple braised in a flavorful cider sauce; and, to finish, a sensational glazed fig tart followed by the best Colombian coffee we have ever found in New York.

Each visit is a brand new experience, and if you could come here every two weeks for dinner, you would never find the same dish twice. This accomplishment alone is a tour de force. One time, for example, you may find lobster consommé, salmon with asparagus, squab roasted with golden oak mushrooms, Kentucky limestone lettuce and an apricot tart with crème fraîche. Another time it could be canapés of smoked salmon and caviar, consommé with mushrooms, baby red snapper with a confit of zucchini, suprème of duck with red wine sauce and a chocolate and vanilla charlotte. And Cellar in the Sky is famous for its wines; its cellar is not only the highest in New York (no doubt in the world) but is certainly one of the richest and best composed, thanks to two expert sommeliers, Kevin Zraly and his assistant, Ray Wellington. With each course you are served a different wine chosen from among the best growths of the world. It is an exciting way for amateurs to discover new wines, and it's also excellent for more advanced wine students, because one could have the pleasure of tasting, in the same evening, the superb Edna Valley '81 Chardonnay, the '78 Aloxe-Corton Hautes Chapelles, a Barbaresco, the Angelo Gaja '71 and a '76 Sauternes Chateau Climens. At $65 per person (everything included), dinner here is nearly a present. And if you want to pursue your wine studies even more seriously, you need only enroll in the Windows on the World wine school; eight lessons and 100 wines later, you will know almost as much as your professor, Kevin Zraly (for information call 938-1111, ext. 344).

12/20

The Market Dining Room
5 World Trade Center
Main Concourse
938-1155
Lunch Mon. to Fri. 11:30 A.M. to 2:30 P.M.; dinner Mon. to Sat. 5:00 P.M. to 10:00 P.M.
All major credit cards
American

Once you forge your way through the unattractive, busy concourse café and past the active bar inside, you'll find yourself in a bustling dining room filled with a lunchtime business crowd. The decor has a vague Belle Epoque look, the noise level is high, and the ambience has the flavor of middle-management deal makers. The straightforward menu has something for everyone, from diet plates for the overtaxed executive to hearty dishes for healthy working appetites. They do a good job here with such simple things as corned beef hash, broiled swordfish, steak tartare, a nice country pâté with white radish salad, a thick (but salty) mussel chowder, a brochette of succulent swordfish and overcooked scallops, a tender and massive pork loin and an excellent pear tart. Portions are generous, the American wines are plentiful, and the price is fairly reasonable for upwardly mobile business lunchers—about $20 per person, without wine.

15

The Restaurant
1 World Trade Center
107th floor
938-1111
Dinner Mon. to Sat. 5:00 P.M. to 10:00 P.M., Sat. brunch noon to 2:30 P.M., Sun. noon to 7:30 P.M.; lunch Mon. to Fri. noon to 2:15 P.M., $7.50 cover charge for nonmembers at lunch only
Continental

As you ascend to Windows on the World, you may have the feeling that you are on your way to heaven ... in a quantum leap. The view is spectacular, and the city lights create a decor unmatched anywhere else; there's a certain headiness that comes with viewing Manhattan's skyline from above it. The vast space (seating over 350) has a certain intimacy and serenity that transcends the normal frenzy of serving so many customers. When you combine the spectacular view with the gracious welcome of Alan Lewis and the guiding light of Blake Johnson, sommelier for The Restaurant, with a four-course $26.95 prix fixe menu filled with inventive dishes, you may think you

18

actually have landed in paradise. You, and so many of the other customers who have traveled across bridges and through tunnels to celebrate on a Saturday night, will be catered to by a professional staff serving such temptations as roast duckling with artichokes and mushrooms, sea trout sautéed with capers and anchovies with a confit of zucchini and tomatoes, salad of bay scallops with corn and broccoli flowers, a tart lemon tart, and sorbets with fruit coulis. The wine list is rich with marvelous California wines priced as reasonably as they are in California, along with selections from the wine countries of the world, including Greece, Switzerland and Israel. There's something for everyone on the à la carte menu from sirloin steak sautéed with sun-dried tomatoes and sage, swordfish with orange tarragon butter, and veal chops with braised leeks and a mustard sauce. Toni Aigner and Alan Lewis see to it that things are done right here, and you will never be disappointed each time you make a mecca to lower Manhattan for yet another night to remember. A la carte, about $45 with wine.

Chinatown Little Italy

10/20
Ballato's
55 E. Houston St. (Mulberry-Mott sts.) 226-9683

Lunch Mon. to Sat. noon to 2:30 P.M.; dinner Mon. to Sat. 5:30 P.M. to 8:45 P.M.
No credit cards

Italian

The quality has deteriorated a little since our last visit, but the rich and famous continue to arrive—according to Mrs. Ballato. Cannelloni di casa are tame and so soft they seem to be blenderized, but the slightly peppery aftertaste helps. Broiled baby lamb steak (a nice change to see on a menu) has a good flavor, but is too chewy and arrives with string beans crawling with garlic. On the plus side, the roasted potatoes that accompany the entrees are great. And—we save the best for last—the sea squab alone is enough of a reason to make the trip downtown. A small school of blowfish comes swimming into sight in a very light white wine sauce with oregano—it is exquisite. The one dessert once worth ordering, zabaglione, is now disappointing. Having loved the place when John Ballato was alive, we hope it will return to its former status. Dinner for two, with wine, will run about $40.

7/20
Benito's II
**174 Mulberry St.
(Hester St.)
226-9007**
*Dinner nightly 6:00 P.M. to 11:00
P.M. (Benito's I open Fri. and
Sat. only)*
No credit cards
Italian

Don't be fooled by the white tablecloths; this has become a fast-food restaurant, complemented by an incredible high-tack decor (it could be considered kitsch, but they're serious). Once seated, you can reflect on the portrait of the owner, enshrined on the wall next to orange plastic octopuses. As your eyes wander into the small, open kitchen, you may catch a glimpse of la proprietaria dabbing her underarms with a dish towel. Perhaps it is she who presides over the pots of French-style, Roman-style or Sicilian-style sauces. Everything, no matter what it is, seems to be French style, Roman style or Sicilian style, with an occasional Alfredo. The decor has much more majesty than the food. Dinner for two, with wine, will run about $50 to $60. If you must, Benito's I across the street at 163 Mulberry (226-9012) has the same menu on Friday and Saturday nights (minus the shrine and the octopuses).

10/20
Cam Fung
**20 Elizabeth St.
(Canal St.)
964-5256**
*Breakfast and lunch daily 7:30 A.M.
to 4:00 P.M.; dinner nightly 7:30
P.M. to 11:30 P.M.*
All major credit cards
Chinese

Built like a Chu Chin Chow version of Versailles, this traditional Cantonese restaurant enjoys a vast following, especially at dim sum time. A large menu, ambitious bar service and willing staff combine to make it an agreeable experience. The fare is above average; both the Peking duck and the steamed sea bass in a ginger and scallion sauce are extremely good. Otherwise the menu ranges from pork tripe in oyster sauce and an agonizing dish described as stir-fried frog to more conventional Cantonese specialties, such as dragon and phoenix shrimp and lobster in black bean sauce. Cam Fung iron steak is quite tender, served on a red-hot griddle. A pair of enormous plastic dragons adorn one of the walls, eyes flashing at regular intervals, like traffic lights. If you want to experience Chinatown in one fell flourish, this is the place. About $15 per person, with a generous Polynesian cocktail.

10/20
Il Cortile
**125 Mulberry St.
(Hester St.)
226-6060**
*Lunch and dinner daily noon to
midnight (Fri. and Sat. to 1:00
A.M., Sun. from 1:00 P.M.)*
All major credit cards
Italian

Well-to-do customers used to come here for the generally high level of cooking and the handsome SoHo-looking decor, but popularity can be a bad thing for a restaurant. In this case, the management has chosen to expand the place to absorb the overflow of clients. The result is that the kitchen has suffered. The expansion alone is dramatic: a great atrium in the back exposes a beautifully designed brick wall with brick supporting columns and a second-level dining area with a balcony. Il Cortile has become a busy and noisy place that caters more to tourists exploring Little Italy than to diners looking for refined Italian dishes. Pastas by and large lack excitement, though one or two are outstanding—the spaghetti with fresh basil is an example. The brodetto is pedestrian, and the mussels in a white wine sauce (quite tasty) are not as carefully cleaned as one has a right to expect. Veal (a simple piccata or with peas and prosciutto) is tenderized and not of the best quality. Desserts don't add anything except calories. If you choose to skip dessert, don't count on a refreshing cappuccino: it is topped with make-believe cream from a can. About $40 per person, with wine.

10/20
Forlini's
93 Baxter St.
(Canal St.)
349-6779
Lunch and dinner daily noon to
midnight (Fri. and Sat. to
2:00 A.M.)
AE, MC, V
Italian

If you can stand the culture shock of the plastic and Formica bar combined with an ornate rococo dining area, by all means arrive early for your reservations at Forlini's. We say "reservations" advisedly: judges from the nearby courts and reporters covering the murders and divorces keep it continuously crowded. You have to be in the right mood for the bar—Elvis is on the jukebox while the ball game blares on TV, tables are cluttered with dirty glasses, and it's apparently self-service for drinks; but even the nuns at the table behind us one evening were having fun with this brand of casual chaos.

As you proceed into the red, red, very red restaurant, be prepared for the celebratory flashbulbs and happy birthday chants. The menu is huge; the "gourmet dinner for two" must have been designed for Adam and Eve, judging by its lack of freshness. The appetizers of stuffed mushrooms, artichoke hearts, mussels, shrimp and eggplant (all with their respective sauces) are unappealingly mixed on the same plate. The tortellini, panserotti and gnocchi get the same treatment, and they all taste the same. For the main course there's veal piccata, shrimp rolatini and chicken Marsala—or perhaps it's veal Marsala, shrimp piccata and chicken rolatini. Who can tell?

To be fair, we have had good lunches here, so if you order à la carte, sit back and enjoy the lively crowd, you may do well. Dress is casual, and there is a wine list for all wallets. Plan on $60 for two, with wine.

11/20
Great Shanghai Restaurant
27 Division St.
(Market St.)
966-7663

Clean, spacious and airy, this restaurant is staffed by pretty, friendly young Chinese women in red brocade jackets. For a change from the southern Chinese dim sums, try the Shanghai and northern varieties. Steamed little bao buns in a basket, plump with pork and juices, and pork dumplings are both excellent. You can make a meal of them, washed down by bottles of cold Tsingtao

*Lunch and dinner daily 11:30 A.M.
to 10:00 P.M. (Fri. and Sat. to
11:00 P.M.)*
All major credit cards
Chinese

beer. There is a full menu, with the now-obligatory Szechwan specialties printed in red. Though this cuisine tends to be reduced to a fiery banality it doesn't merit, both the sea spice shrimp and the eggplant in garlic sauce are excellent, and the pan-smoked fish is outstanding. The only disappointment is the steamed sea bass, fresh but waterlogged in a thin, poorly flavored sauce. There is a choice of set feasts, notably a Peking duck dinner at $10.95. About $17 per person for an overindulgence with beer.

5/20

Hee Seung Fung
46 Bowery
374-1319
*Breakfast and lunch (dim sum) daily
7:30 A.M. to 4:00 P.M.; dinner
nightly 5:00 P.M. to 11:00 P.M.*
No credit cards
Chinese

This erstwhile dim sum shrine appears to have been recently deconsecrated. The range is still staggering, but the quality has deteriorated, possibly because of the proliferation of similar outlets in midtown and the Hamptons. We picked dispiritedly at our oversteamed offerings, watched over by two toads and an eel from the nearby fish tank. About $10 per person, with tea.

12/20

Home Village
20 Mott St.
(Mulberry St.)
964-0381
*Lunch and dinner daily 11:30 A.M.
to 1:30 A.M.*
No credit cards
Chinese

It's been spruced up and air-conditioned, but the Home Village has not lost its rural charm. Hakka cuisine is famed for its seafood, and here there are more than 50 dishes to choose from, ranging from steamed pomfret in black bean sauce to excellent baked prawns with chili and spiced salt—so nicely cooked you can eat the shell. Squid, conch, abalone and scallops abound in amazing permutations of flavor and color, and there are such marine mysteries as stewed triple seafood with fish maws for the valiant. Baked crab with curry proves an agreeable surprise, and steamed sea bass in soy and scallion or sweet and sour sauce is as delicately cooked as you can find in Chinatown.

But the real uniqueness of Hakka cuisine lies in the preparation of offal, which you will find in a section entitled "Exotic Hakka Dishes." This is why, on a busy day, there is the nostalgic and pervasive aroma of a good French triperie floating about the place. Tripe with chili and black bean sauce is good, the tiny, honey-colored combs braised with green peppers and onions. Sautéed pig's stomach with squid, we feel, is best eaten in the winter, but whatever the weather, don't miss the deep-fried fresh pig's intestines. Forget that you are eating pig's entrails—these crispy red sausages with their meltingly soft innards arrive couched on a bed of cabbage and certainly merit the Golden Offal of the Year Award.

In the less exotic department we enjoy the moist and

subtly flavored salt-baked chicken, tender and pink at the bone, which is served with a soy and scallion sauce or, as we prefer it, with a salt, pepper and cinnamon dip. A certain tendency to flirt with American ingredients results in such bizarre combinations as lobster topped with processed cheese sauce and chicken à la king in a nasty white sauce. Although the pork chops could be a disaster, they are surprisingly delicious, crunchingly crisp yet tender and served in a honeyed sauce, just enough to glaze the meat without drowning it.

There are set feasts for parties, but with a menu as large and intriguing as this it pays to be adventurous. About $17 per person, with Chinese beer.

9/20
Hwa Yuan Szechwan Inn
40 E. Broadway (Market St.)
966-5534
Sun. to Thurs. noon to 11:00 P.M.
All major credit cards
Chinese

Everything seemed to augur well at the Hwa Yuan Szechwan Inn, housed in a starkly functional hall like some commune canteen in the People's Republic of China. The restaurant once enjoyed a reputation for regional specialties, and the Spartan setting seemed to proclaim, "All our effort goes into the food!" Alas, it is not so. The extensive menu simply does not live up to its promise, though a starter of finely sliced kidney with bamboo shoots is quite delicious. Pork dumplings lurk in thick, heavy pastry, and the "wonderful taste" chicken is merely ordinary. Shredded pig's ear in a scallion sauce proves to be a high-risk dish, so tough and cartilaginous we could have sworn we had bitten into a hearing aid. Sautéed beef with carrots is soggy and chewy, and the moo shu pork, with thick, overlarge pancakes, appears to have been coarsely hacked by the hand of a kung fu chef. But tough and salty string beans are atoned for by delicious eggplant braised in a sea-spice sauce. Three senior-looking chefs seem to spend most of their time out front, so who is minding the woks, we ask ourselves? The rest of the staff, friendly, helpful and thoroughly uncorrupted, proves to be the best thing about the Hwa Yuan. About $15 per person, with wine.

12/20
Patrissy's
98 Kenmare St. (Mulberry St.)
226-8509
Lunch and dinner daily noon to midnight
All major credit cards
Italian

With its art-adorned red walls and tuxedoed waiters, this is Little Italy at its best—at the least it's a little slice of Rome. The ambitious menu relies heavily on central and southern Italian specialties. Half portions are available so you can sample any of the honest and sometimes exceptional offerings, such as spiedini alla romana (breaded mozzarella, fried and served with lemon herb sauce), paglia e fieno alla papalini and bass livornese (fresh sea bass baked with tomatoes, capers, olives and garlic). Other specialties are eggplant alla Patrissy and veal scaloppine. It's a shame that the respectable Italian wine list has no specifics, such as producer and vintage. Dinner for two, with wine, will run $50 to $60.

10/20
Peking Duck House
22 Mott St.
227-1810
Lunch daily 11:30 A.M to 3:00 P.M.; dinner nightly 3:00 P.M. to 10:30 P.M. (Fri. and Sat. to 11:30 P.M.)
AE
Chinese

Perhaps it is the hordes of people frequenting this restaurant that is responsible for the decline of the food since our last visit. At any rate, we feel compelled to lower the rating. The hot and sour soup resembles giblet gravy, and we have had better steamed dumplings (these are heavy and soggy). But Peking duck is the real disappointment. The sauce, which we usually adore, has no pep to it at all. And the duck could use one of those treatments for skin that is both oily and dry—it is greasy on the outside and like sawdust within. Service is of the inscrutable kind. About $40 for a duck dinner for two.

13 🍴
Say Eng Look
1 E. Broadway
(Canal St.)
732-0796
Lunch and dinner daily 11:15 A.M. to 10:30 P.M. (Fri. and Sat. to 11:30 P.M.)
AE, MC, V
Chinese

There have been changes at this old and reputable Chinese restaurant. The facade looks like a crazy pavement, and waiters wear smart dark waistcoats. You can now select a bottle of wine from a minuscule list; two years ago we had to make do with beer. The place has been thoroughly redecorated and the household goods perched atop the bar have been given a good dusting. The food is Shanghai-style, as both owners and staff come from Ningpo; Chinatown loyalists flock here, for the cooking is still sound and consistent. The never-changing "special" menu offers fillet of eel, scallops with crab and king sea cucumber with shrimp seeds—a dauntingly slimy delicacy for those who like the real thing. Tai-chi chicken is as good as ever, though we have detected a shake or two of the catsup bottle in the sauce. Jumbo lion's head meatballs are subtly flavored with star anise pepper, and an entire croaker, tender and moist under its crispy skin, arrives dredged in a spicy, unctuous macédoine of vegetables. The saucier—if such a creature inhabits Chinese kitchens—has a very good palate: Say Eng Look is strong on flavor. In cold weather try the generous and sustaining range of casseroles and remember that the chef boasts of five different ways of preparing duck (to be ordered in advance). Clear your palate with Italian ice cream, Marco Polo's way of saying thanks for his discovery of China.

At 10:30 P.M. on our last visit, the otherwise serene and shuffling staff underwent a dramatic transformation. We seemed to be witnessing an acrobatic troupe from mainland China: ten waiters tossed chairs and tables in the air in a dazzling display and pulled the red plastic tablecloths from under the noses of remaining customers. At one point we could have sworn there was a vacuum cleaner crawling up our legs. In no time we were surrounded by artistically stacked pyramids of furniture, and it would have been churlish not to break into applause. The message was unmistakable and the check arrived promptly, weighted down by fortune cookies. Could it be that the staff was clearing the decks for action? After all, *say eng look* means "four-five-six," a winning hand in mah-jongg. A meal will run $20 per person, with wine.

12/20
Silver Palace
50 Bowery
(Canal St.)
964-1204
Breakfast and lunch daily 8:00 A.M. to 4:00 P.M.; dinner nightly 4:00 P.M. to 11:00 P.M.
Chinese

On the Bowery, where winos sleep off the effects of lesser vintages, you will find this enormous barn of a dim sum emporium, one of the best of its kind. Situated on the second floor, it is reached by Chinatown's ultimate status symbol—an escalator. Upstairs, pandemonium reigns as red-coated waiters rush around with stainless steel teapots and cozily diminutive trolleys of bite-size delicacies. On most days it hosts a teeming mass of humanity, from breast-fed babies getting their first whiff of soy sauce to venerable grannies sucking on spareribs; this is uninhibited eating, shorn of all niceties save pleasure. The recently installed new management promises long overdue renovations, and an eminent chef who has just defected from a famous uptown establishment is expected to revitalize the menu. Prices, we have been assured, will stay cheap and cheerful. For a real taste of the place try Sunday brunch, when, in seven frantic hours, nearly three thousand mouths are fed. About $12 per person, with beer.

12/20
Wong Kee
113 Mott St.
(Hester St.)
966-1160
Lunch and dinner daily 11:00 A.M. to 10:00 P.M.
No credit cards
Chinese

One of our favorite New York rituals is to go to Chinatown around 11:00 or 12:00 on a Sunday morning, preferably with a group of at least four and usually with a whole family in tow, to sample a variety of unfamiliar dishes at any of a number of Chinese restaurants that serve either dim sum or more home-style fare than one ordinarily looks for at dinner. Wong Kee is a perfect Sunday morning divertissement, for it is small, always crowded with Chinese and cheap beyond belief for good and abundant Shanghai-style food. We recently spent a hazy Sunday morning here and consumed four enormous dishes with tea for less than $12 (and one dish was $4). Be prepared for the rushed atmosphere and for waiters whose English is restricted to repeating whatever you order plus the word *good*. You sit at spanking clean Formica tables set with one canister of forks and another of chopsticks. The place is sleek, and the outside is a handsome gray steel. It's popular, and if you get here two minutes after noon you'll have to wait for a table. But not for long: the turnover is very fast.

As for our specific recommendations: we love the beef with sour cabbage, the crisp-skinned duck seasoned with star anise powder and the shrimp with steamed bok choy. The shredded pork with pan-fried noodles tends to be somewhat gloppy and tasteless. In places like this, unfortunately, you are bound by your inability to read Chinese, for the menu has scores of dishes listed in that language and in no other. But you can always point to the next table and tell the waiter, "I'll have whatever they're eating." It is unlikely that Wong Kee will disappoint you—and at $2.10 a dish, does it much matter if you choose one or two not to your liking?

SoHo

13
Abyssinia
**35 Grand St.
(Thompson St.)
226-5959**
*Dinner nightly 6:00 P.M. to
10:30 P.M.*
No credit cards
Ethiopian

On a quiet corner in SoHo lurks a charming little restaurant with excellent Ethiopian food. The small, cheerful dining room is decorated with tribal paintings on its bamboo walls; you sit on surprisingly comfortable three-legged stools around colorful baskets that double as tables. The crowd is a mix of adventurous uptown and in-the-know downtown, and everyone seems to enjoy the ambience and the food. Ethiopian cooking is hearty, spicy and stewy; the small menu lists its standard dishes: yegomen wot, a delicious dish of kale and potatoes sautéed with onions, green peppers and spices; doro wot, tender pieces of chicken cooked in a hot berbere sauce, served with a hard-boiled egg; zegeni, beef in a marvelous blend of garlic, ginger, onions and spicy berbere; and ye 'beg alitcha, a fragrant, delicious lamb dish with turmeric, onions, garlic and white pepper. Ethiopians prefer not to bother with utensils, so the friendly waitress will keep you supplied with plenty of injera, a crêpelike bread that you use to scoop up morsels of the dishes, which are served family style on one big tray. Bring your own wine (unless you want beer or questionable Ethiopian honey wine), and expect to pay about $13 per person.

10/20
Carumba!
**684 Broadway
(3rd St.)
420-9817**

Even if you can manage to find your way through the hot bodies swarming around the bar to tell the hostess, who must be Charo's sister, that you have arrived, you will continue waiting until any of the hundreds of diners have

Lunch and dinner daily noon to midnight
All major credit cards
Mexican

finished their last bites of burritos and their last sips of Dos Equis and made space for you. The acoustics are something like those of an echo chamber, and if you like to eat mediocre Mexican food and scream at your friends, this is your place. It's a superb location for struggling actors to learn how to practice voice projection. Noise aside, Carumba! is one of the more entertaining places in town: it's the darling of Upper East Siders for dinner and local SoHo residents for late supper. The menu is predictably Mexican and disappointingly bad. Chalupas are unusually heavy (but the chorizo is tasty), the burritos boring, the green chicken enchilada leaden and the chimichanga as nondescript as the rest of the dishes. Don't come to eat—come to have fun and drink along with the rest of the attractive people, who at least know a good bargain when they see one. About $20 per person, with several beers.

15
La Chanterelle
89 Grand St.
(Greene St.)
966-6960
Dinner Tues. to Sat. 6:30 P.M. to 10:30 P.M.
AE, MC, V
American/French (nouvelle)

There is a starkness here that must reflect the owners' idea of refined elegance in the nondecor genre. Its simplicity comes from pale yellow walls, early American chandeliers, Queen Anne chairs, a dozen tables with fresh white linens and a somewhat glazed-looking hostess, who spends the evening at her desk busily preparing your handwritten bill to match the handwritten menu, which is often just as illegible. It's all so civilized and refined that it comes as a jolt to look out the large windows at the shabby street scene (which is no doubt why Chanterelle is open only for dinner—the contrast by day would probably strain the guests). Uptowners gather here to enjoy American cuisine of the nouvelle persuasion. Chef David Waltuck is quite talented, and he has a deft hand with sauces (although there are a few too many on the menu) and cooking times. Wild mushrooms in puff pastry arrive looking something like a tennis ball; the terrine of duck is excellent, as is the warm foie gras salad; the seafood sausage in a shallot beurre blanc is delicious; but the oysters with country bacon are remarkably salty. Mr. Waltuck's creativity is evident, but the emphasis on rich and overreduced sauces tends to take the nouvelle out of nouvelle. Entrees are satisfying: a fricassée of seafood in beurre blanc, soft-shell crabs with sorrel, noisettes of lamb with tarragon, a veal chop with chives and cucumber, squab with a red wine sauce, and haddock with mustard. The cheese board is especially attractive, and you are invited to take as much as you'd like from the mostly imported selections, good news for diners who find the portions here slightly on the stingy side. The wine list is limited, but you'll find a nice Lakespring Chardonnay from California and classic Burgundies from France at somewhat elevated prices. Desserts are superb: a warm apricot tart, sinful chocolate pavé with crème anglaise, good crème brûlée or chocolate reine de saba. That handwritten bill may cause a few heart attacks, as the total rises to astronomical proportions with little effort. There is a $42.50 five-course prix fixe meal, which comes to about the same amount as an à la carte meal ($65 per person, with wine). At these prices, you have good reason to expect a three-toque meal, but unfortunately La Chanterelle has not yet arrived, and the prices far outdistance the quality of cuisine. Apparently no one cares, because the place is full. We, however, wish to lodge a formal protest: Bring into harmony the price-quality ratio, and don't take such a noblesse oblige attitude in a place where local starving artists peer through the windows while limousines wait to take their affluent owners back uptown.

9/20
Cinco de Mayo
349 W. Broadway
(Broome-Grand sts.)
226-5255
Lunch and dinner Tues. to Sun. noon to midnight
All major credit cards
Mexican

If this is the new revolution in Mexican food, then we should all head for the hills instead of for SoHo. In spite of the loftlike space, the brick and pink-painted walls and the harpist, the only thing elevated about your dining experience may be you leaping from your chair after a bite of whole, raw jalapeño innocently skewered with Mexican sausages. From the "guacamole treat" (it isn't) to boudin to a tortilla preparation (layers of corn tortillas and chicken, tasting like a Mexican pot pie), all is sloppy and smacks of shortcuts. Good nachos are still hard to find. Dinner for two, with wine, will run about $50.

12/20
Greene Street
101 Greene St.
(Spring St.)
925-2415
Dinner nightly 6:00 P.M. to 11:45 P.M. (Fri. and Sat. to 12:45 A.M.); brunch Sun. noon to 3:45 P.M.
All major credit cards
American

We always enjoy returning to Greene Street, if for no other reason than to admire the WPA-esque wall mural, the large plants illuminated with tiny white lights, the antique rattan seating and the intimacy that is created by sheer determination in this cavernous garage space. The bar scene is lively, and many attractive local SoHo residents meet here for drinks and to listen to the nightly entertainment. When you first arrive, the jazz pianist may frazzle your nerves somewhat; the music is amplified so loud it precludes normal dinner conversation. After a bottle of Chamisal Chardonnay from Edna Valley, however, the music sounds better. Executive Chef Lawrence Vito has prepared an ambitious menu with intercontinental tastes and uptown prices. It sounds promising, and the daily specials offer many enticing possibilities. But alas, the dishes are slightly out of his reach, from a domestic underseasoned salad to an international bouillabaisse terrine—an odd concoction of seafood en gelée served with a decent rouille mayonnaise (if only the gelée had more of a bouillabaisse flavor). The hot scallop mousse in fennel butter sounds light and refined; it is light, but the presentation is more akin to scrambled eggs than a pleasantly firm mousse, although the taste is delicately good. You can choose from veal chops with baby turnips and onions in a red wine butter sauce; breast of chicken filled with spinach and red peppers in a ginger sauce; a lackluster scallop of veal with scallions and a potato pancake; sweetbreads with mushrooms and spinach that are described as "roasted" but arrive seemingly steamed, with a good basil cream sauce; and a rather mushy red snapper served with an excellent saffron sauce, perfectly cooked broccoli and delightful sweet red pepper slivers. Desserts are good, as befits a cuisine that leaves you hungry because you'll send your plate back to the kitchen half full. The fresh fig tart is an inspiration, and a fairly good raspberry mousse is brightened with an excellent bittersweet chocolate sauce. We feel obliged to take Tony Goldman's toque away until the kitchen achieves the balance and harmony essential for the sort of precise cooking it is trying to offer. About $35 per person, with wine.

13 ♟

Omen
**113 Thompson St.
(Prince St.)
925-8923**
Lunch Thurs. to Sun. noon to 2:30 P.M.; dinner Tues. to Sun. 5:30 P.M. to 10:45 P.M.
AE

Japanese

This attractive, relaxed restaurant with a rural feeling is owned by a family with two hostelries in Kyoto. The patriarch, whose artifacts adorn the walls, is a famous calligrapher and poet. Were he in residence he would doubtless have sung some of his verses for us. As it was, we had to make do with wind chimes and ethnic electronic music. Mikio Shinagawa, the charming young owner, set the tone by giving a demonstration of flower arranging at our table. Everything about the Omen, from the handmade tableware to the sake flasks, is exquisite. The porcelain of our thin, shallow cup with an oyster-shell glaze was said to contain the ashes of an ancestor.

Omen offers the same fare as the family inns in Kyoto. The restaurant is named for the house specialty, an elaborate and ritualistic mating of assorted vegetables, broth and wheat udon noodles. At $7.25 it's a meal in itself and is strongly recommended. All the dishes are beautifully presented, from mixed sashimi of tuna and an unusual chicken and cucumber salad to eff tofu (another specialty) and a potpourri of pickles and relishes tastefully arranged on a tile. Vegetables are a strong point here, with an accent on originality. Grated burdock and carrot sautéed in sesame oil, spinach and mushrooms lightly dusted with toasted sesame seeds and asparagus in sesame cream are all delightful. In spite of the strong sesame connection, all taste refreshingly different. Sashimi or chicken dinners are a good value, but the tempura dinner is a disappointment. We like the informal and nonreverential approach to Japanese eating at the Omen. The young, attractive staff actually communicates and mixes with the customers. Mikio himself is a genial sophisticate and a readily identifiable host, with the authority only two inns can bestow. Though frivolity is not exactly a Japanese attribute, Omen is great fun—and, significantly, not at the expense of the food. About $25 per person, with sake.

12/20
Paradis
**260 W. Broadway
(Sixth Ave.)
925-8463**
Lunch Mon. to Fri. noon to 3:00 P.M.; dinner nightly 6:30 P.M. to 12:30 A.M. (Sun. to 11:00 P.M.); brunch Sun. noon to 3:00 P.M. AE, MC, V
American/Continental

You may think you have climbed into some post-modernist heaven when you find yourself in this lofty pastel room with its 22-foot ceilings, endless columns and cloudy paint job. You're brought back to terra firma with the bargello patterned chairs, the silly crystal chandelier overwhelmed by the space and the view out the window that makes you wonder if TriBeCa is purgatory in disguise. The contrasts are fairly unsettling, and a few casual glances at the street life will remind you that you could do worse than to find yourself in this latter-day paradise. The cuisine, with its nouvelle intentions, is not what we would describe as the nectar of the gods, but it is an honest attempt nonetheless. You won't be unhappy with a garlic soufflé, mussels in green mayonnaise or angel hair pasta with basil. Less interesting is the marigold served on the salad, which is edible but perfectly tasteless. The entrees are interesting ideas: ravioli with a truffle-essence sauce, tournedos with a truffle-Madeira sauce and chicken with bleu de Bresse and a walnut stuffing; but roast duckling with garlic cream, noisettes of lamb with onion sauce and veal medallions with smoked salmon and sorrel sauce are all overcooked. The chef needs to work on his cooking times and stop trumping up good food with gimmicky sauces, for there are some good possibilities here. Desserts will restore your positive mood: good papaya cream puffs, walnut apricot torte and mocha praline pie. And if all else fails, there is the marvelous '81 Edna Valley Chardonnay, which will make your morale ascend even if your palate is a touch disappointed. About $35 per person, with wine.

11/20
Raoul's
**180 Prince St.
(Sullivan St.)
966-3518**

This cheerful neighborhood place seems more like an extended family's home than a restaurant. The decor is classic New York—tin ceilings and walls, a rather personal collection of photos and prints and booth

Dinner nightly 6:30 P.M. to 11:30 P.M. (Sat. and Sun. to midnight)
AE, MC, V
French (classical)

seating made more intimate by the golden light from the small bistro lamps—and you'll get a warm welcome from the young French people who run this place. It has everything going for it, including good wines, a lovely old bar and provincial home cooking that is, although not ambitious, safe, reliable and comfortable. We are concerned, however, about one minor point: the chef appears to spend more time socializing with his friends than he does working in the kitchen. The blackboard menu changes daily, offering fresh products, and there are a few surprises: miniature artichokes steamed in beef broth with a light vinaigrette, escargots served in a traditional thick brown sauce with mushrooms, fillet of bass grenobloise, calf's liver with vinegar, a nice chilled sweetbread salad with homemade mayonnaise, poulet chasseur, overcooked turbot with béarnaise and a provencale côte d'agneau with olives. As in classical cooking, most everything is oversauced; the menu de marché can often be disguised underneath one sauce after another. Desserts are good, particularly the fruit tarts, and you will be sure to pass a pleasant evening in this unpretentious place—so much so that no doubt you'll return often enough to become yet another member of the happy family. About $80 for two, if you submit to the '81 Puligny Montrachet for $37.

10/20
Tamu
340 W. Broadway
(Grand St.)
925-2751
Dinner Mon. to Fri. 6:00 P.M. to 11:30 P.M., Sat. and Sun. 4:00 P.M. to midnight
All major credit cards
Indonesian

Getting to Bali requires a voyage. Getting to Tamu simply requires a subway token. This Indonesian restaurant, installed in a former SoHo shop, has a certain colonial charm with its bamboo furniture, wicker lamps, lovely prints and remarkably friendly staff dressed in white, with batik head scarves. Unhappily, the exotic, spicy fragrance diffused by sticks of incense finds its way only weakly into the kitchen and is sweetened by American tastes in the process. If you have had the chance to eat a genuine rijsstafel in Bali, Java or even the Netherlands, you will be indifferent to the one served here. Nevertheless, two among the twelve dishes that comprise the rijsstafel of Tamu have nearly authentic flavors: udang tumis (shrimp with ginger and onions) and rendang (beef with spices and coconut milk). If only they were served separately— you could have a nice little quasi-Indonesian meal without having to deal with the other ten rijsstafel-à-la-SoHo dishes. About $20 per person, with a glass of very conventional house white wine.

10/20
Wings
76 Wooster St.
(Spring St.)
966-1300

The cuisine in this very pink place (from the grand piano to the giant soft-sculpture calla lilies to the neon tube snaking its way across the ceiling) has not exactly been winging its way aloft since our last visit here. The menu

*Dinner nightly 6:00 P.M. to
midnight; brunch Sun. noon to
4:00 P.M.*
AE, CB, DC
American

still echoes American nouvelle, but after a tired meal of
nearly inedible steamed mussels (three-quarters of them
looked wizened and dangerous), poached oysters
obliterated by the strong taste of pancetta and spinach, an
al dente tortellini in an insipid basil cream sauce, an
acceptable watercress salad with Roquefort, an
overcooked duck in port sauce, a tasteless and
overcooked rack of lamb with black currant–cassis sauce,
an overcooked, tasteless and banal fillet of beef with red
wine shallot sauce and too-sweet banana and strawberry
sorbets, we had to comfort ourselves with the marvelous
Kistler '81 Chardonnay from California and enjoy the
pretty people who love Wings. We have watched this
restaurant spiral downward over the years—a pity,
because it was so promising at first, and it's still one of
our favorite places in New York for the highly personal
decor and trendy crowd. Perhaps in our next edition we'll
be able to report that Wings is on the ascendant. About
$30 per person, with wine.

Greenwich Village

12/20
Angelina's
41 Greenwich Ave.
929-1255

*Lunch Wed. to Mon. noon to 3:00
P.M.; dinner Wed. to Mon. 5:00 to
11:00 P.M.*
AE, DC
Italian

Don't look for trendy pasta combinations at Angelina's;
she has been serving fine, home-style Italian dishes since
she opened her own place in 1936. (She's carrying on a
tradition: before then, Angelina's mother ran the family
restaurant on MacDougal Street.) Still spry and gracious,
she greets guests, including a great many regulars, from a
central table in front of the compact bar. The ground-
floor restaurant, as well as its spacious, year-round
garden, has the nostalgically intimate feel of a past era.
The authentic antique lighting of the dining room and
the pink stucco walls, together with the ersatz ferns on
the fireplace mantels, create a pleasing, homey
atmosphere. The food is homey, too. The bountiful plate
of spaghetti with anisette-flavored meatballs is as
outstanding as are the meat ravioli and the linguine.
Lasagne is served in its pure state—not in a casserole
overwhelmed by liquified cheese, as in so many other
Italian places, but freestanding and plump. Veal dishes,
such as veal and peppers or veal Marsala, are extremely
good. If you are especially hungry, try one of the special
dinners. An appetizer of lasagne, ravioli, minestrone
soup or shrimp cocktail is followed by fried scallops,
shrimp marinara, oysters or calamari. There's also veal

milanese, chicken cacciatore or shrimp parmigiana. Portions are generous and seasonings delicate. Homemade Italian cheesecake finishes the meal. Wines are reasonably priced, too: Corvo white, Ruffino, Valpolicella and Verdicchio are about $10 a bottle. Expect to have a quiet, restorative evening among civilized people with friendly service. Where else can you dine so inexpensively and so well? About $20 for two, without wine.

10/20
Arnold's Turtle
51 Bank St.
(W. 4th St.)
242-5623
Lunch and dinner daily 11:30 A.M. to midnight
MC, V
American (vegetarian)

Arnold's Turtle is the quintessential Greenwich Village vegetarian café (it is perhaps the *only* Greenwich Village vegetarian café). It is located on a pretty, tree-lined street and has a wooden bench outside to accommodate the overflow, as it is nearly always crowded. This is the right place to go if you don't mind tables very close together or occasionally curt waiters and waitresses, if you are a vegetarian or must restrict your dairy or egg consumption (the menu is coded) and/or if your taste in food runs to no taste. Unfortunately, the cuisine here is less than inspired and is somewhat of a mishmash (a perfect description of the lentil cheeseburger, complete with catsup). Salads are fresh and seem to have something to say for themselves, but spinach-tofu-mushroom casserole and similar concoctions are best left unspoken of. And anyone who says that the fruit pies, made without sugar and with canned fruit, are delicious is crazy. Cheer up—the chocolate desserts are made with sugar. Dinner for two, with wine (thank goodness), will run about $40.

11/20
Black Sheep
342 W. 11th St.
(Washington St.)
242-1010
Dinner nightly 6:00 P.M. to 11:00 P.M. (Fri. and Sat. to midnight, Sun. to 10:30 P.M.); brunch Sun. noon to 4:00 P.M.
All major credit cards
French (provincial)

True to its "genuine Greenwich Village bistro" roots, Black Sheep is tucked away on a quiet street and has brick walls, awful op art paintings and lace curtains. The decor and the food are both an attempt at French provincial, and the prix fixe menu (priced according to the entree) begins with crudites that are perhaps a little too "rustique." So are the leek soup with stringy celery and the crumbly, underseasoned pâté de campagne. Entrees may vary from grilled striped bass with a mustard herb glaze to grilled leg of lamb provençale to rolled sole fillets flamed in Pernod with tomatoes and cream. Desserts are plentiful; among them you'll find double chocolate cake and hazelnut cheesecake. The wine list is extensive and enthusiastic, and equally enthusiastic is the service. On the whole, nothing has changed since we last wrote about the Black Sheep—expect no gastronomic spasms of delight, but a friendly, relaxed atmosphere that's somehow right for the neighborhood. Dinner for two, with wine, will run about $55 to $60 (a ten percent discount is given to cash-paying customers).

12/20
Café Espanol
**172 Bleecker St.
(Sullivan–MacDougal sts.)
475-9230**
Lunch and dinner daily 11:30 A.M. to 1:00 A.M.
All major credit cards
Spanish/Mexican

Squeezed between Bleecker Street's dress shops and falafel stands, unassuming Café Espanol is a real culinary find. The mood is festive and the motif flamenco; the food gets better and the portions larger with every visit. NYU students, couples and groups of celebrating friends boisterously down copious amounts of Mexican beer and Spanish wine with the house specialty, paella with lobster. A seafood and sausage paella valenciana is equally impossible to finish, and the mariscada creole, overflowing with scallops, shrimp, lobster and mussels, is gargantuan. Shrimp is prepared in creole, green or diablo sauce and served with extra platters of rice. If so much seafood overwhelms you, choose a traditionally prepared chicken dish or feast on combination Mexican platters. For about $35 (with beer), two can feel that they've eaten enough for three days.

12/20
Café Loup
**18 E. 13th St.
255-4746**
Lunch Mon. to Fri. noon to 3:00 P.M.; dinner Mon. to Sat. 6:00 P.M. to 10:30 P.M.
All major credit cards
French (classical)

Café Loup is a small, bohemian bistro in the lower level of a Greenwich Village brownstone. Stucco walls are decorated with obligatory artwork, and the subdued lighting in the evening creates an intimate atmosphere that's a sharp contrast to lunch, which draws the credit card crowd in search of good, simple French food. For the most part, you'll find it here. The menu is classic French (roast duck, tournedos, escargots, pâté, onion soup) interspersed with the chef's daily "inspirations," which may run the gamut from calf's brains to the ubiquitous swordfish steak with a flavored butter. What's odd is that the specials are dutifully recited by the waiters, when the menus consist of handwritten chalkboards paraded to each table; couldn't they take the extra effort to write down everything? The wine list is well priced, the service is friendly, and dinner for two, with wine, will run about $70 to $75.

13
Café New Amsterdam
**284 W. 12 St.
242-7929**
Dinner Mon. to Sat. 6:00 P.M. to 11:00 P.M.
AE, MC, V
American/French (nouvelle)

Every effort is made to please in this extremely attractive, pleasant restaurant on a relatively quiet corner in the West Village. Handsome antique prints and drawings are well displayed on the burgundy walls; classical music plays unobtrusively in the background. The young, casually dressed waiters are attentive and intelligent, and their advice is worth listening to. The brief, interesting menu changes occasionally, but there's always an excellent country pâté to start, served with a good mustard; other starters may include a chilled melon soup or cold shrimp with basil on a bed of arugula—good, but a bit oily. Entrees range from a veal chop with ginger and chives and a fantastic halibut fillet, perfectly cooked and delicately seasoned with beurre rouge, to a cold loin of pork with apples and currants and a tender, moist chicken breast sautéed with cherries, served in an excellent brandy-cream sauce. The cooking times are scrupulously observed in the kitchen—overcooking is an unknown vice here—and sauces are prepared with a light hand. Care is also taken with vegetables (baby asparagus, new potatoes) and desserts, in particular the peach-raspberry tart. With a good, simple California or French wine, you'll be happy to pay the relatively modest bill of $65 for two.

11/20
Caffé da' Alfredo
17 Perry St.
(Seventh Ave.)
989-7028
Lunch Thurs. to Sat. 12:30 P.M. to 3:00 P.M.; dinner Tues. to Sat. 6:00 P.M. to 10:45 P.M., Sun. 3:00 P.M. to 9:45 P.M.
No credit cards
Italian

A casual, young, typical Village crowd subjects itself to stereotypical Italian service—brusque and impatient—at Caffé da'Alfredo, a tiny, attractive Italian bistro. The small menu offers the Italian classics, some of which are better than others. Stuffed zucchini is flavorful, the marinara sauce on the pastas is well made and delicious, and shrimp in a butter-garlic sauce is good. But the pastas are often soggy, the veal in the veal piccata is dry, and the calamari in the seafood salads is far too chewy. All in all, it's decent New York Italian food, no more and no less. Bring your own wine, make sure to have reservations and plan on spending $40 for two.

13
Cent'Anni
50 Carmine St.
(Bleecker-Bedford sts.)
989-9494
Dinner Wed. to Mon. 5:00 P.M. to 11:30 P.M.
AE
Italian

In Italy, as elsewhere, it is increasingly difficult to find well-prepared regional specialties. It has even been predicted that some of the best Italian food in the next few years will be served in the United States. New York has such a sanctuary: a small, unpretentious restaurant in the Village. The decor is contemporary and pleasant but simply serves as a backdrop for the real emphasis of the restaurant—lusty Italian food in the Florentine tradition. Ingredients from mozzarella to seafood are superbly fresh and prepared to their best advantage. Salads, pastas, seafoods and meats are simple and full of flavor, and daily specials sometimes replace the standard menu items. True to Italian form, the desserts are slightly cloying, including the well-prepared zabaglione. Come here to see friends greeting one another or the host taking a load off his Italian loafers and sipping a glass of wine with friends between greeting customers. Above all, come for honest, delicious food. Dinner for two, with a fine Tuscan wine, will run about $70.

13 👨‍🍳

John Clancy's Restaurant

181 W. 10th St.

242-7350

Dinner Mon. to Sat. 6:00 P.M. to 11:30 P.M., Sun. 5:30 P.M. to 11:00 P.M.

All major credit cards

American (seafood)

If you can't get out to Montauk or up to the Cape, where you can watch the fishing boats unload their catch and pick out the fish for your enjoyment that same day, take a cab to John Clancy's in the Village. It's not far, and you can count on Clancy—an ex-fisherman—to select fresh fish for you. But don't expect fish nets and lobster buoys: this is an elegant restaurant, even if the neighborhood might suggest otherwise. Start with the absolutely wonderful fresh clams and oysters on the half shell. They are as good as you'll find at the seashore. Clancy has made an art of grilling seafood on skewers over mesquite, which imparts an intriguing, smoky flavor to swordfish, fresh tuna (a rarity in New York), sole and sea scallops. Simply sautéed shrimp and tiny bay scallops are also exceptional. Make certain you don't fill yourself before dessert, for each is rich, sweet and quite fabulous; we recommend a chocolate velvet cake in particular and an English trifle that is so good it should be shipped to a friend in London, because he or she has certainly never tasted anything like it. One word of caution: If you hanker for a steak, you're in the wrong place. This is a seafood restaurant pure and simple, and there is no meat to be had. About $30 to $35 per person, with wine.

11/20

Coach House

110 Waverly Pl.
(Sixth Ave.)

777-0303

Dinner Tues. to Sat. 5:30 P.M. to 10:15 P.M., Sun. 4:30 P.M. to 9:30 P.M.

Jacket and tie required

All major credit cards

American/Continental

The Coach House is one of New York's early American antiques; even the loyal clientele, which keeps coming back for more of this boring but authentic American cuisine, has that antiquated look. The incredible reputation of the Coach House has always been a mystery to us. Under the pretext that black bean soup (good), Maryland crab (passable), smoked turkey with horseradish sauce (adequate), chicken pot pie (a faithful rendition of a classic), chocolate cake (very tired) and Mississippi pecan pie (overly sweet and mealy) have been on the Coach House's menu forever, scores of gastronomy critics have tried to pass off Leon Lianides and his chef as the popes of American cuisine. But these two have made no effort over the past 30 years to enlarge their repertoire or to give a precise and exciting image to regional American cuisine, which has been revived during recent years by enthusiastic, curious chefs. Moreover, if the Coach House is truly *the* temple of American cuisine, you have to ask yourself why it holds onto such specialties of old Europe as little inspired as Gruyère quiche, champignons à la grecque, escargots de Bourgogne and shish kebab. To place the Coach House at the top of the list of New York restaurants is a big joke. But that is not to say that what you eat here is bad. It is possible to dine well on striped bass poached in court bouillon and perfumed with anise, crab cakes with lemon, duck with green peppercorns, and apple pie. You'll be served in a cozy decor cluttered with paintings depicting horses and the glory of the hunt. All that being said, there is very little to justify the legendary reputation of the brave Leon Lianides. About $50 per person, with an American wine from the limited list.

14 🍳
Ennio and Michael
504 La Guardia Pl.
677-8577
Lunch Tues. to Thurs. noon to 3:00 P.M.; dinner nightly 5:00 P.M. to 11:00 P.M. (Fri. and Sat. to 11:30 P.M., Sun. to 10:00 P.M.)
AE
Italian

Perhaps it was only a myth that Greenwich Village was once home to dozens of small, family-run trattorias serving good, basic Italian-American food; the evidence suggests such places were actually serving bad imitations of real Italian food. There is no doubt, however, that Ennio and Michael is a neighborhood favorite, and its reputation has outgrown Greenwich Village, for it is always crowded with residents and out-of-towners who come here on Fridays and Saturdays for some of the best Abruzzese cooking in the city. The room is simple, large and quite striking in its gray tones and blond woods. The shirt-sleeved service seems just fine with the shirt-sleeved crowd here, but we advise you to pull either Ennio or Michael over by the elbow and tell them you want your food cooked the way they cook it for themselves and their families. Then you will get platters of red peppers with anchovies, fragrant steamed mussels and a delicately seasoned insalata di mare full of octopus, shrimp and calamari. Pastas are lusty and never subtle, from the linguine with clam sauce to the wonderful pasta e patate—a blend of starches that would fortify a mountain goat. Also try the gnocchi with fresh basil in season. Chicken all'arrabiata is hot, spicy and golden brown, without a trace of oiliness, while shrimp francese—which we find in every Italian restaurant in America—is here an exemplary form of the dish, delicately sautéed and then doused with garlic. As is usual in New York Italian restaurants, the desserts are no more than afterthoughts, and with cheesecake and cannoli as the offerings, they are clichéd afterthoughts at that. But the espresso—when made by Ennio or Michael—is excellent. About $40 for two before wine, tax and tip.

13 🍳
Frank's Restaurant
431 W. 14th St.
243-1349
Breakfast and lunch Mon. to Fri. 2:00 A.M. to 3:00 P.M.; dinner Tues. to Thurs. 5:00 P.M. to 10:00 P.M.; Fri. and Sat. to 11:00 P.M.
AE, MC, V
Continental

Frank's Restaurant has been in the family for 70 years (there never was a Frank). Now George and Gloria Molinari have been joined by their son, a recent graduate of The Culinary Institute of America, and have opened for dinner. As always, Frank's opens at 2:00 A.M. to serve "coffee and ..." to the bustling meat district and remains open for breakfast and lunch. For those who eat to live, there are such lunch items as sliced steak, pot roast, omelets and deli-style sandwiches. But dinner here is for those who live to eat. Though the wholesale meat district is rather desolate in the evenings, the ambience inside the restaurant is lively in the tradition of Les Halles. There is a long, ornate bar under plasterwork ceilings, and the old tile floor is covered with sawdust as if they mean it. George is Italian and enthusiastically urges you to do what you want with his food. Have an entree as an appetizer, try a half portion or ask for something different altogether. Fresh pastas are superb, as are sweetbreads, tripe and the catches of the day. Whatever you do, try the beef. In residence here is one of the finest fork-tender filet mignons in the city. Frank's is very good food in a wonderful tradition. Dinner for two, with wine (wines are only slightly marked up, as George likes to encourage customers to enjoy wine with their food), will run about $70.

9/20
Garvin's
19 Waverly Pl.
(Broadway)
473-5261
Lunch daily 11:30 A.M. to 3:30 P.M.; dinner Mon. and Tues. 5:00 P.M. to 11:00 P.M., Wed. and Thurs. to 11:30 P.M., Fri. and Sat. to midnight
AE, MC, V
Continental

The handsome 1900s decor, the comfortable bar, the well-dressed uptown crowd and the excellent wines by the glass might seduce you into thinking Garvin's is a good restaurant. True, it's a pretty place with very good service; but the food is singularly lacking. If you must eat here, stick to the clams, oysters, salads and hamburgers. The soggy seafood linguine has a tasteless tomato sauce, veal française is tough and dry, and the steaks are often overcooked. The simpler dishes (also the best) can be ordered at the bar, making Garvin's a good place for a late snack. Expect to spend $68 for dinner for two, with an excellent, reasonably priced California wine (the Iron Horse Chardonnay is outstanding).

15
La Gauloise
502 Sixth Ave.
(13th St.)
691-1363
Lunch daily noon to 3:00 P.M.; dinner nightly 5:45 P.M. to 11:30 P.M.
All major credit cards
French (classical)

Because there are so many opportunities to eat abominably in Greenwich Village at any of the chic brasseries that more or less resemble this one, you may be hesitant to open the door to La Gauloise. But this lovely place escapes that sad fatality (pretty decor equals bad cuisine), and you will find in this charming restaurant, decorated with art deco lamps and mahogany mirrors, meals of an exemplary honesty and regularity. Jacques Allimann and Camille Dulac, the two French associates who alternate duties here morning and night, have given a new impetus to their menu to keep up with the times, but they haven't jeopardized the quality of true bistro fare devoted to onion soup, mussels ravigote, grilled chicken, choucroute (on Wednesdays) and entrecôte béarnaise. These classics are enriched with new dishes that are more intricate but that do not make concessions to either the eccentricities or the pretensions of fashionable cuisine today. The products are of the highest quality, and it is not often you'll find, even in Paris, a little place equivalent to this that serves a saddle of veal as juicy and tender, a stuffed rabbit with cream as flavorful or sweetbreads with endives as full of finesse. And you musn't forget the excellent pâtés offered as hors d'oeuvres, nor the outstanding fruit tarts, marquise au chocolat or bombe pralinée. Count on about $40 to $50 per person, with the house wine or, even better, the California Vichon Chardonnay.

12/20
Horn of Plenty
91 Charles St.
(Bleecker St.)
242-0636
Dinner nightly 6:00 P.M. to 12:30 A.M. (Sun. to 11:30 P.M.)
All major credit cards
American (regional)

This Greenwich Village restaurant/bar/nightclub features one of the city's most popular garden restaurants. The setting is pleasant and lush, complete with a refreshing fountain, but it suggests a poor man's Kon Tiki room. This is a restaurant with an identity crisis, despite the staff of cheerful, efficient Broadway hopefuls. An evening's menu may feature attempts at steak house fare, nouvelle American cuisine, French/Continental and soul food. You can't please all the people all the time—so to please yourself, stick to any one of the good, honest soul food specialties, such as Cajun crab and eggplant, barbecued spareribs ("hot" it's not), pork chitlings and pan-fried chicken, all served with candied yams and collard greens. It all makes for an animated evening, but the crowds in the restaurant probably can't compare to the traffic at the service entrance, delivering what we can only assume to be the prepared salad dressings, the white cake mix for the corn bread, the breaded and frozen fish for the catch of the day and the canned fruit for the cobblers. About $25 to $30 per person, with one of the moderately priced table wines.

11/20
Janice's Fish Place
570 Hudson St.
(11th St.)
243-4212
Dinner nightly 6:00 P.M. to 11:00 P.M. (Fri. and Sat. to midnight)
All major credit cards
American (seafood)

Janice's Fish Place (formerly called Fish Place) has changed a bit since our last review. For one thing, not just Villagers dine here anymore; word has spread, and the place is usually crowded with New Yorkers from all over. It's refreshing to be brought a plate of crudités with a good sour cream dip when you are seated; they serve admirably as an hors d'oeuvre. Consider skipping the appetizers (though the littleneck clams are excellent), only because the entrees are so huge. The food here is still good, but we have taken away one point because the simplicity that was so endearing is now missing. The salmon steak, for instance, would be perfectly good plain, but here it arrives covered with mushrooms and sauce that are more a detraction than an asset. The swordfish teriyaki is tasty but unnecessarily buried in snow peas and peppers. It's still a friendly and reasonably priced restaurant, and we hope to be able to upgrade Janice's in our next edition if it gets the message that there is nothing wrong with simplicity. About $22 per person, without wine.

11/20
K.O.'s
99 Bank St.
(Greenwich St.)
243-0561
Dinner Tues. to Sun. 6:00 P.M. to 10:30 P.M. (Fri. and Sat. to 11:30 P.M.)
AE, MC, V
American

This is a smart, informal establishment—clean lines, floor-to-ceiling windows, light woods, brass railings and a small bar—catering to West Villagers and their friends. The menu is short (steaks, chops, grilled fish, with a touch of the Orient in one or two sauced dishes), and the service is amiable. If you are not counting on a memorable gastronomic experience, you surely can spend an enjoyable evening in these pleasant surroundings. About $30 per person, with wine.

11/20
Marylou's
21 W. 9th St.
533-0012
Lunch Mon. to Fri. 11:30 A.M. to 3:30 P.M.; dinner nightly 5:30 P.M. to 11:00 P.M. (Fri. and Sat. to 2:00 A.M., Sun to 10:00 P.M.); brunch Sun. 11:00 A.M. to 4:00 P.M.
All major credit cards
American (seafood)

The lower level of a lovely Village brownstone provides the space for this popular restaurant, and a successful seafood market, also owned by restaurant owner Marylou Baretta, provides the source of supply for the predominately seafood menu. The decor of the three dining rooms and bar is eclectic (to say the least), the noise level nearly unbearable and the service rarely attentive. Perhaps most disappointing of all is that some of the seafood recently showed evidence of having been frozen, appearing at the table looking for all the world like a sloppy blue-plate special. Fresh, seasonal fish simply prepared, such as soft-shell crabs and coho salmon, are good choices, but overseasoned, oversauced specials such as turbot with dill sauce are disappointing. Somewhat misplaced on a menu that features sole amandine are sea bass Thai style, roast duck, filet mignon and Dover sole in chicken pot pie. Also misplaced is the pastry chef, who poorly executes such desserts as lemon mousse, pecan roll and rice pudding. Dinner for two, with wine, will run $70 to $75.

12/20
La Metairie
189 W. 10th St.
989-0343
Dinner nightly 6:00 P.M. to 11:00 P.M.
MC, V
French
(classical/provincial)

Yes, that's Craig Claiborne in the corner devouring with enthusiasm a plate of steaming couscous. He likes hot harissa, and it's just spicy enough here. This is New York's most authentic couscous, and people are drawn to it from all over the city. But this tiny Village landmark (seating only 22) also serves other good dishes, some with a hint of the Belgian cooking that once characterized the kitchen, such as the excellent salad liegoise with a warm dressing incorporating bits of onion and bacon. Other dishes are influenced by nouvelle: a feuilleté of prosciutto and leeks in a cream sauce, a fish terrine, an unsuccessful lotte or turbot poached in an orange and cream reduction, grilled salmon with chives. On the other hand, you can order perfectly acceptable traditional dishes, such as poulet Vallée d'Auge, coquilles Saint-Jacques provençale or canard rôti au poivre vert. Desserts are pedestrian (mousse, crème caramel, bombe pralinée) because, according to Sylvain Fareri, the affable proprietor, there isn't room to prepare or to store something more interesting! There's a good wine list for such a small place. About $35 per person, with wine.

12/20
Il Mulino
86 W. 3rd St.
(Bleecker St.)
673-3783
Lunch Mon. to Fri. noon to 2:30 P.M.; dinner Mon. to Sat. 5:00 P.M. to 11:15 P.M.
AE
Italian

Behind the lace curtains at 86 West 3rd Street, a pleasant surprise awaits you—an oasis of civility secreted amid the carnival of pizzas, heros and Italian ices south of Washington Square. For some strange reason this area is popular with tourists, although the real charm of the Village is further west, where you will find lovely eighteenth-century and Federalist-period townhouses.

Il Mulino is filled with plants and tables at which you'll find immaculate linens, glistening stemware and seemingly happy, gregarious diners. The papardelle (large egg noodles) with tomato and basil are of good texture and are served with a captivating sauce, the tiny soft-shell crabs are carefully sautéed and are excellent, and the veal piccata is quite acceptable, although we suspect that the animal from which it was taken was not on a liquid diet when it drew its last breath. The dessert of fresh fruit is refreshing and obviously only recently prepared, and the espresso (the filter pot is kept warm for a second cup on a réchaud on the table) is strong and full of flavor. This is a lovely place to hide from the tourist hordes, and you'll eat well. About $25 per person, with a Pinot Grigio.

11/20
The Old Homestead
56 Ninth Ave.
(14th–15th sts.)
242-9040
Lunch Mon. to Fri. 11:00 A.M. to 3:00 P.M.; dinner nightly 6:00 P.M. to 10:45 P.M. (Sat. to 11:45 P.M.)
All major credit cards
American (steaks)

The Old Homestead claims to be New York's oldest steak house. It's located in the wholesale meat district, and its indisputable claim to fame must be the nearly life-size steer that is perched on the roof over the entrance and painted with the declaration "We're tops in beef." The statue is a monument to the ambience inside: mounted moose heads, cuckoo clocks, gold leafed mirrors, a collection of beer steins and chandeliers. The bar is crowded with men whose jackets never match their pants and entire families waiting to stuff themselves. If you're there later in the evening, you'll have the pleasure of hearing the pounding percussions of various rock groups who rehearse upstairs.

The emphasis is on quantity rather than quality. Surely, the sheer portions are another claim to fame. Appetizers, such as herring in sour cream and stuffed clams, are reasonable in quantity, while servings of prime rib au jus, sirloin steak and whole lobsters are obscene. Preparation of the "tops in beef" is adequate but secondary to the magnitude. We were advised by our waiter not to order the complete menu, as we'd never make it through until the end, a dubious goal of strawberry cheesecake or chocolate fudge cake, among other things. Count on about $60 for two; that will get you all you can eat and so much more, plus wine.

12/20
One Fifth
1 Fifth Ave.
(8th St.)
260-3434
Lunch and dinner daily noon to 2:30 A.M.
All major credit cards
American

The boat decor is still intact, looking something like a cross between a white tiled kitchen and one of the original New York subway stations. The serving staff is outfitted in black vested bistro garb, and an overdressed maître d' flutters around in a morning suit. The restaurant is fairly quiet, since most of the action here is at the bar, where a string of pianists entertains a lively crowd. The menu has changed to update One Fifth's cuisine in a nouvelle direction, and the well-written menu sounds enticing: sautéed scallops on julienne vegetables, duck liver flan with marinated artichokes, smoked chicken with apples and arugula, breast of duck with pear vinaigrette, grilled tuna with braised fennel and roast loin of pork with chestnut sauce. The results are not bad. Duck with gooseberries is well prepared, and rack of lamb is tender and perfectly cooked, as is red snapper with enoki mushrooms. Desserts, on the other hand, are weak. This is a place to come with friends for a good time; if you don't expect any culinary discoveries, you won't be disappointed. About $30 per person, with wine.

12/20
One if by Land, Two if by Sea
19 Barrow St.
(Seventh Avenue South)
255-8649
Daily 6:00 P.M. to 11:00 P.M.
All major credit cards
American/Continental

This marvelous place will probably win our "Most Romantic Restaurant in New York Award" with little competition. You will instantly fall in love with this former coach house (once owned and reportedly haunted by Aaron Burr) with brick walls, Colonial brass chandeliers and wall sconces, a marvelous long bar, beautiful bouquets of silk flowers, naïf wall paintings depicting Americana, a crackling fire in the winter, a two-tier dining room and a cheery ambience created by a pianist who keeps things lively at night. Everything here is conducive to intimacy, contentment and all the possibilities that a new (or old) romance offers. As for the food: Well, the food is an accessory to the atmosphere, certainly not the focal point. Choose a nice bottle of Montrachet or, even better, the excellent Lambert Bridge Chardonnay, and settle in with the uninspired but safe American cuisine. You won't be disappointed (nor will you leap for joy) with the chilled shrimp cocktail, homemade pâté, simple but well-dressed salads, oversauced medallions of veal with reconstituted morels, steak with herb butter, red snapper with hollandaise, duckling à l'orange or sautéed shrimp. Things look up with the excellent rack of lamb and the perfectly cooked al dente vegetables that accompany main courses; the desserts are less memorable. Everyone looks pleased with themselves after a dinner here as they strike out via taxi to their Upper East Side homes. About $50 per person, with wine.

10/20
Le Paris Bistro
48 Barrow St. (7th Avenue South) 989-5460
Dinner nightly 6:00 P.M. to 11:30 P.M. (Sun. 5:00 P.M. to 10:30 P.M.)
All major credit cards
French (provincial)

We had high hopes for this converted brownstone: a nice, Parisian-style bistro in the Village. Mais non—at least not a good one. Our spirits (and stomachs) fell as we passed from an attractive front dining room through the kitchen into a less than charming garden. When a kitchen has something to be proud of, being visible can add an interesting dimension to dining—but in this case, we lost our appetites.

The simple, freshly prepared dishes are good, such as potato salad, Jersey tomatoes with smoked mozzarella and sautéed calf's liver. Others, such as pâté, cold bisque, fillet of sole meunière and chicken sautéed au pistou, taste old or frozen and are weak attempts at simple French food. Desserts from Chelsea Bakery were wonderful in their day but were not when they were presented to us. Service is a loose term when discussing the waiters—perhaps the food becomes stale before they can manage to get it to the table. About $70 for dinner for two, with wine.

14 ♙
Le Petit Robert
314 W. 11th St. 691-5311
Dinner nightly 6:00 P.M. to 11:00 P.M. (Fri. and Sat. to 11:30 P.M., Sun. to 10:00 P.M.)
AE
French (provincial/ nouvelle)

This lovely little white-on-white restaurant with gazebo detailing and golden light is a small island of civility floating in the middle of the Village street scene. Little Robert himself has left, but his one-time partner, owner-Chef James Peterson, does quite a good job with a cuisine that hovers somewhere between nouvelle and classic, all with a personal touch. The charming host will introduce you to such interesting possibilities as mussel soup with tomato and saffron, a very rich Madeira-ed chicken liver mousse, excellent sautéed wild mushrooms on a bed of greens and exquisite bonsai-size soft-shell crabs served with a good hollandaise and an equally good leek sauce. Entrees are simple, to the point and well prepared. There is an absolutely fabulous grilled tuna that's just the Western side of sashimi, served with a garlicky rouille. There is an equally wonderful cold grilled lamb with a stunningly simple presentation and perfect flavor. The filet mignon with a dense mushroom sauce spiked with Marc de Bourgogne is a bit heavy and the noisettes of veal with peppers a trifle boring. Vegetables are served family style, and the thinly sliced gratinéed potatoes are delicious. Desserts are a major disappointment after the finesse of the starters and entrees. The chocolate cake is banal, and the baba looks like a sad, oversize sponge (and doesn't taste much better), although there is a pleasant ginger pot de crème. The wine list is filled with French selections for very reasonable prices, particularly the Rully white Burgundy. There is a $25 prix fixe meal or the slightly more expensive à la carte route if you submit to some of the extras. This is a civilized surprise, and although we can't promise happiness, you will certainly feel content after spending a quiet evening chez Robert.

11/20
Pirandello
7 Washington Pl.
(Mercer St.)
260-3066
Dinner Mon. to Sat. 5:30 P.M. to 11:00 P.M. (Fri. and Sat. to 11:30 P.M.)
AE
Italian

In the works of Luigi Pirandello, who gave—in spite of himself—his name to this very popular restaurant, you never know where the truth hides. After a single meal in this restaurant, which is uncomfortable and unbelievably noisy, we have cautiously decided to keep from deciding whether the cuisine is worth the compliments others give it, or whether it deserves the criticisms we are tempted to crush it with. If the pasta Alfredo was correct, the pasta with clams was banal, not to say a nothing, the cold antipastos so-so, the bass livornese much overcooked and the veal with artichokes equally overdone and suffering visibly in a white sauce that was as sticky as glue. Finally, the best moment of the meal, other than a look at the chic restaurant-boutique decor and the Village clients who are always so amusing, was a very good apple walnut tart and an excellent espresso, brought to us with a smile because the service is so nice. We will come here another time to see if the zuppe di pesce "tutto mare" and the scampi alla spumante, which have received such flattering commentaries, are capable of making us change our minds. About $30 per person, with wine.

14
La Ripaille
605 Hudson St.
(12th St.)
255-4406
Dinner Mon. to Sat. 5:30 P.M. to 11:30 P.M.
AE, MC, V

West Village intellectuals who read the *Voice* and listen to WQXR know a good restaurant when they find one, and they are not apt to let their uptown friends in on the secret. But we have no such compunctions: There's an absolutely enchanting little French restaurant (45 seats) where the price is right and the food quite exceptional.

French (nouvelle)

The French name La Ripaille means a festive occasion when one dines sumptuously and well. This place is well named. Behind an unremarkable exterior, you'll find a tiny bar built on wine casks, bare brick and stucco walls, graceful vases of fresh flowers, an ancient grandfather clock, a well-executed reproduction of a medieval tapestry and huge cross-beams overhead—in a word, tasteful. All of this was accomplished by brothers Patrick and Alain Laurent, who provide a friendly welcome and attentive service. Patrick's wife, Theresa, supervises the kitchen. There's a touch of nouvelle in the cuisine, but the good lady is not afraid to use a little flour or arrowroot, as her mother taught her, to give body to her sauces. The menu changes weekly; among the appetizers, the mousses of broccoli or fish are particularly light and appealing. Care in preparation continues through the main courses, whether duck (slices of the breast with an exquisite, slightly sweet fig sauce), lamb (chops nicely perfumed with herbs) or fish (perfectly poached with vegetable purées or wine reductions). If you are a chocolate addict (most New Yorkers seem to be), you'll appreciate the white chocolate mousse with a crème anglaise. On the other hand, if the secret gets out before you read this, you may not be able to try it. So by all means call ahead for a reservation. About $30 per person, with a modest Coteaux du Tricastin.

11/20
Ristorante Ponte Vecchio
206 Thompson St. (Bleecker St.) 473-9382
Dinner Mon. to Sat. 5:00 P.M. to 11:00 P.M., Sun 3:00 P.M. to 10:00 P.M.
AE
Italian

Some evenings there is as much Italian spoken around the tables as English, but these visitors from overseas don't come because they expect the best food in town or food as good as they are used to at home. They come because this is such a friendly place and there is just enough in the unpretentious decor (Leonardo prints, white stucco arches) to make them feel comfortable. The menu is standard New York Italian (north and south): cannelloni, linguine, manicotti and chicken and veal parmigiana. Some daily specials are more interesting. The gnocchi could be lighter, although the pesto is everything it should be. Appetizers of stuffed mushrooms with a cream sauce and stuffed eggplant with a tomato dressing are acceptable, though underseasoned for our taste; the medley of seafood is quite good. All in all, we suspect the chef is not sure whether he is to cook Neapolitan or Milanese, and that if he made up his mind to stick with the former the proportion of Italian to English around the tables would be even greater. But whether the chef takes our advice or not, we hope he continues to make the espresso the same way—it is one of the best in town. About $30 per person, with wine.

15

Sabor
20 Cornelia St.
243-9579
Dinner nightly 6:00 P.M. to 11:00
P.M. (Fri. and Sat. to midnight)
AE, MC, V
Cuban

You will most assuredly leave this unprepossessing little place with a smile on your face and a good memory of simple cuisine that is sincerely and honestly prepared. The narrow dining room lacks any distinctive charm, but the Cuban music and exotic drinks will no doubt get you into the proper spirit. Ask your waiter for guidance; you won't be led astray with suggestions for starting with a zesty marinated calamari salad, excellent empanadas filled with spicy chorizo or a fabulous white bean soup. Entrees are equally delicious and imaginative. Try the exquisite red snapper with its marvelous pungent green sauce of parsley, garlic and lime juice; nor will you regret trying the shrimp in lime sauce, the impressive baked chicken scented with cumin, the chilled marinated fish, the spicy roast stuffed with chorizo, olives, raisins and prunes, in a surprising sauce of puréed vegetables, sherry and orange, and the chicken in prune sauce seasoned with curry. As wonderful as these taste treats are, save room for the ethereal baked coconut dessert with cinnamon and sherry, served warm with a dollop of whipped cream—it is sheer perfection. Sabor is clearly one of the best little restaurants in New York, and it's worth a visit to the Village to sample this inventive cuisine. About $30 per person, with wine.

14

Texarkana
64 W. 10th St.
254-5800
Dinner nightly 6:00 P.M. to 4:00
A.M. (Sun. and Mon. to midnight);
brunch Sun. noon to 4:00 P.M.
AE
American (regional)

If you've had enough of cream sauces, shiitakes and ravioli stuffed with air currents, then go to Texarkana to find the simple and even unpolished tastes of real food. Abe de la Houssaye dedicates his restaurant, noisy and full of life, to the cuisine of the Gulf Coast. Under the ceiling fans and in front of the brick fireplace and brass of this adobe-walled place with an open balcony, nice, inexperienced young people serve you dishes that are solid and steady but that also have a certain finesse. Sure, not everything is perfect: crawfish bisque with onion is well done but so spicy it leaves you breathless, and whitefish accompanied with okra and peppers has so little taste you'd think it was raised in Central Park. On the other hand, fresh shrimp sautéed with lemon, garlic and scallions is delicious, fried okra is a marvel, catfish with tartar sauce is good, barbecued tenderloin is juicy and remarkably cooked, and if you order the pig and eat only the crackling skin (the meat is scarce and fatty), you will regale yourself. Everyone is stealing Paul Prudhomme's blackened redfish, and Texarkana makes it just as crisp and spicy as it is in New Orleans. Other unusual choices include barbecued venison, hot chili steak and foie gras from upstate New York. Approach carefully the insipid whipped cream that weighs down an otherwise good bittersweet chocolate cake; even better, end with black-bottom pie or robust pecan pie. You'll have to wait for them to serve you your bottle of Jordan Cabernet Sauvignon, which unfortunately arrives at the temperature of purgatory. About $30 per person, with wine.

17

La Tulipe
104 W. 13th St.
691-8860
Dinner Tues. to Sun. 6:30 P.M. to 10:00 P.M.
All major credit cards
American

It has been several years since we discovered a marvelous woman in Paris who, after having spent ages in the kitchen for her husband and children, opened a little restaurant on the Rive Gauche where the dishes that change daily had the incomparable flavor of home cooking. We wrote so many good things about her that soon there was a line at her door, and that was a catastrophe. Tante Madée, as the place is still named, wanted to prepare everything herself, always at the last minute. Each meal would go on as long as a Wagnerian opera, and her clients would leave furious.

If she doesn't watch out, Sally Darr, owner and chef of La Tulipe, a simple, charming restaurant with mirrors and Belle Epoque lamps, will come to the same end as our dear Tante Madée. Formerly in test kitchens at Time-Life and food editor at *Gourmet,* Sally is also a perfectionist, but she's poorly organized and incapable of serving you a meal at normal speed. It is important to be perfectly exact, but only up to a point. Michel Guérard, Roger Vergé, Andre Soltner and Freddy Girardet do most of their cooking at the last minute, but they don't make you wait 45 minutes between courses. The explanation? They are organized and properly assisted. At La Tulipe, there are only three people in the kitchen to serve two seatings of nearly 40 covers each. Sally had better revamp her system, or she is going to be faced with some serious problems.

All of this leaves us unhappy, because since the first meal we ate here four years ago, we found an exceptional talent, nearly equal to Alice Waters in Berkeley. Sally gives everything she touches an air of grace and an irresistible naturalness, as charming as a springtime bouquet. Her prix fixe menu at $45 is not very long, but each dish will send you immediately to the angels. There isn't another place in New York where one can eat the same gratin of eggplant and tomatoes, salad of warm shrimp with ginger and green onions (one word: the lettuce leaves in this dish are useless), sliced grilled squab with couscous and spinach, rack of lamb with mustard butter, red snapper cooked in paper or even the onion rings accompanying the steak marchand de vin that approaches perfection in its simplicity. But Sally and her charming waitresses take so long to bring you these jewels that you will have already finished your bottle of Côtes de Beaune (at $20) or your Marques de Carceres '79 (at $19). The exquisite desserts make the end of the meal equally memorable, mollifying slightly the interminable wait: apricot soufflé, crème brûlée and the fabulous layered chocolate cake with chocolate tiles are our favorites.

Perhaps we are playing a bad trick on Sally by giving her three toques. But it is possible that, to the contrary, we will incite this terribly obstinate and stubborn lady to react and put her kitchen in order. When we left after a recent meal, we spoke with her charming husband, who powerlessly watched over this marathon of slowness. We said, "Give our felicitations to Sally but tell her, at the same time, she is overindulgently excessive." He responded, as dignified as a fine diplomat, "It would be more appropriate if you told her yourself." As you see, we've done just that.

13 ♟
24 Fifth
24 Fifth Ave.
475-0880
Lunch and dinner daily 11:00 A.M. to 11:00 P.M. (Sun to 10:30 P.M.)
All major credit cards
French (nouvelle)

Talent is like everything else; you musn't abuse it. A painter, an architect and a cook understand their art when they know at what precise moment they should stop elaborating on their work. To go beyond this is to achieve excess and eventual error. The young Michel Fitoussi, in spite of his gifts and clear professionalism, did not always succeed in escaping this trap when he was in charge of the kitchens of the extravagant Palace. He did too much and doted too much over the special-effects presentations that gave his dishes, which otherwise would have been exceptional, a nouveau riche look.

He is now installed in this restaurant of a totally different style, which is actually more seductive, with its discreet art deco decor, rose-beige tones and furiously "in" clientele. He changed his style but, unhappily, didn't correct all of his mistakes. In his attempt to be modern and fashionable, he makes taste mistakes that are quite regrettable: for example, when he serves you large cactus leaves that are far too thick in a red wine sauce of shallots and tomato (green peppers would be infinitely better); or when he adds wine to an undercooked cream of morels; or when he serves the same vegetable garnish (with green beans so raw they are inedible) with three different dishes—not to mention a really stupid dish composed of kohlrabi without any taste, fresh figs and green peas. And what need is there to bury an exquisite chocolate cake under a mountain of Chantilly cream and fresh raspberries?

If by multiplying these unnatural marriages, Michel

believes he is creating nouvelle cuisine, he has been temporarily blinded. The result is that he gives nouvelle a bad character. And this is so sad, because he is an enthusiastic and charming young man who is full of talent, which he proved to us at earlier meals: a delicious salmon with beurre rouge and cucumbers, a marvelous veal chop napped with a delicate mushroom cream sauce and a simple but savory rack of lamb with herbs. Perhaps a little session with Girardet, Guérard or Alice Waters would help him recall that the secret of good cuisine resides in purity of tastes, not in the triumphal welcome that New York gives almost automatically to this chic restaurant. He knows that if we didn't have the highest esteem for him, we wouldn't take the trouble to tell him all of this. About $45 per person, with wine.

10/20
The Ukrainian Restaurant
140 Second Ave. (8th–9th sts.)
533-6765
Lunch and dinner daily noon to 11:00 P.M. (Fri. and Sat. to midnight)
No credit cards
Russian

Nothing has changed here since our last review except the food; fortunately, it is better. The challah bread is certainly worth a mention, as it's delicious. Hot borscht remains good, although the sour cream we requested at a recent meal never arrived. The real sleeper here is the shrimp cocktail. Ordered on a pure whim, the shellfish is tender and fresh, in a spicy horseradish sauce. Even the cabbage pirogis, formerly very nasty indeed, are enjoyable, and the stuffed cabbage is cooked just right, with a real tomato zing. Brightening our evening was the herd of stamping elephants overhead, which upon investigation turned out to be a wedding party dancing their hokeypokey hearts out. The Ukrainian cocktails help you ignore the phlegmatic service. Prices haven't changed here in two years, so even the bill (about $35 for two) will not dampen your spirits.

13
Vanessa
289 Bleecker St. (Seventh Avenue South)
243-4225
Dinner nightly 6:00 P.M. to 11:30 P.M. (Fri. and Sat. to midnight)
All major credit cards
American

Piped-in jazz only improves the ambience of this charming place, with a turn-of-the-century decor and sweet floral arrangements. Vanessa proved immediately popular, owing no doubt to the restauranting skills of owner Bobby Shapiro (whose other ventures include Uzies and Hoexter's Market) and the impressive culinary talents of Ann Rosenzweig. She developed an intelligent, original, nouvelle-style menu, but has now left the kitchen in the hands of her apprentices, and the cooking has suffered for it. While starters and desserts are exceptionally good, the entrees are disappointing. Perhaps ordering two starters is the way to eat well here. The seafood flan is noteworthy, as is the fennel-flavored pasta with everyone's favorite friend, California goat's cheese. The shrimp and scallop mousse in an intense lobster sauce is light and full of flavor; lobster bisque is all it should be. But the middle of the meal falls short of the mark: duck with cassis is tough, stuffed lobster is a glorified version of deviled lobster, and the medallions of veal have that distinct waterlogged taste of less-than-excellent veal. Hurry on to the heavenly flourless chocolate cake, inspired crème brûlée and the ethereal dacquoise. About $40 per person, with wine.

11/20
Village Green
551 Hudson St.
(Charles St.)
255-1650
Dinner Tues. to Sat. 5:30 P.M. to 11:30 P.M.; brunch Sun. noon to 5:30 P.M.
AE, MC, V
Continental

This is still one of our favorite places for a drink, especially in the winter, with the snow falling outside, the pianist plucking your heartstrings and the lights twinkling in the plants. If the cooking continues to improve, as it has since we were last here, it may also become a good place to dine. Perhaps it is because we took care to avoid everything we had ever tried before or because we were expecting so little that we were pleasantly surprised. Cheese ravioli with a sausage sauce is an interesting combination; the ravioli itself is banal, but with the sausage sauce, voilà—you have a good marriage (though one not necessarily made in heaven). Shrimp rémoulade is fresh, but just plain boring. A small green salad arrives between courses and, as far as we're concerned, is the best part of the meal. Crab imperial is only so-so (even though the waiter proudly informed us at our most recent meal that he had cooked it himself), but the loin of lamb in cucumber and mint sauce is good. Hot crème brûlée is a taste treat, the only one we can recommend from the dessert list. All in all, we would term this a fairly good dining experience if it were only less expensive. As it is, prices are pretentious: expect to pay around $100 for two, with one of the least expensive wines. We love the atmosphere but resist paying so highly for it—come for just a drink, and you'll leave less impoverished.

11/20
Ye Waverly Inn
16 Bank St.
(Waverly Pl.)
929-4377
Lunch Mon. to Fri. 11:45 A.M. to 2:00 P.M.; dinner nightly 5:15 P.M. to 10:00 P.M. (Fri. and Sat. to 11:15 P.M.); brunch Sun. noon to 3:30 P.M.
All major credit cards
American (regional)

This nineteenth-century tavern in Greenwich Village serves pleasant, simple American food in an atmosphere of the same persuasion, complete with working fireplaces in the winter and a small, open terrace in the summer. Perhaps the kitchen takes its cue from the decor. Its best efforts are slices of Americana: Southern fried chicken, apple fritters with bacon and maple syrup, chicken pot pie, barbecued ribs, rice pudding, pecan pie and fresh fruit cobblers. The prices seem slightly antique as well: Sunday brunch is $6.95 per person, and dinner for two, with wine, will run about $35 to $40.

12/20

Z

117 E. 15th St.
254-0960
Lunch and dinner Mon. to Fri.
11:30 A.M. to 11:00 P.M., Sat. from
1:00 P.M.
AE
Greek

Z has much to recommend it. It's an attractive place: a series of cheery, white-walled rooms decorated with colorful Greek rugs and folk art. While bouzouki music plays unobtrusively in the background, Greek families and young couples from the Village enjoy authentic cooking and good Greek wines, all at very low prices. All the classics are here, and most everything is good: saganaki (kefalotyri cheese cooked in butter and lemon) or spanakopita (spinach and feta in a crisp crust) to start, and such entrees as lamb yuvestsi (baked lamb and tomato sauce on a bed of Greek pasta), delicious, aromatic souvlaki, Greek-style fried squid and a beautiful moussaka that is smooth but a bit bland. The baklava is respectable, and there are some delicious, unusual Greek wines (try the retsina, a white wine aged with resin). A meal will run $35 for two, with wine.

11/20

Zinno

126 W. 13th St.
924-5182
Lunch Mon. to Fri. noon to 2:30
P.M.; dinner nightly 5:30 P.M. to
11:30 P.M. (Sun. to 10:30 P.M.)
AE, V
Italian

Yet another variation on the chic Italian restaurant theme, Zinno holds its own with nicely prepared food, an attractive and open atmosphere complete with piano bar and the style and sophistication unique to Greenwich Village. The menu features additions to the standard steamed mussels, pasta primavera and zuppe di pesce, with the likes of superb fried zucchini, good tortellini in brodo and hearty chicken and sausage contadina. Several other veal (scaloppine and otherwise) and seafood entrees round out the menu, as do a number of well-chosen Italian wines. This establishment will appeal even to those who think they don't like Italian food. Dinner for two, with wine, will run about $60.

West 18th to 42nd Streets

13

Bistro Bordeaux

407 Eighth Ave.
(30th St.)
594-6305
Lunch Mon. to Fri. noon to 3:00

This unpretentious place is located in a questionable neighborhood, but fear not—there is a handsome suit of armor at Bistro Bordeaux to help you negotiate Eighth Avenue. Surprisingly enough (surprising because the immediate area is a culinary wasteland, with delis and coffee shops catering to the Madison Square Garden

51

P.M.; dinner nightly 5:00 P.M. to 10:30 P.M. (Sun. to 10:00 P.M.)
All major credit cards
French (classical)

crowd), you can get some very good and very honest bistro fare here, served by pleasant young Frenchmen who do their best to accommodate your requests. The wine list is infinitesimal, but you'll find a Sancerre, a Chablis, a reasonably priced Montrachet (at $34) and some good red Bordeaux to accompany your grilled sole, paillard de boeuf, chicken with mustard, any of the steaks poivre, bordelaise or moutarde (if you request it specially) or excellent scallop of veal with a tasty herb sauce. Starters are basic: a good homemade pork pâté, smoked trout, vegetable terrine, escargots and a salade frisée aux lardons that is enhanced with additional oil and vinegar. Desserts will round out your evening: chocolate mousse, crème caramel, tarte tatin or a light apple charlotte that looks something akin to a slice of bread with a luscious crème anglaise. The coffee is good, the clientele rather down-home and the decor of beams and bricks virtually invisible. At $30 per person, with wine, you'll want to rush right over to Bistro Bordeaux, as we intend to do on our next dining marathon in New York.

11/20
Café Seiyoken
18 W. 18th St.
620-9010
Lunch Mon. to Fri. noon to 3:00 P.M.; dinner nightly 6:00 P.M. to midnight (Fri. and Sat. to 1:00 A.M., Sun. to 11:00 P.M.)
All major credit cards
Japanese/French

If you don't want to be deafened by this room, in which you couldn't even hear a squadron of kamikazes, stop at the sushi bar and ask for two pieces of sushi to put in your ears. We suspect the waiters at Café Seiyoken take this precaution, too, because when you call them they generally don't come, and if they do come it is to bring something other than what you ordered. In any event, the dishes they bring are so bizarre, you are given the impression that the menus of two restaurants—one French, the other Japanese—were mixed up by accident. But what you really have here is the practical application of a huge secret plan that will allow the Empire of the Rising Sun to assure itself of the total domination of worldwide gastronomy in several years. As it becomes increasingly difficult to openly impose a foreign influence abroad, the Japanese have decided to use the ultrasophisticated art of camouflage. The first stage has begun: you enter a French restaurant named Chez Tante Louise or La Tour Eiffel. There are views of Paris or Périgord on the walls, waiters wear Basque berets, and right away you're feeling confident. Whoops! The trap closes around you: the kitchen is two-faced. A Japanese spy concocts quenelles of lyonnaise pike with wasabi, coq au vin with shiitakes and cassoulet with tofu. Soon Italian, Indian and Chinese restaurants, even delis, will be disguises for Japanese enterprises. McDonald's, captured at last, will serve you hamburgers with octopus and soy pâté.

But it would be wrong not to take Café Seiyoken seriously. You must recognize that Toni Tokunaga is onto something exceptional. For years we have not seen in New York a decor so successful: large black columns with translucent tops diffuse the light, mirrors in geometric shapes make you think of Mondrian, and there are immense vases of flowers, blond wood paneling, a huge, furiously New Yorkese bar, a spectacular sushi bar with an active staff wearing traditional Japanese dress (in contrast to the aprons and bow ties of the young waiters, who look like students or unemployed comedians) and astonishing paintings, naïf yet ultrasophisticated, of a whale with the New York skyline in the distance; and all of it is bathed in the thundering music of Japanese-American rock. This is the prototype of a new race: the chic-chic, art deco, New York–Paris–Tokyo brasserie. All the formidable "in" people from the fashion, show-biz and advertising worlds who make and break reputations in New York are here, lending a minimum of attention to what one is served and a maximum of attention to watching one another.

The cuisine, in the dodecaphonic style, is an incredible mixed bag, where the worst is jumbled alongside the less good and even the best. The best is incontestably the sushi, served as an appetizer or main course, which is perfectly fresh and appetizing. Shrimp tempura in ginger sauce is equally excellent, and calamari "à la niçoise," so-called, are remarkably tender; these dishes prove that the Japanese haven't lost their mastery over the seas. All is spoiled, unhappily, with Japanese basil pasta; the chiso leaf and wild mushroom sauce has a good taste, but the pasta itself is terribly dry, and if its chef were in Italy he would be scorned by the entire neighborhood. Sliced beef with baby green onions in a teriyaki sauce has a supreme tastelessness, which the Japanese adore; the roast rack of lamb is submerged under rosemary; the suprème of chicken en croûte with Madeira sauce should be classified as an unidentifiable object; and strawberry cheesecake, sweetish and nauseating, should oblige the pastry chef to commit hara-kiri. So you can see that at Café Seiyoken one hasn't a second to be bored. Expect to pay about $25 to $40 per person, with wine (there is a small but acceptable list of French and American wines).

11/20
Cajun
**129 Eighth Ave.
(16th St.)
691-6174**
Lunch Mon. to Fri. noon to 3:00

"Attention Playboy Card Holders" is the sign that greets you at the door and sets the tone for your meal. The first impression is favorable—soft lighting and tables thoughtfully spaced—making it seem a nice oasis in Chelsea. Unfortunately, this feeling is fleeting, as lunch is

P.M.; dinner nightly 6:00 P.M. to 11:00 P.M. (Fri. and Sat. to 11:30 P.M., Sun. to 10:30 P.M.); brunch Sun. noon to 4:00 P.M. All major credit cards

Creole

14 👨‍🍳

Claire's

156 Seventh Ave. (19th–20th sts.) 255-1955

Lunch and dinner daily noon to 1:00 A.M. All major credit cards

American (seafood)

continually interrupted by loud knockings and buzzings at the back door, with delivery boys marching their cargo through the room and people wandering about, coats in hand, looking for a table. Efficient management is not a strong suit here.

But it's the desire for Creole cooking that draws people here, not the ambience. Jaundiced-looking coleslaw is surprisingly pleasant. Appetizers look quite unappetizing: oysters Rockefeller arrive with a snap, crackle and pop of steaming rock salt and look remarkably unappealing, although they taste better than they look. Garlic lovers adore the shrimp rémoulade. Cold boiled crab is good and spicy if you don't mind working hard for your meal. Creole bread pudding looks a bit like turkey stuffing, but try it anyway—the whiskey sauce is great. The margaritas are lovely, and the lawyerish-looking crowd seems to be happy. We might return sooner if something were done about the surly service. About $10 per person, without wine.

A relatively new offshoot of the Key West original, this elegant, spacious and laid-back place serves middling to excellent seafood prepared by Thai chefs. The decor is semitropical, with lots of green and white and a ceiling of whirring fans. "Waitpersons" in shirts by J.G. Hook and Lenny are both charming and quick. You'll be surrounded by hordes of fashionably attractive young men who appear to love gossiping and eyeing one another across the room. Long Island oysters are succulent, and home-cured gravlax has its creamy pink flesh rimmed with green dill. The famous New Orleans specialty, blackened redfish, charred in a cast-iron skillet with assorted peppers and spices, proves remarkably tasty under its crisp, dark crust—it's almost as good as Paul Prudhomme's. Our main grouses are the undercooked and tasteless vegetables—more a garnish than for eating—and the nasty little plastic cups of characterless white sauce that come with most of the cold dishes. Sweets are enormously fattening and quite superb. It's hard to choose between fresh Key lime pie, peach cobbler or the amazing Mississippi mud, a chocolate pudding bathed in whiskey sauce and crowned with whipped cream. Good, strong espresso or Celestial Seasons herb tea will pull you around afterward. About $30 per person, with wine.

12/20

Keens

72 W. 36th St. 947-3636

Lunch Mon. to Fri. 11:45 A.M. to

The proprietors, who also operate One Fifth Avenue, renovated these ancient premises in 1981 with good results. They rearranged the thousands of pieces of memorabilia—clay pipes, theater posters and programs,

4:00 P.M.; dinner Mon. to Sat. 5:00 P.M. to 11:00 P.M.
All major credit cards
American

photographs of royalty and otherwise, early American prints and paintings, and front pages of 1900s newspapers—giving this New York institution (founded in 1885) a brighter and seemingly more authentic turn-of-the-century air. There are numerous dining rooms, upstairs and down, where the pace is as leisurely as we imagine it was a hundred years ago. In the taproom at street level, on the other hand, you will find all the hustle and bustle of today's New York, particularly at midday and after five in the afternoon, when executives and hired hands from the Seventh Avenue garment district, Macy's and Gimbel's on Herald Square jostle one another for a place at the bar.

There are rarely enough patrons to fill all the dining rooms in the evening, which is just as well for those who choose to eat here: the kitchen staff is able to give great care and attention to grilling meats exactly as ordered, something we doubt would be possible if the kitchen had to serve a few hundred diners. But in any event, the mutton chop for which Keens has been known over the years truly is thick, juicy and flavorful, accompanied by its juice with just the right touch of mint. The steaks and rack of lamb are excellent, though the calf's liver is not nearly so good. We suggest you start with the wonderfully fresh oysters and clams, or the poached oysters in a cornmeal batter, not as bizarre as we first suspected they might be, with a mayonnaise-style dressing. After your main course, try the cheese tray, which is limited but good, particularly the perfectly ripe Stilton. Desserts include the usual cheesecake and some cakes and mousses that will be to the liking of New Yorkers addicted to sugary chocolate.

A banner headline on a turn-of-the-century newspaper hanging on the wall proclaims: "Man Commits Suicide to Keep Out of Jail." If the thought of putting an end to it all crosses your mind, please resist until you've visited the new old Keens. You can expect a pleasant and leisurely evening (the service is slow, even in view of the need to cook the meats to order), and it is not likely that you will soon forget the succulence of the mutton chops. About $35 per person, with wine.

13
Lavin's
23 W. 39th St.
921-1288
Lunch seatings Mon. to Fri. noon and 1:00 P.M.; dinner nightly 6:00 P.M. to midnight
All major credit cards
Continental

This attractive restaurant, with lace curtains, wood paneling, bentwood chairs and fresh roses on starched white table linens, welcomes you as you enter from a nondescript, deserted street. Once inside, you'll be tempted by the cruvinet-equipped wine bar, which has some very good selections, both American and European, offered in tiny tastes or in glasses as well as by the bottle. It's a good way to experience new wines without making a big investment. Once you sit down in the long, narrow room, you are confronted with a menu that is ambitious in its conception as well as its length. It changes every few months, to take advantage of fresh products and, no doubt, the chef's and Mr. Lavin's current whims. The prospects are engaging: sliced lamb with crushed peppercorns, capers and julienne vegetables; veal terrine with spinach; carpaccio with mushrooms, scallions, capers and Emmenthal; mussels provençale; duck with lemon. Certainly this is a broadly based repertoire that seems to be focused primarily on unusual combinations and obscure interpretations of nouvelle. Well, we think there may be a slight split-personality problem when in the same dinner we are served a delicate and exquisite-looking gravlax rolled around julienne vegetables, à la sushi, and a boned Cornish game hen spread-eagled onto an oversize plate surrounded with a mountain of delicious shoestring potatoes—on the one hand, elegance and understatement; on the other, something from a Falstaffian banquet. We would not make such a point if the quality of the food were superb. Alas, the game hen is indeed tender and good, but the marmalade-tasting sauce is overwhelmingly sweet. The grilled liver is impeccable, but it too is overrun by those potatoes, as are the mounds of lamb riblets that are tender and tasty, although a bit overshadowed by the sweetish marinade that reminds us of unsuccessful barbecue sauce. The tortellini gratinati is lovely, however, and the homemade veal sausage is quite flavorful, if somewhat dry. Desserts are a blessing: one of the best crème brûlées we have ever encountered, its crispy crust delicious, and a marvelous warm apple tart. The wine list is a delight for anyone in love with California wines, and the prices are actually reasonable. The Acacia Chardonnay and the superb Trefethen Cabernet Sauvignon will help make a perplexing dinner more enjoyable. We feel compelled to leave Mr. Lavin's toque in place but take away a point. He simply must do something about those presentations and the obsession with so many sweetish sauces. Choose wisely, and you will have a most enjoyable dinner here for about $35 per person, with wine.

13 ♟

The New York Restaurant School
27 W. 34th St.
947-7105

We have generally been suspicious of dining rooms in cooking schools. It tests first the students' knowledge and then the clients' patience when things go poorly. Not only does one have to deal with the sincere attempts of soon-to-be-graduating chefs, but the service, also performed by students, can be tentative at best. Happily,

*Lunch Mon. to Fri. noon to 3:00
P.M.; dinner Mon. to Fri. 5:30 P.M.
to 9:30 P.M.
All major credit cards*
American

these problems do not exist at the extremely attractive
New York Restaurant School, which rivals smaller,
professional restaurants in almost every way. The decor is
classic, simple and appealing, with rotating art
exhibitions and contemporary furnishings. The menu is
all-American, a fact that must thrill American food
journalists looking for further evidence of the new
American cuisine. There are a few dishes here whose time
has not yet come (notably the green pepper soup spiked
with jalapeño that would be better off as a dip for
nachos), but the creative attempt is to be commended.
You can have a most pleasant lunch of country pâté
(outstanding), grilled mussels with coriander and
scallions (sometimes lukewarm), Bibb lettuce with
mustard vinaigrette (refreshing) or roasted eggplant with
olive oil and thyme (a classic). Entrees are also well
conceived: a light omelet filled with chutney and country
ham, a New Englandesque brochette of tender swordfish
with large vegetable chunks, a tasty flank steak stir-fry or
a somewhat bland but good veal chop spiced with ginger.
Desserts are not the students' strong suit: although even a
fiercely loyal Southerner could not fault the rich and
delicious bourbon pecan pie, less interesting are the stiff
apricot bread pudding and the pear and port sherbet. The
chocolate chestnut cake, however, will not disappoint.
Three cheers for American classics, updated and made
more interesting by a touch of innovation and good taste.
Our only complaint is that there are not more American
wines to accompany this satisfying cuisine. About $25
per person for lunch; if you still have money to burn, stop
in at the gift store filled with irresistible kitchen
tools and gadgets.

10/20
Lou G. Siegel
**209 W. 38th St.
921-4433**
*Lunch and dinner Sun. to Fri. noon
to 9:00 P.M. (Fri. to 3:00 P.M.)
All major credit cards*
Central European
(kosher)

If you're looking for a 100 percent kosher meal, run right
over to Lou G. Siegel to join the business people who
meet here over sanctioned matzoh ball soup, meatballs
with noodles and peas, lamb chops and roast chicken.
This garment center institution has been turning out its
brand of Jewish-momma food (mushroom barley soup,
gefilte fish, deli platters) since 1917. Old-world tradition
is the rule here, and you may find that most everything is
overcooked and lacking in taste, though the salads are
passable, as is the fluffy kasha. All is prepared under the
watchful eye of the Union of Orthodox Jewish
Congregations of America. We are *still* waiting for this
venerable restaurant to reach its goal of being the pride
and joy of its ethnic roots. If only the kitchen would learn
to cook them better. About $10 to $15 per person for
lunch, without wine.

12/20
Supreme Macaroni
511 Ninth Ave. (38th St.)
244-9314
Lunch Mon. to Fri. noon to 3:00 P.M.; dinner Mon. to Sat. 5:00 P.M. to 11:00 P.M.
No credit cards
Italian

The history of New York's immigrant Italians lives on the walls of this old pasta shop and restaurant (also known as Guido's), in the photos of family and friends, from the present back to the earliest tintypes. Though this neighborhood of Italian groceries and fruit stands is rundown, it's not far from the Manhattan Plaza and its surrounding off-off-Broadway theaters, so in addition to Italian families and longtime regulars you'll see young actors, writers and theater people here enjoying the good, hearty, inexpensive food. It's always noisy, bustling and convivial (owing in part, no doubt, to the inexpensive Italian wines). There are no surprises on the menu, just well-prepared Italian standards: an honest antipasto, fettuccine with a light, delicious marinara sauce, linguine with shrimp and clams, admirable scampi, good (but too dry) chicken with mushrooms, and several veal offerings. You won't be overwhelmed, but you'll have a good dinner in a cheerful, old New York atmosphere. A meal for two will run $45, with wine.

12/20
Woods
148 W. 37th St.
564-7340
Lunch Mon. to Fri. 11:45 A.M. to 3:00 P.M.; dinner nightly 5:15 P.M. to 9:30 P.M.
All major credit cards
American

This stunning restaurant is an exercise in post-constructivist design. The starkness and simplicity of carmine reds, grays and industrial tones is brightened with pleasant color photography posters and softened with banners of packing blankets that cover the ducts on the ceiling. There are lots of mirrors to expand the narrow space and reflect the well-dressed clientele, many of whom hail from the garment center. The honest attempt at innovative cuisine may fall short of its mark, but at least it tries for something out of the ordinary. A basil and shallot custard with fresh tomato sauce and sliced lobster sounds like a catastrophe but proves to be a refreshing dish, particularly if you adore fresh basil. The buckwheat noodles with hot sesame sauce and peanuts are overcooked and sticky (delicate Oriental noodles would be more appropriate than the heavier buckwheat), although the sauce is excellent; the accompanying slices of avocado have absolutely nothing to do with the dish and are an oddity at best. The amateur who prepares these things is a composer; perhaps his music is a bit more refined than the cuisine. There are a handful of entrees: a grilled veal chop with fresh rosemary (for a whopping $26); steamed vegetables served hot or cold with tricky sauces, such as sherried soy or apple-lemon mayonnaise; cold poached salmon with crème fraîche; sautéed calf's liver with prosciutto and the ubiquitous shiitakes—an update on momma's liver and bacon that is good (but after the third slice of liver even Paul Bunyan would be full); and tender, tasty fillet of beef totally

All major credit cards
French (provincial)

order and return with the bottle and the menus. The food is acceptable but lacking the touch of finesse that characterizes this sunlight-filled cuisine. You will be happy, however, with a hearty cabbage soup (a bit generous with the potatoes) spiked with Roquefort, Bay scallops provençale served with their corals intact, marinated mushrooms or ratatouille. We recommend that you skip the eggplant filled with ricotta and spinach— it arrives as a cheesy mass, the delicate eggplant taste obliterated by the other ingredients. Entrees are pleasant: salmon with lemon cream, linguine with sun-roasted tomatoes, a good chicken with pesto cream (the sauce is a bit subtle), bass provençale that is incredibly salty (no matter how much we love Mediterranean black olives), roast duck with a black currant sauce and paillard of beef. Desserts are heaven-sent, especially the excellent blueberry flan with an angelically light crust. You will be sure of a pleasant evening here and will spend about $35 per person, with a nice Chablis Premier Cru.

12/20
Company
365 Third Ave.
(26th St.)
532-5222
Lunch Mon. to Fri. noon to 3:00 P.M.; dinner nightly 6:00 P.M. to 1:00 A.M. (Fri. and Sat. to 1:30 P.M.); brunch Sun. noon to 5:00 P.M.
All major credit cards
American

If Fellini were looking for a Manhattan movie set, this would be the place he'd choose. Disco music and pulsating lights in the bar and front dining area lead to a black-lacquered and mirror-lined room in the back. With man-eating flower arrangements and punked-out, space cadet waiters and waitresses in pink jumpsuits, the effect is reminiscent of an exclusive Parisian beauty salon. The clientele is mostly male and the food, as affected as the atmosphere, runs the spectrum from Jersey tomatoes with mozzarella and basil vinaigrette to sea scallops with orange butter and (unbelievably) kiwi. Perhaps the chef is also a space cadet just back from a voyage that took him far, far away. Do not—repeat, do not—go to Company from the suburbs to celebrate your 25th wedding anniversary. Dinner for two, with wine, will run about $55 to $60.

11/20
Francesca's
129½ E. 28th St.
685-0256
Lunch Mon. to Fri. noon to 3:00 P.M.; dinner Mon. to Sat. 6:00 P.M. to 11:00 P.M.
All major credit cards
Italian

You can't miss Francesca's exterior painted with cheerful naïf garden flowers. Once you step down into this little basement restaurant, the mood changes: it's an upgraded grotto with brick walls, a tin ceiling, fresh white linens and a small bar. This is a good place to come for a simple, home-cooked lunch, although it won't be prepared by Francesca, who will be at her home, cooking her own lunch. The basic cuisine is neither pretentious nor exciting, but it is satisfactory in an honest sort of way. Young men who look like they ought to be playing in a

New Wave band will bring you an excellent dish of sautéed mushrooms with tomato and onion (the mushrooms perfectly al dente), less interesting tortelloni with a too-creamy pesto sauce, a tasty veal rollatine with a mountain of freshly sliced mushrooms and pleasant sautéed sweetbreads with a cache of mushrooms (someone here seems to have a fixation). You can also choose from traditional eggplant, veal or chicken parmigiana, sautéed scallops, bluefish with ginger (perhaps from the Far Eastern shores of Italy), zuppe di pesce, calamari or a host of pastas. Lunch will run about $20 per person, without wine, and dinner slightly more.

14

Hubert's

102 E. 22nd St.

673-3711

Lunch Mon. to Fri noon to 2:30 P.M.; dinner Mon. to Sat. 6:00 P.M. to 10:30 P.M.

AE, MC, V

American

With its twenty little tables, highly varnished parquet floors, bentwood bistro chairs, almost naked walls and warm, romantic lighting, Hubert's is typical of the little restaurants that have flourished in the last decade in New York, Paris and London. These places are of the genre born when dozens of young amateurs believed it was enough to have a good recipe book and good intentions to be successful. Most of these men and women have disappeared without a trace, but some have become true professionals, still conserving a little touch of amateurism that doesn't lack charm. Karen Hubert and Len Allison are two examples of the latter, though when researching our New York guide two years ago, the cuisine first enchanted, then terribly disappointed us. But Len has returned to the ovens after a long absence, and Hubert's has recovered its grace, freshness and creativity. The choice is limited to a half dozen appetizers and seven or eight entrees, all changed daily. And though certain dishes are less inspired than others (we have had enough of raw fish and lamb salads), Len creates happiness with his chilled Russian cucumber soup, Long Island steamers with lemon grass, and tender sweetbreads with lemon in a fine cream sauce (accompanied, unhappily, by tasteless pasta and pretty but insipid carrots). The savory rack of lamb with herbs and lemon is married to perfection with eggplant, spinach and, above all, a fricassée of tomatoes that is certainly one of the successes of the house. The same tomatoes are served with excellent soft-shell crabs, whose finesse, unfortunately, is erased by the powerful taste of an excellently prepared chili sauce. Be that as it may, this cuisine has precise flavors and is lightened with a seductive touch of Provence—it's a style not unlike that of Alice Waters in Berkeley. This "sun cuisine" is better than the raw tuna and boring shiitakes that are invading America. We do wish that the desserts would have more personality and would not disappear under so much whipped cream. About $40 per person, with wine.

11/20
Joanna
18 E. 18th St.
675-7900
Lunch and dinner daily noon to 1:00
A.M. (Sun. to midnight)
All major credit cards
Continental

This is unquestionably the prettiest restaurant in New York: a belle Epoque decor with aqua-green walls, ivory trim, overgrown floral photo murals, vintage lighting, lace curtains, heaven-bound columns, brasserie partitions and a fashionable clientele to match. The noise level can be somewhat disturbing once things get going at night, but the ambience is lively and is designed to make the people who come here feel they are among the most "in" of trendy New York (Joanna's brother, Café Seiyoken down the street, is competing for the same crowd and is doing a brisk business). We love to come here to admire the decor, people watch and drink some wine. The cuisine, alas, is not quite as successful as the atmosphere, although there are a few bright spots. Starters are internationally eclectic: good old California potato skins, good old French-Japanese tuna tartare, good old Italian penne with cayenne and tomatos (excellent), good old bistro smoked trout or gravlax and good old nouvelle duck salad. Entrees are less thrilling: overcooked and tasteless paillard of veal, overcooked hamburgers, decent omelets, acceptable steak au poivre, lightly battered fried calamari and the roast chicken that the menu still announces is served at room temperature (appropriate for any season). Desserts are unmemorable. Joanna's is, in spite of everything, a pleasant rendezvous for lunch if you have two and a half hours to spare; the service is so slow you may want to run into the kitchen yourself to whip up an omelet or pound a paillard. About $25 per person for lunch with wine, slightly more at dinner.

13
La Louisiana
132 Lexington Ave.
(29th St.)
686-3959
Dinner Mon. to Sat. 6:00 P.M. to
11:00 P.M. (Fri. and Sat. to
midnight)
No credit cards
American (regional)

Many residents of Murray Hill and Gramercy Park, tired of dining on second-rate French or Italian cooking in pretentious surroundings at pretentious prices, can be found weekday evenings at La Louisiana (on weekends a crowd of similar disposition comes from farther afield). La Louisiana is the original creation of Alene and Abe de la Houssaye, who are more often seen at Texarkana in the Village, their more ambitious undertaking. Nonetheless, La Louisiana continues to offer the same genial, good service, and the Gulf Coast specialties (gumbos, beans and rice, catfish, crayfish, fried chicken with honey butter and Cajun mustard) seem to be as good now as when Alene and Abe were more frequently on the premises. All of this speaks well for the training they provided the kitchen and serving staff. The boudin with a horseradish sauce (a bit mild for our taste), the crayfish cocktail with a cayenne sauce and the snapper in a spicy crust are all exceptional. The crayfish étouffée (a special) with perfectly prepared rice is authentic, if a bit less zesty than what you might expect in New Orleans. But then you'll find a bottle of fiery hot pepper sauce (available for purchase) on your table, and you can season this or any other dish to your heart's delight—or dismay. Desserts consist primarily of pies (not bad at all), but they seem like an anticlimax to the spicy and intriguing dishes that come before. This is a plain little nondecor place for diners looking for regional taste sensations. We don't believe you will be disappointed, because the food is good and the price is right—about $30 per person, with wine.

13 Mr. Lee's

**337 Third Ave.
(25th St.)
689-6373**

*Lunch Mon. to Fri. noon to 2:30
P.M.; dinner Mon. to Sat. 6:00 P.M.
to 11:00 P.M.
Jackets required
All major credit cards*

Continental

The menu hasn't changed since we were last here, but the cuisine has certainly taken a turn for the better. It's a pleasant place, with a tiny bar, beautiful flowers, a wood and stained-glass ceiling and art deco mirrors. Soothing background music and excellent service help while away the two to three hours you will wait here. According to Mr. Lee, food shouldn't be rushed. The menu warns, "Fine cuisine takes time to prepare, so please be patient," and you should take his advice.

Smoked trout from Scotland looks remarkably like smoked salmon and is every bit as good. The duck salad is enjoyable once you find the dressing lurking on the bottom. Bouillabaisse Marseilles style is not the usual recycled fish thrown into a pot; it is elegant, with mussels, shrimp and lobster. Beef Wellington has a satisfying, flaky crust, even though the flavorful beef is slightly stringy. Poached fresh asparagus is delightful. Peaches in Grand Marnier may be all you can manage after this feast, and they are adequate. The coffee, however, is excellent. As we mentioned in our last edition, an eighteen percent service charge is added to the bill, but it's well deserved. Courses may be slow in arriving, but they are slow in the old-fashioned, gracious way one expects when having a civilized dining experience. No one is too rushed to answer any questions and no one is about to rush you, which certainly adds to the romance of the evening. The bill is, as we said before, staggering: expect to pay $175 for two, with a decent bottle of wine. But if you are prepared to spend that much, why not spend it on an evening you'll always remember with culinary sentimentality?

13 Mon Paris

**111 E. 29th St.
683-4255**

*Lunch Tues. to Sat. noon to 2:45
P.M.; dinner Tues. to Sat. 5:30 P.M.
to 10:00 P.M.
AE, MC, V*

Plus ça change, plus c'est la même chose: the chef and Roger Stephan, his partner of twenty years, had a falling out; the chef left but Roger remained, and neither the customers nor the food changed in the slightest way. Both publishing and neckwear executives (one particular man comes every day of the week) still crowd the place at

French (provincial)

lunch; the same francophiles, hungry for honest bistro fare, still find their way here for dinner. They can still count on carefully prepared (and fresh) calf's brains with capers, tender rognons with mustard sauce, an earthly and well-seasoned boeuf bourguignon, steak au poivre and, on Fridays, a quite acceptable bouillabaisse. The decor has no more surprises than the menu: crystal lamps and chandeliers, huge mirrors and heavily framed oils. After a hearty meal in these surroundings, served by friendly expatriates from Brittany, you may walk out quietly whistling the *Marseillaise*. About $35 per person, with wine.

13

El Parador
325 E. 34th St.
679-6812
Dinner Mon. to Sat. 5:00 P.M. to 11:00 P.M.
No credit cards
Mexican

El Parador is the happy exception to the rule that you can't get good Mexican food in New York. It's certainly one of the friendliest restaurants in town: Carlos, the owner, greets every guest with great warmth, has an amazing, near-total recall for names and will remember the name of a patron he has met only once and hasn't seen for years. His charm and good cheer is contagious, and the service is exceptionally congenial and efficient. This alone would keep people coming back to the bustling three-story restaurant, decorated in a cozy, rustic Mexican fashion, but fortunately there is also a menu full of good, bona fide Mexican dishes. For the unadventurous there are the standard nachos, tacos and enchiladas, but it would be a crime not to try the more unusual (and more authentic) dishes: menudo, a hearty tripe soup; a good ceviche; mole poblano, one of Mexico's national dishes, consisting of chicken in a rich, pungent mole (a dark sauce flavored with chocolate, chili and spices); delicious crab enchiladas topped with a green chili sauce, sour cream and almonds; and another Mexican classic, ropa vieja ("old clothes"), a delicious, spicy dish of shredded beef, served with fried bananas. For dessert, there's classic flan, guava with cream cheese, Mexican mangoes topped with Amaretto, and sopapillas, delicious pastry puffs served with honey. The wine list has a few interesting bottles, but most people stick to margaritas or Mexican beer. Expect to spend $50 to $60 for dinner for two, with margaritas.

11/20
Pesca
23 E. 22nd St.
533-2293
Lunch Mon. to Fri. noon to 3:00 P.M.; dinner nightly 6:00 P.M. to 11:00 P.M. (Sun. to 10:00 P.M.)
AE
Italian (seafood)

This lovely seafood café has a lot going for it: subdued salmon-colored walls with antique marine lithographs, a long, inviting bar, a restored tin ceiling and hardwood floors, freshly cut flowers, a professional staff and a personable host-owner. The ambience is pleasant, but it's a shame the wisdom of restraint that gives the decor its elegant simplicity is not always evident in the cuisine, especially in the daily specials (presented to each table in written form, for which we are grateful). Perhaps a wiser hand in the kitchen would have removed the whole garlic cloves from the seafood risotto with soft-shell crabs; would not have substituted black beans for the traditional white with the fusilli, shrimp and pancetta; would have chosen more appropriate fish than tilefish and bluefish for the resulting grainy seafood pâté; and would not have spread tapenade on tuna carpaccio. Sometimes innovations and embellishments aren't improvements—grant the chef the wisdom to know the difference. With the decor in such good taste, the varied selection of seafood should simply taste good. Dinner for two, with wine, is about $70 to $80.

9/20
The Tibetan Kitchen
**444 Third Ave.
(30th–31st sts.)
684-9209**
*Lunch Mon. to Fri. noon to 3:00
P.M.; dinner Mon. to Sat. 5:30 P.M.
to 10:30 P.M.
No credit cards*
Tibetan

This hole-in-the-wall, with seven tables and a minimal ethnic decor, must be the only Tibetan restaurant in captivity. Two delightful Nepalese sisters serve food that is a cross between Chinese and Indian cuisines, though it lacks the finer points of either. Like Tibet, however, it is worth exploring, if only once. The meat and vegetable dumplings (momos), heavier and coarser than the Chinese variety, come with a red-hot dip of chili, garlic and coriander. Shamdeh, a Tibetan lamb curry that is fragrant with anise, is agreeable and is complemented by a sharp salad of cabbage and carrot. Best of all, however, is a kind of Tibetan steak sandwich called shaphali, with meat juices and onions that soak into the hot Oriental bread. There is a revolting rice pudding that is served, the menu tells you, at Tibetan religious festivals; it is simply cold rice and raisins with a yogurt topping. Our request for Tibetan buttered tea (bocha) brought on a wonderful pantomime from our waitress, with much face pulling and stomach clutching. We ordered it nonetheless and found it rather soothing—at least it was not made authentically, with rancid yak's butter. A further entertainment is the demonstration of csamba making at the table. The gruellike paste, which propels Sherpas up Everest, is ground millet and tea, kneaded by hand into a long brown sausage that tastes the way it looks—repulsive. One can see why it's not on the menu. There are a yogurt drink called thata and free Tibetan black tea, but you are advised to bring your own wine. About $10 per person.

12/20
The Water Club
**500 E. 30th St.
(East River)**

Michael O'Keefe, the happy owner of the River Café, spent a small fortune to transform an old barge that had fallen to pieces at the foot of 34th Street into an elegant restaurant with a panoramic dining room that opens onto

683-3333

Lunch Mon. to Sat. noon to 2:30
P.M.; dinner nightly 5:30 P.M. to
11:15 P.M.; brunch Sun. 11:30
A.M. to 2:30 P.M.
All major credit cards

American

the river, a terrace and a topside deck that has the discreet charm of a yacht club. Success was immediate, and now you'll meet the most "in" New Yorkers here. After a first meal that was hopelessly bad, we have had several more that, although not exceptional, were much more satisfying. It's true that the young waitresses are so pretty that we could be indulgent; this indulgence is encouraged by the good Pacific Northwest smoked salmon, steamed Maine lobster with drawn butter and deep-dish apple pie. The number of covers served at The Water Club certainly can't help the chef, but if he is able to maintain an honest quality and serve his fish ultrafresh (which wasn't the case in the beginning), this could become one of the top tourist spots and stay that way for a long time. About $35 to $40 per person, with wine.

West 42nd to 59th Streets

7/20

Algonquin Hotel

59 W. 44th St.
840-6800

Lunch daily noon to 3:00 P.M.;
dinner nightly in the Oak Room 5:30
P.M. to 7:45 P.M., in the Rose Room
6:00 P.M. to midnight
All major credit cards

Continental

Whether you choose the frivolous Rose Room, with its enthusiastic clientele seated on vintage red vinyl, or the more sober, power-oriented Oak Room, with its predominantly male clientele and deal-making aura, you'll be served the same tired food in the tradition of men's grills from your grandfather's era. Corned beef hash, broiled sweetbreads on toast, fried shrimp, lobster Newburg, seafood creole: all the classics are here. The grainy Welsh rarebit has the lightness of glue, the crab au gratin has the finesse of a peanut butter and jelly sandwich, the Caesar salad is as refreshing as a lead weight, but the rice pudding, thank God, is wonderful. The food, however, isn't really the point here. You'll feast on the crowd and the tradition, with hopes that maybe just once the mixed seafood grill, the steak tartare, the calf's liver, the coconut snowball and the baked apple will taste good. About $25 per person for an entertaining lunch with a glass of wine.

11/20

Barbetta

321 W. 46th St.
246-9171

You will doubtless be seduced by this lovely old establishment, which claims to be the city's oldest Italian restaurant. The welcome is gracious, the outdoor garden

Lunch and dinner Mon. to Sat. noon to 11:30 P.M.
All major credit cards
Italian

is romantic, and the marble dining room has a serene elegance. The decor is what only Italians consider to be intense good taste, complete with a chorus of naked putti. Even though it may transport you, you could end up as anxious as the manager, who ate at the table next to ours recently—edginess can result from the laborious and inattentive service and some of the less than stellar dishes. The antipasto, although large, is hardly memorable, the cima alla genovese is dry and overpriced for three small slices of cold stuffed veal breast, the risotto alla primavera is respectable, the tagliarini verdi alla bolognese is acceptable, and the bagna cauda with pepperoni, rather than being a "hot bath," as it is literally translated, borders on room temperature. And so it goes: bland sweetbreads alla Marsala and a slightly boring, if well-prepared, paillard of veal; even the zabaglione is a disappointment. But we can't help but give this pre- and posttheater spot high awards for set design. The people are entertaining, the ladies border on beautiful, and the impressive wine list is a saving grace. With wine, it's about $50 per person, which we think is about $20 too much for such mediocre food.

13
The Bombay Palace
30 W. 52nd St.
541-7777
Lunch daily noon to 3:00 P.M.;
dinner nightly 5:30 P.M. to 11:30
P.M. (Sun. to 10:00 P.M.)
All major credit cards
Indian

There have been a lot of improvements here in the last few months. The walls, previously a sinister vindaloo brown, are now a classy kulfi beige, some of the dustier ethnic objects have disappeared, and comfortable velvet banquettes have been installed. Piped-in sitar music—strangely alternating with "My Darling Clementine"—is mercifully unobtrusive. Thankfully, you'll still see the massive wooden doors and the even more massive turbaned doorman, who can make the meanest mortal feel like a pukka sahib. Less fortunately, we have found it to be almost a law of nature among restaurants that when the decor goes up the cooking goes down. Although the Palace is still one of the most reliable Indian restaurants in town, it has lost that edge of excellence that so delighted us earlier.

Among the better main dishes are buttered chicken (tandoor roasted and finished in a creamy sauce with tomatoes, onion and ginger), a mildly spiced minced lamb keema and a very fresh-tasting eggplant bharta. Of the hot breads, Palace naan stuffed with chicken and almonds is savory, but the limp onion and mango khulcha bears the flavor of neither. Sweets include a delicious, natural-tasting mango ice cream and a chewy, too-sweet rasmalai. Tandoori dishes, once the restaurant's main attraction, are overcooked and dry. Plan on spending $25 to $30 per person, with wine.

9/20

Café des Sports

329 W. 51st St.
974-9052

Lunch Mon. to Fri. noon to 3:00
P.M.; dinner nightly 5:00 P.M.
to 11:00 P.M.
AE

French (classical)

For years the Café des Sports has been said to be a bastion of simple French cuisine—so good, in fact, that a number of the city's French chefs are rumored to gather here on Sundays when their respective establishments are closed. Since the Sunday meal is a sacred ritual, we can only assume that the food is substantially better when chefs cook for each other. The atmosphere is homely and comforting, in the tradition of small French country restaurants. In the same spirit, the menu features such appetizers as pâté maison, maquereaux au vin blanc, escargots de Bourgogne and saucisson à l'ail. Entrees are standard fare: coq au vin, tête de veau vinaigrette, frog's legs provençale and escalopes de veau à la crème; desserts are of the pêche melba, crème caramel and mousse au chocolat persuasion.

The stage is set, but French tradition ends with the shortcuts: canned button mushrooms, floury-tasting sauces, distinctly over- and underseasoned items, canned peaches and jam instead of fresh fruit purée. We advise those chefs to try sushi on Sundays. Dinner for two, with wine, will run about $55.

11/20

La Caravelle

33 W. 55th St.
586-4252

Lunch Mon. to Sat. 12:15 P.M. to
2:30 P.M.; dinner Mon. to Sat. 6:00
P.M. to 10:30 P.M.
All major credit cards

French (classical)

If after twenty minutes the maître d' still has not pried himself away from his regular clientele to take your wine order and after another ten minutes still has not found time to interrupt his conversation with the waiters to open your bottle, you have every right to protest loudly enough to wake up this sleepy place, which seems to be dying from lethargy. The triste, old-fashioned decor with aesthetically affronting wall murals, little Belle Epoque table lamps, plentiful and inefficient service and outdated cuisine with too many sauces (often overreduced) and too little imagination will make you want to take a nap. We can assure you that even the technical prowess and experience in the kitchen will not raise your morale with escargots en surprise (a surprise indeed: little snails encased in puff pastry on top of an artichoke heart—a marriage made in purgatory); an acceptable but dull mousseline of squab with a too-heavy watercress sauce; a tomato-mint soup served either hot or cold (a soup for all seasons); a lackluster terrine of salmon and crab studded with morels, which is overpowered by a mayonnaise-based sauce; an overcooked but otherwise tasty maigret of duck in a sweetish sauce with the unusual combination of celery purée and chestnut purée (with the consistency of peanut butter); a good lamb chop with watercress sauce; a pleasant fillet of bass with cucumbers in red wine butter; tender scallops with two caviars; and a tasteless veal roast. Desserts look like temptations from the underworld, but an intercession from the angels is needed to revive their flavors: the apple tart has a tasteless crust, the fruit tart is slightly better and the vanilla charlotte with chocolate is more sweet than flavorful. It's time Caravelle wake up and look to the future instead of the past. Clearly, the talent is available, but the spirit is weak. About $65 per person, with a redeeming Chablis Grand Cru.

12/20
Carolina
355 W. 46th St.
245-0058
Lunch Mon. to Fri. noon to 3:00 P.M.; dinner Mon. to Sat. 6:00 P.M. to midnight, Sun. 5:00 P.M. to midnight
AE, MC, V
American (regional)

This relatively recent arrival to West 46th Street is stark, with a chichi nondecor filled with pretheater hopefuls and posttheater survivors. The bare brick walls, mirrors, gray fake suede banquettes, raw wood beamed ceiling with a slight creosote fragrance and the lone Amish-design quilt hung on the wall surround a clientele sampling down-home cooking. And it must be said that this updated Americana cuisine seems slightly out of place in such a slick decor. A rustic shack design might be more appropriate, but heaven knows the well-dressed clientele that visits Carolina would be somewhat put off by such unpretentious humility. In any case, the kitchen could use some assistance from a Southern mama to get things right here. This sort of regional cuisine is best when it's prepared with a lot of love. At Carolina, you get the impression that it's hard work to make barbecue on lettuce (rather dry and dull), green chili soufflé (a total misconception), Carolina pizza (thank you, Wolfgang Puck) and smoked salmon and fillet of beef with a caper sauce—these are hardly Southern classics. We have to give these good people credit for trying; Southern food *can* be bland, but it becomes a matter of pretension when basic food is tricked up or, even worse, made boring instead of messily delicious. Such is the case with the tedious "hot smoke" ribs, with a sauce that does little to enhance the insipid beef, or the more encouraging crab cakes, a personal interpretation with snow crab caked into sautéed patties. There are selections from the grill (beef, salmon, lamb chops) and plenty more "hot smoke" for people nostalgic for the Southwest. The corn pudding accompanying the ribs is a quichelike affair, quite delicate and custardy, the slaw nothing special, the corn bread tasty and the desserts absolutely superb; lemon meringue tartlet and blueberry cobbler are both in the best home-cooked tradition. The wine list is equally impressive, with a lovely selection of American wines, including Trefethen, Grgich Hills, David Bruce and Château St. Jean along with the Hargrave from New York. Dinner for two, with a California wine, will run about $85, lunch slightly less. This charming place has loads of potential, but the cuisine is simply a little too chic and too removed from its roots to be successful (not to mention the fact that it needs a chef who can cook these dishes better).

13

Castellano
138 W. 55th St.
664-1975
Lunch Mon. to Fri. noon to 2:30 P.M.; dinner Mon. to Sat. 6:00 P.M. to 11:30 P.M.
All major credit cards
Italian

This decor is charming enough (though not sober and refined), with black and white photos covering the terracotta walls, the clientele is young and elegant, and the atmosphere on the whole is warm and engaging. The cuisine, on the other hand, is far from even, and in fact we haven't had a meal in this place that hasn't reminded us of a roller coaster. For reasons that elude us, the chef succeeds with certain dishes and massacres others. Does he suffer from an allergy, perhaps? Be that as it may, Harry's Bar carpaccio, still tasting of the inside of the refrigerator whence it comes, is an abomination, fish soup chokes you with an excess of garlic, and calf's liver sautéed with onions and polenta is so dry you could play the drums on it. On the other hand, the milanese cutlet, which is so often a disaster, here is perfectly tender and tasty; risotto with fresh vegetables is perfect; green noodles gratinée are excellent; and rack of veal simply served in its juice is velvety and truly delicious. There's not much to choose from in desserts that are only so-so, the wine list is terribly poor, and the service, if it must be remarked on at all, is negligent and ineffective. About $40 per person, with wine.

11/20

Century Café
132 W. 43rd St.
398-1988
Lunch and dinner Mon. to Sat. 11:30 A.M. to 2:00 A.M.
All major credit cards
Continental/American

This attractive restaurant/bar looks quite modern despite its attempt to evoke early Hollywood, with a neon Loew's marquee sign over the bar, a bold black, white and red decor and large, bright celebrity photos on the walls. Chic young models, advertising executives and shoppers come here for a late lunch of anything from a basic hamburger, to classic French dishes (calf's liver Madeira, country pâté, salmon beurre blanc), to such regional American creations as Tex-Mex fried won tons, leg of lamb with a mint barbecue sauce and ribs with a West Indian sauce. Some of these more inventive dishes are failures; the touted blue nachos—artfully presented blue corn tortilla strips topped with dollops of guacamole and cheese—are a soggy disappointment, served with a bland, catsuplike salsa. But many of the simple dishes are decent: roasted chicken with fines herbes, New York steak, fresh fish and tender scallops with toasted pistachios. There's always an interesting dish on the specials menu, which changes daily, and the worthwhile desserts are homemade. The wine list is tiny but well chosen, and the female service is attentive. It's $25 for a light lunch for two, with a glass of wine, and a too-steep $80 for a full dinner for two, with wine.

11/20

Charley O's
Rockefeller Center
33 W. 48th St.
582-7141
Lunch and dinner daily 11:45 A.M.
to midnight (Sun. to 6:00 P.M.)
All major credit cards
American/Irish

New York's myriad Irish pubs, from blue-collar saloons to elegant East Side watering holes, have one thing in common (apart from the brogue): almost all of them serve good, sturdy food. Charley O's goes beyond the corned beef and cabbage standard, but not uncomfortably far. The lamb stew, not easy to find in Manhattan, is peasant perfection. Prawns in beer batter are usually crisply satisfying. The fish is an exception to the rule that you don't order seafood in pubs—and it is best on Fridays. The Irish coffee ice cream beats the disappointing Irish coffee. There are meaty, no-blarney sandwiches for stand-up liquid lunchers, which spares them the genial but erratic table service. Charley O's Bar and Grill and Bar, to give the place its proper name, does not, of course, cater to hard hat Hibernians but draws its mob from the even thirstier populace of nearby television, magazine and ad shops. Hence the decor: blowups of the famous, lots of mahogany and etched glass dividers. Free parking across the street at night, with theaters a short walk away. Dinner for two with house wine will be about $60.

12/20

Chez Napoléon
365 W. 50th St.
265-6980
Dinner Mon. to Thurs. 5:00 P.M. to
10:30 P.M. (Fri. and Sat. to
11:00 P.M.)
All major credit cards
French (provincial)

There are a dozen inns in France that will proudly show you the bed in which Napoléon slept or the table at which he dined. Did he make a detour to West 50th Street? There are many signs that make us seriously consider the possibility, such as the presence of so many portraits of the emperor in this little bistro, as well as the dish of mussels named for him. Nevertheless, if any doubts persist about this critical historical point, you will have no questions about the authenticity and honesty of this bourgeois cuisine. In this brave little restaurant you'll find the dishes also found in a neighborhood place in Paris or Lyon. Everything is here: pâté maison, rillettes from Tours, onion soup, snails from Bourgogne, tripes niçoise with tomato (well prepared), grilled boudin (perfectly seasoned, which is a rare find in New York), rabbit in white wine sauce, slowly simmered and tender, or beef bourguignon accompanied with buttered carrots. Service is erratic, and the comfort is rather perfunctory. Chez Napoléon is not the place to come to impress your future spouse. But for a 100 percent French meal that is inexpensive ($20 for two for lunch with a glass of wine), it's difficult to find anyplace better.

12/20
Frankie and Johnnie's
269 W. 45th St.
245-9717
Dinner Mon. to Sat. 5:00 P.M. to 11:30 P.M.
All major credit cards
American (steaks)

This is quintessential old New York. You go past an undistinguished entryway, climb up a rickety flight of stairs and find yourself in an old, plain room with cheap paneling, linoleum floors and posters from Broadway plays on the walls; the diners (theatergoers and business people) and the middle-aged black-tie waiters are much better decorated than the restaurant. It's an honest, old-fashioned steak house, with no pretension and with surprisingly good food. The steaks and chops (about the only things to have here) are of excellent quality and are very well cooked, seared on the outside and exactly as rare as you request on the inside. Naturally, the portions are much too large, and the accompaniments are very simple (but better than at most such places): grilled mushrooms, good lyonnaise potatoes, average salads and onion rings. It isn't particularly exciting food, but it's honest and tasty—which makes Frankie and Johnnie's one of the better places in the theater district. Expect to spend $75 for a meal for two, with a bottle of simple Italian wine.

13
Gallagher's
228 W. 52nd St.
245-5336
Lunch and dinner daily noon to midnight
All major credit cards
American (steaks)

This large room has a good sense of old New York (wood paneling and photos of Broadway stars and sports heros); during the evening it's a favorite hangout for the Broadway crowd. At noon, however, this former speakeasy is filled with a primarily masculine clientele that comes here to engulf the monstrous steaks that are aged in the large windowed refrigerator at the entrance. Start with oysters, ask for onion rings with your meat and finish with cheesecake; you'll be left with your stomach full and your wallet lightened of $30 to $40. The secret of Gallagher's meat is that owner Jerry Brody buys from kosher butchers, who, as we all know, have the most tender beef.

10/20
Jockey Club
Ritz Carlton Hotel
112 Central Park South
664-7700
Lunch daily noon to 2:15 P.M.; dinner nightly 6:00 P.M. to 10:30 P.M.
All major credit cards
Continental

Lady Charles Churchill selected the paintings and prints; John Coleman selected the chef. It was the best that this Boston millionaire, empassioned with a strong sense of English chic, could do. Even in London, the mediocrity of the cuisine at the Jockey Club wouldn't pass quite as unnoticed as it is here. It must take some talent to transform products that were originally good into such ungratifying foods. If, for example, they poured water on the capelletti it would have the same taste effect as this tomato sauce. In reading the Jockey Club's menu, you can discern the cautious intentions of its owner, who evidently does not seek to compete with the grand New York restaurants, except in price. Instead he has chosen to

73

maintain a sure and conservative standard, so the assorted hors d'oeuvres, prosciutto and melon and pepper steak would be as safe as the beluga caviar, Dover sole and filet mignon. Within these limitations, however, these dishes can and should be good, but here they are unfortunately mediocre. But all of this is without any importance, for the beautiful people who fill these ravishing rooms, haloed in exquisite rose light, only have eyes for one another. They are accessorized by portraits of racehorses, young lords, prize-winning sheep and very distinguished dogs, all hung on blond South Carolina pine paneling. About $50 per person, served by a very professional part-French, part-Italian staff.

13

Keewah Yen
50 W. 56th St.
246-0770
Lunch and dinner Mon. to Thurs. noon to midnight (Fri. and Sat. to 1:00 A.M.); dinner Sun. 5:00 P.M. to midnight
All major credit cards

Chinese

This elegant restaurant, soberly and somberly Chinese, is jammed at lunchtime, not only because it is close to the Fifth Avenue offices but because the cuisine, under the influences of Canton, Szechwan, Peking and Hunan, has a remarkable finesse. In one of the three rooms decorated with large, traditional paintings or at the bar, you will be served a delicious assortment of fried or steamed appetizers; a gimlo won ton, composed of firm shrimp, chicken and pork in a delicious, slightly acidic orange sauce; shrimp shantung (shrimp is one of the great specialties of the house) prepared in a light coating with water chestnuts; a remarkable Mandarin pork accompanied with a pungent cabbage; or a sliced loin of lamb braised with fresh ginger and white leeks. In general, we would for good reason scorn a Chinese restaurant so well situated in an elegant neighborhood, but there are always exceptions, and Keewah Yen is one. About $25 per person, with wine.

14

Kitcho
22 W. 46th St.
575-8880
Lunch Mon. to Fri. noon to 2:30 P.M.; dinner Mon. to Fri. 6:00 P.M. to 10:30 P.M.
AE, CB, DC

Japanese

Kitcho means "good omen" in Japanese, and it is still good news. Set in a busy midtown side street with an understated, austere decor of black, white and orange panels, it is possibly the most uncompromisingly genuine Japanese restaurant in New York. Service is distinctly maternalistic. Expect no giggling geishas here, for you will be under the wing of stern but benevolent governess figures, ladies of a certain age who, like nanny, will see that you eat what is good for you. Already familiar with Kitcho's menu, we asked our guide Kyio to lead us gently away from the beaten track. The meal she selected was memorable. We started with a superlative sashimi of four different fish, including toro, the marvelously marbled middle cut of tuna. This was followed with a light broth of Japanese mushrooms (matsutake) served in an exquisite, tiny teapot, full of seafood tidbits, seaweed fungi and ginkgo nuts; it is excellent with a squeeze of fresh lime juice. To cleanse the palate (as if this were necessary) we were served a slender, tiny goblet of homemade raspberry sorbet made with white wine and topped with fresh berries. The main course, ishiyaki ("steak on a stone"), was a real coup de théâtre and is probably one of the most spectacular dishes on record. The centerpiece was a red-hot volcanic rock set on the table in a stoneware casserole. The thick, perfectly marbled steak was dissected quickly into cubes. We dipped each piece into a bowl of soy, ginger and chili and cooked it to simple perfection on the hot rock. Next, Kyio suggested tatsetage of chicken—pieces marinated in soy and sweet mirin sake, then delicately fast fried after a dusting of potato flour. This lunchtime feast for two came to $95, all-inclusive, with two flasks of sake; we didn't regret a yen of it. For those poor souls in more of a hurry, there is a choice of good tempura, teriyaki and sashimi lunches, all at around $10. At night the "chef's choice" enables you to sample a seven- to ten-course gourmet dinner, priced between $30 to $60 per person. In light of our experiences at Kitcho, we feel perfectly justified in recommending these dinners unseen and untasted.

11/20
Landmark Tavern
626 Eleventh Ave. (46th St.)
757-8595
Lunch and dinner daily noon to midnight (Fri. and Sat. to 1:00 A.M.)
No credit cards
Irish/English

This part of town (the theater district and its environs) is not especially noted for good food, which makes the Landmark seem somewhat better than it really is. It's one of the oldest taverns in town, and a few years back it was lovingly restored to its original 1880s Irish charm and comfort: rich mahogany, brick walls, antique lighting and a classic wood-burning stove that warms patrons in the winter. It has a relaxed ambience that sets you immediately at ease, with a clientele that can't be pigeonholed—some theatergoers, some longtime regulars, some young Upper West Siders. The menu offers a mixture of Irish, English and American home cooking that is honest and well prepared. The standout is the marvelous, slightly sweet Irish soda bread, made fresh every hour, that is set on the table when you sit down; this and a bowl of Irish potato soup makes an excellent simple and hearty supper. If you're after a more substantial meal, try the savory, well-made shepherd's pie, the thin-sliced roast leg of lamb in its own juices (served with good roasted potatoes and canned peas) or the authentically British fish and chips. There's usually a chicken dish, which can be dry and overcooked, along with steaks, prime rib and fresh fish, all simply prepared. For dessert, try the good pecan pie topped with freshly whipped cream. There are no wines other than the house brand—this tavern caters more to a whiskey- and beer-drinking crowd. A meal will run $46 for two, with drinks.

11/20
Luchow's
**1633 Broadway
(51st St.)
582-4697**
Lunch and dinner daily noon to midnight (Sun. to 10:00 P.M.)
All major credit cards
German

In our last edition we were unable to report on Luchow's because it had not yet opened at its new location, after being on 14th Street for the past hundred years. We noted the generous portions of standard German fare (roast goose, sauerbraten, etc.) and the floury sauces that had marked the cooking, and wrote that only time would tell whether Luchow's can make it into the twenty-first century. Well, the new menu is practically the same: Wienerschnitzel, a platter of wursts, smoked pork, sauerbraten, goose, potato pancakes, linzer torte, apple strudel and so on; there is a good-value pretheater dinner for $18.50. The cooking hasn't changed much, but then there's probably not much that can be done when a kitchen has to turn out 300 dinners per seating. We'll have to wait until our next edition to predict whether Luchow's can still make it into the twenty-first century. About $30 per person, with wine.

12/20
Meson Botin
**145 W. 58th St.
265-4567**
Lunch Mon. to Fri. noon to 3:00 P.M.; dinner nightly 5:00 P.M. to 11:00 P.M. (Sun. from 4:30 P.M.)
All major credit cards
Spanish

It has always puzzled us that a city with New York's large Hispanic population is not home to dozens of good Spanish restaurants. Meson Botin, near Carnegie Hall, is the best of a small handful that does exist on the West Side. It also has one of the best lists of Spanish wines in the country, most of them very reasonably priced, especially some older Riojas.

We must assume owner José Russo supposes most Americans think Spanish restaurants should be decorated with martial paraphernalia, such as crossbows, shields, swords and suits of armor, but it makes us feel as if we are eating our last meal before the Inquisition. The front barroom is much prettier than the main dining room, while the dreary rear room is completely undesirable. The food has spice to it, and we enjoy the crema de alubias pintas (a light black bean soup full of flavor), the gambas al ajillo (shrimp sautéed in garlic) and the lomo de cerdo a la baturra (loin of pork with a zesty Spanish ham and wine sauce). There is a classic paella a la valenciana for two ($18.50) worth ordering, and the rich, eggy flan is the best in the city. Avoid the gelatinous strawberry shortcake made off the premises. Dinner will cost about $40 for two, without wine.

10/20
Orsini's
41 W. 56th St.
757-1698
Lunch Mon. to Fri. noon to 2:00
P.M.; dinner Mon. to Sat. 5:30 P.M.
to 1:00 A.M.
All major credit cards
Italian

We are happy to report that Orsini's is still here and is still mediocre. The rustic-looking upstairs room is filled with business lunchers by day and an older guard by night. The ambience is friendly if you are among those in the inner circle; first-timers (unless you are an unabashedly attractive lady) may play the waiting game. And if you are impatient because it has been 35 minutes since you ordered lunch and still haven't been served, you have every right to ask if the chef has taken off for a matinee. And when you receive your lackluster pasta, overcooked scampi or banal baked clams, you may wonder, as we have, how the venerable Orsini's continues to stay in business. The cuisine is just as unmemorable as we described in our last edition. Veal piccata is tough and borders on the tasteless, the osso buco is still uninteresting, the sorrentina scaloppine is a hodgepodge of cheese and eggplant, but the fried zucchini is surprisingly good. Come here, if you must, to pay about $30 per person (with wine) for a truly banal lunch. At least at dinner the crowd is more visually interesting, ensuring that your evening will have some sparks of excitement.

13
Orso
322 W. 46th St.
489-7212
Lunch and dinner daily noon to
11:45 P.M.
MC, V
Italian

This very white, very bare trattoria has a charming trompe l'oeil painting that makes its simplicity seem sophisticated. Named after a Venice gondolier's dog, of whom the owners were quite fond, Orso is a good place to come pre- or posttheater for honest, home-cooked food prepared the way momma made it in the Italian countryside, cooked with sincerity and care by a young, all-American staff. These nice people have a gentle hand with such classics as penne with four cheeses, tortellini with butter and Parmesan, tagliarini with bacon, tomatoes and hot pepper, zuppe di pesce, osso buco, sea bass with fennel, grilled red snapper and a tender calf's liver. Desserts are pleasant, particularly the polenta cheesecake and zuppa inglese. You will find one of the city's best price-value ratios here, including the wines. Everything is served on lovely country floral crockery, which helps warm up the slightly frigid decor. When you reserve, ask for a table against a wall—otherwise you'll be floating in the middle of a highly varnished wood space in an echoing abyss. About $30 per person for a generous, simple dinner with wine.

12/20
Pantheon
689 Eighth Ave.
664-8294

Thirty-five years ago, when Pantheon opened, it was in the center of an almost exclusively Greek neighborhood—Greek ships literally came in at the docks

*Lunch and dinner Mon. to Sat. noon
to 10:45 P.M.*
All major credit cards
Greek

not too far away. Now it is on the edge of a district whose pleasures aren't quite as innocent as a decent piece of baklava. Nevertheless, the menu is still printed in Greek on one side, the chefs and waiters are still Greek (perhaps there since the restaurant opened), and the wines are all Greek. The strong Mediterranean blue decor is pleasant if a little worn, and while such daily specials as lamb fricassée with egg-lemon sauce, moussaka, stuffed cabbage and roast leg of veal appear at the table looking a little like a Greek blue-plate special, they are delicious. The restaurant is now frequented by the theater crowd and people looking for good Greek food. Dinner for two, with wine, will run about $40.

12/20
Patsy's
236 W. 56th St.
*Lunch and dinner daily noon to
10:30 P.M. (Fri. and Sat. to
11:30 P.M.)*
All major credit cards
Italian

They've been standing in line at Patsy's for nearly 40 years (the restaurant does not accept reservations), but you get the feeling that the party's over. Patsy's has slipped into the status of an institution, still frequented by the old guard and theatergoers. Good Neapolitan food is served in both upstairs and downstairs dining rooms, each with its own kitchen. Downstairs, the Mediterranean blue walls are lined with photos of celebrities (never mind that we don't know who many of them are), and the waiters banter back and forth in Italian. The staff is professional and will guide you through both an extensive wine list and a menu that offers antipasti, soups, spaghetti, eggs and omelets, lobster, mussels, squid, grilled meats, veal in every way, shape and form, potatoes, vegetables, salads and cheeses, as well as daily specials. Desserts are of the Italian cheesecake and cannoli variety. Patsy's isn't a great restaurant, but it's certainly a good one. Dinner for two, with wine, will cost about $60.

7/20
Pearl's
38 W. 48th St.
586-1000
*Lunch and dinner Sun. to Fri. noon
to 10:00 P.M.*
No credit cards
Chinese

Perhaps someone told these people that if you dig a tunnel long enough, you'll reach China. This long, narrow, one-room restaurant with a rounded ceiling appears to be the first leg of a journey home. The decor doesn't suffer from the bright red banquette syndrome common in Chinese establishments; indeed, the decor in the Pearl tunnel is virtually nonexistent, but no matter— the poor lighting prevents you from seeing much anyway.

The Cantonese-style food is an adulterated American version and is generally poorly prepared. Broths, such as in the won ton soup, taste canned; egg rolls are indigestible; shrimp foo young is greasy and tough; lemon chicken tastes cloyingly sweet; pork with black bean and garlic sauce is tough and salty. The yook soang, a sort of Chinese soft taco with pork and water chestnuts wrapped in lettuce, was the best offering at a recent visit.

Desserts are nearly as nonexistent as the decor; the liquor and wine list features lots of the former and only one bottle ("imported") of the latter. We can only speculate that the loyal patrons from the television and advertising worlds continue to frequent this restaurant in the hopes that if they come often enough, they'll earn a free trip when Pearl's breaks through to China. Dinner for two, with wine, is about $50.

10/20
Pierre au Tunnel
250 W. 47th St.
582-2166
Lunch Mon. to Sat. noon to 3:00 P.M.; dinner Mon. to Sat. 5:30 P.M. to 11:30 P.M. (Wed. and Sat. from 4:30 P.M.)
AE

French (classical)

Pierre Pujol's kitchen isn't what it was when he started in the restaurant business more than 30 years ago, but the pretheater dinner crowds don't seem to care too much; they pack the place nightly. Every New York French cliché is on the menu (moules ravigote, artichauts vinaigrettes, pâté, grenouilles provençale, coquilles Saint-Jacques), and none of it seems to have any inspiration whatsoever. A vegetable soup is floury, a nicely poached lotte is not helped by a poor sauce americaine, slices of duck breast are flavorful but the sauce is heavy, and the fruit tarts are not special. The cassoulet (a Thursday special) has been cooked so long that the meat falls apart, and the thin sauce has no character. Maybe it's time for M. Pujol to give way to some young hands who need a challenge. About $35 per person, with a modest wine.

13 ♟
René Pujol
321 W. 51st St.
246-3023
Lunch Mon. to Fri. noon to 3:00 P.M.; dinner Mon. to Sat. 5:00 P.M. to 11:30 P.M.
All major credit cards

French (provincial)

René Pujol grew up in the back country between Toulouse and the Pyrénées. Today, he and his family operate a successful restaurant in the middle of New York's theater district; he attracts hordes of theatergoers as well as tourists looking for a not-too-expensive, solid French restaurant. With his son-in-law, Claude Franques, in the kitchen and various other members of the family in other roles, René makes certain that ingredients are fresh, sauces are properly prepared and that the kitchen and staff do not falter. He offers commendable versions of traditional bourgeois dishes, such as rognons de veau moutarde, boeuf bourguignon and entrecôte marchand de vin. At the same time, he includes among his specials each day several nouvelle-style dishes. The poached salmon in feuilleté, for example, with its finely flavored white wine reduction, is superb. The fruit tarts and pastries (made on the premises) are acceptable enough. The decor—bric-a-brac from the French countryside, false wood beams—holds no surprises and doesn't add much excitement to the pleasure of eating here. But what is surprising is the authenticity of the nineteenth-century bourgeois cuisine and the success of the handful of ventures into the twentieth century. About $30 per person, with a simple wine.

12/20
Raga
57 W. 48th St.
757-3450
Lunch Mon. to Fri. noon to 2:45
P.M.; dinner nightly 5:30 P.M. to
11:00 P.M.
All major credit cards

Indian

Nothing has changed here, from the stately grandeur of the setting, with its carved wooden pillars and silken wall hangings, to the mediocrity of the cooking, apparently designed not to offend Western tastes. The service is attentive, the seating comfortable, and the twanging of the sitars not too obtrusive, but nothing really sears or surprises the palate. Among the acceptable, if not exciting, dishes are murg tikke makhani, tandoor-cooked chicken finished in a butter sauce, and the gosht vindaloo, a piquant Goanese preparation of lamb garnished with potatoes and pickled onions. Only one dish is outstanding: the murg ki chat, chicken and potatoes in a marvelously tasty sauce of tamarind, coriander and a curious dark brown herbal salt. Known as the Alka-Seltzer of the East, this salt is apparently good for upset tummies, and quite a few dishes feature it—as a precaution only, one hopes. You are, in any case, advised to avoid seafood in Indian restaurants. Here the oysters, which the waiter assures us are fresh, turn out to be frozen, the crab Goa watery and stringy and the shrimp from the tandoor oven tough. There are an executive luncheon at $15 (on which eight items bear a surcharge!) and a downstairs buffet for people in a hurry. The evenings are more glamorous, and pricier—ideal for entertaining visiting VIP's. Not a load of fun, but they might be impressed by the ambience and the attentions of charming sari-clad ladies. About $25 per person for dinner with wine.

15
Raphael
33 W. 54th St.
582-8993
Lunch Mon. to Fri. noon to 2:00
P.M.; dinner Mon. to Fri. 6:00 P.M.
to 11:00 P.M.
AE, DC, V

French (nouvelle)

You are not obliged to congratulate the owner for the masterpieces on the walls—Raphael Edery is not a descendant of the Master of Urbino but, more prosaically, is a former bartender from one of the Rothschild hotels in Paris. Moreover, it suffices to glance at the reproductions to know there is no risk of them being stolen by museum thieves. On the other hand, the intimate atmosphere of this long, narrow room with a garden in the rear, the charming welcome of Raphael and even the cuisine prepared by a former Lenôtre chef provide every reason for gourmands to return here regularly, as long as they have no fear of paying $65 per person per meal. There is no prix fixe; a short French menu varies according to season and to daily market finds. At lunch, the price of the entrees is about $24, including soup or an appetizer. The delicate cuisine is light and imaginative but without eccentricity or overelaboration; the products are left with their natural flavors. It's difficult to do better than the lobster soup with mussels; magret of duck with ginger, not too fat under its crispy skin, and accompanied by baby vegetables and exquisite wild rice; a sautéed chicken with tarragon, perfumed with Xerxes; or a bittersweet chocolate mousse with orange peel. And it is here that, for the first time, we made a discovery that was hard on our nationalistic French honor: Raphael presented us with a duck liver from Wisconsin that was so satiny and pretty we would have sworn it came from Landes! It's true that we weren't displeased, since for some time we have predicted that one day America would produce foie gras as good as our own.

10/20
La Reserve
Swiss Center
4 W. 49th St.
247-2993
Lunch Mon. to Fri. noon to 3:00 P.M.; dinner Mon. to Sat. 5:30 P.M. to 10:30 P.M.
All major credit cards
French (classical)

It is difficult for us to be reserved about La Reserve when, after having ordered a grilled fillet of bass with purée of endives, we receive some sort of gray-flannel-colored fish that should never have been released from the refrigerator except to be tossed into the garbage. Our reserve falters even more when this dish is replaced with a steamed salmon with vegetables that looks better but proves to be mushy and banal. The same reproach could be given to the Bay scallops with tomato and chive cream, which on top of everything else is served lukewarm. You can undoubtedly understand why this French restaurant doesn't unchain our enthusiasm, in spite of its comfort, its pleasant if a bit wan decor of a Venetian chandelier and naturalistic wall paintings of birds, flowers and the countryside, its excellent service and a reasonable prix fixe lunch for $24. Everything is set up to make La Reserve a success—except for the food.

10/20
Rio de Janeiro Boat 57
41 W. 57th St.
935-1232
Lunch and dinner daily noon to 11:00 P.M.
All major credit cards
Brazilian/Portuguese

This serviceable and pleasant restaurant near Carnegie Hall is one of the few Portuguese-Brazilian dining rooms in the city. It is a cheery place to go for its enormous portions of seafood stews and fairly priced lobsters, but we find that most of the offerings lack the kind of authority and seasonings we suspect the senhoras y cavalheiros who frequent the place demand. As a matter of fact, the only seasoning the chef seems enamored of is salt, which dominates a good shrimp soup and ruins an already overly reduced lobster bisque. The avocado and shrimp appetizer is quite good, however, and the complimentary slices of sausage placed on your table are a delightful surprise. The menu is as confusing as Brazil's debt management, with pages of appetizers and salads, followed by "specialties" and seafood, followed by more pages of meats and the notation to consult the "posted menu" on the wall for even more specialties. Many of the dishes are described as being prepared in the "Bahiana" style, meaning with peppers, onion, tomato and white wine, and you could feed the multitudes with the good, zesty dish of lobster, shrimp, scallops and clams that arrive in a large pot with a side order of white rice and black beans. Shrimp sautéed in what is called a "hot, spicy Portuguese sauce" has none of those qualities, while shrimp dipped and grilled in a similar sauce are completely dull. A half-inch-thick slab of swordfish is cooked as if it were a two-inch-thick slab of swordfish— it's dry as a bone and served with a little dish of that same not-hot, not-spicy Portuguese sauce. Such desserts as brandy Alexander pie seem out of place here, but then that would be out of place anywhere. The Brazilian coffee, however, is excellent. Your bill for two, without wine, tax or tip, will come to about $50. Stick with a light Vinho Verde white wine at $12 a bottle.

10/20
Romeo Salta
30 W. 56th St.
246-5772
Lunch and dinner Mon. to Sat. 5:00 P.M. to 11:00 P.M.
All major credit cards
Italian

Not so long ago, sophisticated New Yorkers with money to spend flocked to Romeo Salta, believing it to be one of the city's best Italian restaurants. We don't know whether Romeo Salta was ever as good as its reputation, whether what comes from the kitchen today is less inspiring than it once was or whether the restaurant simply cannot stand comparison with the dozens of newer Italian establishments offering more interesting and more carefully prepared dishes—as well as more amiable service. Whatever the case, Romeo Salta still attracts a moneyed crowd that looks as jaded as the place itself. The clientele apparently doesn't recognize that the pastas are pedestrian, that the traditional Italian specialties (scaloppine di vitello, pollo scarpariello) lack distinction—and that the heavy-handed wall paintings haven't improved with the passage of years. About $35 per person, with wine.

12/20
The Russian Tea Room
150 W. 57th St.
265-0947
Lunch and dinner daily 11:30 A.M. to 12:30 A.M.
Jacket required
All major credit cards
Russian

The Russian Tea Room is such a busy place that its fantastic decor tends to be overlooked. Lunch, when the entertainment and communications worlds dominate the scene and the service, is not the best time to take in the 100 gleaming samovars, the 100 paintings and the chandeliers festooned with Christmas balls and tinsel. Dinner is a little more calm, particularly in summer; if you really want peace, dine in Siberia upstairs, where you find neither the people nor the scenery.

All that glitters is not gold plate, however, though with help from the RTR's sixteen imported vodkas it can be made to seem so. As always, the RTR serves the best borscht in town, and the chicken Kiev spurts butter like a new oil well. The other standards are all they should be: blinis with red caviar and sour cream, Caucasian shashlik, Pojarski veal cutlets, beef Stroganoff (though it's a little bland), kasha Gourieff (hot farina and puréed fruit), and, of course, strawberries Romanoff. Dinner for two can top $70 with a vodka and a carafe of house wine. No charge for the pretty postcards.

10/20
Sardi's
234 W. 44th St.
221-8444
Lunch and dinner daily 11:30 A.M. to 12:30 A.M.
All major credit cards
Continental

Thank God there are still things you can rely on. If we were ever to lose those venerable, slightly boring but timeless traditions, what would we do? So we take solace in the knowledge that nothing at Sardi's has changed: you can rely on the same lineup of star caricatures, recognizable to the chosen few who are these actors' peers; you can rely on the same Belle Epoque chandeliers, the same dazed-looking tourists, the same captains, the same slow service, the same cannelloni au gratin, the same red caviar served with Wonder Bread toast points, the same Sardi hot shrimp swimming in a garlic-laden sauce, the same overlarge portions of tasteless pasta, the same tired veal piccata, the same heavy crab with Mornay and asparagus tips, the same good pepper steak and the same tasty creamed spinach. Only the bill is slightly higher, to keep up with the times. The wine list offers Italian, California, French and New York selections; the desserts are plentiful and just as reliable as the rest of the menu. About $50 per person for a posttheater dinner with wine; slightly less for a late supper.

11/20
Sea Fare of the Aegean
25 W. 56th St.
581-0540
Lunch and dinner Mon. to Sat. 11:30 A.M. to 11:00 P.M.; dinner Sun. 4:00 P.M. to 11:00 P.M.
All major credit cards
Greek (seafood)

The decor of this large Greek seafood restaurant is supposedly modeled on the famous palace at Knossos, on Crete, and it houses the owner's collection of Greek art. It looks more like Dino de Laurentis's version of *The Poseidon Adventure,* so don't expect to see Nike of Samothrace, and don't expect fabulous food either. Appetizers, such as taramo salad (red caviar spread) and fish soups, are nicely prepared, but the Greek seafood specialties lose something in the translation. The seafood is fresh, but it suffers from an overly ambitious menu and a kitchen trying to serve three dining rooms, which together are the size of a luxury liner. Dinner for two, with wine, will run about $70 to $75.

8/20
Seeda Thai
204 W. 50th St.
586-4513
Lunch Mon. to Fri. 11:30 A.M. to

The uninspired decor of this tacky little place is not redeemed by the quality of the food, which lacks all the delicacy normally associated with this cuisine. Service is unhelpful; at a recent meal a waiter, asked to elucidate the

3:00 P.M.; dinner Mon. to Fri. 4:00 P.M. to 11:00 P.M.
All major credit cards
Indonesian

mishmash of brown objects on our plate, replied with a shrug, "Well, you've got a 92, a 25 and an 86." The satay, a major fire hazard, is soused in vodka and set alight. Large, uncouth slabs of sirloin hang from skewers, forcing us to attack them with a knife and fork instead of employing the more usual nibbling technique. The deep-fried snapper appears to have committed suttee on its oval platter, its blackened sauce charred and smoking at the edges. Hacking with difficulty through the incinerated skin, we finally excavated a few shreds of overcooked fish. Mee krob, those usually wonderful crispy noodles, are flabby and markedly lacking in the promised prawns and pork. Some rubbery coconut cake and a cup of bad instant coffee rounds off a very nasty experience. About $25 per person, with wine.

12/20
Tastings
144 W. 55th St.
757-1160
Lunch Mon. to Sat. noon to 2:30 P.M.; dinner Mon. to Sat. 5:30 P.M. to 11:00 P.M. (Fri. and Sat. to 11:30 P.M.)
AE, MC, V
American

When you go to a place with a name like Tastings you expect at the very least to taste some great wines. But the Burgundy Chassagne Montrachet duc de Magenta that was served to us was absolutely undrinkable. We admit it could have been an accident. In any case, it's amusing to be able to choose from among 30 or so wines of both great and small growths. You can order them by the glass, thanks to a French invention that infuses nitrogen into opened bottles, allowing them to keep for several days (The Wine Bar and Lavin's, among others, are also blessed with this device). We caution this wine bar/restaurant, in the same building as the international wine center, to choose its wines with more discernment, although its staff seems to know its wines very well. As for the cuisine served in this charming little dining room decorated with mirrors mounted on the brick walls and green glass lamps suspended over the tables, it is of surprising quality and is unpretentious. A selection of generous sandwiches changes daily, and the tortellini with a lemon-scallion sauce is worth trying. A pâté de campagne, chicken pot pie with Madeira, exquisite sautéed scallops or beef tenderloin wrapped with Westphalian ham, a chocolate ganache cake and two glasses of Mercury or an excellent Prieure-Lichine '76, all for less than $25, gives you a meal that is quite agreeable.

12/20
21 Club
21 W. 52nd St.
582-7200
Lunch and dinner daily noon to 1:00 A.M.

Sheldon Tannen is a good sport. To prove to me (this is Christian Millau speaking) that he didn't resent my having written in our previous edition of this guide, "Cuisine at the 21 is irregular; one time it is bad, the next time it is worse," he invited me and my wife to dine with

All major credit cards
American

him and his wife. It was one of the rare times I accepted, as a meal with a restaurateur is nearly always a catastrophe. Or perhaps I have an evil eye and bring bad luck to the chef, who becomes paralyzed and completely forgets how to do everything. This time, to my great regret, the meal was nearly perfect from beginning to end; delicious whitefish quenelles in light cream sauce had a remarkable finesse, young roast turkey was full of flavor, and the all-American dessert finishing this dinner, just like a real family holiday meal, was most satisfying. I therefore give you a tip: If you want to dine deliciously at the 21, simply publish a guide, write two or three disagreeable things about the cuisine and wait for the invitation of Sheldon Tannen or Charlie Berns, who are among the most charming and amusing hosts I know. If, however, the invitation is late in coming, you will not go wrong by eating, at your own expense, a cold Senegalese consommé, Malpeque oysters, poached fillet of lemon sole, delicious tarragon lamb, excellent rice pudding or a very satisfactory cheesecake, and in choosing from the most magnificent wine list in New York a wine that, even if modest, has every chance of being good.

Nevertheless, you still have to be able to get into the 21; the door of this former speakeasy is open to everyone but not just anyone. When the doorman replies, "We have no more room," you must understand that to mean, "We have no more room for the likes of you." But there is always space for the regulars who jam these rooms, where in a brownstone, black beamed and varnished wood decor that has developed a lovely patina, there still floats the nostalgic perfume of Prohibition under an extravagant forest of miniature trucks, buses and other toys suspended from the ceiling. And, as in a socialist paradise, even once one is admitted to the 21 there are stratified classes. The "21," the first room you come to, is reserved for the apparatchiks of finance, politics, journalism and the arts; at noon one sees more and more women (from business as well as the beautiful society ladies) entering this macho temple. The "19" is a little less brilliant, but it's still no Gulag; that definition is reserved for "17," baptized "Siberia" because everyone who is not known is parked there. Don't miss climbing the stairs to open, indiscreetly, the private salon doors— you will always find some famous faces. And visit the little room to the right of the entrance to see the Remington paintings, which must have cost a small fortune. And if the day arrives when you are no longer asked for a credit card but are simply asked to sign the check, then you'll know you truly belong to the 21 Club. About $45 per person, with wine.

11/20
United States Steakhouse
Time-Life Building
120 W. 51st St.
757-8800
Dinner Mon. to Sat. 5:00 P.M. to 11:30 P.M. (Sat. from 4:30 P.M.)
All major credit cards
American (steaks)

A very popular rendezvous with the staff of Time-Life, who come to admire the superb news photos covering the light wood walls. The cuisine is clearly less enthusiastic than the photojournalism. Nevertheless, with some oysters or a tomato-basil salad and fried scallops or sirloin steak with béarnaise, accompanied by bad french fries, a chocolate mousse pie and good espresso—all served without many smiles by a staff who has little time to devote to you—you can feed yourself correctly for less than $25.

9/20
Wharf 56
127 W. 56th St.
957-8020
Lunch Mon. to Fri. 11:30 A.M. to 3:00 P.M.; dinner nightly 6:00 P.M. to 11:00 P.M.
All major credit cards
Continental (seafood)

This may be Wharf 56, but we feel lost at sea. The staff is Oriental, the decor is updated Kon Tiki (the boat, not the bar), the music eeking out from tiny speakers sounds like a long ride in an elevator, and the menu ranges from pasta primavera to New England clam chowder to fish and chips. Specials feature such weary items as red snapper with saffron butter sauce. Seafood is the specialty here, and while most of the fish tastes fresh, some are definitely not. Unfortunately, what might well be the catches of the day (or at least the last few days) are uniformly doused with seafood seasoning, heavy in paprika. You may get a nibble, but the fishing is not good at Wharf 56. Dinner for two, with wine from a very limited list, will be about $50.

11/20
Wo Lee Oak of Seoul
77 W. 46th St.
869-9958
Lunch and dinner daily 11:30 A.M. to 10:30 P.M.
AE, DC, V
Korean

In a decor a little sad but as clean and proper as a Korean cafeteria, cooks grill, at your table, slices of chicken, pork or beef marinated in herbs and served with green onions, cabbage leaves (also marinated), bean sprouts and a bowl of sticky rice that is totally devoid of taste. Or, if you prefer, the same beef, chicken or pork is served in a hotpot. In truth, there isn't much to say about this cuisine, which is rather primitive, except that the products are of good quality. Other than the beef tripe, everything tastes the same. About $13 per person, with beer.

East 42nd to 59th Streets

10/20
Altri Tempi
237 E. 58th St.

It's a shame you can't eat the menu here. The cover bears a reproduction of an elegantissimo painting by Giancarlo

752-2113
Lunch Mon. to Fri. noon to 3:00
P.M.; dinner Mon. to Sat. 6:00 P.M.
to 11:30 P.M.
AE, CB, DC
Italian

Impiglia (the original is on the wall); this is the most successful element of this Italo-chichi restaurant, decorated in a meticulously spiritless art deco fashion. The good news, as proclaimed by the menu, is that for the first time, Americans have the privilege of discovering at Altri Tempi the "secret recipes" of the great aristocratic Italian families, prepared on command with the "freshest ingredients possible." The bad news is that the maestro of the kitchens must have found the ultrafatiguées clams accompanying the completely insipid linguine in the refrigerator by accident, that his macaroni with mushrooms and ham would certainly not earn compliments from the Italian aristocracy and that his chicken "alla fiorentina" fried with parsley and Parmesan has a taste so strange it would win the grand prize at the Bienniale of Culinary Horrors. The vegetables, on the other hand (spinach, baby carrots and artichokes with olive oil and white wine), are perfectly prepared and juicy, and the chocolate cake is decent enough. But there is nothing here to encourage us to return too quickly, even though the staff is friendly. In any case, there is no urgency for the chef of Altri Tempi to fly to Italy to get additional recipes from Italian families: if they aren't any better than the ones he already has, we can wait several more centuries. There's a prix fixe lunch at $17.50; à la carte, with a simple wine, will be about $30 to $40 per person.

10/20
Anche Vivolo
222 E. 58th St.
308-0112
Lunch Mon. to Fri. noon to 3:00
P.M.; dinner Mon. to Sat. 5:30 P.M.
to 11:30 P.M.
All major credit cards
Italian

Like most sequels, Anche Vivolo (*anche* is Italian for "also") does not compare well with Vivolo on East 74th Street, its bustling progenitor. Since the menus are mostly the same, the difference can be attributed only to careless (or uncaring) management—even though Anche Vivolo's location, on fiercely competitive East 58th Street. (a.k.a. Via Vitello), would seemingly dictate unremitting concern for quality. The restaurant's main fault is that the fish and seafood are not consistently fresh, even on Friday. There can be few more venal sins. The kitchen is slow, and the service, though amiable, is unpolished. With many dishes, on the other hand, Vivolo, Jr., does quite well. Among the antipastos, mozzarella deep fried in batter and the eggplant rolatini with ricotta (also offered as a main course) are good. Pasta dishes, served as either a first or a main course, include savory linguine with clams and better-than-average fettuccine with tomatoes and onions. Broiled steak, grilled veal chops and shrimp fra diavolo (when the shrimp is fresh) are all properly prepared. Nuova cucina this is not. Run-of-the-mill desserts, which would seem to be supplied from outside, include spumoni, which has disappeared from most Italian menus in recent years. The prices are among 58th Street's lowest: $60 for a three-course lunch for two, with an aperitif and a glass of house wine.

8/20
Beijing Duck House
144 E. 52nd St.
759-8260
Lunch and dinner Mon. to Sat. noon to 11:00 P.M. (Fri. and Sat. to midnight)
AE, MC, V
Chinese

Little has changed here since our last review, including, unfortunately, the fat in which the duck appears to have been deep fried. It still has the same strange, greasy smell. Peking Duck should be a ceremonial feast (it can never be an assembly-line operation), starting with the arrival of the Duck Blower, whose job it is to loosen the skin of the duck by blowing into one of its orifices. But complaints that this was ruining the blowers' social lives resulted in the introduction of the bicycle pump in many establishments. We preferred not to ask which method was currently in vogue here. After being scalded and hung up to dry, the duck should then be rubbed with honey and spices and roasted to order in a special hot oven. With dozens of roast ducks flying in at twenty-minute intervals (preceded by their webbed feet, in the form of a rather nasty cold appetizer), it appears that this process had been speeded up here. Neither did we approve of the way our bird was hacked to pieces (no nonsense about carving you thin slices of crispy skin) and served up as an unwieldy package in a tough, doughy pancake. Other dishes, notably the spring rolls, fried dumplings and stuffed eggplant, are also heavy and oily. A place to be avoided by anyone who has experienced the real thing—sheer culinary quackery! Dinner with drinks will run $30 per person.

9/20
Beijing Pavilion
220 E. 46th St.
661-8275
Lunch daily noon to 3:00 P.M.;
dinner nightly 6:00 P.M. to 11:00 P.M.
All major credit cards
Chinese

You have the feeling of being lost in a gray pavilion here: it's one large room (gray) with a huge pillar in the middle and a large, gray-toned mural along the back wall depicting mountains and the Great Wall of China. We hope you like cloisonné—we'll leave our opinion of the cloisonné flamingos open to conjecture. This is an elegant if somewhat somber room, and so it is quite a surprise to see the menu, which is pink, wrinkled, stapled and spotted with grease, with some items simply crossed out and reinserted in a quite amusing style. For those of you wondering about the fate of Lot's wife, wonder no more: we are fairly certain she is hard at work in the Beijing Pavilion's kitchen. Tangy, spicy young chicken would be good if not coated with salt. Crystal shrimp—more like a shrimp cocktail than anything else— is good but also too salty. Scallops in ginger sauce are quite pleasant, but taste more of salt and pepper than of ginger.

And the rubbery barbecued lamb seems to have been in the kitchen since Lot's wife arrived.

Běijing Pavilion tries hard, and there is the feeling of a missing ingredient that, if found, could pull it all together. Perhaps it is too Americanized: there are handles on the teacups, no chopsticks on the tables and mostly American business people here for lunch, although the menu has enough exotic items (jellyfish, frog, sea cucumbers) to make you want to return and experiment. Service is friendly and helpful—in fact, there's more staff than clientele. Expect to pay around $50 for lunch for two, with wine.

12/20
Benihana
120 E. 55th St.
593-1627
Lunch Mon. to Sat. noon to 2:30 P.M.; dinner nightly 6:00 P.M. to 11:00 P.M. (Fri. and Sat. midnight, Sun. to 9:45 P.M.)
All major credit cards

Japanese

At the risk of being stoned to death with umeboshi plums by Japanese food purists, we have to admit to quite enjoying this chain of fast-food Japanese steak houses. It may not be a luminous gastronomic experience, but it's cheap, cheerful and good theater. Chefs in high hats chop, slice and season with a juggler's skill, searing the assorted meats, seafood and vegetables on the hot plate that forms the centerpiece of your table. Anything that can be thrown into the air— from a pepper mill to a handful of sesame seeds—most certainly will be, and you may as well share a table, since the ambience is so convivial. All this is not a smoke screen to disguise inferior ingredients; steak is of the best quality, scallops are fresh and tender, and even the green salad, with its thick garlic and ginger dressing, is remarkably crisp and tasty. The stir-fried vegetables (zucchini, mushrooms, onions and bean sprouts) are uninspired, and fried rice, tasting of burned fat, is to be avoided at all costs. With ice cream for dessert and a couple of Japanese beers to wash the whole thing down, you can be in and out in 40 minutes—which, of course, is just how the management likes it. About $16 per person, with beer.

12/20
Le Bistro
827 Third Ave.
(50th St.)
759-8439
Lunch Mon. to Fri. noon to 3:00 P.M.; dinner Mon. to Sat. 6:00 P.M. to 10:00 P.M.
All major credit cards

French (provincial)

Wedged between office skyscrapers, Le Bistro is jammed at lunch with business types more interested in their white wine or martinis and their business deals than in what they are eating. Le Bistro is at its best after dark. The only thing missing is a striking Toulouse-Lautrec lady of the evening and her dapper escort. Everything else is here: the metal bar, red-backed banquettes, dark wood paneling and etched glass partitions. If New York has a Belle Epoque bistro, this is it.

We were not around to sample bistro food at the turn

of the century, so we can only guess how it compares with today's renderings. We suspect, however, that some of the lustiness that marked the cooking of that era (not often found in France today) is not always apparent in Le Bistro's cassoulet, cuisses de grenouilles, tripes à la mode de Caen or bouillabaisse (Fridays only). But still you will enjoy these old standbys, even if they don't always excite you to quite the degree that you anticipate. After all, the ambience is absolutely delightful and the service totally professional (are there more affable hosts on the New York restaurant scene than Georges and Henri?). About $30 per person, with a fresh Beaujolais.

10/20
The Box Tree
250 E. 49th St.
758-8320
Lunch Mon. to Fri. 12:30 P.M. to 2:00 P.M.; dinner seatings nightly 6:30 P.M. and 9:30 P.M.
No credit cards
French (classical)

When you enter the foyer of the new Box Tree, you may have the inclination, as we have had, to run as quickly as possible in the opposite direction. There is something disheartening about being confronted by a dollhouse version of an English manor house, complete with a badly painted oil portrait. The once bright and cheerful decor of the former Box Tree has given way to a serious, sober dark green and wood paneled decor, relieved faintly by an interior courtyard that looks something like a decorated shaft way. There is a pompous air here, from the tuxedoed waiters to the atmosphere of false luxury that we can only assume is for the benefit of the nouveau riche clientele that doesn't know the difference. On top of these small trifles, we're sorry to report that the cuisine has not improved with the move. A quasi-nouvelle approach is misunderstood to the point of quiet desperation (ours). The Wedgwood china, sparkling stemware, Christofle flatware and rosebuds pinned onto each diner cannot salvage the $47 prix fixe dinner. It offers plenty of courses; the question is whether you will enjoy them, particularly with 20-minute waits in between. The menu changes seasonally, which may give you the questionable good fortune to sample a rather gelatinous smoked haddock mousse (it looks like a midwestern housewife's recipe contest winner), snails in Pernod, exquisite calf's brains en croûte (they're actually inside hollowed-out French bread), a passable artichoke with Dijon dipping sauce, an excellent although tart sorrel soup, good chilled cucumber and yogurt soup or a morel bisque that is unbelievably rich. The chef here has a penchant for sauces, liberally ladeling them over everything. The poached salmon is drowning in hollandaise (the menu says it's a mousseline), and the striped bass is floating in beurre blanc (with a too-healthy dose of vinegar)—although the rack of lamb is good, the calf's liver pleasing and the duck with green peppercorn sauce worth ordering. Dinner also includes a salad with Stilton and desserts that are quite flavorful, as we expect in places where the food fails to rally our spirit. The vacherin is filled with raspberries, the crème brûlée a bit soupy but good nonetheless, the délice au chocolat a sinful luxury and the cocotte of raspberries a strange concoction of whipped cream and a berry purée. The filtered coffee is weak, and the bill climbs to Olympian proportions with all the extras, particularly with the expensive, limited wine list. You might want to become a member of The Box Tree club, if you have the misguided desire to eat here often: no credit cards, but the restaurant will bill you if it's prearranged.

9/20
The Brazilian Pavilion
316 E. 53rd St.
758-8129
Lunch Mon. to Sat. noon to 4:30 P.M.; dinner Mon. to Sat. 5:00 P.M. to 11:00 P.M.
All major credit cards
Brazilian

This cool green and white restaurant is best known for its feijoada, Brazil's national dish, a hearty and far from subtle combination of black beans with various cuts of pork, smoked tongue and sausage, which is sprinkled with manioc flour and eaten with rice, sliced fresh oranges and collard greens. This is a dish you'll either like or loathe, but aficionados assured us that we would find the genuine article here. Our own experiences were not so happy. We have sampled thin bean soup (presumably the water from the feijoada beans), a dried up piece of chicken with a grayish sludge masquerading as mashed potato and an indescribably nasty mariscada, Brazil's answer to bouillabaisse. This odd dish resembles an abandoned aquarium full of sea creatures, each of which contributes a certain je ne sais quoi to the broth, the large, pleated flaps of chewy octopus being particularly daunting. From what the menu describes as the "rolling dessert cart" you can choose from four different kinds of egg custard or a soggy banana cake. Drinks here are powerful and delicious, based mainly on rum, fresh lime and coconut, and as the service is mercifully slow you may well be in a state of happy and uncritical oblivion by the time your food arrives. About $25 per person, with tropical cocktails.

12/20
Bruno's
240 E. 58th St.
688-4190
Lunch Mon. to Fri. noon to 3:00 P.M.; dinner Mon. to Sat. 5:00 P.M. to midnight
All major credit cards
Italian

Yet another restaurant on the 58th Street Little Italy row, Bruno's is popular with a clientele of regulars who bring their spouses and lovers to be pampered by good service and Italian food of the home-cooked genre. You will not find much spirit or imagination in the kitchen, but the cuisine is satisfactory in a safe sort of way. If you splurge and order the Gavi San Pietro wine (at $34—hefty for

Italian wines), your dinner will be better than average, because Bruno's has possibilities if you're under the influence. Start with the tortellini ai quattro formaggi or the angel hair pasta with seafood and move onto a good Caesar salad, then to an acceptable saltimbocca or slightly overcooked seafood dish (calamari, snapper, scampi, bass and sole), ending with an excellent zuppa inglese. Nothing will overwhelm you, but you will pass a pleasant evening among nice people—particularly the Yugoslavian bartender, who is enthusiastic and friendly, making your turn at the bar a pleasant diversion rather than an interminable wait. About $40 per person, with wine.

12/20
Café 58
232 E. 58th St.
758-5665
Lunch and dinner Mon. to Sat. noon to midnight; dinner Sun. 5:00 P.M. to 11:00 P.M.
AE, DC, V
French (provincial)

We were so thrilled at discovering a little corner of Paris in New York (as regulars describe it), where you can find authentically grilled pig's trotters and drink the first Beaujolais nouveau, that we can forgive certain culinary peccadilloes: densely sticky rillettes, sandy moules marinière and scrappy tripe à la mode de Caen, which tastes as if consommé has been poured in at the last moment. On the credit side, there is a beautiful cold striped bass with a green mayonnaise, an unctuous oeufs en gelée (the aspic is flavored with fennel and topped with finely diced chicken), a flaky, well-caramelized apple tart and feather-light oeufs à la nage. The prix fixe lunch, at $17 for three courses, is an excellent value. Otherwise count on spending about $20 to $30 per person, with a bottle of Blanc de Blanc.

13 ♟
La Camelia
225 E. 58th St.
751-5488
Lunch Mon. to Fri. 11:30 A.M. to 3:00 P.M.; dinner Mon. to Sat. 5:00 P.M. to 1:00 A.M.
Jackets required
All major credit cards
Italian

Perhaps you will run into a member of your family—let's say your godfather—in the crowd that comes to this Italian restaurant, which has a flashy elegance but doesn't lack charm, with its imposing chandelier and plants hanging from the ceiling. The chef, if he received threats after the bad criticism he got in our previous edition, deserves a reprieve after our most recent meal here. A very good pasta moistened with the juice of wild game was a bit too salty but had a wonderfully powerful taste; agreeable clams and mussels in a saffron sauce were well done; gnocchi with broccoli were light and flavorful; and, above all, a remarkable spinola al forno (baked whole sea bass) was perfectly cooked and served with a lemon sauce; to finish, a chocolate mousse cake, although a bit pale in taste, was good nevertheless. During the evenings, an orchestra feels obliged to make some music, but after midnight, the chef comes out with his hot plate to prepare pasta on the piano—we prefer the chef's music. There's a spectacular exclusively Italian wine list with several bottles that are priced crazily but others that are quite reasonable. About $45 per person, with wine.

13 Captain's Table

860 Second Ave.
(46th St.)
697-9538

Lunch Mon. to Fri. noon to 3:00 P.M.; dinner Mon. to Sat. 5:00 P.M. to 11:00 P.M. (Sat. to midnight)
AE, MC, V

American (seafood)

The last time we visited the Captain, he had lost his rudder. Perhaps he had gone fishing for lunch. In any case, after we selected a striped bass and loup, presented in a basket filled with many other pretty fresh fish, he made us wait 45 minutes before anyone wanted to serve us. Moreover, our fish were cold and their flesh a bit insipid, which naturally left some doubt about their degree of freshness. The soft-shell crabs were nothing extraordinary, and our meal, all summed up, confirmed some sort of deception. It was certainly not at the level of our previous meals here, nor a justification for the high prices. When you pay $20 for soft-shell crabs and $25 for loup, you have every right to hope for something exceptional. Certainly an accident is always possible, and our optimistic nature invites us to leave his toque in place. We continue to love the amusing jumble of Belle Epoque that slightly evokes Maxwell's Plum in its liveliness, the extremely energetic atmosphere and its praiseworthy ambition to serve only fresh fish from the Atlantic and the Mediterranean. But it is dangerous if success allows owners Gino and Sabine Musso to relax their surveillance.

15 La Cascade

Olympic Towers
645 Fifth Ave.
(51st St.)
935-2220

Dinner nightly 5:30 P.M. to 10:00 P.M.
All major credit cards

French (nouvelle)

When you wander through the gallery of the Olympic Towers, it would be most improbable to suspect that there is a marvelous restaurant hidden away downstairs, facing the cascade of water that gives this public area its distinctive architectural charm. This little place is a jewel, calm and tranquil despite its curious photographic wall mural. The service is excellent, the ambience slightly relaxed and the cuisine a surprise. We have always loved La Cascade, and things are improving even more; you can expect a superb meal prepared with imagination, sensitivity and delicacy. Pass up the bistro-type starters (smoked salmon, snails, smoked trout) for one of the lovely dishes of pike quenelles, scallops en feuilleté or marvelous lobster bisque. The entrees are supplemented with specials, but you will not be unhappy if you sample the astonishing sweetbreads, housed in a crown of smoked chicken and topped with chanterelles; these sweetbreads are whole, tender and absolutely delicious. Nor will you be disappointed with the poached turbot, the salmon with sorrel sauce or the breast of duck. There is real prowess in the kitchen, and, happily, it is reflected in your plate. Desserts are supplied by Guy Pascal Les Délices, and if you have only one dessert to try, don't miss the délice cake made with layers of meringue, mocha cream, almond butter cream, chocolate mousse and toasted almonds—it is a gift from the gods. There are plenty of other temptations, including exquisite ice cream concoctions. The wine list is modest but adequate, and you will leave mesmerized not only by the constant flow of water reflected in the mirrors but also by this deft cuisine, which doesn't deserve to be as sheltered as it is in this pretty basement. About $45 per person, with wine.

16

Le Chantilly
106 E. 57th St.
751-2931
Lunch Mon. to Sat. noon to 3:00 P.M.; dinner Mon. to Sat. 6:00 P.M. to 11:00 P.M.
All major credit cards
French (classical)

If Swiss owner Paul Dessibourg and French Chef Roland Chenus, who is his associate, were less modest and had a more developed sense for public relations, you would know that Le Chantilly is one of the very good French restaurants in New York. If you are tired of the excessive eccentricities of chichi cuisine, and if you've had enough of restaurants that are too pretty to be honest, then it's time for you to discover, or rediscover, this place. It is ultratraditional, and its less-than-inspired appearance gives you all sorts of good reasons to believe that it is boring—but when professionalism attains such heights as Chantilly's kitchen does, a meal here becomes a veritable celebration. While so many fashionable restaurants disguise the most mediocre cuisine with ridiculously seductive names, it is a point of honor here to give the delicious dishes a banal description. When, for example, you order shrimp with Russian dressing (one of the old war-horses in second-class hotels), you don't expect to find shrimp with perfect texture and a tomato mayonnaise flavored with celery that is equally excellent. The calf's liver with grapes is thick, rosy and velvety; kidneys flamed in Armagnac are delicate; lotte steak with paprika is flavorful; and the loin of veal with fresh tarragon and thyme merits a place in gastronomic anthologies. Roland Chenus, who worked in Switzerland with the father of the famous Fredy Girardet, poses some questions. A traditional chef, he asks himself whether his cuisine is passé and whether he should join the vanguard of more modern tastes. But he should rest assured. Creativity doesn't consist of inventing just anything; it gives cuisine a proper distinction and personality. And he knows how to do this, even with a simple salad. He doesn't need kiwi to prove his talent. We give him one more toque, which he greatly deserves. The lunch prix fixe menu is $21.50; the dinner menu is $36.50.

14 👨‍🍳
Le Cherche Midi

936 First Ave.
355-4499

Lunch Tues. to Fri. noon to 2:30
P.M.; dinner Mon. to Sat. 6:00 P.M.
to 11:00 P.M.
MC, V

French (provincial)

Sally Scoville has looked for the Midi, and has clearly found it. This tall New Yorker, as beautiful as she is shy, studied family cooking in Provence for some time; she was so inspired by it that she prepares a fresh, appetizing and often most successful cuisine in this simple, elegant little bistro, where the tables are decorated with garden flowers in the summer and the atmosphere is warm and cozy in the winter. The duck pâté, a touch mushy, is not her chef d'oeuvre. On the other hand, the pissaladière niçoise with anchovies and onions has an authentic taste, even though Sally betrays the traditional recipe by substituting feuilleté pastry (which is excellent) for the bread dough. Arriving piping hot from the oven, Sally's pissaladière agreeably excites the appetite and opens the way to a delicious leg of lamb in its natural juices and fresh parsley, accompanied by a delicious ratatouille, which she is wrong, in our opinion, to serve cold. One can equally recommend the sweetbreads with wild mushrooms and tarragon cream or the seafood ragout, lightly perfumed with Pernod. These dishes are more convincing than the roast chicken stuffed with zucchini, ham, herbs and chèvre, which reminds us of the gimmickry of amateur chefs. Sally would also do well to take a little more care with desserts; the hazelnut chocolate cake and lemon tart do not give an ideal finish to a meal that, without being grandiose, has all the charm of authenticity and things of value. Espresso here is excellent, and the smallness of the wine list belies a real care in research. Sally, like us, has a predilection for Rhone wines, so unknown and so inexpensive in view of their quality. This is the place to discover these red wines that are full of sunlight, such as the Crozes-Hermitage, Saint-Joseph, Côte Rôtie, the admirable Châteauneuf-du-Pape Château Rayas or the more modest house reserve Vacqueyras, well priced at $14. About $30 to $40 per person, with wine.

11/20
Christ Cella

160 E. 46th St.
697-2479

Lunch and dinner Mon. to Sat. noon
to 10:30 P.M. (Fri. and Sat. to
10:45 P.M.)
All major credit cards

American (steaks)

If even the steaks are not good at Christ Cella, something is going wrong in the world. The one served to us, enormous as usual, had so little taste that we felt it our right to ask the waiter if the cow or bull who so generously provided it hadn't died a slow death from anemia or from a broken heart. The fat french fries didn't make anything better, leading us to the recommendation that the chef be sent for an urgent refresher course at McDonald's. We were grateful to see the honor of this institution saved with a good mixed salad and a striped bass, which, in spite of being overcooked—as usual—was excellent. Despite our having said all that, our criticisms certainly won't empty the three little rooms with highly varnished floors and white walls hung with engravings and paintings, all of which is plunged into a sad light like that found at a club for aging gentlemen. Nor will our criticisms make the sluggish, undeceiving waiters surprised when they return plates three-quarters full to the kitchens. Nor will they inspire the owner to present a wine list that is more exciting and a bit less expensive. About $40 per person, with wine.

17

La Côte Basque
5 E. 55th St.
688-6525
Lunch Mon. to Fri. noon to 2:30 P.M.; dinner Mon. to Sat. 6:00 P.M. to 10:30 P.M. (Sat. to 11:00 P.M.) All major credit cards
French
(classical/nouvelle)

After passing through the glorious epoch of Henri Soulé, who 40 years ago was the initiator of grand French cuisine in New York, the Côte Basque had become a dismal copy of what it once was. Its renaissance is the result of its new owner, Jean-Jacques Rachou, a French chef who passed his tests at Lutèce and the Colony. Wisely, he hasn't touched the provincial decor, the slightly naïf trompe l'oeil wall painting depicting the port of Saint Jean de Luz or the false beams that make the place look like a Basque farm. He did make it so warm and comfortable, however, that the cream of the financial and business worlds found their way very quickly to Côte Basque. At the same time, Rachou gave his most classic dishes a personal touch, a new attractiveness and marvelously precise tastes. He still cedes a bit too much to the temptation of rich sauces, truffles and foie gras, but if you know how to choose from the extensive menu, you will be sure of a superb meal: for example, scallops with grapefruit or, even better, Bay scallops in a fabulous beurre blanc with Sauternes, lightened with thyme and chives; feuilleté of lobster with morels; roast duck with two sauces; or a fantastic veal chop with cream, topped with a rather mediocre scallop of foie gras, which doesn't add anything to the veal—but the marriage of wild rice and an exquisite purée of white onion and celery is absolutely ideal. Rachou is a master of purées, and you need only taste these creations to discern the difference between them and the baby food that has been fashionable for the past three years and is an obsession of gastronomy critics. These well-meaning people have tried to create a reverse trend by scorning this whole category of cuisine. Imagine if, under the pretext that one mediocre artist abused aesthetic principles, all the grand masters of the Renaissance were forbidden to paint angels, crèches and the baby Jesus!

The dessert cart is a temptation sent by the devil in person, and even the simple île flottante with its caramelized topping leaves a marvelous memory. The wine list is superb, the service is prodigiously efficient and pleasant, and the tables are sufficiently separated so you are not forced to participate in your neighbors' conversations. And although the evening's prix fixe menu at $40 doesn't give you much hope of leaving without spending less than $150 for two, the lunch prix fixe at $24 is almost a deal. You can see how it would be impossible to refuse a third toque to Jean-Jacques Rachou, even if in serving no less than 350 meals a day, he occasionally has mishaps.

16

Le Cygne
53 E. 54th St.
759-5941
Lunch Mon. to Fri. noon to 2:30 P.M.; dinner Mon. to Sat. 6:00 P.M. to 10:00 P.M. (Fri. to 10:30 P.M., Sat. to 11:00 P.M.)
All major credit cards
French (provincial)

In its new nest, supremely elegant and decorated with fresh floral paintings in the style (albeit remotely) of Claude Monet, which brighten the walls with their tender colors, this swan has taken a renewed flight, and without hesitation we salute it with a second toque. Originally from Nantes, the port where beurre blanc was created, Chef Jean-Yves Piquet is less inspired by the Atlantic than he is by the Mediterranean (which is not too surprising, since one of the two owners, Michel Crouzillat, is a child of Grasse—a little town near Cannes celebrated for its perfumes—who told his chef of his fascination for herbs and the fresh fragrances that are the charm of provençale cuisine). The menu still lists the old-fashioned international cuisine, with such dishes as calf's kidneys Beauge or pepper steak flamed in Cognac, but if you choose the exquisite fricassée of baby Maine shrimp sautéed in olive oil, tomato and basil, cream of mussels, frog's legs sautéed in garlic butter, striped bass with cucumbers, fillet of silver salmon with herbs or braised squab with olives and artichokes, you will be embraced by the sunlight of Provence that so overruns this place. These tastes are subtle and marvelously light; products are left with their natural flavors, and they give a fabulous whet to the appetite. You will find at Le Cygne one of the most authentic successes of regional French cuisine, and the most sure advice we can give Jean-Yves Piquet is for him to steer resolutely toward the Mediterranean, which is evidently his best inspiration. But don't leave before tasting the fresh California raspberry soufflé, with its light texture and irresistible fragrance—it is one of the best desserts we could possibly dream of. There's just one lonely American wine, but a pretty choice of French wines, among which is the excellent Chassagne-Montrachet Morgeot, a great deal at $26. The lunch prix fixe menu is $25.50, and the dinner menu is $42.75.

10/20
Enoteca Iperbole
137 E. 55th St.
759-9720
Lunch and dinner daily noon to midnight
AE, DC
Italian

Enoteca Iperbole has the feel of a book-lined library at an exclusive Fifth Avenue club (the quiet is disturbed here and there by the intermittent clatter of forks on plates instead of the rustle of newspapers). You are, in fact, surrounded by the most complete collection of Italian wines in the city, instead of musty, leather-bound sets of Dickens and Thackeray—but this does not, however, ensure that the handful of occupants is less formal or more exciting. After all, there are many New York business people so intent on the next merger, contract or lawsuit that they are oblivious to where they are or what they are eating; you will be sure to find some of them here at lunch and more of them (with their spouses) at dinner. The kitchen perfectly reflects this clublike setting: unimaginative pastas, listless renderings of other Italian dishes and unsmiling service—at prices that will ensure the continued exclusivity of the place. About $35 per person, without wine.

16
Felidia
243 E. 58th St.
758-1479
Lunch and dinner Mon. to Fri. noon to midnight; dinner Sat. 5:00 P.M. to midnight
All major credit cards
Italian

Lidia is one of those Italians whose generous shape, radiant gourmet face and joie de vivre make you love her the minute you see her; you say to yourself that if she would only invite you into the kitchen to share her dinner, you would be among the happiest people in the world. But fear not! You will not be among the most unhappy in the narrow little room on the ground floor or upstairs in the less well lit gallery. The moment you sit down, one of the two captains, Nino or Dante, is at your side to detail with a rare enthusiasm all the daily specials and the regular menu, and to advise you with such an art that you'll feel you couldn't compose your own dinner better. It's a grand moment—and what follows is no less exciting. Lidia and her partner Felix come from one of the Italian regions where you can eat the best—Friole, near Trieste, close to the Yugoslav border. In the nearly ten years they have been in New York, they have scarcely forgotten the authentic flavors of regional cuisine, and each meal at Felidia is a celebration. (It is a fête when they receive from Italy fresh white truffles or porcini mushrooms, which they lightly sautéed in olive oil and serve still crunchy.) The fresh pasta is a marvel, whether it be gnocchi al pesto or the amazing fusilli in duck sauce. It would be impossible not to find something good on the menu or among the twenty or so specials proposed each evening. It is nearly impossible for us to tell you how to decide between the Florentine tripes, Roman saltimbocca, Istrian zuppe di pesce, fillet of red snapper with polenta, veal chop stuffed with broccoli or chicken roasted with rosemary. But don't make the choice yourself. Nino and Dante know much better than you do what you want, and it's impossible to resist them. Let them also select a wine from the extremely rich list, which contains many delicious bottles for less than $20. In our previous edition, we left hope for a second toque for Lidia and Felix; they didn't have to wait long. About $45 per person, with wine.

12/20
Fonda La Paloma
256 E. 49th St.
421-5495
Lunch Mon. to Fri. noon to 3:00 P.M.; dinner nightly 5:00 P.M. to midnight (Fri. and Sat. to 1:00 A.M., Sun. to 10:30 P.M.)
All major credit cards
Mexican

Twenty years ago, long before what passes as Mexican food caught on in New York, Dinna and Sal Hernandez opened this peppy (and sometimes noisy) little place with stucco walls, tiles, earthenware pottery and intriguing primitive oil paintings by Agapito Labios. The crowd continues to be livelier than the food. That is not to say that the nachos with frijoles, the guacamole, the rellenos or the mole poblano (with excellent chicken under the sauce) are not acceptable enough. What we find is that the dishes are a little bland and not very stimulating. In a word, the warmth of Sal and Dinna as hosts (to say nothing of the handsome, mustachioed maître d') is not always reflected in what comes from the kitchen. This is nonetheless a place to have fun. And if you like things spicier, you can always add a bit more jalapeño. About $30 per person, with refreshing Mexican beer.

16
Four Seasons
99 E. 52nd St.
752-9494
Bar room: lunch Mon. to Sat. noon to 2:00 P.M.; dinner Mon. to Fri. 7:30 P.M. to midnight
Pool room: lunch Mon. to Fri. noon to 2:30 P.M.; dinner Mon. to Sat. 5:00 P.M. to 11:30 P.M.
All major credit cards
American/Continental

The advantage of restaurants that serve many covers is that if it works, the owner makes a lot of money. The inconvenience for the client is that it is extremely difficult to maintain the same level of quality from one year to the next. For the past fifteen years, we have visited this extraordinary place fairly regularly. Its sublime coldness, signed by Philip Johnson and Mies van der Rohe, still doesn't show a wrinkle, and we have no doubt that one day it will be proclaimed an historical landmark.

We have had many experiences here, both admirable meals and meals that have been terribly disappointing, if not in totality, at least in part. In spite of our admiration for owners Paul Kovi and Tom Margittai and Chef Seppi Renggli, we have to admit that our most recent meals fell into the latter category. We hope next time we will be luckier and will find them at their best. This spectacular and grand dining room is around the pool; the service is impeccable and the atmosphere refined and romantic enough to drive even the most sensible of men to marriage proposals. We hope that next time we will be enchanted again by such seasonal dishes as shrimp ceviche, salmon and pike terrine, crisped shrimp stuffed with mustard "fruits," superb breaded and fried calf's

brains, fettuccine with crabmeat, steamed bass with Sauternes, delicious fillet of pompano with macadamia nuts, scallop of veal with ginger, breast of squab with Merlot, braised duck with green peppercorn sauce, rack of lamb with rosemary, a sinful chocolate cake, a marvelous bourbon and maple syrup soufflé and fruit sorbets. The products are of exceptional quality, and Chef Renggli is capable of pulling them all off, but it would be a tour de force to succeed every day. For the most part, however, the cuisine is delicate, and we prefer to remember our good experiences instead of the bad ones.

The Four Seasons has made a big point about its spa cuisine; the menu enthusiastically proclaims that Chef Renggli has developed these dishes for health-conscious customers in accordance with the latest nutritional developments. It takes a highly refined palate to appreciate the nutritious taste of bland spinach with poached oysters (although the truffle topping gives us hope), steamed lamb with cabbage, or whole wheat pasta. But all is not lost—the self-indulgent can pass by the spa and feast instead on wonderfully tender pheasant stuffed with green mustard, or perfectly cooked venison served with a luscious chestnut purée.

In any case, what will never disappoint you is the exceptional atmosphere of the Four Seasons, the perfection of the welcome, the professional service and the prodigious richness of the wine cellar, where both the biggest and the most modest French, California, Italian, German and Hungarian wines are among the best. About $65 per person; the fare is slightly less in the grill, where New York's powerful meet for lunch.

11/20
Girafe
208 E. 58th St.
752-3054
Dinner Mon. to Sat. 5:30 P.M. to 10:30 P.M.
All major credit cards
Italian

Traditional Italian cuisine served in a traditional Italian restaurant decor. The pink light is flattering to diners of all ages, particularly since the place is so dark it takes some adjusting if you choose Girafe for lunch. The flowers are graceful, the service is attentive, and the cuisine is boring. There's a certain lack of love here, although the results are not unsatisfactory, simply a little tired. Tortellini in cream is a baked affair with a gratin crust, and the homemade pasta melts in your mouth. The linguine with clam sauce is tasty, as is the baked ravioli. A salad of arugula, endive and radicchio is fresh, with a well-seasoned dressing, and is a refreshing alternative to the heavy pastas. Entrees are predictable: grilled snapper, five classic veal dishes, such specials as breast of chicken with eggplant, prosciutto and mozzarella, and chicken with pepperoni. The zuppa inglese is luscious and the cheesecake worth trying. All in all it's a nice experience, even though you may leave feeling a little cheated of the sincerity and care you find in the less chichi mamma and papa places. About $30 per person for lunch, nearly double at night.

12/20
Gloucester House
37 E. 50th St.
755-7394
Lunch daily noon to 3:00 P.M.;
dinner nightly 5:30 P.M. to
10:30 P.M.
All major credit cards
American (seafood)

If you venture into this male bastion for lunch, you will be surrounded by executives entertaining their clients and each other in a boring boat decor, complete with benches reminiscent of those on the Martha's Vineyard ferry. Nantucket blue, nautical details (thank God no nets), a dramatic stairway perfect for a small luxury liner and a seafood menu complete the Cape Cod scene. Unfortunately, the menu is deceptive, and much of what you may order may not be available—and not for seasonal reasons. On our last visit, only one family of oysters was available (of the five varieties); nor was there red snapper or anchovy butter. No matter, there are enough seafood choices to please even the most finicky appetite. The quality is superb, but we really have to object to the astronomical prices (salmon at $22.50, snapper at $23.50, English sole at $27.50, lobster for two at $67.50), when you can get even more superb food at half the price down the street at the Oyster Bar. The wine list is decent, with a few unremarkable California whites tossed in with French Bordeaux and Burgundies. Desserts are as all-American as apple pie, blueberry slump and a strawberry shortcake overwhelmed with sugary syrup, with strawberries nested on the same good homemade biscuits served with your meal. If you're on an expense account, join the men here and be prepared to pay about $65 for lunch for two, without wine.

11/20
La Grenouille
3 E. 52nd St.
752-1495
Dinner Mon. to Sat. 6:00 P.M. to
10:30 P.M.
AE, DC
French (classical)

The La Grenouille that we used to know as such a chic place no longer sparkles. It's sad to see it dragging itself around in the same large room, with its almond-green walls and slightly faded luxury, when for so many years it was the scene of success. After having lunched on an oversalted salmon pâté that was insipid, a tough, overcooked breast of veal soaking in an overly thick herb sauce and accompanied with noodles that are more suitable for a school cafeteria, a noncommittal fig tart and a pineapple sorbet with no flavor of pineapple, you could ask yourself what illness has stricken this frog. Perhaps it is simply the fatigue that comes with getting old, which engenders bad habits and uncomplicated tastes. In Paris we have witnessed the same decline at

Laperouse and Lucas-Carton, and if older New Yorkers remember the glory of Henri Soulé's Pavillon with emotion, they must also recall that at the end, the cuisine was no longer glorious. Even the best restaurants end eventually, from aged arteries. In any case, former owner Charles Masson would never have dared to let his cuisine descend to this level, with hastily prepared dishes that cost no less than the good cuisine of Lutèce, La Côte Basque or Le Cirque. The overall feeling of ennui is spared on the maîtres d' and waiters (they continue to be willing and excellent), but it reverberates through the wine list. While more and more New York restaurant owners go to the trouble to hunt out good wines, often moderately priced and off the beaten track, here you find a collection of great names—Lafite, Latour, Petrus—sold at inflated prices. And as for the others, they are represented by one or two negotiants for whom the most we can say is that they will not bore you to death. This is perhaps only a small detail, but the composition of a wine cellar in a restaurant is more revealing than you might think, for when fatigue hits downstairs, there is a good chance it has also affected the upstairs. The lunch prix fixe menu is $27.75; dinner is $45.75.

14

Hatsuhana
17 E. 48th St.
355-3345
Lunch Mon. to Fri. 11:45 A.M. to 2:30 P.M.; dinner Mon. to Fri. 5:30 P.M. to 9:30 P.M., Sat. 5:00 P.M. to 9:30 P.M.
All major credit cards
Japanese

Hatsuhana is exceptionally bright and clean, even by Japanese standards, all varnished pine with big, colorful cutouts on the walls; there is something almost childishly gay and cheerful about his ultramodern and efficient sushi bar and restaurant. Downstairs it's a pleasure to watch the specially trained Japanese chefs press and mold the sticky, slightly sweet rice with its adornments of raw fish and dark green seaweed, or slice the superbly fresh fish for the sashimi. Our favorite remains the deep pink tuna, particularly the marbled, fatty variety known as toro. A selection of all these on a round lacquered tray makes a fascinating kaleidoscope of red, black, green and yellow; it is served with hot green mustard, pickles and lacy spirals of grated white radish. As an added bonus there are some excellent hot and cold dishes for appetizers: nuta, raw tuna and steamed scallions in a silky yellow bean and sake sauce; chawan-mushi, a melting egg custard studded with green ginkgo nuts, prawns and vegetables; scallops broiled in butter; and even raw squid with Japanese apricots. Sweets are almost nonexistent, but hot mugs of green tea make a soothing finale. No reservations are taken, so be prepared to stand in line for about twenty minutes at peak hours. About $25 per person, with sake.

Bruce Ho
116 E. 57th St.
421-4292
Lunch and dinner Mon. to Sat. noon to midnight, Sun. 3:00 P.M. to midnight
All major credit cards
Chinese

We had optimistically believed that Chinese restaurants of this ilk had gone out with chop suey, but one whiff of the menu at this dinosaur of a restaurant and we knew we were back in pu-pu-platter land. Even the descriptions of the dishes are unappetizing, as if penned by some apprentice fortune cookie writer. What can you make of a dish—unmusically named subgum won ton—that the menu describes as "a real yum-yum"? This unholy concoction contains tough chicken, crustaceans with an ammonialike taste, ancient, leathery shreds of char-siu pork and incinerated won tons, the whole doused in a cornstarch sauce lightly tempered with soy. As for the final garnish, it takes real talent to produce limp prawn crackers. Whatever happened to the proverbial flavor, freshness, color and texture of Chinese cuisine? Or is it all some sinister conspiracy by the tongs to destroy American digestive systems? No wonder the head of the bronze Buddha above our table kept his eyes discreetly shut. This place gets the Gault Millau Greasy Chopsticks of the Year Award. About $20 per person, with beer.

10/20
Hunam
845 Second Ave.
(46th St.)
687-7471
Lunch daily noon to 3:00 P.M.; dinner nightly 3:00 P.M. to midnight (Fri. and Sat. to 1:00 A.M.)
AE, CB, DC
Chinese

Having done New Yorkers a major service by introducing them to the fiery joys of Hunanese cooking in the '70s, this restaurant seems to be resting on its rather dusty laurels. The fact that you eat in a cold, gray room reminiscent of a third-class saloon on a minor cruise ship could be overlooked if the food sparkled, but we find it remarkably lackluster.

To start with, the good news: cold appetizers are delicious, composed of a threesome of crunchy jellyfish salad, sliced shrimp in an impeccable dressing flecked with brown Szechwan pepper and thinly sliced duck in five spices. This is followed by a passable chicken soong, finely minced with pine nuts and cradled in a leaf of limp lettuce. The so-called turnip cakes are a bit of a fraud, more like rubbery shrimp balls with hardly a hint of the honorable root, though an excellent hot and sweet dip helps make them palatable. On our last visit, the orange beef we wanted was hijacked by the waiter, who had other ideas. "You no like," he assured us persuasively. So it had to be crispy beef and carrots, an unacceptable version of this classic, with limp, raw carrots and chewy, shredded meat. Hunan lamb with scallions in a hot pepper sauce is passable, but spareribs in a bamboo steamer, a great regional dish, are a disaster. To make matters worse, everything is piled onto the same plate with the most unaesthetic results, especially since most dishes seem to be the same unappealing brown. So be sure to ask your waiter to serve you Chinese style, with each dish arriving separately; that, like asking for wooden chopsticks, is the mark of a true Mandarin. Friends have warned us about the torpedolike honey bananas, so we prefer to finish with a refreshing pot of oolong tea. This once-good restaurant seems to have lost its way. About $25 per person, with wine.

14

Inagiku
Waldorf-Astoria
111 E. 49th St.
355-0440
Lunch Mon. to Fri. noon to 3:30 P.M.; dinner Mon. to Sat. 5:30 P.M. to 10:00 P.M.
All major credit cards
Japanese

In marked contrast to the fussy, grandiose lobbies of the Waldorf-Astoria, this cool, elegant Japanese restaurant is modeled on a fifteenth-century shrine. We found the bronze and brown decor as restful as ever, the sake martinis as lethal as ever, the waiters as inscrutable as ever and the food as exquisite as we remembered. Only the cacophony of business deals being struck at surrounding tables slightly mars the Oriental calm. At the central tempura bar, a corps de ballet of cooks produce feather-light fritters of seafood and vegetables under the stern gaze of the master chef. They wear maroon happi coats and what appear to be black tea cozies on their heads. The sushi served in the main restaurant is both decorative and exceptionally light; the raw fish in the sashimi is ultrafresh, though cut, we feel, a trifle too thick, in deference to American tastes. Try the deep red, almost meaty tuna, crispy squid or tender sea bass, dipped in a hot green wasabi relish. More adventurous eaters should ask for the Japanese menu (the manager, Mr. Haura, will help you here) and try a divine combination of finely cut raw fluke wrapped in a green, verbena-scented leaf, or the lobster sashimi: the white meat is eaten raw, and the claws are cooked in a hot butter sauce. Another outstanding dish that is well suited to the American palate is negimayaki, strips of charcoal-broiled steak wrapped around finely cut scallions and basted with sweet sake. For busy executives, the best choice is the carved wooden luncheon tray with a choice of tempura, sirloin steak (New York or teriyaki style), sushi or sashimi; soup, salad, rice, sherbet and green tea are included in the price. There is a small, quite adequate wine list, but green tea, sake or Kirin beer seem best to suit the fresh, light style of this food. About $25 per person for dinner with sake.

12/20

Joe & Rose
747 Third Ave.
(46th St.)
355-8874
Lunch and dinner Mon. to Fri. 11:30 A.M. to 10 P.M.; dinner Sat. 6:00 P.M. to 11:00 P.M.
AE, DC

Joe & Rose has been in approximately the same Third Avenue location for 70 years and has inevitably acquired the atmosphere of an unassuming neighborhood bistro. Though it has its regulars from nearby office buildings, it is much more than that: an excellent, assuming restaurant that draws guests from far beyond its environs with first-rate meats, top-drawer pastas, a selection of fairly

Italian/American
(steaks)

standard Italian specialties and several fish dishes. It is basically a steak house, however, and its roast prime ribs of beef, filets mignons, sirloin for two and lamb chops are all beyond reproach, as are the hash browns and cottage fries. Servings are so generous you will probably not crave dessert, though the cheesecake is above average. Salads tend to be limp and watery. Unlike many of their steak house confrères, the waiters are friendly. They recite the menu, but not the prices, which put Joe & Rose far, far out of the bistro category: lunch for two, with an aperitif and a glass of house wine, will run $85.

13

Kurumazushi
423 Madison Ave.
(48th St.)
751-5258
Lunch Mon. to Fri. noon to 2:30
P.M.; dinner Mon. to Fri. 5:30 P.M.
to 10:00 P.M.
AE, DC

Japanese

This discreet, almost anonymous sushi bar is a great find. It's situated over the Larmen Dosanko noodle restaurant; you have to sneak up a narrow staircase and through people gorging on noodles and pot stickers to locate an almost invisible sliding door that finally admits you to the sushi bar. You are well advised to have made reservations. This is a tiny, modest place with a bar used mainly by waiting customers. There are a few small tatami rooms for private parties and a diminutive sushi counter where three virtuoso chefs ply their ancient art under a canopy of paper lanterns. Dark and pale pink tuna cuts, neatly trimmed octopus, abalone, porgy, fluke, shrimp and bass are all manifestly fresh and laid out in an oceanic mosaic before you. Start with the lightest of consommés, full of objets trouvés (such as are found on deserted beaches); it will keep you going while you watch the chefs mold and form lightly vinegared rice and fish with lapidary skill. The deluxe selection includes rice, fish and pickle rolled into ribbons of dark seaweed, sushi rolls topped with pale gold keta caviar or coral red smelt roe, and a maki-sushi of delicate sea urchin roe. It's enough to make you reach for a brush and toss off a haiku. Sushi can, of course, be ordered by the piece, including one custom-rolled special containing crisp, slender carrot sticks and that ubiquitous but hauntingly fragrant shiso leaf with its verbena aftertaste. It is immensely gratifying to see the wide acceptance sushi bars have won among the discerning public. At our most recent visit here, we spotted a tatami room full of sake-quaffing business execs lunching Japanese style. Could sitting cross-legged be good for stress? About $22 per person, with sake.

13

Lello
65 E. 54th St.
751-1555
Lunch Mon. to Fri. noon to 3:00

Has success turned Lello's head—so much so that it can purchase an entire page in the *New York Times* to boast of its own merits? In any case, when we returned with pleasure to this nice place, where the decor on the

*P.M.; dinner Mon. to Sat. 5:30 P.M.
to 10:30 P.M. (Fri. and Sat. to
11:00 P.M.)
All major credit cards*
Italian

18
Lutèce
249 E. 50th St.
752-2225
*Lunch Tues. to Fri. noon to 1:45
P.M.; dinner Mon. to Sat. 6:00 P.M.
to 9:45 P.M.
AE, CB, DC*
French
(classical/nouvelle)

ground floor disappears into obscurity (at least this prevents you from seeing the unsightly paintings), we didn't experience our former enjoyment. The service was frantic, the daily specials were of little interest, and above all, mistakes were made that are difficult to forgive. Hard and tasteless baby artichokes were doused with mediocre olive oil, ham with no tenderness accompanied an unripe cantaloupe, too-dry tortellini were stuffed with leathery meat, and veal piccata was overcooked. Happily, there were delicious grilled scampi with fresh tomato, a perfect zuppe di pesce and an excellent chocolate-topped Napoleon to raise our morale and encourage us to leave Lello's toque in place, even though we are lowering the ranking by one point. In short, this is a place to watch from the corner of your eye—one in which we do not have total confidence. About $45 per person, with wine.

When we gave a fourth toque to Haeberlin in Alsace, Paul Haeberlin sent us the following telegram: "Thank you for this distinction. Now our problems begin." With much wisdom, he understood that being propelled to the forefront would require him to pay the price of success. When we took the well-thought-out risk of giving André Soltner the highest ranking in this guide two years ago, we knew he would run into difficult moments. Apparently he has surmounted them; you may believe the inevitable detractors of Lutèce, who complain about the slow service and even the downright unsuccessful dishes, but Soltner has never had to turn away so many people. It is easy to ask yourself how he and his team can serve so many meals without falling into the laziness of commercial cuisine. The answer is very simple: André Soltner is one of the most honest and rigorous chefs there can be. These typically Alsatian virtues have not been tarnished by his spending the last twenty years in Manhattan. If, for example, one criticizes him justifiably, instead of shrugging his shoulders and taking you for an imbecile (a reaction of so many chefs, who try to persuade us that that have as much value as God), he listens and does whatever is necessary to fix his mistake. If there were more men like him in American and French kitchens, gastronomy critics would be able to take more vacations. One of the secrets of Soltner's success is that instead of strutting through the dining room or giving seminars in Los Angeles or Tokyo, he spends most of his days in the kitchen, a worker among his workers. His other weapon is that he is one of the rare chefs who has a veritable brigade in the kitchen. If you are ever curious enough to look in through the doors of most large New

York restaurants, you'll be enlightened to see how very few have sufficient staffs. This evidently explains why they cannot cook to order and why most dishes are prepared so far in advance, which is contrary to the laws of good and true gastronomy. A mise en place is certainly necessary if a chef doesn't want to keep customers waiting for hours for their dinners, and Lutèce doesn't overlook this procedure. But it is also one of the rare establishments where most of the work is done at the last moment, as in the great kitchens of Guérard, Girardet, Vergé, Troisgros, Chapel and others.

The big question is: Is Lutèce better at lunch or dinner? The unambiguous answer is that you must go for lunch and dinner. These are experiences so different that both are worth trying. A $27 prix fixe lunch is a true gift, particularly if you compare prices in other New York restaurants. Our last lunch was a pure marvel: we shared an exquisite cold shrimp terrine and a saucisson chaud en croûte that was wonderfully light and one we would love to find in Lyon; then a mousseline of pike, which miraculously tasted of pike; an extraordinary fricassée of milk-fed lamb, slowly simmered with garlic cloves, carrots, onions, tomatoes, celery and bay leaves and accompanied by fresh pasta (absolutely sensational; Italian chefs in New York, so proud of their pastas, would do well to borrow the recipe), which is a great Alsatian specialty; and then, for dessert, a praline glazed cake and a Prélat chocolate cake that will make you fall to the floor.

In the evening, the choice is more extensive and the mini dégustation menu (eight courses at $60 per person) allows Soltner and the chief of his kitchen, Christian Bertrand, to let their fantasies soar with such superb dishes as salmon with bacon poached in milk and barely cooked in the center; Bay scallops with a lightly tomatoed cream sauce that feels like satin in your mouth; little rock rougets with olive oil that are so fresh they seem to move on your plate; and an incredibly tender pigeon (even in Bresse it's hard to find birds as fine as these, raised on a Pennsylvania farm) posed on a nest of chanterelles and snow peas. If you order from the menu, which offers a scallop of fresh salmon with sorrel, veal kidneys with red wine and an exquisite orange chocolate, it will also cost you about $60. You must take care also to choose a great Bordeaux or superb Burgundy, offered on a short but remarkably selected wine list. In any case, one doesn't come to Lutèce to save money. If you cede to the lobster sauté, duck liver with morels and cream, and Chambertin, you will leave, no longer in the grip of hunger, but fresh, spruced up and lightened of $250 for two.

9/20
Madras Woodlands
310 E. 44th St.
986-0620
Lunch Wed. to Mon. noon to 2:30
P.M.; dinner Wed. to Mon. 5:30
P.M. to 10:00 P.M.
All major credit cards
Indian (vegetarian)

Indian vegetarian cuisine must be something of a contradiction in terms, for as every good Indian cook knows, his first duty to a fresh green vegetable is to hack it, pulverize it, boil it in hot oil or seethe it in fiery spices until its identity is suitably obliterated. The vegetable thali at Woodlands is no exception—apart from the relishes, the thali's ingredients consist of six object lessons in how to disguise the true taste of a vegetable. Creatively thwarted in this direction, the cooks have lavished their talents on the grains and legumes, producing every variety of starchy artifact known to man. Uppathans and poppadums, pulkas and iddlis, pakoras and pooris, baturas and bajis—all are made from lentil, rice or wheat flour. These pancakes, dumplings and breads come in every shape and form, from huge golden balloons to lacy white crêpes. The very apotheosis of starch is, of course, the famous masala dosai, a huge envelope of lentil flour wrapped around spicy potatoes. The curries and hot chutneys that alleviate this heaviness are strangely similar in flavor: a blend of fiery chili, ginger and black pepper tempered with the sourness of lime and tamarind. They first intrigue, then numb the palate. As you may have gathered, you will either love or loathe this cuisine, depending on how your stomach reacts to a diet of unalloyed carbohydrates. Service is willing but often marred by a complete and mutual noncommunication between diner and staff. An interpreter may be needed to get you a cup of coffee. About $10 to $15 per person, without wine.

12/20
Manhattan Market
1016 Second Ave.
(54th St.)
752-1400
Breakfast 7:00 A.M. to 10:00 A.M.;
lunch Mon. to Fri. 11:45 A.M. to
3:00 P.M.; dinner Mon. to Sat. 5:30
P.M. to 11:30 P.M. (Sat. to
midnight); brunch Sun. 11:00 A.M.
to 3:30 P.M.
All major credit cards
American

David Liederman liked what he tasted in the Troisgros kitchen in France, so much so that he gave up the law and eventually opened Manhattan Market. In our last report we described it as one of the "nicest, smartest little restaurants" in the city. On the basis of what he had learned in France, David used his imagination and fresh ingredients to produce a stylish New York counterpart to French nouvelle cuisine, and he became an instant success with his young, upbeat clientele, who perfectly complement the refined dining room, which has a lovely carved wooden bar and black and white cityscapes on the wall. But David discovered that there is a far richer future in chocolate chip cookies (David's Cookies), and he no longer has time for the Manhattan Market's kitchen. While the menu of simply prepared light American dishes still has promise, its execution is uneven. You won't go wrong with the smoked trout, the shell steak or the salads, and the chicken coated with pecans and served with a mustard-sour cream sauce is glorious. But the shrimp pâté is an ill-conceived notion, the grilled lamb chops are tough and tasteless, and the sautéed duck is not as tender as it should be. There is something suspicious about a place that charges $3.50 for an order of toasted French bread, but David is happy to have found another best-seller for his bakery. The dessert offerings include, naturally, David's cookies with ice cream, for a premium price. About $35 per person, with wine.

10/20
Mariana's
986 Second Ave.
(52nd St.)
759-4455
Lunch Mon. to Fri. noon to 3:00
P.M.; dinner Mon. to Sat. 5:00 P.M.
to 11:00 P.M. (Sat. to 1:00 A.M.)
All major credit cards
Continental (seafood)

At street level, a bar and some stools (as well as a beautiful barmaid and some beautiful people) fill a small corridor, and upstairs a handful of tables overlook the sidewalk and the stairwell. Yet the architect, Juhn Tudda, has fashioned from this unlikely space one of the most dazzling restaurant settings in New York: a veritable botanical garden at the entrance, with mirrors everywhere to give freedom, add dimension and reflect the ingenious stage lighting, chrome-frame Breuer chairs and light wood paneling.

We find it all the more deplorable that the kitchen is not up to producing anything nearly as interesting. The menu is short (mainly seafood) and lists Japanese tempura, Italian pasta, New England clam chowder (a special), bluefish en papillote and some tasteless chocolate desserts. In a word, something for every taste, but nothing very good. We suggest that Mariana send her architect to the kitchen. With his keen eye and sense of proportion, he could straighten things out right away. About $30 per person, without wine.

12/20
Il Nido
251 E. 53rd St.
753-8450
Lunch Mon. to Sat. noon to 2:15
P.M.; dinner Mon. to Sat. 5:30 P.M.
to 10:15 P.M.
All major credit cards
Italian

There's a wonderfully warm and cozy feeling in Il Nido. The business-suited clients look happy, the service is cheerful, the farmhouse decor is comforting, and the happy noise level makes it seem that everyone is having a wonderful time. And they probably are, although we doubt it is due to the cuisine. Brother to Il Monello, Il Nido is tasting a little tired these days, and we have fond memories of when the food was considerably better, back when we were researching our first edition of the New York guide. Unhappily, things have changed, and, with the exception of a perfectly prepared paglia e fieno, most of the dishes here lack spunk. Scampi milanese is prettily presented with its wreath of crustaceans, but the tender shrimp are overcooked. The sausage and peppers are acceptable, but the veal chop stuffed with cheese and prosciutto is dry and lifeless. Baked clams are tolerable, the pasta special is banal (although the tortellini with a hint of Gorgonzola is tasty), and the mussels marinara are quite good. Desserts are as uneven as the entrees: zabaglione is not quite complete, as a large shot of Marsala sits in the bottom of the goblet; zuppa inglese is not as lush as we love it; but the cheesecake is nice. The wine list is a mirror of Il Monello's; there are many reasonably priced Italians, and the Chianti riserva will make an admirable accompaniment to a slightly overpriced meal ($50 per person).

15

Oyster Bar
Grand Central Station (Lower level)
Lunch and dinner Mon. to Fri. 11:30 A.M. to 9:30 P.M.
All major credit cards
American (seafood)

The best and freshest fish in New York can always be found in this astonishing white tiled restaurant located in the basement of Grand Central Station and resembling a métro station in Paris. The noise of dishes, silverware and hundreds of pairs of jaws do not make this the ideal spot for a business lunch or a romantic tryst. But the fish is so extraordinary that you'll soon forget these minor inconveniences. From the sea, stream, lakes and river, the fish is never frozen , and the menu depends on daily arrivals. You will always have a difficult choice from the 30 or so varieties of bluefish, pompano, brook trout, striped bass, salmon or wolf fish. And this is without mentioning the dozens of varieties of oysters as fresh as the ocean, as well as the clams, crabs and lobsters. Order your fish as natural as possible (meunière, grilled or fried), because they are best when simplest. But don't forget the salmon, smoked here in apple wood, which gives such a special flavor, or the clam chowder. Nor should you ignore the chocolate mousse or the cheesecake: both are delicious. Plunge happily into the wine list; there are more than 120 varieties of white American wines, chosen with great discernment and all nicely priced. When you realize that the Oyster Bar serves more than 2,000 meals daily, you can only be stupefied by the evenness of the kitchen. If fish offered medals to restaurateurs, Jerome Brody would deserve first place. About $30 per person, with wine.

9/20

Oyster Bar
**Plaza Hotel
Fifth Avenue and 59th Street
759-3000**
Lunch and dinner Mon. to Sat. 11:30 A.M. to 12:30 A.M.
All major credit cards
American (seafood)

Don't confuse this Oyster Bar with the real one. The cuisine is without interest, judged easily by a poached Boston scrod and a red snapper marseillaise. Both are overcooked, and the latter is poorly garnished with boiled potatoes. What is more successful is the decor of this Victorian pub with its large rectangular bar, its somber woods and its etched glass. We'll refrain from comment about the painted murals in a Belle Epoque style; if you look at them too long, they make a mess out of everything else. Good draft beer, excellent coffee and a chic enough clientele, but much too expensive for what you get. Expect to spend about $40 per person, with a glass of wine.

13

Palm
**837 Second Ave.
(44th St.)
687-2953**

*Lunch and dinner Mon. to Fri. noon
to 11:30 P.M.; dinner Sat. 5:00
P.M. to 11:30 P.M.
All major credit cards*

American (steaks)

With all the mountains of meat, Maine lobsters, onion rings and potato chips that customers leave on their plates or take home in doggie bags, one could open a third or even a fourth Palm. But let's not dwell on the excess of this monstrous mess: it is the trademark of this New York institution, which since 1926 has attracted generations of journalists, sportsmen and politicians. Their caricatures liven up the walls and amuse all the nameless who shuffle through the sawdust on the floor and come here to satisfy their hungers with a carnivorous instinct inherited from the Stone Age, amid the infernal noise of a commissary. We doubt this steak house is in the spirit intended by its Italian founders (it should have been called Parm, but a city clerk made an error and it was named Palm), and if you think you might detect the fragrance of garlic or Marsala as you climb the stairs, pay no attention; the chef lost the secrets of Italian cuisine a long time ago. He has no need to reclaim them, however, as he has mastered the art of cooking sirloin steak, filet mignon, prime rib and lamb chops. The meats are generally (not always) of exceptional tenderness and perfectly flavored, even if they are brought to the table on cold plates. With a single T-bone at $20, you can easily eat enough for three people; but the waiters show no excessive enthusiasm when you order half portions or ask to share. Nevertheless, if you insist, they may yield to more conventional servings. Don't forget to ask for the onion rings, which are crispy and tender, among the best in New York. As for the rest of the menu, except for the gargantuan slices of cheesecake, forget it. Shrimp are spoiled with a formidable cocktail sauce, clam chowder is so bland it could be served in a hospital, overcooked broiled lobster (at $34 for four and a half pounds) resembles a paper carton. The old faithfuls of the Palm wouldn't run over to Palm Too (across the street at 840 Second Avenue) for anything in the world. In their minds, it is a little too new and prim. But the food there is rigorously the same, in both its qualities and its faults. About $100 for two, with wine.

16

Le Périgord
**405 E. 52nd St.
755-6244**

*Lunch Mon. to Fri. noon to 3:00
P.M.; dinner Mon. to Sat. 5:30 P.M.
to 10:30 P.M.
All major credit cards*

French
(classical/nouvelle)

Antoine Bouterin felt lost after leaving the Quai d'Orsay in Paris and finding himself in New York without understanding a single word of English. Today, however, he is a happy man. He learned Spanish in his kitchens, as an accessory to English, and became coowner of Périgord. With a little trouble he convinced his associates to make the place more comfortable and elegant (the floral fabrics on the walls are no wonder, but the coral velvet banquettes and the lighting system on the new ceiling are a triumph). Encouraged by a rapid success, he had the good idea to lengthen his menu by nearly half. His classical background restrains him from extravagances, but his cuisine is not boring or lazy. Bouterin is a young chef full of potential, and his personal style is becoming liberated little by little. Certain dishes succeed better than others; among the former, we must mention his cold crab and cucumber soup, the marvelous fillets of squab with juniper berry gelée, fillets of duck with fresh fruit, warm confit of duck that is crusty and velvety and wild mushroom mousse served in a lightly flavored lemon cream sauce. He seems to be happier with dishes of well-defined taste than with more subtle nuances, as is in the case with the turbot with its natural sauce, cooked to perfection but a bit banal. And if the warm pear tart napped with a strawberry sauce is a true delight, his version of cheesecake needs a serious revision. Even so, Périgord deserves one more point. And if you have read elsewhere that the service is not the best, don't believe a word of it. The staff takes great care with clients, and if this were not the case, they wouldn't come in such numbers from the United Nations for lunch and from Sutton Place and all the other beautiful neighborhoods for dinner. Menus at dinner are prix fixes of $36, $40 and $46. It's rare to find great vintages at reasonable prices in a luxury restaurant, but you will here: $94 for Château Lafite Rothschild or a Cheval Blanc '76, $32 for an excellent Gevrey Chambertin or a Domaine Geoffroy '78 or $16 for a marvelous Saint-Emilion Château Simard '76. But if you are tempted by the extravagant Chassagne Montrachet from Marquis de la Guiche or the grandiose Bonnes Mares '72 from Comte de Vogue, that's your business.

11/20
La Petite Marmite
Beekman Hotel
6 Mitchell Pl.
826-1084

Lunch Mon. to Sat. noon to 12:30 P.M.; dinner Mon. to Sat. 6:00 P.M. to 10:00 P.M. (Sat. to 10:30 P.M.) All major credit cards

French (classical)

This rather tired-looking restaurant is trapped in a time warp. The dowdy decor of marbelized mirrors, provincial fabric walls and red velvet banquettes appeals to the U.N. crowd that rushes here to escape the Delegates' Dining Room. For that same reason, they surely find this cuisine immensely appealing, although we can only report that it has all become a little tiresome. There's nothing really wrong with smoked salmon, an artichoke vinaigrette or a cassolette d'escargots, but they're old hat and rather boring. Even the delicate Bay scallops served with fresh sage and the seasonal soft-shell crabs cannot liven up the menu. But there are decent classics, such as rognons dijonnaise, grilled chicken with diable sauce, fillet of sole meunière and filet mignon with sauce choron to feed the habituées who come here for business lunches and early dinners. We urge our compatriots who run Marmite to return to France and update their cuisine with selections that are more inspired, up-to-date and innovative, or to take a tip from their new sibling, Prunelle, where the cuisine is all it should be. You can expect steadiness, good service and a bill that will easily climb beyond the $25 prix fixe luncheon menu with any of the expensive French wines or supplements on the menu, which offer potentially more interesting choices.

14

Prunelle
18 E. 54th St.
759-6410
Lunch daily noon to 3:00 P.M.;
dinner nightly 5:30 P.M. to 11:30
P.M. (Sun. to 9:30 P.M.)
All major credit cards
French (nouvelle)

If you're looking for an ultrachic decor in which, miraculously, good cuisine is offered (a combination that is nearly nonexistent), rush over to Prunelle, where you will be welcomed by a happy staff intent on making your evening a delight. You will dine surrounded by veneer of French birch maple, creating a cozy effect not unlike being ensconced in a Mark Cross humidor. This is one of the new jewels of New York's restaurant scene, and the design is truly stunning. Prunelle's sibling, La Petite Marmite, could take a few lessons from this new kid on the block—in the kitchen as well as in the look of that venerable but aging grandmother. Here, things are cheerful and up-to-date. For a pricey $42 prix fixe dinner, you can enjoy an excellent watercress flan with frog's legs, a marvelous Alsatian pâté, an equally good seafood soufflé and a light feuilleté of asparagus. Entrees are well prepared, and you may return often to sample the Bay scallops à la nage, the salmon with a tomato fondue, the perfectly cooked rôti of lamb, the acceptable veal with asparagus and hollandaise, the marvelous crisped duckling or any of the nightly specials that make the most of a seasonal market. Desserts crown a pleasant dinner with, for example, a lovely, crispy apple tart, a lemon charlotte or a sinful chocolate cake. The wine list offers many good French selections, making Prunelle one of the most pleasant new finds in New York.

17

Quilted Giraffe
955 Second Ave.
(50th–51st sts.)
753-5355
Dinner Mon. to Fri. 5:45 P.M. to
10:00 P.M.
All major credit cards
American/French
(nouvelle)

Four years ago, we had no need to return ten times to Barry Wine's to be persuaded that the Quilted Giraffe was already, in spite of some youthful errors, one of the best and most passionate places in New York. At the time, the critics didn't take this young lawyer seriously. He became a chef when he opened this restaurant with a decor devoted—almost to the point of obsession—to every possible representation of the giraffe, making us inevitably think of a nursery. Having finally grown up and having become well-known, Barry and his wife Susan liberated their giraffes, leaving only a porcelain souvenir downstairs and a tapestry upstairs, and redid their place with a sophisticated, elegant air, one more compatible with the cuisine. Their success was brilliant, and you now have to plan ahead to have a table downstairs surrounded by art deco etched glass and the nineteenth-century Chinese-motif ceramics that once decorated the ovens of Lyon's silk factories, Japanese glassware and floral arrangements, all of which is a testimony to refined taste. Even the sumptuous rest rooms upstairs are an experience, and the dining room on the second floor is especially pleasant for private parties. The young people who make up the serving staff, including the excellent sommelier, look more like they have graduated from the better East Coast schools than from the pantry, but they have none of the affectation that makes so many luxury restaurants resemble funeral parlors. These young people are in love with their work and are a perfectly soldered team with the kitchen staff around Barry Wine.

The departure of Mark Chayette, trained in the Guérard school, would have been a cruel blow if Barry had not, over the years, become a true professional who is perfectly capable of mastering one of the most frequently changing and inspired menus in New York. Each evening, in addition to a tasting menu of $75, which we do not advise for small appetites, there is a $52.50 prix fixe that gives you a choice of eight appetizers, seven or eight main courses, a beautiful selection of cheeses and ten or so desserts. Constant change is one of the principal charms of the Quilted Giraffe, and it is impossible for us to guess in advance what your choices might be. In any case, you will have a marvelous dinner: perhaps a superb, rich-bodied consommé, followed by ravioli stuffed with wild mushrooms, and sweetbreads of an unimaginable tenderness, accompanied by Chinese cabbage, delicious green beans and a debatable cauliflower in a wondrous sauce in which soy and sesame provide a sweetness and exceptional profundity (Barry seems recently inspired by French-Japanese cooking). Another night you may have a memorable meal of lobster with lightly smoked scallops, served scarcely cooked in a delicious mustard cream sauce, and fillets of duck with ginger and lime. Or a dinner that you would remember for eternity: beluga caviar beggar's purses, rack of lamb with Chinese mustard and a grand dessert, for which you may be charged supplements of $20, $7.50 and $5, respectively, but without regret. All this will make you pass the hat for the $100 per person tab, particularly if you cede to the always brilliant advice of the sommelier and offer yourself a Mt. Eden '78 Cabernet Sauvignon, which is a small miracle.

15

La Récolte

**Inter-Continental
Hotel
110 E. 49th St.
421-4389**

*Lunch Mon. to Fri. 11:30 A.M. to
2:30 P.M.; dinner Mon. to Sat. 6:00
P.M. to 11:00 P.M.*
All major credit cards

French (nouvelle)

What we have come to expect in New York is that everything can change overnight. La Récolte's original chef left for New Jersey, his second went to Garden City, and the present chef arrived from Florida via Dubai to dish up the complicated, sophisticated cuisine that puts this elegant restaurant in contention with the finest places in New York. The room is pretty in a striking sort of way, the service is impeccable in its grand manner, and the clientele is business oriented at lunch and equally well-heeled in the evening, when the ladies dress up to complement the luxurious decor. There are the occasional random hotel guests who stumble into La Récolte, not expecting the first-class experience or the outer-space prices. But they will not be disappointed if they order from the seasonal menu carefully. The cuisine is ambitious, as befits an haute dining experience, but there are weaknesses in the kitchen here and there—we suspect more from its reliance on recipes from some of the best places in France than from a lack of technical prowess. Needless to say, most chefs feel more comfortable with recipes they have developed themselves, but learning from the great masters is always a good way to improve and enhance one's own repertoire. And when things are working well here, your meal can be a delightful experience. We cannot fault the superb pheasant consommé that is subtly rich, although its pastry crown does more for its decor that for its taste. The poached oysters with saffron and julienne vegetables are overpowered by the broth, although the endive salad is refreshing and lightly dressed. The artichoke soup is worth sampling, as is the mussel soup with watercress. When it comes to the main course, you can be assured you'll have a good meal if you order seafood; the brill with sea urchin cream is as lovely as the salmon with lime sauce and the classic Troisgros braid of fish. If you are visiting La Récolte during the autumn, the venison may be a little gamy, the gambas sautéed with whiskey a little tough and the magret of duck to be avoided at all costs. Most things work here, but we have to draw the line at nouvelle when potatoes are served al dente. Desserts merit the chef a reprieve: marvelous sorbets, an excellent mocha mousse with bittersweet chocolate sauce and a host of other tempting trifles that will spoil any diner who has penchant for sweetness. If you accompany your meal with the extraordinary Trefethen Chardonnay, you may not register the cold reality that dinner at La Récolte will run at least $60 per person, and lunch only slightly less. We urge the good people at the Inter-Continental to bring the cuisine up to the same standards as the elegance of La Récolte, giving us a three-toque cuisine to match the prices.

13

The Rendez-Vous

Berkshire Place
21 E. 52nd St.
753-5800
Breakfast, lunch and dinner daily
7:00 A.M. to midnight
All major credit cards
French (nouvelle)

Madison Avenue account executives, Chemical Bank vice-presidents, headhunters, litigators, planners of vast estates and trusts and a sprinkling of footloose out-of-towners fight with one another for drinks at the rectangular four-sided bar that dominates the enormous room. This hectic time, between 5:00 and 8:00 P.M. every weekday evening, reminds us of the frenzy of last-minute quotes at the New York Commodity Exchange. After 8:00 P.M., the bulls and bears have departed, some now paired off for the evening, and you become aware of the muffled conversation of serious diners around you and of the beauty of your surroundings. The brightly polished brass railings that separate you from the bar area (a couple of steps below) remind us of the Left Bank, which is in fact the mood intended for the late supper menu (after 10:30 P.M.) and for brunch on weekends.

Dinner at The Rendez-Vous, however, is not a bistro experience. The menu, prepared by Didier Busnot, is French nouvelle, extensive and expensive: tiny Bay scallops in a tomato concasse (delicious), snails in puff pastry surrounded by an enchanting herb sauce, lobster cassoulet with a brioche topping (excellent), succulent medallions of veal with a watercress purée and, for dessert, a delightful apple sorbet, well laced with Calvados. The rich chocolate mousse cake, fast displacing fruit tarts on French menus in New York, is not so much to our liking. You will rarely eat better in a hotel dining room, but make your reservation after the close of trading at the bar. About $50 per person, with a respectable California Cabernet.

14

Restaurant Jean Pierre

405 E. 58th St.
751-2790
Dinner Mon. to Sat. 6:00 P.M. to
10:00 P.M.
AE, MC, V
French
(nouvelle/provincial)

Perhaps you remember the Dodin-Bouffant: its decor as joyous as that of a Bulgarian army commissary, the moods of its young hostess unpredictable and the reputation of its amateurish cuisine incomprehensible. After this exciting episode, there was Pierre François, a young, aristocratic French-Czech who had the good idea to redo the decor of this charming little Victorian home entirely and to team up with a really professional cook, Jean Pierre Lauret, who spent time at Taillevant in Paris. Then, taking his turn, Pierre François disappeared into the blue, leaving behind his chef, who is now sole master, assisted by his wife, a sweet Colombian, who takes charge of your welcome. There are about twenty tables in the adjoining rooms, with paisley-fabric-covered walls in roses and beige, filtered light, pretty bouquets of flowers and the tastefully discreet atmosphere of a private home. You are put into the best possible disposition to taste the cuisine of Jean Pierre Lauret, who presents a short menu plus three to four specials. His products are superb and his dishes prettily presented; the only reproach we can make is that for the sake of elegance his cuisine is sometimes affected. This is the case, for example, with Bay scallops with cream of leeks and tomato sorbet. The leeks are exquisite, but the scallops would be better if they were warm, and the fresh tomato, although excellent, overwhelms everything else. It is also not evident that feuilleté pastry adds anything great to the sweetbreads with cream and parsley, which are tender and delicious. But besides the errors, there are incontestable successes: the cold terrine of rabbit with black currants, carrots and onions, which is a small marvel; red snapper with mushrooms in a cream tomato sauce; or the delicious milk-fed lamb, thinly sliced, cooked very rare and served in its natural juices with baby carrots, turnips and a very good potato gratin. The terrine of bittersweet chocolate with orange doesn't leave imperishable memories. Altogether the check comes to about $100 for two, with an excellent Château Fuissé. Nothing is missing for Jean Pierre Lauret, except for him to give his cuisine a little more distinctive personality.

10/20
Restaurant Laurent
111 E. 56th St.
753-2729
Lunch Mon. to Sat. noon to 3:00 P.M.; dinner nightly 6:00 P.M. to 10:30 P.M. (Sun. from 5:00 P.M.)
AE, CB, DC
French (classical)

There is something cathedralesque about Laurent, with its solemn wood paneling, stained glass windows and ceremonial service, but there is little inspiration in the cuisine. The traditional French menu is classically dull, to match, we presume, the dull captains-of-industry crowd interspersed with the ladies who lunch. Habituées line the walls, perched on their velvet banquettes and attended to by tuxedoed waiters who fuss over them, giving them the impression they are somebodies. The rest of the clientele is nearly ignored by comparison; it may take you as long to receive the menu as it does eventually to pay your check, which at $30 per person for lunch without wine is steep. But no one seems to care much, as most of the successful-looking diners are on expense accounts and appear to enjoy the vintage '50s menu offering smoked trout, salmon mousse with dill sauce, céléri rémoulade, eggs Benedict, paillard de veau, sauté de boeuf Tolstoï and salade niçoise. It is disheartening at the least to be served a tasteless artichoke with vinaigrette spiked with capers, cornichons and chopped egg; an only passable avocado stuffed with crab; or a sea bass that is virtually tasteless. Things look up slightly with well-prepared sautéed sweetbreads on a bed of spinach. The île flottante can only be made with what looks and tastes like whipped cream and an excessive degree of sugar, although the strawberry tart allows you to leave with some optimism. Come here if you must; the room is pretty, and it's a good place to talk business. Don't, however, expect the food to approach any sort of divine experience. Dinner for two will run $85 without wine.

13 ♟️
Restaurant Nippon
145 E. 52nd St.
355-9020
Lunch Mon. to Fri. noon to 2:30
P.M.; dinner Mon. to Sat. 5:30 P.M.
to 10:00 P.M. (Fri. and Sat. to
10:30 P.M.)
All major credit cards

Japanese

Nobuyoshi Kuraoka came to New York from Japan some twenty years ago, opened Restaurant Nippon and then started the somewhat less formal Hyo Tan Nippon on East 59th Street. Now, in a reverse migration pattern, he is planning a restaurant in Tokyo. A high proportion of his customers here are Japanese tourists and business people, which speaks well for the authenticity and excellence of what he serves. Perhaps he is counting on having them as patrons on their return to their homeland.

The menu at Restaurant Nippon offers a bewildering (to Western eyes) collection of Japanese specialties. But Mr. Kuraoka also offers a single page of dishes he says are popular with Americans in Japan and can serve as an introduction to a broader sampling of Japanese dishes. There is no reason to content yourself here with tempura, teriyaki and sukiyaki, dishes that are available (if not always as well prepared) at other Japanese restaurants around town. This is the place to challenge your palate with more unusual ingredients and preparations: sea cucumbers, seasoned seaweed, fish roes, sea urchins, seafood in sake and a myriad of items you won't encounter elsewhere. The sushi counter, the small dining rooms and the tatami sections (with wells for long-legged Westerners) are as pleasant as ever, although the little running stream has inexplicably dried up. We trust that Mr. Kuraoka's venture in Tokyo will bring to Japan the happiness he has brought us here. But can even this man of such obvious talent keep a firm hand in kitchens a world apart? About $25 per person, with sake.

11/20
The Russian Bear
139 E. 56th St.
355-9080
Lunch Mon. to Fri. noon to 4:00
P.M.; dinner nightly 5:00 P.M. to
11:30 P.M.
All major credit cards

Russian

Nothing changes at The Russian Bear—neither the faded, folkloric murals, the fiery, homemade pepper vodka, the kohl-eyed gypsy fortune-teller nor the violinist with a slight case of fiddler's elbow, launching on his umpteenth rendering of "Kalinka." Everything seems stuck in the same cozy, nostalgic time warp. Plump, blond Valia is still in the kitchen, and her cooking has, if anything, improved. She produces a near-perfect borscht that is dark, sweet and flecked with sour cream, eaten with the flakiest of meat piroshkis. There are a delicately smooth and sharp aubergine purée, pele memi (tiny dumplings) in a fragrant chicken and dill broth, eaten Siberian style dipped in mustard and vinegar, and, of course, the pièce de résistance, blini. They arrive crisp, fluffy and golden under their folded napkin, and are greedily devoured with melted butter, sour cream and a huge helping of red salmon roe. Stuffed cabbage is unexciting, but the well-marinated shashlik is always good. Try to avoid the more boring vegetables, such as fried potatoes and frozen peas, and ask for the dark brown, earthy-tasting buckwheat kasha. Sweets are unimportant, vodka is powerful—indeed, mandatory— and the service, by charming young women fresh from Moscow or Leningrad, is better than anything you'll find in the old country. About $30 per person, with vodka.

13 ♟

Shinbashi
**280 Park Ave.
(48th St.)
661-3915**
*Lunch Mon. to Fri. 11:30 A.M. to 2:30 P.M.; dinner Mon. to Sat. 5:30 P.M. to 10:00 P.M.
All major credit cards*

Japanese

Shinbashi means "new bridge," and there is a nice introduction to the menu expressing the hope that this restaurant will become part of the cultural span between the Japanese and American people. If different cultural groups arrive, contemplate the lovely rock garden awhile and then move on to dine in one of the exquisite tatami rooms; the calm and peaceful atmosphere is sure to bridge any cultural gaps. The general dining room is also spacious and comfortable, though more functional than romantic, with its straightforward traditional Japanese nondecor and cooking.

Start with the sushi, but don't be misled into thinking the sushi okonomi is sushi economy style. Okonomi is sushi as you like it, and you'll like this so much you may just keep ordering. The tuna, octopus and sea urchin roe are all impeccably fresh and just as cool as they are supposed to be, not jellied or ice-cold as in most Japanese restaurants. This allows you to appreciate the true flavor. Negimayaki (sliced beef rolled around scallions and broiled with mirin sauce) is good, as is salmon teriyaki, but after the sushi they seem to lack excitement. Beef sukiyaki for dinner will revive your spirits. (Speaking of spirits, the Sapporo draft beer is the perfect accompaniment.) Your waitress immerses the well-marbleized, thinly sliced beef in the boiling broth at your table; the sukiyaki sauce blends in with the bean curd, shirataki, bamboo shoots and noodles and is delicious. Ingredients are all top quality. Service is professional, although you may feel rushed toward the end of your dinner—it does close promptly at 10:00 P.M. Expect to pay $70 to $80 for dinner for two, with beer (more with cocktails).

8/20

Sparks Steak House

Sparks continues to attract steak-happy New Yorkers, but frankly we don't know why. When we last reported, we gave credit to the vast wine list and at the same time

210 E. 46th St.
687-4855
Lunch Mon. to Sat. noon to 3:00
P.M.; dinner Mon. to Sat. 5:00 P.M.
to 11:00 P.M.
All major credit cards
American (steaks)

12/20
Les Tourne- broches
Citicorp Center
153 E. 53rd St.
935-6029
Lunch Mon. to Sat. 11:30 A.M. to
3:00 P.M.; dinner Mon. to Sat. 5:00
P.M. to 10:00 P.M.
All major credit cards
French (provincial)

found the food mediocre. Now that other restaurants have become serious about wine and offer selections comparable to those at Sparks, along with passable food at more modest prices, we are at a loss to explain the continuing popularity of this place. The steak described at once as prime sirloin and a boneless shell steak is small and acceptable, no more. The appetizers (baked clams, broiled shrimp) are absolutely undistinguished. Among the main courses, the bass comes in a coat of flour and is dry and tasteless, the Bay scallops are supposed to be broiled but swim in a liquid that suggests a recent defrosting, and the medallions of beef come in a sauce whose relationship to the classic bordelaise we fail to detect. The hashed brown potatoes (everything is à la carte) contain burned bits and offer not the slightest suggestion that they are freshly prepared; the side order of spinach (of good quality, as is the spinach salad) lacks seasoning of any kind. "Fresh" strawberries are overripe and mushy. If you insist on going to Sparks, choose the '76 Château La Grange St. Julien, avoid the other, overpriced, listings and count on spending at least $40 per person.

If Presidents Reagan and Mitterand can't agree on anything else, perhaps they can agree that Les Tournebroches serves the interests of their respective countries. The president of the United States would surely like the plain cooking over an open fire, but beyond that he would be even more pleased to find that Charles Chevillot, the proprietor and a compatriot of M. Mitterand, is such a stalwart inflation fighter: a special dinner of soup, entree, salad and coffee is priced at $8.75. On the other hand, M. Mitterand would no doubt be happy to applaud M. Chevillot (and Alain Jardin, his chef) for bringing to America the basic, straightforward cooking that will almost certainly persuade those Americans who are disenchanted with tricked-up nouvelle cuisine to fall in love with France again. You will find filet mignon with béarnaise, entrecôte with herbed butter, grilled veal sausages, roast chicken with a taste of Calvados, seafood and mixed grill brochettes and rack of lamb. The fruit tart is quite acceptable, too. The grill and spit (tournebroche) are right in the center of the small (if slightly disjointed) dining area; a skylight brings cheer from the street above; and service among the handsome tiled tables is pleasant. What's more, à la carte prices at night are no more than at lunch, and sometimes less. This happy alternative to the saucy, pretentious cooking that seeks to pass itself off as French in New York could do more for Franco-American relations that a new spate of cables between Foggy Bottom and the Quai d'Orsay. About $25 per person, with a carafe of the Mirabeau house wine.

14 ♟
Tre Scalini
230 E. 58th St.
688-6888
Lunch Mon. to Fri. noon to 3:00 P.M.; dinner Mon. to Sat. 5:00 P.M. to midnight
All major credit cards
Italian

The lighting in this long room, with low ceilings, mirrors and green plants, is so lugubrious that you wonder if the place wasn't commissioned by the director of a funeral parlor. Happily, there is the formidable captain, Celestino, to electrify you; obliging and amusing, he plays the comedy of grand service as only Italians know how to. And then there's the cuisine. To explore in detail this interminable menu, you'd have to take a sabbatical and move to Tre Scalini. You will pardon us for limiting our experiences to several meals, which were a bit uneven but sufficiently good to give us no doubt about the quality of this place: delicious bresaola (air-dried beef) in ultrathin slices, pepperoni abbracciati con alici (pimientos and anchovies) that melt in your mouth without setting fire to it, very good fettuccine della casa, remarkable gnocchi, red snapper cooked to perfection and served in a very fine tomato sauce with capers and black olives, flavorful beefsteak alla fiorentina, very good chicken alla cacciatore and several desserts, such as zabaglione and ricotta cheesecake. On the other hand, the sweetbreads alla ciociaro, the veal special (in spite of its good laurel sauce) and the ganache cake were most uninteresting. About $45 per person, with wine.

12/20
Tse Yang
34 E. 51st St.
688-5447
Lunch daily noon to 3:00 P.M.; dinner nightly 6:00 P.M. to midnight
All major credit cards
Chinese

As you walk through the magnificent portals of Tse Yang and are stopped in your tracks by the dazzling decor, you will have an uneasy feeling that you'll somehow have to pay for all this. The service and setting are perfection. The large and interesting menu promises much, and you may soon unfurl in the sybaritic ambience like paper flowers in a mai tai. The rainbow-colored appetizers have class: tiny poached shrimp and scrumptious hacked chicken are tastefully arranged on a bed of hot and tangy cabbage salad. The famous Peking dumplings, couched on lettuce leaves in a bamboo steamer, are as fine as you'll get anywhere in New York. (It is advisable to be blissfully ignorant of the price, at $14.50 per dozen of the tiny fellows.) Scallops, described as "dans leur sauce Ravigote," are tantalizing; what streak of Taoist lunacy could have dreamed up this Sino-French misalliance? Wanton curiosity may prompt you to try the calf's liver, at a draconian $21. It will prove to have an identical sauce to the scallops, with an even heavier hand on the hoisin bottle. Most dishes are well prepared but suffer from a certain sameness. On the whole, Tse Yang is evolving into an agreeable and popular restaurant; the menu is original and intriguing, and nothing here will attack your tastebuds. It's absolutely perfect for expense account bandits and equally good for giving a treat to your rich maiden aunt, especially if there's a legacy in the offing. Prices on the whole are exorbitant, and inevitably your expectations will fall short of the final bill: just under $120 for five dishes and two drinks. Never have so few been charged so much for so little.

11/20
Zapata
330 E. 53rd St.
223-9408
Lunch Mon. to Fri. noon to 2:00 P.M.; dinner nightly 6:00 P.M. to 11:00 P.M.
All major credit cards
Mexican

This small, dark neighborhood Mexican restaurant looks like it was designed to be a replica of one of Zapata's mountain hideouts. Brick and white stucco walls are decorated with saddles, pottery and other miscellaneous Mexican revolutionary decor. It may be hideaway size, but the restaurant is clean and well ventilated, and the service is professional. The food is better than average and the menu more sophisticated than at the standard Americanized Mexican restaurant. Such specialties as mole poblano and Swiss enchiladas are very good, but the combination plates still suffer from the run-together, soggy taco syndrome. Desserts are terrible—but how much can you expect of a restaurant with an enlarged glossy photo of Anthony Quinn as its hero? Dinner for two, with wine, sangria, margaritas or beer, will run about $40 to $45.

West 59th Street and Up

13
Café des Artistes
1 W. 67th St.
877-3500
Breakfast Mon. to Fri. 7:30 A.M. to 9:30 A.M.; lunch Mon. to Sat. noon to 2:30 P.M.; dinner nightly 5:30 P.M. to midnight (Sun. to 8:30 P.M.); brunch Sun. 11:00 A.M. to 2:30 P.M.

The titillating, divine creatures on the walls of Café des Artistes must certainly go elsewhere for their Sunday brunch. We wish they didn't have such pink cheeks, soft skin and bouncing derrières, which show off a rich diet of the highest order. It's hard to imagine being swept into this manifestly sensual scene when you are served four minuscule pieces of smoked salmon, as thinly sliced as cigarette paper, smoked leg of lamb accompanied by unpeeled tomatoes and fat, stringy green beans, pecan ice

All major credit cards
Continental

cream with little taste, and a carafe of insipid white wine. We were served just this one Sunday by a waiter who is destined for a role in a comedy. With a serious delivery he announced to us: "We are very proud of our chocolate mousse pie. Unhappily, we don't have any." Then, an instant later: "We are very pleased with our blueberry tart, but we don't have any."

Fortunately, all is not lost. We have been happy enough with an excellent charcuterie platter with sausage, crunchy pâté, tasty prosciutto and rilettes. The toasted steak tartare, which has the curious appearance of a very rare hamburger, is good, with piñolas and curry. The calf's brains are lovely and light, and the bourride with aïoli is satisfying in a bourgeois manner. Desserts are nothing special, although it's a relief to see an alternative to sugar-saturated dessert menus, with offerings of dates and papaya with Stilton and nuts. There is an unevenness here; owner George Lang, who is one of the best restaurant consultants in the country, as well as a marvelously gifted gastronomy writer, might consider disguising himself and eating here secretly to diagnose his own place. This might result in a consistency that reflects the rapture on the walls. About $40 per person, with the "George Lang selection" wine.

14 ♟
Café Luxembourg
200 W. 70th St.
873-7411
Dinner nightly 5:30 P.M. to 12:30 A.M. (Sun. from 6:00 P.M.); brunch Sat. and Sun. 11:00 A.M. to 3:00 P.M.
AE, MC, V
American

This uptown Odeon is a welcome addition to the West Side Lincoln Center scene. The menu, designed by Odeon chef Patrick Clark, is an echo of its original version; the Wellfleet oysters poached in Champagne sauce are still delicate and tasty, the sautéed scallops in lime butter are delicious, the steak and frites are good, and the fettuccine al pesto is marvelously fragrant. You'll have a wonderful time in this deco setting that is as attractive as the clientele, as casual as neighbors who have stopped in for supper and as dressed to the hilt as opera fans. No matter what your fashion code, you'll enjoy the chicken liver terrine with a good red onion marmalade, the chicory salad served with Roquefort and country bacon, the seafood sausage wrapped in spinach and served with beurre blanc and the California classic, warm chèvre on a mâche salad (the French notwithstanding). Entrees are consistently good, from the tender mesquite-grilled lamb chops and marinated red snapper to the somewhat chewy duck in its glaze of honey and coriander and the salmon in ginger sauce. Desserts are a bit uneven (the lemon tart is an unrealized idea), but you'll be delighted with the white and black chocolate mousses with bittersweet chocolate sauce, the walnut tart, the cheesecake and the simple crème caramel. The wine list is fairly limited and unfortunately doesn't offer many interesting selections—French or American. Plan on about $30 per person, without wine.

12/20
Dimitri Restaurant
152 Columbus Ave. (66th–67th sts.) 787-7306

Lunch Mon. to Fri. 11:45 A.M. to 2:30 P.M.; dinner Mon. to Sat. 5:00 P.M. to midnight, Sun. 4:00 P.M. to 11:00 P.M.

All major credit cards

Italian/Greek

It's not easy to find a decent, unpretentious place to eat in the Lincoln Center area before or after an opera or concert. Dimitri's is such a place, however, and regulars at Lincoln Center already seem to know about it. The cooking is uncomplicated, the service smiling, and the value quite good. Despite what the name Dimitri might suggest, the menu here is basically Italian, although there are Greek appetizers, such as spinach pie or a traditional Greek salad. The real finesse here is seen in the pastas (particularly seafood linguine) and the fish dishes. Both the whole steamed bass in a ginger-scented broth (a touch of the Orient) and the simply grilled whole red snapper are extremely well prepared and recommended. (How often are you served a whole fish in New York— especially at affordable prices?) Other good main courses are veal piccata and chicken scarpiello.

There is no decor to speak of, and the noise level can be rather high when the place is crowded. But what comes from the kitchen is prepared with such sincerity that you will be happy you chose Dimitri, especially if you spent the better part of your paycheck for your tickets to Lincoln Center. About $25 per person, with wine.

9/20
Ernie's
2150 Broadway (76th St.) 496-1588

Lunch daily noon to 3:45 P.M.; dinner 5:30 P.M. to midnight

All major credit cards

Italian

The darling of the West Side, Ernie's is an exercise in patience and indulgence: patience because it may take two days to give your order and then be served, indulgence because it's impossible not to be seduced by the insanity of this place, which makes Maxwell's Plum look like kid's play once the singles here get into gear. We have a soft spot for these American places that take pride in their expensive, interior-designed nondecor. It's hard to tell if the owners ran out of money and decided to leave the brick walls bare, decorating missing chunks with pastel splatter painting, or if some designer is being hailed as a hero for his or her discovery of decorator-oblige poor simplicity. In any case, you will undoubtedly be as amused as we have been watching the calculated casual-chic crowd fight its way to the bar in a din that can only be described as competition for a Cape Canaveral flight pad. *Architectural Digest* may no longer be interested in the passé Corinthian columns that demark the freestanding bar, but it would undoubtedly celebrate the snakelike patterns of ceiling ducts and conduits, all painted in au courant colors—as well as the wall of pay phones tastefully integrated into the bare-wall decor. All of this has a sort of innocent charm, except we simply cannot forgive the cuisine. When you order it, and when you finally receive it, you will be faced with one inexplicable dilemma after another. The safest thing you can choose is the pizza with duck sausage, leek and sage, although we think a refresher course at Spago would certainly help the chef. As for the rest of this freely interpreted Italian cuisine: the fried calamari is passable (although the sauce reminds us of Russian dressing), the deep-fried mozzarella lukewarm and hard as a rock inside, the raclette with smoked mozzarella and grilled radicchio not bad if you push the excess oil to the side; the decent pesto pasta an economic liability with its two-inch layer of pine nuts, the angel hair pasta with goat's cheese rather strong, the baked loin of pork with garlic wine sauce overrun with tomatoes, the seafood with vegetables on pasta insipid and the veal piccata overcooked. We didn't have the heart for dessert at our last meal and chose instead to make a beeline for the door to escape the singles screaming for one another's phone numbers. About $35 per person, with a just-acceptable carafe of house wine.

11/20
The Gingerman
51 W. 64th St.
399-2358
Lunch and dinner daily 11:30 A.M. to 1:00 A.M.
All major credit cards
American

This charming bistro has by far one of the most attractive bars in New York City, filled with pre- and posttheater crowds and some interesting-looking people in between hours. There is a series of honeycombed rooms filling a converted warehouse space, with low ceilings and eccentricity intact. The front room, however, is *the* place to sit, so you're free to people watch when actors and actresses come here to dine in unnoticed peace. The menu is pretty basic, but if you have good company who enjoys any of the better California wines, you can have a romantic evening and not worry about the food. Roast duckling, fettuccine, calf's liver, a good smoked trout, tender rack of lamb, broiled fish, steak tartare or a passable scampi will bring a moderate level of contentment, as will the cheesecake, chocolate hazelnut torte or homemade ice creams. A good place to visit if Lincoln Center is in your evening's plans and you have about $40 to spend per person on dinner with wine.

11/20
Milestone
70 W. 68th St.
874-3679
Dinner Tues. to Fri. 5:00 P.M. to

A restaurant of this sort seems out of place in Manhattan—it would fit in much better in Portland or Denver. It's quite charming in a rustic, late '60s way, with rough wood booths, little shelves of books, dried

10:45 P.M., Sat. 4:30 P.M. to
10:45 P.M.
AE, MC, V
Italian/Continental

flowers on the walls and an antique wood-burning stove—rather like the living room of some former flower child in Colorado. In spite of the negligent, dim-witted service by earthy young women, Milestone is popular with neighborhood residents of all ages, no doubt because of the reasonable prices and generally decent cooking. The emphasis is on Italian, and the dishes are well-meaning but not inspired. The antipasto can be good, the garlic bread is delicious, the chicken Marguerite (with tomato, prosciutto and mozzarella in a wine sauce) is tender and very tasty, and the Italian-style zucchini is spicy and perfectly cooked. But the whitefish in an Oriental-style black bean sauce is most disappointing, overcooked and overwhelmed by the taste of ginger. There are several veal dishes that are well prepared but suffer from the common problem of poor-quality meat. But, all in all, you'll get honest food at very fair prices: less than $40 for two, with house wine.

11/20
Nishi
**325 Amsterdam Ave.
(75th St.)
799-0117**
Dinner nightly 6:00 P.M. to 11:45
P.M. (Sun. to 10:45 P.M.)
No credit cards
Japanese

You've never seen a Japanese restaurant like this one: it's fun and it's relaxed, with friendly, casual Uruguayan waiters serving breaded pork chops and Mandarin chiffon pie. It also has that trendy, all-black look, with the tiny spotlights much favored by Oriental restaurants bent on breaking the mold (Auntie Yuan is another example). Appetizers are the high spot: lovely sake-steamed mussels, a flaming conch shell filled with tender meat in a fragrant broth, moist little prawn dumplings and crisp eggplant slices in a dark miso sauce topped with crunchy shavings of bonito. Sushi and sashimi are perfectly fresh and acceptable, though lacking the brilliance you'd find at a good sushi bar.

Then there are the Europeanized entrees, which are a big letdown. Pork chops, chicken casserole and fillet of sole are all sloppily presented; the sauces have a monotonous similarity, with sake and soy predominating. If nouvelle cuisine is the art of taking Western ingredients and giving them a delicate, almost Oriental gloss, then the reverse is true here: Japanese specialties are given the meat-and-two-vegetables treatment. Your teriyaki comes dwarfed by a dollop of rice, a slurp of heavily sauced vegetables and the mandatory mound of wilted bean sprouts, army-canteen style. The Japanese restaurateur who dreamed up Nishi obviously wanted to make his American diners feel at home, but we can't help feeling that a more gracious presentation would lose him no face. Nevertheless, if you like Japanese food but hate the chilly ceremony that so often accompanies it, you'll probably enjoy Nishi. About $30 per person, with sake.

10/20
Santa Fe
72 W. 69th St.
724-0822
Lunch daily noon to 3:30 P.M.;
dinner 5:00 P.M. to midnight
AE, MC, V
American (regional)

This extremely attractive renovated townhouse gives customers a touch of Southwest chic with salmon-pink walls, Indian artifacts, clean-line chairs and small candles that enhance everyone's pallor. We keep searching for Tex-Mex food in New York, but unfortunately the cuisine here is as trendy as the decor. It would be a good place, however, for a visit from Chef Sedlar from St. Estèphe in Los Angeles, who is perfecting his own curious brand of nouvelle Southwest cuisine. Perhaps these two places are in cahoots with the grilled trout with pine nuts and coriander or sole broiled with avocado butter. We didn't have the heart to sample the more precious dishes and instead concentrated on nachos that are a cross between a Mexican pizza and a Southwest casserole, a burrito that doesn't deserve to be served in our favorite dive in Laredo, a tostada that makes this simple dish seem even more boring and chilis rellenos so thickly battered that the chilis slip out of their shells (but they are passable without the thick masa). These nice people mean well, but the attempt at authentic tastes is somewhat of a travesty. It's packed at night, and the well-heeled young crowd doesn't seem to care about the cuisine as they quench their thirsts with frozen margaritas and enjoy one another's company while eating a relatively inexpensive dinner that is filling and, after all, not the worst meal to be had on the West Side. About $10 per person for lunch, with a Carta Blanca.

12/20
Sidewalkers
12 W. 72nd St.
799-6070
Dinner nightly 6:00 P.M. to 11:30
P.M. (Fri. and Sat. to midnight,
Sun. from 5:00 P.M.)
All major credit cards
American (seafood)

New Yorkers who adore Maryland crabs invade Sidewalkers just as boldly as the tabloid menu announces, "Crabs Invade New York." These diners sit in casual comfort at paper-covered tables, wearing the ubiquitous bibs and cracking crabs to their hearts' delight. You will too, as they are quite good here. Seafood is prepared over a mesquite grill, there is Texas barbecued shrimp, the Sunday "crab bash" lets customers cash in on one of the best deals in town, and the wine list is full of California wines, among which the Sonoma River West Chardonnay is a good choice. The desserts are worth waiting for, particularly the raspberry torte with Grand Marnier. The price is right: plan on about $45 for two, with wine.

12/20
Simons
75 W. 68th St.
496-7477
Dinner nightly 6:00 P.M. to
11:30 P.M.
All major credit cards

Some things haven't changed at former food critic Jon Simon's restaurant. It is still an uncomfortable little room, whose decor veers from trapper's cabin to art deco, in an unpleasant basement near Lincoln Center. The restaurant is probably still always crowded and still

American/French
(nouvelle)

"in." The menu remains in the nouvelle cuisine style, although somewhat simplified and by no means inspired or inventive—this is nouvelle cuisine in a time capsule. Meats and fish appear frequently with such butters as saffron, lemon-chive and shallot. But perhaps Mr. Simon heeds the comments of former colleagues, because some things have changed. He seems to have found a chef who can not only make compound butters but can successfully prepare a seafood terrine with leek sauce, broil fresh salmon and sauté medallions of veal, using fresh products. Certainly someone has an experienced hand with sorbets, if not the pastries. All in all, nothing's nouvelle under the sun. Dinner for two, with wine, is slightly expensive for what is offered: about $75.

7/20
Tavern on the Green
Central Park West and 67th Street
873-3200
Lunch Mon. to Fri. 11:30 A.M. to 3:30 P.M.; dinner nightly 5:30 P.M. to midnight; brunch Sat. and Sun. 10:00 A.M. to 3:00 P.M.
All major credit cards
Continental

The main reason among the many that we love Tavern on the Green is that there are never any surprises: the cuisine is always bad. In spite of the comings and goings of so many chefs, it is remarkable that this place can attain such regularity of mediocrity. Nothing is perfect, however, and it happens from time to time that a small error manifests itself. The last time, for example, we were served a quite edible chicken. The chef, happily, must have noticed it; thank heaven, at the last minute he placed it on a bed of thick Gruyère, which saved the situation by transforming the whole thing into a sort of poultice. In any case, we admire the iron-willed determination here: clients are enthusiastically served basil pasta with an unidentifiable taste, the rémoulade sauce separates on the plate; mealy red snapper that we suspect was raised in a goldfish bowl; eggs Benedict that you could easily confuse with shaving cream; or sliced fillet of beef that would be perfect for resoling shoes. The admirably trained staff is always on top of things. Our waiter asked, "How was the meal?" with a magnificent smile, while our four plates remained three-quarters untouched. Then several minutes later, after our coffee, he asked, "What else can I do for you?" We replied, "Bring us more coffee." And with another radiant smile he responded, "Impossible for twenty minutes." As you can see, you'll never be bored at Tavern on the Green. And if you are, all you need to do is look around you to contemplate the enchanting decor, which resembles both an outlandish carnival and a Viennese cake for a giant bar mitzvah. Surrounded by midwestern tourists who swoon with emotion when faced with so much amassed beauty and older women who are treating their grandchildren, you'll find a taste of lost innocence here, and you may well ask yourself at what time the curtain closes on *Alice in Horrorland*. About $25 to $35 per person for lunch with a glass of wine.

12/20
Teacher's
2249 Broadway
(80th St.)
787-3500
Lunch and dinner daily 11:00 A.M. to 2:00 A.M.; brunch Sat. and Sun. 11:00 A.M. to 4:00 P.M.
All major credit cards
Continental/American

Teacher's continues to please its loyal clientele as a neighborhood pub grown up. In fact, it grew so much that Teacher's Too has opened at 2271 Broadway, near 82nd Street (362-4900), for those who prefer a newer, slightly Oriental pub atmosphere. The menus are nearly the same (perhaps with the difference of a fettuccine here and a gazpacho there), and both feature an eclectic cuisine inspired by the talents of an apparently classically trained Thai chef who supervises both restaurants. A weekend brunch includes several versions of eggs Benedict and omelets, as well as baked smoked trout with ratatouille and sautéed onions, fettuccine with broccoli, a good chicken milanese and several excellent Thai specialties, including gai khoong pad khing (just tell them you'd like the delicious chicken, shrimp, pepper, black bean, mushroom and ginger dish). Dinners feature such classics as escargots, chicken Kiev, duckling à l'orange, sautéed calf's liver and prime rib. Menus change daily, but there is always a hamburger to be had as well as reasonably priced wines and beers. Desserts (orange pound cake, praline ice cream cake, chocolate layer cake, cheesecake and pecan pie) are just plain good. Never mind that the menu, atmosphere and kitchen collectively represent the United Nations; it's an easy place to be, and the food is fine. Dinner for two, with wine, will run about $40 to $45.

13 🍳
The Terrace
400 W. 119th St.
666-9490
Lunch Tues. to Fri. noon to 2:30 P.M.; dinner Tues. to Sat. 6:00 P.M. to 10:00 P.M. (Fri. and Sat. to 10:30 P.M.)
All major credit cards
French (classical)

The first time you come to The Terrace it might be a little like a blind date with someone who's described as "not great looking, but has a terrific personality." The decor of this restaurant at the summit of Columbia University's Butler Hall is nothing special, and during the day it's even rather banal looking. But at night when the candles are lit, you'll notice the mirrors scintillating and the floor-to-ceiling windows overflowing with plants. This is when the magic begins in this long dining room that becomes one of the most romantic in New York. If you have a sentimental young man or woman to seduce, a wedding anniversary to celebrate or an intimate evening to spend with a friend, this is the place, even if the chamber music lacks discretion and the service is erratic. The cuisine of owner-Chef Dušan Bernic is in the same image as the atmosphere—that is to say, discreet elegance. Don't expect anything extraordinary or too original, but the dishes with their French accents have a certain finesse, particularly the delicious steamed shrimp with baby vegetables, lobster salad, baby scallops sautéed with watercress and fresh salmon. The sweetbreads with port are firm and well cooked but the sauce is too rich, and the red snapper is overcooked and rather banal. Try the always excellent rack of lamb, though you have every right to be allergic to its mint purée. The lack of interesting desserts is compensated by the very acceptable wine list: the exquisite red Hermitage is a gift at $20. About $50 per person, with wine.

12/20

Tovarisch
38 W. 62nd St.
757-0168
Lunch and dinner Mon. to Sat. noon to 11:00 P.M.
All major credit cards
Russian

Opulent reds, gilded mirrors and patterned wallpaper create a Dr. Zhivago mood in the friendly bar and two narrow dining rooms, which attract theatergoers, émigrés and other personalities combing Lincoln Center for classic czarist cooking. Talk immediately centers around the impressive caviar selections. It's wise to spend an additional $3.75 to spread Tovarisch's own Pausnaia pressed black caviar, $14.75 the ounce, on warm buckwheat yeast blinis. If you're feeling extravagant, pamper yourself with beluga caviar, at $34.75 the ounce. Melted butter, sour cream, egg and onion prolong the experience. There is the usual assortment of Russian zakuska appetizers: maatjes herring in wine or tomato sauce, exotic-sounding Georgian wind-dried beef. A zakuska supper is available after 10:30 P.M. Tovarisch features lamb and pork kebabs as well as more imperial dishes, such as Norwegian salmon and chicken tabaka or fried baby chicken served with tkemali or plum sauce. Prices are imperial as well. The quail, roast young kid, goose, baby lamb Uzbeck, partridge and Georgian hen appear on the menu without prices, which gives you an idea of their cost. Unhappily, the chicken Kiev is unexciting, and the swordfish kebab tastes of grilled meats. Entrees are served with rice or moist, deeply satisfying kasha. Tovarisch's politics are patriotic; there are no Russian vodkas, but there's a large selection of potato vodkas, and wines are predominantly French. The house dessert is an overwhelming meringue concoction named for the ballerina Anna Pavlova, but the chocolate cake with Grand Marnier satisfies less baroque tastes. This is the place where New York University professors can impress out-of-town academicians or where anyone can indulge Anna Karenina fantasies. You'll pay for the privilege, though: dinner for two, including caviar and wine, will cost you around $80.

East 59th Street and Up

9/20
Adam's Rib
23 E. 74th St.
535-2112
Lunch Mon. to Fri. noon to 4:00 P.M.; dinner nightly 5:00 P.M. to 10:45 P.M. (Sat. to 11:00 P.M.) All major credit cards
American (steaks)

To quote the amusing menu, which you must read, "This is a roast beef house." Off the lobby of the old Volney Hotel in the heart of the gallery district, Adam's Rib looks like the perfect setting to serve the quintessential Yorkshire pudding: an English-style dining room with dark wood walls, mirrors with ornate gold leaf frames, wood and leather chairs (try to ignore the potted dead branches with tiny Christmas lights blazing from several corners of the restaurant). But read the menu more closely: "A Yorkshire Pudding ... somehow this flavorful pastry puff sounds better than it tastes." Trust the menu. The gospel according to Saint Nicholas (N.A. Nicholas, proprietor) quotes Genesis 1:26: "Man has dominion over ... the cattle," and he says that, frankly, the nonbeef entrees (roast duckling, lobster tails and broiled fillet of gray sole) are a compromise. Again, in the menu we trust. The Caesar salad is sublime but desserts are a blasphemy, and while we don't need to preach the merits of prime midwestern cattle, it is somewhat disappointing as prepared here. Lunch features omelets, hamburgers and sandwiches. Dinner for two, with one of several reasonably priced wines, will be about $50.

17
An American Place
969 Lexington Ave. (70th St.)
517-7660
Dinner Mon. to Sat. 6:00 P.M. to 10:30 P.M.
AE, MC, V
American

very good

All that seems to be missing is the American flag. There's a celebration of Americana here that gives Larry Forgione's own little restaurant a certain uniqueness in New York, the city's handful of all-American places notwithstanding. This place is chic in an understated way, with hand painted fabric walls that remind us of the paintings of Southwest Indians; the Indian influence is only reasonable in such a regional American milieu. It is refined, elegant and fairly sedate, with earnest waiters who take it all pretty seriously. It's too bad, because this sort of Forgione-branded American cuisine lends itself to a certain sense of humor that would liven up the place.

We have to hand it to Forgione, who weathered through several years at The River Café, where the

131

cuisine was generally superb, although the kitchen conditions were lamentable. Ever since we discovered him when we published our first guide to New York and encouraged him to open his own establishment, we have been waiting for him to come into his own with no restraints, no excuses and fewer clients, which would be appropriate for his type of cooking. The menu certainly lives up to those expectations, reminding us of some of the lovely meals we had across the bridge in Brooklyn, for which we awarded three toques in our previous edition for his imagination, creativity and enterprise. Those qualities are still being nourished. Where else in this urban theater can you find Virginia ham with a sweet potato and pea salad, Washington State Willipa oysters that remind us of colonial oyster pan roasts, pasta with the ubiquitous California goat's cheese (marvelous with the crispy artichokes), veal with Montana beef jerky (which looks like a small hedgehog), wild duck with blackstrap molasses, blackened redfish à la Prudhomme (less spicy and firm than its namesake—Larry's version suffers from a touch of pallor) and good old lamb from America the beautiful? Even the amber waves of grain are represented, with home-baked breads that are served warm and fresh.

Sometimes, though, the idea is better than the reality. We hope that certain dishes we have sampled are not indicative of an overdose of ambition. We fear that at times he is perhaps trying a bit too hard to reclaim the currently chic American cuisine. While we have no desire to hold chefs back from their roots, we *are* concerned that they cook them properly. We do not doubt Forgione's talent, but a little restraint is called for in his mixed-metaphor tortilla dish, made with layers of wild duck and surrounded by a lackluster salsa. Partridge, so lovely when presented rare and tender, is sometimes overcooked and is accompanied by a too-sweet, maple syrupy stuffing. The shrimp salad arrives looking like a Christmas wreath, unhappily, neither the shrimp nor the scallops are particularly tasty. All is not lost, however. The lobster and frog's leg salad with a lentil and ham hock garnish is wonderful, as is the smoked fish terrine and the refreshing light salad. The breast of wild duck is superb, and so is the perfectly cooked lamb—the best we've found in New York.

Desserts are not An American Place's strong suit; the quality varies according to the pastry chef's inspiration. The huckleberry shortcake, for example, is a waterfall of berries, but there is a pronounced aftertaste that is not particularly pleasant. The fig custard tart is tasty, the simple apple tart delicious and the poached pear with crème anglaise a delight. The American wine list offers several affordable selections (the overall list is stratospheric in its pricing), particularly the Trefethen '80 Pinot Noir. The $42 prix fixe menu changes seasonally. We once again award Larry with his three toques and feel sure that when things have settled down, his cuisine will become even more refined and adventurous, leaving the overly manipulated and handled creations behind and letting his simplicity and good taste shine through.

14

Andrée's Mediterra- nean
354 E. 74th St. 249-6619
Dinner Tues. to Sat. 6:30 P.M. to 9:30 P.M.
No credit cards
Mediterranean

The New York friend who helped us discover Andrée, who at the time was virtually unknown, could not have imagined that his favorite little restaurant would become invaded by so many people after the publication of our first guide to New York. Today, we have to reserve a table weeks in advance. In spite of this success, however, the pretty Andrée, who is always so gay and smiling, holds onto her cool and continues to prepare all these good dishes herself in her sparkling clean little kitchen. We suggested that she open another room on the second floor, but perhaps it wasn't such a great idea after all: the service is a bit inexperienced and slow, and you may even have to ask yourself if Andrée has problems serving more meals than she ought to. Several signs make us worry. It is nothing irreparable (one dish arrives nearly cold, sign of a poorly monitored cooking time), and we adore her too much not to put her on her guard. This said, this French-Egyptian amateur cook, who lived in Cairo and Marseilles before immigrating to the United States, possesses a particular grace that she transmits to her cuisine, which is full of freshness, flavor and spontaneity. It is a Mediterranean cuisine in the largest sense of the word, because you will find a little bit of Lebanon, Egypt, Turkey, Algeria and even Italy (in a delicious fettuccine al pesto with shrimp and broccoli) and provincial France, all illuminated by sun and warmed by spices. But Andrée has added her own original ideas to traditional recipes. Her couscous, for example, unorthodox but still light and of a remarkable flavor, is one of our favorites, along with babaganoutch, hummos, moussaka, striped bass Corfu and, above all, an exquisite rack of lamb coated in garlic and fresh herbs—it has a crusty skin and juicy meat that leaves an indescribable perfume in your mouth. On the other hand, we have to ask what a salmon mousse and cold turban of sole with herb mayonnaise are doing on the Mediterranean scene; even if Andrée is proud of them, they do little to add to her glory. Bring your own wine from home and save space for dessert: crème caramel, mocha crème royale and Oriental fruit salad are just a few of Andrée's miracles. For $37.50 per person, you will have a happy evening and will instantly make a reservation for your next visit.

12/20
Auntie Yuan
1191A First Ave.
(64th St.)
744-4040
Lunch and dinner daily 11:45 A.M. to midnight (Sun. to 11:00 P.M.)
AE
Chinese

This dazzlingly chic new Chinese restaurant is totally black, with cunningly placed spots highlighting the pink orchids and the beautiful people. It is the brainchild of Ed Schonfeld, who has installed not one but four aunties in the kitchen, instructing them to give an international touch to their own specialties. You'll find such unusual ingredients as quail and salmon, and with Caucasian waiters, Mozart on the stereo and fruit sorbets replacing lychees, this might well be described as a Chinese restaurant for those who don't like Chinese restaurants.

Along with the à la carte menu, there are three set menus, including a tasting dinner—a kind of magical mystery tour of strangely assorted offerings, some great, some awful. We like the scallion pancake, the pretty if somewhat impregnable crayfish, Auntie's up-market version of ants climbing a tree (beef and glass noodles wrapped in a pancake) and the delicious sautéed mussels. Not so exciting are a dish of custard studded with musty-tasting ham, tough, stringy orange beef and some pallid joints of boiled chicken that have already given their all to the stockpot. The duck dinner is more mystery than magic, the high spot being a two-bite crispy pancake enfolding a two-inch square of crispy skin; at a recent meal, the promised shredded duck meat never materialized. The centerpiece of the lobster dinner, on the other hand, is a tasty if rather minor-league crustacean that is moist, delicious and still inhabiting its carapace—unlike the token shell you sometimes get in less reputable places.

The idea here is a good one, though the cooking still lacks any consistent style (one too many aunties in the kitchen, perhaps?). On the one hand you'll enjoy an exquisite, almost nouvelle cuisine arrangement of black mushrooms and bok choy in the shape of a flower, served with, on the other hand, coarse and oily greens that would be more at home in a Harlem soul food kitchen. But these are doubtless only teething troubles; with so many of the older, established Chinese restaurants stuck in the stalest of regional ruts, any attempt to add a fresh dimension can only be good news. About $30 per person, with wine.

13
Bistro
Bambouche
1582 York Ave.

This sweet place has what we have always dreamed of discovering: sincere owners, a charming ambience, a lighthearted menu and a prix fixe dinner for $19.50.

26.

(83rd St.)
249-4002
Dinner Tues. to Sun. 6:00 P.M. to
11:00 P.M.
No credit cards
French

Very good

What more could you ask for? The lovely family that runs this slip of a bistro (a handful of tables, exposed brick walls, warm lighting and contented neighborhood clients) does its best to produce a simple cuisine that is both refined and honest. The four-course menu includes a marvelous scallop mousse, lightly creamed chicken in profiterole (the pastry dough is too sweet for this sort of marriage), a lovely sorrel soup and caviar blinis as starters. A light salad will refresh you before you sample the delicious steamed red snapper, perfectly sautéed scallops presented with sparkling brown butter, a nice although slightly overcooked stuffed chicken and a simple and tasty entrecôte. If these offerings aren't enough, the desserts are the crowning glory: the lemon tart, apple tart, apricot soufflé and luscious ice cream with hot chocolate sauce will finish a delightful dinner. Bring your own wine and return often. This place is a rare jewel in a city infested with overpriced, pretentious, self-conscious places.

12/20
Bravo Gianni
230 E. 63rd St.
752-7272
Lunch Mon. to Fri. noon to 2:30
P.M.; dinner Mon. to Sat. 5:30 P.M.
to 11:30 P.M.
All major credit cards
Italian

An evening at Bravo Gianni is not unlike a film premiere in Rome. The bejeweled women, exotically attractive in their sequins, veiled cloches and all-black ensembles (including, of course, the stone-encrusted pumps and stockings), are accompanied by handsome, dark-suited older men. There is much greeting and whispering in the Italian tradition, as successful-looking hosts welcome extended family members into their arms and then onto the rose-striped banquettes. It is only with great regret that *we* have to pay more attention to what's on our plates than to the meteor shower around us, for without a doubt this glitter show is more a feast for the eye than the palate. It is a cheerful place, with enough theater and drama to make Orsini's look like a funeral parlor by contrast. You will be advised, pampered, taken care of and served with flourishes and macho Italian sincerity. And chances are you won't be disappointed by the pastas—particularly the tender tortellini in cream sauce, the tagliatella with a light tomato-herb sauce and the spinach-filled ravioli in pesto served, oddly, with green beans and potatoes. As in many Italian places, the pasta whets the appetite, but the entrees are disappointing by comparison. You want these people to succeed because the place is so friendly and happy, but more energy could be directed to finesse in the kitchen rather than to ambience in the dining room. The red snapper with tomatoes and shellfish is overly complicated, the grilled veal chop is tender but lacking taste, and the scampi, although presented as a work of art, is disappointing, because the poor shellfish are overwhelmed by salty garlic butter and are overcooked as well. The menu is filled with classics, but you might need an interpreter to help decipher the Italian terminology. Desserts are nothing special, although the homemade cheesecake is pleasant; most of the pastries are from Désirs la Côte Basque and are what you expect. The wine list has depth, and the prices are eminently reasonable. Come here for an amusing, decorative evening, but bring realistic culinary expectations. About $40 per person, with wine.

15 🍳
Café Lavandou
134 E. 61st St.
838-7987
Lunch Mon. to Sat. noon to 2:30 P.M.; dinner Mon. to Sat. 6:00 P.M. to 10:30 P.M. (Fri. and Sat. to 11:00 P.M.)
All major credit cards
French
(nouvelle/provincial)

In our last guide, we judged La Côte Basque worthy of two toques and Le Lavandou worthy of only a 12/20 rating, even though both were operated by the same talented nouvelle cuisine chef, Jean-Jacques Rachou. Perfectionist that he is, he decided it was impossible to supervise the kitchens in both places and maintain standards that would satisfy him—and the critics (us among them). So in mid-1983, he closed Le Lavandou, with the intention of converting it into a brasserie serving ragouts, cassoulets and other dishes that demand less of his personal attention. To go along with this simplified menu, he started to install rustic posts, overhead wood latticework and copper pots and pans. Apparently, though, before the work was complete, he had second thoughts about the type of restaurant he wanted, and the result is a somewhat curious combination of a bistro with the more formal banquettes and watercolors one is apt to see in a restaurant serving elegant meals. And the short menu that is now in place reflects this shift in emphasis: the light sauces, delicate preparations and eye-appealing presentations associated with nouvelle cuisine, with only a few throwbacks to the earthy cooking that Jean-Jacques originally projected for Café Lavandou. These traditional dishes are outstanding: a superb lapereau, moist and tender; a cassoulet toulousain (M. Rachou is from Toulouse); and excellent rognons, prepared either with the traditional mustard sauce or with green peppercorns.

What is of more interest, however, is the generally high level of the nouvelle dishes, many of which are also prepared at La Côte Basque. He has solved the problem of maintaining standards at two restaurants by installing Jacques Coustar as chef at the café (he served under M. Rachou at La Côte Basque and also under André Soltner at Lutèce). M. Coustar's seafood appetizers are an absolute delight: succulent Bay scallops, quenelles, a soup of mussels, scallops and shreds of leek, a salad of crabmeat and a seafood pasta with a nantua sauce that is truly exceptional. Main courses are not quite so close to the picture-perfect dishes of his mentor at La Côte Basque, but we can find no fault with the duck breast, the rack of lamb or the lobster with a sauce américaine. All in all, Café Lavandou seems to be in good hands. Before too long, you may not be able to tell the difference between Jean-Jacques's two places—except in the price, which today is still much less at the café. We trust that difference will continue. About $40 per person, with wine.

11/20

Café San Martin

1458 First Ave. (75th St.) 288-0470
Dinner nightly 6:00 P.M. to midnight; brunch Sun. noon to 4:00 P.M.
All major credit cards
Spanish

Café San Martin makes a wonderful first impression. The atmosphere is sophisticated: parquet floors, a piano bar and an elegant dessert table greet you as you are ushered into the small dining room. Part of the kitchen is visible, and you can only hope that the copper pots aren't just for show and will produce some authentic Spanish cuisine. As the restaurant fills up, however, people are crowded next to you, the piano only increases the noise level, the waiters become frantic and sloppy, and you have to search for Spanish specialties amid duck pâté with cumberland sauce and Waldorf salad, fillet of sole amandine, veal scaloppine du chef and roast duck with cherries and chestnut purée. Appetizers, such as gazpacho and garlic shrimp, are ordinary, but some of the search is worth it—the paella is delightful, with all of the necessary accoutrements. A similar search through the wine list will yield some good Spanish wines. Ramon Martin is most gracious and sincerely tries to please all of the people all of the time. What results is a Continental restaurant with Gershwin melodies and Spanish overtones. Dinner for two, with wine, will run about $65.

10/20

Casa Brasil

406 E. 85th St. 288-5284
Dinner Mon. to Sat. 6:30 P.M. to 10:00 P.M. (Sat. to 11:00 P.M.)
No credit cards
International

You might assume, as we did, that Casa Brasil would offer some of the Brazilian specialties that we have become accustomed to enjoying when visiting Rio during Carnival. The cuisine here falls more into the mélange category, with such offerings as beef Wellington, prosciutto and melon, crabmeat salad and roast duck. Brazilian owner Donna Helma continues to prepare the undefinable cuisine that we last reported on in our first New York guide, so we cannot truthfully say that things have improved. Perhaps you should venture here for dessert amid the remotely famous and local residents who seek out this basement-level retreat; her tapioca with wine and vanilla sauce gives some semblance of hope. It's too bad that the $30 prix fixe dinner offers so little nourishment—for either the soul or the appetite.

12/20
Chatfield's
208 E. 60th St.
253-5070
*Lunch Mon. to Sat. noon to 3:30
P.M.; dinner nightly 6:00 P.M. to
11:30 P.M. (Sun. to 11:00 P.M.)
AE, MC, V*
American

Shoppers weary from their dedicated forays into Bloomingdale's come to this unpretentious place with dark wood paneling, heavily framed mirrors, a brick fireplace and a friendly bar to sample the imaginative American cuisine. Sometimes the nouvelle goes too far (or not far enough), so it may be safer to stick to the handful of straightforward fish and meat preparations. If you're feeling adventurous, go ahead and try the caviar pie, mussels with apples and onions or the basil-lemon sorbet. You will be pleasantly surprised that these unexpected marriages succeed as well as they do. On the more conservative side, the pasta with clams is perfectly al dente, the grilled shrimp (in their shells) are excellent, and the poached sea scallops with a butter-lemon sauce are delicious. Chatfield's is definitely worth a visit, if for no reason other than to be served good food at reasonable prices—something that's hard to come by in this absurdly overpriced neighborhood. About $30 per person for dinner, with wine.

15
Chez Pascale
151 E. 82nd St.
249-1334
*Dinner Mon. to Sat. 6:00 P.M. to
midnight
All major credit cards*
French (classical)

If you are considering falling in love, bring your prospective partner to Chez Pascale. This is quite possibly the most romantic restaurant in New York. The lighting is golden, cleverly hidden behind bleached wood wall panels, the floral prints are charming, and the well-dressed service is pleasant. But above all, the ambience creates an intimacy that makes the rest of the well-heeled Upper East Side clientele disappear into the bare brick walls. The candles on the tables simulate the lighting of Lescaux, but you only need illumination to read the enticing provincial menu. Starters are tempting, from scallops and oysters poached in Champagne sauce and fresh pasta with basil to a salad of green beans and truffles and a seafood pâté. The escargots in cream of garlic are superb, as is the wild game pâté. Entrees are equally tasty: bouillabaisse, bass en croûte, Cornish hens with tarragon and veal kidneys with mustard sauce. If you have the chance to try the soft-shell crabs provençale, don't miss it; the tender shellfish are perfectly partnered with a marvelous fresh tomato sauce. The veal chop with morels is also tender and, mercifully, tastes like veal. Finish your meal with a melt-in-your-mouth raspberry mousse, accompany everything with superb '79 Meursault, and you won't even think twice when your bill comes to $120 for two. After all, what does price matter when the prospect of love is at hand?

16
Le Cirque
58 E. 65th St.
794-9292

There are no more than five or six restaurants in the world where it is absolutely unthinkable not to be between the hours of 1:00 and 2:30 P.M. We are only

*Lunch Mon. to Sat. noon to 2:45
P.M.; dinner Mon. to Sat. 6:00 P.M.
to 10:30 P.M.
AE, CB, DC*
French
(classical/nouvelle)

speaking, obviously, of those people who can't afford not to be seen traveling by Concorde and buying leather goods from Gucci and cat food dishes from Tiffany. A chic restaurant is clearly one that has the power to bring together the greatest possible number of celebrity faces, but this alone is not enough. From Gianni Agnelli to Gloria Vanderbilt, from Marisa Berenson to Barbara Walters, from Hugh Carey to Malcolm Forbes, all the habituées of Le Cirque also go to Côte Basque, Lutèce or Four Seasons, and although these are no longer chic-chic restaurants, Le Cirque still is. Why? First of all because the journalists say so, and secondly because it's absolutely true.

After twenty years of research and studies we have conducted in Paris, London, Milan, Geneva, Madrid, Dar es Salaam (that was our travel agent's mistake), Palm Beach, Tucson (another mistake), Rio de Janeiro and New York, we have come to the conclusion that chic-chic restaurants have a number of points in common:

1. You can recognize a chic-chic restaurant, not by dinner, but by lunch. For example, Maxim's in Paris can still be considered a chic-chic establishment because its lunches attract the crème de la crème, even though during the evening you run the risk of bumping into your hairdresser or the most recent lottery winner. At Le Cirque, each lunch is a social event, except on Saturdays during the summer, when "no one" is there (which means the 2,000 people who count in New York have left for the weekend).

2. In a chic-chic restaurant, there are more women than men. Le Cirque is one of those rare places that has the privilege of attracting society ladies who come to discuss things that are of no consequence but without which life would be unthinkable. In the large restaurants where the clientele is 98 percent masculine, the spectacle is somewhat demoralizing. You think you are in a canteen for executives, and it would be more appropriate to serve them their lunches under a stockmarket display board.

3. A chic-chic restaurant generally has an Italian owner and an ancient maître d' or bartender who has been there for years. This was certainly the case at The Colony, where Sìno Maccioni, a Florentine whose father was a concierge of a grand hotel, practiced his talents; also of Cecconi's in Paris and, of course, Harry's Bar in Venice. The superiority of veteran maîtres d' over all restaurant owners is demonstrated by the fact that they know one never sits at the table with clients. They have mastered the very specialized art of being both friendly and distant, which also gives the impression to these multimillionairesses (who could buy the restaurant on a

whim simply by signing a check) that they are privileged individuals. When maître d' Sino brings a basket of fresh Italian truffles to Ivana Trump or Pierre Cardin, the gesture becomes as significant as if the Queen of England were to take out the crown jewels.

4. In a chic-chic restaurant, it is extremely vulgar to seem interested in the cuisine. The true chic lunch on a slice of smoked salmon and a salad, or, even better, they vary their pleasures with melon and Parma ham, an omelet, grilled chicken or fish without sauce, all washed down with Perrier. You could easily ask yourself what is the fate of the 43 entrees and half dozen specials presented each day to the clients at Le Cirque. Perhaps they are meant to feed the many employees—if so, they must be very happy, because even if the cuisine of Chef Alain Sailhac doesn't have an overflowing imagination, it has developed a remarkable quality over the years. Like a good tailor-made suit, it has the supreme elegance not to draw attention to itself. But the awakened palate senses immediately the excellence of the products and the perfection of the cooking. When a rabbit pâté with rosemary, a duck terrine, a vegetable cake en gelée, a pasta primavera or even a simple salad of céléri rémoulade is this good, you overlook Alain Sailhac's lack of boldness. He has prepared for us the best soft-shell crabs we have ever eaten, accompanied by fresh tomato and large green peas; his masterpiece is veal kidneys grilled with green onions and lemon thyme, served with an upside-down cake of eggplant. These creations are followed with one of the fabulous desserts. The most popular one, crème brûlée, would be even better with a touch of orange or lemon. But this is the only reproach we can make to pastry chef Joseph Jensen, for his mocha cake with chestnuts and his fruit tarts will make you fall to the ground. The espresso is nothing, and apart from a beautiful selection of Bordeaux, the wine list isn't very impressive—which is not to say that the simple Bourgogne served as the house wine in carafes isn't excellent, nor that the Nobile di Montepulciano at $19 isn't nearly a gift. As you know, the rich don't like to spend their money, and with lunches at a $22.75 prix fixe, no one can accuse Sino of abusing his millionaires. In the evening, however, you can get trapped into spending no less than $120 for two with ease.

14 Claude's
205 E. 81st St.
472-0487
Dinner nightly 6:00 P.M. to
10:45 P.M.
All major credit cards

If you don't have a minimum of two hours to spend over dinner, it is useless to come to Claude Bailes's. Just as when he was at The Palace, he prepares everything to order, and that takes time. Contrary to those restaurants where they are content to reheat dishes prepared in

French (classical)

advance, everything here is done at the last minute. Although Claude is a traditional rather than creative cook, he brings several personal touches to a repertoire that, while engaging, has as its greatest weakness being too static. We would love it if this menu, where we find year after year the same specials (Bocuse's truffle soup, striped bass stuffed "paquelot France," bouillabaisse catalane or rack of lamb baked in a crust), would move a little more. And we would love above all for Claude, who is Catalan by origin—from a region known for its spices and powerful tastes—to give more contrast to some of his dishes, such as his very beautiful rack of lamb stewed in a juice that would be even better if it were more vigorously seasoned. It's true that you can add your own pepper, but it's not the same thing. The cold platter of New Jersey vegetables à la grecque is a bit pale. On the other hand, the grilled beef with Brouilly is excellent, the vegetable or fish feuilletés are delicious, and the pastries, particularly the chocolate cake, are of the first order. A good cellar of French and California wines, very professional service and an elegant decor of red lacquer and mirrors give this little room a holiday air. There's a prix fixe dinner for $45 and another menu of seven courses for $60.

14 ♟

Contrapunto
200 E. 60th St.
751-8616
Dinner Mon. 4:00 P.M. to 11:00 P.M.; lunch and dinner Tues. to Sat. noon to midnight
AE
Italian

"Our philosophy is counterpoint to other restaurants specializing in Italian cuisine. Master Chef Angelo Serpe has unusual pasta dishes you will not generally find elsewhere." Thus proclaims the menu of Pasteria Contrapunto. This type of literature is generally a prelude to catastrophe. But Contrapunto, a relative newcomer located over Yellowfingers, is, to the contrary, a complete success. You feel it when you enter the immaculately tidy room with its white walls, spotlit round tables, open kitchen with chefs busy at their ovens and charming staff in long aprons, all of which gives you a feeling of well-being and a sense of confidence. This is an accurate first impression, because everything served to you here is indeed perfectly fresh, scrupulously honest and of the quality we would love to find in other Italian restaurants in New York more well-known than this modest pasteria. The menu is limited to four appetizers (two salads, mushrooms alla romana and thinly sliced dried beef with Parmesan and olive oil), three imported pastas and eight fresh pasta dishes, all prepared at the last minute. They are altogether delicious, making any choice a good one: rigati ai quattro formaggi (tubular pasta with four cheeses), tagliarini alla conga d'oro (thin ribbon pasta with yellow and red peppers, zucchini, eggplant and fresh garlic), pappardelle boscaiola (white ribbon pasta with mushrooms, Marsala and pecorino) or malfatti con granchio (pasta squares filled with crab). There are also three meat dishes, of which the grilled T-bone veal with spinach appears most appetizing. But we recommend you save space for the marvelous chocolate cake, lightly meringued and served with homemade ice cream; the praline alone would make you die while crying, "Viva Italia!" About $20 per person, with a glass of honest house white wine and an excellent espresso. Now you have a good pretext to rush over to Bloomie's across the street to shop off your lunch.

12/20
La Crémerie
1053 Lexington Ave.
(74th–75th sts.)
535-6541
Lunch and dinner Mon. to Sat.
10:00 A.M. to 11:00 P.M.
No credit cards
French (provincial)

The well-scrubbed kitchen look promises good country cooking, and so it proves. The twelve marble slab tables and the rattan chairs, the tiled walls and the simple dishes and cutlery go well with the choice of food: pâtés, salads and snails to start; beef bourguignon, veal normandie or chicken chasseur as entrees, served with tiny vegetables prepared to the right degree of doneness; a tarte tatin or crème caramel to finish. These rustic pleasures come in a $19 prix fixe dinner, extra for specials, espresso, wine or beer. Croissants, muffins and danish are served before lunch, soup, salads, omelets and sandwiches come at noon, and tea and dessert are served from 3:00 P.M. to 6:30 P.M. The young French staff is eager to please.

15 🖐
Devon House, Ltd.
1316 Madison Ave.
(93rd St.)
860-8294
Dinner Mon. to Sat. 6:00 P.M. to
1:00 A.M.
All major credit cards
French/Continental

Even New Yorkers who can afford to pay a million dollars for an apartment on Fifth or Park Avenue may have trouble finding someone to cook dinner. These unfortunates need no longer be concerned, because they can now walk a block over to Madison Avenue, where they can get the same personal attention they would expect at home—and in surroundings altogether in keeping with what they are used to.

Devon House is the creation of Yvonne Scherrer, a native of Jamaica (Devon House is the name of an old manor house there), and it is more like a private club than a conventional restaurant. But unlike some clubs we know, there is nothing seedy or musty here: rather, you'll find refined, understated good taste. Everything is elegantly appointed from the tiny mahogany bar and tables; well spaced and set with beautiful crystal and linens. Unobtrusive chamber music in the background adds to the sense of gentility. And, happily, Mrs. Scherrer's cooking is every bit up to this setting.

Her style is basically French (not much influenced by nouvelle), but she also gives vent to her own imagination. The result is an extremely personalized cuisine that doesn't stray far from traditional French but sometimes incorporates unusual and intriguing herbs and taste sensations. (She imports herbs and some condiments from Jamaica.) This ability to combine the best of tradition with her own innovation is perhaps best realized in a delicious peppery sauce with fresh ginger and guava that accompanies a tender roast loin of pork. Another interesting flavor is the pickapepper sauce (a condiment bottled in Jamaica) that accompanies the fillet of beef. But you will also find the more traditional renditions of French sauces equally enchanting: Madeira with sweetbreads in puff pastry, Grand Marnier with roast duck or Marsala with veal. Mrs. Scherrer gives extraordinary care to everything she prepares, and that means you may have to wait between courses. But in these surroundings it's not a hardship. In any event, when your first order arrives and you've sampled what is before you, the next interlude will turn into pleasant anticipation.

For personalized attention in a civilized environment, you can expect to spend $60 per person à la carte, without wine, or you can opt for the prix fixe: appetizer, entree, salad, cheese (a superb, though small, selection), desserts (from the Dumas and Bonté pastry shops) and coffee for $42.50.

14 🎩 Divino Ristorante

1556 Second Ave. (81st St.) 861-1096

Lunch daily noon to 3:00 P.M.; dinner nightly 5:00 P.M. to midnight (Sun. 1:00 P.M. to 10:30 P.M.)
All major credit cards

Italian

Divino is not one of those Upper East Side Italian restaurants where the name of the game is to see and be seen, usually in the latest from Saint Laurent, Givenchy or Versace. This is a serious place to eat; fashion at the next table is secondary. Conversation is apt to be about how the gnocchi or the broiled veal chop here compares with the same fare enjoyed in Milan last summer. What accounts for the excellence of this little restaurant is no doubt the strict attention to detail given in the kitchen as well as in the dining room by the proprietors, Antonio Bongioanni (from Turin) and Mario Balducci (from Genoa). One or the other is always present to see that standards are not relaxed. Pastas with accompanying garnishes and sauces are outstanding (try the gnocchi special with asparagus tips, prosciutto and cream). Nine months of the year, the owners are able to get Golden Oak mushrooms from West Virginia, which are delicately sautéed in oil, garlic and herbs. Veal, whether scaloppine or chops, is of top quality and carefully prepared. Fish (red snapper or swordfish) is fresh and nicely seasoned (the snapper is deboned at the table). Desserts include the usual fruit tarts, zabaglione and tartufo, and there's an exceptional hazelnut cake. Given these unpretentious but cozy surroundings (tiny bar, white stucco arches and bare bricks with a few hanging knicknacks) and prices (about $30 per person, with wine, somewhat less than midtown), you are all but assured a pleasant evening. But the word is already out about Divino, so you may have to wait even with reservations. Wait; you won't be sorry. If you're in a hurry, go next door to the Café Divino (under the same management), where the menu is shorter, the prices more modest and the service quicker.

8/20
Elaine's
**1703 Second Ave.
(88th St.)
534-8103**
*Lunch Mon. to Sat. noon to 4:00
P.M.; dinner Mon. to Sat. 5:30 P.M.
to 2:00 A.M.*
AE
Italian

The ardent look with which Woody Allen contemplates for an hour or two his plate of spaghetti or osso buco proves, if it still needs to be, that Elaine's is really one of the best restaurants in the world. By the way, we're going to tell you a secret: Elaine, who possesses, as everyone knows, a palate of extreme delicacy, recently trained with the great Girardet and returned from Switzerland with admirable recipes for overcooked clams, reheated calf's liver Venetian and tomato sauce with an exquisite burned taste. These are a few of the little marvels that regale one of the most difficult clienteles in New York each evening. Elaine, charming and voluptuous, welcomes them with an eternal radiant smile, in a decor full of chic in this delicious snug little house, which it always seems they have forgotten to clean for the last ten centuries. About $25 per person, with wine.

11/20
Elio's
**1621 Second Ave.
(84th–85th sts.)
772-2242**
*Dinner nightly 5:30 P.M. to
midnight*
AE
Italian

If you find comfort in numbers, this is the place. And if you're a regular, you'll probably even be seated in the *right* place. Elio's, owned by Elio Guaitolini (formerly of Parma restaurant), is an attractive restaurant, but its interior, framed by standard white plaster walls and wood floors, is much better appreciated when it's not crowded and you are forced to sit elbow to elbow with the next tables. If you can hear above the cocktail-party noise level, your waiter will tell you about the specials of the day. Or if he can hear you, you can order from the unimaginative menu, featuring such predictable items as vitello tonnato, seafood salad, risotto, spaghetti and so on. This is standard Italian restaurant fare, some of it less than standard in preparation. Dinner for two, with wine, is about $65.

14
Erminia
**250 E. 83rd St.
879-4284**
*Dinner nightly 5:00 P.M. to 11:00
P.M. (Sun. to 10:00 P.M.)*
No credit cards
Italian

If you are planning to have dinner at Trastevere and they give away your table because you are late, if you arrive with an extra person in your party or if you're just having one of those days, you may be shuttled down the street to mamma's place, Erminia. The Lattanzi family now has three restaurants within a block or so of each other, and customers happily dine at any one of them, feasting on recipes developed by momma. This latest addition to the group is absolutely charming, with rough wood paneling, lace curtains, hanging bistro lamps shaded with what looks like hand-crocheted fabric shades and the same unpretentious atmosphere that has made Trastevere so successful. The service is cheerful, as are the clients (primarily a neighborhood-looking group), who dine on Erminia's simple menu. Starters include baked tiny artichokes with garlic and olive oil, superb fresh mozzarella with plum tomatoes and generous servings of pasta (orecchiette alla Erminia with fresh broccoli is as wonderful as the vermicelli alla pizzaiola with veal and tomatoes). Entrees are equally uncomplicated and delicious, particularly the grilled chicken with its seasoned, crispy skin, the homemade sausages and the calamari with scampi. There is a limited wine list, with a very good Bollino Pinot Grigio, and the desserts are good but unmemorable. The prices are as honest as is this intimate little place; dinner for two, with wine, will run about $60.

12/20
Fortune Garden
1160 Third Ave. (68th St.) 744-1212
Lunch and dinner daily noon to 11:00 P.M. (Wed. to Sat. to midnight)
All major credit cards
Chinese

An agreeably comfortable restaurant with the ubiquitous lacquered screens and chandeliers, plus a statue of the old sage Lao-tse himself. Reliable hot and cold appetizers include various dumplings and won tons in a chili and sesame dressing. Crab-stuffed mushroom caps in a creamy sauce have an almost French flavor, and we like the finely minced vegetables and bean curd packaged in lettuce leaves. As for the rest of the menu, Chef Cheng appears to have taken on too many specialties, and some, such as the much-raved-about rainbow lobster, just don't work. This dish has the mandatory red carapace presiding over two lots of meat, one white and bland, one brown and spicy. Neither tastes in the least like lobster—could the shell be a prop, we ask ourselves? In any case, it's exorbitant at $26.25—so try the lobster in garlic sauce at half the price. The also much-touted velvet scallops with a coronet of broccoli tastes of absolutely nothing. Where Chef Cheng does score is with the spicier dishes, such as the delicious orange beef, seared to a miraculous crispness, in a rich, dark sauce flavored with dried orange peel that would do credit to a French duck. Shredded pork in garlic sauce, an often abused Szechwan specialty, is impeccable here; also recommended are Hunan lamb and tea-smoked chicken. Sweets are run-of-the-mill; the Chinese themselves prefer a platter of fresh fruit to round things off. The thoroughly attentive and intelligent staff do the Fortune Garden credit. Consistently underrated by many Chinese food fans, the cuisine here scores because Chef Cheng has not quite forgotten how things tasted back home. About $30 per person, with wine.

14 🍳
The Gibbon
24 E. 80th St.
861-4001
Lunch Mon. to Fri. noon to 2:30 P.M.; dinner Mon. to Sat. 6:00 P.M. to 10:30 P.M.
All major credit cards
French/Japanese

This lovely upstairs restaurant is a favorite lunch place for the Metropolitan staff and visitors from across Fifth Avenue. When you come to The Gibbon, insist on sitting upstairs; you'll be surrounded by pretty Oriental screens, daylight from the large windows and crisp white linens. Downstairs is a triste affair, somewhat of a cross between a teahouse and Polynesian bar decor. Lunch here can be a delight (we prefer it to dinner, since the atmosphere is even more serious at night) to sample some of the exquisitely presented works of art from the kitchen. The Japanese-European trend that has slowly (very slowly) swept across the nation has given us such treasures as La Petite Chaya in Los Angeles (where it is done right) and a growing number of Oriental chefs who blend traditions arbitrarily and with great inventiveness (even if some of their experiments fall a bit short). The Gibbon has this same mysterious consciousness, and you won't be disappointed by whitefish sashimi, presented as a field of snowdrops, traditional veal chops with a cress sauce, perfect little tofu blocks floating in sauce, symmetrical wilted cucumbers and crab (the seafood is far too salty), the sashimi platter that celebrates form and function, the tataki fillet that is basically steak tartare, classic baked chicken, superb sakura mushi rolls of salmon with soba noodles, rack of lamb and the simplicity of soft-shell crabs with ginger. It's all minimalist food of the East with the merchandising of the West. The Oriental names give mystery to the dishes, the American service tries hard to please, and the very Western prices (about $25 per person for lunch, without wine) keep the balance of trade operating.

12/20
Gino's
780 Lexington Ave.
(60th St.)
223-9658
Lunch and dinner daily noon to 10:30 P.M.
No credit cards
Italian

When you enter the small, somewhat shabby room that is Gino's you'll feel plunged into deepest, darkest Italy. The tacky decor is early Italian safari, but the clientele seems oblivious to the red lacquer trim and the zebra-covered walls, as if they'd been coming here for years. And, in fact, they have. The restaurant attracts fashionable, savvy regulars, especially at lunch. Sunday lunch is particularly pleasant. Regulars shake hands with the tuxedoed owner and are known by name. The elite may meet but they also come to eat. The vast, eclectic Italian menu is generally well executed. The linguine with frutti di mare is fresh and full of fragrant shellfish. Fettuccine alla romana is a perfectly acceptable Alfredo, veal piccata is tender, with just the right lemon accent, and the calf's liver alla veneziana melts in your mouth, with onions and a nice tang of vinegar. Neither desserts nor wines are a strong point, but the comfortable atmosphere makes up for it. About $55 to $60 for two, with wine.

7/20
La Goulue
28 E. 70th St.
988-8169
Lunch Mon. to Sat. noon to 3:00 P.M.; dinner Mon. to Sat. 6:30 P.M. to 11:30 P.M.
All major credit cards
French (classical)

This is without doubt one of the most authentic-looking French bistros in New York. The traditional white-aproned service, the simple menu and the pretty noontime crowd brighten up the handsome wood paneling in this charmingly decorated place. But they still can't get things right here, and would be better off serving plain chicken salad than an inedible calf's liver with shallots, an overcooked cold bass with green sauce, an insipid duck terrine and the determinedly risky kidneys, duck, salmon or saddle of lamb. Even the apple tart here is beyond hope. Come for a drink to watch the well-heeled crowd, but don't come to eat. Lunch with a glass of wine will run an outrageously excessive $25 per person.

10/20
Greener Pastures
117 E. 60th St.
832-3212
Lunch and dinner daily noon to 9:30 P.M. (Sun. to 8:30 P.M.)
No credit cards
American (vegetarian)

This looks like a typical health food store, with walls of vitamins, herbal teas and whole grains. But is it? Actually it is Greener Pastures, a natural food restaurant; if you continue through the retail store you'll find three dining rooms, two of them especially attractive, including an airy greenhouse room. The entire meatless, saltless, sugarless, kosher menu is available for takeout. It includes papaya cocktails and banana smoothies, 26 sandwiches on good dark bread, salads, vegetarian entrees, nicely prepared seafood and such desserts as deep-dish fruit delight and frozen yogurt.

Next question: What looks like meat, is shaped like meat, has the texture of meat, but isn't? It's a vegetable cutlet made from "protein." And when it's served in monstrous portions, smothered with tomato sauce and mozzarella cheese, smells and tastes for all the world like a deluxe pizza but isn't, it's the vegetable cutlet alla parmigiana. This is the home of the Vegetarian Whopper. At Greener Pastures, salt won't tempt you, and neither will meat, poultry or refined sugar. You can even take a rabbi to lunch. What could seriously endanger your health, however, are the gigantic portions and touches of inconsistent overkill, such as a ladle of whipped cream served on a slab of rich (albeit refined-sugar-less) cheesecake. One final question: If all this is so good for you, why do they think they must serve three times as much as other places to satisfy you? Very reasonable prices make dinner for two about $20.

15 🍳
L'Hostaria del Bongustaio
108 E. 60th St.
751-3530
Lunch Mon. to Thurs. noon to 3:00 P.M.; dinner Mon. to Sat. 5:30 P.M. to 10:30 P.M. (Fri. and Sat. to 11:00 P.M.)
AE, MC, V
Italian

In its smart new location, installed on two floors, with creamy white walls and flowered banquettes, this relatively recent Italian creation confirmed our previous good impressions with its debut. The welcome is warm, the service is very efficient, and the authenticity of the cuisine indicates that it is prepared with care and concern. The extensive menu merits a detailed exploration, but be sure to sample the rigatoni with five cheeses, pasta with porcini mushrooms, green gnocchi with cream sauce, zucchini and almonds (this dish alone makes the trip worthwhile), red shrimp grilled to perfection and doused with very fine cooking juices, and the breast of chicken with artichokes, tender and well perfumed with fresh herbs. Or try the marvelous penne with an exquisite tomato-basil sauce, tortellini with peas that is just as good, and superb salmon poached in a pungent herb and wine sauce. The zabaglione with raspberries is the answer to your prayers, and the Italian cheesecake is creamy and light at the same time. All this will convince you that the Hostaria deserves its good name. About $35 per person, with an honest house wine.

13 🍳
Hyo Tan Nippon
119 E. 59th St.
751-7690
Dinner Mon. to Sat. 5:30 P.M. to 10:00 P.M. (Fri. and Sat. to 10:15 P.M.)
All major credit cards
Japanese

Sometimes singles have a problem in New York (as elsewhere): Where is it comfortable to eat alone? Nobuyoshi Kuraoka, proprietor here and also at the more formal Nippon Restaurant, installed a huge, circular counter with comfortable chair-level seats, where everyone (particularly shoppers from nearby Bloomingdale's) can feel at ease and enjoy marvelous, freshly prepared Japanese staples—tempura (both vegetables and seafood), beef sukiyaki and chicken yakitori—as well as sushi and sashimi. In the evening there are seafood specials: shrimp (mercifully, it tastes fresh) and fish, both tempura and charbroiled, with mushrooms and crunchy, flavorful broccoli. For the care given these preparations, Mr. Kuraoka is certainly entitled to a toque (he didn't receive one for this establishment in our last report). With an excellent sake, a full-course meal will be about $20 per person.

13 🍳
Jack's
1022 Lexington Ave.
(73rd St.)

This upstairs restaurant is a newcomer on the chichi scene, recently discovered by Upper East Side residents and a few commuters from the West Side. The downstairs

628-5300
*Lunch daily noon to 3:00 P.M.;
dinner nightly 6:00 P.M. to 11:00
P.M. (Fri. and Sat. to midnight)
All major credit cards*
American

is charming, with a black-and-white tiled floor, an old bar and an elegant, clublike feeling. Up the tiny winding staircase you'll find a pleasant room, although the tables are too close together, making the evening uncomfortable for long-legged friends and intimate conversation. We also advise you to refrain from wearing black (New York's most fashionable color), because if you do you will fade directly into the black-moiré-covered walls. Simple engravings of racing dogs repeat the black and white theme, and friendly, amateurish service adds to the clubby, relaxed atmosphere. The menu changes daily; it's a bit ambitious for nouvelle preparations, but the kitchen is doing well so far. On a given evening you could sample California cuisine classics, such as warm goat's cheese salad or buffalo mozzarella salad; French-Japanese mussels; regional American Cajun sausage with summer squash; and Continental duck livers on arugula, calamari fritters, Blue Points and scallops with hollandaise, ravioli in garlic cream, and foie gras and morels in port wine aspic. For entrees, there are lots of American possibilities: Long Island duckling with Oregon blackberries, a veal chop with New Jersey tomatoes, Colorado steak with Sonoma Zinfandel sauce, a Maine lobster and scallop fricassée, Maryland soft-shell crabs with American caviar, braised chicken with Maryland oysters and buttermilk biscuits, and pork with truffles and figs. All of it is well prepared, the creativity refreshing, the American wine selection only adequate and the prices uptown: $40 per person, with wine. Desserts still have a way to go to achieve the same culinary levels.

12/20

Jacqueline's
**132 E. 61st St.
838-4559**
*Lunch Mon. to Sat. 11:00 A.M. to
2:30 P.M.; dinner Mon. to Sat. 6:00
P.M. to 11:45 P.M.
All major credit cards*
French (provincial)

In this plush, sophisticated neighborhood just steps from Bloomingdale's, a vivacious, petite French-Swiss from Lausanne has created an inviting, informal little bar and restaurant that is practically irresistible. At noon, ladies from the area who have the time but not the inclination to prepare their own lunches (and who could well afford to eat at La Côte Basque) fill the few tables and chat leisurely over their omelets, salads and pastas. In the evening, their husbands arrive to relax at the bar over well-selected Champagnes and sparkling wines by the glass. Jacqueline is a charming hostess as well as a good cook, and a number of ladies and gentlemen will be persuaded to stay on for a perfectly acceptable dinner: chicken breasts with a Dijon mustard sauce, exquisite Bay scallops or a near-perfect filet mignon with a peppery sauce. Don't pass up the ricotta cheesecake, even if cheesecake is not on your preferred dessert list. About $25 per person, without wine.

10/20
Kavkasian Restaurant
1638 Second Ave.
(85th St.)
861-0595
Lunch and dinner daily 11:00 A.M.
to midnight
No credit cards
Russian

We originally discovered this restaurant on a hot tip from a Russian taxi driver, a profession not generally renowned for its gourmet tastes. But the ethnic connection was reassuring, and it proved, in fact, to be a bright, pleasant place serving tasty Georgian food of the type you might expect to find in Tiflis, the capital of one of the more laid-back Soviet republics. On the bandstand, Grisha on the piano and Lenya on the balalaika perform their heart-searing and vodka-exacting repertoire of Russian folk songs. Grisha is not only Rasputin's namesake, he is also a dead ringer for the mad monk in his prime. One night, just to stir the ethnic mix a bit, a black diner in a skullcap joined the act with his clarinet (which happened to be handy). He gave a moving and mellifluous rendering of "Moscow Nights" and "Kalinka," with everyone joining in, after which the resident orchestra burst into "My Yiddish Momma." As the old immigrant saying goes, "Only in America!"

The Kavkasian started life as the Caucasian, until protest calls came in from black and human rights groups. To clear up the semantic confusion, it was respelled with a *K*. There is a vast range of Georgian specialties ranging from chakhomili, a chicken casserole rumored to have been Stalin's favorite dish, to a shashlik of ribs of lamb strung on a two-foot skewer, served with tkemali, a fiery chili and coriander sauce. Also noteworthy are the various nourishing soups and the grilled shashlik of sturgeon. The Kavkasian will not restore you to the glories of the czar's table; it better recalls Russian slumming in Paris in the twenties, when ethnic taxi drivers—Russian officers to a man—could be relied upon to take you to the right place at the right time. About $30 per person, with vodka.

12/20
Luscardi's
1494 Second Ave.
(77th St.)
249-2020
Lunch Mon. to Fri. noon to 3:00
P.M.; dinner nightly 6:00 P.M. to
midnight
AE
Italian

No doubt about it—this is a lovely restaurant. White walls, dark wood and a gracious staff set the tone of comfortable elegance. An already substantial menu of pastas, seafood, chicken and veal dishes is supplemented with daily specials that require repetition by already overworked waiters. They are professionals, however, and will repeat with feeling such specials as moules marinière, rigatoni with tomatoes and basil, vitello tonnato (a superb example of how this classic should be prepared), ravioli with spinach al pesto and bass with mussels and clams. Our only complaint is that in several instances mussels are carelessly cleaned and raw vegetables garnish cooked dishes. Desserts, including mocha meringue cake, tartufo and chocolate mousse cake, are fresh and appealing. What the food may sometimes lack in finesse is more than compensated for by the ambience and the staff. Dinner for two, with wine, will run about $70.

12/20
Madame Romaine de Lyon
32 E. 61st St.
758-2422
Lunch daily 11:00 A.M. to 3:00 P.M.
No credit cards
French

When Madame Romaine was a little girl, her mother ran the Hotel Terminus in Lyon. At the age of fifteen she was presented with her first omelet pan, and she has not stopped frying since. Her menu, a list of 600 omelets (plain, not so plain and positively Lucullan), all handwritten in faded blue ink, makes the right choice agonizingly difficult. Faced with such an embarras de richesses—chicken, sweetbreads, quenelles, kidneys, brains (there's even an awful-sounding concoction of foie gras, grapes and strawberries in Champagne sauce)—your best bet may well be the plainest. The omelet Savoyarde (sautéed potatoes, onions, garlic and cheese), for instance, is delicious, whereas the more elaborate ones seem more like a messy way to present an entree. The omelet tour de pin, a mound of truffles, chicken, artichokes, foie gras and walnuts in a sauce royale, is only lightly encased in egg and is hardly an omelet at all. The great specialty, omelet lyonnaise, with onions, black butter, vinegar and parsley, is described on the menu as "very unusual"—a phrase that often denotes something you probably won't like much. Possible accompaniments are a simple green salad or an oversweet hot croissant. Some brave souls even find room for the sweet omelets, with apples, chestnuts or walnuts in brandy sauce, but we prefer the lovely chocolate mousse and apricot tart. Waitresses are friendly, and the cozy provincial decor is reminiscent of maman's front parlor at the Hotel Terminus. About $15 to $20 per person, with wine.

11/20
Maxwell's Plum
1181 First Ave.
(64th St.)
628-2100
Lunch Mon. to Fri. noon to 4:30 P.M.; dinner nightly 5:00 P.M. to 12:45 A.M.; brunch Sat. noon to 4:30 P.M., Sun. 11:00 A.M. to 4:30 P.M.
All major credit cards
Continental

If you like baroque boudoirs, easy-listening music, tourists from Kentucky and Rouen, balloons on your birthday and dining inside an Italian wedding cake, you'll adore Maxwell's Plum. It remains one of the better examples of high camp in the Western world. The clientele by day enjoys light lunches as they watch the Upper East Side world walk by outside, and by night the bar is packed with secretaries making a stab at becoming upwardly mobile. The food is of little interest here, but you can get by with a paillard of beef, burgers, hot chicken salad, a somewhat soggy and garlicky Bay scallop sauté, an overgrilled swordfish, a reasonably grilled red snapper with an insipid dijonnaise sauce and a surprisingly good tarte tatin for lunch. Customers love to wine and dine themselves by night, if they can get through the throngs that make the bar here one of the most visual mating games in town. If you come with less than great expectations, we can assure you that you won't be disappointed. We caution you to take your time touring the place; the highly varnished floors make ice-skating in your winter boots a cinch by comparison. About $25 per person for lunch with wine, and much more for dinner (watch out—you'll be charged for the bread unless you read the fine print and reject it).

11/20
Meat Brokers
1153 York Ave.
(62nd St.)
752-0108
Dinner Mon. to Sat. 5:00 P.M. to midnight, Sun. 4:00 P.M. to 11:00 P.M.
All major credit cards
American (steaks)

If you are curious how Americans eat (and how so many become overweight) you simply must visit Meat Brokers, a steak house like many thousands of others across America (once inside you'll have trouble remembering what city you are in—the appearance of the informally dressed patrons won't help much either). Perhaps it was with this geographical identity crisis in mind that the management installed an overhead electronic ticker tape to announce impersonally what is available from the kitchen—no printed menu here. This means of communication suggests that you are not too far from Wall Street; but actually these people have simply capitalized on the brokerage theme uptown. If the dark wood bar, the brass trim, the ceiling spotlights and the good-looking, friendly waiters and waitresses don't give you a clue as to what city you are in, the food certainly won't be of any help: a salad bar with a standard assortment of condiments (artificial bacon bits, chopped hard-boiled eggs) and gooey dressings (cheese and otherwise), thick, tenderized steaks, bottled sauces from Heinz and Heublein, baked potatoes smothered in sour cream and cheesecake heavy enough to be compatible with what came before. Yet the steak is good (not always the same cut as quoted, however), the rack of lamb is perfect (all seven or eight chops served), meats are cooked the way you order them, and prices are 30 percent less than you'll find in midtown. So Meat Brokers is not altogether a bad risk, something like investing in G.M.: no expectations of fantastic rewards, but a good prospect of long-term growth, at least in the midriff. About $25 per person, without wine.

11/20
Meson Madrid
1394 York Ave.
(74th St.)
772-7007
Dinner Mon. to Sat. 5:00 P.M.

East Siders with copious appetites find this an attractive alternative to the busy and often frantic Italian restaurants that dominate the neighborhood. There is a spacious, unhurried air (dishes are cooked to order), and the white stucco, bare bricks, iron grillwork and soft

to 11:00 P.M. (Fri. and Sat.
to midnight), Sun. 3:00 P.M. to
10:00 P.M.
All major credit cards

Spanish

music from the piano by the bar evoke memories of another continent and another era. The menu is predictable: parrillada de marisco, zarzuela de marisco and an acceptable paella with well-prepared seafood, chicken and chorizo (a bit bland). Sometimes angulas (baby eels flown in from Spain), sizzling in hot olive oil, are available as an appetizer; other times lechona asada (roast suckling pig) is on the menu. The effort that goes into making these specials available reflects the management's wish to do something different—and better—than the other Spanish restaurants around town. But we wish they would not compromise quite so much in seasoning the dishes, which we recall to be spicier (and more interesting) on the other side of the Atlantic. About $25 per person, with a good Rioja Cabernet.

10/20

Il Monello
1460 Second Ave.
(76th–77th sts.)
535-9310

Lunch Mon. to Sat. noon to 3:00
P.M.; dinner Mon. to Sat. 5:00 P.M.
to midnight
All major credit cards

Italian

The decor is so nondescript it is nearly invisible: a benign backdrop for a well-fed clientele as interested in impressing their new girlfriends and boyfriends as they are in reminiscing about their most recent trip to Burgundy. In any case, they seem to be completely oblivious to the cuisine, which is prepared and presented by a rather surly troop of maîtres d' who could use a little basic training at a friendliness camp. As a matter of fact, the chef could possibly use more training: it might bring the life and joy we love so much in Italian cuisine to Il Monello. The menu is filled with interesting possibilities, most of which do not live up to their traditional reputations. It makes us sad when tortellini ai quattro formaggi arrives with its four cheeses stringy and undercooked. It makes us happier when the bresaola turns out to be an acceptable rendition of air-dried beef—Italian beef jerky. The succulent-sounding (albeit breaded) rack of veal is a disappointment: the butterflied, overcooked veal looks not unlike a flattened catcher's mitt. Broiled scampi with a sweetish anchovy-caper sauce is also a letdown; the lightly breaded shellfish is tender but lacks the fresh taste that usually makes this dish so refreshing. But there are so many other choices: more than 22 pastas, an appetizing grilled red snapper, sautéed sweetbreads with wine and mushrooms, brains and a host of chicken, veal and beef dishes. Zabaglione is whipped up tableside by one of the less than cheerful staff members. The wine list is excellent, with many reasonably priced Italian wines and a choice of rare vintages at rare prices. The dinner, however, will not be as reasonably priced as you would imagine for such mediocre food. When spending $100 for two, you have a right to expect something better.

12/20
Christopher Myles
208 E. 73rd St.
737-7677
Dinner Tues. to Sat. 7:00 P.M. to 11:00 P.M.
No credit cards
Continental

If you're particularly sensitive to tacky objets d'art and violent bright green, be forewarned that Christopher Myles has an abundance of both. This odd little place looks as though it might be a gift shop run by a couple of small-town matrons. But don't be put off by the decor—you'll find a good deal more taste on your plate than in your surroundings. The waitresses, dressed in black and white maids' uniforms, recite the night's several offerings to the handful of tables. The dishes are honest and light; red meat is rarely offered, with fresh seafood and fowl taking center stage. With luck, you'll be offered as starters a near-perfect spinach salad, fresh oysters Rockefeller or good, classic escargots in a shallot and white wine sauce. Entrees might include a delicious baked trout, stuffed with plump scallops and served with a light cream sauce; a Cornish game hen stuffed with cream cheese, scallions and radishes; perfectly seasoned shrimp with butter and garlic that, unfortunately, can be overcooked; or duck in a plum sauce. Accompaniments range from slightly old snow peas to excellent thinly sliced potatoes. Skip the bland cocoa mousse pie, but don't pass up the fantastic chocolate mocha cheesecake. There is a sure and steady hand in this kitchen, and while the dishes may lack a certain joie de vivre, they are well prepared and flavorful. Bring your own wine and expect to spend about $75 for two.

10/20
Ottomanelli's Steak and Wild Game Restaurant
439 E. 82nd St.
744-9600
Dinner Mon. to Sat. 5:00 P.M. to 11:00 P.M.
All major credit cards
American (steaks)

Even the affluent on Manhattan's Upper East Side are having trouble these days finding domestics who can cook a decent meal or will even stay late enough to prepare it. When Ottomanelli (a 1900s butcher shop in the Village) opened a satellite at 82nd Street and York Avenue, it ran head-on into this problem. Alas, so many of its potential customers, tired after a tension-filled day at the office, had no one at home to grill the steak or clean up afterward. But the butcher boys were not to be daunted, and one of the clan (probably with an M.B.A. behind his apron) came up with the solution: organize vertically. He opened a cooking school next door to teach basic cooking and then an adjacent steak house to snare those either too busy or unable to learn to cook. Upstairs at the tiny 37-seat steak house, these hungry souls can now relax without dressing for dinner, have a few drinks at the bar under a cylindrical skylight and enjoy an Ottomanelli steak here or downstairs in even more cramped quarters, where you could easily succumb to claustrophobia. The meats are superb (supplied as needed from the retail shop), the wild (?) game, such as venison, pheasant or quail, is less satisfactory (though prepared by a Swiss chef practiced in the art of snaring hare), and the chef's exotic creations are to be avoided. You could make a grievous mistake if you pass up the excellent steak, veal, lamb chops or filet mignon. About $35 per person, with wine.

15 Pamir
**1423 Second Ave.
(74th St.)
734-3791**
*Dinner nightly 5:30 P.M. to
11:00 P.M.*
MC, V
Afghanistani

The only good fortune resulting from the Soviet invasion of Afghanistan is that the Bayat brothers (now six) fled their homeland and opened a wonderful little restaurant in New York. Without previous experience in the business, they recreated an enchanting setting bounded by exquisite Pakistani rugs and such subtle yet exhilarating flavors and aromas from the kitchen that in our last report we awarded them a toque. Today, the service is just as friendly, and the kitchen is even better. A growing number of adventurous New Yorkers seems to agree with us, because the place is now packed.

Appetizers consist of delicate turnovers, dumplings and fried pastries, each with a different combination of meats, vegetables and spices. We recommend an assortment to experience the full range of taste sensations, plus the two dips, one of mint, peppers and coriander, the other a tart yogurt. Skewered marinated lamb is grilled perfectly, and the result is marvelously juicy and tender meat. A combination grilled lamb preparations is offered, with brown rice and vegetables (the pumpkin is particularly good). As wonderful as these grilled lamb preparations are, there is a sautéed lamb with brown rice that you must not miss. Called norange palaw, it consists of seasoned (but not marinated) cubes of lamb sautéed with onions and served on a mound of brown rice, topped with slivers of orange rind, almonds and pistachios, and bathed in rose water and cardamom. It is absolutely delicious. If you crave dessert, try the straightforward Afghan pudding or the paper-thin gosh-e-feel (elephant's ear) pastry dusted with powdered sugar, a not-so-distant cousin of the Italian sfogliatelle. Then sip a cup of nicely scented herbed tea. If the single toque that the brothers shared caused any rift among them, we trust it will not be exacerbated if we award them two. About $20 per person.

15 Parioli Romanissimo
**24 E. 81st St.
288-2391**
Dinner nightly 6:00 P.M. to

Happily ensconced in its new location, Parioli Romanissimo is doing the same brisk business it did on First Avenue. Our advice is to let your maître d' guide you in selecting your dinner; chances are he will do a better job than you will, especially if he suggests the three varieties of marinated eggplant served with slivered

11:30 P.M.
AE, DC
Italian

peppers, a marvelously refreshing dish. Then let him prepare you a superb pasta with porcini (French!) and wild mushrooms that is refined in its subtlety. Next, sample the mâche salad with fresh mint and tamarillos; it's a wonderful contrast of tastes, even though the greens are overdressed. You are now ready for a superb rack of lamb with rosemary, cooked to perfection, although the serving could easily feed a family of four. Since the desserts are banal, let yourself be persuaded to delight in the aged Parmesan, Gorgonzola and other Italian cheeses served with sliced pears and pomegranates. After a bottle of Pinot Grigio and then a Chianti Classico Reserve (both perfectly priced at under $25), you will leave smiling and happy, having filled yourself with marvelous food and lightened your wallet of a staggering $150 for two.

14 ♕
Pari Passu
147 E. 60th St.
832-8972
Lunch and dinner Mon. to Sat. noon to 10:00 P.M. (Fri. and Sat. to 10:30 P.M.)
AE, MC, V
French
(classical/nouvelle)

Pari Passu (formerly La Cocotte) is under the new management of Raoul Garino, a restaurateur, and Theodore Kheel, a prominent New York attorney with lots of friends in the city's power elite. Mr. Garino ensures totally professional service and a much improved kitchen offering contemporary and appealing, if not revolutionary, dishes, while Mr. Kheel ensures that the place is filled with his acquaintances and their acquaintances day and night. The pair have given the premises a facelift, providing more space in the front by the bar (and less noise) and in the attractive refurbished closed-in garden in the back. The menu, too, is almost totally revised: appetizers of foie gras in a watercress salad, a fish terrine, quennelles and a paupiette of sole with a crayfish farcie, bathed in a Champagne sauce; and meat and fish entrees that reflect Chef Pierre Koehler's prior experience under the tutelage of Jean-Jacques Rachou. Nothing extraordinary in concept, but everything is well prepared and presented. The sauces in particular are light, intense and sometimes memorable. On the whole, what comes from the kitchen, together with the ambience and service, makes for a pleasant experience. When you pay your check (at least $40 per person, without wine), you can leave secure in the knowledge that everyone engaged in this enterprise will share your munificence equally, which is the meaning of *pari passu* in Mr. Kheel's legal dictionary.

10/20
Parma
1404 Third Ave.
(79th St.)

Upwardly mobile advertising agency vice-presidents, business types and a few doctors and lawyers continue to favor Parma—one of the first of the new-breed, bistrolike

535-3520
Dinner nightly 5:00 P.M. to midnight
AE
Italian

Italian restaurants—with boundless enthusiasm, but alas, the kitchen is unable to respond in kind. The standard fettuccine Alfredo is gluey in too much cheese, the chicken francese is mushy and some days past its prime, and the crust on the raspberry tart shows signs of imminent petrification (though the fruit is fresh and tasty). With this state of affairs we are perplexed to explain how the kitchen (which also serves Uzies next door) produces an entirely acceptable spaghetti all'amatriciana and a luscious veal chop. We can report, however, that the converted gas lamps and the posters of the Lagos di Garda, Como and Maggiore are no more thrilling than most of the dishes. But, then, this has become a neighborhood institution where the people at the bar and at the next table are much more important than the cuisine. About $30 per person, with house wine.

13
Le Périgord Park
575 Park Ave.
(63rd St.)
752-0050
Lunch Mon. to Fri. noon to 2:00 P.M.; dinner Mon. to Sat. 6:00 P.M. to 10:30 P.M.
All major credit cards
French
(nouvelle/classical)

This mastodon is looking very, very tired—and it has a clientele to match. The trompe l'oeil decor is sad and out of date, and the service appears to have been resurrected from some school of imitation grand service. It's not that things are bad here; they are just dreary. And when you pay $140 for dinner for two, you have every right to expect the best. On that note, we cannot protest too much about the exorbitantly priced wine list (only a very few are under $30), the table d'hôte menu, most of whose dishes have supplemental prices, and the audacity of the maître d', who may outright ask for a larger tip after you have paid the service on the basis of merit. If you were us, you'd hesitate a long time before visiting this place to sample any of the nouvelle-slanted cuisine, even though the medallions of lamb with tarragon are excellent, the wild duck is superb, the ballotine of sweetbreads with ham and duck is tasty, and the creamed morels are sinfully rich and good. Less interesting is the fish tartare, the vapid vegetable pâté with tomato coulis, a gamy and overcooked venison and an overcooked pheasant stuffed with foie gras, which is no revelation in the culinary arts. But there are plenty of other choices that give us hope, and the pastries are quite nice, particularly the apricot tart, the light cassis cake, the strawberry tart and the dense chocolate cake. There is clearly talent in the kitchen, but the overall ambience and unprofessional staff make Périgord Park a touch disappointing.

15
La Petite Ferme

If you are looking for a faultless provençale meal served in a charmingly unpretentious atmosphere somewhat

**973 Lexington Ave.
(70th St.)
249-3272**

*Dinner Mon. to Sat. 6:00 P.M. to
10:30 P.M. (Fri. and Sat. to
11:00 P.M.)*
AE

French (provincial)

reminiscent of a country farmhouse (white stucco walls, rough-hewn beams, blond wood tables, random antiques, a pretty summer garden), La Petite Ferme is your haven. The menu changes twice daily, depending on market availability and Chef David Kinch's fancy (having trained with the Troisgros and Bocuse, his simple fancies are small miracles). You may be offered, among the three or so starters, a cream of watercress soup or a platter of various hors d'oeuvres (presented sushi style on a wooden tray), of which the marinated red cabbage, mushrooms and pearl onions provençale, marinated leeks and fresh mussels are delectable. Entrees are equally limited: a tomato omelet, cold poached salmon, a superb fricassée of chicken perfumed with vinegar and equally wonderful scallops provençale. But try to save space for dessert; if you have the chance to taste his chocolate-walnut rum cake, you will surely think you have ascended to heaven along with the pair of turtle doves cooing in their cage in the back. You will adore the cuisine so much that no doubt you'll rush right back for dinner to try superb mussels vinaigrette, an excellent volaille à l'estragon, a wonderful poached salmon and a sinful fruit tart, all delightfully accompanied by a reasonably priced Meursault. Things were a bit rocky here when we published our first New York guide, but owner Charles Chevillot now has things firmly in hand, and you couldn't hope for a more pleasant experience. About $30 per person for lunch and $40 for dinner with wine.

10/20

Les Pleiades

**20 E. 76th St.
535-7230**

*Lunch Mon. to Sat. noon to 3:00
P.M.; dinner Mon. to Sat. 5:00 P.M.
to 11:00 P.M.*
All major credit cards

French (provincial)

Madison Avenue art dealers and their customers make this their luncheon headquarters, which is strange because the paintings depicting French country scenes, the red-plastic-covered banquettes and the traditional French provincial dishes do not reflect any particular artistic quality. In the evening, the place is taken over by Fifth Avenue dowagers and their families, which is not so strange, because it is only a few steps from their apartments.

The predictable New York French menu (artichoke or leeks vinaigrette, chef's pâté, frog's legs and fruit tarts) would not *have* to be this boring (and disappointing), if only quality ingredients were used and care exercised in preparation. In this plush neighborhood (and at $40 per person with a modest Medoc), one would expect this to be the case. The crafts people in the kitchen here would probably improve their skills if the lunch crowd would give some critical attention to what is on their plates. Sending a dish back once in a while might do wonders.

15 ♟

The Polo Bar and Restaurant

(Hotel Westbury)
Madison Avenue and
69th Street
535-2000
Lunch daily noon to 2:30 P.M.;
dinner nightly 6:30 P.M. to
10:00 P.M.
All major credit cards
French (provincial)

The metamorphosis of this very chic English-club-style dining room with dark wood walls, orange-tone paisleys and horse engravings makes the old Polo doubly unrecognizable. Having decided to forget the banal meals that used to be served here, Henri Manassero hired a brilliant pair of French chefs: Patrice Boely worked quite a long time with Roger Vergé at Moulin de Mougins, and his second, Daniel Boulud, trained with Guérard and Vergé. The press saluted The Polo as soon as it opened as a disciple of nouvelle cuisine, but this does not stand up, because Boely, to the contrary, presents a classical menu, one that is even a bit too timid for our tastes. It is true, however, that he is in the process of evolving and gives his dishes a slight provençale accent, close to the "sun cuisine" of Vergé. Something tells us that this straightforward cuisine, as appetizing and joyous as the countryside whence it comes, should find a great success in the States. The moment has come—and people are ready—to appreciate the flavors of vegetables, fresh herbs, spices and condiments that give spirit to even the lowliest dish. Certainly Madison Avenue isn't Mougins, and the cuisine de marché presents several problems—but most of the products can be found locally, and Patrice Boely shows you the proof in the delicious provençale hors d'oeuvres, such as a rabbit gâteau en gelée almost as flavorful as Vergé's; in a red snapper of perfect finesse, grilled in saffron oil, a good turbot with baby vegetables, a delicious rack of lamb with green peppercorns served in its tarragon-perfumed juices and a tender and juicy côte de veau sautéed with mushrooms and tomatoes; and in a delicious gratin of raspberries with almonds. On the other hand, smoked salmon is mediocre, the feuilleté escargots with Pernod is nothing special, and the sole pâté is served with a neutral-tasting cocktail sauce. But these are merely details, and the most important task now is to make the menu as exciting as the daily specials. Service is first-rate, the chic Madison Avenue clientele has style, and the whole experience leaves you with the feeling of success. About $50 to $60 per person, with a Château Smith Haut Lafite '80 or a nice Brouilly Château de la Chaize; if you want to drink American, the Far Niente Chardonnay is a true delight.

13 ♟

Primavera

1570 First Ave.
(81st St.)
861-8608

So much charm and so many beautiful people are always crowded into this lovely little Italian restaurant with somber brick walls, tulip-shaped lamps and pretty paintings. There is also a lot of noise, but the simple

Dinner nightly 5:30 P.M. to
midnight
AE, DC, V
Italian

cuisine is fresh and has taste. Escape the boring hors d'oeuvres and order instead linguine al pesto, tortellini with ham and peas, a perfectly tender chicken in a delicate sauce and, above all, a roast kid with crackling skin. The cheesecake is forgettable, but the zuppa inglese is very well made. About $35 per person, with wine.

12/20
Quo Vadis
26 E. 63rd St.
838-0590
Lunch Mon. to Sat. noon to 3:00
P.M.; dinner Mon. to Sat. 6:00 P.M.
to 11:00 P.M.
All major credit cards
French
(classical/nouvelle)

If you are 80 years old, live on Fifth Avenue at 64th Street, have a collection of Chanel suits (the originals) and have a husband who has been wearing Brooks Brothers for decades, then you undoubtedly lunch at Quo Vadis on Wednesdays. This rose-tinted restaurant is nearly a Disney replica of a past age when ladies had gentleman callers, when granddaughters certainly went to Chapin and when Europe was a sailing destination every September. Quo Vadis is still flourishing, with its rococo ceilings, rococo ladies and baroque service. There's a certain consolation in knowing that some things never change, and it appears that Quo Vadis is happy to be trapped in its time warp. It's a pleasantly decorative place with crystal chandeliers, bordello-burgundy velvet banquettes, putti flying around on the ceiling and sober, nearly too-attentive tuxedoed service.

The cuisine, mercifully, is not trapped in the same historical era, and Chef Michel Bourdeaux, formerly of Maxwell's Plum, is doing his best to give these elegant dowagers and their consorts something updated, light and relatively interesting. You can lunch peacefully on barely cooked warm scallops on a bed of spinach with the tasty touch of marinated strips of ginger (sort of Quo Vadis French-Japanese sushi), a salade composé of duck, blueberries, mangos, sliced hearts of palm and green beans (sort of a Quo Vadis California health salad), a marvelous classic rognons de veau with a lovely Meaux mustard sauce and an equally delicious fillet of sole with beurre rouge (although the fish is dominated by the sauce). There are also traditional favorites, such as calf's liver with shallots, scallop of veal with morels, tortellini with cream sauce, crab soufflé and the ladies' favorites: egg dishes and light salads. Of course, this simple food leaves enough space for the exquisite desserts by Dieter Schorner, who makes a crème brûlée that approaches something this side of divinity. His pastries, crème anglaise, chocolate mousse and chocolate cake are lovely, although the sugary mocha meringue may prompt the clientele to stand up and march home with the energy of a troop of scouts. Dinners, when the jewels come out, are equally decorative. Lunch for two, without wine, will run about $60.

11/20
Red Tulip
439 E. 75th St.
734-4893
Dinner Wed. to Sun. 6:00 P.M. to
midnight (Sun. from 5:00 P.M.)
AE
Hungarian

The Red Tulip looks like the sort of place where
American schoolchildren studying Germanic cultures
would go on a field trip. It is both a beer hall with
community-style tables and a Disney-esque version of
"It's a Small World Goes to Hungary." Still, there are
lanterns on the tables, hand painted crockery hanging on
white brick walls and a string band of gypsies playing
rhapsodies (if more Frank Sinatra than Hungarian at
times). The menu is strictly Hungarian and will surely
satisfy any need to have food that will stay with you all
week. Menu items include gulyas (goulash), Hungarian
sausage, roast duckling with braised cabbage, chicken
and veal paprikas and stuffed cabbage just like the
owner's grandmother used to make. Crêpes filled with
apricots, poppy seeds, cheese or walnuts will top off a
robust meal. Although better Hungarian food could be
found, the Red Tulip is a favorite for its atmosphere and
charm. A very respectable selection of Hungarian wines is
available. Dinner for two, with wine, will be about $50.

12/20
Le Refuge
166 E. 82nd St.
861-4505
Lunch daily noon to 3:00 P.M.;
dinner nightly 6:00 P.M. to
10:30 P.M.
No credit cards
French (provincial/
nouvelle)

Dozens of new Italian and Oriental restaurants flourish
on Manhattan's Upper East Side. But where are the
French? Only Claude's, Chez Pascal and Le Refuge have
withstood the assault. Le Refuge holds itself out as a kind
of neighborhood bistro, and, in fact, most of the smartly
dressed crowd has to walk only a block or two to get
there. But don't let the plain exterior or the interior brick
walls, checkered napkins and bare tabletops fool you: this
is a pricey place with a cuisine that attempts a certain
sophistication but does not always come off. So we find
as appetizers nicely garlicked snails with raisins or
sautéed chicken livers with blueberries. When the chef,
whose non de plume is Pierre Saint Denis, controls his
impatience to be different, he is much more successful:
mussels in a pastry shell are in a worthy wine reduction, a
vegetable terrine is acceptable, roast veal is excellent, and
chicken and duck dishes cannot really be faulted. The
bouillabaisse (a bit skimpy) is accompanied by a zesty and
authentic rouille. Plan to spend $35 per person, without
wine, and you'll have saved cab fare to a midtown
restaurant if you live in the neighborhood.

12/20
Le Relais
712 Madison Ave.
(63rd St.)
751-5108
Lunch Mon. to Sat. noon to 3:00
P.M.; dinner nightly 6:30 P.M. to
10:30 P.M. (Sat. and Sun. from
7:00 P.M.)

There are at least some French who are happy about the
exchange rate. These are the refugees of after–May 10th,
Mitterand and his austere joys of socialism. You will find
them on the sidewalk café or around the small bar of Le
Relais, which they have made into their neighborhood
headquarters. These playboys with their flashing white
teeth and gold chains (more probably gold plated) on

AE, MC, V
French (classical)

their well-tanned chests dream about all they could buy in France with their dollars, and for a moment, as they are offered their chairs for lunch, they have the sensation of being rich. The crowd of models, photographers, designers, Madison Avenue shop owners, idle rich and pretty young women who work when they feel like it is clearly the attraction of this lovely restaurant decorated with mirrors and old engravings. It's the same group you'll find in Saint Tropez. But even though the cuisine is only a pretext to meet and to be seen, it's not as bad as some people say it is. The products are of good quality, and with chicken salad, endives with Roquefort, grilled entrecôte with beárnaise, cold leg of lamb, chocolate mousse or crème caramel you can have an engaging meal for about $35 per person, with wine, served by mostly French waiters who have the air of having just arrived at the restaurant the moment you did.

12/20
The Restaurant
(Carlyle Hotel)
35 E. 76th St.
744-1600
Lunch daily noon to 2:30 P.M.;
dinner nightly 6:00 P.M. to
11:00 P.M.
All major credit cards
Continental

If it is your chef's day off, if your maître d' left you to go work for Lady Di or if you've simply had enough lunches at home facing a pair of Cézanne apples, ask your chauffeur to get out the Rolls and drive you to the Carlyle. This is the only shelter worthy of welcoming a person such as yourself. In three little dining rooms ornamented with hunt engravings, precious china and dreamlike bouquets of flowers, you will feel right at home with a staff that is somewhat more eager when they know you and can serve you such distinguished dishes as a vegetable tourte, a ballotine of salmon and sole, oeufs périgordine or chicken curry, to which you must add a little salt and pepper for a satisfying taste. In the event that you are tired of drinking Château Latour '53 at $300, the house, which cares very much about its wine list (as well as its desserts), has previewed for you some excellent Bordeaux: a Margaux Prieure Lichine '76 at $28 or an excellent Château Bouscaut of the same year at $21. Not having spent more than $40 or $50 per person, you need only cross the street to Sotheby's to complete your afternoon.

10/20
Sahib
222 E. 86th St.
535-6760
Lunch and dinner daily noon to
11:00 P.M. (Sun. to 10:30 P.M.)
AE, MC, V
Indian

This is uptown Indian. The decor is slick, sophisticated and attractive, but the tables are close together, and the result is a noisy, rather congested restaurant. Add to this several waiters (walking, not running) with sizzling trays of sometimes smoking food, and the result is chaos. Could it be an attempt to capture the true ambience of Bombay?
    Would that the true spirit of India evidenced itself in

the cuisine. It is disappointing that a restaurant presenting a cuisine so fragrant with the subtle use of herbs and the exciting employment of spices could present so many dishes that are not only mediocre but are bland and boring. The menu is more than complete, but the appetizers and entrees are overly oily and sometimes hopelessly oversalted. Desserts, however, include better-than-average preparations of such specialties as kulfa, a sweetened cream flavored with cardamom and pistachio, and kheer, a rice pudding with honey and raisins. On the whole, the food simply does not do justice to this interesting cuisine. Dinner for two, with wine, will run about $50.

8/20
Sign of the Dove
**1110 Third Ave.
(65th St.)
861-8080**
Lunch Tues. to Sun. noon to 3:00 P.M.; dinner nightly 6:00 P.M. to midnight
All major credit cards
Continental

If you find yourself floating on a deserted island in a wash of peach color, surrounded by hanging plants, crowded by a too-close-for-comfort staff and serenaded by an enthusiastic pianist, you can be sure you have arrived at the Sign of the Dove for lunch. Sitting at your peaceful but lonely vigil, reflected in the strategically placed mirrors that make it look like there are more of you than there really are, you may come to the conclusion that the rest of New York City knows something you don't. It's true that this elegant restaurant, with its lace curtains and officious service, has received some of New York's least encouraging reviews; a simple lunch of overcooked lamb chops in a surprisingly good fennel sauce, or a tepid lobster salad with too-tough meat, or a curious chicken salad with a macadamia nut garnish and strong soy sauce will make you agree that the Sign of the Dove is no culinary refuge. It is indeed unfortunate that such a pretty place is the victim of such mediocre cuisine. But then you have so much to choose from—smoked goose, steamed red snapper, carpaccio, poached salmon, game hen scented with garlic and bay—that perhaps you'll hit the culinary jackpot and find yourself with a passable meal before you. About $35 per person, with wine, which is about $20 too much for us.

13
Szechwan East
**1540 Second Ave.
(80th St.)
535-4921**
Lunch and dinner daily noon to 11:30 P.M. (Fri. and Sat. to 12:30 A.M.)
AE, DC
Chinese

This is still one of the most reliable and popular Chinese restaurants in New York, with a cuisine that has not been corrupted by overpandering to American palates. The food is determinedly Szechwanese, and the menu is dotted generously with red stars that signify hot and spicy specialties. Among the appetizers we like the diced chili chicken with peanuts and the sliced kidneys in soy and sesame dressing. Dumplings with a fiery yet subtle dip are a delight, to be enjoyed harmoniously with a bowl of hot and sour soup. The hot or cold combination platters or mixed hors d'oeuvres provide a sensible way to start your meal. Sautéed shrimp with hot pepper sauce (two red stars!) are a triumph of freshness and flavor, as is the carp in hot bean sauce. Ta chien chicken and chicken "showered with ginger sauce" are both to be recommended, and you'll hear Peking duck being noisily enjoyed at neighboring tables. Both double sautéed and moo shu pork are authentic versions of these much vulgarized favorites. There is a list of daily specials, a welcome touch in Chinese restaurants, where menus tend to petrify with age and inertia. Also try the ongoing chef's specialties, which include memorable versions of scallops in garlic sauce and orange beef. This reassuring consistency of cuisine has impressed us over many visits.

A good-natured clientele comprising entire families and young couples make Szechwan East a friendly, sociable place. Appropriately, the staff is both affable and approachable, no mean achievement in a Chinese restaurant. A large, efficient and workmanlike bar takes the pain out of waiting for a table. Expect to spend $25 per person, with wine.

12/20
Table d'Hôte
44 E. 92nd St.
348-8125
Dinner Tues. to Sat. 6:30 P.M. to 9:30 P.M.
No credit cards
American/Continental

When the weather is pleasant, the door is left open and a frayed cloth band laden with little bells bars the entrance. Once you unhook this contraption and admit yourself to the tiny premises (the cramped tables seat only 24), you are expected to refasten the curious barrier. We still don't know whether it's intended to discourage people from coming in or to discourage people from leaving before they have paid their bill. Whatever the case, the device is some indication of the amateurism that characterizes this quaint establishment, which is run by three diverse personalities (one hailing from New Delhi), and caters to the neighboring affluent. What they find here is a plain decor (a few antiquities hanging from white walls, oil lamps on the tables) and almost no service (you pour your own water).

In view of the rather bizarre setting, the food is surprisingly well prepared. A ceviche of tiny Bay scallops with bits of red pepper is refreshing and enchanting, the crostini (chicken liver on fried bread) with a hint of fresh rosemary is more exciting than in most Italian restaurants, and the salad (with a not-so-exciting dressing) is as fresh as can be. Salmon with a decent-enough white wine reduction is excellent, liver with green olives and mushrooms not quite so good (but acceptable enough) and the veal chop disappointing, though the sorrel sauce stands up well. Desserts (a lemon tart and a kind of chocolate roll) are not up to the level of what comes before. Guests here don't seem to mind putting up with what amounts to an off-off-Broadway performance, and they are willing to pay first-row Broadway prices. Who knows, if the place lost its amateurism, it might lose its customers as well. About $40 per person, with the remarkable '78 St. Michelle Cabernet from Washington State.

13
Tour de France
1428 York Ave. (76th St.)
744-7844
Dinner nightly 5:00 P.M. to 11:30 P.M.
All major credit cards
French (provincial)

The curtains are drawn wide open so you look right into this engaging little neighborhood place, with its starched white linens and pretty fresh flowers on each table. Above is a bicycle sign advertising the Tour de France, which is something like the World Series and the Super Bowl rolled into one. All of this, including a straightforward French menu, suggests you will be greeted inside by a Gallic cycling champion (René Dreyfus, one such French hero, presided over a midtown bistro for many years), or at least by someone with a French accent. This is not the case. The maître d' does not understand French and has some difficulty with English; he and the chef, Veera Promon, are from Thailand. One waiter, from Argentina, speaks Italian and Spanish but no French. Yet what comes from the kitchen are the same dishes (and often as good) you would expect on the Left Bank or at Mère So-and-so in Lyon: escargots en croûte (excellent), saucisson chaud (nicely perfumed with garlic), demi poulet (plump and hot from the oven) and a sorbet of cassis (clean and refreshing). We don't know about the rabbit stew or the gigot, but we will certainly sample these on our next visit. It is still a mystery how a Thai chef can learn to cook traditional French dishes in Thailand, cross the Pacific and prepare them with such honesty here, while so many French chefs cross the Atlantic and immediately forget everything they learned at their mothers' knees. For this phenomenon we have no explanation, but Tour de France is certainly the place to investigate it. About $30 per person, with a splendid René Junot "21" Brands house wine.

14
Trastevere
309 E. 83rd St.
734-6343
Dinner Mon. to Sat. 5:00 P.M. to 10:30 P.M. (Fri. and Sat. to 11:00 P.M.)
AE

Gloria Vanderbilt, Robert Redford and Elizabeth Taylor are among the few who warrant having their publicity photos on the brick walls of this tiny, welcoming establishment. We can't vouch for their palates, but we can certainly add our praise to the Lattanzi family, who runs this excellent, unpretentious place. They continue to

Italian

dish out excellent food: the classic and delicious spiedino alla romana (cheese with prosciutto that is breaded, fried and covered with an anchovy sauce), an excellent muscoli in brodetto (mussels with tomatoes and wine) and some of the best capellini primavera we've had outside of Italy. It is hard to resist the entrees, even with such generous home-cooked portions for starters: the calamari with plenty of garlic and tomatoes is a delight, as is the chicken with peppers, traditional veal piccata and garlicky scampi. If you are fortunate enough to live in the neighborhood, you will be sure to become an habituée here; if not, it is worth the commute to sample honest food prepared with lots of care. We just wish the Italian wine list, though reasonably priced, was more complete. Dinner for two, with wine, will run about $80.

9/20
Tre Amici Ristorante
**1294 Third Ave.
(74th St.)
535-3416**
Dinner Mon. to Sat. 5:00 P.M. to midnight (Sat. to 12:45 A.M.)
All major credit cards
Italian

Patrons (mostly old-timers from the neighborhood) don't seem to notice that the oil paintings hanging in ornate frames in the dimly lit premises have lost some of their luster over the years; the same can be said about what comes from the kitchen. A flavorful but mild marinara sauce does not dispel our suspicion that several of the bivalves in our cozze posillipo expired several moons before their internment in the bowl before us. The sautéed veal lacks both texture and taste, the sea bass with mussels and clams consists largely of the black, fatty tissue, and the clams and mussels are overcooked. Redeeming features are a good linguine, acceptable enough French pastries and unusually intense and fragrant espresso. The heavy wine book, with its handful of labels behind soiled see-through dividers, is a tip-off of what to expect here: a bit of show and very little substance. It will take more than tuning the piano bar up front to bring cheer to Tre Amici: It needs some new, lighthearted music from the kitchen. About $35 per person, with a modest Italian wine.

Tucano
**333 E. 60th St.
308-2333**
Dinner Mon. to Sat. 7:00 P.M. to midnight
AE, DC
French

We French are always a little concerned when French restaurateurs open a second front in America. Only God, and even then not always, is capable of being perfect simultaneously on both sides of the Atlantic. However, Jacques Maximin is no ordinary person. This young thirty-five-year-old man, who was elected "Top Young Chef" by a jury comprised of chefs awarded three or four toques by Gault Millau (Paul Bocuse, Michel Guérard,

Roger Vergé, Alain Chapel, Alain Senderens, etc.) has the gift like Bonaparte, whom he oddly ressembles, to know how to organize his battlefield and lead his men to victory. It's still too soon to tell if Tucano, where Maximin has installed a team of three of his closest assistants, will be able to compete with the quality of his restaurant, Chantecler, in the Hotel Negresco in Nice where he is executive chef. For this reason, we prefer to withhold our ranking for the moment. But we are sure, in any case, that there is a very good chance for Ricardo Amaral, the flamboyant king of the night and owner of Club A, to have one of the most interesting restaurants in New York.

Jacques Maximin, who was paradoxically born in the fogs of Pas de Calais, established himself on the Côte d'Azur nearly by chance, and he knows better than anyone else how to capture the spirit of Mediterranean cuisine, which is the most flavorful, fragrant, and joyous of all the regional French cuisines. And because he is a true creator, he revitalized his classic repertoire entirely and has never stopped inventing new dishes and marrying new tastes. Maximin's cuisine is like a small ray of sunlight on your plate. His grilled scallops with caviar cream accompanied with greens, his pigeon salad laced with almonds served with mushroom mousseline, his shellfish soup with pistou, his fresh pasta timbale filled with fricasseed lobster, his fresh salmon roasted in a crust of coarse salt served with tomato-basil fondue, his squab risotto perfumed with saffron, his sautéed sliced lamb flavored with olive butter, his chocolate mousse served with hot caramel coulis and his fresh raspberry gratin flavored with Grand Marnier butter gives us the never-ending desire to make a pilgrimmage to Nice. New Yorkers are luckier than the Parisiens because they are able to taste Maximin's cuisine in their own home town, with the hope that it will always be faithful to the original.

They also have even better luck; at Chantecler in Nice, the decor is relentlessly tedious, whereas at Tucano, the opposite is true. from the moment you enter, you are on stage of a theater before the curtain rises. The play could be called, "Caviar in the Tropics;" in this highly civilized tropical forest with its mahagony-framed mirrors and parrots and parakeets showing off their multicolored plumage on the walls, you'll find explorers dressed in Giorgio Armani or Yves St. Laurent. You almost think you are at Carnival in Rio—and this is certainly more exciting than Carnival in Nice! About $60 per person with wine.

13 🍳
Uncle Tai
1059 Third Ave.
(62nd St.)
838-0850
Lunch Mon. to Fri. noon to 3:00
P.M.; dinner nightly 4:00 P.M. to
11:00 P.M.
AE, CB, DC
Chinese

Many chefs have inhabited the persona of the quasi-mythical Uncle Tai over the years. The latest incumbent to lurk behind the avuncular facade is Mr. Kung. Despite frequent changes, this Hunan-style place has remained one of the best of the old, established Chinese restaurants in New York. The menu is long and ambitious, with spicy-hot dishes noted in red type. Cold appetizers include "wonderful taste" chicken, five-flavor beef and thousand-year eggs with shredded jellyfish. A tasty deep fry of minced chicken and pine nuts comes with leaves of wraparound lettuce. There are a good, thick hot and sour soup and a delicate fish broth with the same flavor. Orange beef is crusty and tender under its aromatic glaze. Vegetable rolls turn out to be crisp, waferlike sandwiches filled with fresh-tasting, lightly cooked vegetables and served with a perfect dark brown sesame sauce. Scallops in garlic sauce are outstanding, and frog fanciers will enjoy toying with few slender legs, Hunan style. Vegetables are excellent, especially broccoli in garlic sauce and the pretty tricolor mushrooms. Only the duck with green ginger disappoints; it lacks the flavor, consistency and character of the bird and could easily pass for pork. Also avoid the sesame bananas, which are heavy and tasteless, rather like bad nursery fritters. But, carping aside, we are immensely reassured by the continuing dedication of "Uncle Tai" to the cause of honest, authentically seasoned and delicious Hunanese cooking. About $25 per person, with wine.

12/20
Il Valetto
133 E. 61st St.
838-3939
Lunch Mon. to Fri. noon to 3:00
P.M.; dinner Mon. to Sat. 5:30 P.M.
to 11:30 P.M.
All major credit cards
Italian

There is no danger of going unrecognized at Il Valetto. The pretty back room is so well lit that you have a good view of diners well across the way lining the banquettes, who look more cheerful after they have finished their bottles of Pinot Grigio, Bardolino or Chianti. The beige striped walls covered with smoked glass mirrors and illuminated with crystal chandeliers flatter the predominantly middle-aged clientele, although the room looks more like the bridal dressing room at Neiman-Marcus than a luxury restaurant. None of this seems to faze the macho maîtres d', who go about their business with little of the love and enthusiasm we see in other Italian places. In fact, there is little spirit of any sort here; the wealthy clientele pays a fortune for mediocre pasta and entrees, apparently oblivious to the fact that the Italian wines are as overpriced as the food. It is possible to eat well under the watchful eye of the Renaissance tapestry that looks out of place here, if you choose the fresh Caesar salad, the eclectic antipasto, the capelletti with a creamy tomato sauce, the passable gnocchi, the tender and plump scampi cooked perfectly, the reasonably good saltimbocca, the refreshing striped bass and all the veal classics that Americans so adore in Italian restaurants. Finish your evening with a fragrant and beautifully made zabaglione, which will send you out onto the streets with a good memory, obliterating the fact that you have spent $55 per person (with wine) for a less than stellar experience.

10/20
Vasata
339 E. 75th St.
988-7166
Dinner nightly 5:00 P.M. to 10:45 P.M.; brunch Sun. noon to 5:00 P.M.
All major credit cards
Czechoslovakian

Tastes may have changed, but you can rely on Vasata to offer the same old-world cuisine that could use some spicing up. You will be joined by distinguished-looking diners in this brightly lit dining room with exposed beams and decorative plates; they appreciate the unpretentious, simply prepared, generous dishes. Traditional appetizers include ham suvorov or eggs à la Prague, served hard-boiled with caviar, mayonnaise and ham. Entrees will fill you up: schnitzels, boiled beef, chicken livers, a bland roast chicken, veal with duck livers and bacon and an underseasoned veal paprika. The boring vegetable offerings are made up of the expected cabbage, dumplings, boiled potatoes and a curious creamed spinach that needs inspiration. The Hungarian Egri Bikaver red wine is a good accompaniment that may cheer you up after a lackluster meal. About $35 for two, with wine.

11/20
Veau d'Or
129 E. 60th St.
838-8133
Lunch Mon. to Sat. noon to 2:30 P.M.; dinner Mon. to Sat. 6:00 P.M. to 10:15 P.M.
AE
French (classical)

For the past twenty years, the escargots Bourgogne, saucisson chaud en croûte, tripes à la mode de Caen, Toulouse cassoulet, mussels marinières, civet of rabbit and all the other good old bistro dishes that have been the specialty of Veau d'Or have been a benediction for those wanting to escape steak Diane and tournedos Rossini in New York's big French restaurants. Today, this fare is on the menus of dozens of restaurants, and you are compelled to make comparisons. These dishes are no longer to the advantage of this little place that we continue to love for the provincial atmosphere, an idiotic but rather charming decor and service that is very active. The cuisine, unhappily, has lost its flavor and authenticity. Traditional dishes require just as much attention and talent as others, but this fact has been ignored when one is presented with an insipid saucisson chaud surrounded by a mushy crust and made with no finesse, potatoes that are hard and tasteless, artichoke hearts à la grecque that are equally unappetizing or a roast leg of lamb that is of good-quality meat, but with a so-called juice made into a thick sauce that has been overreduced and that surrounds white beans already drowning in tomato sauce. Nothing catastrophic, but nothing memorable. The huckleberry tart is acceptable, even though it is wrongly called "clafoutis." The white house wine, passed off as a Burgundy, is very ordinary, but the filtered coffee is excellent. At about $25 per person for lunch with a glass of wine, it's easy to find a better meal elsewhere.

15 ♟
Vienna Park
35 E. 60th St.
758-1051
Lunch Mon. to Fri. noon to 3:00 P.M.; dinner Mon. to Sat. 6:00 P.M. to 11:00 P.M.
All major credit cards
Austrian

Most restaurants, even the best, have one weak point. Here it is the unevenness of the cooking. After a recent lunch that bordered on perfect banality, we asked ourselves if this could truly be the celebrated Vienna Park, whose praises certain critics never seem to tire of singing. With a few exceptions, the menu is the same as the one at Vienna 79, which would not be a serious problem if we could rely on consistently good food. It has been nearly impossible for us to forget this lunch, which rivaled airport cafeteria cuisine: a glutinous mass of Gruyère in a mushy feuilleté, insipid cold poached salmon that needed a light mustard sauce instead of the dill sauce that resembled diluted yogurt, and the catastrophic goulash that we can only believe was meant for octogenarians dining in a tea room—even a trained police dog would have been unable to sniff out the slightest trace of paprika. The only saving graces were the excellent späetzle and a broccoli mousse with lemon butter, a dish that would have been more appropriate as an accompaniment for meat or fish than as an appetizer. Even the topfentorte (Viennese cheesecake) was nothing but a lemony spongecake that left us unamused. Perhaps the lunch chef needs to return to Austria to rediscover the robust, sincere flavors of true Austrian cuisine, rather than continue this poor imitation of haute cuisine. Apparently the elegant lunchtime clientele that fills this chic khaki and gray room, ornamented with etchings of Lippeizaners and a panoramic view of Vienna, is not knowledgeable in Austrian cuisine. But we *can* understand why they come for dinner: to sample the excellent venison, cooked until just pink, the good rack of lamb and one of the most extraordinary desserts you could hope to find in the New World—a cheese strudel studded with lightly poached raspberries, which will convince you that you have died and ascended with the angels. How can Vienna Park have such a split personality? The lunches are mediocre, but the dinners will make you want to regularly join the pretty diners who keep this place one of the most talked about in New York. The wine list offers the best possible selection of Austrian whites; with wine, lunch will run about $35 and dinner about $50 per person.

12/20
Vienna 79
320 E. 79th St.
734-4700
Dinner Mon. to Sat. 5:30 P.M. to 11:00 P.M. (Sat. to 11:45 P.M.)
All major credit cards
Austrian

The Viennese, who dote on romantic lighting and a gemütlich ambience, would certainly not swoon over this long room decorated in gray and khaki with stingy lighting that irresistibly evokes a civil defense shelter. It would take an overzealous imagination to find any charm in this austere place. For those not familiar with the true charms of Austria, we have been publishing a guide to Austria for the past five years, filled with addresses in that exquisite country that are so much more seductive and picturesque than Vienna 79. Even so, the welcome and service of this restaurant are imprinted with the civility and gentleness that are Austria's greatest traditions, and you can spend some agreeable moments here as long as you don't wait for any culinary miracles. A new breeze (albeit a still timid one) has been blowing over Austrian cuisine for the past two or three years, which is fortunate since this culinary tradition has never had the reputation of being one of the best in Europe (unlike the superior Hungarian cuisine). Today, in Vienna, Salzburg, Linz and several other cities, a handful of old regional recipes are being adapted to today's tastes and an Austrian nouvelle cuisine is being created that is very flavorful indeed. If you have the chance to visit Salzburg and dine at Restaurant Eschelbach on Lake Mondsee, you will understand the reasons for our enthusiasm and optimism.

This movement, however, has not yet reached the kitchens of Vienna 79, where the chef pays a particularly discreet homage to the motherland's gastronomy. A good part of the short menu could be found in any Continental restaurant serving scallops with lobster sauce, tournedos with foie gras or sweetbreads with basil. The Austrian accent here is placed on a well-made pâté of pork's head with celery, marinated salmon with dill, served with an excellent mustard sauce, Viennese stuffed

171

chicken with its tender, fat skin (although you could skip the cheesy potatoes—they are dry and heavy) and tafelspitz, reduced, unhappily, to its most basic expression—which means it is simply a slice of tasteless boiled beef, carrots and potato pudding, all napped with a sauce of Roquefort and chives. In Vienna, this dish has been a must since the reign of Emperor François-Joseph; tafelspitz at Vienna 79 is priced at $17.95, but it wouldn't begin to impress a Viennese concierge, who cooks it every Sunday. The recipe must have been lost between Vienna and New York, along with that of the Sacher torte, which is dry and tastes very little of chocolate. Instead, select the palatschinken, crêpes with chestnut purée and whipped cream, which is essentially faithful to the authentic recipe.

Unknown to many foreigners, Austrian white wines are excellent, light and fruity (with two or three exceptions, the reds are not worth drinking). Vienna 79 is a good opportunity to taste the Granzinger-Nussberger or the Kremser Grüner Veltimer. Austrians succeed far better than Italians with coffee, and it is delicious here. Vienna 79 is certainly not the mecca of Austrian cuisine, and you musn't hope for any revelations. It is, all the same, a serious house that is very professional, if a little boring, and it will neither cause you great joy nor offer you any gross deceptions. About $50 per person, with wine.

12/20
Wilkinson's 1573 Seafood Cafe
1573 York Ave. (83rd St.)
535-5454
Dinner nightly 6:00 P.M. to 11:00 P.M.
AE, DC
American (seafood)

This is a small, attractive neighborhood bar/restaurant (light woods, etched glass partitions and pretty trompe l'oeil paintings on bare brick walls in the tiny dining area in the rear) that appeals to the Upper East Side affluent who can afford midtown prices but prefer to stay closer to home. The seafood dishes prepared by Shirley King, a transplanted Englishwoman, are essentially in tune with the imaginative and refreshing decor: oysters in a watercress purée, mussels in a white wine reduction, striped bass with a hint of the Orient in the dressing and good salmon with a red wine sauce. But sometimes Shirley goes too far, as in a sweet pepper concoction that serves as a garnish for a combination of shrimp and scallops—they could swim well enough on their own. Desserts are worth mentioning: an intense chocolate cake, moist and rich, and a hazelnut cake, a perfect blend of texture and flavor. With a dearth of good seafood houses in New York, this is a welcome—if a bit saucy—addition. About $35 per person, with wine.

10/20
Woods
**718 Madison Ave.
(63rd St.)
688-1126**
*Lunch Mon. to Sat. noon to 3:00
P.M.; dinner Mon. to Sat. 6:00 P.M.
to 11:00 P.M.*
All major credit cards
American

The chichi Madison Avenue lunch bunch still comes here to bask in the palest pink nondecor and sample uninspiring American cuisine. But the food is not the point here, as Woods is simply a stopping-off place between meetings and boutiques. The cuisine is simple: a generous breast of chicken salad, curious chilled cucumber and chicken with glass noodles, a light trout with a depressing watercress sauce, a perfectly cooked fillet of beef with whiskey and pepper, passable salmon with sorrel, dreadful chocolate mocha roulade, bland strawberry-rhubarb tart and harmless fresh fruit. The wine list is extremely limited, the conversation bountiful, the people pretty and the prices high for third-rate food—about $20 per person for lunch without wine.

Other Boroughs

THE BRONX

16 🍴
Amerigo's
**3587 E. Tremont
Ave.
The Bronx
792-3600**
*Lunch Wed. to Mon. noon to 3:00
P.M.; dinner nightly 5:00 P.M. to
11:00 P.M. (Fri. and Sat. to
midnight)*
All major credit cards
Italian

When Amerigo and Millie Coppola opened their little pizzeria in the Bronx more than 40 years ago, the neighbors little suspected they were harboring the Ludwig of Bavaria of the pasta belt. To Amerigo, small was never beautiful, and he achieved his dream palace in two large dining rooms, where he served some of the best Italian food in the city. Since our last visit, the Coppolas have retired, and the restaurant has been taken over by Tony and Anna Cortese, who have not only maintained Amerigo's high standards of food (Tony was the headwaiter for fifteen years) but have improved the service (which was once lead footed) and, by the slight application of talent, have made once-good dishes even better and added new dishes only after thoroughly testing and retesting. Amerigo's is even better than we remembered it.

Everything in the decor is crimson—the carpet, the tablecloths, even a twenty-foot-wide waterfall, fronted by a broken pillar and a statue of an athlete scratching his foot, no doubt a gesture toward classical grace. Nevertheless, the somewhat more formal main dining room has a distinctly amiable ambience, with tables well separated and lighting quite pleasant.

Portions here are enormous, so watch out for the scrumptious Abruzzese bread and crunchy, sesame-coated grissini placed on the table at the start. The key to dining wisely at Amerigo's is to ask to share appetizers and first plates: superb antipasto caldo, a large pot of mussels alla marinara or a greaseless spiedino alla romana with a well-wrought anchovy sauce. Scampi sautéed in garlic and oil make a fine primi piatti, but it would be an insult to forego one of the kitchen's exquisite—and very rich—pastas: tender potato gnocchi with a true bolognese sauce, capellini provinciale (a house specialty of such spicy seasonings as onion and capers), fettuccine Alfredo (one of the richest we've ever had and also one of the best) and a verdant seasonal pesto. The entrees include not only standard items (chicken scarpariello and a myriad of veal dishes) but also some of the finest steaks, chops and other grilled meats and fish to be found in the city. The beautifully aged shell steak is at least a pound, and the veal chops with vinegar peppers are not to be improved upon. Dessert pastries are brought in from Manhattan's esteemed Dumas Patisserie, but don't neglect the homemade cheesecake, either. Wines represent most of the Italian regions (though not always the best labels) and are fairly tariffed. Amerigo's is well worth the trip from midtown. And don't worry: the neighborhood is very safe. About $40 per person, with wine.

13 Mario's Restaurant

2342 Arthur Ave.
The Bronx
584-1188
Lunch and dinner Tues. to Sat. noon
to 11:00 P.M.
All major credit cards
Italian

The Migliucci family—Mario and Clemente in the kitchen and affable Joe out front—must be doing something right: patrons with hefty appetites and a yearning for good Neapolitan cooking come from all over metropolitan New York. On weekends they are willing to line up on the sidewalk for a chance to enjoy excellent pastas with zesty sauces based on such fresh ingredients as peppers, eggplant and tomatoes (in season only); stews of calamari and congilli that sing with the taste of the sea; and more or less standard scaloppini and rolatini of veal and chicken that would bring credit to a midtown establishment offering them at twice the price. Everything is cooked to order (except the exceptional cannoli from a local baker), and you will have to wait. But the vitality of the place is contagious, and you will no doubt join in the fun and the conversation at the next table. So you won't notice the delay, or the physical setting about you: faded pastoral scenes under glass, unconvincing columns, arches, brick and miniature copies of recognized Roman and Italian nude sculpture.

But the preparations that come from the kitchen are convincing and authentic, and this is what Mario's is all about. About $25 per person, without wine.

Brooklyn

10/20
Gage and Tollner
**372 Fulton St.
(Jay St.)
Brooklyn
875-5181**
Lunch and dinner Mon. to Fri. noon to 9:30 P.M.; dinner Sat. 4:00 P.M. to 10:30 P.M.
All major credit cards
American
(steaks/seafood)

Gage and Tollner may be New York's oldest restaurant: it claims continuous operation in downtown Brooklyn for 105 years. In any event, its handsome appearance is one of permanence: dark wood paneling, damask walls, a decorated tin ceiling, and the original gas (now electric) lamp fixtures. Lawyers, politicians and business people cut their deals around well-spaced tables as they have for the decades since Brooklyn was an independent city. What is served to these high-powered diners has not changed (or improved) with the passage of time. Simply grilled fish, steak and chops are acceptable enough, but side dishes of potatoes or vegetables are no better than you'll find at a corner diner. Our advice: start with fresh clams or oysters on the half shell (avoid the cocktail sauce), order the broiled scrod (forget the tartar sauce) and save room for the Nesslerode pie. After this meal, accompanied by a glass of imported beer, you could even leave with a favorable impression of a part of old New York that has seen much better days. About $30 per person.

12/20
Nightfalls
**7612 Third Ave.
Bay Ridge
748-8700**
Lunch daily noon to 3:00 P.M.; dinner Mon. to Sat. 6:00 P.M. to 11:00 P.M. (Fri. and Sat. to midnight), Sun. 5:00 P.M. to 9:00 P.M.
All major credit cards
American

If Manhattan has its West 46th Street restaurant row, then Brooklyn has its counterpart on Third Avenue in Bay Ridge. Some of the newer establishments here are surprisingly sophisticated, drawing patrons from miles around. Nightfalls is a case in point. Voorsanger & Mills (Le Cygne and other Manhattan eateries are to their credit) designed a stunning brick terrace with a wall of falling water, a terra-cotta interior, miniature Mediterranean blue Roman villa columns and an exciting upstairs balconied atrium.

Although what's delivered from the kitchen does not altogether live up to the lofty expectations inspired by these surroundings, it is better than much of the so-called new American cooking proliferating throughout the country. Seafood is perfectly poached; both an appetizer of cold mussels in a New Orleans–type dressing of green pepper, onion, celery and mustard seeds and a main course of scallops, baby lobster, snapper and salmon in a saffron broth are good. There are also down-home creations (honey-glazed baby back ribs for an appetizer) and standard Italian items (mozzarella and roasted sweet peppers and a pasta primavera), as well as some with a nouvelle influence (sautéed chicken and wild mushrooms with a red wine reduction, neatly presented on an oversize plate). For dessert, we recommend the old-fashioned Indian pudding. All in all, there is something of an accomplished amateurism reflected in these dishes, which we find refreshing—and encouraging, when we contemplate the future of American cooking. About $35 per person.

13 🍳 Peter Luger

**178 Broadway
(Driggs Ave.)
Brooklyn
387-7400**
*Lunch daily noon to 3:00 P.M.;
dinner nightly 5:45 P.M. to 9:45
P.M. (Fri. and Sat. to 10:45 P.M.)
No credit cards*
American (steaks)

At midday, Wall Streeters in their vested pinstripes make the taxi ride over the Williamsburg Bridge to gorge themselves on huge steaks, German-fried potatoes, creamed spinach and cheesecake. In the evening they come back, in shirt sleeves and jeans, with their families in Cadillacs and Mercedes. This no-nonsense steak house, with beautiful oak tabletops and wood-handled knives and forks, has survived and prospered in a rundown neighborhood by offering absolutely first-rate meats, cooked simply and carefully (the loin lamb chops and roast beef are as good as the steaks). There's a good selection of imported and domestic beers (some on draft) and a limited wine list. If you want to find out what it is that attracts New Yorkers to this unlikely corner of Brooklyn, order the single steak and share it with a friend, or order the steak for two and share it in a party of four. You won't leave disappointed or hungry. But a word of caution: If you drive here, park your car in the lot by the bank across the street or along the curb in front of the entrance. If you do not heed this advice and instead park it on a side street, it may not be there after your meal. Then you'll have to wait for the doorman to call for a cab as you search in your wallet (now lighter by at least $35 per person, without wine) for the number of your insurance company. This little chore could leave you with a bad taste in your mouth, your good dinner notwithstanding.

13 🍳 Restaurant Lisanne

**448 Atlantic Ave.
Brooklyn
237-2271**
Dinner nightly 6:00 P.M. to 10:00

Joel Wolfe gave up television commercials for his greater love, the kitchen, five years ago, creating this handsome restaurant among the antique shops that predominate along this slowly reviving part of Atlantic Avenue. Behind a small, see-through kitchen, he installed overhead track lighting, cordoned off a section of the

P.M. (Sun. to 9:00 P.M.)
AE, MC, V
French (provincial)

room for green plants with strings of tiny Christmas tree lights and painted the fleur-de-lis-patterned tin walls a stark white. His patrons are residents of Brooklyn Heights and Park Slope—as well as a growing number from farther afield—who place greater value on the quality of what they are eating than on where they are eating it, and they find the dishes here as light and refreshing as the neighborhood is somewhat dreary.

The menu is basically French, but Joel is not afraid to impress his own jovial personality on some of the dishes: excellent calf's brains in a light batter with a caper-flavored mayonnaise, poached salmon with an interesting fennel sauce and an acceptable enough breast of duck with a medley of crisp vegetables. Desserts are exceptional: delicious fruit sorbets, a flavorful cappuccino ice cream and a rich crème brûlée. There is no printed menu: the handful of dishes are presented on a blackboard, which permits Joel to change dishes on the basis of what's available at the market or what is on his mind at the moment; you might say everything is a special. We suggest you drive right up to Restaurant Lisanne (there's parking along the curb in front) and hurry in. This way you won't notice the seediness of the neighborhood, and you'll enjoy what you find inside all the more. About $30 per person, without wine.

12/20
The River Café
1 Water St.
(Cadman Plaza West)
Brooklyn
522-5200
Lunch daily noon to 2:30 P.M.;
dinner Sun. to Thurs. 6:30 P.M. to
11:30 P.M., Fri. and Sat. 7:00 P.M.
to 11:30 P.M.
AE, MC, V
American

The view is still superb, the flowers are a bit less dramatic, and the clientele is looking slightly more Brooklyn brownstone than Upper East Side carriage house. The menu sounds familiar, and Chef Charles Palmer is manning the wheel in Larry Forgione's wake after he sped across the river to his own little American place. On the surface, things look and feel the same at The River Café. It's possible that you won't be disappointed with the terrine of pike with a fragrant roasted sweet pepper sauce, the lamb carpaccio, its rare meat complemented with yellow pepper relish, or the tuna sashimi marinated in lime and ginger with a too-sweet, insipid horseradish sauce. Nor will you refuse a fresh, all-American green salad, smoked salmon or those stunning Wilippa oysters from Washington State. Beginnings here will give you reason for hope. After the appetizer plates have been whisked away by the abrupt waiters, you have more than twenty minutes to contemplate the view before the entrees arrive, looking lovely and optimistic. The fascination for things American, so chic throughout the country these days, is self-evident in this place's obsession with making every dish regional or a creative interpretation of traditional culinary roots. Chicken from the plains states is teamed up with California cashews, Long Island duckling makes an appearance in the old-world tradition, rare and confited, Western veal is sauced with California Champagne, and Northwest salmon is filled with oyster mousse and touched with caviar. The intentions here are honorable, and with a little more discipline and attention to cooking times, you could be happy with a tuna steak in ginger port that is otherwise cooked to tastelessness; pheasant with marvelous chanterelles, its overcooked meat nearly inedible; and an Idaho lamb that is indeed rare and tender, served with an ill-conceived package of carrots and mushy apples that looks like a Purina checkerboard in bondage.

But all is not lost. For the $40 prix fixe you can have the six American cheeses that are au courant (produced by "small American farmers," which leads us to believe they must live in Oz), or any of the well-prepared desserts, such as the ultrarich chocolate terrine that may have you tap dancing all the way home, an apple and cranberry crumb pie that will wake you right up or a highly personal praline charlotte served with ladyfingers that remind us of macaroni. The wine list is acceptable, with lots of American selections, and the ambience is still as lovely as ever. It will get better here, we hope, making the pilgrimage to Brooklyn worthwile.

QUEENS

11/20
Le Capon
94-09 63rd Dr.
Rego Park
Queens
459-3939
Lunch Mon. to Fri. noon to 3:00 P.M.; dinner nightly 4:00 P.M. to 10:00 P.M. (Sun. from 3:00 P.M.) AE, MC, V
French (provincial)

No one is sure how many Bretons work in Manhattan's French restaurants, but whatever the number, most of them and their families live within a block or two of Queens Boulevard in Queens. Patricia and Michel Gallic, tired of commuting to work, did the rational thing: they opened their own little bistro right near home. Originally, only French was heard around the tables, but now the word is out that you don't have to go to Manhattan for boeuf bourguignon or coq au vin, and American voices abound. The moules marinière are a triumph, the stuffed mushrooms are not so good, and a mixed green salad is beautifully fresh (if a little drowned in vinaigrette). The rack of lamb and grilled veal chop are all they should be, but the béarnaise with the sliced filet mignon has no elegance whatsoever. The complete dinner (except on weekends), including appetizer, main course, salad, dessert and coffee, is under $15, so perhaps a lapse or two in the kitchen is pardonable.

14 Manducati's

1327 Jackson Ave.
Long Island City
Queens
729-4602

*Lunch Mon. to Fri. noon to 3:00
P.M.; dinner nightly 5:30 P.M. to
10:00 P.M.*
No credit cards
Italian

Don't be discouraged by the neon Budweiser sign in the window or the unfortunate siding on the outside of this building. Walk in, avoiding the bare, cavernous barroom, and proceed to the dining room in the rear, with its huge fireplace, aglow whenever the weather is the least bit chilly. Here among the cheery brick walls, chandeliers and a few plants, there is warmth whether the logs are burning or not. The simple Italian offerings from Ida Manducati's kitchen are so well prepared and Vincent Manducati's welcome is so radiant that serious diners from miles around have become regulars; reservations are a must.

There is spontaneity in the cooking here, an honesty and directness that is all too rare in this era of mass feeding and inflated prices. Pastas that would cost twice as much at a pretentious mid-Manhattan restaurant are nicely sauced, sometimes with imported ingredients such as porcini mushrooms. The usual chicken and veal dishes found on Italian menus everywhere reflect Ida's personal touch. She also makes her own manicotti, cannelloni, lasagne and gnocchi. A grilled orato (a Mediterranean fish sometimes called a gilthead) is served whole and is boned at the table. Vegetables are much more than an afterthought—crisp and tasty, in excellent oils and flavorful herbs. Only the desserts—tartufo, rum cake, cheesecake—are humdrum, but they are prepared elsewhere. About $25 per person, with a simple Italian wine.

14 Water's Edge

44th Drive and the
East River
Long Island City
Queens
392-4055

*Lunch daily 11:30 A.M. to 3:00
P.M.; dinner 5:30 P.M. to
11:30 P.M.*
All major credit cards
American

One of the best ways to appreciate New York City is to get far enough away (some people think Los Angeles isn't far enough) to get a clearer perspective than is possible in town. You can do that quite nicely in this latest riverside attraction in the unlikely location of Long Island City. (The owners would do well to develop a water-bus service to transport diners more easily to and from the East Side.) In any case, you can generally rely on a stunning view of the city when the sun sets behind Citicorp, its dormant solar panels blazing as you watch Con Ed light up the town. This is the perfect place to visit with a poor conversationalist, because there's always the view to spark speculation, comment and even romance. The understated decor here is medium-tech in tasteful desert tones; there's a casual ambience, beautiful fresh flowers and very friendly service.

The cuisine is American, with a trendy Japanese influence that looks and tastes out of place. The wine list is hardly a celebration of American growths, but there are a few expensive California selections to accompany superb mussels with basil on spinach, an equally good shrimp mousse with watercress sauce, cured fish with fennel, a warm vegetable salad and good curry soup with salmon and cilantro. The chef still needs a little more finesse to carry off this inventive cuisine, but in updating American classics, he is definitely on the right track. There is a very good grilled swordfish with a mustardy mint sauce, a decent duck with raisins and pears (also good when served with sorrel), a classic leg of lamb with rosemary, overcooked sea scallops with beurre blanc, red snapper with basil and ginger (also delicious with a tarragon beurre blanc) and a passable veal chop with chanterelles. The tempura vegetables are indistinguishable, although the salads are refreshing. The rich crème brûlée is good, the homemade sorbets better and the rich cakes and tortes best when shared by two.

There's loads of promise here, and we predict that Water's Edge will flourish as more and more New Yorkers venture across the 59th Street Bridge to discover the delicious cuisine and bask in the pleasant ambience. Dinner with the superb Far Niente Chardonnay will run about $40 per person.

STATEN ISLAND

12/20
Framboise
585 Forest Ave.
Staten Island
981-5725
Dinner Tues. to Fri. 6:00 P.M. to 10:00 P.M., Sat. 5:30 P.M. to 11:00 P.M., Sun. 3:30 P.M. to 8:30 P.M.
All major credit cards

Italian

If you should find yourself in the wrong lane in speeding traffic and end up in Staten Island at dinner time, all is not lost: there is an interesting restaurant in this otherwise dull (and most remote) part of the city. It is called Framboise, not because the food is French, but to distinguish it from the hundreds of undistinguished Italian establishments on the Island. The young chef and owner, Frank Puleo, is of Italian origin, and by selecting a French name he hoped to distance his cooking from the veal parmigiana and spaghetti dishes that are the standards surrounding him. He succeeds in more than name: he has a fine hand with pasta—for example, capellini with shrimp (imported from Ecuador) is flavored with a delicious tarragon-scented sauce. Sweetbreads in a mustard sauce are excellent, and the duck with a tangerine sauce and red snapper on a bed of sautéed watercress are delicious though quite disarming. Desserts, we regret to tell you, are not up to Mr. Puleo's own creations; he relies on outside help for these. A former schoolteacher who spent his summers at DeMarco in Nantucket, Mr. Puleo is a newcomer to running his own restaurant. This explains the inconsistencies that are apparent from time to time, particularly on weekends, when he has trouble giving a personal touch to all the dishes coming from the kitchen. But we find it refreshing and exciting to discover that such an effort is being made at all in Staten Island. Mr. Puleo could be wearing a toque before our next guide is out. About $35 per person, with wine.

Toque Talley

18/20

Lutèce $60 per person without wine $27 ea - lunch

17/20

An American Place 42 ea
Cellar in the Sky 65 ea
La Côte Basque - 40 ea

Maxime's
Quilted Giraffe 52.50
La Tulipe

16/20

Amerigo's
Le Chantilly 36.50 ea
Le Cirque 22.75 lunch 60 dinner
Le Cygne 42.75 ea

Felidia 45 ea
Four Seasons
Le Périgord - 36, 40, 46 ea.
Guy Savoy

15/20

Auberge Maxime
The Box Tree (Purdys)
Café Lavandou
La Cascade
La Chanterelle
Chez Pascale
Le Délice
Devon House, Ltd.

Oyster Bar (Grand Central Station)
Pamir
Parioli Romanissimo
Pear Tree
La Petite Ferme
The Polo Bar and Restaurant
Raphael
La Récolte

La Gauloise
L'Hostaria del Bongustaio
L'Hostellerie Bressane

Sabor
The Tarragon Tree
Vienna Park

14/20

The American Bounty Restaurant
Andrée's Mediterranean
Café Luxembourg
Le Cherche Midi
Chez Catherine
Claire's
Claude's
Contrapunto
La Côte d'Or
Divino Ristorante
Ennio and Michael
Erminia
The Gibbon
Hatsuhana

Hubert's
Inagiku
Kitcho
Manducati's
The Odeon
Pari Passu
Le Petit Robert
Prunelle
Restaurant Jean Pierre
La Ripaille
Texarkana
Trastevere
Tre Scalini
Water's Edge

13/20

Abyssinia
American Harvest Restaurant
The American Hotel
Bistro Bambouche
Bistro Bordeaux
The Bombay Palace
La Bonne Bouffe
Bridge Café
Buffet de la Gare
Café New Amsterdam
Café des Artistes
Caliban
La Camelia
Captain's Table
Castellano
Cent'Anni
René Chardain
John Clancy's Restaurant
Frank's Restaurant
Gallagher's

La Louisiana
Peter Luger
Mario's Restaurant
Mr. Lee's
Mon Paris
Mona Trattoria
The New York Restaurant School
Omen
Orso
Palm
El Parador
Le Périgord Park
Primavera
Rene Pujol
The Rendez-Vous
Restaurant Lisanne
Restaurant Nippon
Saint Jean des Prés
Salerno's Old Town Coach House
Say Eng Look

La Grange at The Homestead Inn
Harralds
Hyo Tan Nippon
Jack's
Keewah Yen
Kurumazushi
Lavin's
Lello

Shinbashi
Szechwan East
The Terrace
Tour de France
24 Fifth
Uncle Thai
Vanessa

12/20

Angelina's
Auntie Yuan
The Balkan Armenian Restaurant
Benihana
Le Bistro
Bravo Gianni
Bruno's
Café Espanol
Café 58
Café Loup
Capsuoto Frères
Carolina
Chatfield's
Chez Napoleon
La Colombe d'Or
Company
La Crémaillère
La Crémerie
Dimitri Restaurant
Fonda La Paloma
Fortune Garden
Framboise
Frankie and Johnnie's
Gino's
Gloucester House
Gordon's
Greene Street
Home Village
The House on Toilsome
Jacqueline's
Joe & Rose
Keen's
Luscardi's
Madame Romaine de Lyon
Manhattan Market

Christopher Myles
Il Nido
Nightfalls
One Fifth
One if by Land, Two if by Sea
Pantheon
Paradis
Patrissy's
Patsy's
Quo Vadis
Raga
Le Refuge
Le Relais
The Restaurant
The River Café
Russian Tea Room
Sammy's Roumanian
    Jewish Restaurant
1770 House
Sidewalkers
Silver Palace
Simons
Supreme Macaroni
Table d'Hôte
Tastings
Teacher's
Tenbrooks
Les Tournebroches
Tovarisch
Tse Yang
21 Club
Il Valetto
Vienna 79
The Water Club
Wilkinson's 1573 Seafood Café

The Market Dining Room
Meson Botin
La Métairie
Il Mulino

Wong Kee
Woods
Z

11/20

Apricots
L'Auberge de France
Barbetta
Black Sheep
Café San Martin
Café Seiyoken
Caffé da'Alfredo
Cajun
Le Capon
La Caravelle
Century Café
Charley O's
Christ Cella
Coach House
Elio's
Francesca's
The Gingerman
Girafe
Great Shanghai Restaurant
La Grenouille
Janice's Fish Place
Joanna
K.O.'s
Landmark Tavern
Luchow's
Marylou's

Maxwell's Plum
Meat Brokers
Meson Madrid
Milestone
Nishi
The Old Homestead
Pesca
La Petite Marmite
Pirandello
Raoul's
Red Tulip
Restaurant Laurent
Ristorante Ponte Vecchio
The Russian Bear
Sea Fare of the Aegean
Stonehenge
The Three Village Inn
United States Steakhouse
Veau d'Or
Village Green
Wo Lee Oak of Seoul
Ye Waverly Inn
Zapata
Le Zinc
Zinno

10/20

Acute Café
Altri Tempi
Anche Vivolo
Arnold's Turtle
Ballato's
The Box Tree (Manhattan)
Cam Fung
Carumba!
Casa Brasil

Il Monello
Orsini's
Ottomanelli's Steak and Wild Game
    Restaurant
Le Paris Bistro
Parma
Peking Duck House
Pierre au Tunnel
Les Pléiades

Il Cortile
Delphi
Enoteca Iperbole
Forlini's
Gage and Tollner
Gosman's Dock
Greener Pastures
Horn of Plenty
Hunam
Jockey Club
Kavkasian Restaurant
Lobster Inn
Mariana's

La Réserve
Rio de Janeiro
Sahib
Santa Fe
Sardi's
Lou G. Siegel
Tamu
Tapestries
The Ukrainian Restaurant
Vasata
Wings
Woods (Madison Ave.)

9/20

Adam's Rib
Beijing Pavilion
The Brazilian Pavilion
Café des Spòrts
Le Chambord
Cinco de Mayo
Ernie's
Fraunces Tavern Restaurant

Garvin's
Hwa Yuan Szechwan Inn
Madras Woodlands
Oyster Bar (Plaza Hotel)
The Tibetan Kitchen
Tre Amici Ristorante
Wharf 56

8/20

Beijing Duck House
Elaine's
Seeda Thai

Sign of the Dove
Sloppy Louie's
Sparks Steak House

7/20

Algonquin Hotel
Benito's II
The Fishmarket Inn

La Goulue
Pearl's
Tavern on the Green

6/20

Romeo Salta

5/20

Hee Seung Fung

No Ranking

Bruce Ho   **Tucano**

The World's Cuisines

Afghanistani

Pamir

American

The American Bounty Restaurant
The American Hotel
An American Place
Apricots
Bridge Café
Café Luxembourg
Café New Amsterdam
Carol's
Cellar in the Sky
Century Café
La Chanterelle
Charley O's
Chatfield's
Coach House
Company
Le Délice
Four Seasons
Fraunces Tavern Restaurant
The Gingerman
Greene Street
Hubert's

Manhattan Market
The Market Dining Room
The New York Restaurant School
Nightfalls
Odeon
One Fifth
One if by Land, Two if by Sea
Paradis
Quilted Giraffe
The River Café
Salerno's Old Town Coach House
Simons
Table d'Hôte
Tastings
Teacher's
Tenbrooks
The Three Village Inn
La Tulipe
21 Club
Vanessa
The Water Club

Jack's
K.O.'s
Keens

Water's Edge
Wings
Woods

American (regional)

American Harvest Restaurant
Carolina
Horn of Plenty
La Louisiana

Santa Fe
Texarkana
Ye Waverly Inn

American (seafood)

Captain's Table
Claire's
John Clancy's Restaurant
The Fishmarket Inn
Gage and Tollner
Gloucester House
Gosman's Dock
Janice's Fish Place

Lobster Inn
Marylou's
Oyster Bar (Grand Central Station)
Oyster Bar (Plaza Hotel)
Sidewalkers
Sloppy Louie's
Sweet's
Wilkinson's 1573 Seafood Café

American (steak)

Adam's Rib
Christ Cella
Frankie and Johnnie's
Gage and Tollner
Gallagher's
Joe & Rose
Peter Luger

Meat Brokers
The Old Homestead
Ottomanelli's Steak and Wild Game
    Restaurant
Palm
Sparks Steak House
United States Steakhouse

American (vegetarian)

Armenian

Austrian

Vienna Park   Vienna 79

Belgian

Saint Jean des Prés

Brazilian

The Brazilian Pavilion   Rio de Janeiro

Central European (kosher)

Lou G. Siegel

Central European

Sammy's Roumanian Jewish Restaurant

Chinese

Auntie Yuan   Hwa Yuan Szechwan Inn
Beijing Duck House   Keewah Yen
Beijing Pavilion   Pearl's
Cam Fung   Peking Duck House
Fortune Garden   Say Eng Look
Great Shanghai Restaurant   Silver Palace
Hee Seung Fung   Szechwan East
Bruce Ho   Tse Yang
Home Village   Uncle Tai
Hunam   Wong Kee

Continental

Algonquin Club   Milestone
Café des Artistes   Mr. Lee's

Century Café
Coach House
Devon House, Ltd.
Four Seasons
Frank's Restaurant
Garvin's
Gordon's
Harralds
The House on Toilsome
Joanna
Jockey Club
Lavin's
Maxwell's Plum

Christopher Myles
One if by Land, Two if by Sea
Paradis
The Restaurant
Sardi's
1770 House
Sign of the Dove
Table d'Hôte
Tapestries
Tavern on the Green
Teacher's
Village Green

Continental (seafood)

Mariana's

Wharf 56

Creole

Cajun

Cuban

Sabor

Czechoslovakian

Vasata

English

Landmark Tavern

Ethiopian

Abyssinia

French (classical)

Acute Café
Auberge Maxime
Bistro Bambouche
Bistro Bordeaux
La Bonne Bouffe
The Box Tree (Manhattan)
The Box Tree (Purdys)
Buffet de la Gare
Café Loup
Café des Sports
Capsuoto Frères
La Caravelle
Le Chambord
Le Chantilly
René Chardain
Chez Pascale
Le Cirque
Claude's
La Côte Basque
La Crémaillère
Devon House, Ltd.

La Gauloise
La Goulue
La Grange at The Homestead Inn
La Grenouille
Lutèce
Maxime's
La Métairie
Le Périgord
La Périgord Park
La Petite Marmite
Pierre au Tunnel
Quo Vadis
Raoul's
Le Relais
La Réserve
Restaurant Laurent
Stonehenge
The Terrace
Tucano
Veau d'Or
Pari Passu

French (nouvelle)

Acute Café
Café Lavandou
Café New Amsterdam
Café Seiyoken
Caliban
La Cascade
Cellar in the Sky
La Chanterelle
Chez Catherine
Le Cirque
La Côte Basque
La Côte d'Or
Le Délice
The Gibbon
L'Hostellerie Bressane
Lutèce
Pari Passu

Pear Tree
Le Périgord
Le Périgord Park
Le Petit Robert
Prunelle
Quilted Giraffe
Raphael
La Récolte
Le Refuge
The Rendez-Vous
Restaurant Jean Pierre
La Ripaille
Guy Savoy
Simons
The Tarragon Tree
24 Fifth

French (provincial)

L'Auberge de France
Le Bistro
Black Sheep
Café 58
Café Lavandou
Le Capon
Capsuoto Frères
René Chardain
Le Cherche Midi
Chez Catherine
Chez Napoleon
La Colombe d'Or
La Crémaillère
La Crémerie
Le Cygne
L'Hostellerie Bressane

Jacqueline's
Madame Romaine de Lyon
La Métairie
Mon Paris
Le Paris Bistro
Le Petit Robert
La Petite Ferme
Les Pléiades
The Polo Bar and Restaurant
René Pujol
Le Refuge
Restaurant Jean Pierre
Restaurant Lisanne
Tour de France
Les Tournebroches
Le Zinc

German

Luchow's

Greek

Delphi
Dimitri Restaurant

Pantheon
Z

Greek (seafood)

Sea Fare of the Aegean

Hungarian

Red Tulip

Indian

The Bombay Palace
Raga

Sahib

Indian (vegetarian)

Madras Woodlands

Indonesian

Seeda Thai

Tamu

International

Casa Brasil

Irish

Charley O's

Landmark Tavern

Italian

Altri Tempi
Amerigo's
Anche Vivolo
Angelina's
Ballato's
Barbetta
Benito's II
Bravo Gianni
Bruno's
Caffè da'Alfredo
La Camelia
Castellano
Cent'Anni
Contrapunto
Il Cortile
Dimitri Restaurant

Girafe
L'Hostaria del Bongustaio
Joe & Rose
Lello
Luscardi's
Manducati's
Mario's Restaurant
Milestone
Mona Trattoria
Il Monello
Il Mulino
Il Nido
Orsini's
Orso
Parioli Romanissimo
Parma

Divino Ristorante
Elaine's
Elio's
Ennio and Michael
Enoteca Iperbole
Erminia
Ernie's
Felidia
Forlini's
Framboise
Francesca's
Gino's

Patrissy's
Patsy's
Pirandello
Primavera
Ristorante Ponte Vecchio
Romeo Salta
Supreme Macaroni
Trastevere
Tre Amici Ristorante
Tre Scalini
Il Valetto
Zinno

Italian (seafood)

Pesca

Japanese

Benihana
Café Seiyoken
The Gibbon
Hatsuhana
Hyo Tan Nippon
Inagiku

Kitcho
Kurumazushi
Nishi
Omen
Restaurant Nippon
Shinbashi

Korean

Wo Lee Oak of Seoul

Mediterranean

Andrée's Mediterranean

Delphi

Mexican

Café Espanol
Carumba!
Cinco de Mayo

Fonda La Paloma
El Parador
Zapata

Portuguese

Rio de Janeiro

Russian

Kavkasian Restaurant
The Russian Bear
The Russian Tea Room

Tovarisch
The Ukrainian Restaurant

Spanish

Café Espanol
Café San Martin

Meson Botin
Meson Madrid

Thai

Seeda Thai

Tibetan

The Tibetan Kitchen

THE DIVERSIONS

The Diversions

THE SIMPLE PLEASURES

New Yorkers are capable of arguing for hours about the best pizza, deli or hamburger in town. While we have no desire to jump into the middle of these never-ending disputes, we do have some personal favorites (and some we avoid). No matter what one's financial means, one can't dine at Lutèce every day; sometimes a simple salad and an espresso at a modest café can be most soul-satisfying. New York is rich with culinary diversions, from Italian caffès to high-tech ice cream parlors to late-night diners, and you would do Manhattan a great disservice if you didn't explore them with great gusto.

Barbecue

Dallas Jones Bar-B-Q
27 W. 72nd St.
873-2004
Daily noon to midnight (Fri. and Sat. to 1:00 A.M.)
AE, MC, V

This huge place resembles a pleasantly decorated mess hall: tables are packed close together in a big, high-ceilinged room, and it's always teeming with young families, students and those who appreciate a good bargain. And what a bargain it is: if two come for dinner before 6:30 P.M., they can each have half a barbecued chicken, soup, corn bread and potatoes, with a tab of just $6.95 for the both of them. Prices after 6:30 P.M. aren't too much more than that. For the most part, the food is satisfactory. While it isn't the most authentic barbecue around, the ribs and chicken are tender and fall right off the bone. Ribs and chicken are about the extent of the menu, except for the accompaniments: homemade chicken soup, decent corn bread, corn on the cob, a greasy, ridiculously huge "loaf" of fried onions and homemade desserts. Service is prompt, the atmosphere is cheerful, and there's a booming takeout business (great for picnics in nearby Central Park). Dinner for two (after 6:30 P.M.) will come to $25 with beer. There's another location at 336 East 86th Street (772-1616).

Smokey's Pit
230 Ninth Ave.
(24th St.)

The standard fast-food chain vinyl decor won't put you off once you catch the aroma that wafts onto the Chelsea streets outside. The tender ribs and chicken are dark with

924-8181
*Mon. to Fri. 11:00 A.M. to 11:00
P.M.; Sat. and Sun. noon to
11:00 P.M.
No credit cards*

delicious sauce (mild, medium or hot—and hot is searing). There are also messy, spicy chicken wings, barbecue sandwiches, chili (also sold at Bloomingdale's), hot links and adequate potato salad and baked beans. Skip the pecan pie, but try "Mrs. Smokey's" icebox cake. A barbecue feast for two is $22 with beer. Another location at 685 Amsterdam Avenue, near 94th Street (865-2900).

Wylie's
**891 First Ave.
(50th St.)
751-0700**
*Daily 11:30 A.M. to midnight
All major credit cards*

Most people insist that Wylie's has the best ribs in New York City. To make your own decision, be prepared to wait here with an attractive crowd that spends as much time waiting at the bar or on the sidewalk as they do feasting on servings of ribs and chicken designed for herculean appetites. The baby back ribs are tender and tasty, as is the chicken. The beef ribs are also delicious , although a bit fatty, and you will be supplied with a pitcher of barbecue sauce to make a messy meal even messier. One of the favorite traditions here (other than singles meeting singles) is what Wylie's calls an onion brick. This mass of fried onions is good where it's crispy, but by the time you get to the center of this curious dish it resembles Jabba the Hutt more than some down-home culinary inspiration. The ribs are worth the wait, and for $20 per person, with beer, you will be well fed.

Cafés

WALL STREET · SOHO

Café Fidelio
**195 Spring St.
(Sullivan St.)
334-9522**
*Daily 8:00 A.M. to midnight (to
8:00 P.M. in winter)
AE, MC, V*

After visiting the SoHo galleries and shops, rest your feet outside or in this cheerful café and have a cappuccino, hot chocolate, iced coffee or fresh squeezed orange juice and a piece of delicious homemade pie or cake or an ice cream sundae. Our favorites are a delicate Russian mazurka (hazelnut cake, whipped cream and fresh orange slices) and fudge walnut pie, with a taste of rich brownies. The most popular are a flaky two-crust fresh peach or apple pie with whipped cream. The cheesecake is light as a feather and topped with fresh strawberries.

Swiss owner Alex Kimche prepares authentic Bircher-muesli, the oat-based cereal that is as delicious for a light lunch as for breakfast; it's made the traditional way with yogurt, milk, fruits, nuts and heavy cream. After noon, the menu offers soups, salads, sandwiches, light entrees and those fantastic desserts. You can read copies of the popular papers (*Interview, New York Beat, New York Times, Wall Street Journal* or even Zurich's *Tages Anzeiger*) and linger as long as you like. And you will.

Central Falls

**478 W. Broadway
(Houston St.)
475-3333**
Daily noon to 2:00 A.M.
AE

Central Falls is an absolutely charming place for SoHo pretties and their uptown counterparts to meet for Saturday lunch. The lofty recycled box-factory space is sweetened by the strains of chamber music performed by serious musicians. The highly polished mahogany bar is impressive, the seating is comfortable, and the walls are white to show off the series of temporary exhibitions that brighten up the place. The menu, unhappily, is not as appealing as the decor or the clientele. There seems to be something for everyone, which leaves us perplexed and slightly out of focus. Bistro fare is the standard, with sandwiches, good omelets (although one is filled with canned artichoke hearts), a very good two-toned pasta with pesto, barbecued ribs, carpaccio or excellent spinach ravioli in cheese sauce. Dinner gets slightly more ambitious with the perfunctory veal scaloppine, a chicken Cordon Bleu–ish presentation, lamb chops and dubious sole with black beans, soy and snow peas. Don't expect great food, but you will have a pleasant lunch here fueling up for the inevitable shopping spree just outside the door. About $12 per person for lunch without wine.

Elephant and Castle

**183 Prince St.
(Sullivan St.)
260-3600**
*Mon. to Thurs. 8:00 A.M. to
midnight; Fri. 8:00 A.M. to 1:00
A.M.; Sat. 10:00 A.M. to 1:00
A.M.; Sun. 10:00 A.M. to midnight*
All major credit cards

The hangout for artists, hustlers and all SoHo aficionados. The atmosphere is warm and relaxed, with fans circulating on the painted tin ceiling. There's a wood-paneled wall with uncomfortable benches; it's better to take a small wooden table by the white-paned windows. The breakfast menu includes oatmeal with currants and walnuts, huevos rancheros and espresso. All day long there are 25 omelets to choose from. An Elephantburger, charcoal grilled, is topped with curried sour cream, bacon, cheddar, tomato and scallions and has to be one of the best burgers in town. Most desserts are made with Häagen-Dazs ice cream and sport grandiose names: Magnificent Obsession, Heart of Darkness, Velvet Underground, Garden of the Gods (with prices to match: $4.75 to $5.50). There's another branch in Greenwich Village, at 68 Greenwich Avenue, near Seventh Avenue. Dinner with a glass of wine and a sweet dessert crêpe will cost $15.

Gianni's

South Street Seaport
15 Fulton St.
608-7300
Daily noon to 2:00 A.M.
All major credit cards

Watch the Wall Street and tourist worlds walk by from your perch on the sidewalk café at Gianni's; the visual feast will not disappoint even if your lunch leaves you a little hungry. The grilled shrimp and fish prepared by energetic Japanese chefs are generally good, the salads are fresh, the accompanying peppers are tasty, and for $18 you'll have a decent lunch. You can also choose from chicken with rosemary, cold mussels with an herb-tuna sauce, seafood salad and cold pasta. Indoors, the menu is more extensive.

J.S. Van Dam

150 Varick St.
929-7466
Nightly 7:00 P.M. to 12:30 A.M.
(Fri. and Sat. to 3:00 A.M.)
AE, MC, V

The Brooks Brothers contingent comes slumming here in TriBeCa hoping to run into recording artists, local craftspeople or any of the very pale, costumed New Wavers who make the bar scene here. In a retro decor (which is slightly sad) in deep reds and browns, the pace picks up the later it gets, when there is enough body heat to warm up the place; the loud music impairs any attempts at normal conversation. The bistro menu offers little hope for nourishment; the tortellini is passable but the salmon is absolutely desolate. The duck can be good, although its preparation tends to be uneven, the roast chicken with tarragon is edible, and there are the more ambitious lamb chops with Pernod and rosemary, and the good kidneys. This amusing establishment seems to have lost some of its luster, but it's a good location for a snack before a workout at Heartbreak just down the street. About $35 per person for dinner with wine (there's a $10 food minimum per person).

Washington Street Café

433 Washington St.
(Desbrosses–Vestry
sts.)
925-5119
Dinner Tues. to Sat. midnight
All major credit cards

There must be a general warehouse from which would-be restaurateurs can order prefabricated trendy restaurants. It is as if a giant crane dropped just such a package in a forgotten corner of TriBeCa, where it was promptly painted pink and black, given track lights for appropriate drama and filled with a serviceable but unknowledgeable staff and disappointing, eclectic bistro/wine bar cuisine. A redeeming feature of the café is the now-prerequisite cuvinet contraption, which allows samplings of wines by the glass, making the wine list far more interesting than the menu. Dinner for two, with several tastings of wine, will run about $50.

The Wine Bar

422 W. Broadway
(Prince St.)

A serious-looking crowd comes here to enjoy light lunches of quiche, salad and pâté and to sample French and domestic wines by the glass. There is no wine

431-4790
Daily noon to 2:00 A.M. (Fri. and Sat. to 4:00 A.M.)
AE

machine; the good wines are gassed with nitrogen overnight to keep them alive. The building is typically old New York, with lofty ceilings, brick walls and a beautiful bar. If you want some decent wine, this is the place. The crowd gets livelier at night.

GREENWICH VILLAGE

Caffé Reggio
119 MacDougal St.
(W. 3rd St. and
Minetta Ln.)
475-9557
Daily 11:00 A.M. to 2:00 A.M. (Fri. and Sat. to 4:00 A.M.)
No credit cards

Two blocks from Washington Square you'll find the best espresso (hot or iced) in New York, in an Italian Renaissance setting, plus cappuccino and hot chocolate as creamy as can be, perfumed teas and, for the starving, toasted prosciutto and cheese sandwiches and Italian pastries. This is not so much a spot for gourmets as for aesthetes, with a trendy crowd in a very romantic setting. Absolutely the place to go for an after-dinner coffee and to be encircled by the intellectual fringe of fashionable New York.

The Cloister
238 E. 9th St.
777-9128
Daily noon to midnight (Sat. and Sun. to 1:00 A.M.)
No credit cards

This unpretentious neighborhood espresso bar is frequented by Lower East Side artists, actors and the underemployed. Avoid the dull room inside and (when the weather permits) take a table in the large brick courtyard, lit with strands of tiny white lights, that is reminiscent of Rome. The only merit of the food is its low cost, but few come here to eat; they come for espresso, bowls of good café au lait and decent desserts, all at very low prices ($4 for café au lait and cheesecake). The service moves with glacial speed.

Cottonwood Café
415 Bleecker St.
924-6271
Nightly 5:00 P.M. to 11:30 P.M.; brunch Sat. and Sun. 10:30 A.M. to 2:00 P.M.
No credit cards

Join the neighborhood regulars and the attractive preppies who make their pilgrimages here for Tex-Mex food that is plentiful and inexpensive. The decor is down-home plain, with a few cowboy classics lining the walls and music in the Del Rio Room Monday through Saturday. You'll enjoy the mesquite-smoked ribs, crisply fried okra and chili. Perhaps less fascinating are the overcooked pork chops, chicken-fried steak with traditional pan gravy, boring black-eyed peas and simple pintos. But it's good, honest food and tastes pretty respectable when washed down with a bottle of chilled Rolling Rock beer. About $12 per person with good but soggy nachos.

Front Porch
253 W. 11th St.
675-8083
Daily noon to 11:30 P.M.
No credit cards

This friendly restaurant lets you sample its soups before ordering. It even lets you preview the moist, slightly sweet meat loaf in gravy just like mother used to make. Front Porch is aptly named—there's a homey, country feeling, with a decor so like grandma's kitchen, you almost expect a plump little white-haired lady to enter with a smudge of flour on her cheek. This is more a café than a restaurant, although there's a fairly large menu after 6:00 P.M.; before that mostly soups, salads, and omelets. Try the excellent Mom's chicken soup (made with turkey) and the equally good chili Mallorca (chili in pita bread with onions and cheddar cheese). Service is friendly, the crowd youngish and the parade of Villagers outside the window entertaining. Other locations uptown. About $6 per person for lunch.

MIDTOWN

Beggars Banquet
125 W. 43rd St.
997-0959
Mon. 11:30 A.M. to 8:00 P.M.;
Tues. to Sat. 11:30 A.M. to
11:00 P.M.
AE, CB, DC

A popular midtown lunch spot with a pub atmosphere and good, simple, homemade food. Secretaries and junior executives come here for the excellent quiches (try the provençale or seafood varieties), the good salads, the different daily soups (Dutch split pea, pistou, cold cucumber and beet) and the hearty chili and stews. The delicious bread on the table is baked fresh daily, and the desserts are worth trying. This is an honest, unpretentious, friendly place that would also be perfect for a simple before-theater meal. Lunch for two with a glass of wine comes to $15.

The Café Between the Bread
145 W. 55th St.
581-1189
Mon. to Thurs. noon to 10:00 P.M.;
Fri. and Sat. noon to 11:00 P.M.
AE, V

After the success of Between the Bread's self-service bistro on the East Side, owner Riki Eisen opened this very attractive café next door to a small Between the Bread muffin bakery. The fare is similar to that on the East Side: marvelous sandwiches that combine fresh breads (raisin, German pumpernickel, French, pita) with such delights as Black Forest ham, Scotch salmon, prosciutto with Brie and egg salad with herbs. There are also excellent salads and desserts—the seasonal fruit muffins and tarts are outstanding. All this is served by attentive young men in a handsome, modern decor of gray and red. There's a charming outdoor patio in back, and if a dessert particularly strikes your fancy you can order it next door to take home. One of the best lunch bets in the area. About $12 per person without wine.

Café Madeleine
405 W. 43rd St.
246-2993
Daily 11:00 A.M. to midnight (Sun.
to 11:00 P.M.)
No credit cards

An adorable little French café in the theater district, with brick walls, lace curtains and on the menu a platter of assorted fish pâtés, cheese, delicatessen items and good salads. The dishes are fresh, delicate and inexpensive: $15 to $25 for a simple meal for two.

Café Rififi

1070 First Ave.
(58th St.)
No telephone
Daily 11:00 A.M. to midnight (Fri. and Sat. to 1:00 A.M.)
No credit cards

This attractive room is dominated by a wonderful old brass Cimbali espresso machine, which dispenses the coffees, heats the cider and steams the hot chocolate for customers seated on bentwood and cane chairs at small marble-topped tables. Brunch on Saturday, Sunday and holidays is only $5.95; it includes a small garden salad, Nova Scotia salmon and cream cheese, French bread and butter, a choice of entree (omelet or frittata primavera, or waffle with Frusen Glädjé ice cream) and a cup of brew from the great machine. Save room for the delicious chocolate Ganache from Désirs la Côte Basque or the hazelnut cake from Vienna Desserts.

Café Un Deux Trois

123 W. 44th St.
354-4148
Mon. to Fri. 11:00 A.M. to 12:30 P.M.; Sat. and Sun. 5:00 P.M. to 12:30 P.M.
AE, MC, V

If you are celebrating your birthday at Un Deux Trois (although we can't imagine what would prompt you to), you'll be serenaded with an enthusiastic anvil-chorus rendition of "Happy Birthday" performed by the international staff. The traditional brasserie is still intact, the pretentious chandeliers are still lit up, the crayons are still on the tables to test the clientele's creativity and sobriety, the Pompeiian-ruins decorative effects are still on the walls, the beautiful bar is still popular, and the food is still mediocre. The kitchen seems to have a little trouble getting their French right. Boudin blanc is remarkably like Italian sweet sausage (served with delicious apples), the moules are so overcooked they are nearly inedible, the pepper steak is of very poor quality even though the sauce is passable, but the frites are wonderful. You can try the chicken breast with mustard sauce, the third-rate mixed grill, the good green salad vinaigrette, the awful profiteroles and the worse charlotte. It's such a shame, because it could be a good pre- and posttheater alternative to the snob scene at Joe Allen's. Our suggestion, however, is to come here to drink, people watch and draw your pictures. Leave the food to the desperate. About $35 per person for dinner with house wine.

ddl Bistro

Trump Tower
725 Fifth Ave.
(57th St.)
832-1555
Mon. to Sat. 8:00 A.M. to 6:00 P.M.
All major credit cards

Tucked away in this awesome quarry of pink marble, behind the unnerving pianist and violinist, hidden from the hordes of tourists, shoppers, security guards and boutique owners, ddl has created an elitist bistro that gives the impression of a touch of class. Waiters and waitresses clad in traditional bistro garb attend to an unusual variety of customers seated on red velvet banquettes or attractive Italian-designed chairs at small marble-topped or white-linen-covered tables. All of this is well and good, particularly since the food is actually surprisingly decent, especially compared with the consummately inedible open buffet across the lobby, where unsuspecting innocents are served mediocre pasta salads, bread as hard as rocks and pastries that could be used as sea-to-land missiles. The bistro dishes up more elegant and, fortunately, more palatable fare, such as assorted antipastos, a plate full of radicchio, cold poached fish, an excellent minted eggplant and lamb terrine, veal medallions with basil and a delicious gnocchi in a tomatoey gorgonzola sauce. The ricotta cheesecake is a bit too sweet, but the espresso custard is refreshing. Lunch for one will run an exorbitant $10 at the buffet and an outrageous $33 at the bistro, without wine.

Hard Rock Café
221 W. 57th St.
489-6565
Open daily 11:30 A.M. to 4:00 A.M.
AE, MC, V

The Hard Rock is not for the fainthearted. If you've been one of the sturdy souls lined up on 57th Street for endless hours waiting your chance to pass under the fin-tailed, rearend salute to New York that serves as an awning and sneak by the Cerberus at the gates, only to find yourself packed among the attractive L.A.-chic outfitted young people who look like they have just found their bicoastal way here, you know you have made it into New York's hottest new nightspot. The Hard Rock has mastered the art of giving its clientele the impression that they are special enough to get in. It's hard to estimate how special anyone can feel when pressed up against all the other special hot bodies stacked at the bar. But these patient people wait over two hours for a table and the chance to eat burgers, steaks, pig sandwiches, St. Louis cut ribs, dreadful fries and surprisingly good milkshakes, floats, sundaes and other all-American desserts. All of this is dished out amidst deafening hard rock and a visual fashion show that would slake the appetite of a starving animal. Which is an advantage since it takes another two hours to be served here by apologetic, sweet young men. It does give you time, however, to make a dent in the Café's supply of Rolling Rock and Lone Star, drunk macho style from the bottle. The eclectic decor has a early '70s theme when the Beatles were gods and life somehow seemed simpler. Of course, you may be fortunate enough as we were to visit the Hard Rock on Billy Cohen's birthday when Moët and Chandon flowed as freely as the catsup on his guests' cheeseburgers. A rare experience in any case to watch New York's youth in action, all night long; about $20 per person with beer.

UPPER WEST SIDE

All State Café
250 W. 72nd St.

On a cold, wintry day the fireplace in this small café and bar welcomes you, creating a warm coziness that

874-1883
Daily 11:30 A.M. to 1:00 A.M.
No credit cards

enhances the bare-bones decor and simple environment. The All State is an actors' hangout, and you'll more than likely run into interesting characters and literaryesque conversations. The food is basic, plentiful and inexpensive at lunch; a blue-plate special for the meat-and-potatoes crowd runs under $5, slightly more at dinner. A good address on the West Side, particularly for the budget conscious. About $7 for a burger, fries and beer.

Café Central
384 Columbus Ave.
(78th St.)
724-9187
Daily 11:45 A.M. to 3:00 A.M.
AE, MC, V

The loyal regulars have emigrated from what they called "Das Boot" (the original Central on Broadway) and now find themselves in the very attractive new location, surrounded by a deco decor, beautiful mahogany walls and an understated, elegant atmosphere. Lunch is simple but satisfying, with hearty soups, good burgers and the ubiquitous pasta dishes that New Yorkers seem to expect. Dinner is a bit more ambitious: sautéed scallops with saffron, a good fillet steak, game hen, Italianized veal and basic chops. It's a pleasant place for a leisurely lunch or a high-energy dinner, surrounded by good-looking people who clearly have made their life in the arts. One of the best choices on the West Side; rarely will you find this much character elsewhere. About $12 per person, with a beer.

Cantina
221 Columbus Ave.
(70th St.)
873-2606
Daily 11:30 A.M. to 1:00 A.M.
AE, MC, V

Young Upper West Siders fill Cantina's sidewalk tables in the summer, just as they fill every other sidewalk café along Columbus. Like several of these places, Cantina serves Mexican food, and like many of them the food is without merit. Though the portions are huge, the prices are high for Mexican food, and the preparation is not very authentic. Stick to the passable enchilada and taco plates and avoid the overcooked, often inedible Mexican-style seafood dishes (usually red snapper or shrimp). The service is prompt, the margaritas are decent, and the atmosphere is pleasant enough, with a typical Columbus-Avenue café decor spiced up with cactus and a few paintings of Mexico. Dinner for two with margaritas will come to $45.

Noodles
40 W. 72nd St.
873-3550
Mon. to Thurs. 5:00 P.M. to 11:30 P.M.; Fri. and Sat. 5:00 P.M. to 12:30 A.M.; Sun. 4:00 P.M. to 11:30 P.M.
All major credit cards

You might think you're taking your chances in this little restaurant, secreted away in the rear of a residential hotel with a lobby full of residents who look to be in the advanced stages of their last hurrah. Noodles is a sweet place with bentwood chairs, checked tablecloths, a pleasant bar and an active clientele that packs the place at dinner. And for good reason: the noodle dishes are offered at Depression-vintage prices. If any of the sixteen or so Italian selections (gnocchi, linguini, ravioli, tortellini) don't appeal to you, there are some Far Eastern preparations: soba, chow fun (Chinese noodles with shredded beef), Korean cellophane noodles and an Indian curry dish. Even the desserts are pasta based, with a variety of homemade strudels. Dinner for two with a carafe of the house wine will run about $25. A new location at 75th Street and First Avenue, 737-3328.

O'Neal's Baloon
48 W. 63rd St.
399-2353
Daily 11:30 A.M. to midnight (Sun. to 11:00 P.M.)
All major credit cards

O'Neal's is always bustling with local office workers, Columbus Avenue shoppers, tourists and those coming or going from Lincoln Center across the street. It's a place for drinking, not eating, as evidenced by the uninteresting menu offering the most banal hamburgers, omelets, club sandwiches and fried foods, all of which are prepared carelessly. Salads are sad and soggy, hamburgers are overcooked, and the chicken pot pie is a tasteless, gluey mess. But there are some very good beers on tap and lots of atmosphere and opportunity for people watching in this vast turn-of-the-century tavern (which, by the way, claims to be New York's first saloon). A simple dinner for two with beer will run $23.

West Side Storey
700 Columbus Ave.
(95th St.)
749-1900
Daily 7:00 A.M. to 11:00 P.M.
No credit cards

This neighborhood restaurant is an oasis in the increasingly upscale Upper West Side. Much of the clientele eats here daily, and the atmosphere at the sit-down counter is friendly. Families with children usually come before 8:00 P.M. and are seated in booths with upholstered banquettes; lines start to form later in the evening. The cuisine reflects the origins of the different chefs: Thai, Moroccan, Egyptian, American. We are particularly fond of the chicken gai yang, good even without its Thai hot sauce. Sandwiches, soups and salads join a variety of entrees in what makes for a well-chosen menu. Two can enjoy a delicious meal with wine and espresso for $30.

UPPER EAST SIDE

Abbondanza
1647 Second Ave.
(86th St.)
879-6060
Mon. to Fri. 11:30 A.M. to 3:00 P.M. and 5:00 P.M. to midnight; Sat., Sun. and holidays 11:00 A.M. to midnight
AE, MC

This inviting white and red tiled café looks like an overgrown ice cream parlor, an oasis of taste in this hearty once-German district. The members of a talented Italian family have combined their culinary skills in pasta and salad preparation, using the freshest quality ingredients. At lunch, selections are spread out buffet style; in the evenings table service includes a choice of pastas and traditional dishes. Desserts are produced by a Sicilian, and ice cream is churned by the owner. All items can be wrapped to take home, a reminder that this successful establishment began in the takeout business. Dinner for two, with wine and espresso, will come to $35.

The Beach Café

**1326 Second Ave.
(70th St.)
988-7299**
Daily 11:30 A.M. to 1:30 A.M. (Fri. and Sat. to 2:00 A.M.)
No credit cards

This café/gallery is a very civilized, relaxed place for lunch, a snack or a drink. It's all brick and rich wood, with bentwood chairs, classical music in the background, the ever-popular glassed-in sidewalk patio and uninteresting art on the walls. The hamburgers are juicy and quite good, and there's the usual array of quiches, omelets, salads and grill items, along with some more ambitious Italian dishes. Service is friendly and prompt. Lunch with a glass of wine will come to $8 per person.

Camelback and Central

**1403 Second Ave.
(73rd St.)
249-8380**
Lunch Mon. to Fri. 11:30 A.M. to 3:00 P.M.; dinner Mon. to Thurs. 5:00 P.M. to 11:00 P.M.; Fri. 5:00 P.M. to midnight; Sat. 6:00 P.M. to midnight; Sun 6:00 P.M. to 11:00 P.M.; brunch Sat. 11:30 A.M. to 3:30 P.M.; Sun. 11:30 A.M. to 4:00 P.M.
All major credit cards

This place tries hard to be chic but falls short of the mark. It makes a stab at a New Wave/high-tech decor, with gray brick walls, unattractive functional black and steel chairs and hard, high-backed booths. But the awful Muzak in the background and the bordering-on-elderly crowd give it away: this is just another omelet/quiche/salad lunch spot for weary shoppers. The lunch fare is perfectly passable (particularly the hamburger and the tiny roast chicken with herbs), though hardly memorable. We didn't run the risk of dinner here, which gets suspiciously elaborate: tournedos béarnaise, roast duck in a port and currant sauce, tempura. There's a pleasant little bar to one side. A hamburger lunch for two will cost $20; dinner for two will be $45 without wine.

Demarchelier

**808 Lexington Ave.
(62nd St.)
223-0047**
Lunch Mon. to Sat. noon to 3:00 P.M.; dinner nightly 6:00 P.M. to 11:00 P.M.
All major credit cards

This charming bistro is so welcoming, with its wood paneling, back room salon, sidewalk seating and marvelous old bar, that you'll be ready to settle in for lunch after a morning at Bloomingdale's or for a romantic dinner. The slow French staff is in traditional bistro dress, the mood is intimate, and the crowd is Continental chic. But watch out! The inedible cuisine ranges from a bizarre mushroom salad with an acidic sour cream dressing and a banal house pâté to a reasonably flavorful saucisson chaud with tasteless steamed potatos and overcooked, boring chicken with a passable tarragon sauce. Desserts, as is to be expected when the food is inedible, are not bad; the tarte tatin and crème caramel are admirable examples of traditional cuisine. Your best bet? Come here for a drink or a late-night dessert. About $20 per person for lunch without wine.

Desirs la Côte Basque

This Lexington Avenue café with its rustic charm offers a large selection of exquisite pastries prepared in the French manner. Fortunately it opens early for leisurely

**1032 Lexington Ave.
(73rd-74th sts.)
535-3311**
Daily 7:30 A.M. to 7:30 P.M.
All major credit cards

breakfasts. Pâtés and quiches join salads and cheeses at lunch; the same light fare is served until closing. If one slice of its delicious ganache chocolate cake isn't enough, take home a whole cake.

Kleine Konditorei
**234 E. 86th St.
737-7130**
Daily 10:00 A.M. to midnight (Fri. and Sat. to 1:00 A.M.)
AE, DC

There remain but a few reminders of the German character of this neighborhood. Kleine Konditorei is one, with a menu laden with specialties only a hearty Teutonic palate could love: suelze, herring, goulash, sauerbraten, schnitzel. The pastries, on the other hand, are made with a delicate hand and are rigorously authentic: rigo torte, gugelhupf, rum punch torte, Schiller locken (those curls of light pastry filled with whipped cream the moment you order them), apple strudel, Black Forest cake and, of course, Sacher torte. We prefer to come here from 3:00 to 5:00 in the afternoon, when things quiet down, for Viennese iced coffee or cake. Complete dinners cost under $15.

Jim McMullen
**1341 Third Ave.
(76th–77th Sts.)
861-4700**
Daily 11:30 A.M. to 1:45 A.M.
AE

The snobbism of this place is equaled only by the snobbism of its clients. By night it's ablaze with handsome young men, pretty young women and successful-looking people of indeterminate ages. By day, the bright room is filled with septuagenarians, Madison Avenue–clothed mothers with their pained-looking children, somewhat self-conscious-looking men meeting their perfectly coiffed girlfriends, and an entourage of models who hike up here for a light lunch. All of this is watched over day and night by the always charming and ever youthful Mr. McMullen, who is making a fortune watering successful athletes and feeding New Yorkers chic food that is no doubt what is keeping them fashionably thin. There's no risk gaining weight with an insipid steak tartare, a sharp, bitter gazpacho or an overcooked lemon sole with chives. But there are plenty of sandwiches and the view is pretty, so settle in with a beer and dream about these attractive people, who always look slightly bored in that honorable East Coast establishment tradition. About $15 per person for lunch.

Mortimer's
**1057 Lexington Ave.
(75th St.)
861-2481**
Daily noon to midnight (supper menu Tues. to Sat. to 2:30 A.M.)
All major credit cards

The attractive middle-aged crowd that lunches at Mortimer's is replaced at night by the attractive middle-aged crowd that brings the place to life. It's a chic spot for lunch, although the food is hardly the draw. The neighborhood supplies a clientele of gallery staffers, shoppers and local residents in retirement. The fare is standard: burgers, chicken hash, entrecôte, overcooked chicken paillard, salads and some very good shoestring potatoes and fried onion rings. It's a decorative place to eat, and you'll notice quite a few of the regulars admiring themselves in the mirrors that line the walls of this brick café. There's outdoor seating for the sandwich crowd. About $25 per person for lunch, more at dinner, although the real scene is at the bar, not at the bentwood chairs around the small tables.

Andrew William
1340 First Ave. (72nd St.)
570-0060
Lunch daily 11:30 A.M. to 4:30 P.M.; dinner Sun. and Mon. 5:30 P.M. to midnight; Tues. 5:30 P.M. to 1:00 A.M.; Wed. to Sat. 5:30 P.M. to 2:00 A.M.
All major credit cards

Don't look for much more than another First Avenue café/bar filled with the sort of people who make these nondescript places their hangouts. Lunch is pleasant; you are surrounded by trelliswork, flattering pink walls, lots of mirrors reflecting the ladies who lunch and an enclosed sidewalk seating area that offers good people watching, particularly if you like to keep track of nearby New York Hospital staffers. Evenings are more lively, with singles sharing drinks and an occasional dinner, and local residents sampling some of the safe but not overly imaginative cuisine. You will be agreeably surprised, however, if you order the passable calf's liver with lingonberry sauce, the paillard of chicken on fresh spinach with an acceptable mustard herb sauce, the satisfying cream of broccoli soup and the good (though a bit too sweet) crème brûlée. There are few wines to speak of, but the St. Michelle Merlot from Washington State will improve your mood considerably. About $15 per person for lunch without wine.

Delis

Carnegie Delicatessen
854 Seventh Ave. (55th St.)
757-2245
Daily 6:30 A.M. to 4:00 A.M.
No credit cards

The most famous, and one of the oldest, of the midtown delis. Not far from Times Square and the big Broadway shows, it attracts both audience and actor. Owner Leo Steiner is a celebrity in his own right, as is headwaiter (now coowner) Milton Parker. The sandwiches are standard fare; you can also enjoy homemade matzoh ball or meatball soup and the fresh pastrami. Expect long lines Sunday morning. A deli lunch will cost $10.

The New York Delicatessen
104 W. 57th St.
541-8320
Daily 6:30 A.M. to 1:30 A.M.
AE, V

David Wolf sold the restaurant bearing his name across the street and opened here in what was once a Horn and Hardart automat, beloved by Carnegie Hall musicians. The decor has been revitalized, and the art deco setting is the best thing about this establishment (but be careful not to eat on the balcony, which vibrates when the air conditioning is on). You'll enjoy the dish of cole slaw, pickles and peppers that arrives while you're waiting for your enormous sandwich, large enough for two to share, but you'll be less fond of the barely chopped chicken liver and the just-fair pastrami. The food here has yet to tempt the orchestra members back to their old haunt.

Ratner's
**138 Delancey St.
(Essex St.)
677-5588**
Daily 6:00 A.M. to 11:00 P.M. (Sat. to 2:00 A.M.)
No credit cards

Opened in 1905, Ratner's is the most famous deli on the Lower East Side and probably in all of New York. Vast (it resembles the waiting room in a Central European train station), it can serve close to 200 people at any one time—Dustin Hoffman, Mayor Koch, Elia Kazan and Jackie Mason have all been spotted here. But why they come, we can't imagine. The waiters' motto is apparently "The customer is rarely right," and nearly everything here is bad, from the tasteless borscht to the spongy gefilte fish. The Israeli army could use the blintzes in their cannons. The specialty, kasha varnishka (kasha with onions and small noodles), is dense to the point of being, in our opinion, barely edible. The enormous cakes, especially the cheesecake, are tasteless and too sweet. All in all, it's a spot typical of the Lower East Side, to be visited for a sandwich but otherwise to be avoided, unless you relish reliving the gustatory experiences of stetl cuisine a century ago. Lunch for two will run $17.

Second Avenue Deli
**156 Second Ave.
(10th St.)
677-0606**
Daily 11:00 A.M. to 11:00 P.M.
No credit cards

On the boundary of the Lower East Side, this is one of New York's most famous kosher delis, and also its best. The Lebenwohl family (father, mother and two daughters) have taken great pains to recreate a 1900s Lower East Side atmosphere, reflecting the days when immigration was at its height. In a nostalgic setting, big, motherly waitresses unload chicken soup (excellent) with matzoh balls, boiled beef, goulash, Rumanian-style steak with chili peppers. New York humorist Sam Levenson claimed that the reason the Second Avenue Deli's cooking is so salty is that the Jewish mothers sob while cooking at the stove. All the dishes are accompanied by kasha, kugel (noodle pudding), knaidlach (dumplings) and kishka (stuffed beef intestine). The gefilte fish deserves special attention: it's made of whitefish or carp seasoned with onions and served with horseradish. Considering the psychological pressure exerted by the waitresses, it's difficult not to order the chopped liver ($3.50) as an appetizer. It's a tradition, and Abe Lebenwohl claims he serves the best chopped liver in the world—the only one made according to the rules: liver (fresh daily), vegetable oil, chicken fat, eggs and onions. He's so proud of it that if you ask, he'll let you taste it for free. You'll pay $25 for a deli feast for two.

Fast Food

The Big Kitchen
World Trade Center Concourse level
938-1153
Mon. to Fri. 7:00 A.M. to 7:00 P.M.; Sat. 9:00 A.M. to 5:00 P.M.

If the words *fast food* evoke for you the smell of burning grease, a prison atmosphere and gastric punishment, you owe yourself a visit to the complex of restaurants that takes up most of the concourse in the World Trade Center. You'll see that it's entirely possible to feed the multitudes good, healthy food simply prepared and offered in a relaxing atmosphere at ridiculously low prices. What strikes you at first is that although thousands of meals are served here daily, you never get the impression that there's a crowd. The space is divided into a number of warm and intimately lit zones in attractive colors with comfortable seats, each zone arranged around a particular stand. From hamburgers to roast chicken, from seafood (including oysters that Europeans will find staggeringly inexpensive) to pastries (167 different sorts), from international delicatessen fare to the 42 different types of bread available at the bakery, you're offered hundreds of hot and cold dishes prepared the same day, which you can take out or eat at the attractive tables. In short, for about $6 (provided your willpower is strong enough to resist temptations) you can lunch at The Big Kitchen—lightly, it's true, but in a remarkably appetizing manner. Owners of assembly-line-type restaurants would do well to spend some time studying under Toni Aigner, the manager of this extraordinary restaurant giant.

Dosanko
135 E. 45th St.
697-2967
Daily 11:00 A.M. to 9:30 P.M
No credit cards

Japanese cuisine calls to mind delicate, perfumed soups, noodles fried with soy, spicy dumplings ... and that's exactly what you'll find here, served with the politeness and efficiency characteristic of the Far East. Japanese wines and beer, tea and coffee are served, along with copious but light and tasty dishes, which leave no unpleasant memories. The only thing fast food–ish are the prices (under $6 per dish). Takeout service. Various locations.

Ice Cream

Agora
1550 Third Ave.
(87th St.)

In ancient Greek *agora* means "marketplace," a place where people buy and sell just about everything. Here the word refers especially to clothes and ice cream, because

369-6983
Daily 11:30 A.M. to 12:45 P.M.
All major credit cards

this extraordinary shop is divided into two entirely distinct sections: a men's and women's clothing store on one side and an ice cream parlor and restaurant on the other. You can enjoy the best ice cream sodas in town (25 varieties, from the most classical to the most unlikely, and 21 very good ice cream flavors) in an authentic late-nineteenth-century setting: stained-glass windows, frosted mirrors, beaded chandeliers, beautiful hand-carved mahogany cabinets and an onyx soda fountain at the entrance. All of this makes for an unusual spot to eat ice cream and more (the window terrace restaurant offers a complete menu). Certainly worth a visit.

Dmitri's Café
156 Spring St.
(W. Broadway)
334-9239
Mon. to Thurs. 7:30 A.M. to midnight; Fri. and Sat. 9:00 A.M. to 2:00 A.M.; Sun. 9:00 A.M. to midnight
No credit cards

Dmitri's is a charming place to refresh yourself after an afternoon of prowling through SoHo's shops. The very attractive white and gray café serves very good ice creams from Vermont's acclaimed Ben and Jerry's, along with espresso and homemade pastries (try the beautiful baklava). There are some unusual ice cream flavors, such as Dastardly Mash (chocolate chips, almonds, raisins and more), white Russian (Kahlua and cream) and Oreo mint.

Gelato Modo
464 Columbus Ave.
(82nd St.)
663-0942
Daily noon to midnight (Fri. and Sat. to 1:00 A.M.)
No credit cards

One of the most recent additions to New York's bevy of ice cream parlors, Gelato Modo is already immensely popular and is planning to expand. This is authentic Italian gelato, rich and made fresh daily, with such flavors as mocha, zuppa inglese and zabaglione. There are also excellent fruit sorbettos—the strawberry is marvelous. Some sundae-type concoctions are made with Dilettante sauces; these can be eaten at tables in the attractive gray and green room, accompanied by a variety of espressos and other coffees.

Le Glacier
1022 Madison Ave.
(78th–79th sts.)
249-2975
Daily 11:00 A.M. to 10:00 P.M.
No credit cards

Frozen yogurt (vanilla, chocolate, raspberry, lemon, peach) made on the premises is exceptional. But the owner is Austrian, so you might want to try his hot fudge sundae (Sedutto ice cream) topped with whipped cream—it will bring back memories of your last visit to Vienna.

Minter's Ice Cream Kitchen
551 Hudson St.
(Perry St.)
242-4879
Mon. to Fri. 8:30 A.M. to midnight; Sat. 1:00 P.M. to 1:00 A.M.; Sun.

This is the kind of stuff children dream of—mixing your favorite ice cream with your favorite fresh fruit, candy or cookie. The hand-mixed ice cream idea comes from Boston (as does the ice cream itself, Bassetts). There are more than a dozen ice cream flavors, all smooth and good, and more than 20 mixings, from fresh blueberries to crumbled Heath bars to brownie bits. The old Village shop is minuscule and charming, with a small corner

1:00 P.M. to midnight
No credit cards

devoted to selling homemade gifts. Fresh pastries are brought in daily for breakfast, and for the snowbound (or lazy), Minter's will deliver free in the West Village area.

Old-Fashioned Mr. Jennings
12 W. 55th St.
582-2238
Mon. to Sat. 11:00 A.M. to 11:00 P.M.
No credit cards

The women who shop at Bonwit's and Saks adore Mr. Jennings. You'll see them here in abundance every afternoon, setting their shopping bags down on the black and white tiled floor to have an ice cream soda, shake or sundae (sometimes preceded by a light salad lunch). Mr. Jennings ran the ice cream shop for many years at Bonwit's before its move to Trump Tower; he's moved around himself several times since then, but seems to be settled here for awhile. The ice cream itself isn't stellar, but his creations are: sundaes with lots of fresh fruit and/or delicious fudge; rich, thick shakes, and all manner of ice cream concoctions. And the real reason these ladies come here is Mr. Jennings himself, who runs the place like a hawk and visits with all his guests, reassuring them that their double malteds won't *really* set them back on their diets. There's a full menu of salads and sandwiches for lunch, along with omelets for supper.

Peppermint Park
666 Fifth Ave.
581-5938
Mon. to Fri. 8:00 A.M. to 7:30 P.M.; Sat. 10:00 A.M. to 6:30 P.M.
No credit cards

A classic ice cream parlor, modern, light and appropriately decorated in peppermint green, for pies, ice creams and homemade chocolates of only average quality. A pretty spot nonetheless. There's another, larger Peppermint Park with an outdoor café at 1225 First Avenue, near 66th Street (879-9484).

Sant Ambroeus
1000 Madison Ave. (77th St.)
570-2211
Mon. to Sat. 9:30 A.M. to 10:30 P.M.; Sun. 10:30 A.M. to 7:00 P.M.
AE, MC, V

A fashionable Milanese pasticceria and gelateria has moved to Madison Avenue; the Italian flair for flamboyance is evident in the decor and the fancifully iced cakes, the elegantly packaged chocolates and homemade cookies. It all looks too good to eat. At tea time, you can sip espresso from the Richard-Ginori cups, have an ice cream sundae ($5 to $7) or try the overly sweet cakes and tarts. The bizarre, tentlike-ceilinged dining room is also open for breakfast, lunch and dinner. Better yet, take out a sorbetto or gelato in a cup—no tasting allowed—for a mere $1.25.

Late Night

Brasserie
100 E. 53rd St.
751-4840

This institution is still going strong. It's New York's place to meet for breakfast at 3:00 in the morning, for lunch at the counter (the always attractive flowering-plant display

Daily 24 hours
All major credit cards

holds forth above the counter island) or for a pretheater supper. The simple menu is fairly reliable, with a decent onion soup gratinée, quiche, grilled meats, good eggs Florentine, a popular monte cristo sandwich, a proper choucroute, a light salad nicoise and less interesting, more ambitious dishes that should best be avoided. The ambience is cheerful, the noise level high enough to give you the impression that everyone's having a terrific time, the service fairly friendly and the bill about $11 per person for lunch without wine.

Corner Bistro
331 W. 4th St.
(Jane Street and
Eighth Avenue)
242-9502
Daily 24 hours
No credit cards

A good, old-fashioned neighborhood bar in Greenwich Village that is always filled with regulars who come for the beer, Irish coffee and burgers. The crowds spill over into the back room, with its straight-backed wooden booths, chow-down chili and "bistro burgers," half pounders with cheese, bacon, onion, lettuce and tomatoes, prepared in a minuscule open kitchen by an Indian cook. The kitchen closes at 3:30 A.M. About $6 per person.

Electra Restaurant
949 Second Ave.
(50th St.)
421-8425
Daily 24 hours
No credit cards

The Greeks have taken over the city's luncheonettes, and nearly every New Yorker has developed a taste for their salads, moussaka and souvlaki. At the counter or in one of the booths, the service here is quick and efficient. Cheeseburgers, immortalized on "Saturday Night Live," are available, of course, along with standard Greek and American dishes. Try a feta cheese and tomato omelet, a jumbo bagel with lox and cream cheese or a quiche and salad. Wine (domestic and Greek), beer, cappuccino and espresso are available at all hours. About $6 per person without drinks.

Empire Diner
210 Tenth Ave.
(22nd St.)
243-2736
Daily 24 hours
AE

The Empire is an art deco railway car that welcomes a mixed bag of superb cover girls, leather-jacketed bikers and establishment types from the area who are willing to swallow anything as long as there's ketchup on it. The elderly Queen of the Piano, Miss Bea, resurrects prewar hits from 11:00 A.M. to 3:00 P.M. (other pianists entertain during dinner, and until 4:00 A.M. on Saturday nights). Highly recommended for breakfast around 4:00 or 5:00 A.M. About $12 per person.

L'Express
169 Eighth Ave.
(18th St.)
255-3887
Daily 24 hours
AE

If you're in the area and you're hungry for bistro food at 3:00 A.M., stop off at L'Express for reliable though uninspired cuisine. If you're awake enough, you'll appreciate the stunning metro decor à la deco. The wooden seating in the front section is a bit uncomfortable, but the atmosphere is a nice throwback to the '20s. You can find everything from a scallop salad and smoked chicken to red snapper and chicken with mustard sauce. Desserts will give you the sugar hit you need to make it home after an all-nighter at the Roxy. About $30 per person for dinner with wine, for food that is overpriced for its quality.

Kiev
117 Second Ave.
(7th St.)
674-4040
Daily 24 hours
No credit cards

This overheated, overbright luncheonette is safe at all hours for a breakfast with a Russian-Jewish flavor. Stick to scrambled eggs with delicious kielbasa or the French toast made with challah. Other specials include blintzes, matzoh brie, potato or cheese pirogis (kreplach) and varnishka. About $4 per person.

Market Diner
572 Eleventh Ave.
(43rd St.)
244-6033
Daily 24 hours
MC, V

The decor here, vintage plastic and aluminum, was immortalized by painter John Baeder. Typical along-the-highway diner fare is served, to the delight of taxi drivers, patrolling police and others for whom an hour's free parking is of primary importance. You can eat and drink here for under $12 a person and never know you are in New York. Additional locations at 256 West Street and 411 Ninth Avenue, near 33rd Street.

103 Second Avenue
103 Second Ave.
(6th St.)
533-0769
Daily 24 hours
No credit cards

The Village atmosphere is great here at every hour, but it's at its best from 3:00 to 5:00 A.M., when punk locals, party goers and disco dancers are joined by off-duty local bartenders. The Japanese owner is responsible for the neat and clean look: butcher block tables are set at angles to the long bar, which serves drinks (until 4:00 A.M.) at one end and food at the other. Service is quick and pleasant. The 24-hour menu of sandwiches, burgers, chili, guacamole, omelets, granola with yogurt, homemade pies and cakes, espresso and so on is augmented by daily dinner specials from 5:30 to 10:45 P.M. The food is good, the noise level is high, and on weekends there may be lines to get in—but dinner will be fun, at $15 per person, with wine or beer.

Richoux of London
1373 Avenue of the Americas
(55th–56th sts.)
265-3090
Daily 24 hours
All major credit cards

The decor lives up to comfortable English standards—but, alas, so does the cuisine. The waitresses in their demure white caps and aprons smile sweetly while serving breakfast (from 2:00 A.M. to 11:30 A.M.), lunch and dinner. The food is overpriced and banal; rarebits and shepherd's pie are disappointing. Britain's culinary reputation has not been damaged—or improved—in the colonies' version of this popular London chain. Dinner for two with wine and Godiva chocolates will run about $40.

Tony Roma's A Place for Ribs

This chain of inexpensive barbecue restaurants, begun in Florida and California, has a distinctly middle-American, family restaurant flavor, down to the plastic plates and paper menu place mats. The miniuniformed waitresses

400 E. 57th St.
308-0200
Mon. to Sat. 11:00 A.M. to 4:00
A.M.; Sun. 4:00 P.M. to 4:00 A.M.
AE, MC, V

receive three weeks' training in balancing up to six plates of tasty baby back ribs, chicken or steak up their arms; it's just what you'd expect from the man who managed Playboy bunnies twenty years ago. His Las Vegas pals, Frank Sinatra and Tony Bennett, seem to enjoy the casual atmosphere and hearty food. The onion rings are reputed to be "world famous," and we can report that this is not far from true. Bobby Cole entertains on the piano after 9:00 P.M. for those downing huge $2 drinks at the bar. Dinner is about $25 for two, with wine by the glass. Another location at 450 Sixth Avenue, near 10th Street (505-7000).

Silver Star Restaurant
1236 Second Ave.
(65th St.)
249-4250
Daily 24 hours
AE, MC, V

Near all the East Side first-run movie houses, this overgrown Greek coffee shop, with enclosed outdoor seating, has made the big time. It found the right combination to make it popular with the neighbors, who come here regularly for dinner. The decor is nautical, and the accent is on seafood, with live lobsters and soft-shell crabs in season. The menu also has every conceivable sort of sandwich, burger, salad, steak and chop, egg and omelet dish. There's a full bar with ouzo and retsina, of course. Don't touch the "tempting" desserts, revolving helplessly in an illuminated display case; they look lovely, but their taste is infinitely sad. About $10 per person for dinner.

Texarkana
64 W. 10th St.
254-5800
Supper Tues. to Sat. midnight to
4:00 A.M.
AE

After the late-night movie crowd has come here for dinner and the last of the three-piece-suit set has left, Texarkana takes on a more casual air. The bartender plays Motown music, and a younger crowd congregates at the bar. Performers and musicians come for the supper menu of Southern specialties after their shows close and savor the Gulf shrimp, barbecued pork, catfish sandwiches and fried chicken. The imaginative kitchen is not for the timid of palate or pocketbook, however. A simple supper for two will run about $30 per person.

Pizza

The American Pie
68 W. 70th St.
787-5446
Tues. to Sun. 11:00 A.M. to 10:00

Think of *mamma mia* and apple pie, and you've got it! Thick, crusty, warm-from-the-oven pies—your choice of whole wheat or white crusts—are filled with fresh, natural ingredients: cheese (sometimes too much), tomatoes, pepperoni, anchovies and so on. All the regular

P.M. (Fri. and Sat. to 11:00 P.M.)
AE, MC, V

pizza-type combinations are here, plus pesto, shrimp, ham, Swiss and tomato, garden vegetable and ricotta varieties. Tiny pies, about the size of a chicken pot pie, are $2.95; ten-inch pies are $8.50 to $13. Open-face pizzas and large stuffed pizzas are also made. It's mostly takeout, though there are one or two small tables.

Goldberg's Pizzeria
996 Second Ave.
(52nd–53rd sts.)
593-2172
Daily noon to 11:00 P.M.
No credit cards

Larry Goldberg tried 44 jobs (salesman, radio/TV announcer, stand-up comic, etc.) before he discovered that for him pizza was the total experience. Today, he is described as the Pizza King of New York, and his distinctive neon sign was selected to be part of the Smithsonian permanent collection in Washington, D.C. What distinguishes the Goldberg pizza is fresh, tasty ingredients baked in a deep pie tin, to be eaten with knife and fork. Try the SMOG pizza—sausage, mushroom, onion and green pepper—at this or two other East Side locations: 1443 York Avenue (76th Street) or 253 Third Avenue (20th–21st streets).

Pizzapiazza
785 Broadway
(10th St.)
505-0977
Daily 11:30 A.M. to 1:00 A.M. (Fri. and Sat. to 3:00 A.M.)
MC, V

On an unexpected corner in the Village you'll find this pretty, modern restaurant; its pink and white checked tablecloths, pink and green menus and pink and green sculptures dictate that this place should appeal to preppy college grads. It serves ten bland varieties of deep-dish pizza, all with a thick whole wheat crust (too heavy for our taste), a mixture of Gruyère, Locatelli Romano and mozzarella cheeses and chunky tomatoes. The bizarre assortment of toppings includes chili, "all-white" (with onions) or chicken Parmesan. Burgers, salads, soups and desserts round out the menu, with espresso and full bar choices available. The weekday lunch specials include basic pizza, salad and a drink for $4.95.

Pizza Pino
981 Third Ave.
(58th–59th St.)
688-3817
Daily 11:30 A.M. to 11:00 P.M.
MC, V

This place serves acceptable pizzas cooked in a wood oven before your eyes and a good choice of Italian dishes, all in a very New York setting: brick walls, mirrors and green plants. The pastas are recommended; you can choose from six types of sauces, including a very tasty seafood sauce. Try to be seated at the back on the ground floor, as it's much more pleasant than in front or on the second floor. Takeout service is available. A pizza dinner for two will cost $20.

Pizzeria Uno
391 Avenue of the Americas
(8th St.)
242-5230
Daily 11:00 A.M. to 1:00 A.M.

Chicago's contribution to fast food is the deep-dish pizza, and here it is. The thin-crusted, one-and-a-half-inch-high pizza comes in three sizes and more than a dozen varieties. It is baked in 20 minutes on a conveyer belt (not unlike David's cookies) in a three-story oven. A tasty individual pie with cheese is $2.45, and the special

(Thurs. to 2:00 A.M., Fri. and Sat. to 3:30 A.M.)
No credit cards

(with extra cheese, sausage, pepperoni, mushrooms, onions and green peppers) is delicious at $4.75 for one very hungry person. The young crowd orders beer or sangria by the pitcher and starts with a dish of crudites. A full menu of salads and sandwiches is served at the bar or in the main dining room until the wee hours. The place is attractively designed with dark green banquettes and ceiling, black and white tiled floors and walls, and lamps hanging above each table. Dinner for two will run from $12 to $20. Pizzas can be taken out frozen or partially or fully baked.

Ray's Pizza
**465 Avenue of the Americas
(11th St.)
243-2253**
Daily 11:00 A.M. to 2:00 A.M. (Fri. and Sat. to 3:00 A.M.)
No credit cards

In the Village, this is one of the best pizzerias among the hundreds in New York. More than two thousand people eat pizza whole or by the slice every day. This is *the* original Ray's; there are other locations throughout New York.

Sandwiches

Between the Bread
**141 E. 56th St.
888-0449**
Mon. to Fri. 8:00 A.M. to 8:30 P.M.; Sat. 8:00 A.M. to 4:00 P.M.
AE

Despite the self-service and the paper plates, these are very elegant sandwiches: filet mignon with mustard sauce on French bread, prosciutto with Brie on German pumpernickel, smoked chicken salad on raisin bread. You pick the kind of bread and what you want on it; prices run from $3.65 to $7.95. The desserts are outstanding, and the muffins with fruit are justly famous. For the same fare in more elegant surroundings (including service), visit The Café at Between the Bread, 145 West 55th Street (581-1189).

Jackson Hole Burgers
**232 E. 64th St.
371-7187**
Mon. to Sat. 10:30 A.M. to 1:00 A.M.; Sun. noon to midnight
No credit cards

Our thanks to Gerry Frank (*Where to Find It, Buy It, Eat It, in New York*) for having singled out these burgers. We won't go so far as to proclaim, as he does, that they are the best in New York. Still, they are very thick, very juicy and very well prepared—in a word, excellent. Good sandwiches too. Various locations.

Manganero's Hero Boy Restaurant

Lovingly prepared by Italian hands, these sandwiches are among the most famous and the biggest in New York. (The Champion can feed 25 people, and must, of course, be ordered in advance.) Several hot Italian dishes, rather

**492 Ninth Ave.
(38th St.)
947-7325**
Daily 6:30 A.M. to 7:30 P.M.
No credit cards

Nathan's Famous

**1482 Broadway
(Times Square at
43rd St.)
382-0620**
*Daily 7:00 A.M. to 2:00 A.M. (Fri.
to Sun. to 4:00 A.M.)*
No credit cards

Nyborg Nelson

**Citicorp Center
153 W. 53rd St.
223-0700**
*Mon. to Fri. 11:30 A.M. to
9:00 P.M.; Sat. and Sun. noon to
6:00 P.M.*
All major credit cards

nondescript (although the place boasts of having served Frank Sinatra a meal), are also offered.

When Eddie Cantor and Jimmy Durante, singing waiters at nearby night spots, used to drop in after work at Ida and Nathan Handwerker's pint-size snack bar in Coney Island, the all-beef hot dog was five cents. Sixty-five years later, Nathan's is big business (a dozen locations in the metropolitan area and franchises in Florida and California), and the original hot dog is 89 cents.

At the cavernous Times Square location, cafeteria-style counters offer hamburgers, pizzas, chili con carne, fresh littleneck and cherrystone clams, deep-fried chicken and seafood, deli meats, ice cream (Good Humor), domestic beers and soft drinks. The meats are available to take out either in sandwiches or by weight, a quarter pound and up. Everything is self-service, but there is table seating on street level and, by escalator, a floor below. Prices are right, even if the environment is a bit tawdry and some of the fried items are not as crisp as they might be. Stick to Nathan's original and a cold glass of beer.

A cornucopia of smoked fish (herring, salmon, trout), Scandinavian cheeses, open-face sandwiches and Viennese pastries are dished up in a hurry for the Citicorp lunch crowd. Some rush in for takeout, but the more sensible ones have their gravlax at the comfortable tables. A Scandinavian sandwich and a glass of wine will set you back $8.

Tea Rooms · Pastries

The Barclay Terrace

**Hotel
Inter-Continental
111 E. 48th St.
755-5900**
*Tea Mon. to Sat. 3:00 P.M. to
5:00 P.M.*
All major credit cards

Yes, the parrots still squawk in the famous bird cage of the former Barclay Hotel lobby. The balcony comfortably seats 100, overlooking the quietly sedate room with plush leather sofas and beautiful flower arrangements on gilt-leg tables. Afternoon tea, at $9.50 a person, is handsomely served in individual Rosenthal china pots; forgettable finger sandwiches come on silver platters, scones are accompanied by whipped cream and strawberry jam, and the huge pastries are excellent. The

Barclay blend, a Darjeeling tea, is the best, and it's available in eight-ounce tins from the maître d'hôtel. This is the place to come with your banker, your broker or the executor of your rich uncle's estate.

Eclair
141 W. 72nd St.
873-7700
Daily 8:00 A.M. to midnight
No credit cards

Middle Europeans have been coming here since World War II for authentic pastry in the Austro-Hungarian tradition. Follow their lead, make your way to the back room and indulge in at least one helping of opera torte, rigo torte (if you can pass by the temptations spread before you on the bakery counter) or Grand Marnier cake. No one will flinch if you ask for a side order of whipped cream with your Sacher torte and coffee. The older clientele starts coming for dinner at 4:30 P.M., when the menu adds more substantial entrees. We prefer to come for dessert after a concert at Lincoln Center or in Central Park. About $6 for two people.

Furnished Room
(American Stanhope Hotel)
Fifth Avenue and 81st Street
288-5800
Tea daily 3:00 P.M. to 6:00 P.M.
All major credit cards

The only reason to come here is to see how Laura Ashley might furnish your wood-paneled living room. The blue-gray wall coverings, shirt-fabric-slipcovered chairs and charming curtains go perfectly with fresh flowers and English ironstone dishes. The waitresses, dressed in tidy black dresses and white pinafore aprons, don't hold up the high English tea standard, and neither does the food. There's a choice of six tea bags with a half pot of water, scones without cream, dry, thick tea sandwiches and pastries we have had little desire to try. If you must come here, relax on the sofas and enjoy a light snack or drink. Sandwiches and tea will run about $8 per person.

Helmsley Palace Hotel
455 Madison Ave.
(50th–51st sts.)
888-7000
Tea daily 2:30 P.M. to 5:30 P.M.
All major credit cards

The Gold Room is an opulent setting for afternoon tea. Gilt in Renaissance style from the floor to the spectacular arched ceiling, it served as financier Henry Villard's music room at the turn of the century. Today a harpist plays on the balcony from 2:30 to 5:30 P.M. while weary Fifth Avenue shoppers unwind on golden settees. The $12 prix fixe menu includes a choice of fifteen teas, undistinguished sandwiches, correct scones served with whipped cream and raspberry jam, excellent fruitcake and modest fruit tarts. If it's available, try the superb nut cake. Tea can be taken in the adjacent noisier and brighter Madison Room, once Villard's drawing room. Both rooms are also open for breakfast, lunch and late evening snacks.

The King's Angel
119 E. 74th St.

The Parish House of the Church of the Resurrection may seem a most unlikely place to have tea. But it's the best spot for a cuppa in the city. For an incredible $3.75, an English lady—the rector's secretary—prepares traditional

879-4320
*Tea Sat. and Sun. 3:00 P.M. to
5:00 P.M.*

scones with strawberry jam and with whipped or Devon cream, lemon curd, fruit tarts and shortbread. In cool weather, tea is served in the rector's living room, with its warm fireplace, overstuffed furniture and soft classical music. On sunny summer weekends, the tables are moved outdoors.

The Konditorei
Fay & Allen's Food Halls
1241 Third Ave. (71st St.)
794-1101
*Daily 8:00 A.M. to 11:00 P.M. (Fri. and Sat. to 12:30 A.M., Sun. to 10:30 P.M.)
All major credit cards*

It's hard to choose among 150 desserts, from 25 New York bakers, when they all look so fresh and appetizing. Suppliers include Gindi, Carousel, Eclair, Ratchik (four varieties of rugalach), Taste (chocolate walnut cake), Warren (ten-layer cinnamon mousse cake, apple ginger tart) and son Mark's own chocolate soufflé cake. For sweet-toothed customers watching their weight, there are even dietetic cherry and apple strudels. Frozen yogurt and tofutti, omelets, croissant sandwiches, platters from the takeout delicatessen and cheese section next door and soda fountain treats round out the menu. About $4.50 per person.

Lanciani
271 W. 4th St. (Perry St.)
929-0739
*Tues. to Thurs. 8:00 A.M. to 11:00 P.M.; Fri. and Sat. 8:00 A.M. to midnight; Sun. 8:00 A.M. to 7:00 P.M.
No credit cards*

On a quiet street in the West Village, this delicious bakery now has thirteen tables for the faithful customers who line up before 8:00 A.M. to have croissants, danish, muffins and pains au chocolat with their morning cappuccinos or espressos. It's hard to resist the pastry, cookies or cakes in the spanking clean, white tiled shop. The truffles (at $20 a pound) are notorious, and we have developed a hopeless addiction to the Sacher torte. About $4 per person.

The Mayfair Lounge
The Mayfair Regent Park Avenue at 65th Street
288-0800
*Tea daily 3:00 P.M. to 6:00 P.M
All major credit cards*

The Mayfair Regent has to be one of the most elegant places to have tea in the city. The coffered ceiling, tufted love seats and comfortable chairs in burnt sienna, deep coral and champagne harmonize with the beautiful floral centerpiece. Tea is as it should be—a choice of seven blends, accompanied by paper-thin finger sandwiches and scones with whipped cream and raspberry preserves, for $8 a person. The waitresses, attractively dressed in long black skirts and high-necked white blouses, serve tea in Richard-Ginori china, and thoughtfully provide a tea cozy to keep the pot warm. French pastry, cakes, ice cream, excellent coffee and cocktails are also available.

Palm Court
Plaza Hotel
Fifth Ave. and 59th St.
759-3000
Tea Mon. to Fri. 3:30 P.M. to 8:00 P.M.; Sat. and Sun. 4:00 P.M. to 8:00 P.M.

A tantalizing display of cakes, mousses, fresh strawberries and whipped cream greets you as you enter the columned court off the well-trafficked hotel lobby. The leisurely strains of the violin and piano remind you that no one is in a rush here. You can linger over your cocktails or tea, pastries or uninspired open sandwiches, sundaes or cakes until dinner time. Schmaltzy music

All major credit cards

Guy Pascal les Délices

939 First Ave. (51st-52nd sts.) 371-4144

Daily 8:00 A.M. to 10:00 P.M.
AE, DC

Very good

Rumple-mayer's

46 Central Park South 755-5800

Daily 7:00 A.M. to 12:30 A.M.
All major credit cards

St. Honoré

235 E. 57th St. 355-6478

Mon. to Fri. 9:00 A.M. to 7:00 P.M.; Sat. 9:00 A.M. to 5:00 P.M.
No credit cards

lovers seem happy in the pseudo-Viennese atmosphere until closing at midnight, when they must finally venture forth from underneath the ubiquitous potted palms. About $8 per person.

The former pastry chef of La Côte Basque has brought his exquisite cookies and cakes to the site of the old Elysée pastry shop and added ten tables for snacking and a hardy espresso machine. He opens early enough for a Continental breakfast of fresh orange juice and wonderful apple turnovers, switching to salads and sandwiches at lunch and dinner, with ice cream sundaes and pastries in between. The best dessert is still the Délice cake, with its layers of almond meringue, chocolate mousse, whipped cream and mocha butter cream frosting, topped with toasted almonds (at $3.75, it's worth every penny). After splitting up with his partner (who continues to serve the same savories and sweets at Désirs la Côte Basque on Lexington Avenue), Pascal continues to maintain his patisserie at the Olympic Tower, a disappointing concession at Zabar's and a new branch at Madison Avenue and 89th Street. Given all these choices, we still prefer the Lexington Avenue locale for its rustic ambience. About $6.50 per person.

This kitschy 1950s pink tea room offers pastries, ice cream and winsome waitresses in pink and red pinafores. The fake marble and real mirrors please the little girls and boys who ogle the stuffed animals by the soda fountain or drool over ice cream sundaes. The best buy is the superb hot chocolate served in a silver pot with a bowl of real whipped cream. At other times the menu includes soups, salads and sandwiches for those who prefer the atmosphere and prices to those of the more pompous restaurants in the nearby St. Moritz Hotel. About $13 per person.

At last, a Swiss patisserie/café has opened in New York. Not as sweet as French pastry, these cakes are often laced with liqueurs. Individual Mont Blanc and St. Honoré pastries are prepared to perfection; cakes, tarts, cookies and excellent chocolates (André Bollier, a Swiss, produces these in Kansas City) can be eaten here or taken home. At breakfast, the danish are particularly popular, especially puffed cheese buns, preserve-filled almond crescents and pinwheel schnecken. During the day you can enjoy fine salads, cold meats and pâtés, smoked trout and—joy of joys—the famous paper-thin air-dried beef from the Grisons. Expect the Swiss to serve Grapillon grape juice, Moussy (alcohol-free) beer and Perrier water, as well as cappuccino, espresso, tea and hot chocolate. About $5 per person for tea and $12 for lunch.

The Waldorf Cocktail Terrace

(Waldorf-Astoria Hotel)
Park Avenue and 50th Street
872-4818
Tea daily 2:30 P.M. to 5:00 P.M.
All major credit cards

Tea is now served on the art deco terrace overlooking the restored Park Avenue lobby of the Waldorf, with its mosaic floor and painted murals. The tea trolley, brought to your sofa and table, has an exotic choice of loose teas: apple mint, apricot, black currant, Darjeeling, mango or "amorous almond." The pinwheel tea sandwiches and petits fours are unexciting; the fruit tart is a more satisfying choice than the gugelhupf or coffee cake. Clearly no English lady has counseled this noble hotel, as there is no strawberry jam or cream to accompany the scones. Cocktails and piano music also soothe ruffled sensibilities on the terrace from 2:30 P.M. to 1:00 A.M. Expect to pay $7 for tea and sandwiches.

THE NIGHTLIFE

The Nightlife

All Night Long

Many visitors think New York's nightlife is about as safe and amusing as Calcutta's is. These people would never venture downtown, preferring to play it safe in the uptown clubs and cabarets. We can report that not only is most of the action downtown, it's also safe to commute there to tap dance the night away. The visual stimulation is enriching (if you don't mind the punked-out style still hanging on in the above-ground underground), and the music can be fantastic; a sense of humor is always helpful. We love New York at night, because the city never sleeps—even if you're thrown out of your favorite club at 4:00 in the morning, there are still the all-night diners and cafés to keep you from going home. We would love to write about everything New York's night has to offer, but it would fill an entire book, which would be out of date as soon as it was published. It is our sincere regret that so many wonderful places may have closed by the time this guide is printed. But rest assured: their replacements will no doubt be just as entertaining and provocative. If some of our favorites have already passed on to the other side, we apologize for building up your expectations; always be sure to call first!

Bars

Joe Allen's
326 W. 46th St.
581-6464
Daily noon to 3:00 A.M.
MC, V

Thespians and partisans alike pack the bar and tables of this New York institution. They come to see and be seen by each other and to exchange views (reviews?) of the Great White Way.

Auction's
1406 Third Ave.
(80th St.)
535-2333
Nightly 5:00 P.M. to 1:00 A.M.
(Sun. to 11:00 P.M.)
Two-drink minimum
All major credit cards

A very civilized bar complete with piano entertainment and walls covered with Sotheby Parke Bernet catalog pages. The older, more sophisticated Upper East Side crowd here no doubt chooses Auction for its tranquil alternative to the driving primal beat of the singles scene.

Beach Café

**1326 Second Ave.
(70th St.)
988-7299**

*Mon. to Thurs. 11:30 A.M. to 1:30
A.M.; Fri. and Sat. 11:30 A.M. to
2:00 A.M.*
No credit cards

If you wear your oxford cloth shirts buttoned down, your shetland sweaters knotted around your shoulders, your jeans authentically faded, your blond hair in a ponytail and your Topsiders scuffed, then you'll feel right at home at the Beach. This neighborhood place is filled with attractive local residents who meet under the ceiling fans and around the old wood bar to swap stories about the office and the Hamptons.

Bowlmor Lanes

**110 University Pl.
(12th St.)
255-8188**

Mon. to Wed. midnight to 5:00 A.M.
Admission charge varies
No credit cards

You can bowl all night long at this shabby, low-lit bowling alley, and there are two bars and lots of loud music to help you keep your mind off the game. The crowd is mixed—everything from celebs to debs—and one thing is certain: no one comes here to strike out.

Café Central

**384 Columbus Ave.
(78th St.)
724-9187**

Daily 11:45 A.M. to 3:00 A.M.
AE, MC, V

You'll find all the old regulars in the front room and squeezed in at the bar at the new Café Central; they faithfully migrated north to the handsome new roost on Columbus. The decor is simple but chic: beautifully finished mahogany details deep red ceilings and the standard exposed brick walls. The attractive actors and actresses that frequent the Central are still sought after by hopeful groupies of both sexes. The classic scene continues to continue, and you'll no doubt have a great time observing and becoming a part of it any night of the week.

Carumba!

**684 Broadway
(W. 3rd St.)
420-9817**

Daily noon to midnight
All major credit cards

You have to squeeze your way through the throngs of pinstriped young men and women in order to find your way to the bar and sample one of the birdbath-size margaritas. The noise level is deafening, the atmosphere highly kinetic and the crowd very pretty. We can only assume Upper East Siders come here to meet their neighbors and share taxis back uptown.

Charley O's

**33 W. 48th St.
582-7141**

*Mon. to Fri. noon to 3:00 P.M. and
5:00 P.M. to 11:30 P.M.; Sat. 4:30
P.M. to 11:30 P.M.*
All major credit cards

A sign outside proclaims "Bar, Grill and Bar," which gives you an idea of the priorities here. It's an attractive, typically New York saloon frequented by the happy-hour set from the office buildings on Madison and Fifth. The crowd is handsome and cheerful; the men hover near the bar, while women cluster at the tables off to the side. A food bar serves sandwiches and snacks to accompany the liquid refreshments.

Chinese Chance

**1 University Pl.
(8th St.)**

Struggling artists found a safe harbor in this downtown bar/restaurant, and some of their works eventually appeared on its walls. This is the last in a long line of famous and infamous watering holes started by the late

677-4440
Daily noon to 4:00 A.M.
All major credit cards

Mickey Ruskin, founder of Max's Kansas City. The crowd here often includes luminaries of the art and music worlds, who hold court at the comfortable but bland and unadorned tables. The music played on the scratchy stereo is excellent . It's worth a late-night visit, but the regulars say things won't be the same without Mickey.

City Lights Bar
World Trade Center
938-1111
Daily 3:00 P.M. to 1:00 A.M. (Sun. to 9:00 P.M.)
Cover charge varies
All major credit cards

A drink. Soft music. Plush comfort. A view from atop New York's tallest, offering a unique geographic perspective. Some say it's a long way to go for a drink, while others come again and again. We think the latter group shows the better judgment.

P.J. Clarke's
915 Third Ave.
(55th St.)
355-8857
Daily noon to 4:00 A.M.
No credit cards

How long will owner Daniel Lavezzo be able to refuse the offers to buy his landmark New York saloon? Doesn't he feel a little lonely in this small brick house, dwarfed among the megabuildings in the neighborhood? We hope he doesn't lose his resistance, because we would then lose one of the most typical of New York places, which continues to charm us with its genuine character. Apparently we're not alone, because so many East Side types pack this place at lunch, at happy hour and on into the evening. In fact, everybody in New York has gone, is going or will go to P.J. Clarke's: writers, bankers, executives, artists from all neighborhoods.
Why not you?

Costello's
225 E. 44th St.
599-9614
Mon. to Fri. 11:30 A.M. to 2:00 A.M.
All major credit cards

Costello's is a nondescript drinking man's bar whose claim to fame is regular Jimmy Breslin. It fills up after work with a noisy crowd from the *Daily News* and other nearby offices.

Dobson's
341 Columbus Ave.
(W. 76th St.)
362-0100
Daily 11:30 A.M. to 12:30 A.M. (Fri. and Sat. to 1:30 A.M.)
AE, MC, V

While the upwardly mobile chichi fill up Ruelle's, a more casual crowd keeps Dobson's busy. This East Side-looking establishment with its brick walls, sidewalk seating and substantial bar is popular with West Siders who drop in after work or come out prowling for conversation and company during the evening. It's a lively place with a pleasant clientele. The food is predictably bar boring.

Ernie's
2150 Broadway
(76th St.)
496-1588
Daily noon to 1:00 A.M.
All major credit cards

This West Side restaurant/bar has a noise level so high that sign language is the only effective way to communicate. Yet the crowds keep coming for table space, bar space—any space—in this popular hangar-size establishment. Is it the food? (Pizzas, pastas and other things Italian.) The conversation? (Raise one finger for yes and two for no.) Our best guess would be that they come here for each other, which means this could become the new champion of the West Side singles scene.

Garvin's
19 Waverly Pl.
473-5261
Daily 11:30 A.M. to 12:30 A.M.
AE, MC, V

A cozy, comfortable Village bar with lots of burnished wood, green plants and mirrors. A well-dressed, uptown crowd comes here to nibble on clams and oysters while listening to the pianist play the usual show tunes. There's a different house wine every month, and it's usually very good. A pleasant place for a relaxed drink.

Gramercy Park Hotel Bar
2 Lexington Ave.
(21st St.)
475-4320
Daily 11:00 A.M. to 1:00 A.M.
All major credit cards

Few will go out of their way to come to this neighborhood sanctuary, and that's one of the reasons we find it interesting. Once opulent, now slightly seedy, this off-key watering hole caters to the tastes of neighborhood regulars and eccentric hotel guests. The music is off-key too: an old trouper murders all the old favorites while accompanying herself on an out-of-tune piano. Sometimes it's the last place in the world you would want to be. But other times it all comes together, making this a perfect spot for an early- or late-evening rendezvous.

Hard Rock Café
221 W. 57th St.
489-6565
Open daily 11:30 A.M. to 4:00 A.M.
AE, MC, V

Is it possible that these stylishly dressed young people with their blasé looks and roving eyes have nowhere else to go? The throngs here are as immobile as the Port Authority at rush hour, but these night owls apparently don't care, and prefer to pack themselves in at the bar where conversation is impossible because of the sonic boom soundtrack. It seems they are content with seeing and being seen as they down yet another long-necked bottle of beer in the hopes that Mr. Right or Ms. Perfect will wander into their periphery. It's an entertaining show here run by the youthful entrepreneurs who staff the place and are gracious and cheerful as they help you squeeze the troops in the entry after you have finally gained passage from the queue on the street. For the lowdown on what's really happening here, send a friend to ladies' room to catch a conversation of high school vintage on how to handle a hungry man and the prospects of dating one's father's friends. The Hard Rock is a place whose time has come to infuse New York with some good old-fashioned teenage Americana.

Harvey's Chelsea Restaurant
108 W. 18th St.
243-5644

Dick Harvey has done a commendable job of restoring this old Chelsea saloon so it glows with an abundance of rich mahogany and good cheer. The woodwork and etched glass behind the bar are especially beautiful. It's a lively and friendly spot that has become a popular after-

Daily noon to midnight
No credit cards

work meeting place; the three-piece-suit set shares the bar with local artists and intellectuals. The back room serves good English/American pub fare for those who require more than liquid sustenance.

Hoexter's Market
1442 Third Ave.
(81st-82nd sts.)
472-9322
Nightly 5:30 P.M. to 4:00 A.M.
All major credit cards

This market is of the meat variety. The place is packed with dark-suited, Paul Stuart–tied young men lining the bar and silk- and pearls-dressed women hugging the walls. They get together on the dance floor, at one of the round tables for inedible food or at the bar to scream at each other over the music with their distinctive singles' mating calls. Upper East Siders at their best.

Holbrook's
1313 Third Ave.
(75th-76th sts.)
734-2050
Nightly 6:30 P.M. to 2:00 A.M.
AE, MC, V

A sophisticated decor ('20s posters, black columns and an illuminated bar) makes Holbrook's a tranquil island of urbanity. You'll find some attractive people here, from after-work socializers to black-tie revelers. It's not the most active singles bar in town, but a pleasant place to regroup for the next round of Third Avenue bars.

Landmark Tavern
626 Eleventh Ave.
(46th St.)
757-8595
Daily noon to midnight (Fri. and
Sat. to 1:00 A.M.)
No credit cards

The Landmark is quite the place to be on Saturday afternoon, when uptowners stop by after a day of shopping and settle in by the wood-burning stove to quench their thirsts. It's a beautiful, classic Irish tavern that was carefully restored by Dick Harvey, owner of Harvey's Chelsea Restaurant. Built in the 1880s, this congenial pub is worth a visit for both the handsome decor and the convivial crowd.

Lion's Head
59 Christopher St.
(Seventh Avenue
South)
929-0670
Daily noon to 4:00 A.M.
All major credit cards

Don't turn away when you enter the Lion's Head and at first see only a small bar filled with rather scruffy local oddballs. Continue on into the comfortable, simple back room, where a very Village crowd discusses art and ideas—or the latest gossip—over good tap beers (McSorley's, Bass and Guinness, to name a few). There's a surprisingly complex blackboard menu that offers the likes of gazpacho, Chinese-style conch soup, roast duck with black currants and fettuccine with vodka and caviar.

Maxwell's Plum
1181 First Ave.
(64th St.)
628-2100
Daily noon to 1:30 A.M.
All major credit cards

An acquaintance of ours was waiting for his friend recently at Maxwell's, which, as usual, was packed with lively (desperate?) singles. After ten minutes, a young lady who had been eyeing him snapped, "What's the matter with you? You're not talking to anyone." Maxwell's bar is an absolute must for anyone's debut in New York. The word *shy* isn't in the vocabulary here, and people will talk to you whether you're interested or not. It's a one of a kind, and we've seen far too many imitators.

Jim McMullen
**1341 Third Ave.
(76th-77th sts.)
861-4700**
*Daily 11:30 A.M. to 4:00 A.M.
AE*

This lively bar would have been the perfect place for a scene in a Woody Allen movie during his *Annie Hall* stage. You can just imagine him here meeting his current passion, who is enjoying herself among some very tall and beefy gentlemen. McMullen's is a favorite hangout for basketball, football, hockey and tennis players. Sports fans and ex-models are welcome; dwarf-size intellectuals might prefer to stay home. The place is always crowded, popular and full of pretty girls.

McSorley's Old Ale House
**15 E. 7th St.
473-8800**
*Daily 11:00 A.M. to 1:00 A.M.
No credit cards*

Perhaps the most amusing and entertaining bar in New York. No singles scene here—it's devoted to the hard-core enjoyment of McSorley's ale, which goes down like water. The neighborhood clientele loves to get singing on holidays, and we love the hard-boiled eggs and sandwiches, the crazy, cluttered decor, the marvelous bartenders and its taste and touch of old New York. One of our favorites.

Meriken
**162 W. 21st St
620-9684**
*Nightly 6:00 P.M. to midnight
(Sun. to 11:00 P.M.)
Minimum $7.50
AE*

The cuisine is Japanese. The decor is New Wave. The nose is unbearable. Dilettantes and "Old Wavers" in new clothes love it here, but the table turnover is extremely slow, and so is the endless line at the one-person-at-a-time restrooms. What you need most here is patience.

Odeon
**145 W. Broadway
(Thomas St.)
233-0507**
*Daily noon to 4:00 A.M.
AE, MC, V*

The "real hip" come here to trade insults and compliments. It's a favorite hangout for artists and dealers (and their groupie attendants); veterans of "Saturday Night Live" have been spotted here too. The bar and table scene is active yet low-key, though it's becoming more frantic all the time as more and more people strive to be "real hip."

One Fifth Avenue
**1 Fifth Ave.
(8th St.)
260-3434**
*Daily noon to 1:45 A.M. (Fri. and
Sat. to 2:45 A.M.)
Minimum $6.50 Fri. and Sat.
All major credit cards*

This nautical wonderland takes itself too seriously, but, fortunately, the people who come here don't. The too-noisy crowd (there always seems to be a crowd) is a pleasant mix of young singles and couples; music is usually supplied by an endearing jazz trio (with vocalist Phoebe Legere) or pianist. No one goes overboard.

Oren and Aretsky
**1497 Third Ave.
(84th-85th sts.)
734-8822**
*Nightly 6:00 P.M. to 4:00 A.M.
AE*

A handsome purple neon sign guides you into this attractive gray Belle Epoque watering hole, which is brightened with art posters. On some nights the crowd is the hottest in town; on others it seems that everyone has left to check out Hoexter's or Wilson's. A good place nonetheless to see attractive uptown singles work it out in style.

Pete's Tavern

129 E. 18th St.
(Irving Pl.)
473-7676
Daily 9:30 A.M. to 2:00 A.M. (Fri. and Sat. to 3:00 A.M.)
All major credit cards

As the menus, matches and several signs continually remind you, this is the tavern "O. Henry made famous." It's also the oldest original tavern in New York (established in 1864). Young SoHo denizens, local priests and middle-aged regulars love Pete's for its comfort, history and unpretentiousness; you won't find lots of hustling singles here. In the back there's a dining room serving Italian food, but we prefer to stay in the handsome bar to nibble on good potato skins while soaking up a little of old New York.

Prince Street Bar

125 Prince St.
(Wooster St.)
228-8130
Daily noon to 2:00 A.M. (Fri. and Sat to 3:00 A.M.)
No credit cards

You'll find SoHo residents lunching on sandwiches (many prepared in pita), snacking on everything from ceviche and guacamole to burgers and ribs, and dining on a selection of Indonesian dishes. The high ceilings, maroon walls, mismatched mirrors and ceiling fans provide the decor, and the clientele provides the high energy level. You can get Prince Street Bar T-shirts here, if you're so inclined. You're bound to run into someone interesting, particularly in the late hours of the night.

Redbar

116 First Ave.
(7th St.)
No telephone
Nightly 4:00 P.M. to 4:00 A.M.
No credit cards

This place has stayed "in" for an unusually long time—trendy young New Wave places often have a very short life expectancy. It's a corner bar not far from St. Mark's Place that has the ultimate in chic—no sign or identifying marks outside—and looks more like an abandoned diner than a bar. The patrons are young but surprisingly diverse, from button-down preppies to purple-haired punks. It's crowded and uncomfortable, but it's one of *the* places to be.

Rick's 181 Lounge

181 Eighth Ave.
(19th St.)
691-9845
Nightly 4:00 P.M. to 4:00 A.M.
AE

Step back into the '50s with live popular piano music (from 6:00 P.M.) and a witty decor that's all in fun—pink and white clouds and lots of mirrors. The waiters and waitresses move about the crammed tiny tables in tacky black outfits, serving serendipitous Tex-Mex food in appetizer and full-scale portions. The big drinks have questionable names: a Creamsicle contains vanilla Häagen-Dazs, orange juice and vodka; Montezuma's Secret is prune juice and tequila; Janitor in a Drum has vodka, brandy and crème de cacao. Susan Trilling's praiseworthy kitchen closes at midnight Sunday to Thursday, at 1:00 A.M. on Friday and Saturday.

Ruelles

321 Columbus Ave.
(75th St.)
799-5100
Daily 11:00 A.M. to 2:00 A.M. (Fri. and Sat. to 4:00 A.M.)
All major credit cards

Once upon a time there was a modest clothing and gift boutique with a small area on the second floor serving desserts, cappuccino and teas. But the little West Side boutique couldn't resist the chance to become *the* East Side–style singles bar. It gobbled up space from surrounding businesses and grew into a large, gaudy bar/restaurant that attracted so many people they spilled onto the sidewalks (which were eventually glassed in). This is still *the* place, and it might be worth checking out before it loses its title.

Le Saloon
1920 Broadway
(64th St.)
874-1500
Daily 11:30 A.M. to 4:00 A.M.
All major credit cards

Location is everything, and this bustling bar/restaurant has it. Just across the street from the Lincoln Center complex, it attracts hordes of theatergoers, actors and on-the-town tourists. In an effort to please them all, the menu lists scores of items and the loud music bounces from one genre to another. It's crowded, colorful and noisy—and sometimes it works, sometimes it doesn't.

Swell's
1439 York Ave.
(76th St.)
879-0900
Mon. and Tues. 6:30 P.M. to 2:00 A.M.; Wed. 6:30 P.M. to 3:00 A.M.; Thurs. to Sat. 6:30 P.M. to 4:00 A.M.
AE, MC, V

Another popular preppy bar filled with trust fund babies taking it easy after a hard day of high finance. The polo theme coordinates with the clientele's fashion code, and most serious drinkers here have their own brands ready and waiting. The '50s music from the jukebox keeps everyone rocking 'n' rolling, and the slightly noblesse oblige downscale decor lets these pretty people sparkle like their Tiffany diamonds in the rough.

Tap a Keg
330 Columbus Ave.
(75th-76th sts.)
874-8593
Daily 2:00 P.M. to 4:00 A.M.
No credit cards

This is the kind of neighborhood bar you'd expect to find in Montana. It occasionally gets down and dirty, but its pool-playing, beer-drinking clientele calls it home, and the management calls it "a hell of a joint." In any case, it's full of local color and is a good place to visit if you're stouthearted.

T.G.I. Friday's
1152 First Ave.
(63rd St.)
832-8512
Daily 11:30 A.M. to 1:30 A.M. (Fri. and Sat. to 3:00 A.M.)
All major credit cards

This venerable institution is still going strong, catering to the bridge and tunnel crowd. It does an impressive business, with a fairly young clientele filling the Belle Epoque place and eating the burgers and specials. The fashionably chic avoid this spot, but the ambience is lively if you go for basic tradition.

Top of the Sixes
666 Fifth Ave.
(53rd. St.)
757-6662
Mon. to Thurs. 11:30 A.M. to midnight; Fri. and Sat. 11:30 A.M. to 1:00 A.M.
All major credit cards

This senior citizen still offers an excellent bird's-eye view of New York, but that's about all. The entire interior was recently redesigned to attract a broader and younger crowd. It worked, but everything still feels dated: the decor, the food and even the young crowd. Fortunately, you can have the view for the price of a drink.

Uzie's
1442 Third Ave.
(82nd St.)
744-8020
Nightly 6:00 P.M. to 12:30 A.M.
All major credit cards

Everyone in this beautiful, low-lit establishment is beautiful and low lit. We thought we might have to audition before buying a drink. If you like that feeling (many do), you will enjoy yourself here.

Wilson's
1444 First Ave.
(75th St.)
861-0320
Nightly 6:00 P.M. to 4:00 A.M.
AE, CB, DC

One of *the* hot places on the Upper East Side. You may have to wait outdoors to get into this little turn-of-the-century-style place, always crowded with attractive people who have a hungry look in their eyes. The music is loud and the crush rather like the subway's, but with so much body heat you're bound to meet someone to drink with.

Cabarets · Comedy

Asti
13 E. 12th St.
741-9105
Tues. to Thurs. 5:00 P.M. to 12:30 A.M.; Fri. and Sat. 5:00 P.M. to 1:00 A.M.
No cover charge
All major credit cards

Drop in here for a touch of old-time charm, when the waiters and regulars take their stands and sing Broadway and operatic classics. It's a good time, and the clientele loves to join in and sing a few rounds, too. The walls are completely covered with photos of past divas and opera stars, the coloring is very red, the service is friendly, and the evening will be a lark if you bring some good friends who have a sense of humor.

The Ballroom
253 W. 28th St.
244-3005
Tues. to Sun. noon to 1:00 A.M.; shows 6:30 P.M., 9:00 P.M. and 11:00 P.M.
Cover charge varies
AE, MC, V

In its new, expanded quarters, this former SoHo cabaret/restaurant has become a miniature entertainment complex. A large cabaret is in the back, with a theater downstairs. Up front is the restaurant, with its grand two-tiered bar. It's all done with style and a lot of class. Certainly worth a visit.

Caroline's
332 Eighth Ave.
(26th St.)
924-3499
Tues. to Sun. 5:00 P.M. to 3:00 A.M.
Cover charge varies
AE, MC, V

This handsome comedy club is generally filled with very attractive young people who have a healthy sense of humor. The comedians who play here are first-rate, and you may see some of the "Saturday Night Live" crowd (audience as well as performers). There is a two-drink minimum and cover, but if the talent is good the 90-minute show will make your time and money well spent (call ahead to see who's scheduled). The active bar scene here attracts Chelsea residents and good-humored people from all over town.

Dangerfield's
1118 First Ave.
(61st St.)
593-1650
Shows Mon. to Thurs. 9:00 P.M. and 11:15 P.M.; Fri. 9:00 P.M. and 11:30 P.M.; Sat. 9:00 P.M. and midnight; bar closes at 4:00 A.M.
Cover charge varies
All major credit cards

There are many places where comedian Rodney Dangerfield gets no respect, but this isn't one of them. Here he is king and frequently holds court before SRO crowds that need only to laugh more than anything else. The place isn't the same when Rodney isn't present, but the singing and comedic talents who fill in deserve their share of respect.

Duplex
55 Grove St.
(Christopher St.)
255-5438
Nightly 4:00 P.M. to 4:00 A.M.
Cover charge $5; two-drink
minimum
No credit cards

A lot of nobodies became somebodies at this famous Greenwich Village cabaret/piano bar—Woody Allen, Joan Rivers, Rodney Dangerfield and so on—so naturally it's a magnet to the many unknown talents looking for a break. You might see some of tomorrow's stars here, or even become one yourself if you take part in the sing-along that unfolds every Saturday night around the downstairs piano bar.

Freddy's
308 E. 49th St.
888-1633
Nightly 6:30 P.M. to 4:00 A.M.;
shows nightly 8:30 P.M. and
11:00 P.M.
Cover charge varies
AE, MC, V

Female impersonator Charles Pierce gets top billing at this cabaret, and he deserves it. With his dazzling display of comic disguises and impressions, he steals the show. Even the real females who perform here sometimes look to Mr. Pierce for pointers.

O'Neals' 43rd Street
147 W. 43rd St.
764-6200
Shows Tues. to Thurs. 8:00 P.M.;
Fri. and Sat. 8:00 P.M. and
10:30 P.M.
Cover charge varies
All major credit cards

Some mighty big talents have taken over the small stage of this midtown cabaret. Martin Charnin, the director and lyricist of the award-winning *Annie,* staged his long-running musical revue *Upstairs at O'Neals'* here. Downstairs, the bar/lounge teems with theater types.

Palsson's
158 W. 72nd St.
595-7400
Nightly showtimes vary
Cover charge and minimum vary
All major credit cards

This delightful cabaret seems misplaced, surrounded by fast-food joints and pedestrian traffic that sometimes looks like it belongs in Times Square. Fortunately it's better than its environment, particularly the musical comedies, which are far above average. Once inside, you'll quickly forget the outside.

Panache
Magic Pan
1409 Sixth Ave.
(57th St.)
765-5080
Shows 8:30 and 11:30 P.M.
Cover charge varies
AE, MC, V

The musical revues and solo acts at this large cabaret/restaurant serve as a showcase for the talented multitudes who beat the pavements of New York City. It's a great place for them to show what they can do and a fair place to spend a rather predictable evening.

Pyramid Club
101–103 Avenue A
(6th–7th sts.)
No telephone
Daily 4:00 P.M. to 4:00 A.M.

It is advisable that when visiting this tourist attraction (the tent sign outside the obscure entry invites all tourists to come on in), one should be well versed in the intricacies and finer points of *Chang in a Void Moon*. This cosmic soap opera (performed in the back room) has captured the hearts and imaginations of a loyal young following dressed primarily in black and sporting crewcuts, '50s oversized shirts and that slightly bored New Wave demeanor. It is also not advisable to wear

233

white, as the ultraviolet lights will make you look like some sort of huge floating cloud. It will also compete with the tropical decor of tastefully hand-painted animals and zebra stripes, and one wall filled with what may only be described as subway graffiti. You will be sure to run into someone interesting with whom to have a disjointed but rather stimulating conversation and drink tap beer crowded next to other members of the Pyramid Club.

Sweetwater's
**170 Amsterdam Ave.
(68th St.)
873-4100**
*Nightly 4:00 P.M. to 3:00 A.M.
Cover charge $5 weeknights, $10
weekends
All major credit cards*

Located in the Lincoln Center area, this beautiful multilevel cabaret/bar/restaurant could easily have been done by the same designer as the center. People dress up to come here and look at each other or themselves (there are mirrors everywhere), and sometimes they even pay attention to the entertainers, who are always good and deserve to be looked at.

Dancing · Nightclubs

CBGB
**315 Bowery
(Bleecker St.)
982-4052**
*Nightly 8:30 P.M. to 2:30 A.M.
Cover charge varies
No credit cards*

Punk rock first surfaced in New York at this Lower East Side club, and for many current name acts, this was once the only place they could play. It's now an institution that is listed in tourist guides, and people who never even knew New York had a Lower East Side can be found here. Not to worry—the club still features some of the best up-and-coming avant-garde rock and punk groups around. The crowd is young and dedicated to the eccentricities of the modern rock movement. Interesting to observe or be a part of, depending on your preference.

Chippendale's
**1110 First Ave.
(62nd St.)
935-6060**
*Shows Wed. to Sat. 8:30 P.M.
(women only); disco Wed. to Sat.
10:30 P.M. to 4:00 A.M. (men
invited)
Admission $15–$18*

You can take the boy out of California, but you can't take California out of the sunshine boys who titillate the mobs of women who have made New York's Chippendale's an arousing success. The former Magique (redubbed Tragique during its death throes) has been given new life with the same stage show that keeps Los Angeles ladies entertained on a nightly basis. This classy strip show, for women only, is as harmless as it is good, clean fun. Girlfriends embarrass one another by tipping the attractive, athletic young men, who stuff their tributes into their minuscule G-strings and thank the ladies with kisses; the women respond in kind with a fair amount of manhandling. These men dance, strut, strip and smile their dazzling Southern California smiles as they win the hearts and imaginations of a clientele largely composed of bachelorette and birthday parties, the enthusiastic curious and married ladies out on the town for an innocently good time. The show is slick and a bit silly, but anyone with a healthy sense of humor will enjoy. The boys hawk an endless series of merchandise during the show so the smitten can take home a bare-bones wall calendar, playing cards of men au naturel or any of the other Chippendale's novelties.

City Limits
125 Seventh Avenue South
(10th St.)
243-2242
Nightly 8:00 P.M. to 4:00 A.M.
Cover charge varies
No credit cards

During the week, this is the most authentic neighborhood country-western dance bar in town, with great live music and a dance floor big enough to allow you to kick up your heels properly. On the weekend, the crowds grow larger, and penny loafers compete with cowboy boots for dance floor space.

Club A
333 E. 60th St.
308-2333
Mon. to Sat. 10:00 P.M. to 4:00 A.M.
Cover charge Mon. to Wed. $20, Thurs. to Sat. $30
AE, V

Ricardo Amaral has one-upped Régine. This Brazilian entrepreneur knows how to operate nightclubs; he ought to, with his background in running the successful Hippopotamus clubs in Rio and throughout Brazil. This clever man found a formula with a superb contrast: questionable location versus chic clientele. He has opened a very sophisticated disco that for the moment is all the rage. The international jet-set clientele isn't much different from that at Régine's, but this place has a spirit and style that makes it worth a trip. And the food in the bistro next door is quite good, so you can make an entire one-stop evening of it here.

Danceteria
30 W. 21st St.
620-0515
Nightly 9:00 P.M. to 5:00 A.M.
Cover charge varies
No credit cards

Three levels, three types of music. Everything and everyone is au courant, dressed to the New Wave hilt. You'll enjoy listening to the rock, New Wave, rhythm 'n' blues and every other recent and revived musical trend. The food is so-so, but the people are a visual feast; be warned that a suit and tie (except perhaps a '50s sharkskin) will keep you out of here.

Heartbreak
179 Varick St.
(Charlton St.)
691-2388
Nightly 10:00 P.M. to 4:30 A.M.
Cover charge Tues. and Wed. $10, Thurs. to Mon. $15
No credit cards

During the day, this is just another truck-stop diner, but in the evening the tables are pushed aside, unveiling a large dance floor that vibrates to '50s rock 'n' roll (live bands play on Mondays). A lot of stars come here, which attracts people who just like to be where stars congregate—but one could come just for the dancing. The music never stops from dusk to dawn, and only the sun drives everyone home.

Les Mouches
260 Eleventh Ave.
(26th St.)

In spite of its location (so far west, some think it's in New Jersey), this cabaret/discotheque continues to be a stellar attraction. The cabaret entertainment is superb, the dance

695-5190
*Wed. to Sat. 10:00 P.M. to
4:00 A.M.
Cover charge $10
All major credit cards*

floor is large and uninhibited, and the crowd subscribes to the motto, "Live and let live." Yes, it's a long way to go for fun, but the fun is guaranteed.

Paradise Garage

**84 King St.
(Varick St.)
255-4517**
*Fri. and Sat. midnight to
10:00 A.M.
Cover charge $8 for members, $15 for
nonmembers
No credit cards*

This renovated parking garage is so enormous that you'd think it would be a cinch to get in. It isn't. But the owner is understanding. The clientele—young blacks and Latinos—is mostly gay, and the music here is among the most terrific in New York, thanks to a fabulous disc jockey and an incredible sound system. This is no jet-set place; it's better, because it's a truly authentic New York dance club. One year's membership will cost you $70.

Rainbow Room

**30 Rockefeller Plaza
757-9090**
*Tues. to Sat. 8:00 P.M. to 2:00
A.M.; Sun. 7:00 P.M. to midnight
Cover charge $4.50; minimum before
10:00 P.M.
All major credit cards*

It's about time some New York millionaire gave the party of the century in this fabulous dinner-dance club that overlooks Rockefeller Center. The view alone is stupendous. The theme would be the '30s, of course, the big band led by the Room's Sy Oliver and the guests ideal and smooth. There is food here, but it's better that we not talk about it.

The Red Parrot

**617 W. 57th St.
247-1530**
*Wed. to Sun. 10:00 P.M. to
4:00 A.M.
Cover charge $15
No credit cards*

The only nightclub in New York that occupies the surface of an entire city block! It is indeed gigantic, and the red parrots are no subtlety: they are on full display in dramatic plumage, inhabiting their large cage. But the best part of this place (a bit passé at this point) is a fifteen-piece orchestra that can play anything but seems to love '40s and '50s classics—and apparently so does the crowd. It's worth a visit because it is so different from any other place in the city.

Régine's

**502 Park Ave.
(59th St.)
826-0990**
*Nightly 6:00 P.M. to 4:00 A.M.
Cover charge $15 weeknights, $20
weekends
All major credit cards*

Is Régine here? You'd better ask before you shell out your $15 or $20 and step into this very French discotheque that still manages to hold onto its glamour and drama. Régine's name has been franchised, and the Parisienne Empress of the Night is not always in town, as she travels all over the world to oversee her nocturnal domain. When she is in New York, this place can be very amusing. She knows everyone with a name and continues to give fabulous dinner parties that are quickly reported by the local columnists. Husband Roger Choukroun is the resident host, along with Régine's sister, Evelyne. Most gentlemen (of the aging variety) wear the requisite coat and tie.

Ritz
119 E. 11th St.
254-2800
Nightly 10:00 P.M. to 4:00 A.M.
Cover charge varies
No credit cards

This very large dance club is a haven for a very young crowd of rock 'n' rollers (if you're over 30, you might feel ancient here). The live music features some of the best unknown and known rock talents, including many of the new British bands. Many more top stars perform in absentia via an enormous video screen. The ambience is everything that goes along with youth. In other words, it's possible to have a good time here, but don't expect a classy evening.

Roxy Roller Rink
515 W. 18th St.
691-3113
Sun. to Tues. 8:30 P.M. to 2:00 A.M.; Wed. 8:00 P.M. to 3:00 A.M.; Thurs. 10:00 P.M. to 4:00 A.M.; Fri. 11:00 P.M. to 6:00 A.M.; Sat. 2:00 P.M. to 7:00 P.M. and 11:00 P.M. to 6:00 A.M.
Cover charge varies
No credit cards

It's huge. It's dark. It's jammed. It's smoky. It's loud. And it's great fun. Young people of all sexual and racial persuasions join under this enormous roof to dance and skate their hearts out, choreographed by a sensational disc jockey. They slam dance when the mood is right, but otherwise expect a bit more conventional musical ritual on the dance floor (break dancing was first brought into the limelight here). The costume show is terrific, the music riveting and the beer not too expensive.

The Saint
105 Second Ave.
(St. Marks Pl.)
674-8369
Sat. 11:00 P.M. to 11:00 A.M.; Sun. 8:00 P.M. to 8:00 A.M.
Members and their friends only; cover charge varies
No credit cards

Many nightclub owners in America and the rest of the world consider The Saint to be the most beautiful nightclub they have ever seen. They could be right, but how do you get in to see it yourself? You don't if you are female or are with your wife or girlfriend; women are not too welcome here. But if you have a gay friend who is a member, it shouldn't be too difficult. Straights are tolerated, and no one will interrogate you to determine whether or not this is your first trip out of the closet.

S.O.B.
204 Varick St.
(W. Houston St.)
243-4940
Tues. to Thurs. 7:00 P.M. to 2:00 A.M.; Fri. and Sat. 7:00 P.M. to 4:00 A.M.
Cover charge $7 weeknights, $10 weekends
All major credit cards

How can you resist the beating drums that pull you through the doors of S.O.B.? The sounds of Brazil liven up this desolate area that some New Yorkers call "limbo" (between SoHo and the Hudson River). As everyone knows, Brazilian music would wake up a cemetery. This is a truly original night spot. Fridays and Saturdays are dance nights (sometimes with Pe de Boi's combo), and weekday evenings are a bit tamer. S.O.B. is a real treat—a must for out-of-towners as well as for entrenched New Yorkers.

Studio 54
254 W. 54th St.
489-7667
Tues. to Sun. 10:00 P.M. to 4:00 A.M.
Cover charge $15 weeknights, $18 weekends
No credit cards

Once the darling of the jet set, this grand disco is now just another place to dance. It's still grand, with its incredible lighting system and enormous dance floor and balcony, and the new management strives for some of the old exclusivity. But the word is out that 54 is now closer to 65 (retirement age). If you've never been, it's a must. If you have, then you know it's still a good place to dance even without the famous faces.

Xenon

124 W. 43rd St.
221-2690
Mon. to Sat. 10:30 P.M. to
4:00 A.M.
Cover charge $12 weeknights, $15
Fri., $18 Sat.
No credit cards

This large disco never did achieve the status that 54 once had, but it held its own through the difficult times of disco's decline and is now one of the leaders of the dance club resurgence. Housed in an old theater (including a balcony), this survivor continues to draw a large, diverse crowd to its laser-lit dance floor. It's not the same star-studded group of old, but no one seems to miss them.

Jazz

Eddie Condon's

144 W. 54th St.
265-8277
Nightly 8:30 P.M. to 2:00 A.M.
Cover charge varies
All major credit cards

Long before jazz became fused, progressed and modernized, it went through eras of swing and bebop. These periods were characterized by small (and large) bands playing a very high energy music that had fans tapping their feet and even dancing. You can still hear that music at this New York institution, and it sounds just as good now as it did then.

The Cookery

21 University Pl.
(8th St.)
674-4450
Daily 11:00 A.M. to 1:00 A.M.
Cover charge varies
AE, MC, V

Eighty-eight-year-old Alberta Hunter is still the queen at this downtown jazz club/restaurant. She performs here whenever she feels like it, and when she doesn't, a host of other very good jazz artists fill in. It's not the hottest jazz scene in town, but it is one of the most reliable.

Fat Tuesday's

190 Third Ave.
(17th St.)
533-7900
Nightly 8:30 P.M. to 2:00 A.M.
Cover charge $7.50
AE, MC, V

Those who know their jazz come here to be entertained by the top names in the business. It's elegant and comfortable with sincere acoustics. If you're one who knows, you'll certainly appreciate this club; if you're not, it's not a bad place to get a good education.

Gregory's

1149 First Ave.
(63rd St.)
371-2220
Nightly 5:00 P.M. to 3:00 A.M.
Cover charge varies; two-drink
minimum
All major credit cards

Candlelit and laid back on the far East Side, this cozy, modern little jazz club offers an excellent way to go gently into (or out of) the night.

Jazzmania Society

40 W. 27th St.

This smartly recycled loft (it's decorated in a warm, living room fashion) features great jazz performed by many of the jazz greats and dancing in a spacious yet intimate

532-7666, 684-8196
*Thurs. 9:00 P.M. to
1:00 A.M.; Fri. and Sat. 9:00 P.M.
to 3:00 A.M.
Cover charge varies
No credit cards*

environment. Lots of private parties are held here, so one can never be sure when the place is open to the public, but it's worthwhile to find out.

Michael's Pub
211 E. 55th St.
758-2272
*Mon. to Sat. 5:00 P.M. to 2:00 A.M.
No cover charge; $10 minimum
All major credit cards*

This bar/restaurant is newer than most of the jazz clubs around, but it features old-fashioned jazz for a middle-aged, establishment crowd. Tourists abound on Monday nights, when the ragtime band that often includes Woody Allen plays. If you come on a Monday, don't go to the late show: it lasts less than a half an hour, which hardly gives you time to drink your $10 worth.

Mikell's
760 Columbus Ave.
(97th St.)
864-8832
*Nightly 4:00 P.M. to 4:00 A.M.
Cover charge varies
All major credit cards*

Jazz lovers come from near and far to this uptown club because the musicians on the constantly changing roster are usually giants in the field. It's a diverse crowd that sometimes appears to have nothing in common but the music. That's enough.

Red Blazer Too
1576 Third Ave.
(88th St.)
876-0440
*Mon. to Thurs. 9:00 P.M. to 1:00
A.M.; Fri. and Sat. 9:00 P.M. to
3:00 A.M.; Sun. 9:00 P.M. to
midnight
No cover charge; $7.50 minimum*

Nostalgia is king at Red Blazer Too, a very friendly club that relives the days of Benny Goodman, Billie Holiday and Fred Astaire. It draws an older crowd that misses those good old days, along with young sophisticates who are just discovering big band and dixieland-style music. There's a small dance floor that's put to good use; the show there (past-their-prime couples cha-cha-cha-ing and swinging) is often more interesting than the show onstage.

Jimmy Ryan's
154 W. 54th St.
664-9700
*Daily 3:00 P.M. to 2:00 A.M. (Sat.
to 3:00 A.M.)
No cover charge
AE, MC, V*

The chairs are hard and uncomfortable, the drinks are $6 apiece (at tables), and the club is unattractive and rather grimy—but ah, the music! Once Spanky Davis and his band start up, you'll quickly forget these little inconveniences, and you'll leave with a smile on your face (until you pay the bill—the drinks are wildly overpriced to compensate for the lack of a cover charge). Ryan's is one of New York's oldest jazz clubs, and the music you'll hear is old-fashioned jazz, a happy mix of swing, dixieland and bop. Spanky is an exceptional trumpeter, and he and his band clearly love to play. They perform Tuesday to Saturday (there's another band Sunday and Monday), and they really get going during the second show (about 10:30 P.M.), when the place fills up.

Seventh Avenue South
21 Seventh Avenue

Aside from the music, which is always first-rate and always performed by first-class musicians, the most appealing thing about this lovely two-tiered jazz club is

South
(Bleecker St.)
242-4694
Nightly 10:00 P.M. to 2:00 A.M.
Cover charge varies
MC, V

the people it attracts: a colorful group that seems just as interested in each other as they are in the music. Reservations are a must.

Sweet Basil
88 Seventh Avenue
South
(Bleecker St.)
242-1785
Nightly 9:00 P.M. to 3:00 A.M.
Cover charge varies
AE, MC, V

Aficionados of jazz seldom look around to see where they are; their main concern is the music. They rarely notice how small or crowded a room might be—that is, if the music is good. The music here is very good, and the room is small and crowded. It's an especially fine place to hear excellent, infectious salsa.

Village Gate
160 Bleecker St.
(Thompson St.)
475-5120
Nightly 9:45 P.M. to 2:30 A.M.
Cover charge varies
All major credit cards

More of a concert hall than a club, the Village Gate draws many top names from the jazz world. The downstairs showroom is spacious, with chairs packed closely together, and there's an area in back for dancing, unusual in a jazz club. For those who prefer their jazz in the background, a pianist and bassist play in the upstairs bar/café for a noisy, young Village crowd.

Village Vanguard
178 Seventh Avenue
South
(11th St.)
255-4037
Nightly 9:30 P.M. to 2:00 A.M.
Cover charge $7.50
No credit cards

Much of what we know about jazz today was discovered in this dark, smoky basement. All the greats have performed here (many of them started here), adding their essence to this jazz monument. After almost 50 years, very little has changed: the greats still perform here, and it's still dark and smoky.

West Boondock
114 Tenth Ave.
(17th St.)
929-9645
Nightly 7:00 P.M. to 1:30 A.M.
No cover charge
All major credit cards

You will never find yourself in this part of town unless you plan it. Plan it. This low-key, out-of-the-way establishment rewards every wayfarer with good Southern cooking (ribs, chicken, black-eyed peas) and live modern jazz. It's not the best food or the best jazz, but together the combination is just right.

West End Café
2911 Broadway
(113th St.)
666-9160
Nightly 8:00 P.M. to 2:00 A.M.
AE, MC, V

Students from neighboring Columbia University are the primary patrons at this huge, chaotic, rather messy bar/rib joint/jazz club—which means it's one of the best deals around. There's no cover in the music room, where good local bands play straight-ahead jazz, and drinks are quite reasonable. You'll see starving young people swallow large quantities of pizza and barbecue dishes that are notable more for low prices than for high quality.

Music

The Bottom Line
15 W. 4th St.
228-6300
Shows Sun. to Thurs. 8:30 P.M. and
11:30 P.M.; Fri. and Sat. 9:00 P.M.
and midnight
Cover charge varies
No credit cards

In its heyday, this was the number-one rock palace in town. Now the playbill features everything from jazz to New Wave, country-western to reggae. It's still popular, and there are still two shows each night. Tickets are sold in advance, so you should check local listings for coming attractions.

Chelsea Place
147 Eighth Ave.
(17th St.)
924-8413
Nightly 5:30 P.M. to 4:00 A.M.
All major credit cards

It's amusing. It's a bit touristy. It's so alive that any latent (or confirmed) snobbism disappears shortly after you enter this place. You encounter a fairly traditional room to begin, then pass through a closet that leads you to a second, larger room where everyone enjoys the live musical entertainment. It's crowded, it's smoky, it's noisy and friendly. What else could you ask for?

Folk City
130 W. 3rd St.
254-8449
Mon. to Sat. 8:00 P.M. to 3:00
A.M.; Sun. 3:30 P.M. to 3:00 A.M.
Cover charge varies
No credit cards

This landmark Village spot was possibly the most influential club in America when folk was king. It was the first in New York to showcase Bob Dylan, Simon and Garfunkel and Joan Baez, among others. Not much has changed since those days (it's still scruffy, with a dark, bordellolike red flocked wallpaper); though Folk City isn't as hot as it once was, you can still hear fine folk, rock and blues talents here, along with some unimpressive local bands.

Lone Star Café
61 Fifth Ave.
(13th St.)
242-1664
Nightly 7:30 P.M. to 3:00 A.M.
(Fri. and Sat. to 4:00 A.M.)
Cover charge varies
All major credit cards

A little bit of Texas, New York style, is what this country-western music bar offers. The entertainment is top-notch and everyone is family in this beer-drinking, chili-loving cowboy oasis, where you don't have to be a Texan to feel like one. Leave your city pretensions at the door—though no one will notice if you don't.

O'Lunney's
915 Second Ave.
(49th St.)
751-5470
Nightly 9:00 P.M. to 2:00 A.M.
(Fri. and Sat. to 3:00 A.M.)
Cover charge $3 and $3 minimum
(at tables only)
All major credit cards

You've just spent the whole day plowing the back 40; you're hot and hungry. What you need are a few tall ones and some food that sticks to the ribs. And some country-western music, the kind that keeps your foot tapping and head bobbing. It's all here ... except the back 40. The crowd is young and loud.

S.N.A.F.U.
676 Avenue of the Americas
(21st St.)
691-3535
Tues. to Sun. noon to 1:30 A.M. (Fri. and Sat. to 2:30 A.M.)
Cover charge varies
No credit cards

The clientele at this bar/cabaret varies from night to night, depending on who's performing; the entertainment ranges from jazz to rock, cabaret to theater, and each draws its own type of audience. People come to this dark, cozy little club to have fun and really don't pay attention to which crowd they belong to—neither should you.

Tramps
125 E. 15th St.
(Irving Pl.)
777-5077
Nightly 10:00 P.M. to 4:00 A.M.
Cover charge $4; two-drink minimum
No credit cards

A lot of old rhythm 'n' blues greats perform here, as well as many current reggae stars. When it fills up, which it does all the time, there's hardly room to move (unless it's to the beat), but it's a friendly crowd, and everyone has a good time.

Trax
100 W. 72nd St.
799-1448
Tues. to Sun. 9:00 P.M. to 4:00 A.M.
Cover charge varies
All major credit cards

Still hidden downstairs behind a nondescript street door, this dark, comfortable club still showcases some of the best new rock talents. The mystique is gone but the colorful crowd remains, and if you're lucky, you still might bump into your favorite rock star.

Piano Bars

Beekman Tower
3 Mitchell Pl.
(First Ave.)
355-7300
Nightly 5:00 P.M. to 2:00 A.M.
No cover charge
All major credit cards

What we love most about New York is a room with a view. You can survey the majesty of New York in its twilight state of grace when perched on the perimeter of this vintage 1928 tower, indoors or out, joined by after-work business drinkers, romantic couples and the random tourist. The interior is a bit triste, although a piano player tries his best to liven things up. The real scene, however, is on the terrace, where you can watch New York go from day to night—looking to the west or toward the East River and the graceful, old-fashioned apartment complexes on Sutton Place.

Bemelmans Bar
Carlyle Hotel
35 E. 76th St.
744-1600
Mon. to Sat. 9:00 P.M. to 1:00 A.M.
Cover charge $5
All major credit cards

The intimate bar of the Carlyle Hotel is named for the painter of its classic murals; it attracts a more relaxed crowd than the well-heeled fashionables next door at the Café Carlyle. Barbara Carroll plays and sings all year long.

Bradley's
70 University Pl.
(10th St.)
228-6440
Nightly 9:45 P.M. to 4:00 A.M.
Minimum at tables $5
AE, CB, DC

This long, narrow, dark-paneled room is well established among the young devotees who cram into the bar to hear some of the best jazz piano-bass duos in the world. Such musicians as Richie Beirach, Kirk Lightsey, Tommy Flanagan, Kenny Barron and Larry Willis consider it a prestigious place to perform, even though the crowd is talkative; about 25 diners squeeze into the back room and barely listen to the music. The food, served until 12:30 A.M., is good and reasonable. The bar is always lively until closing time at 4:00 A.M.

Café Carlyle
Carlyle Hotel
35 E. 76th St.
744-1600
Music nightly 10:00 P.M. to midnight
Cover charge $20
All major credit cards

This supper club housed in the Carlyle Hotel is home to pianist Bobby Short most of the year. Bobby sings a specialized gamut from Lorenz Hart to Cole Porter, in a style that is at once witty and poignant, suave and sentimental. In his absence, such greats as Peter Nero or George Shearing hold forth. Dinner is served from 6:00 P.M.

Carnegie Tavern
165 W. 56th St.
757-9522
Mon. to Fri. 9:00 P.M. to midnight
No cover charge
All major credit cards

Ellis Larkin makes his home here for most of the year. The grand man who accompanied Ella Fitzgerald and Mabel Mercer now lightly skims the ivories in his refined, impeccable style. Sit close to the stage-lit piano for the delicate music, or if romance is your desire, select one of the dark corners and enjoy the music with a friend. This is a class act, popular with out-of-town visitors from nearby hotels and with seasoned New Yorkers after Carnegie Hall concerts.

Hanratty's
1754 Second Ave.
(91st St.)
289-3200
Sun. to Thurs. 8:30 P.M. to 12:30 A.M.; Fri. and Sat. 9:00 P.M. to 1:00 A.M.
Cover charge $5
AE

Walk through a typical Upper East Side bar into another world. In a tasteful green felt and wood-paneled room, subtly lit, with plenty of green plants, you sit comfortably and hear fine solo jazz pianists, such as Dick Wellstood, Ralph Sutton, Dave McKenna and Jay McShann. The sophisticated audience may include William F. Buckley, Jr., Paul Newman or Alistair Cooke, or any number of the well-groomed lawyers, stockbrokers or doctors who come to eat, listen and too often talk. Hanratty's is a handsome place to hear prerock classics: ragtime, swing and tunes by Fats Waller, Scott Joplin, Irving Berlin and Cole Porter.

The Hors d'Oeuvrerie
1 World Trade Center
938-1111
Nightly 4:00 P.M. to 1:00 A.M. (Sun. to 9:00 P.M.)
Cover charge $3
All major credit cards

The view from the 107th floor can distract you from admiring the spectacular multilevel interior designed by Warren Plattner. Phil Della Penna alternates at the piano with a jazz trio (which comes in at 7:30), and the small dance floor never seems to get crowded. The hors d'oeuvres are just fine. Jackets required.

Knicker- bocker Saloon

33 University Pl. (9th St.) 228-8490

Nightly 10:00 P.M. to 1:30 A.M. (Fri. and Sat. to 3:00 A.M.) Cover charge varies in restaurant; minimum at bar tables $5 All major credit cards

This neighborhood restaurant/bar draws those who appreciate fine contemporary jazz piano-bass combos. Billy Taylor, a world-renowned pianist, plays here when he is in New York; other nights it's Ron Carter, Hilton Ruiz, Sir Roland Hanna or Joanne Brackeen. There's a low murmur of conversation, usually more subdued by the second set. Regular patrons come singly or in groups; the serious listeners get their drinks at the bar and stand behind the piano to absorb the music. A young crowd of all ages comes for the reasonable food (entrees from $8 to $17) in the comfortable, large room with its turn-of-the-century decor and good sight lines to the musicians.

One if by Land, Two if by Sea

17 Barrow St. (Seventh Avenue South) 255-8649

Mon. and Tues. 8:00 P.M. to 1:00 A.M.; Wed. to Sun. 6:00 P.M. to 3:00 A.M. No cover charge All major credit cards

No sign identifies this charming landmark carriage house once owned by Aaron Burr. However, cognoscenti come from all over town for the piano music and the lively ambience in the handsome bar. Primitive American paintings, spectacular flowers and working fireplaces decorate the room. Norman Linscheid plays show tunes and light classics during the dinner hour, Paul Edwards plays and sings after 11:00 P.M., and Leslie Lipton fills in with jazz and contemporary music. Black-tied waiters serve the classy diners in the restaurant, while the bartender serves the 26 keyboard aficionados seated in the front room.

Peacock Alley

Waldorf-Astoria Hotel 49th Street and Park Avenue 355-3000

Sun. and Mon. 8:30 P.M. to 12:30 A.M.; Tues. to Sat. 6:00 P.M. to 2:00 A.M. No cover charge All major credit cards

The lobby bar in the Waldorf is a New York institution, and Cole Porter's piano is kept in tune for some fine pianists. Jimmy Lyon plays with verve and style from 6 to 10:00 P.M., Lynn Richards sings familiar songs after 10:00 P.M., and Penny Book fills in on Sunday and Monday.

Regency Lounge

Hotel Regency 61st Street and Park Avenue 759-4100

Nightly 6:00 P.M. to 1:45 A.M. No cover charge All major credit cards

Jimmy Badger plays popular music in the handsome bar of this proud hotel. The atmosphere reeks of sophistication, the clientele often seems to have walked out of advertisements in *Town and Country*, and the music plays second fiddle to the experience.

The River Café

1 Water St.

Yes, it's quite a trip from midtown Manhattan to this barge/restaurant with piano bar and cocktail lounge beneath the Brooklyn Bridge. The extraordinary view of

Brooklyn
522-5200
Nightly 8:00 P.M. to 1:00 A.M.
No cover charge
AE, CB, DC

lower Manhattan and the East River make it thoroughly worthwhile. It's crowded and full of life and is always a good place to impress a companion.

Ruppert's
1662 Third Ave.
(93rd St.)
831-1900
Daily 11:30 A.M. to 4:00 A.M.
No cover charge
All major credit cards

The music here is incidental, a pleasant backdrop to the conversations at the small tables. The piano is on the balcony, and its sounds drift down to those seated at the 35-foot-long antique bar and yet more tables below. The casual Upper East Side patrons pay little attention to the pianists who play Wednesday through Saturday nights or the guitarist who accompanies Sunday brunch. There's a very reasonable menu at dinner (until 12:45 A.M.) and libations appropriate for a place named after a former local brewery. It's a pretty place, with brick and mirrors, flowers and candles and an easy atmosphere.

Surf Maid
151 Bleecker St.
(La Guardia Pl.)
473-8845
Sun. to Thurs. 9:30 P.M. to 3:30 A.M.; Fri. and Sat. 9:00 P.M. to 3:30 A.M.
No cover charge
All major credit cards

Ignore the busy outdoor terrace and the fairly noisy bar, overlook the nonexistent decor and the gentle smell of fish, and pull up a stool by the piano or sit at one of the four tables nearby. Here the public is quiet and attentive—serious listeners these. Claude Garvey, Nipsey Russell's accompanist, plays piano here during the week, and fine jazz duos take over on weekends. The Villagers may come here for the shrimp and salad bar, but we prefer the music.

Village Corner
Bleecker Street at
La Guardia Place
473-9762
Music nightly 9:30 P.M. to 2:00 A.M.
No cover charge or minimum
No credit cards

The tables are minuscule, the ceilings high and the decor a bit seedy, but the jazz piano of Lance Hayward has been drawing people to this Village bar since 1969. He may not see the keys, but he certainly feels the music. Jim Roberts takes over with music from the '30s and '40s on Wednesdays and Thursdays. Both have records on sale at the huge bar. The place attracts an attentive young crowd, and the conversation is respectfully low. Food is of the burger, chili and cheesecake variety; beer comes by the mug, bottle or pitcher.

Village Green
531 Hudson St.
(W. 10th St.)
255-1650
Tues. to Thurs. 8:00 P.M. to 1:00 A.M.; Fri. and Sat. 9:00 P.M. to 2:00 A.M.
No cover charge
AE, MC, V

The lounge is upstairs and the restaurant downstairs in this beautiful West Village townhouse. Murray Grant is at the keyboard most nights, singing his own songs and playing other contemporary favorites. Friends from nearby Christopher Street and uptown chitchat around the piano, listen at the bar or relax at the green-cloth-covered tables. The interior designer deserves applause for the effective use of mirrors, exposed brick, beamed ceilings, fireplaces and flattering lighting—even the ladies' room is done artfully.

THE HOTELS

The Hotels

═ SOPHISTICATED TOUCHES ═

New York's urban landscape continues to remold itself on almost a daily basis. Whenever we return to the city, we are amazed by changes in the skyline; we look for old buildings we remember, only to find replacements that are making New York start to rival Texas, the land of the mirrored skyscrapers. Is New York becoming (even more) narcissistic after all these years?

The hotels are taking better care of themselves these days. Venerable institutions have been upgraded, refurbished, renovated. The scenery continues to change from the inside out. And new monuments will be adding their sophisticated touches to the hotel skyline: the luxurious Plaza Athénée from Trusthouse Forte will be ensconced on 64th Street near Madison; we are still waiting for the nouveau-elegante Nova Park to open; and the circular Hyatt in the theater district is propelling itself skyward. Business is booming: the streets are filled with visitors, hotel lobbies are alive with activity, and the weekend packages are attracting locals who want to pamper themselves for two days of first-class treatment.

On the lower end of the scale, you'll get what you pay for, so choose your hotel wisely and insist on changing your room if it doesn't please you. We have attempted to include hotels in most price ranges, to help you make the best seletion for your taste and pocketbook. The prices listed are before taxes; weekend package prices are for doubles, unless otherwise noted. Nearly all hotels accept the major credit cards, unless noted. The dot symbols are relative; they indicate our own judgment of the quality and what pleases us. Thus an expensive landmark that disappoints us might be ranked the same as a charming but modest out-of-the-way "find."

Luxury

••••
American
Stanhope

A jewel of a little hotel that is frequented by knowledgeable members of the art world who are frequent flyers to the Metropolitan Museum of Art. The

995 Fifth Ave.
(81st St.)
288-5800

lobby is charming in its old-world style, with a remarkable collection of American art. The rooms (some of which overlook Central Park) are comfortable and tastefully done with lovely antiques, Laura Ashley touches and a look that makes the upper-crust clientele feel they are in their own homes away from home (the comfortable, upper-class decor is no doubt intended to remind guests of their summer retreats). One of the brightest stars in the Stanhope galaxy is the open-air café, which is perfect for people watching and is a great premium in a walking city that is far too short on outdoor cafés.

Singles: $135–$165; doubles: $155–$185; suites: $300–$450.

••••
The Berkshire Place
21 E. 52nd St.
753-5800

Unquestionably one of the most attractive lobbies in New York, this is a perfect place to arrange a rendezvous, business or otherwise. The atrium mirrors reflect the beautiful floral arrangements and contemporary furnishings, all of which give the space an understated elegance. A smaller hotel, the Berkshire is a study in refinement and modest luxury. The rooms are prettily furnished and comfortable, the services professional and the welcome friendly. You will no doubt run into some of the very attractive Berkshire clientele in the lobby or elevators. It's a cheerful place, and the staff makes a sincere effort at personalized attention. Outside the hotel, you are conveniently located in midtown, a quick walk from business as well as boutiques. Highly recommended.

Singles: $125–$175; doubles: $145–$195; suites: $225–$1,500; weekend package: $120.

••••
The Carlyle
35 E. 76th St.
744-1600

You may feel the urge to whisper when you enter the hallowed halls of The Carlyle. The welcome is so serious and the atmosphere so solemn that perhaps you might wish you had brought the Queen along with you to justify the restraint. The limousines with their owners' vanity plates continue to line 76th Street, waiting patiently for the grandes dames and old-money tycoons to make their rendezvous with their couturiers and portfolio analysts. This elegant establishment continues its tradition of luxury accommodations and services, with The Restaurant holding court for New Yorkers who find their passport cases at Mark Cross and their crystal ashtrays at Cartier. Bobby Short still commands the Café Carlyle. This is the "only" place to stay for a strata of clients who find The Carlyle just like one of their homes and who keep the reputation of this elegant place discreetly intact.

Singles: $160–$195; doubles: $180–$215: suites: $325–$500; dogs: $2.50 per day.

••••
The Inter-Continental
111 E. 48th St.
755-5900

(handwritten: 4 star Mobil; Very attractive lobby; Well located, friendly service; Rooms nice/both small)

This grande dame upholds the Inter-Continental group's tradition of old-world elegance, refinement, luxury and professionalism. We love the hotel for its old-fashioned rooms that make us nostalgic for New York when life was simpler. The suites are similar to elegant New York apartments, with impeccable furnishings and decor. For the modern minded, there are newly renovated rooms complete with mini spas. Everything at The Inter-Continental is done with finesse and style, from the personalized service, the two restaurants (La Récolte and the Barclay) and the elegant Continental lobby to the highly professional staff and the constant attention to detail. If you need to have your hair done, Leonard of London will give you a quick makeover; if you need to contact your office overseas, there is a complete communications system; and if you need to translate a guidebook, such services are available on 24-hour call. We're not alone in loving this marvelous place—you may bump into the likes of James Michener, Robin Williams, Henry Cabot Lodge, Gloria Vanderbilt, Twiggy or Bjorn Borg, who make The Inter-Continental their home. This is unquestionably one of the best hotels in New York.

Singles: $125–$165; doubles: $145–$185; suites: $225–$800; weekend packages: $99–$129. *(handwritten: 160–200)*

••••
The Mayfair Regent
610 Park Ave.
(65th St.)
288-0800

(handwritten: 3 star)

What a pleasure to know that The Mayfair Regent continues to retain its luxuriously high standards in this highly technological society. This jewel offers an exceedingly pleasant welcome in a European style that makes us feel as if we are entering a hospitable mansion. The fireplace, lovely salon lounge and pretty rooms decorated in an old-world English style give the Mayfair its warranted feeling of exclusivity. It's a small hotel where personalized attention and recognition of a civilized existence often charm guests into becoming residents.

Singles, doubles: $144–$200; suites: $230–$730.

••••
Parker Meridien
118 W. 57th St.
245-5000

The rather cold lobby might be better suited for an aerobics class or a roller derby, but don't let these trifles bother you; the extraordinary exotic flowers more than compensate for the chill. The Meridien, one of the most coveted addresses in New York, is one of the best places to stay in the city. For a large hotel, the service, staff and ambience are personally attentive, all watched over by the charming, highly professional Robert Bergé. There's a good chance you'll bump into an au courant rock star, a team of tennis pros during the U.S. Open, an entourage of European visitors and any number of chic guests. They come here for the luxury and to admire the extraordinary view of Central Park from one of the well-appointed suites. The rooms, furnished in a contemporary decor, are cozy in a comfortable way. When you tire of the Fifth Avenue shops, you can destress yourself at the health club, on the running track on the roof, in the indoor pool or on the sun deck alongside the regulars who come here to relieve their urban pallor during the summer. After you have recovered, don't delay in making a reservation at Maurice, which offers a superb example of Alain Senderens's nouvelle magic. Some New Yorkers love the Meridien so much they check in for weekends to be pampered in an elegant, refined tradition.

Singles: $125–$185; doubles: $145–$205; suites: $225–$450; weekend package: $110. ~~155~~-2/5

Three Star

●●●● The Pierre
2 E. 61st St.
838-8000
(800)828-1188

A rather subdued lobby with Empire expectations greets you as you enter The Pierre, and you will probably run into some odd (albeit rich) birds—on our last visit we saw a couple taking their Burberry-clad poodles out for a walk, and a diva sporting an aqua-blue mink rushed past us to her waiting limo. The atmosphere may be a little tired here, but you can be sure of tranquility and will be surrounded by professional, efficient service and a sort of ambitious grandeur that makes this little château one of the nicer hotels in New York. The rooms, each with a different Empire decor, are spacious but fairly modest. Those commanding a view of Central Park are the most pleasant. There is a calming influence here that makes many visitors return regularly for a touch of ultra-luxurious sanctuary in this fast-forward city.

Singles: $175–$225; doubles: $200–$280; boudoirs, suites: $390–$685.

●●● The Regency
540 Park Ave.
(61st St.)
759-4100

Did you just walk into Le Petit Trianon? You might think so with this abundance of Empire furniture, tapestry wall hangings and an obsession with gilt—all contrasted with contemporary stark marble paneling. This exercise in luxury, which offers attractive rooms and an efficient staff, attracts a sophisticated traveler. If you go for baroque, you'll come to The Regency. The piano bar, its questionable red floral panels notwithstanding, is a pleasant place to sip Champagne (Moët et Chandon) before dinner, while the melodic piano man sings most agreeable Cole Porter renditions. The clientele is just this side of the geriatrics ward, but the service is friendly and the ambience comforting.

Singles: $130–$190; doubles: $150–$210; suites: $250–$650.

••••
Ritz Carlton
112 Central Park South
757-1900

You'll find a lot of Vuitton and brocaded luggage at the Ritz; the clientele is chic and clearly affluent. There is an elegance that comes from a self-assurance in the decor here. The early American motif rivals that of the more elegant private clubs in New England, with a welcoming fire in the Jockey Club bar during the winter and beautiful fresh flowers in the lobby to brighten up every season. The rooms are handsomely decorated in Americana antique replicas and brightened with cheerful chintz. Good taste and refinement abound, and no detail has been spared to make the appointments anything less than first-class. One of the best addresses in New York and another jewel in Coleman's Crown. Some of the weekend packages include meals, theater tickets and limousine service.

Singles: $195–$155; doubles: $215–$175; suites: $195–$630; weekend packages: $135–$700.

••••
United Nations Plaza Hotel
1 U.N. Plaza (44th St.)
355-3400

When you enter this luxury hotel, you may think you've wandered into an apartment lobby for narcissists. There are so many mirrors, it can be a distraction simply to check in. The U.N. Plaza, however, is one of the most exclusive and chic addresses in the city. Although some people prefer to be in the midtown area instead of off the beaten track near the United Nations, the rooms here are beautifully furnished and snug, the clientele can be very interesting when it travels with its diplomatic entourage, and the services make fitness fans feel right at home. On the top floor you can play tennis or swim laps nearly 24 hours a day. If you think the lobby provides one too many mirror images, take your chances at the Ambassador Grill downstairs, where even Alice in Wonderland would be amazed at the labyrinthine corridors created by the mirrors and light tricks. A stunning piece of hotel design.

Singles: $100–$165; doubles: $145–$185; suites: $400–$645; weekend package: $99.

•••
The Waldorf Towers

Presidents stay here. Ambassadors entertain here. Wealthy out-of-towners play here. And a privileged few live here. The Towers is a separate annex of the Waldorf

100 E. 50th St.
355-3100

that offers better security, more personalized service and deluxe accommodations. It is quiet, tranquil, civilized and a touch frumpy, in the way that makes many old New York hotels seem like home. The suites are spacious, the antiques more or less authentic and the bathrooms wonderfully big and old-fashioned. If you're going to stay at the Waldorf, treat yourself like royalty and choose the Towers to escape from the big city business of it all.

Singles: $150; doubles: $230–$270; suites: $700–$2,000.

••••
The Westbury
15 E. 69th St.
535-2000

The nouveaux riches go to the Palace. The arrivistes go to the Ritz. The self-assured affluent make The Westbury their temporary home; they love being surrounded by understated wealth, refinement and a civilized ambience, all overseen by the ever-present, ever-suave Pierre Constant. The Westbury is undergoing a revival, and its renaissance makes it without doubt one of the most agreeable hotels in New York. The small lobby is an exercise in restraint and good taste. The staff is polite and professional. The rooms are superbly done, with a provincial charm that belies their elegance. The service is reliable. And the hotel is located just temptation's throw from the fashionably chic Madison Avenue boutiques and watering holes that make this neighborhood a sophisticated European-style community not without its glamour. To our great satisfaction, the Polo Lounge has reopened, which adds to the charm of this venerable hotel. Come here if you want a small place that takes pride in personal attention. It's not for the big-business convention crowd, nor for the financially fainthearted. It *is* for individuals who recognize and live for quality.

Singles: $135–$195; doubles: $155–$215; suites: $300–$650; weekend packages: $110–$142.

First Class

••••
The Drake
400 Park Ave.
(56th St.)
421-0900

The Drake has undergone a facelift. Unfortunately, we were unable to see the ambitious plans come to fruition before the publication of this guide, but we can be sure that Swisôtel will have done a first-class job. The new lobby area has been expanded to create more meeting places and to add a dash of excitement to the previously sedate space. In any case, The Drake continues to be an elegant hotel with cheerful, spacious rooms preferred by such personalities as Jane Fonda and Jack Lemmon. Services are excellent, and the staff is extremely helpful. A very civilized place of understated luxury, this is one of our favorites.

Singles: $120–$165; doubles: $135–$180; suites: $280–$400; weekend package: $135.

•••
Essex House
160 Central Park South
484-5100

This big hotel is the perfect place to visit when traveling undercover. The large lobby is attractive, with wood paneling, crystal chandeliers and a world-traveling clientele. The hotel is impersonal in that sleeping-factory way, but the rooms are nicely furnished; some are quite large with views of, naturally, Central Park. Some weekend packages include meals, Champagne and bicycles. Business guests, honeymooners, out-of-towners on holiday shopping sprees and Marriott faithfuls keep the place busy on a constant basis. One of the best of the large, first-class hotels.

Singles: $120–$175; doubles: $140–$195; suites: $175–$625; weekend packages: $175–$275.

••
Grand Hyatt
Park Ave. at Grand Central
883-1234

As with all Hyatts, this branch features drama in the hotel school of design. The theatrical lobby is spacious, dominated by an enormous astrophysics contemporary sculpture and a smaller piano, a style typical of this popular chain. There is plenty of lobby seating in this latter-day palace, and the solarium sprinked with trees softens the megalithic space. The Hyatt is popular with no-nonsense business travelers who don't seem to notice the trademark Hyatt invisible room decor. We have to give the designers credit for making this 1,350-room hotel as eclectic as possible. In the echo of the waterfall, you'll find a diorama complete with stuffed exotic birds peering out at guests from their protective foliage (at The Inter-Continental, the birds of paradise are for real.)

Singles: $125–$155; doubles: $145–$175; suites: $300–$1,500; weekend package: $88.

•••
The Harley
214 E. 42nd St.
490-8900

You are greeted with a dramatic, modified North Dallas decor, with stainless steel columns and lofty ceilings in the lobby. The unsinkable Queen Leona has papered the place with her graceful image, assuring guests that they will be served in the Helmsley style with all the amenities due them. The rooms are pleasant, decorated in that invisible, contemporary style, and guests are well taken care of, with careful attention paid to detail (although we've never been crazy about scales in hotel bathrooms, particularly when preparing a guidebook). A slightly weary-looking business clientele peoples the lobby bar, and the staff tries its best to keep their spirits high.

Singles: $125–$175; doubles: $145–$195; suites: $270; weekend packages: $47–$54.50 per person.

••
Helmsley Palace
**455 Madison Ave.
(50th St.)
888-7000**

It may be your questionable fate to run into Queen Leona when you are passing through the Palace. No doubt the world is intrigued with seeing this multimillionairess doing her best to fold towels, arrange flowers, greet guests and taste the hotel's cuisine, all the while decked out in one of her many dramatic evening gowns. Clearly personal service is her m.o., with her face beaming from all of the promotional literature as well as the endless series of Helmsley (and Harley) ads.

In any case, it is impossible to overlook this petite Versailles, which has become a copy of a copy (originally Henry Villard's private home, it was modeled after La Cancelleria in Rome). The collection of gilt, marble, wood paneling, crystal and miles of desperate-looking garish carpeting would make any nouveau rich financier proud. Above all, the Palace is an exercise in conspicuous consumption. Bewildered-looking tourists roam the halls, as there is virtually no public seating (no doubt to discourage loitering by any neighborhood bag people). The rooms are housed in the Erector Set structure looming over this neophyte *hôtel,* decorated in Queen Leona's regal style, and guests love them for their comfort and view.

We must commend the Palace for its noble civic-mindedness; the trees lit up like Tivoli Gardens are charming, enlivening Madison Avenue, and how can we thank them enough for the laser beam that simulates moonlight on Saint Patrick's every night?

Singles: $165–$205; doubles: $185–$225; suites: $275–$1,400; weekend packages: $67.50–$73.74 per person.

•••
Lowell
**28 E. 63rd St.
753-8600**

This well-located hotel has recently been refurbished, and many corporations now have permanent apartments here. The makover is admirable; each room is equipped with a full kitchen, the plumbing and windows have all been replaced, and you'll find a phone in every room. There are excellent conference rooms, a tea room and library exclusively for guests and many rooms featuring wood-burning fireplaces—the last word in chic in New York. Prices have risen considerably, as befits the new level of comfort, elegance and discretion.

Singles, doubles: $150–$250; one-bedroom suites: $300–$450; two-bedroom suites: $400–$600.

••
Park Lane
**36 Central Park
South
371-4000**

The commercial-looking lobby of the Park Lane is decorated in understated Texas chic. Red, gold, polished marble and ersatz crystal provide the big-hotel decor that is just this side of nouveau riche taste. It's big and impersonal, but it's a favorite of business people, who like its location, services and rooms decorated in contemporary styles. The staff is courteous—some speak enough foreign languages to keep guests on the right track in the city—and the suites, 46 stories up at the pinnacle of this ultramodern tower, offer a romantic view of Central Park. Weekend packages include breakfast and wine.

Singles: $125-$195; doubles: $145-$215; suites: $375-$610; weekend packages: $70-$100.

••
The Plaza
**768 Fifth Ave.
(59th St.)
759-3000**

The best thing about The Plaza is its stunning location. Dominating the corner of Fifth Avenue and 59th Street, it represents all the romance and history of a past age, which this constantly evolving cityscape is doing its best to forget. Even the tourist-trap hansom cabs look attractive, and although there are plenty of new-age musicians making their own personal brand of music on the square, The Plaza still reigns over the park with the grace of an aging dowager. Entering this mastodon, however, is another matter. You'll be on your own when you try to master the intricate maze of hallways and deal with the tired-looking Continental splendor that is obscured by hordes of Midwestern tourists, weekend couples, afternoon pleasure seekers and the old guard that still comes here because it's tradition. The old-world rooms can be shabby and cramped, although the suites are spacious and pleasant. The Palm Court still serves tea to grandmothers and their granddaughters, The Oak Room attracts a business clientele more interested in conversation than cuisine (mercifully, since the cuisine is not the attraction here), and The Oyster Bar still dishes up its sad seafood cuisine. Despite all its faults, however, we cannot help but love The Plaza—simply because, against all odds, it's still there; it's old New York at its best and worst.

Singles: $95-$265; doubles: $155-$285; suites: $350-$600; weekend packages: $190-$420.

•••
St-Regis
Sheraton
**2 E. 55th St.
753-4500**

One of the best things about the St-Regis is the Maxfield Parrish "Old King Cole" mural in the dining room. This alone is worth a trip to this turn-of-the-century institution built by John Jacob Astor. The opulence, so essential in the early 1900s, is still going strong in the eclectic decor that mixes the boudoir with Empire pretensions. It's an impressive place with charming rooms, attracting a clientele of successful business travelers and people who enjoy the good life. The St-Regis is in a terrific location with easy access to all of the Fifth Avenue temptations.

Singles: $120–$175; doubles: $140–$195; suites: $195–$450.

•••
Sherry Netherland
781 Fifth Ave.
(59th St.)
355-2800

The Sherry Netherland is a touch of old Europe. The lobby is still elegant in an old-world, civilized way, and the spacious rooms are lovely. Many people make the Netherland their home in one of the co-op apartments. It used to be *the* place to meet for a cocktail or nightcap, but nowadays the fading bar tends to be filled with dazed-looking out-of-towners planning their theater dates. The location is superb, and you won't be disappointed with the helpful staff and aging, elegant ambience.

Singles, doubles: $130–$200; suites: $225–$500.

••
Vista International Hotel
3 World Trade Center
938-9100

At last there is a first-class hotel in the city's financial district. Vista, operated by Hilton International, has 829 pleasantly furnished rooms, many overlooking the Hudson River and the construction of Battery Park City. It's close to Chinatown, the art galleries of SoHo and TriBeCa and the stock exchanges. In addition to housing the excellent American Harvest restaurant, the hotel offers guests an "executive fitness center" with a heated indoor pool, racquetball, jogging track, Nautilus equipment, massage services and saunas. The 20th and 21st floors house the "executive rooms," with such extras as a private lounge with complimentary bar, free newspapers and a concierge to attend to your needs. The business service center provides secretarial help, a telex operation, reference materials and individual meeting rooms.

Singles: $105–$185; doubles: $135–$215; suites: $250–$390; weekend packages: $79–$178.

••
The Waldorf-Astoria
301 Park Ave.
(49th St.)
355-3000

Things are looking brighter and prettier here. The continuing deco refurbishment is casting a new glow on this enormous, 1,850-room institution. It is still cavernous and you still might get lost trying to meet someone in the lobby, but there are plenty of Waldorf staffers to help you. An attempt at more personalized attention is afoot, and the international concierge and attractive lobby hostess will do their best to keep you on the right track. The rooms are pleasant, varying from old-world spacious suites with marvelous bathrooms (as big as many New Yorkers' studio apartments) to comfortable yet snug rooms with provincial charm. The clientele is a bit touristy, but heads of state still make The Waldorf home, along with the American presidents. There are two sides to The Waldorf's coin: the Towers is luxury par excellence.

Singles: $95–$160; doubles: $130–$195; suites: $280–$415; weekend packages: $82.50–$197.

Comfortable

•••
Barbizon Hotel
140 E. 63rd St.
838-5700
(800)223-1020

This former residential hotel for women has been converted into a fine hotel in the European tradition, catering to every whim, to the delight of its discriminating clients. The rooms are on the small side, but no one seems to mind, since they include Continental breakfast (via room service) and a welcome basket of fruit. A restaurant is slated to open in the summer and a health spa in '85. This well-kept secret is not to be confused with the Barbizon Plaza.

Singles: $85–$115; doubles: $95–$115; suites: $175; weekend package: $79.

Barbizon Plaza
106 Central Park South
(Avenue of the Americas)
247-7000
(800)223-5493

Not nearly as classy as some of the other hotels overlooking Central Park, the Barbizon Plaza has been around for quite a while and has a devoted following. All-new double-pane windows keep out the cheerful noise of the hansom cabs and the rush-hour traffic. The airline crews prefer the quieter courtyard rooms. Larger tower rooms (from the 31st to 36th floors) have cold pantries and the same modest furnishings.

Singles: $89–$110; doubles: $99–$135; suites: $165–$375; weekend packages: $75–$95.

••
Beverly
Lexington Avenue and 50th Street
753-2700
(800)223-0945

We like the uncrowded, family-owned Beverly for its old-world character and personal attention, which is assured by the resident concierge. Past the elegant lobby are attractively decorated rooms, mostly suites and junior suites with fully equipped kitchenettes. Our only caveat is that the outside noise level is high; light sleepers should

bring earplugs and ask for an upper floor.
Singles: $79–$119; doubles: $89–$119; suites: $150–$300; weekend packages: $54–$79.

Blackstone
50 E. 58th St.
355-4200

Next door to Gaylord's Restaurant, the undistinguished entrance to the Blackstone is easy to miss. The staff is devoted and the rooms are clean, albeit furnished in a Spartan manner. They're redecorating the rooms one by one, so ask for a refurbished one. A nice touch: a free copy of the New York *Times* every day except Sunday.
Singles: $64–$74; doubles: $74–$89; suites: $95–$150.

• Doral Inn
49th Street and
Lexington Avenue
755-1200
(800)223-5823

The Doral has just redecorated its 700 rooms, which are now attractive and comfortable. Just across the street from The Waldorf, it has squash courts, saunas, a do-it-yourself laundry room, a 24-hour coffee shop and a helpful, multilingual staff. Well worth a visit, except when the place is overrun by large groups and the lobby and two elevators clog up. The weekend package includes breakfast and wine.
Singles: $82–$100; doubles: $94–$112; suites: $175–$400; weekend package: $75.

•• Dorset
30 W. 54th St.
247-7300

There is something sure and steady about the Dorset. Its welcome is pleasant, although the wood-paneled lobby is a bit somber; the luxury is discreet and the location perfect for Museum of Modern Art fans. Although it's not a particularly memorable place, it's comfortable and reasonably priced.
Singles: $75–$125; doubles: $95–$140; suites: $240.

•• Halloran House
525 Lexington Ave.
(49th St.)
755-4400
(800)223-0939

Five years ago this handsome building was converted to a hotel, and the oak-paneled lobby and leather upholstery give the place the look of an expensive private club. The 652 rooms feature closet safes, bedside remote controls for the color televisions, peephole doors and extension telephones in the bathrooms. Behind the front desk, an efficient computer makes for speedy check-ins. The weekend package includes breakfast.
Singles: $89–$116; doubles: $98–$129; suites: $185 and up; weekend package: $76.

Lexington
Lexington Avenue
and 48th Street
755-4400
(800)228-5151

The pink Spanish courtyard lobby is often busy with United Nations visitors or airline crew members. The decor is a bit garish, the rooms are small (some have refrigerators), but the convenient location and multilingual staff make the Lexington acceptable. The weekend package includes dinner at Raga, the posh Indian restaurant, plus breakfast.

Singles: $82–$86; doubles: $94–$98; suites: $200–$250; weekend package: $55 per person.

Loews Summit
51st Street and Lexington Avenue
752-7000

Every one of the 800 rooms at this hotel has the same monotonous modern decor—terrific if you like brown. But phones in the bathrooms, mini refrigerators in the bedrooms, Nautilus equipment in the health club, the Jacuzzi and the sauna make up for some of the shortcomings. Don't take an even-numbered room: these face the street, with its fire and police department sirens. The computer age has given the hotel unwanted wrinkles and made tempers short at the registration desk. The weekend package includes breakfast and dinner.

Singles: $84–$100; doubles: $99–$115; suites: $135–$250; weekend package: $162.

••
Lombardy
111 E. 56th St.
753-8600

This smaller hotel offers nothing of great distinction, but the rooms are pleasant, and the service is efficient. The somber lobby is not terribly inviting, particularly with the staff caged behind glass, reminding us of New York's partitioned taxicabs. No matter—the studio-apartment rooms are acceptable, and the location is perfect for yet another Bloomingdale's run.

Singles: $90–$105; doubles: $105–$120; suites: $195–$245.

••
Madison Towers Hotel
Madison Avenue and 38th Street
685-3700
(800)225-4340

A marvelous example of what five million dollars can do to an old hotel in Murray Hill. The old Lancaster has been reborn, with nice rooms modestly decorated. It's a great find at sensible prices. The weekend and holiday package includes an American breakfast in its coffee shop, and a drink at the delightful, cozy Whaler Bar (with a wood-burning fireplace and a piano).

Singles: $65–$75; doubles: $75–$85; suites: $150–$275; weekend package: $65.

•
Mayflower
15 Central Park West (61st St.)
265-0060
(800)223-4164

The Mayflower is a simple but very pleasant hotel, so close to Lincoln Center that it is likely your next door neighbor will be a well-known dancer, musician or singer. (Nota bene: They keep late-night hours and may rehearse by day). Request a room overlooking the park and don't be afraid to join the morning joggers.

Singles: $75–$105; doubles: $90–$125; suites: $145–$160.

Milford Plaza
270 W. 45th St.
869-3600

Behind the shiny, modern Best Western lobby of the Milford Plaza, with its pushing and shoving, are the old, cramped rooms of the Royal Manhattan hotel, which

(800)221-2690

have been glossed over in this reincarnation. The low prices (thanks to the city's cooperation in improving the Times Square area) make it all bearable. The hotel is full of group tours and airline crews, who like being near the Broadway action. There's a choice of weekend, sightseeing and theater packages; the weekend package includes breakfast, cocktails and dinner.

Singles: $56–$76; doubles: $70–$90; suites: $150–$325; weekend package: $86.

••
New York Hilton
**1335 Avenue of the Americas
(53rd–54th sts.)
586-7000**

Book a "double double" on a "new floor," and you'll find the Hilton rooms spacious, tastefully redecorated and clean. You may be able to overhear the conventioneers partying next door, but that has to be expected from a place that boasts more than 2,000 rooms, including the new "executive tower" and accommodations for handicapped guests. Thirty-five languages are spoken by the Hilton personnel; one hopes these include English. The weekend package includes breakfast and cocktails.

Singles: $125–$155; doubles: $150–$175; suites: $290–$435; weekend package: $99.

New York Penta Hotel
**Seventh Avenue and 33rd Street
736-5000
(800)223-8585**

Yes, this is the former Statler, with the same phone number made famous by Glenn Miller, PEnnsylvania 6-5000. Convenient to Madison Square Garden and the garment district, it's a big (1,700 rooms), old hotel with some redecorated units and a helpful staff. Ask for an "alcove" room, which is more spacious than the others. The weekend package includes breakfast.

Singles: $78–$106; doubles: $95–$123; suites: $175–$360; weekend package: $59.90.

Park Central
**Seventh Avenue and 56th Street
247-8000
(800)325-3535**

In the midst of being refurbished, this former Sheraton is like most of its relatives: very huge, very popular, very busy and very ordinary. This one is well managed, has 200 suites and caters to conventions and airline crews. It's well located for theatergoers and sightseers, and it's close to Central Park and the Coliseum. The weekend package includes breakfast and is good for four nights.

Singles: $79–$120; doubles: $99–$140; suites: $205–$400; weekend package: $79.

Ramada Inn
**48th Street and Eighth Avenue
581-7000
(800)228-2828**

The name says it all. This place has all the comfort and Formica you've come to expect. It is, however, in the theater district, and there's an extra bonus in having on-premise parking and an outdoor rooftop pool (nice during the muggy summer months).

Singles: $59–$89; doubles: $71–$101; suites: $120–$195.

St. Moritz
**50 Central Park
South
755-5800**

It's seeming a little tired at the St. Moritz these days; there is a vestige of old-world elegance that attracts a clientele with a merchant-mentality look. The rooms, some of which are the size of closets, are decorated in understated bad taste, although the hotel-style decor often becomes invisible. But there is always Rumplemayer's to save the day: its charming retro pink-vinyl seating, wall of stuffed animals and ice cream sodas remind us of the time when the St. Moritz was a luxurious giant to be reckoned with. Some weekend packages include breakfast, cocktails and theater tickets.

Singles: $95–$145; doubles: $105–$170; suites: $165–$575; weekend packages: $40–$89.

Salisbury
**123 W. 57th St.
246-1300
(800)223-0680**

One of the city's older hotels, the independently operated Salisbury is near Central Park and Carnegie Hall. Its 320 rooms are on the small side and are not always the brightest, but they're clean and well outfitted.

Singles: $69–$78; doubles: $79–$88; suites: $120–$150; weekend package: $58.

Sheraton Centre
**52nd Street and
Seventh Avenue
581-1000
(800)325-3535**

Yes, this is the old Americana in a new cloak. The Caffè Fontana in the lobby offers buffet lunches and piano entertainment in the evening. You *and* your pets are welcome in the 1,835 roons, with all the expected amenities. Weekend packages include Champagne and caviar and are good for up to three nights. The top five floors, under the Sheraton Towers label, are filled with luxury suites and rooms. Note: Employee rows with management have led to arson, theft and unannounced room cancellations. Until the staff is satisfied, the Sheraton Centre is a risky booking.

Singles: $85–$150; doubles: $95–$160; suites: $280 and up; weekend packages: $69–$75.

Sheraton City Squire
**790 Seventh Ave.
(51st St.)
581-3300
(800)325-3535**

Somehow, the City Squire doesn't appear to be the convention motel it is. The 720 rooms are nicely furnished, and there's nothing to irritate the discriminating eye. A glass-enclosed pool makes year-round swimming a feature. Minibus service is available to the city airports. Pets are allowed, and there's on-premise parking for a fee. One of the better choices in the theater district.

Singles: $79–$115; doubles: $89–$135; suites: from $210; weekend package: $67.

Shoreham
**33 W. 55th St.
247-6700**

In a small, well-located brick building a stone's throw from Fifth Avenue, rooms are adequately furnished in a bare, modern style. You can hear the neighborhood building construction through the old windows, when you're not distracted by the noisy air-conditioning units. An adequate accommodation for the price.

Singles: $58–$68; doubles: $72–$82; suites: $90–$125.

Tudor
304 E. 42nd St.
986-8800
(800)221-1253

Near the United Nations, this peaceful and quite pleasant hotel has an international clientele. There are 500 indifferently decorated but well-maintained tiny rooms, each with a bathroom and television. A few triples and quads are available.

Singles: $65–$70; doubles: $80–$85; suites: $130–$250.

••
Warwick
54th Street and
Avenue of the
Americas
247-2700
(800)223-4099

The Warwick has large rooms that are tastefully furnished; be sure to indicate your preference for a bath or a shower. The place seems smaller than its 500 rooms, but it is well kept up and has recently installed double windows to cut down on the traffic noise. We prefer the Warwick's traditional, Continental atmosphere to that of the impersonal Hilton across the street.

Singles: $105–$125; doubles: $120–$140; suites: $150–$250.

••
Windsor
Harley
100 W. 58th St.
265-2100
(800)321-2323

Leona Helmsley has done it again: her familiar preference in decor (flowered bedspreads and curtains), large beds (kings or two doubles) and presto! the Manger Windsor becomes a Harley hotel. It's convenient to Central Park and Carnegie Hall.

Singles: $90–$100; doubles: $100–$110; suites: $150–$250; weekend package: $65.

Small · Charming

••••
Algonquin
Hotel
39 W. 44th St.
840-6800

You are nearly sure of running into a few literary types, if not the real thing, when you check into the Algonquin. The marvelous men's-club lobby is steeped with tradition and evokes a time when writers were not made-for-TV personalities. This charming hotel is a welcome change of pace from the newer, more contemporary and more frigid hotels dotting this urban landscape. The refurbished rooms are lovely and comfortable, and regulars who come here wouldn't dream of staying anywhere else. We adore the Algonquin—but please understand that you are under no obligation to eat here!

Singles: $78–$100; doubles: $81–$100; suites: $154–$372.

• Bedford
118 E. 40th St.
697-4800
(800)221-6881

Convenient to midtown offices and the garment district, this smaller hotel (like its neighbors) is packed during market week. But it has reasonable prices on weekends and during holiday periods. All rooms are large and well maintained and have complete kitchen facilities.

Singles: $79–$99; doubles: $89–$99; suites: from $120; weekend packages: $59–$99.

Chelsea Hotel
222 W. 23rd St.
243-3700

Artists and writers are drawn to this hundred-year-old landmark hotel. It has character—we'd call it rundown and seedy. If you thrive on a bohemian atmosphere and memories of eccentric geniuses passing out in its musty halls, the Chelsea is for you. Thomas Wolfe, Arthur Miller, Brendan Behan, Virgil Thompson, Mark Twain and Janis Joplin all found inspiration and privacy here. The 400 dingy rooms range from tiny singles with a bath down the hall to five-room apartments on long-term leases. All are soundproof, and some have wood-burning fireplaces.

Singles: $50–$150; doubles: $55–$155; suites: $125–$175.

•• Doral Park Avenue
70 Park Ave.
(38th St.)
687-7050

This modest little hotel has a very pretty rotunda lobby with a touch of the baroque. Alas, this crystal-chandelier decor is not reflected in the simply furnished rooms. Nonetheless, it's a comfortable place with a nice bar and attractive dining room. There's a pleasant feeling here of visiting New York in a civilized residential neighborhood instead of at the crazed pace of Madison Avenue. A definite find for the sophisticated traveler looking for bargains.

Singles: $93–$110; doubles: $120–$130; suites: $200–$300.

•• Doral Tuscany
120 E. 39th St.
686-1600

Although the lobby with its somber wood paneling is a little triste, the room decor is pleasant, and the staff offers a warm welcome. It's another of the smaller hotels located below Grand Central, and its guests enjoy the quiet neighborhood and restrained pace. The Doral Tuscany is a find for the traveler weary of impersonal, large hotels that lack the charm and understated taste of

this "biggest little hotel" in New York.
Singles: $115–$140; doubles: $140–$165; suites: $200 and up.

••
Elysee
60 E. 54th St.
753-1066

The decor here can be eclectic; some of the rooms have a typical hotel blandness, while others are a bit on the motel garish side. It is advisable to take a quick look at your room before moving in. But the Elysee is a pleasant place that is unpretentious and reasonable. The Monkey Bar is only for those enamored of primate imagery. The location is excellent for midtown pleasures.
Singles: $75–$125; doubles: $85–$135; suites: $175–$275.

Hyde Park
Hotel
25 E. 77th St.
744-4300
(800)847-8483

This once exclusively residential hotel in a quiet neighborhood now takes an increasing number of transient guests who are content with the subdued atmosphere and the respectful treatment. Amid the townhouses and galleries off Central Park, the Hyde Park offers large, modestly furnished, comfortable rooms, each with a mini refrigerator.
Singles: $95–$135; doubles: $105–$145; suites: $160 and up; weekend package: $115.

••
Kitano
66 Park Ave.
(38th St.)
685-0022

Enter the quiet, dignified lobby of the Kitano hotel, and you will know the elegance of Japanese hospitality. Halls and rooms are harmoniously decorated, the furniture is simple, and throughout there's an aura of peace and serenity. Try the tatami suites and sleep on the floor as the Japanese do (at $160 a night).
Singles: $85–$100; doubles: $100–$120; suites: $160–$275.

••
Middletowne
Harley
148 E. 48th St.
755-3000
(800)221-4982

This apartment-house-turned-hotel offers a kitchenette in every one of its 190 traditional rooms. The decor features Leona Helmsley's favorite floral spreads and curtains. As at many East Side hotels, minibus service is offered directly to the airports. The minuscule lobby may get busy, but there's something to be said for the at-home, calm feeling of the place.
Singles: $90–$100; doubles: $100–$110; suites: $150–$170; weekend package: $65.

•••
Sheraton
Russell
45 Park Ave.
(37th St.)
685-7676

This little hotel has few tangible signs of a Sheraton management, outside of the green-blazer uniforms. It is absolutely charming and is a far cry from the sleeping-factory look of most Sheratons. The ersatz library lobby offers a pleasant welcome, and there's a European feeling to its design. The pretty dining room and handsome bar

265

are popular at lunch with the local business crowd. The Americana room decor is tastefully done, each with a different style and ambience—some even have fireplaces! It's a veritable jewel that makes staying below 42nd Street a real possibility.

Singles: $120–$150; doubles: $140–$170; suites: $205–$295; weekend package: $199.

•
Surrey Hotel
20 E. 76th St.
288-3700

Located on an elegant, quiet street of townhouses near the Whitney Museum, the Surrey is a fine, older residential hotel with large, well-maintained rooms equipped with serving pantry or full kitchen and traditional furniture. Nothing splashy, no bus tours and no conventions. Just a home away from home, with someone else to make the beds.

Singles: $95–$115; doubles: $105–$125; suites: $135–$250.

•••
The Wyndham
42 W. 58th St.
753-3500

One of the most comfortable and handsomely furnished lobbies in town greets you at The Wyndham, a small, older apartment hotel, with cheerfully decorated rooms, just off Fifth Avenue and Central Park. At last we've found a place to meet, sit and talk in this age of barren lobbies. The clientele, knowing it has found a good thing, keeps coming back for the friendly service and quiet ambience.

Singles: $74–$80; doubles: $84–$90; suites: $120–$150.

Economy

Century-Paramount
235 W. 46th St.
246-5500
(800)223-9868

In the heart of the theater district, it's difficult to find a quiet room. Here the 650 rooms are tiny and dark, and thin walls let you follow the adjacent conversations; window air-conditioning units add to the noise level. But the low prices make it hard to complain. The furnishings are adequate, the rooms are clean, and every one has a color television and private bath or shower. There's a coffee shop and cocktail lounge off the lobby.

Singles: $45–$60; doubles: $50–$70.

Edison
228 W. 47th St.
840-5000

For budget-conscious theatergoers, the Edison offers clean, comfortable rooms with ample closet space, cable television and individual air conditioning. It's a favorite with those on group tours, who are invariably found hanging around the lobby with packed suitcases, waiting for the next bus.

Singles: $46–$50; doubles: $56–$60; suites: $72–$80.

Esplanade
305 West End Ave.
(74th St.)
874-5000

West End Avenue was once one of New York's finest addresses, and it is still an elegant residential boulevard. The Esplanade, a reminder of what it once was, has spacious suites with kitchenettes at prices that bespeak the modest furnishings. It's all neat and tidy, with a family atmosphere—isn't that your great-aunt from eastern Europe, one of the permanent residents, sitting in the lobby? Behind the desk confusion reigns; a knowledge of Yiddish will help you communicate. No credit cards.

Singles, doubles: $40; suites: $60.

Executive Hotel
237 Madison Ave.
(38th St.)
686-0300

The Executive promises to be more glamorous and expensive when the construction and refurbishing is completed in 1984. In the meantime, it offers incredible weekend rates for modest older rooms, as well as redecorated ones, that include breakfast and admission to Studio 54.

Singles: $60–$70; doubles: $68; suites: $95; weekend packages: $45–$75.

Gorham
136 W. 55th St.
245-1800

Just opposite City Center, with its excellent modern ballet companies, the Gorham is not inspiring, but it has earned a faithful following thanks to its good location, modest prices and the honest comfort of its rooms. The furniture cries for upgrading, the mattresses remind us of Italy, and the kitchenettes could be newer. But, alas, that seems to be standard for the price.

Singles: $53–$70; doubles: $58–$80; suites: $75–$90.

Henry Hudson Hotel
353 W. 57th St.
265-6100

Once known for its pool (now a private health club), the Henry Hudson today offers basic accommodations and little more. There are phones without dials, window air-conditioning units and simple furnishings, but very reasonable long-term rates. Convenient to Lincoln Center and the Coliseum, and just above Channel 13's offices.

Singles: $40; doubles: $55.

International House
500 Riverside Dr.
(123rd St.)
678-5000

The Rockefellers donated this large building overlooking the Hudson River, and those over age nineteen who are students, researchers, faculty members, interns or trainees at corporations can use it from late May to early August. All rooms are doubles and rent by the day, week or month ($260–$320). Showers, a cafeteria, TV rooms and a gym are offered.

Doubles: $20 first night, $13 thereafter.

International Student Center
38 W. 88th St.
787-7706

In the tradition of European overnight youth hostels, the ISC provides foreign students with $6-per-night dormitory accommodations in this location near Central Park. Each dorm has shower facilities. In the summer, there's a five-night maximum stay. The second location, at 210 W. 55th St. (757-8030), has four-to-a-dorm accommodations at $8 per night.

Dormitory beds: $6–$8.

Murray Hill Hotel
42 W. 35th St.
947-0200

An older hotel near Herald Square that's functional and not much else. It's inexpensive, clean and friendly, with a mini fridge and television in every room. We wish they'd fix the peeling plaster, however. Rock-bottom weekly rates for stays longer than two weeks.

Singles: $35; doubles: $40.

Pickwick Arms
230 E. 51st St.
355-0300

A bargain hunter's hotel, including clean rooms without bath for $20 a night, in a fine East Side location. Across the street from a charming vest-pocket park, it attracts colorful characters and penny-wise tourists. Families should request a studio with kitchenette. No televisions in the rooms, however. The friendly staff requires daily payment in advance.

Singles: $24–$32; doubles: $45–$55; triples: $55 and up.

Wales
1295 Madison Ave.
(92nd St.)
876-6000

This small hotel off museum mile has 150 simple rooms with bath. They are comfortable enough, but be sure to ask for a quiet room. It's clean, with a coffee shop next door. Because of the out-of-way location, it has very reasonable prices.

Singles, doubles: $45–$90.

Wellington
Seventh Avenue and 55th Street
247-3900

The Wellington is a large, older hotel with small rooms, but it's a good value and is well kept up. Ask for a room in the "new" section. If a blizzard traps you in town overnight, it's worth a try.

Singles: $50–$60; doubles: $60–$70; suites: $95–$135.

• Wentworth
59 W. 46th St.
719-2300
(800)223-1900

Convenient to the theaters and jewelry district, this small, older hotel faces the city's newest park, People Plaza. The 240 rooms have big old tubs, cheerful floral wallpaper and curtains, cable television and air conditioning. Ask for the larger, sunny rooms facing south. Modest, but obviously well maintained.

Singles: $50; doubles: $60; suites: $80.

THE SHOPS

The Shops

CONSUMMATE CONSUMERISM

It's not hard to come to the conclusion that New York City is simply one big advertisement: there is always something new to buy and something impossible to live without. New Yorkers may be the consummate consumers: the ladies who lunch always seem to sport new wardrobes, and their affluent homes, whether they be in SoHo or Sutton Place, display the latest at-home accessories, often just featured in chichi design magazines. But there are millions of bargains in New York, and it's generally unnecessary to pay full price for anything. If all else fails, the street vendors may have just what you're looking for. It's a shopper's dream and a spendthrift's nightmare—New York is the consuming capital of the New World!

Antiques

We haven't attempted the impossible: to assemble a comprehensive list of all of the antique dealers and secondhand shops in New York City. Instead we have listed what we feel are the most promising shops. You might want to do some exploring on your own and find your own special place.

The Downtown Antique District

The highest concentration in New York of antique dealers, both retail and wholesale, are scattered throughout an area bordered by Broadway and University Place, from 10th to 13th streets. What were once strictly import shops, to the trade only, now have found themselves next to shops selling Mickey Mouse watches or '50s moderne. The shops are too numerous to list individually, and our recommendation is that you wander about the area, checking both sides of the street—you're bound to find something of interest.

Walking the Streets

Madison Avenue has shops scattered on both sides, from the low 60s up through the 80s. Look up, because many are one flight above. Prices are generally high, but the quality is good.

Fifty-seventh Street from Third to Fifth avenues is for the more affluent. Shops border both sides of the street, and some are even hidden away in office buildings, preventing common passersby from gawking.

Lexington Avenue from the high 60s to the low 80s has a smattering of shops, but not very many. The same goes for the Chelsea area (Ninth Avenue in the twenties).

Second Avenue has shops in the twenties, 50s and 60s, spaced quite erratically.

In Greenwich Village, the majority of antique shops are concentrated on Bleecker Street from Seventh Avenue to 11th Street. Hudson Street has several shops, though they are generally of a secondhand-shop nature.

Columbus Avenue (the high 60s to 80s) is the up-and-coming urban renewal candidate, with lots of chic restaurants and boutiques. Look for more antique shops to appear there. Also check out the SoHo area. More than likely you'll get to chatting with an antique dealer who will suggest another shop. Happy hunting!

AMERICAN

America Hurrah
766 Madison Ave.
(66th St.)
535-1930
Tues. to Sat. 11:00 A.M. to 6:00 P.M.

Hooray for America Hurrah! After fifteen years in the business it has moved to a bigger and better location, with two floors filled with country Americana: more than 400 old quilts, game boards, black rag dolls, grain-painted furniture, splint baskets, needlepoint samplers and teddy bears. This is the real thing—not the "country look" made popular by decorating magazines, but honest-to-goodness antique country items. One of the top Americana dealers in New York, America Hurrah has had many of its more important pieces purchased and exhibited by major museums and private collections. It offers restoration consultation as well as quilt mounting and framing.

Laura Fisher/ Antique Quilts & Country Things

Gallery 73
1050 Second Ave.
(55th St.)
838-2596
Daily 1:30 P.M. to 6:00 P.M. and by appt.
(866-6033) from 9:00 A.M.

Laura speaks several languages and will be only too happy to tell you anything you want to know about her antique quilts ($275 to $700) and collection of folksy arts and crafts. Her gallery, at the back of the third floor in the Manhattan Antiques Center, is worth tracking down. Crammed into every corner are baskets, tables, toys, folk art (decoys, primitives, needlework samplers) and all sizes of quilts. She arranges for quilt repair and restoration, finds antique textiles and folk art for collectors and lectures on quilt care and collecting.

Funchies, Bunkers, Gaks and Gleeks

Gallery 71
1050 Second Ave.
(55th St.)
980-9418
Mon. to Sat. 11:00 A.M. to 6:00 P.M.; Sun. noon to 6:00 P.M.

What at first glance might seem like a confusing, chaotic jumble, jammed to the rafters with a thousand things, is actually quite cleverly organized by subject, object, color or material used in the making. Choose among hundreds of patchwork and appliqué quilts (each one photographed in an album for easy selection), a huge number of delightful duck and goose decoys, cast-iron doorstops, metal chocolate and ice cream molds, lead soldiers by the regiment, tin windup toys, cast-iron still and mechanical banks and a multitude of other collectible items.

The Gazebo

660 Madison Ave.
(61st St.)
832-7077
Mon. to Sat. 9:00 A.M. to 6:30 P.M.; Sun. 1:30 P.M. to 6:00 P.M.

Sugar and spice and everything nice—that's what The Gazebo is made of. Pastels set the tone, from the old and new patchwork and appliqué quilts and hooked and woven rag rugs to pillows, place mats, pot holders and painted baskets. Everything is color coordinated—there are no nasty dark colors to cast gloomy shadows in this candy-colored fantasy shop. Each item is designed to make you smile, especially the doggies, kitties, bunnies and duckies that are totally devoid of teeth, claws or any of the true grit usually found in old Americana. The Gazebo is charming and delightful in a studied manner.

Kelter-Malce

361 Bleecker St.
(W. 10th St.)
989-6760
Mon. to Sat. noon to 8:00 P.M. (closed Sat. in July and Aug.)

One of the more important American folk-art shops in New York, with a huge selection of patchwork quilts, hooked rugs and rag runners, whirligigs, weather vanes, checkerboards, black rag dolls, carved folk figures and toys. There is also a large selection of old Christmas tree ornaments year around. The decor is country barn siding and beams, and there's a country kitchen with an old stove to display its collection of sponge-decorated pitchers, bowls and agateware.

Bernard and S. Dean Levy
Carlyle Hotel
981 Madison Ave.
2nd floor
(76th St.)
628-7088
Tues. to Sat. 10:00 A.M. to 5:30 P.M.; (open Mon., closed Sat. in summer)

The highest-quality American antique furniture and decorations are here in a showroom larger than some museums' American wings. It specializes in furniture from the late seventeenth through the early nineteenth centuries, along with the complementary silver, export porcelain, pottery and paintings of the same period. Levy is also known for special painting exhibitions, such as that of the work of Cecil B. Bell, who has been compared with Reginald Marsh and John Sloan. Serious collectors consider Levy the top name for American antiques of investment quality.

Made in America
1234 Madison Ave.
(88th St.)
2nd floor
289-1113
Mon. to Fri. 10:30 A.M. to 6:30 P.M.; Sat. 11:00 A.M. to 5:30 P.M.

Country antiques and quilts are the specialty of this attractive boutique. The quilts date from the late nineteenth through the first half of the twentieth century. There are a few contemporary articles made in the old-fashioned manner, along with evening classes in quilting and quilts (call for information). Summer hours may vary, so you might want to telephone before visiting.

Random Harvest
60 W. 75th St.
799-0134
Daily noon to 7:00 P.M. (Wed. to Fri. to 9:00 P.M.)

Beth Genther and her associates spent years as runners, wholesaling antique quilts to many of the larger, well-known antique dealers in New York. It was hard work, and when they thought it might be easier to settle down in one location and sell to the public directly, most of their former customers were supportive and offered encouraging advice. Needless to say, the shop was an immediate success, and they are now working twice as hard to keep the shop well stocked. They offer antique quilts, fine linens, vintage clothing, wicker furniture and iron bedsteads in a relaxed, apartmentlike setting. The prices are right.

Israel Sacks
15 E. 57th St.
753-6562
Mon. to Fri. 10:00 A.M. to 3:00 P.M.; Sat. by appt. only (open July and Aug. by appt. only)

At Israel Sacks you'll discover a choice selection of important American furniture dating from 1650 to 1825. William and Mary, Queen Anne, Chippendale, Hepplewhite and Pilgrim items, even a few rare John Seymour pieces, are to be found here. Museum-quality pieces at museum-quality prices.

Thomas G. Schwenke
956 Madison Ave.
(75th St.)
772-7222
Tues. to Sat. 11:00 A.M. to 6:00 P.M. (closed Sat. in summer)

The investment-quality formal Queen Anne, Chippendale, Hepplewhite, Sheraton and early classical American furniture here is guaranteed authentic for the serious collector. Mr. Schwenke shares the space with Child's Gallery (772-6606), which specializes in American paintings, watercolors, drawings and prints.

Thos. K. Woodard American Antiques and Quilts

835 Madison Ave.
(69th-70th sts.)
988-2906
Mon. to Sat. 11:00 A.M. to 6:00 P.M. (closed Sat. in July and Aug.)

Tom Woodard and Blanche Greenstein specialize in antique quilts in excellent condition dating from the early nineteeth to early twentieth centuries, with highly original patterns. Prices range from $80 for an unlined top quilt to $700 for an entire quilt, and more for the rarest pieces. They also carry some antique painted country furniture, baskets and old rag rugs. A large selection of new woven rag rugs in traditional patterns, from runner to room size, and a sizable fabric department with new solids and calico prints in the country look are pushing this shop out of the antique category.

ART DECO · ART NOUVEAU

Added Treasures

577 Second Ave.
(31st St.)
889-1776
Mon. to Sat. noon to 6:00 P.M.

If you're looking for a good time and want to smile while you're antiquing in New York, make Added Treasures a must-see. Deco, nouveau, funky and spunky nineteenth- and twentieth-century American memorabilia, artifacts and serious collector's pieces are abundant. The delightful stock (from $1 to $1,000) changes every day.

Artisan Antiques

999 Second Ave.
(52nd St.)
750-8892
Mon. to Sat. 10:00 A.M. to 6:00 P.M.

Artisan specializes in '20s and '30s frosted glass lighting fixtures (Lalique, Sabino, Degue, Le Leu), perfect accents for the good art deco furniture and bronze sculptures (Le Verrier, Le Faguays) also found in the glowing atmosphere of this shop. A few doors down, at 989 Second Avenue (751-5214), is a larger showroom offering mostly French furniture, bronzes and porcelains. Between these two showrooms we just might be looking at the largest selection of art deco lighting in the world.

Delorenzo

958 Madison Ave.
(75th St.)
249-7575
Mon. to Sat. 10:30 A.M. to 5:30 P.M.
(Closed Sat. in summer)

A good selection of art deco furniture, lighting and decorative objects, mostly French, is featured in this store. Superior quality that is quite costly.

Leo Kaplan

910 Madison Ave.
(73rd St.)
249-6766
Mon. to Sat. 10:00 A.M. to 5:30 P.M.
(Closed Sat. in summer)

An unusual combination of four separate specialties characterizes this interesting shop: art nouveau glass (Daum, Gallé, Webb, Stevens and Williams), eighteenth-century English pottery and porcelain (Prattware, Staffordshire, Wedgwood and Worcester), a huge assortment of antique and modern paperweights (Baccarat, Saint Louis, Clichy) and Russian enamel and porcelain. This curious contrast, which proves to be quite compatible, developed because each of the family members brought his or her own separate interest to the shop. Worth a visit.

Muriel Karasik
1094 Madison Ave. (82nd St.) 535-7851
Mon. to Fri. 10:00 A.M. to 6:00 P.M.

This extraordinary shop deals in one-of-a-kind furniture and decorations—predominately high-style art deco in glass, chrome, lacquer and silver, combined with less formal pieces of folk art, such as turn-of-the-century weather vanes, whirligigs and old oversize advertising display items that are used as pop-art sculptures. Typical of its flair for the unusual is the Egyptian revival bed made as a prop for the film *The Ten Commandments* in the 1950s. Such items as these account for Karasik's popularity with the top interior designers.

Kips Bay Gallery
462 Third Ave. (32nd St.) 685-1364
Mon. to Sat. 11:00 A.M. to 7:00 P.M.

Period art deco and art nouveau of the highest quality are featured here in an ever-changing collection of unusual American and European furniture and decorative accessories, including important signed art glass, light fixtures, paintings, posters and rugs. Congenial proprietor Stuart Sacks makes his selections with a broad knowledge and appreciation of art and a meticulous concern for authenticity. The focus here is on fine and exotic woods, but there are also chrome and lacquer pieces, all exemplifying good design and good taste.

D. Leonard and Gerry Trent
950 Madison Ave. (74th St.) 737-9511
Mon. to Thurs. 11:00 A.M. to 6:00 P.M.; Fri. 11:00 A.M. to 5:30 P.M.; Sat. 11:00 A.M. to 5:00 P.M. (closed Sat. in summer)

Come to this pleasant shop for a good offering of Tiffany lamps and glass, art nouveau furniture, American bronzes, Jensen silver, Mucha lithographic posters and art nouveau and art deco jewelry.

Simon Lieberman
989 Madison Ave. (77th St.) 744-3005
Mon. to Sat. 10:30 A.M. to 5:00 P.M. (closed Sat. in July and Aug.)

Art nouveau and art deco furniture, paintings and glass, all of fine quality, are featured at this establishment. A delightful ambience is created by the contrast of Tiffany, Daum, Gallé and Marinet in objets d'art; Toulouse-Lautrec, Jules Cheret and Emile Grasset in posters; and the large selection of ceramics by Picasso.

Macklowe Gallery, Ltd.

This spacious two-floor showroom is filled with art nouveau furniture and art objects, including Tiffany and French cameo glass vases and lamps. There's also a fine

**982 Madison Ave.
(76th St.)
288-1124**

*Mon. to Fri. 10:45 A.M. to 5:45
P.M.; Sat. 10:45 A.M. to 4:45 P.M.
(closed Sat. in July and Aug.)*

selection of jewelry signed by Tiffany, Cartier, Lalique and other important designers, all of the highest caliber.

Modernism
**984 Madison Ave.
(77th St.)
744-9040**

*Mon. to Fri. 10:45 A.M. to 6:00
P.M.; Sat. 10:45 A.M. to 5:00 P.M.
(closed Sat. in July and Aug.)*

A large gallery, newly opened, specializing in Vienna Secession (an arts and crafts movement from 1900 to 1920) and French art deco furniture and objects. It was a matter of national pride with the French, epitomized by the ocean liner *Normandie*, to show that they had survived World War I with their design leadership intact. High-quality construction, lavish and opulent materials (rosewood, Makassar ebony, sharkskin, palm wood, zebra wood) and a timeless endurance of design are all evident in the fascinating decorative items offered by this gallery.

Lillian Nassau, Ltd.
**220 E. 57th St.
759-6062**

*Mon. to Fri. 10:00 A.M. to 5:30
P.M.; Sat. 10:30 A.M. to 5:00 P.M.
(closed Sat. in summer)*

Tiffany glass and Lillian Nassau are synonymous; you can't think of one without the other. She is credited with creating the resurgence of interest in Tiffany glass in the '50s and paving the way for many other shops—but none match this one, which features probably the largest selection of Tiffany lamps in the world. In business for more than 40 years, she recently retired at age 83, but her son, Paul, still carries on the tradition she started, selling art nouveau and art deco furniture, glass, ceramics, silver and bronze accessories. The stock is too large and too diversified to list, but among the items you'll find are American bronze sculptures by Frishmuth, Hoffman and Hyatt, an interesting selection of Wiener Werkstaette (a European crafts movement) and classic American and European art pottery by Rookwood, Grueby, Newcomb, Zsolnay, Rorstrand and even Sèvres, to mention a few.

Oldies, Goldies and Moldies
**1609 Second Ave.
(83rd St.)
737-3935**

*Mon. to Fri. noon to 8:00 P.M.; Sat.
11:00 A.M. to 7:00 P.M.; Sun.
11:00 A.M. to 6:00 P.M.*

Art deco furniture, decorations and accessories are the current specialties, though Empire pieces can be found here, too. The lighting ranges from hanging fixtures to floor lamps; giftware includes sets of china, glasses, pottery and a good selection of jewelry. The store also offers such special services as restoration and refurbishing of furniture, stained glass, lighting fixtures, clocks and watches; radio repair; and silver plating.

Primavera Gallery
808 Madison Ave.

Art deco is the specialty here: cabinets, chairs, consoles and dressing tables, by such names as Ruhlmann, Sue et Mare, Pierre Chareau and Jean Dunand. There are floor lamps, vases, art glass, silver and lots of other objects for

(68th St.)
288-1569
Mon. to Sat. 11:00 A.M. to 6:00
P.M. (closed Sat. in summer)

art deco fanciers, including a fine collection of jewelry from all the important designers of the period.

Minna Rosenblatt
840 Madison Ave.
(70th St.)
288-0250
Mon. to Sat. 10:00 A.M. to
6:00 P.M.

Recently moved to the newly renovated Westbury Hotel shops, Rosenblatt has a huge selection of decorative art glass, Tiffany lamps and vases, French cameo glass (Gallé, Daum and others), pâte de verre and Loetz, all from the art nouveau and art deco periods.

Rita Sacks/ Limited Additions
Gallery 66
1050 Second Ave.
(55th St.)
421-8132
Mon. to Sat. 10:30 A.M. to 6:00
P.M.; Sun. noon to 6:00 P.M.

An atmosphere of discovery beckons visitors to this delightful shop, which is filled with an eclectic array of often dramatic surprises. Art nouveau and art deco are emphasized here; nineteenth- and twentieth-century signed art glass, art pottery, Orientalia, jewelry and decorative objects abound. Possibly the best surprise (and the reason for a special trip) is the in-depth collection of twentieth-century costume jewelry lovingly shown by owner Rita Sacks, who herself collects outrageous fakes.

Second Hand Rose
573 Hudson St.
(11th St.)
989-9776
Mon. to Fri. 10:00 A.M. to 6:00
P.M.; Sat. noon to 5:00 P.M. (closed
Sat. in summer)

This shop carries a huge selection of moderne furniture and accessories from the '20s through the '50s, from such names as Eames, Frankl, Nelson and Rohde and it also offers a vast amount of period wallpaper. If you like that sort of thing, this is the shop for you, but avoid it if you are a Chippendale type.

Fred Silberman
1162 Madison Ave.
(85th St.)
861-0705
Mon. to Sat. 10:30 A.M. to 6:00
P.M. (closed Sat. in July and Aug.)

Silberman has been in business for more than eighteen years, specializing in Italian moderne and other art deco furniture and decorations from France, Austria and Germany. It services collectors, dealers and museums all over the world, with a keen eye for quality, style, line and proportion taking precedence over names—but the important names (Wiener Werkstaette, Hoffman, Gio Ponti, Picasso) are here.

AUCTION HOUSES

A major portion of the antiques and art trade is transacted over the auction block. You may have an urge to go where the dealers do, thinking you can get it wholesale, but *caveat emptor*—auctions are for neither the timid, the faint of heart, nor the uninitiated. If you do go to bid, make certain you have inspected the merchandise; then decide on your maximum bid before the sale, and stick to that figure. Don't get caught up in the fun and excitement of auction fever—before you know it, your bid will be astronomical!

Christies
502 Park Ave.
(59th St.)
546-1000
Mon. to Fri. 10:00 A.M. to 5:00 P.M. (earlier closing on auction days); viewing to 2:00 P.M. on days preceding auctions

The second biggest name in the auction business, worldwide and in New York, Christies has important weekly specialty sales in Americana, Oriental works of art, art nouveau, paintings and more. Many record prices are set here.

Christies East
219 E. 67th St.
570-4141
Mon. to Sat. 10:00 A.M. to 5:00 P.M.; some Sun. 1:00 P.M. to 5:00 P.M.

A subsidiary branch of Christies, this outfit sells interesting but less important furniture, paintings, glass and china. There are also periodic collectors' sales of toys, dolls and quilts.

William Doyle Galleries
175 E. 87th St.
427-2730
Mon. 9:00 A.M. to 7:30 P.M.; Tues. 9:00 A.M. to 5:00 P.M.; Sat. 10:00 A.M. to 5:00 P.M.; Sun. (during exhibition weeks only) noon to 5:00 P.M.

The third in New York auction sales, Doyle is American owned, with no worldwide branches. It's quite fashionable with the Gucci and Louis Vuitton set, which makes it increasingly difficult for dealers to buy here, as prices often go far beyond retail. There have been interesting estate sales (Hope Hampton, Gloria Swanson), and it's the only auction gallery to have twice-yearly auctions of duck decoys and shorebirds.

Phillips Fine Art Auctioneers
406 E. 79th St.
570-4841
Mon. to Fri. 9:00 A.M. to 5:00 P.M.

The third-largest auction house worldwide, but the fourth in New York sales, has recently moved. The new location (the former Plaza Auction Gallery) should prove to be better suited to auctions than the previous ones. You'll find all sorts of high-quality fine and decorative arts, from paintings to furniture to objets d'art.

Sotheby Parke Bernet
1334 York Ave.
(72nd. St.)
472-3400
Tues. to Sat. 9:30 A.M. to 5:00 P.M.

This is the largest and most important auction gallery in New York and the world. Newly relocated in a luxuriously renovated building, Sotheby's has always been in the news with multi-million-dollar painting sales records. The latest news involves threats of corporate takeover and a disappearing diamond, a story that rivals TV's *Dallas* for intrigue. You too can be part of the excitement—bidding and buying Old Masters, modern or Impressionist paintings, jewelry worth a king's ransom, fine furniture from England, France, China or Japan, African masks, Egyptian sculpture and just about any other sort of valuable you could imagine.

Sotheby's Arcade Auctions

1334 York Ave.
(72nd. St.)
472-3577
Mon. to Sat. 9:15 A.M. to 5:00 P.M.
(call for exhibition hours)

You'll generally find more affordable items than upstairs here, with regular sales each week and specialty sales in toys and dolls twice a year.

Swann Galleries

104 E. 25th St.
4th floor
254-4710
Mon. to Fri. 9:00 A.M. to 6:00 P.M.; Sat. 10:00 A.M. to 4:00 P.M.

At this small auction house sales, arranged around a central theme, are conducted every Thursday. Usually you'll find rare books, autographs, manuscripts, maps, atlases, prints and other graphic arts, and photographic materials. Inspection exhibitions are held the two days preceding each sale.

BOOKS

J.N. Bartfield

45 W. 57th St.
753-1830
Mon. to Fri. 10:00 A.M. to 5:00 P.M.; Sat. 10:00 A.M. to 2:30 P.M. (closed Sat. June to Sept.)

A specialist in bindings, which many top interior designers buy by the yard to give a literary look to a room. That's not to say that the books themselves are devoid of interest; there is a little bit of everything—art, history, philosophy and, of course, fiction, most commonly sold in sets. A yard of Kipling, anyone?

Antiquarian Booksellers Center

50 Rockefeller Plaza
(50th St.)
246-2564
Mon. to Fri. 9:30 A.M. to 5:30 P.M.

A few shelves with rare tomes in all languages and on all subjects. Come here for a listing of the best rare book dealers affiliated with the Antiquarian Booksellers Association.

Appelfeld Gallery

1372 York Ave.
(73rd. St.)
988-7835
Mon. to Fri. 10:00 A.M. to 6:00 P.M.; Sat. by appt. only

This small, old-fashioned book shop has walls lined with rare books and first editions, many illustrated and with leather bindings. Browsers are welcome in Appelfeld's pleasant atmosphere. The store also offers a mail-order catalog subscription ($5 for the year).

Argosy Book Store

116 E. 59th St.
753-4455
Mon. to Fri. 9:00 A.M. to 6:00 P.M.; Sat. 10:00 A.M. to 5:00 P.M. (closed Sat. May to Sept.)

More than just a bookstore—this is a library where researchers come to consult all sorts of documents on all sorts of subjects. The collection of maps is probably the most comprehensive in New York, and you'll also see an excellent selection of old engravings and posters. Prices vary, of course, but there is much here that any browser can afford.

Philip C. Duschnes
699 Madison Ave.
(62nd. St.)
838-2635
Mon. to Fri. 9:45 A.M. to 4:30 P.M.

The quality of what is offered here is beyond reproach: the selection consists almost entirely of illuminated manuscripts, fine press books, fine printings and bindings, and first editions of American literature. An appointment is suggested.

Lucien Goldschmidt
1117 Madison Ave.
(83rd. St.)
879-0070
Mon. to Fri. 10:00 A.M. to 6:00 P.M.; Sat. 10:00 A.M. to 5:00 P.M.

Lucien Goldschmidt was established in New York more than 40 years ago. The collection comprises Continental books exclusively: French, Dutch and Italian, from fifteenth-century incunabula to books from the 1950s. There is a large selection of engravings and drawings by European artists from 1800 to 1950.

Leonard S. Granby
1168 Lexington Ave.
(80th St.)
249-2651
Mon. to Sat. 10:00 A.M. to 6:00 P.M. (Sat. by appt. only in summer)

This is a pleasant little shop filled with rare books and limited editions on almost every subject. Lots to browse through, without pressure to buy, in this amiable and easygoing gallery. Call first, as hours may vary.

Hacker Art Books
54 W. 57th St.
757-1450
Mon. to Sat. 9:30 A.M. to 6:00 P.M. (closed Sat. in summer)

Hacker has one of the largest selections of books on art and architecture—both old and rare—in the world. You will also find a few engravings here.

CLOCKS

William E. Berger Antique Clocks
29 E. 12th St.
929-1830
Tues. to Sat. noon to 6:00 P.M. (closed Sat. in summer) Appt. suggested

Primarily a clock and watch restoration specialist who repairs any vintage timepiece, Mr. Berger comes with good references from museums and antique dealers. He also sells clocks (anything from a small carriage clock to a huge grandfather clock), as well as jewelry and small collectibles.

The Clock Hutt, Ltd.
1050 Second Ave.
(56th St.)
759-2395
Mon. to Sat. 10:30 A.M. to 5:30 P.M.; Sun. 1:00 P.M. to 5:30 P.M.

After twenty years in business, specializing in rare and antique timepieces, Fred and Lila Hutt are in their second generation as a family business, now that their son David does excellent clock repair work. The shop's more than 1,200 square feet houses the largest collection of eighteenth- and nineteenth-century European and American clocks in New York, from miniatures to grandfathers to everything in between.

William Scolnick and Joseph Fanelli
**1001 Second Ave.
(53rd. St.)
355-1160**
*Mon. to Fri. 10:00 A.M. to
5:30 P.M.*

Antique grandfather clocks, wall clocks, carriage clocks, wristwatches, pocket watches and fobs can be found at these specialists, who carry only the best. Customers come from all over the world. Repair service is available, with estimates given free.

CURIOSITIES

Gloria Boscardin
**Gallery 70
1050 Second Ave.
(55th St.)
980-3268**
Tues. to Sun. noon to 5:30 P.M.

Those who like the romantic and the pretty will love Gloria Boscardin's shop. It's a tiny, comfortably cluttered boutique with a mélange of exquisite antique fans, dozens of art deco and Victorian beaded and mesh evening bags, fine jewelry, perfume bottles, enameled, silver, brass and bronze picture frames, delicate laces, linens, paisley shawls, needlepoint pictures, samplers and other sewn collectibles. She is a charming lady who is well liked by her regular customers, but who can be impatient and abrupt at times. Serious browsers, however, are always welcome.

Bottles Unlimited
**245 E. 78th St.
570-6571**
By appt. only

A rather dusty display of good old American hand-blown bottles and historical flasks, as well as glass whimsies and walking sticks is what you'll find in this unpretentious shop. It has everything from pretty colored glass for $5 to historical flasks for as much as $10,000. Whether you are a novice or an advanced bottle collector, you should definitely check out this dealer—it's the only shop of its kind in New York.

Robert L. Brooks
**235 E. 53 St.
486-9829**
*Mon. to Fri. 11:30 A.M. to 5:00
P.M.; Sat. by appt. only*

It's a man's world at Mr. Brooks's shop, a mellow, smoke-filled room with an atmosphere of masculine camaraderie. Women are not excluded, but they tend to steer clear of this store filled with military and nautical accessories. Far from being hawkish, though, Mr. Brooks is an amiable teddy bear. His interests run to the historical aspects of arms, armor and military items; he has a fine selection of American and British percussion and flintlock firearms and edged weapons, peppered with uniforms, drums, flags and other military accoutrements.

Vito Giallo Antiques
966 Madison Ave.

A small shop with a big, eclectic stock of decorative items: Chinese pottery and porcelain, nineteenth-century silver, carved wooden santos figures, majolica, fountain

(76th St.)
535-9885
Mon. to Sat. 11:00 A.M. to
6:00 P.M.

pens and inkwells and even some furniture. There is a substantial turnover, so the selection is continually changing. A good shop for browsing.

Johnny Jupiter
385 Bleecker St.
(Perry St.)
675-7574
Tues. to Sun. noon to 7:00 P.M.

Come to Johnny Jupiter if what you like is kitchen kitsch, and lots of it—salt and pepper shakers, utensils, dish towels and linens, enamel dishes and other objects from 1920 to 1950. The store also carries tons of forgotten amusements: plastic water pistols, tin toys, jokes, novelties and those tricks children used to order from the back pages of comic books. A true nostalgia trip.

Phyllis Lucas Old Print Center
981 Second Ave.
(52nd St.)
755-1516
Tues. to Sat. 9:00 A.M. to 5:30 P.M.

Whether you're looking for a woodcut, aquatint, etching, engraving, lithograph or any other form of print, visit this shop, which specializes in all of the above. Lucas has periodical exhibitions of different artists or themes, and there are prints available in most subjects; golf, medicine, law, sports, the military, maps, Audubon, Currier and Ives. All are suitable for framing, which Lucas also does.

Man-Tiques, Ltd. Gallery 69
1050 Second Ave.
(55th St.)
759-1805
Mon. to Sat. 11:00 A.M. to 6:00
P.M.; Sun. noon to 6:00 P.M.

Elly Zelin and her mother, Margaret Hirsch Weiss, have been business partners for eighteen years. The antique shop evolved from the family hat business, when momma used to decorate the window displays with fancy canes and other manly accessories. Changes in fashion found them selling more accessories than hats, and thus Man-Tiques was born. The name says it all—antiques for men. Special-interest collectibles in many media, such as canes and walking sticks, occupational shaving mugs, postcards and stereopticon slides, are always in stock. The themes and subjects range from ocean liner and coronation commemorations to Napoleon, Dickens and Shakespeare to tennis, golf and other sports. Steins, medical instruments, cigar cutters, match safes, scales and cameras are just a few examples of the exceptionally varied choices here for both novice and advanced collectors.

Nelson's Folly
152 E. 79th St.
(2nd floor)
755-0485
Mon. to Sat. 11:00 A.M. to
6:00 P.M.

Nautical and marine artifacts are the specialty here: ship models, half hulls, paintings, telescopes, running lights, scrimshaw, ships in bottles. After being in business for more than 35 years, Mr. Cowell doesn't get around quite as well as he used to, so a lot of space has been filled in with more contemporary objects—but the shop is still worth checking out.

Ellen O'Neill's Supply Store

Newly relocated in larger quarters, this shop is predominantly a vintage clothing and linen boutique, with some quilts, quilt tops, textiles, lace, ribbon and

242 E. 77th St.
879-7330
Mon. to Sat. 11:00 A.M. to
7:00 P.M.

Philip W. Pfeifer
900 Madison Ave.
(72nd St.)
249-4889
Mon. to Fri. 10:30 A.M. to 5:30
P.M.; Sat. by appt. only (store open by
appt. only in Aug.)

Ann Philipps Antiques
899 Madison Ave.
(72nd St.)
535-0415
Tues. to Sat. 10:00 A.M. to
5:30 P.M.

Piston's Gallery 92
1050 Second Ave.
(55th St.)
753-8322
Mon. to Fri. 10:30 A.M. to 4:00
P.M.; Sat. by appt.

The Place for Antiques
993 Second Ave.
(53rd St.)

trimmings, buttons and beads. There are also plastic boxes filled with small novelties, erasers, pencil sharpeners and tiny toys, like a colorful penny candy display.

Someone once said, "What separates the men from the boys is the price of their toys." A fabulous assortment of eighteenth- and nineteenth-century toys awaits the men who can afford them here: toys such as remarkable Noah's Ark sets with carved wooden animals marching two by two, brass microscopes and telescopes of all different sizes, magnifying glasses, corkscrews, candlesticks, canes and all sorts of interesting scientific and medical instruments for the professional collector.

This fascinating store specializes in nineteenth- and twentieth-century ephemera and commemorative items. Political buttons and banners; presidential, suffragette and theatrical posters, pamphlets and flyers; military, world's fair and Civil War memorabilia—name any subject, and there's probably an object in this shop that relates to it. The hard-to-find character of these items justifies their premium prices.

Fay Piston is still carrying on the family business. What started 75 years ago as a simple metal repair service has evolved into a shop dealing exclusively in museum-quality pewter-, copper- and brassware ranging from the sixteenth to the nineteenth centuries. English and Dutch pewter tankards and platters sit side by side with early copper kettles and brass candlesticks of worldwide origin. There is a good selection of eighteenth-century American bell-metal andirons, brass fire tools and other fireplace accoutrements. Also of interest is the huge collection of metal and glass curtain tiebacks: clusters of silver mercury glass, bunches of gilded brass flowerettes, lacy-petaled pressed sandwich glass and delicately painted late-eighteenth-century Battersea enamel rondelles cover two walls, making it look like a surrealistic botanical garden. Mrs. Piston is an expert in her field and is well respected by an international clientele, including museum curators and other serious collectors. Prices are commensurate with the quality and importance of the pieces.

There is a rough-hewn, folksy quality to this intriguing shop. Rustic Adirondack twig furniture made from gnarled and twisted wood with the bark still attached, interesting pieces made from steer and elk horn, and

308-4066
Mon. to Sat. 10:30 A.M. to 6:30
P.M.; some Sun. (phone first)

Harmer Rooke Numismatists, Ltd.

3 E. 57th St.
751-1900
Mon. to Fri. 9:30 A.M. to 5:00
P.M.; Sat. 10:00 A.M. to 4:00 P.M.
(closed Sat. in summer)

Sideshow

184 Ninth Ave.
(21st St.)
675-2212
Tues. to Sat. 11:00 A.M. to
6:30 P.M.

Stampazine

3 E. 57th St.
(5th floor)
752-5905
Mon. to Fri. 10:00 A.M. to 6:00
P.M.; Sat. 10:00 A.M. to 5:00 P.M.

Winston House

997 Second Ave.
(53rd St.)
752-2665
Mon. to Sat. 11:00 A.M. to
5:00 P.M.

mounted-antler hunting trophy plaques are displayed against exposed brick, old shingles and weathered plank barn siding, all adding to the store's rugged appeal.

This unique gallery specializes in collectible coins and currency from ancient Greece to the twentieth century (which apparently necessitates the armed guard on duty). The guard and the physical layout of the premises contribute to its banklike, no-nonsense atmosphere. Compatible with the ancient coins is the huge selection of antiquities from Greece, Rome and Egypt, as well as the pre-Columbian artifacts. Another specialty is the amazing assortment of colorful American glass (bottles, flasks and all sorts of jars). All this and more is available across the counter and through a mail-order catalog auction several times a year.

A charming shop in Chelsea (a very up-and-coming district), filled with interesting and decorative tin advertising signs, old kitchen utensils and gadgets, and a diverse selection of nineteenth-century mementos. It also has a nice collection of vintage cast-iron and tin windup toys.

Established in 1937, Stampazine has the largest offering of collectible singles, blocks and sheets of postage stamps in the United States. It also sells through a bimonthly mail-order auction catalog. This shop is more for the serious collector than for the beginner.

This is a rather unpretentious setting for some interesting artifacts. The stock consists mainly of Greco-Roman and Egyptian antiquities and of primitive ethnographic artifacts from Africa, New Guinea and pre-Columbian and North American Indian cultures. The shop is also a source of many curiosities, including a fully articulated human skeleton; particularly macabre are the psychedelically decorated monkey skulls painted by Mr. Winston himself.

ENGLISH

Arthur Ackerman and Son

50 E. 57th St.
753-5292

Arthur Ackerman's collection of exquisite eighteenth-century English furniture and decorations shows a particular penchant for hunting and equestrian motifs— just right for the horsey set. Royal Worcester porcelain figural groups of racehorses and champion jumpers accent the sporting prints and paintings of fox hunters,

Mon. to Fri. 9:00 A.M. to 5:00
P.M.; Sat. to 4:00 P.M.

Judith Amdur Antiques
**950 Lexington Ave.
(69th St.)
472-2691**
*Mon. to Sat. 11:00 A.M. to
6:00 P.M.*

Phillip Colleck of London
**122 E. 57th St.
753-1544**
*Mon. to Fri. 9:30 A.M. to 5:30
P.M.; Sat. 9:30 A.M. to 2:00 P.M.*

La Compagnie Anglaise
**1113 Madison Ave.
(83rd St.)
772-8515**
*Mon. to Sat. 10:00 A.M. to
6:00 P.M.*

Eagles Antiques
**1097 Madison Ave.
(83rd St.)
772-3266**
*Tues. to Sat. 10:00 A.M. to
5:30 P.M.*

Hyde Park Antiques
**836 Broadway
(13th St.)
477-0033**
*Mon. to Fri. 9:00 A.M. to 5:30
P.M.; Sat. 10:00 A.M. to 3:00 P.M.
(closed Sat. in summer)*

dogs and polo ponies. There's also a fine selection of Dorothy Doughty porcelain bird groupings.

Here we have a husband and wife team that works separately at two different locations—a his-and-hers partnership that is probably the envy of other antique dealers. The other location is at 1193 Lexington Avenue, near 80th Street (879-0653). The stock of the two shops seems to overlap; you'll find smaller English furniture and decorations, inkwells, bells, rulers, picture frames, Staffordshire and copper luster. An interesting pair of stores—if she doesn't have what you want, then he probably does.

Established in New York in 1938, this very fine London firm recently moved to its new showroom. It features eighteenth-century English furniture, particularly Queen Anne and Chippendale, as well as a large array of mirrors, lamps, chandeliers and other accessories of the same period.

This tremendously successful Parisian firm specializes in rescuing and revitalizing antique English and Scottish pine furniture through its own special refinishing process. Its two-floor gallery has about 150 pieces on display at all times: armoires, chests of drawers, tables, chairs and sideboards, all refinished to the warm honey glow of the wood's natural color.

Eagles offers predominately English formal furniture of the eighteenth and early nineteenth centuries, together with a few American pieces from the same period. There's a grand array of dining tables and chairs, sideboards, secretaries, desks, chests, highboys, mirrors, drop leaf and card tables, and a good assortment of Chinese vases—both porcelain and cloisonné—mounted as lamps. Prices are high, but for this level of quality they usually are.

Located in the heart of the downtown antique district, these spacious showrooms on several floors are filled with what is probably the most varied and comprehensive collection of fine English furniture in America. Whether it is William and Mary or Regency, you are bound to find it here among the profusion of furniture and accessories and English and Chinese export porcelains, paintings and mirrors. An abundance of stock with an abundance of space to match, so there's no sense of crowding or clutter.

James II Galleries
15 E. 57th St.
6th floor
355-7040
Mon. to Fri. 10:00 A.M. to 5:30 P.M.; Sat. 10:30 A.M. to 5:30 P.M. (closed Sat. in summer)

When the elevator door opens, be prepared to stifle a scream of joy. It's antique heaven here, with everything neatly grouped and arranged, dusted, cleaned and polished. Bristol claret jugs, hyacinth vases, multicolored glass bells, cut and clear decanters, Nailsea glass whimsies; rolling pins, canes and paperweights; brass fireplace equipment, nutcrackers, desk accessories and candlesticks; turned wood objects, boxes, tea caddies, sewing boxes, humidors, gaming boxes and lap desks; tartan ware and tunbridge ware; Mason's ironstone, Imari dishes, Sunderland luster motto plaques, Staffordshire pink luster tea services—the list is endless. Each piece is chosen for its quality, charm and one-of-a-kind character. There's a dreamlike feeling seeing it all together—but the prices will shock you awake.

Marco Polo
1135 Madison Ave.
(85th St.)
734-3775
Mon. to Fri. 10:00 A.M. to 6:00 P.M.; Sat. noon to 5:00 P.M.

Marco Polo is a small shop dealing mostly in small items: porcelain snuffboxes, magnifying glasses, inkwells and other desk accessories, as well as smaller brass optical instruments, such as microscopes, telescopes and binoculars. Space is limited, but it does manage to fit in a nice selection of English bamboo and lacquer furniture, as well as child-scale Windsor chairs. A very pleasant store that is well worth looking into.

Royal Oaksmith
982 Second Ave.
(52nd St.)
751-3376
Mon. to Sun. noon to 9:00 P.M.

Here you'll find turn-of-the-century golden oak, walnut and stripped Irish pine furniture imported directly from Britain. A huge selection of dining tables, pressed back chairs, marble-topped washstands, vanities and nightstands is available, as well as a great number of mirror-front armoires. Of special interest to those looking for office or study furnishings are the legal-style stacking, glass-front sectional bookcases, wooden office files, rolltop desks and swivel chairs. With three other Oaksmith shops around the city, this place seems to be becoming the antique world's McDonald's.

Florian Papp
962 Madison Ave.
(76th St.)
288-6770
Mon. to Fri. 9:30 A.M. to 5:30 P.M.; Sat. 10:00 A.M. to 5:00 P.M. (closed Sat. in summer)

Florian Papp has the distinction of being the first antique store in New York. It opened at the turn of the century and for three generations has offered a marvelous collection of seventeenth- and eighteenth-century English furniture, together with a few American and Continental pieces and an ever-changing selection of mirrors, grandfathers clocks and other decorative accessories.

Trevor Potts Antiques
1011 Lexington Ave.
(72nd St.)
737-0909

This store specializes in English Regency painted furniture, chinoise-style lacquer and bamboo, and fine walnut and mahogany. Potts is also partial to fine needlepoint rugs and pictures, and trays in tole and papier-mâché, but its main love in accessory themes is dogs. Spaniels and pugs predominate the litter in porcelain, paintings and sculpture, but an occasional poodle or bulldog appears as well—a true dog fancier's delight.

Bob Pryor
1023 Lexington Ave. (73rd St.)
688-1516
Mon. to Sat. 10:30 A.M. to 5:30 P.M. (closed Sat. in summer)

Pryor's is a treasure trove of delightful items: predominantly English brass and treen artifacts, along with American and French objects. There is a huge assortment of old copper jelly molds, brass candlesticks, shoehorns, scales, inkwells, letter openers, snuffboxes, tobacco jars, nutcrackers, corkscrews, canes, door knockers, doorstops ... the list goes on and on. The shop is jammed to the rafters with individual items guaranteed to delight the eye as well as the heart.

Mon. to Fri. 9:00 A.M. to 5:00 P.M.; Sat. 10:00 A.M. to 4:00 P.M. (closed Sat. in summer)

Stair and Co.
59 E. 57th St.
355-7620
Mon. to Fri. 9:30 A.M. to 5:30 P.M.; Sat. 10:00 A.M. to 4:00 P.M. (closed Sat. in summer)

Established in 1912, Stair and Company has long enjoyed a trusted and honorable reputation in the field of fine English seventeenth- and eighteenth-century antiques. With five floors, its stock of Georgian furniture, Chinese export porcelains, paintings and other works of art is one of the largest in the world.

Stair's Incurable Collector
42 E. 57th St.
755-0140
Mon. to Fri. 9:30 A.M. to 5:30 P.M. (to 5:00 P.M. in summer); Sat. 11:00 A.M. to 4:30 P.M. (closed Sat. in summer)

Across the street from Stair and Company, this two-floor subsidiary sells the later (eighteenth- and nineteenth-century) English Regency furniture, Chinese lacquer screens and sporting and marine paintings. Everything here is of a high quality and is tastefully understated in the English manner.

Sylvia Tearston
1053 Third Ave. (62nd St.)
838-0415
Mon. to Fri. 9:30 A.M. to 5:00 P.M. Appt. suggested

English furniture and accessories of the Queen Anne, Chippendale and Regency periods are offered here. Decorations include Chinese export porcelain and paintings and a vast selection of American and European framed engravings, etchings and lithographs.

Tiller and King, Ltd.
1058 Madison Ave. (80th St.)
988-2861
Mon. to Sat. 10:00 A.M. to 5:30 P.M. (closed Sat. in July and Aug.)

This luxurious shop is filled with fine eighteenth- and nineteenth-century English furniture and decorative accessories, particularly export ware, Prattware, Wedgwood, clocks and paintings. Everything is tastefully displayed to enhance its elegance.

Vernay and Jussel

This outfit is one of New York's oldest and most respected antique dealers for seventeeth- and eighteenth-

**825 Madison Ave.
(69th St.)
879-3344**
*Mon. to Fri. 9:30 A.M. to 5:30
P.M.; Sat. 11:00 A.M. to 4:00 P.M.
(closed Sat. in summer)*

century English antiques: furniture, clocks, globes, mirrors and china produced in the Queen Anne and Georgian periods.

FRENCH · EUROPEAN

Didier Aaron
32 E. 67th St.
988-5248
*Mon. to Fri. 10:00 A.M. to
6:00 P.M.*

A famous Parisian dealer. The quality of the furniture, objets d'art and paintings on display here is equal only to the setting in which they are presented: a superb five-story townhouse decorated in eighteenth-and nineteenth-century European styles. The lavish collection includes such items as a Roentgen mahogany secrétaire made for Catherine II of Russia, chairs made for Versailles by Jean Boucault and Old Master paintings.

**L'Antiquaire,
and The
Connoisseur**
36 E. 73rd St.
517-9176
*Mon. to Fri. 9:00 A.M. to
5:30 P.M.*

Newly relocated in a brick townhouse, these two antique dealers continue their association, specializing in French and Italian furniture, paintings and decorative accessories from the fourteenth to the eighteenth centuries, with a few pieces from Spain for good measure.

**B.I.R.
Galleries**
**834 Madison Ave.
(71st St.)
737-5688**
*Mon. to Fri. 10:30 A.M. to 6:00
P.M.; Sat. 11:00 A.M. to 5:00 P.M.
(closed Sat. in summer); also by appt.*

A tasteful selection of eighteenth-century French furniture, sculpture and drawings, as well as nineteeth-century paintings, are pleasantly mixed with some knockout art deco pieces. It offers design and decorating consultation and has another shop in Paris.

**Tom Ballan-
Rhona
Lazarus
Antiques**
**1148 Second Ave.
(60th St.)
832-3490**
*Mon. to Fri. 10:30 A.M. to
5:30 P.M.*

A choice selection of Oriental and Biedermeir furniture is mixed with such stylish decorator items as carved blackamoor figures or German carved, polychromed female-figure and antler chandeliers. There is a satisfying selection of excellent enameled and etched colored Bohemian glass, as well as chess sets, mercury glass, cloisonné and screens—a very eclectic stock of items with strong decorative appeal.

**Bartholomew
Brown and
Co.**

Newly relocated, with a garden addition to the rear of the building for additional display space, this unpretentious shop has no particular style or period specialty other than nineteenth- and twentieth-century eclectic. The furniture

357 Bleecker St.
(10th St.)
691-6919
Wed. to Sun. noon to 7:00 P.M.

is serviceable, while the accessories are more stylish. The pleasant proprietor will assist in arranging for reupholstering or refinishing of furniture. Drop in if you're in the neighborhood.

Le Cadet de Gascogne
1015 Lexington Ave.
(73rd St.)
744-5925
Mon. to Sat. 10:00 A.M. to 6:00 P.M. (closed Sat. in July and Aug.)

This fine dealer recently moved to a luxurious, newly renovated showcase, an apartmentlike setting with gray flannel walls that offer the perfect background for the choice selection of French furniture, paintings and accessories. The proprietor, Gilbert Gestas, returns to the southwest of France each year to acquire antiques in his areas of specialty: Louis XIV, XV and XVI, Directoire and First Empire. Everything is authentic and in its original state, without restoration, and prices are reasonable for the quality offered. Mr. Gestas is a former stockbroker with a great deal of charm, and he'll give you a friendly welcome.

Dalva Brothers
44 E. 57th St.
758-2297
Mon. to Sat. 10:30 A.M. to 5:30 P.M. (closed Sat. in summer)

Five floors of carved-paneled rooms are filled with Louis XIV, XV and XVI furniture, covered in luscious brocades and delightful petit point tapestries. Period decorations include Sèvres vases as well as a grand selection of important eighteenth-century bronze and porcelain clocks (several from the Frick Museum exhibition). The objects are costly but not overpriced, and the proprietors are surprisingly pleasant and amiable, without the stiff reserve one might expect to find in such an elegant and opulent shop.

Evergreen
1249 Third Ave.
(72nd St.)
744-5664
Mon. to Sat. 11:00 A.M. to 7:00 P.M.

The Scandinavian penchant for elegantly simple design is abundantly present in these two shops. (The other is at 120 Spring Street, near Greene, 966-6458.) Owner Paul Siegenlaub has assembled possibly the largest collection of authentic eighteenth- and nineteenth-century Scandinavian country furniture anywhere, from currently popular stripped pine pieces (many with delicate hand carving) to singularly beautiful painted clocks, chests, chairs and cupboards. Prices are relatively reasonable, ranging from $300 for a pine side table with white marble top to a rosy painted armoire with original iron hardware, for your widest wall, at $9,500. There's also a good selection of inexpensive rag rugs in lovely heathery colors, with the odd dash of cranberry or bright blue, and gift-worthy salt glaze ceramic pickle jars in several sizes and shapes, from $25 to $100.

Hamilton-Hyre, Ltd.
413 Bleecker St.

This is one of the prime sources of the top interior designers for finding one-of-a-kind furnishings, particularly good bamboo furniture and items made from

(Bank St.)
989-4509
*Mon. to Fri. noon to 7:00 P.M.; Sat.
noon to 6:00 P.M. (closed Sat. in
summer)*

antlers. It's a very popular and busy shop with a huge turnover, so if you like something, buy it then and there—it
will probably be gone the following week.

Madison Galleries
1023 Second Ave.
(53rd St.)
688-1994
*Mon. to Sat. 9:00 A.M. to 5:30 P.M.
(closed Sat. in July and Aug.)*

Known in the design and decorating trade as an excellent
source for distinctive nineteenth-century Continental and
Oriental furniture and decorative items, Madison offers a
huge selection of Imari, Satsuma, ivory, hard stone,
bronze, Sèvres and Chinese lacquer pieces, plus screens
and furniture. Not the rarest of the rare, so prices are
relatively accessible.

Malmaison Antiques
29 E. 10th St.
(University Pl.)
473-0373
*Mon. to Fri. 10:00 A.M. to
6:00 P.M.*

New York's greatest specialist in Empire, Directoire and
Biedermeir styles. Roger Prigent's collection of furniture,
mostly French, is extremely impressive: there are more
than 1,000 pieces, only a few of which, necessarily, are
exhibited in this showroom. The rest can be studied in
photographs and by appointment at a nearby Broadway
showroom. Prices vary from $500 to $100,000 for the
best pieces. The quality of the wares and the welcome go
hand in hand; a visit here is a real pleasure.

Martell and Suffin Antiques
339 Bleecker St.
(W. 10th St.)
675-8764
*Mon. to Fri. noon to 7:00 P.M.; Sat.
noon to 6:00 P.M. (closed Sat. in
summer)*

You'll find a pleasant, eclectic selection of French,
English and Continental furniture and accessories, as
well as Oriental screens and decorations—elegant items
in an unpretentious setting. Uptown designers come
here for downtown prices.

Paul Martini Antiques
833 Broadway
(12th–13th Sts.)
982-5050
Mon. to Fri. 9:00 A.M. to 5:00 P.M.

Paul Martini is considered one of the best sources of
French eighteenth-century furniture and decorations.
There are also some English and Continental antiques
and objets d'art. His three floors of showrooms are well
worth a trip downtown.

J. Garvin Mecking
188 E. 64th St.
688-0840
*Mon. to Fri. 9:30 A.M. to 5:00 P.M.
(closed Mon. and Fri. in summer)*

This truly unique shop is filled with one-of-a-kind
decorative accessories and furniture. Many items are
made from lavish materials and reflect an attention to
detail that is lost today. Furniture is intricately carved and
inlaid with ivory, fancy woods, horn or mother-of-pearl.
Bamboo, lacquer, sharkskin, hand-tooled and decorated
leather and needlepoint abound in this charming
establishment. The accessories are equally luxurious, as
well as being rather whimsical; this has to be the largest

selection of majolica ware we've seen in New York. There's another furniture showroom at 72 East 11th Street (677-4316).

Pierre Deux
369 Bleecker St.
(Charles St.)
243-7740
Mon. to Sat. 10:00 A.M. to 6:00
P.M. (closed Sat. in July and Aug.)

If French provincial is your thing, you'll love this shop filled with armoires, chests, chairs, tables, loveseats and huge painted screens. Another shop, on Madison Avenue, features Pierre Deux's famous country print fabrics.

Juan Portela Antiques
783 Madison Ave.
(67th St.)
650-0085
Mon. to Sat. 10:00 A.M. to 6:00
P.M. (closed Sat. in July and Aug.)

If you're rich and want everyone to know it, visit this dealer for drop-dead decorative pieces that will have your friends and enemies green with envy. Top interior designers find their clients unique eighteenth- and nineteenth-century furniture, paintings and accessories at this luxurious, elegant shop.

Provence Antiques
35 E. 76th St.
288-5179
Mon. to Fri. 10:00 A.M. to
5:00 P.M.

Newly relocated in the Carlyle Hotel, these people continue to offer superb eighteenth-century French period furniture and decorations. Rare lacquer pieces from Europe and the Orient, an excellent selection of important Chinese and Japanese art objects and several magnificent period paneled rooms all are served up with panache and charm by the distinguished owners of this lavish, tasteful gallery.

Joseph Rondina, Ltd.
27 E. 62nd St.
758-2182
Mon. to Fri. 10:00 A.M. to
5:00 P.M.

A delightful shop that is slightly overcrowded with Continental and English furniture, Chinese sculpture and eclectic accessories. Each piece is chosen with great care, with an emphasis on high quality, true luxury and seductive charm. Having sold and shipped to more than 28 different countries, Mr. Rondina can freely admit to being world renowned.

Rosenberg and Stiebel
32 E. 57th St.
5th floor
753-4368
Mon. to Fri. 10:00 A.M. to 5:00
P.M. (appt. preferred)

For more than 100 years, this has been an outstanding source of magnificent works of art: medieval and Renaissance bronzes, European and Chinese porcelains, French and Italian furniture and Old Master paintings and drawings, all of which are consistently of museum quality.

N. Sakiel and Son
1024 Third Ave.
(60th St.)
838-8576
Mon. to Sat. 10:00 A.M. to
5:00 P.M.

N. Sakiel is an old European firm dealing mostly in fine eighteenth-century European and American furniture, ceramics, silver and bronzes. The emphasis here is on quality rather than on quantity.

Matthew Schutz
1025 Park Ave.
(85th St.)
876-4195
By appt. only

This Park Avenue dealer carries high-quality French furniture from the late seventeenth to the early nineteenth centuries. The choice of pieces is abundant, and, considering the quality, prices are fair—in the middle to high range. Lots of Chinese lacquer furniture. An excellent spot.

Peter Spielhagen Fine Arts
372 Bleecker St.
(Perry St.)
741-0489
Mon. to Sat. noon to 7:00 P.M.

A nice selection of small eighteenth- and nineteenth-century Continental furniture, accessories, paintings, prints and other artworks can be found here. We think this is a very pleasant shop for browsing.

Garrick C. Stephenson
50 E. 57th St.
(7th floor)
753-2570
Mon. to Fri. 10:00 A.M. to 5:00 P.M. (appt. suggested)

This store features a luxurious selection of Chinese and Japanese lacquer, as well as French furniture of the seventeenth and eighteenth centuries and a fine assortment of large wall mirrors from various countries and periods. Each piece is individually chosen for its extraordinary quality and craftsmanship, which tends to limit the number of items and give the gallery an uncluttered, almost Spartan atmosphere.

York House Antiques
1150 Second Ave.
(60th St.)
755-9543
Mon. to Fri. 10:00 A.M. to 5:00 P.M.

Not a flashy, decorator-style shop, York House has understated elegance that is classical and tasteful, particularly in its French, English, Biedermeier and other Continental furnishings and decorations, principally from the Empire and Restoration periods. Of special interest is the huge collection of eighteenth-century Chinese blue and white porcelain, from giant vases and garden seats down to delicate little teacups. A shop not located in the mainstream, but worth the effort of a special visit.

JEWELRY

A La Vieille Russie
781 Fifth Ave.
(59th St.)
752-1727
Mon. to Fri. 10:00 A.M. to 5:30 P.M. (to 5:00 P.M. in summer); Sat. 10:00 A.M. to 4:00 P.M. (closed Sat. after Christmas)

The specialty here is imperial treasures of Czarist Russia. There are magnificent pieces of enameled glass, Russian icons and paintings, fabulous enamel plique-à-jour goblets, marvelous carved hard stone animals in rhodonite, nephrite and purpurin (a synthetic mineral used exclusively by Fabergé), gold snuffboxes, enamel frames, cuff links, watch-fob seals and eggs. You'll also see a wonderful selection of French eighteenth-century furniture. Encrusted with gold, diamonds and precious stones, the items here are worth thousands, perhaps millions.

The Antique Buff
**321½ Bleecker St.
(Christopher St.)
243-7144**
Mon. to Sat. 2:00 P.M. to 8:00 P.M.

In this small shop crammed with enough jewelry to fill many treasure chests there are trinkets dating from 1800 to 1900, including a good collection of Victorian rings, silverware and other items from that era.

Ares Rare
**961 Madison Ave.
(75th St.)
988-0190**
*Mon. to Sat. 11:00 A.M. to
5:30 P.M.*

Come here to choose from four thousand years of jewelry, from ancient Egyptian to art deco. There are also periodic exhibitions of works by fine contemporary goldsmiths and jewelers. Prices start at $500.

Ilene Chazanof
737-9668
By appt. only

Her art deco and art nouveau jewelry is every bit as good as that found at her more famous rivals, but there's more. Besides the Jensen, Bakelite and marcasite, Ms. Chazanof offers mission furniture and accessories by Kosta, Orrefors, Roycroft and Rebajes. Old perfume bottles, cigarette cases, match safes and letter openers are just some of the smaller items that round out the stock. Prices are reasonable, and there's even a box of $1 items, just so you don't have to leave empty-handed.

Fred Leighton
**781 Madison Ave.
(66th St.)
288-1872**
*Mon. to Sat. 10:00 A.M. to
6:00 P.M.*

One of two new locations—the other is in the Trump Tower Gallery—housing the rarest, the most beautiful and the most extravagant jewelry (from 1800 to 1950) available in New York. Its collection of art deco jewelry from the '20s is far superior in quality to anything found elsewhere. The Cartier pieces are pure marvels. High quality at high prices.

Jan Skala
**1 W. 47th St.
246-2814**
*Mon. to Fri. 9:30 A.M. to 5:00
P.M.; Sat. 10:00 A.M. to 4:00 P.M.*

This jeweler on the outskirts of the diamond center has stunning nineteenth-century watches and jewelry, as well as Russian enamels and, as you might expect, diamonds—all at accessible prices.

LINENS

Anichini Gallery
**7 E. 20th St.
12th floor
982-7274**
By appt. only

A complete line of nineteenth- and early twentieth-century bed and table linens has been chosen by Renaissance woman Patrizia Anichini. The linens and antique clothing, presented in perfect condition, are beautiful and usable in modern surroundings. This is surely the largest selection of antique hand-embellished luxuries in town. The gallery also offers exhibitions of work by international contemporary artists and craftspeople, along with performances of drama, music and poetry.

MARKETS

The Annex
Sixth Avenue and 26th Street
Sun. (Apr. to Nov., weather permitting) 9:00 A.M. to 6:00 P.M.

The Annex is a tradition in the New York antiques world. Many of the shop owners listed in this book started out selling here. It's a mixed bag—some quality, some junk and some of everything else in between. Many smart shoppers like to arrive early, when the dealers are unpacking and setting up around 7:00 A.M., to beat the nominal admission charge and get first crack at what's being offered.

The Manhattan Art and Antiques Center
1050 Second Ave. (55th St.)
355-4400
Mon. to Sat. 10:30 A.M. to 6:30 P.M.; Sun. noon to 6:00 P.M.

Ten years ago Glenwood Management built a shopping mall to help replace many small Second Avenue antique shops that were forced out by urban changes. This antique and art center offers one-stop shopping convenience in an attractive, air-conditioned marble and glass setting. Since the center consists of more than 70 individual shops, it has 70 times the idiosyncrasies, including many galleries not being open at regular hours (they're particularly prone to absenteeism on Mondays). Most dealers are knowledgeable, friendly and helpful, though a few are intimidating, indifferent or downright rude. But betwixt and between all this, you'll find a terrific selection. The street level consists mainly of jewelry shops; the first concourse (one flight down) has larger shops dealing in Oriental rugs, clocks, tapestries, quilts, decoys, toys, banks, soldiers, glass, porcelain, bronzes and paintings from many different countries, styles and periods. The second concourse (two flights down) has shops specializing in silver, pewter, brass and African arts, as well as furniture of all kinds. One could (and will) spend hours here.

Walter's World Famous Greenwich Village Emporium
252 Bleecker St. (Sixth Ave.)
255-0175
Thurs. to Sun. 1:00 P.M. to 8:00 P.M.

Wondrous things await the clever shopper at this unusual market, where 52 shops tempt collectors with antique as well as new items in a browsers-welcome, flea market atmosphere.

MUSIC BOXES

Rita Ford
19 E. 65th St.

When you see this amazing array of American and European music boxes dating from 1830 to 1910, all in

535-6717
Mon. to Sat. 9:00 A.M. to 5:00 P.M.

The Last Wound-Up
**290 Columbus Ave.
(73rd St.)
787-3388**
Mon. to Sun. 11:00 A.M. to 8:00 P.M.

working order, you'll want to play each one. Rita Ford also has a huge assortment of contemporary music boxes at more accessible prices; you can sometimes pick the musical theme to go in the box of your choice.

A shop for the young at heart, filled with music and laughter. Nathaniel's music boxes date from 1850. There's also a huge selection of tin windup toys from 1880 to the present. If it has a key, it usually winds up here.

ORIENTAL

Art Asia
**1088 Madison Ave.
(81st St.)
249-7250**
Mon. to Sat. 10:30 A.M. to 6:00 P.M.; Sun. noon to 6:00 P.M.

Art Asia offers a charming selection of Oriental antiques, furniture, folk art and jewelry, including Imari and export porcelain, Tansu chests, screens, ancestor portraits, Tanka and Indian miniatures, wood carvings, woodblock prints, pillows made from Kilim rugs, and delightful Hina dolls and Chinese puppets. The stock here isn't the rarest of the rare and is therefore relatively affordable.

Doris Leslie Blau
**15 E. 57th St.
759-3715**
By appt. only

The serious collector will want to check out this dealer, which specializes in rare antique Turkish, Persian, Caucasian, Indian, Chinese and European rugs, carpets and textiles, dating from the seventeenth to the early twentieth centuries.

Frank Caro
**41 E. 57th St.
2nd floor
753-2166**
Tues. to Sat. 9:30 A.M. to 4:30 P.M.

This very attractive collection of Indian and Chinese art dating from the Shang dynasty to the eighteenth century includes furniture and objets d'art. An appointment is suggested, particularly during the summer months.

Ralph M. Chait Galleries
**12 E. 56th St.
758-0937**
Mon. to Sat. 10:00 A.M. to 5:30 P.M. (closed Sat. in summer)

Established in 1910, this is the oldest shop in the country that specializes in magnificent Chinese treasures in bronze, pottery, porcelain, jade, enamel and silver. Some of the objects date back as far as the Neolithic period (3000 B.C.), while a few are as recent as the nineteenth century; regardless of the date, each piece is chosen for its quality and is elegantly presented in a plum-colored, softly lit gallery. It has a private laboratory equipped for thermoluminescence dating and authentication, as well as one of the largest private libraries on Chinese art in New York.

Barry Chan
**948 Madison Ave.
(74th St.)**

Eighteenth- and nineteenth-century Chinese and Japanese decorative art and artifacts is the specialty of this charming shop. The collection includes lacquer furniture

288-0798
Mon. to Sat. 10:00 A.M. to 6:00 P.M. (closed Sat. in summer)

Felice Fedder Oriental Art
754 Madison Ave.
(65th St.)
348-7497
By appt. only

E&J. Frankel, Ltd.
25 E. 77th St.
879-5733
Mon. to Sat. 10:00 A.M. to 5:30 P.M.

Hartman Rare Art
978 Madison Ave.
(76th St.)
794-2800
Mon. to Fri. 9:30 A.M. to 5:00 P.M.

Koreana Art and Antiques
963 Madison Ave.
(75th. St.)
249-0400
Mon. to Sat. 10:00 A.M. to 6:00 P.M.

Diane Love
851 Madison Ave.
(70th St.)
879-6997
Mon. to Sat. 10:00 A.M. to 5:30 P.M. (closed Sat. in July and Aug.)

and screens, painted screens, cloisonné, garden seats, palace-size vases and a delightful assortment of China trade birds and animals.

Ms. Fedder's shop is of interest primarily to the advanced collector: every one of her pieces of Chinese, Korean and Japanese art is a small treasure. Ceramics, paintings, furniture, screens, lacquer ware, jade ornaments and sculptures are magnificently represented, with each item carefully selected and displayed.

Mrs. Frankel's is one of the most attractive galleries for Chinese and Japanese art in the world. Here you'll find jade ornaments, ceramics, bronzes, jewelry, furniture, paintings, rugs, textiles and robes, dating from the Shang dynasty in China (1700 B.C.) and the Jomon period in Japan (5000 B.C.) to the present. An absolutely stunning collection selected with the expertise that has earned Mrs. Frankel chairmanship of the Far Eastern studies department at the New School for Social Research.

Hartman has probably the largest collection of Oriental art in the United States, with works from the Shang to Ching dynasties. The T'ang Dynasty pottery and the Shang and Chou dynasty bronzes are outstanding; there are also Japanese metalworks, ivory netsuke, cloisonné and Satsuma. The Hartmans own a second gallery in the Manhattan Art and Antique Center, 1050 Second Avenue, between 55th and 56th streets (794-2812). This shop features an enormous and magnificent collection of silver, enamel, porcelain and Oriental accessories, plus a few pieces of French furniture.

The skill and imagination of Korea are perfectly represented by this shop's gingko and elm cabinets with brass fixtures, folk paintings and ceramics of the eighteenth and nineteenth centuries. The proprietor is amiable, and the welcome here is sincere.

Diane is known for her silk flowers and her line of fragrances and potpourri, which permeate everything in the shop. But that's not all that she carries. In her travels she always finds some exotic items to bring home for the gallery. Currently the look is Japanese, evident in furniture, pottery, porcelain and other decorative items, including a number of kimonos (to wear or to hang). The high-tech setting acts as a glorious backdrop for each piece—the effect is almost overpoweringly dramatic.

G. Malina
680 Madison Ave.
(61st St.)
593-0323
By appt. only

No serpentine, aventurine or new machine-carved jades are to be found in this establishment—nothing but the finest authentic antique jade carvings for the discriminating collector. Mr. Malina's expertise extends to important Oriental sculptures and Chinese porcelains, and he is willing to work with novice collectors to help build a selective collection.

Mitsukoshi
461 Park Ave.
(57th St.)
935-6969
Mon. to Sat. 10:00 A.M. to 6:00 P.M.

The New York branch of Japan's largest department store offers a selection of blue and white Imari porcelain and rustic pottery, lacquer trays, cast-iron teapots and other tea ceremony utensils. Most things seem to be related to food and eating, which is understandable, since its restaurant is downstairs. There are painted and lacquered screens as well, but everything is presented in an uninteresting atmosphere; the old and new are mixed together, so there's no sense of anything being antique at all.

Vajra Arts
971 Madison Ave.
(76th St.)
249-1677
Mon. to Sat. 11:00 A.M. to 6:30 P.M.

As you step through the door incense enhances the sense of peace and harmony that this shop, specializing in the art and artifacts of India, Nepal and Tibet, conveys. Bronze figures, ranging in size from three to 40 inches, line the walls, interspersed with Tanka paintings and stone and wooden temple carvings. There is a nice selection of exotic silver jewelry, as well as some interesting ritual objects, all at reasonably affordable prices.

Weisbrod and Dy, Ltd.
906 Madison Ave.
(72nd St.)
734-6350
Mon. to Fri. 10:00 A.M. to 5:00 P.M.

Chinese treasures dating from the Neolithic era to the eighteenth century, archaic bronzes from the twelfth and thirteenth centuries B.C., porcelain, stoneware and other pottery—the selection at this establishment is of high quality, and the range of prices is wide. You might want to call before visiting, as the hours can vary.

POTTERY · PORCELAIN

Ages Past Antiques
1030 Lexington Ave.
(73rd St.)
628-0725
Mon. to Sat. 11:30 A.M. to 5:30 P.M. (closed Sat. in summer)

A charming assortment of pottery and porcelain from England is dominated by a huge number of important Staffordshire figural groups, watch holders and busts. There's also a grand selection of blue and white china and lusterware in copper, silver, pink and canary.

Bardith, Ltd.
901 Madison Ave.
(72nd St.)
737-3775
Mon. to Sat. 11:00 A.M. to 5:00
P.M. (closed Sat. in July and Aug.)

Specializing in mid-eighteenth- and nineteenth-century English pottery and porcelain, English glass, hanging lanterns and papier-mâché trays, Bardith presents its wares in a no-nonsense manner for serious collectors. Not particularly conducive to browsing.

Gem Antiques
1088 Madison Ave.
(81st St.)
535-7399
Mon. to Sat. 10:30 A.M. to
5:30 P.M.

Gem Antiques is a small, well-stocked shop filled with a huge selection of antique paperweights (Clichy, Baccarat, Saint Louis), as well as collectible contemporary paperwieghts (Stankard, Tarsitano, Banford, Perthshire). There's also a large collection of art pottery and porcelain from both sides of the Atlantic: Rookwood, Grueby, Ohr, Van Briggle, Newcomb, Weller, Pilkington, Moorcroft, Martin Brothers, Royal Doulton, Massier, Zsolnay, Gouda, Wedgwood, Worcester and Belleek. You name it, it's probably here. In view of the treasure trove available, the shop is aptly named.

Philip Suval
17 E. 64th St.
794-9600
Mon. to Fri. 9:00 A.M. to 5:00
P.M.; Sat. by appt. only

Breathtakingly beautiful porcelain and pottery await you at one of New York's oldest antique dealers. There are lots of Chinese trade goods, along with enchanting pieces from the best English factories—Worcester, Chelsea, Liverpool and Wedgwood—dating from the eighteenth and nineteenth centuries. A small selection of English and American furniture from the same period rounds out the collection.

RELIGIOUS

Atikoth
16 E. 71st St.
570-2591
Mon. to Fri. 10:30 A.M. to
5:30 P.M.

Atikoth is the hebrew word for "antique," and Hebrew antiques are what you'll find here. Owner Gloria Abrams is world renowned for her expertise in Judaica and Hebraica; her stock includes Bezalel arts, antique embroideries and other textiles, menorahs, ivory, bronze, silver, jewelry, paintings and sculpture, as well as Greek, Roman and Egyptian antiquities. You'll even find a modern painting or two relating to the history, religion or culture of the Jewish people.

Moriah Antique Judaica

There is an admirable display of Jewish ritual and ceremonial art in this gallery devoted to antique Judaica from the sixteenth to twentieth centuries: Hanukkah lamps, Torah ornaments, antique textiles, manuscripts.

298

699 Madison Ave.
(62nd St.)
751-7090
Mon. to Thurs. 9:00 A.M. to 5:00
P.M.; Fri. 9:00 A.M. to 4:00 P.M.

books, wedding rings and illuminated marriage contracts. The quality and quantity are superb.

SILVER

Samuel H. Mintz Straus
870 Madison Ave.
(71st St.)
288-3031
Tues. to Sat. 11:00 A.M. to 5:30
P.M. (closed Sat. in summer)

American sterling silver from the 1870s through the 1940s is primarily what you'll find here, but there's a special emphasis on Scandinavian designers (Georg Jensen, David Anderson). The shop also offers a huge array of small cabinet pieces related to particular themes—such as Napoleon, astrology, theater, medicine, Wall Street or law—as well as jewelry, pillboxes and collectible spoons. A great selection of sterling gifts.

James Robinson
15 E. 57th St.
752-6166
Mon. to Fri. 10:00 A.M. to 5:30
P.M. (closed Sat. in July and Aug.)

Known for the biggest and best selection of tasteful antique Georgian to Victornian silver, Mr. Robinson also has his own exclusive line of contemporary handmade sterling silver flatware. To go with the silver, there is a fine choice of late eighteenth- and nineteenth-century Coalport, Spode, Derby, Minton and Worcester porcelain dinner services. Pick out a centerpiece from the assortment of Georgian cut glass, and your table will be complete. Of course, with such elegance, you'll have to get a few simple baubles from his vast collection of opulent nineteenth-century jewelry to wear over your apron.

S.J. Shrubsole
104 E. 57th St.
753-8920
Mon. to Fri. 9:00 A.M. to 5:00 P.M.

This old English firm specializes in antique English and American silver. The cool reception does not especially inspire one to browse.

S. Wyler
713 Madison Ave.
(63rd St.)
838-1910
Mon. to Sat. 9:00 A.M. to 5:45 P.M.
(Mon. to Fri. 9:00 A.M. to 5:00
P.M. in July and Aug.)

Authors of the standard reference *The Book of Old Silver*, Seymour Wyler and his son, Richard, are acknowledged experts in the field of fine silver. Nor is their expertise limited to that single subject, as their selection of antique porcelain, Sheffield plate and Victoriana proves. One could easily spend a lot of time and a lot of money at their interesting shop.

TOYS · DOLLS

Iris Brown
253 E. 57th St.

This shop should be called "Iris in Wonderland," for though Iris herself is petite, she towers magically over a

593-2882
Mon. to Fri. 11:00 A.M. to 6:00 P.M.; Sat. 12:30 P.M. to 5:30 P.M.

charming world of delicate porcelain Victorian dolls, child-scale furniture, dollhouses and miniature accessories. It doesn't require too much imagination to see one's self shrinking down to fit into a child's chair at a child's table decked out with miniature silver and a porcelain tea service, joined in a mad tea party by two teddy bears bearing a striking resemblance to Sebastian's Aloysius and Christopher Robin's Pooh. A little more magic dust will have you shrinking even smaller, until you are sitting on a tiny velvet sofa in the middle of a Victorian parlor on the ground floor of a shuttered dollhouse. You could easily get caught up in all sorts of fantasies; the prices, however, will jolt you back to reality. Dolls range from one to 42 inches in height, and the price spread is equally wide. Iris Brown is a world-renowned expert on rare and unique dolls and Victorian childhood accessories for the advanced collector. The shop is small and cluttered, so browsing is discouraged, but serious inquiries are always welcome.

Chick Darrow's Fun Antiques
1174 Second Ave. (62nd St.)
838-0730
Mon. to Fri. 11:00 A.M. to 5:00 P.M.; Sat. 11:00 A.M. to 4:00 P.M.

Toys, for grown-up girls and boys. Regardless of your age, you'll be gripped by nostalgia as soon as you step through the door, and you'll see something from your childhood you'll want to recapture: comic characters, such as Lil' Abner, Dick Tracy or Popeye; early television personalities, such as Howdy Doody or the Mouseketeers; Disney watches, toys and games; Beatles collectibles; Kewpie dolls; and cast-iron and lithographed tin wind-up, friction and even battery-operated toys, dating from 1870 through the 1970s. There's also a selection of gumball and gambling slot machines, cash registers, advertising memorabilia and other nostalgic items.

New York Doll Hospital
787 Lexington Ave. (61st St.)
838-7527
Mon. to Sat. 10:00 A.M. to 6:00 P.M. (closed Sat. in July)

If your doll's arm were to fall off, what would you do? Pick up the bits and pieces of your battered child and rush right down for an emergency consultation with Irving Chais, the doll doctor. He has spent more than 35 years repairing, restoring and reviving dolls of all sizes and materials, including wood, plastic, porcelain and cloth. Each job is handled with expertise, sympathy, humor and a bedside manner that we would like to find in our own doctors. Aside from the slightly macabre sight of so many limbs, heads and other body parts lying about, the shop is quite charming, with antique dolls from as far back as the early nineteenth century for sale. Prices on dolls and their repairs vary, of course, and unfortunately aren't covered by Medicare or Blue Cross.

Second Childhood
**283 Bleecker St.
(Seventh Ave.)
989-6140**
*Mon. to Sat. 11:00 A.M. to
6:00 P.M.*

The best toy store in New York is light and clean and has good displays with old and rare tin windup toys from Marx, Lehmann, Bing and Marklin, as well as a huge selection of cars ranging from Tootsie Toy to Buddy L in size. There are soldiers, particularly Nuremberg flats, and a large assortment of contemporary Japanese robots for collectors of the future.

Beauty · Health

BODY SHOPS

Allana of New York
**527 Madison Ave.
(54th St.)
Ste. 520
980-0216**
*Mon. to Thurs. 10:00 A.M. to 7:30
P.M.; Fri. 10:00 A.M. to 5:00 P.M.*

This totally professional, careful and caring company is owned and operated by two enterprising women. Your first visit is always a free consultation, and a medical history is taken before any electrolysis begins. The electrolysis itself is advanced: Allana rids you of unwanted hair by means of an innovative silicon-insulated electric probe, which makes your electrolysis practically painless and virtually eliminates the chance of scarring. Treatment, of course, isn't cheap—$60 per hour ($31 a half hour), and you may end up going for several months. Such is the price of beauty.

Anushka
**241 E. 60th St.
355-6404**
*Mon. to Fri. 9:30 A.M. to 5:30
P.M.; Sat. 9:00 A.M. to 11:00 A.M.*

In these recently expanded surroundings, you can be made over from the inside out. Anushka is devoted entirely to body care: its well-known head-to-toe treatments ($100), consisting of two and a half hedonistic hours of massage, paraffin body sloughing, and cream applications, make you so relaxed you'll find it hard to stay awake. Intensive European facials are $35. Another service is the individualized ten-session cellulite treatment and diet program conducted by a physiotherapist and nutritionist.

Elizabeth Arden Salon
**691 Fifth Ave.
(54th St.)
407-7900**
Mon. to Sat. 9:00 A.M. to 4:00 P.M.

A day spent behind this famous red door is worth every pretty penny it costs. Six hours—steam bath, exercise, massage, facial, makeup, manicure, pedicure, styling and a light lunch, all for $145—will make you feel ten years younger. If you don't have the whole day, opt for the specific treatment you want: a sybaritic massage ($40), a rejuvenating facial ($42) or a wonderful manicure ($12). For another way to feel good, try the series of ten half-hour gymnastic lessons ($94) given by a Marjorie Craig–trained instructor. A full-service, elegant salon on seven floors.

Beauty Checkers

Henri Bendel
10 W. 57th St.
247-2829
Mon. to Fri. and alternate Sat. 10:00 A.M. to 4:00 P.M.

Bring your own makeup, and for $20 you'll get an hour-long lesson on how to, or how not to, apply it. This tiny glass room on Bendel's fourth floor is the ideal place to get an unintimidating change of face. Low-key makeup artists work one-on-one to create a look that suits your lifestyle as well as your face. If your own makeup doesn't do, they'll suggest a color from their line of reasonably priced Beauty Checkers products (try the mascara). The end result is a subtly made up demeanor—a change in cheek color, a few eye tips, a new lipstick. Somehow, it's always an improvement.

Ann Keane

29 E. 61st St.
3rd floor
644-0755
Tues. to Sat. 10:00 A.M. to 6:00 P.M. (Thurs. to 8:00 P.M.)

This slightly old-fashioned but reputable beauty shop offers a pleasant welcome plus good treatment. The specialty is aroma therapy, a face and body massage done with essential natural flower oils, followed by a mask ($35). It's more relaxing than stimulating, but you feel good, so who cares?

Georgette Klinger

501 Madison Ave.
(52nd St.)
838-3200
Mon. 9:00 A.M. to 6:00 P.M.; Tues., Thurs. and Fri. 9:15 A.M. to 4:30 P.M.; Wed. 9:00 A.M. to 7:00 P.M.; Sat. 9:15 A.M. to 3:30 P.M.

A huge, luxurious salon for men as well as women, where you can spend $45 and two hours having a superb facial (herbal steaming, nourishment masks) and ending with an individualized makeup for a clean new look. Before you leave, you'll be given a home care program outlining the necessary steps you should take to maintain your now-wonderful skin, and the products you should use, chosen from among the 350 unscented, minimum-preservative items made in the Georgette Klinger laboratory.

Lancôme Institut de Beauté

(Bloomingdale's)
Third Avenue and 59th Street
8th floor
705-3166
Mon. and Thurs. 10:00 A.M. to 9:00 P.M.; Tues., Wed., Fri. and Sat. 10:00 A.M. to 6:30 P.M.

Its reputation in Paris is high, and for its New York Institut, Lancôme has imported a team of Paris-trained aestheticians. The treatment rooms are very comfortable, the skin care program can be adapted to every type of skin, and the results are entirely satisfactory. A makeover, including a facial and complete makeup, is $45. Special treatments include minifacials (a half hour long) for $14, throat or hand treatments, makeup lessons, waxing and eyebrow shaping. After it all, you can, of course, purchase the excellent house products.

Rosalinda

22 E. 66th St.
737-2788
Tues. to Sat. 9:30 A.M. to 6:00 P.M.

This refreshingly unpretentious beauty shop is run by the ever-charming Rosalinda, who takes a personal interest in each of her customers—service that cannot be beat. The simple pale pink salon with wicker seating is tasteful and cheery. The back room is reserved for many of the body services: waxing, massages and facials. Rosalinda herself takes care of you, and her manicures and pedicures are excellent. It's not Elizabeth Arden, but the welcome is much friendlier, the attention seductive and the prices absolutely reasonable.

Janet Sartin of Park Avenue, Ltd.
480 Park Ave.
(58th St.)
751-5858
Mon. to Sat. 10:00 A.M. to 5:45 P.M.

Behind Janet Sartin's armored door lies a tiny but plush consultation center for her scientific skin care program. No actual treatments are done here, but you do learn how to use her expensive and effective products. When you enter, you are seated at a small couch until one of the two or three Sartin skin experts can examine and evaluate your complexion. This is done at an antique table fitted with a mirror and magnifying glass. Your skin type is then categorized on a scale of –4 to +4, and you are shown how to implement cleaning, correction and consistency—the three Sartin bywords. If it sounds a bit like the Erno Lazlo system, it should: from 1937 to 1946, Janet Sartin worked with the Hungarian doctor until she developed her own spin-off products. Sartin's client list includes Gloria Vanderbilt, Jill Clayburgh, Calvin Klein and a slew of models. If you're very rich and famous, or if your skin is very bad (rarely do the two go hand in hand), Ms. Sartin herself will consent to see you for intensive treatments at her very private uptown office.

Lia Schorr Skin Care
527 Madison Ave.
(54th St.)
Ste. 619
486-9670
Mon. to Fri. 9:00 A.M. to 7:00 P.M.; Sat: 9:00 A.M. to 3:00 P.M.

When you call Lia Schorr for an appointment, don't be surprised if she picks up the phone herself. This hardworking Valmy/Klinger-trained cosmetologist oversees every detail of her business—which after just two years has a star-studded client list and looks as rosy and glowing as the faces she treats. These include teenagers and octogenarians, stars and stargazers, acne sufferers (this is a real specialty) and the peaches-and-creamies. Sixty percent of Lia Schorr's clients are men (Dustin Hoffman and Paul Newman among them). All her products are based with such natural ingredients as aloe, ginseng and vegetable extracts. Her technique is simple but effective: First, she pampers and relaxes each client as she analyzes the skin. A luxurious massage is followed with herbal steaming in a darkened room, a natural mask and, finally, a soothing moisturizer. (Women's facials end with complimentary makeup.) The total 75-minute experience is better than two weeks in Tahiti. A facial is $34, and a six-day deep cosmetic peeling treatment is $300. Paraffin treatments for hands or feet, body waxes and makeup lessons are also offered. Consultations are always free.

Christine Valmy

767 Fifth Ave.
(59th St.)
752-0303
Mon. to Wed. and Fri. 10:00 A.M. to 5:00 P.M.; Thurs. 11:00 A.M. to 6:00 P.M.; Sat. 10:00 A.M. to 4:00 P.M.

A scientific skin care center that uses machines and its own line of Byogenic products to cleanse, clear and care for your skin. A windowed minilab lets you watch the dermaspecialists mix vitamins, oils and extracts into products for you to buy and use at home. A variety of facials and peeling treatments are offered. Other services include eyebrow shaping and tinting, makeup lessons, waxing, body massages, manicures and pedicures. A Valmy Day, which includes everything (even lunch), is $160. Another location at 153 West 57th Street (397-5226).

Diane Young Skincare Center

243 E. 60th St.
753-1200

The holistic approach to skin care. Soft-spoken Diane Young has assembled a high-powered team of experts (a dermatologist, a nutritionist, aestheticians and a makeup artist) who will give yet another perspective on your health and beauty needs. The facial ($40) starts with an intelligent analysis of your lifestyle—including diet, exercise, rest and stress levels—and includes a magnified look at your skin. Then you're whisked away to a pink and white room, wrapped in a luxurious terry robe and laid to rest while light fingers dance across your face. Can something that feels this good actually be good for you? The experts say yes! Afterward, you're instructed in a complete skin care regime and given a bag of Diane Young sample products and a makeup application. All this is done in the most low-pressure, soothing manner imaginable. Diane Young herself is lovely; she treats each client as a special friend. Other services include makeup lessons, nutritional consultations, seminars for teenagers, collagen injections, manicures, pedicures, waxings and Swedish and shiatsu massages.

EXERCISE

Alex & Walter Physical Fitness Studio

30 W. 56th St.
265-7270
Mon. to Fri. 8:00 A.M. to 8:00 P.M.; Sat. 10:00 A.M. to 2:00 P.M.

Alex Jaskewicz reigns over this New York branch of the bicoastal Alex & Walter gyms. Come here and you'll stretch, swing, tumble and stand on your head according to Russian gymnastic techniques. Don't panic—the highly professional instructors know exactly how far to push you, and you may surprise yourself with what you can actually do. Men and women are taught in half-hour private ($20) or semiprivate ($18) sessions, and in hour-long group sessions ($10) of up to six people. While this is definitely a studio for the stars, it's not a designer-leotard place. Everybody is seriously interested in improving his or her body posture. No music, no security lockers and no pretension, but there are showers and changing rooms.

Lotte Berk
23 E. 67th St.
288-6613
Daily 7:00 A.M. to 8:00 P.M.

A well-known women's workout. Developed by Russian dancer Lotte Berk and opened here thirteen years ago by Lydia Bach (who still comes in and out, but no longer teaches regular classes), the Lotte Berk method consists of a strenuous series of movements to stretch and strengthen your muscles, expecially the abdominals. It's particularly good for women with posture or lower back problems, as well as for those who want to develop all-around tone. The highly effective, often imitated exercises borrow techniques from modern dance, ballet and yoga and are done to music. The facility itself is clean and friendly, with three carpeted, air-conditioned studios, an ever-ready coffeepot, sofas, showers and towels. Class size is limited to nine. A series of ten sessions costs $135; the price per class decreases with longer series. Highly recommended.

The Cardio-Fitness Center
345 Park Ave.
(52nd St.)
838-4570
Mon. to Fri. 6:45 A.M. to 8:30 P.M.; Sat. 9:00 A.M. to 3:00 P.M.

The Cardio-Fitness system is the executive's way to exercise. This unique, goal-oriented approach to fitness emphasizes reducing coronary risk—every CEO's concern. By taking care of your heart, however you also take care of the rest of you; building stamina, strengthening your back, toning up and slimming down. Regimens are personalized and extremely well supervised. The nice part about this gym is that everything is ready and waiting for you daily—a clean T-shirt, socks, shorts, towels and shower supplies, even the latest issue of *Fortune* to read while you cycle. The facilities are always immaculate, and the staff is friendly as well as intelligent. Lots of Fortune 500 companies offer membership as a perk. And no wonder: for this top place, you'll pay top dollar. The annual cost is $795, with a $450 initiation fee. Other locations at Rockefeller Center, 1221 Avenue of the Americas, near 49th Street (840-8240), and at 79 Maiden Lane (943-1510).

Exercise Plus
30 W. 57th St.
586-1742
Mon. to Thurs. 9:30 A.M. to 6:30 P.M.; Fri. 9:30 A.M. to 5:30 P.M.; Sat. 10:30 A.M. to 12:30 P.M.

The "Plus" refers to babies. This studio is specially for mothers-to-be and mothers-who-are. Stretching, toning and strengthening exercises help women feel good at precisely the time they tend to feel most out of shape. Hour-long classes—some quite large—are divided into prenatal and postpartum groups. Aside from the carefully monitored instruction, the classes provide a wonderfully supportive meeting place for expectant and new mothers. Another plus is free baby-sitting during classes. There are no showers here, but these exercises are not designed to work up a sweat. One month (eight classes) is $80; three months (24 classes) is $190; and one year (100 classes) is $495.

Harkness Horizons
Harkness House
4 E. 75th St.
570-1505
Call for class schedule

If your mind is younger than your body, former ballerina Joy O'Neill will show you how to get back in tune with a regimen of her own exercises, using only the slant board, the floor and your body. Her small studio atop the Harkness House for Ballet Arts is extremely private and not very well-known outside of an inner circle of wealthy clients. Ten hour-long classes cost $225, and there are several early-morning sessions for those who have to go to work afterward.

New York Health & Racquet Club
110 W. 56th St.
541-7200
Midtown clubs: Mon. to Fri. 7:00 A.M. to 10:00 P.M.; other clubs: Mon. to Fri. 10:00 A.M. to 10:00 P.M.; all clubs: Sat. and Sun. 10:00 A.M. to 6:00 P.M.

The NYHRC gives you everything the Vertical Club does, including the crowded singles scene, at a slightly lower price and with much less glamour. But here, too, you can swim, run, dance, stretch, lift, eat and play among beautiful bodies. For your convenience, there are five locations around town. They all maintain high standards, but the newest club, on West 56th Street, is by far the nicest and cleanest—and hence, the busiest. It's also the only one with an indoor track; the others have jogging machines. While it has racquetball courts, squash is located at 20 East 50th Street (593-1500), and tennis is available in the Village, at 24 East 13th Street (924-4600). All the clubs have daily fitness classes, ranging from yoga to calisthenics to karate, plus a full range of Nautilus equipment, pools, saunas, and showers. Other locations at 132 East 45th Street (986-3100) and 1433 York Avenue, near 76th Street (737-6666).

Nickolaus Exercise Centers
767 Lexington Ave. (60th St.)
355-2693
Mon. to Fri. 10:30 A.M. to 6:30 P.M.; Sat. and Sun. 10:30 A.M. to 12:30 P.M.

Nonaerobic stretching plus a little yoga, a few isometrics and some concentrated breathing add up to the Nickolaus technique. Geared toward toning, slimming and detensing your body, Nickolaus classes are the intellectual's way to keep in shape. Hour-long sessions are conducted in large, unmirrored studios, on plain black exercise mats. There is no music, but the instructor's voice establishes a mantralike rhythm. If you hit it right, there could be as few as three people in a class. On a bad day, the room can be jammed. Members are predominately women. The minimum program is for twice-weekly classes (24 are $200), which you can take at any of the various locations around the city. The six-month, unlimited-class program is $400. Tapes and/or a book are also available for at-home workouts.

Sports Training Institute
239 E. 49th St.
752-7111
Mon. to Fri. 6:00 A.M. to 9:30 P.M.; Sat. 9:00 A.M. to 1:00 P.M.

Stamina and strength are the goals at this very serious non-health-club gym. This is where the Yankees and Giants come off-season, where Jane Fonda works out between workouts and where Chris Evert Lloyd develops upper body strength. It's also the place for nonprofessionals to get into or improve their shape. Here's how it works: When you join the Sports Training Institute, you have a comprehensive physical evaluation. On the basis of that, you're assigned a professional athletic trainer who works with you (by appointment) every time you come to the gym—ideally, two or three times a week. Although stretching and aerobic warm-ups can be done on your own (there are stretching classes every fifteen minutes), the Nautilus equipment and weights always require trainer supervision—and these trainers have no mercy. The gym also offers physical therapy for those who are referred by a doctor. The routine is similar to the regular conditioning, with a qualified physical therapist replacing the trainer. Heat, ultrasound, whirlpool and orthopedic equipment might be used. The facilities themselves are clean and resemble locker rooms with showers and towels available. There is also a wonderful noncompetitive camaraderie among the members, something we didn't find at any other fitness club. Thirty trainer sessions, plus the $75 evaluation, run $525. Physical therapy is $35 a session.

The Vertical Club
330 E. 61st St.
355-5100
Mon. to Thurs. 7:00 A.M. to 11:00 P.M.; Fri. 9:00 A.M. to 11:00 P.M.; Sat. and Sun. 9:00 A.M. to 9:00 P.M.

A favorite sweatshop of models and millionaires, this Scarsdale-in-the-sky has top-notch facilities, with an attitude to match. A predictably slick mirrored entry welcomes the narcissistic members. Downstairs, the small lap pool is rarely crowded, and neither are the whirlpool and juice bar. But the recently added hot tubs, saunas and tanning rooms may change all that. The men's exercise floor looks like a sci-fi fitness lab, with more than 200 machines to pump iron and egos. It's accented with red neon, and rimmed one flight up by the largest indoor running track in the city. A separate women's exercise area houses more machines for the less aggressive. Another room is for weights and bench presses. Aerobics, jazz, yoga and slimming classes are also taught, and personal supervision is available for all members. On the top floor, two tennis courts (by separate membership only) and squash and racquetball courts share space with a bar and a restaurant. Everything—from the modern oak lockers to the rooftop sun deck—is obsessively clean and safe. In the winter, there's even a security coat check for your fur. Membership is only $500 a year, though that's after an exorbitant initiation fee. If you like to work out with the nouveau riche and the semifamous, this is the club for you.

FRAGRANCE

The Bath House

**215 Thompson St.
(Bleecker St.)
533-0690**
*Tues. to Thurs. and Sun. noon to
8:00 P.M.; Fri. and Sat. noon to
10:00 P.M.*

This is the purists' domain. In this tiny Village shop, hundreds of natural oils and extracts are available for you to use in creating a personal fragrance signature. Cindy Annchild, the very knowledgeable owner, will happily discuss the roots of and myths behind various essences, as well as suggest ways to mate different products. Her own blends are extremely popular, as are the zodiac oils, which combine the three traditional elements (flower, spice, tree) of ancient signs. Bubble bath, shower gel, body oil and lotion, massage cream and shaving products, all naturally based, can be custom scented. Soaps, face masks and sea- and mineral-salt bath crystals are also sold.

Crabtree and Evelyn

**30 E. 67th St.
734-1108**
*Mon. to Sat. 10:00 A.M. to
6:00 P.M.*

There's a very olde London atmosphere in this wonderful shop lined with painted shelves imported from England. The products are no less charming: soaps, shampoos and bath oils scented with almond, corn or oatmeal fragrances; seashell soaps and children's soaps in the shapes of Babar and Alice in Wonderland; and marvelous rosewood hairbrushes and shaving brushes, which are among the shop's specialties. All sorts of goodies, such as cookies, jams and unusually flavored and packaged teas, are available in gift baskets. Many other stores sell Crabtree and Evelyn products. Exclusive shops are located on the Upper East Side, the Upper West Side and Citicorp Center.

Dans un Jardin

**143 E. 57th St.
980-1177**
*Mon. to Fri. 10:00 A.M. to 6:00
P.M.; Sat. 11:00 A.M. to 5:00 P.M.*

Soft green and white, with occasional touches of pink: that's the pretty, gardenlike setting conceived by Lucile de Baudry d'Asson, a young Frenchwoman who gave up a vice-presidency at Chase Manhattan Bank for the world of perfumes. In this New York franchise of her international boutiques, owned by Mary Viscountess Rothermere, you'll find her striking collection of ready-made perfumes, all marvelously fresh and different, and a line of 50 exclusive flower, fruit and wood fragrances that you can combine to create your own personal scent, which can then be mixed into eau de toilette, beauty milk, bubble bath or oil. There are also six different lines of soaps, bubble baths, shampoos and more, plus scented lightbulb rings, incense, candles and a skin care collection. Pretty lacquer boxes, bathrobes, embroidered evening bags, china and matching linens, all in green, white and pink, are sold at the back of the store.

Joovay
436 W. Broadway
(Prince St.)
431-6386
Mon. to Sun. noon to 7:00 P.M.

A charming little lingerie store that will also pamper you with a full line of fresh, scented oils, soaps, lotions and skin creams. What you don't see can be specially made up: if, for example, you want a massage cream scented with vetiver, you can have it mixed while you wait. There are a lot of unusual fragrances; aside from the floral and earth scents, you can choose tropical rain, sequoia or vanilla. Colored soaps, which can be ordered by the brick, come with jojoba, aloe, cocoa butter or honey. You'll also find special soaps for shaving. All in all, a delightful store.

Diane Love
851 Madison Ave.
(70th St.)
879-6997
Mon. to Sat. 10:00 A.M. to 5:30 P.M.

The scent of roses and jasmine greets you outside the door of Diane Love's highly personal boutique. Inside, silvery lidded baskets and pastel taffeta bags of potpourri, flickering scented candles and delicately fragranced fabric petals continue to delight your senses—but without ever overwhelming them. Diane Love's fragrance for the home was created to set a welcoming mood, and nowhere does it work better than here. Look around: treasured pieces of china—the antiques from Diane's travels, the modern pieces, her own designs—interplay with unusual quilts and are complemented by the most exquisite fabric flowers (sweet peas, Queen Anne's lace, lilies, cabbage blooms) in baskets old and new, Japanese and American. Up the narrow stairway is another world: a Japanese homelike setting of furnishings, lacquer boxes, basketry and other crafts and an exotic collection of antique kimonos, displayed like the works of art they are. This is a lovely, unusual and totally sensual store.

Scentsitivity
870½ Lexington Ave.
(65th St.)
988-2822
Mon. to Fri. 10:00 A.M. to 6:00 P.M.; Sat. noon to 6:00 P.M.

Inside this recently relocated parfumerie you'll find soaps, potpourris, oils, bath foams and other treats for delicate epidermises. Here, too, you can create your own perfume using any of their 100 varieties of aromatic oils, elegantly presented in one-of-a-kind bottles. Wonderful bath accessories, candles, scented books and ravishing made-to-order gift baskets are also sold.

Soap Opera
31 Grove St.
(Bleecker St.)
929-7756
Mon. to Sat. noon to 7:00 P.M.; Sun. noon to 5:00 P.M.

Soap, soap, and ... well, tea. This small Village store specializes in the English Crabtree and Evelyn products. Delicious fruit-scented soaps, body creams, shaving soaps, jams, cookies and teas are sold in an attractive shop, where the staff's manners wouldn't have delighted nanny.

Soap Scents, Ltd.
245 E. 77th St.

There are soaps of all shapes, colors, scents; bath oils, shampoos and eaux de toilette; potpourri by the ounce; and loads of fragrant gift ideas in this tiny shop located

861-3735
Mon. to Sat. noon to 7:00 P.M.

just below street level. We were charmed by the soap sculptures shaped like birds, butterflies, seashells and animals. Lots of children's soap stuff, including bubble bath fingerpaints and crayon soap. The store will also make up personalized gift baskets.

HAIR SALONS

Children

Michael's
1263 Madison Ave.
(90th St.)
289-9612
Mon. to Sat. 9:00 A.M. to 5:00 P.M.
(Sept. to June)

After Paul Molé's, the most popular children's haircutting salon in town is Michael's. The shop itself has nothing much to offer beyond barber chairs and comic books, but nonetheless it is friendly and pleasant, and there are lollipops for kids to suck on while being shorn. Ask for Dino. Cuts cost $10.50. No reservations.

Paul Molé Barbershop
1021 Lexington Ave.
(73rd–74th sts.)
535-8461
Mon. to Sat. 8:00 A.M. to 6:00 P.M.
(Wed. and Thurs. to 7:30 P.M.)

This is a real turn-of-the-century barbershop, clean and old-fashioned, with comfortable old leather chairs. It deals with an impressive number of children every hour and always seems to be full. Certainly service is fast and efficient, and the barbers are friendly. What more could you ask for? Walk-ins and appointments are $12; $15.70 includes a shampoo.

Men · Women

Bumble & Bumble
56 W. 57th St.
757-3328
Mon. to Sat. 9:00 A.M. to 5:30 P.M.
(Thurs. and Fri. to 6:30 P.M.)

A high-tech, innovative, full-service salon where the stylists are as dramatic as their clients. The atmosphere is fun, charged and experimental, but don't let it fool you: these people are committed professionals, and they are continually being exposed to new ideas and trained in new techniques. Sophisticated, up-to-the-minute (though never bizarre) cuts and color are the trademarks here. Consultations are always free. Suggestions are never lacking, but high pressure is extremely rare. Cuts range from $35 to $60.

La Coupe
694 Madison Ave.
(62nd St.)
371-9230
Mon. to Sat. 9:00 A.M. to 4:30 P.M.

One of the hot spots. This truly dynamic salon boasts some of New York's most gifted stylists. Whether you want your hair cut athletically short, left romantically long or styled into a sophisticated chignon, you're sure to find what you're looking for here. But you have to reserve long in advance (it helps to be famous), as this establishment is well-known to both men and women. La

Coupe also sells some pretty finery for your hair and will do your makeup. Thirty-six dollars to $75 (depending on the stylist) buys a haircut and styling.

Jean Louis David

Henri Bendel
10 W. 57th St.
6th floor
247-1100
Mon. to Sat. 9:30 A.M. to 5:00 P.M.
(Thurs. to 6:00 P.M.)

A prestigious name, yet we do not recommend him very warmly. Jean Louis doesn't cut here, and the team of stylists, though trained on the job in Paris, do not always share the master's talent. Instead, try the Jean Louis David walk-in arrangement: no reservations, but it's only $25—not a bad deal. Full-service salon for men and women.

Davir

30 E. 67th St.
2nd floor
249-3550
Mon. to Sat. 9:00 A.M. to 6:00 P.M.

This elegant European-style salon, overlooking Madison Avenue, boasts an international clientele and discreet French-trained stylists. Claiming to be geared toward a "total look," Davir specializes in hair streaking and color. A cut costs $50 to $75; a blow dry, $20. And you'll be given a relaxing neck and back massage before a stylist begins with a shampoo.

Hair Power

27 St. Marks Pl.
(Second Ave.)
982-6300
Mon. to Fri. 10:00 A.M. to 10:00
P.M.; Sat. 10:00 A.M. to 7:00
P.M.; Sun. noon to 7:00 P.M.

The address should tell you all. Men's and women's styles and color extraordinaire. Nothing tried and true—this is not for the timid! A shampoo, cut and styling is $31 for women and $21 to $26 for men.

Hair Styling by Joseph

113 E. 60th St.
355-6965
Mon. to Fri. 9:00 A.M. to 6:00
P.M.; Sat. 8:00 A.M. to 2:30 P.M.

A salon that specializes in hair styling for blacks, Joseph and son Joseph, Jr., wash, set and style some of the most famous heads in show biz: Diana Ross, Natalie Cole, Bill Cosby, Stephanie Mills. At their homey, three-story shop they will pamper you from top to toe with all kinds of hair treatments, cuts and styling for both men and women, plus a full list of other services, including facials, waxing, manicures, makeup and massages.

Kenneth

19 E. 54th St.
752-1800
Mon. to Fri. 9:00 A.M. to 5:00 P.M.

Kenneth is to New York what Alexandre is to Paris: a famous hairstylist specializing in very elaborate hair constructions—rarely a simple cut, but Kenneth's clients don't do their own hair between visits. Make an appointment several weeks ahead, especially if you want to put your hair in Kenneth's own hands. The salon is located in a superb five-story townhouse; the pampering is equally superb. A shampoo, cut and blow dry/styling is $57.

Linterman's

21 E. 62nd St.
2nd floor

Roget Resca, a lively native of Nice, presides over everything in this small, sunny salon that, although internationally known and respected, retains an almost

421-4560
Mon. to Sat. 9:00 A.M. to 5:30 P.M.
(Thurs. to 7:30 P.M.)

family-style atmosphere. Adept at natural hairstyles that need little care beyond a morning shampoo, he is the unrivaled specialist of the dry cut, which lets him adapt the style to the individual's hair and gives clients advance warning of the final results. A good cut doesn't necessitate a blow dryer—and his don't. Cuts are $70 to $80.

Monsieur Marc
22 E. 65th St.
2nd floor
861-0700
Mon. to Fri. 9:00 A.M. to 4:30 P.M.

Marc de Coster is the coiffeur par excellence for the Reagan set. You can sip a hot cup of his special-mixture tea and gossip among the flowered wall hangings, rococo chairs and undistinguished paintings. As for the methods, the blow dryer plays a negligible role, with curlers and crimping firmly ensconced in this bastion of tradition. The results: you'll head for Le Cirque looking fifteen years younger, with a lovely 1968 creation adorning your head. But that's obviously what many right-thinking ladies are looking for. Likable staff.

Pierre Michel
6 W. 57th St.
3rd floor
757-5175
Mon. to Sat. 9:00 A.M. to 5:00 P.M.
(Thurs. to 6:00 P.M.)

A once furiously fashionable spot for having your hair done in whatever sexy, original or romantic style the moment dictated. This is the sort of ultraplush place where "everybody" went ... last year. Ho-hum. Also serves men. A cut is $35 to $65, depending on the stylist.

Pipino Buccheri
14 E. 55th St.
2nd floor
759-2959
Mon. to Fri. 10:00 A.M. to 6:00 P.M. (Thurs. to 7:30 P.M.); Sat. 10:00 A.M. to 5:00 P.M.

This, too, ranks as one of the top salons of the moment, mostly because of owner Marc Pipino. He and his talented team of young stylists take credit for many of the carefree hairstyles you see in the latest fashion magazines, and what they do for the camera they'll also do for the client. You'll walk out of here looking better than when you arrived, with a good, easy-to-live-with cut. The atmosphere is calm for such a dynamic group, thanks to the pastel artwork, plush carpets, angled alcoves and soft music. A cut by Marc is $72; the other stylists start at $35. A full-service salon.

Raymond and Nasser
747 Madison Ave.
(64th St.)
737-7330
Mon. to Fri. 9:00 A.M. to 5:30 P.M. (Thurs. to 6:00 P.M.); Sat. 9:00 A.M. to 4:00 P.M.

An immense salon with a very modern atmosphere, as much because of the mirrors and bright walls as because of its clients and style of cuts. It's a very efficient place, and in less than an hour (by appointment, of course) you'll leave shampooed and set, without looking as if you were headed for a wedding. Your greeting may be frenetic, but the results are entirely satisfactory. Especially recommended for henna. Manicures, pedicures and makeup are also done, as well as men's styling. Considering the neighborhood, the prices should not come as a surprise (a cut and blow dry is $60).

Le Salon
16 W. 57th St.
2nd floor
581-2760
Mon. to Sat. 9:00 A.M. to 5:30 P.M.
(Thurs. to 6:30 P.M.)

Simplicity and efficiency are the order of the day in this trés chic salon run by Italian master Bruno and his polyglot team of stylists. They cut both men and women, and specialize in tinting. The cuts themselves are like the decor—clean, simple and decisive. Bruno himself can be had for $65; the others start at $45.

Vidal Sassoon
General Motors
Plaza
767 Fifth Ave.
(59th St.)
535-9200
Mon. to Sat. 9:00 A.M. to 5:00 P.M.
(Thurs. to 7:00 P.M.)

Back when this salon was in its prime, straight, carefree cuts were considered very avant-garde. But now that everyone wears carefree hair and waves have usurped angles, Vidal Sassoon has lost its special niche. Vidal himself no longer cuts, although he does stop by every now and then to assess his assets, a complete line of hair care and a new line of nail care products among them. All the stylists are still trained in Sassoon schools. The place itself is done in modern gray, silver and brown, and is comfortable and clean. The clientele is neither young and with-it nor old and without it. (Mostly they look like sophisticated tourists.) And the styles, likewise, are never drastic—just slightly left of classic. All in all, this is a safe bet rather than a best bet. Cuts range from $35 to $55, depending on the stylist.

Suga
115 E. 57th St.
421-4400
Mon. to Sat. 9:00 A.M. to 6:00 P.M.
(Wed. to 8:00 P.M.)

The owner of this dazzling white and mirrored salon is considered to be the best hairstylist presently working in New York (when he's not jetting off on location!) He can do everything, from the most natural to the most sophisticated style, from the simplest to the most extravagent. What's more, this talented Japanese has surrounded himself with a diligent and highly competent staff that caters to a clientele of very up-to-date men and women. A cut by Suga is $100, while the others start at $40 (not counting the shampoo and dry). A full-service salon.

MAKEUP

Citi Cosmetics
643 Lexington Ave.
(54th St.)
752-3505
Mon. to Fri. 8:30 A.M. to 8:00 P.M.; Sat. 9:30 A.M. to 6:00 P.M.

As sparkling and busy as its neighbor, the Citicorp Center, this modern mirrored shop offers every beauty aid imaginable. All the best names in makeup, hair care, treatments and fragrance are represented, and there are also lots of accessories: hair ornaments, travel cases, manicure kits and vitamins. With a $25 purchase you become eligible for a beauty care service, in which you receive advice about makeup and grooming. Experts from different cosmetic companies occasionally give free lessons and beauty analyses.

Make-Up Center
150 W. 55th St.
977-9494
Mon. to Fri. 10:00 A.M. to 6:00 P.M. (Thurs. to 8:00 P.M.); Sat. 10:00 A.M. to 5:00 P.M.

A large, modern and friendly shop-salon, crowded with everyone from fashionable and trendy New York. Models, actors and dancers come here to stock up on theatrical makeup, which is the Center's specialty—including its own famous, moderately priced On Stage line. In addition to its products, the Center offers one-hour makeup lessons—truly personalized—for $25, and gives all sorts of facials using its own custom-formulated products ($35 for one and a half hours). Waxing, nail care, lash dying and eyebrow arching are also done.

Il Makiage
Salon: 107 E. 60th St.
Store: 50 E. 58th St.
371-3992
Mon. to Thurs. 10:00 A.M. to 9:00 P.M. (Tues. and Wed. to 6:00 P.M.); Fri. 9:00 A.M. to 5:00 P.M.; Sun. noon to 6:00 P.M.

The Fiorucci of makeup: a small, very fashionable and slightly eccentric shop that does makeup of all kinds, but excels in the unorthodox. You can receive all the usual full-service treatments—haircuts, manicures, facials—but if in addition you want to have your eyelashes dyed, your fingernails filled in, your hair treated with henna or yourself done over with sparkles and spangles, this is the place to go. Its own line of expensive products features all sorts of extraordinary colors, many of them in hard-to-find matte shades. Makeup lessons are $45 an hour, an eye makeup application is $25, and a full face application is $35; an entire day of beauty costs $150. Other services include on-location makeup and a special program for teenagers.

Merle Norman Cosmetics
5 W. 57th St.
980-6970
Mon. to Sat. 10:00 A.M. to 6:00 P.M. (Thurs. to 8:00 P.M.)

This is where middle Americans learn to look like Miss Americas. The largest cosmetic store chain in the United States, Merle Norman has 30,000 shops across the country. The 57th Street store is modern and spacious, and classical music keeps you company. A team of beauticians waits to advise you on which products and colors suit you best, how to minimize your little flaws (if flaws there be) and how to transform yourself for a special occasion. All these services are free, and you'll be given a personalized instruction guide to take home. Naturally, the cosmetics used—and which you are encouraged to buy—are exclusively from the Merle Norman line.

PHARMACIES

Boyd Chemists
655 Madison Ave. (60th St.)
838-6558
Mon. to Fri. 9:30 A.M. to 7:00 P.M.; Sat. 9:30 A.M. to 6:00 P.M.

You'll find most lines of European beauty products in this very famous very Madison Avenue, drugstore. You'll also find its own line of Fabriella products, plus soaps, shampoos, brushes and barrettes. Several aestheticians are available for makeup consultations (by appointment); a full face is $50 and eyes are $25—both redeemable in products. In short, this is a mecca for beauty products, frequented by the beautiful people and those who would like to be. Over-the-counter and prescription drug service as well.

Cambridge Chemists
702 Madison Ave. (62nd St.)
838-1884
Mon. to Fri. 9:00 A.M. to 7:00 P.M.; Sat. 9:00 A.M. to 6:00 P.M.

Despite its small size, this classic pharmacy is well stocked with domestic and imported cosmetics, beauty products and toiletries. Most of its best lines are from Great Britain, including Cyclax products (used by Her Majesty Queen Elizabeth), Floris fragrances and Geo. F. Trumper men's products. That should give you an idea of Cambridge Chemists' style. If the trip is too much for you, call and ask that you be sent its attractive catalog. And if you do plan a visit, call first—Cambridge is planning a move to 21 East 65th Street.

Caswell Massey Co., Ltd.
518 Lexington Ave. (48th St.)
755-2254
Mon. to Sat. 10:00 A.M. to 6:00 P.M.

The oldest apothecary shop in the United States. Established in 1725, this uptown spot deserves at least one visit. If you'd like to try the eau de cologne used by George Washington and his friend the Marquis de Lafayette, or the special night cream prepared for Sarah Bernhardt, or one of its extraordinary soaps (it has the largest selection of imported soaps in the world), or if you simply want to contemplate the marvelous apothecary jars, some of which date from the eighteenth century, don't hesitate—there's nowhere else like this in the country. Another location at the South Street Seaport, 21 Fulton Street (608-2233).

Clayton and Edwards Chemists
1004 Lexington Ave. (72nd St.)
737-1147
Mon. to Sat. 9:00 A.M. to 7:00 P.M.

Two excellent corner pharmacists, of a type that scarcely exists anymore. These shops' traditionalism is matched by their professionalism. The Lexington shop specializes in beauty products and perfumes, while the store at 1327 York Avenue, near 71st St. (737-6240), deals more in pharmaceutical and surgical items. Both stores carry unmarked brands of products that are excellent in quality and relatively low in price.

Kiehl's Pharmacy
109 Third Ave. (13th St.)
475-3400
Mon. to Fri. 10:00 A.M. to 6:00 P.M.; Sat. 10:00 A.M. to 2:30 P.M.

A long, narrow, fragrant apothecary shop where you're sure to be made welcome, Kiehl's is certainly the most seductive of the New York pharmacies. On the shelves are rows of jars full of the marvelous ointments, potions and drugs Kiehl's has been making since 1851, using herbs and natural products exclusively. Natural henna, musk oil, herbal facials, botanical drugs and everything for men's and women's body care—all of irreproachable quality—are available in jars, bottles or sachets. A full line of homeopathic remedies is also sold. Kiehl's counts among its staunchest clients a good number of people who frequent health stores and who have an ecological frame of mind.

Books · Stationery

BOOKS

Argosy Book Store

116 E. 59th St.
753-4455
Mon. to Fri. 10:00 A.M. to 6:00 P.M.; Sat. 10:00 A.M. to 5:00 P.M.

Argosy is a huge, ancient repository of used books and prints located in the bustle of midtown Manhattan. Wooden stands outside the store contain old bookplates and prints ranging in price from 75 cents to $10. Once inside the store, with its dark wood paneling and brass lamps with green shades, you'll be struck by the age of the place. Books cover three floors of the building and are categorized in the usual manner, although chaos seems to reign. It's an old-fashioned bookstore, in that the material varies greatly in quality, the staff seem to be indentured and the shelves display both dust and discoveries.

Barnes and Noble

105 Fifth Ave.
(18th St.)
807-0099
Mon. to Fri. 9:45 A.M. to 6:45 P.M.; Sat. 9:45 A.M. to 6:00 P.M.; Sun. 11:00 A.M. to 5:00 P.M.

Barnes and Noble claims to be the biggest bookstore in the world, and we've been so overwhelmed by the enormous number of books here that we wouldn't dare challenge it. In fact, we get positively exhausted browsing among the nearly three million new and used hardcover and soft-cover books. The Sale Annex across the street, at 128 Fifth Avenue is a haven for bargains—it offers up to 90 percent off on remainders and overstocks, and 33 percent off on titles from the *New York Times* best-seller list. Record hunters will find a large classical music department, and the textbook selection is unbeatable. Whether you come to buy or look, the offerings are irresistible, which makes the trip downtown all the more attractive. If you've got enough energy left, you can walk back uptown and pass some of the more expensive bookstores, pleased with the money you've saved at this venerable New York institution. There's a midtown location at 600 Fifth Avenue, near 48th Street.

Battledore Books

36 E. 61st St.
832-8231
Mon. to Fri. 10:00 A.M to 5:00 P.M. (by appt. only)

Battledore (formerly Justin Schiller) is arguably the foremost shop in the world for children's books. Battledore carries material (including drawings and prints) from the fifteenth century to the present, including first editions of such classics as *Tom Thumb* (1746), *Cinderella* (1510) and *Robinson Crusoe* (1814) and the Perrault edition of *Mother Goose* (1697). Although material of this nature is directed toward the serious collector and scholar, it is nevertheless a delight to view firsthand books whose readership has been so universal and whose titles bring forth forgotten memories of childhood.

Books and Co.
939 Madison Ave. (74th St.)
737-1450
Mon. to Sat. 10:00 A.M. to 7:00 P.M.; Sun. 11:30 A.M. to 6:00 P.M.

A very special mention for this splendid store, both for its style and for the quality. You won't find just current best-sellers—there are also, carefully presented, the complete works of most good authors, as well as American and foreign poetry magazines and beautiful books on photography, art, architecture and philosophy. The children's books are wonderful, and there's a fine and thorough paperback collection. Not quantity, but quality.

B. Dalton Bookseller
666 Fifth Ave. (52nd St.)
247-1740
Mon. to Fri. 9:30 A.M. to 8:00 P.M.; Sat. 10:00 A.M. to 6:30 P.M.; Sun. 12:30 P.M. to 5:00 P.M.

This flagship store of the B. Dalton chain stocks an impressive array of 200,000 titles. You'll find noteworthy collections of art, fiction, literature, travel, cooking and children's books, as well as a large number of titles in the science and technical sections. A research department will help you find what you're looking for, and the sales staff is competent and cooperative. Other branches are at 170 Broadway, near Maiden Lane, at 109 East 42nd Street and at the corner of Sixth Avenue and 8th Street.

Doubleday Book Shop
724 Fifth Ave. (57th St.)
397-0550
Mon. to Sat. 9:30 A.M. to midnight; Sun. noon to 5:00 P.M.

Doubleday is a browser's heaven day or night. In fact, it's one of the few stores on Fifth Avenue (along with Rizzoli) open late at night, which makes for an interesting after-hours clientele. We've seen everything from weary tourists and dressed-up couples on dates to idle browsers and the occasional serious bibliophile searching for a "must-have" title. This store (as well as its sister on Fifth and 53rd) is cheerful, airy and well lit, so any nocturnal wanderings among the well-stocked shelves are a pleasure. The striking glass elevator will take you to four levels of books, including a basement full of paperbacks and a mezzanine with theatrical books and a large record collection. Elsewhere are good sections of art books, limited editions, history books, remainders and, of course, all current fiction and nonfiction.

Eeyore's
1066 Madison Ave. (81st St.)
988-3404
Mon. to Sat. 10:00 A.M. to 6:00 P.M.; Sun. noon to 5:00 P.M.

A bookstore exclusively for children, this charming, friendly place will delight kids of all ages. There are books and records to enchant youngsters from infancy to adolescence, and every Sunday a captivating storyteller entertains. Go once at least. There's a West Side branch at 2252 Broadway, near 81st Street (362-0634).

Endicott Booksellers
450 Columbus Ave.

You step back in time when you step into Endicott, a spacious, Victorian-style book shop in a restored turn-of-the-century building, complete with oak shelves and brass plaques. Other relics of days gone by are a most

(81st St.)
787-6300
Daily 10:00 A.M. to 9:00 P.M.

knowledgeable and helpful staff, leather-bound and signed first-edition books and monthly readings featuring such top writers as Margaret Atwood and John Barth. You'll find all the latest books here, along with thorough collections of literature, children's books and books on the arts. Endicott is also an excellent place to find titles from small publishers and university presses.

Ex Libris
160a E. 70th St.
249-2618
Mon. to Fri. 10:00 A.M. to
5:00 P.M.

Arthur Cohen's Ex Libris is a mecca for those interested in the major art movements of the twentieth century, and it's the finest shop of its kind in the world. An exquisitely designed space in the basement of an Upper East Side townhouse, Ex Libris carries books, photographs, posters, manuscripts, periodicals, ephemera and works of art from the great art movements: futurism, vorticism, De Stijl, constructivism, Dada, surrealism, German expressionism and the Russian avant-garde. The frequently published catalogs are models of scholarly research, and the stock is worthy of most major museums and institutions. More a fine gallery than a bookstore, Ex Libris is one of New York's great cultural assets.

Forbidden Planet
821 Broadway
(12th St.)
473-1576
Mon. to Sat. 10:00 A.M. to 7:00
P.M.; Sun. 11:00 A.M. to
6:00 P.M.

This temple of science fiction offers an astronomical selection of science fiction books, magazines, drawings, models, gadgets and toys, along with similar items about rock stars. Fan heaven and cultist's delight.

Foul Play
10 Eighth Ave.
(12th St.)
675-5115
Mon. to Sat. noon to 10:00 P.M.;
Sun. noon to 6:00 P.M.

A real find for those who can't get to sleep at night without a good murder mystery. The shop is extremely tidy and well organized, with an excellent selection of mysteries, thrillers, whodunits and so on, from Agatha Christie and Dorothy L. Sayers to John Le Carré and Lawrence Sanders. The friendly women who run Foul Play, devoted fans themselves, are always happy to give the novice mystery reader suggestions.

Four Continents
149 Fifth Ave.
(21st St.)
533-0250
Mon. to Sat. 9:30 A.M. to 5:30 P.M.

Impropaganda? Four Continents is filled with books, magazines and newspapers from Russia, Poland, Czechoslovakia and other eastern European countries; some, not many, are translated into English and Spanish. You'll also find records, comic books, posters and small souvenirs.

Gotham Book Mart
41 W. 47th St.

Gotham is a hub of literary activity, with a huge selection of American poetry (mostly from the twentieth century) and some 250 literary and underground magazines filling the cluttered aisles. This is the place for

719-4448
Mon. to Sat. 9:30 A.M. to 6:30 P.M.

Kitchen Arts and Letters
**1435 Lexington Ave.
(93rd–94th sts.)
876-5550**
*Mon. to Fri. 10:00 A.M. to 6:00
P.M. (Wed. and Thurs. to 7:00
P.M.); Sat. 11:00 A.M. to
5:00 P.M.*

H. P. Kraus
**16 E. 46th St.
687-4808**
Mon. to Fri. 9:30 A.M. to 5:00 P.M.

Librairie de France/ Libreria Hispanica
**Rockefeller Center
610 Fifth Ave.
(49th–50th sts.)
581-8810**
*Mon. to Fri. 9:30 A.M. to 6:15
P.M.; Sat. 10:00 A.M. to 6:15 P.M.*

Madison Avenue Bookshop
**833 Madison Ave.
(70th St.)
535-6130**
Mon. to Sat. 9:30 A.M. to 6:00 P.M.

information on poetry events throughout the city. "Wise men fish here," says the wooden sign over the door, and we won't contest that.

New York now has an all-cookbook bookstore, with a selection of 2,000 titles sensibly arranged into such categories as type of cuisine, desserts, gastronomic memoirs, Christmas, classics, wine guides and so forth. The shop is decorated with old can and crate labels. Original art by cookbook illustrators, suitable for kitchen display, is for sale, as are aprons, potholders and stationery featuring fruit and food designs. The knowledgeable owner, Nahum Waxman, does his best to please.

An internationally known dealer of fine books, H.P. Kraus specializes in rare books and manuscripts published before 1700. The shop once owned and placed a Gutenberg Bible, perhaps the single most important book of all time; in general, it maintains a collection of only the rarest and most sought-after illuminated books and books on scientific and European history. In business for more than 50 years, Kraus publishes two or three catalogs yearly, each devoted to a particular subject or period. Prices are naturally commensurate with the rarity and value of such merchandise: books can exceed $85,000. Appointments are not necessary but are advised—the staff is more than likely to ask you what it is you are doing *there* instead of at B. Dalton.

We can't say that the atmosphere, display or prices are particularly attractive, but you'll nonetheless find a good selection of magazines (not always the current issues), new novels and, on the French side, such Gallic glories as the Astérix comic books. There's another location at 115 Fifth Avenue, near 19th Street (673-7400).

Quality and service are the watchwords at the Madison Avenue Bookshop. You won't find bargain books here— it stocks only the finest art books, gift books and current fiction and nonfiction. The paperback collection on the second floor is outstanding; its emphasis is on the classics, philosophy and poetry. Service is the specialty: the small, friendly staff will provide any personalized service a book buyer might need. They are particularly good at putting together unusual, attractive and/or extravagant gifts. Madison's window displays are without a doubt the finest in the book world; designed by Tiffany's window dresser, they reflect the quality found on the shelves.

Metropolitan Museum of Art Bookstore
Fifth Avenue and 82nd Street
570-3726
Tues. to Sat. 10:00 A.M. to 4:45 P.M. (Tues. to 8:45 P.M.); Sun. 11:00 A.M. to 4:45 P.M.

If you're not tempted by the major reproductions in the Met's gift store on the ground floor, keep walking. You'll surely be interested in the superb collection of art books in the bookstore. Not only is the selection exhaustive (everything from prehistoric to contemporary), but the store is handsome and well organized.

The Military Bookman
29 E. 93rd St.
348-1280
Tues. to Sat. 10:30 A.M. to 5:30 P.M.

The Military Bookman is entirely devoted to out-of-print and antiquarian books concerning military history. As one of the staff so succinctly puts it: "We are not interested in diplomacy, negotiations or politics ... just war." It is a shop for authors, professional historians, collectors and the casual browser. The subject material dates from the earliest record of human conflict up to the Vietnam War. The staff is particularly well versed and solicitous. Books are filed according to the particular war, whether it be the Napoleonic wars or the Battle of Troy, including subcategories with such intriguing headings as "Aircraft Pictorials," "Arms and Armor" and "Biographies of Air-Marshals." The Military Bookman is, without a doubt, one of a kind.

Murder Ink
271 W. 87th St.
362-8905
Mon. to Sat. 1:00 P.M. to 7:00 P.M.

This is *the* place for detective and mystery fiction in New York. Taking its name from Al Capone's nefarious crime syndicate, this small West Side shop not only has the best selection of the current crop of detective writers, such as Timothy Harris and L.A. Morse, but the classics abound as well: Agatha Christie, Dashiell Hammett and the incomparable Raymond Chandler. Patrons exchange opinions and information with an ease that occasionally leads to heated banter over the merits or faults of a particular new title or author. The staff is composed of hard-core fans who know virtually every title in stock. An added mention goes to the host of well-fed, lumbering cats who inhabit the place, providing both amusement and obstruction.

999 Bookshop
999 Madison Ave. (77th St.)
288-9439

The 999 is a bright, airy store with a large selection of titles displayed on handsome oak shelves. It's a good general bookstore, but art books are the specialty—so much so that the 999 now runs the book concession at Sotheby's. The collection of books on decorative arts is

Mon. to Fri. 9:30 A.M. to 6:00 P.M.; Sat. 10:00 A.M. to 5:00 P.M.; Sun. noon to 5:00 P.M.

particularly strong, and there is an excellent choice of out-of-print titles. The staff is friendly, and the shop is service oriented (it delivers locally).

Jaap Rietman
167 Spring St.
966-7044
Mon. to Fri. 9:00 A.M. to 6:00 P.M.; Sat. 10:00 A.M. to 6:00 P.M.

Jaap Rietman carries in-print art books and periodicals and is in many respects a SoHo institution. Rietman caters more to an audience interested in art than to collectors who regard books as fine objects and collectibles. The selection of catalogs from domestic and international museums and galleries is most impressive; many titles not readily available in the United States somehow find their way to Rietman. Catalogs of the stock are published seasonally, and the store's mail-order service is excellent. The staff, however, other than Jaap Rietman himself, is rather surly and uninformed.

Rizzoli
712 Fifth Ave.
(56th St.)
397-3706
Mon. to Sat. 9:30 A.M. to midnight

The wood-paneled walls covered with their freight of multilingual books will make you think you're in a library rather than in a bookstore. There is a perfect art section, as well as European newspapers (in a section at the back to the right), a small art gallery and a department for classical and jazz records (on the mezzanine). You'll browse to the accompaniment of opera or chamber music, a refreshing change from the almost inescapable pop found elsewhere. Rizzoli is now open until midnight, making it great for a late-night stop.

The Scribner Book Store
597 Fifth Ave.
(48th St.)
486-2700
Mon. to Fri. 9:00 A.M. to 6:30 P.M.; Sat. 9:30 A.M. to 5:30 P.M.

This is certainly one of the most elegant bookstores in New York. The architecture is almost cathedralesque, with its multistory windows and ironwork—in celebration of books, we presume. Many customers prefer Scribner for its personal service in a city renowned for the do-it-yourself school of retail services. You may find obscure titles here, although no rare books are offered. No matter—there are nearly 50,000 titles from which to choose, and there's an out-of-print search service. A comprehensive paperback gallery and a collection of leather-bound books round out the selection in this established, reputable store.

South Street Seaport Book and Chart Store
25 Fulton St.
(Water St.)
669-9400
Daily 11:00 A.M. to 6:00 P.M.

A part of the restored South Street Seaport village, this shop has appropriately been given over to the sea. The complete works of Herman Melville take their place among sailing magazines, guides to navigation, travel books, how-tos for building your own boat, and—since the shop is also a government supplier—very attractive charts. Everything is neatly organized—no storms or heavy seas on the horizons here.

The Strand

**828 Broadway
(12th St.)
473-1452**
*Mon. to Sat. 9:30 A.M. to
6:30 P.M.; Sun. 11:00 A.M. to
5:00 P.M.*

"The biggest used-book store in the world" is how The Strand describes itself, and it has eight miles of new and used books to prove it. You'll find everything you might want in the art and history sections. Some current titles are sold at half price. This institution is a must-see for book lovers.

Supersnipe Comic Book Euphoriam

879-9628

As we went to press, this unique shop had closed its Second Avenue doors, with plans to reopen at an as-yet-undiscovered location. But it still has its fabulous stock of more than 250,000 old and new comic books, including rare collectors' items, all of which can be ordered by mail (send your "want list" to P.O. Box 1102, Gracie Station, New York, NY 10028). It also stocks complete sets of books and magazines, as well as first, rare and current editions. Call before sending in a mail order, as a new location may have opened by the time you read this.

Three Lives and Company Books

**131 Seventh Avenue South
(10th St.)
741-2069**
*Mon. to Sat. 11:00 A.M. to 10:00
P.M.; Sun. 1:00 P.M. to 7:00 P.M.*

A friendly little Village bookshop frequented by lovers of literature and art. Three Lives stocks a great variety of titles from the worlds of biography, literature, letters, modern art, design, architecture and gay writing. One of the best features of this store is its readings, held on alternate Thursday evenings, where New York writers hold forth with their stories. It's a casual place, and the hours may vary according to season, weather and whim, so we suggest that you call before visiting in the early or late hours of the day.

Urban Center Books

**457 Madison Ave.
(51st St.)
935-3595**
*Mon. to Fri. 10:00 A.M. to
6:00 P.M.*

Urban Center is located within the Italianate splendor of the Helmsley Palace hotel, and, appropriately, it carries books and periodicals on architecture and design. The shop has high ceilings, Corinthian wall columns and French windows that look onto a charming courtyard facing Madison Avenue. The stock includes domestic and international titles, including out-of-print volumes by and about Richard Neutra, Frank Lloyd Wright and Le Corbusier, and a comprehensive selection of foreign architectural and design periodicals such as *GA*, *Domus* and *Casa Vogue*. Urban Center, concerned with the history of architecture from the time of the Egyptians to the present, also sells many titles on the decorative arts from such major design movements as the Bauhaus, art nouveau and art deco. For the traveler, the store's selection of guides and maps to New York City is unparalleled.

Ursus Books

**39 E. 79th St.
772-8787**

After the bother of being "buzzed" through three separate locked doors, you'll enter New York's most overpriced art bookstore, Ursus. True, there's a

Mon. to Fri. 10:00 A.M. to 6:00 P.M.; Sat. 10:00 A.M. to 4:00 P.M.

tremendous selection, but the books are generally 30 percent higher in price than one should pay. This store is perfect for the most desperate collector who, not having the time to shop around, can purchase an entire body of printed matter on important modern and contemporary artists at a single opportunity—providing he or she is affluent enough. Much of the stock is also worn and tattered and, though catalogued and filed properly, seems neglected.

Waldenbooks
57 Broadway
(Trinity Pl.)
269-1139
Mon. to Fri. 8:00 A.M. to 6:00 P.M.

Waldenbooks is a nationwide chain of small, shopping-mall best-seller houses. But this store near Wall Street is a happy exception to the rule. It's a large, inviting shop with a well-rounded collection on four levels. Like any good bookstore, it reflects its neighborhood—so business and computer books are the specialty here. But you'll also find thorough offerings of travel books, classics, science fiction, current fiction, children's books and cookbooks.

Oscar Wilde Memorial Bookshop
15 Christopher St.
(Waverly Pl.)
255-8097
Daily noon to 7:00 P.M.

This famous gay thoroughfare is home to a shop specializing in printed matter of interest to homosexuals: novels, essays, magazines and poetry, along with T-shirts proclaiming one's affiliation.

Wittenborn Art Books
1018 Madison Ave.
(78th St.)
2nd floor
288-1558
Mon. to Sat. 10:00 A.M. to 5:00 P.M.

This bookstore devoted to the visual arts (painting, sculpture, architecture, tapestry, furniture and so on) looks like an overcrowded archive, but the disorder is only superficial. The classification is rigorous, and the choice is a wonder.

Woman Books
201 W. 92nd St.
873-4121
Tues. to Sat. 10:00 A.M. to 7:00 P.M.; Sun. noon to 6:00 P.M.

This shop is of great interest to women engaged in the struggle for women's rights. It specializes in books written by and for women and carries a selection of nonsexist children's books as well.

Zen Oriental Bookstore
142 W. 57th St.
582-4622

This delightful place sells everything in the way of books about Japan: its philosophy, its culture and its cuisine. There are also records, artistic supplies, toys, prints and crafts in this shop, whose clients are almost exclusively

Mon. to Fri. 10:00 A.M. to 8:00 P.M.; Sun. noon to 7:00 P.M.

Japanese. A small cafeteria on the mezzanine is perfect for relaxation, at one spiritual level or another, over a cup of tea. Another location at 521 Fifth Avenue, between 43rd and 44th streets (697-0840).

STATIONERY

Brandon Memorabilia
222 E. 51st St.
593-2794
Mon. to Fri. 10:00 A.M. to 6:00 P.M.; Sat. 11:00 A.M. to 5:00 P.M.

A tiny card shop filled with some lovely nostalgic cards, stickers and sheets of Victorian angels and Belle Epoque ladies. Alternative cards, a selection for gay men, retro designs, writing papers, little trifles and pop-out cards give nearly everyone a choice here. Pleasant, sweet service.

Ffolio 72
888 Madison Ave.
(72nd St.)
879-0675
Mon. to Sat. 10:00 A.M. to 6:00 P.M.

You'll find everything you need in the way of formal and classic stationery and calling cards at Tiffany or Cartier, but for more original and creative ideas, this shop will print your own stationery to order, along with invitations and business or calling cards—from formal to eccentric, depending on your mood.

Greetings
740 Madison Ave.
(64th St.)
734-1865
Mon. to Fri. noon to 6:00 P.M.; Sat. 10:00 A.M. to 6:00 P.M.

Restrained New Wave background music keeps customers happy as they pore through the alternative greeting cards designed to meet any modern shopper's needs. There are plenty of gay renditions to supplement the straight but still nontraditional designs, most of which are greetingless so you can create your own salutation. You'll also find plenty of stickers, colorful writing papers, attractive giftwraps and a few address books in rainbow hues. Another location at 35 Christopher Street (242-0424).

Hallmark Gallery
720 Fifth Ave.
(56th St.)
489-8320
Mon. to Sat. 9:30 A.M. to 6:00 P.M.

A large, spacious and well-lit shop in which to find party decorations, cards, candles, trinkets, puzzles, albums, frames, plaques and jewelry. You can choose at your leisure from among 500 middle-of-the-road types of cards covering almost any occasion—only divorces seemed to be missing. Many other Hallmark stores throughout the city.

Hudson Street Papers
581 Hudson St.
(Bank St.)
243-4221
Mon. to Fri. 8:00 A.M. to 9:30 P.M.; Sat. 9:00 A.M. to midnight; Sun. 9:00 A.M. to 6:00 P.M.

Card and stationery shops abound in this area, but none have the faultless taste we found here. The selection isn't large, but everything is charming and worthwhile. There's a small, very intelligent collection of paperbacks, a case of pretty jewelry and accessories, art, fashion and literary magazines, unusual postcards and attractive stationery, wrapping papers and cards. Prices are quite reasonable.

The Paper House
**741 Madison Ave.
(64th St.)
737-0082**
*Mon. to Sat. 9:30 A.M. to
6:30 P.M.; Sun. 10:00 A.M. to
6:30 P.M.*

Too-cute cards, posters, novelties, ribbons and wrapping papers are here to supply your at-home gift department. The selection is good, although we cannot vouch for the taste level of all the merchandise. A good address for party planners and frequent gift givers. Several other locations.

Under Attack
**187 Columbus Ave.
(69th St.)
724-6865**
Mon. to Fri. 11:00 A.M. to midnight

Attractive and extravagant cards starting at 40 cents, unusual calligraphy pens and a large collection of T-shirts are carried in this West Side shop.

Untitled Art Postcards
**159 Prince St.
(W. Broadway)
982-2088**
Daily noon to 7:00 P.M.

A minuscule shop that nonetheless houses the biggest collection in the world of international art postcards from all disciplines: photography, painting, science, literature and so on, organized by artist or subject. A very interesting spot.

Children

CLOTHES

Botticellino
**777 Madison Ave.
(65th St.)
628-9001**
*Mon. to Fri. 10:00 A.M. to 6:30
P.M.; Sat. 10:00 A.M. to 6:00 P.M.*

Italian style and quality distinguish these exclusive shoes from babies' size two up to women's size seven and a half. If you have to ask, you can't afford them. Another location in Trump Tower, 721 Fifth Avenue, near 56th Street (308-6402).

Cerutti
**807 Madison Ave.
(68th St.)
737-7540**
Mon. to Sat. 9:00 A.M. to 5:30 P.M.

A reliable classic for children up to age sixteen. The window may not be particularly well arranged or kept up, but the clothes inside are beyond reproach, and the many Madison Avenue mothers who come here regularly can't all be wrong. In addition to an unsurpassed selection of ready-to-wear (not always made in Europe), you can also have clothes made to measure for an additional $20 or $30. Good accessories and all the basics—underwear, socks, tights—plus an extremely elegant choice of shoes and flats. Madison Avenue prices.

Au Chat Botté
0 to 4 years:

The most elegant and expensive children's clothing imaginable, mostly from France and England. Everything

**888 Madison Ave.
(72nd St.)
772-3381
5 to 15 years:
1065 Lexington Ave.
(75th St.)
988-3482**
*Mon. to Sat. 10:00 A.M. to
6:00 P.M.*

is admirable in both taste and quality, whether it's a sailor suit or a taffeta dress, finely embroidered baptismal robes or excellent shoes. You'll find the best European brand names, some exclusive to these shops. Another store, at 886 Madison Avenue specializes in similarly high-quality cribs and infant furniture and accessories—here's where to come for that canopied brass crib you've been wanting. It also carries a selection of clothes for mothers-to-be. If you're not afraid to spend a lot of money, don't pass by these three shops.

The Chocolate Soup
**946 Madison Ave.
(75th St.)
861-2210**
*Mon. to Sat. 10:00 A.M. to 6:00
P.M.; Sun. noon to 5:00 P.M.*

The specialty here is imaginative clothing in colors ranging from the reserved to the frankly audacious, along with reasonably priced smocked Liberty dresses designed especially for the store. There are corduroy overalls with patterns sewn on the front, OshKosh overalls dyed in solids or stripes, an abundance of stretchies and T-shirt sets, plus a wonderful choice of toys and knickknacks: old-fashioned metal mechanical toys, nontoxic painted wooden toys, dinosaurs, dolls and dollhouses. A fascinating, minuscule shop, only a few square yards in size, that is both colorful and crammed with goods.

City Kids
**130 Seventh Ave.
(18th St.)
620-0906**
*Mon. to Fri. 11:00 A.M. to 7:00
P.M.; Sat. 11:00 A.M. to 6:00 P.M.*

Good taste characterizes this charming little shop that sells clothing and toys for small children. The domestic and imported clothes are more for playtime than for Sunday dinner—T-shirts, colorful swimsuits, OshKosh overalls and adorable beaded moccasins for little girls. Prices are reasonable. There's a small, thoughtful selection of simple and unique toys, books and stuffed animals.

Fusen Usagi
**927 Madison Ave.
(73rd St.)
772-6180**
*Mon. to Sat. 10:00 A.M. to
6:00 P.M.*

Now, even before they can walk to wear a Walkman, the tiniest Upper East Siders can show their Oriental savvy with an outfit from Fusen Usagi. This finely made cotton clothing is imported directly from Japan, where the brand is recognized and respected by nearly every Japanese mom. Some of the highlights of this well-laid-out boutique are intricately designed socks with skid-proof bottoms, all-cotton underwear and two-way-snap stretchies. The full layette is designed to last until your baby reaches six months, and it can be ordered with as few or as many pieces as your budget allows. (Prices for prestige, however, are never cheap.) For boys up to size four and girls up to size seven, the clothing is wearable and wonderful, with simple designs. Everything's washable—and the best-selling colors are black and gray! Fusen Usagi also carries kid-size accessories and colorful canvas shoes, as well as a line of handmade (in the U.S.A.) quilts. This is by far one of the most exciting children's shops to open in a long time.

Greenstones & Cie
442 Columbus Ave.
(81st St.)
580-4322
Mon. to Fri. 11:00 A.M. to 7:00 P.M.; Sat. 11:00 A.M. to 6:00 P.M.; Sun. noon to 6:00 P.M.

West Side classics for infants to preteens. Spacious Greenstones & Cie has fun-loving clothes: leather bomber jackets, Meronas, khakis for kids and great appliqúed sweats. Most of the better children's brands are represented, plus a lot of the lesser known (but not lesser quality) names. Prices are nouvelle Columbus Avenue.

Kidz
109 Thompson St.
(Spring St.)
334-9851
Tues. to Sun. noon to 6:00 P.M.

Back in the days when father knew best, kids wore clothes that didn't resemble shrunken adult wear. Today, West Murray has a secret source for just such clothes, and she's gathered them together in her playful SoHo boutique. You'll find Gene Autry rain boots, sailor suits, smocked dresses and saddle shoes, mostly from the '40s and '50s. The sizes range from infant to fourteen, with the biggest concentration in the smaller sizes. Everything's never-worn, totally authentic and practically at yesteryear's prices.

Little Bits
1186 Madison Ave.
(86th–87th sts.)
722-6139
Mon. to Thurs. 10:00 A.M. to 7:00 P.M.; Fri. and Sat. 10:00 A.M. to 6:00 P.M.

A marvelous selection of infants' and children's clothing, including its own special line of jeans and overalls that are embroidered, appliqúed and riveted to the nines. You'll see lots of things you won't find anywhere else: richly textured sweaters, the tiniest ballerina slippers, diamond-studded mary janes, a restaurant survival kit, black-tie stretchies and glow-in-the-dark gloves decorated with the New York City skyline. A small store full of big surprises.

Le Monde des Enfants
870 Madison Ave.
(71st St.)
772-1990
Mon. to Fri. 10:00 A.M. to 5:00 P.M.; Sat. 11:00 A.M. to 5:30 P.M.

Everything for the French schoolgirl—including the blackboard. Pleated wool jumpers in gray or navy, colorful, coordinated play clothes and classic separates for sizes two to sixteen: a charming but limited selection of very good clothes, all imported from France.

Pamper Me
322 First Ave.
(19th St.)
677-0604
Mon. to Sat. 10:00 A.M. to 6:00 P.M.

This good and very friendly store for sizes newborn to fourteen is run by two Hawaiian ladies who don't push you to buy, but try to help you as much as possible—even to the point of suggesting other shops if they can't deliver the goods themselves. The quality and variety of what they do have (mostly American clothes, with some imports), along with the relaxed atmosphere, make this establishment the one we recommend most heartily to people in the neighborhood.

Pinch Penny Pick-a-Pocket
1242 Madison Ave.

This enticing little store carries the largest variety of contemporary children's clothing next to Cerutti. Some of the things are handmade—the charming Nantucket

(89th St.)
831-3819
Mon. to Sat. 10:00 A.M. to
6:00 P.M.

dresses, sweaters, batik "cowboy" quilts—and there's a kit for kids to make their own painted T-shirts. It also carries the entire Baby Bjorn line of Swedish wonders (bibs, travel beds, knapsacks and so forth), which make life easier for both parent and child. The ground floor stocks from infant up to size six for girls and up to size four for boys (after that, head for Tim's under the same ownership), plus an irresistible collection of jewelry and accessories. The downstairs is devoted entirely to girls' sizes seven to preteen. It also carries shoes up to women's size eight.

RG Crumb-snatcher
254 Columbus Ave.
(72nd St.)
724-8681
Mon. to Fri. 11:00 A.M. to 7:00
P.M.; Sat. 11:00 A.M. to 6:00 P.M.

Rita Finkel takes as much delight in her store as the wide-eyed children who come in do. Stocked from floor to ceiling with surprises—puppets hanging from the rafters, a carousel horse, Ol' Bob the uni-seesaw, a mahogany motorcycle—this store also carries terrific clothing for children newborn to age fourteen. Rita likes kids to look like kids, and you won't see a lot of designer names here. Many things are made especially for her (some by her costume-designer sister-in-law), while others she discovers here and in Europe. Her accessories are also irresistible: hand-painted hangers, bandana bibs, soft, infant-sized cowboy boots and angel-winged shoes. Her latest discovery is hats—from motorcycle helmets to Yankee caps. Truly a Never-Never-Land!

Second Act
1046 Madison Ave.
(89th St.)
2nd floor
988-2440
Tues. to Sat. 10:00 A.M. to
5:00 P.M.

The best-known shop in New York for secondhand children's clothing. Second Act is well organized and crowded with hand-me-downs (on consignment) that have been cleaned and are in very good condition, if not actually new. Most are excellent brands at excellent prices. A more-than-useful spot.

Tim's
878 Madison Ave.
(72nd St.)
535-2262
Mon. to Fri. 10:30 A.M. to 6:00
P.M.; Sat. 11:00 A.M. to 6:00 P.M.

Boys will be boys. And no one knows it better than Tim's, where fashion meets function, and tradition meets ... opposition. This tiny, slightly irreverent shop is the most delightful place in the city to outfit your son: in prep-school gray flannel shorts, polo shirts and club ties; in cabled fisherman's sweaters, tweed newsboy caps or down army jackets; in sophisticated double-breasted "business" suits or elegant French velvets. For sizes two to twenty, there's a definite point of view here that we find thoroughly refreshing and certainly unique. Aside from the clothes, Tim's stocks all the basics to go over and under everything your boy wears.

Tru-Tred Shoes

A store that always seems to be jammed with people; it wouldn't be surprising if you had to register before being served. At any rate, patience, and plenty of it, is de

**1241 Lexington Ave.
(84th St.)
249-0551**
*Mon. to Fri. 9:30 A.M. to 5:00 P.M.
(Thurs. to 7:00 P.M.)*

rigueur. But that will give you time to look over all the models and styles offered. If you still can't decide for yourself, one of the efficient salespeople will eventually help you make a wise choice of shoes for your child. You can't go wrong, as all are of excellent quality made by such American manufactures as Sebago, Capezio, Stride-Rite, Nike and Timberland and by their European counterparts. It also sells some shoes for adults—not very stylish, but sensible. Shipment available throughout the nation.

Wendy's Store
**456 W. Broadway
(Houston St.)
533-2306**
Daily 11:00 A.M. to 7:00 P.M.

A SoHo playground where you can find absolutely everything. Wendy's specialties include clothing hand knitted especially for her shop, with delightful animal designs in a rainbow of colors, plus quilts for cribs, hand-painted T-shirts, embroidered sneakers, jeans for the newborn, elegant imported clothing from France and miniature toys. There's also a terrific choice of children's books for all ages. Reasonable prices, on the whole. Sizes from infant to twelve.

TOYS

Mary Arnold Toys
**962 Lexington Ave.
(70th St.)
744-8510**
Mon. to Fri. 9:00 A.M. to 6:00 P.M.; Sat. 10:00 A.M. to 5:00 P.M.

At Mary Arnold Toys you'll find not only stuffed animals, dolls, dollhouses and all sorts of other toys but also stationery, art supplies, helium-filled balloons, books for readers of all ages and a good selection of party favors. This shop is particularly dear to the hearts of younger shoppers, as they can leave their own wish list here for a birthday, Christmas or special occasion.

Childcraft
**150 E. 58th St.
753-3196**
Mon. to Fri. 10:00 A.M. to 5:45 P.M.; Sat. 10:00 A.M. to 4:45 P.M.

Mostly wood educational toys, plus puzzles, construction sets—from Lego to the latest American creations—laboratory equipment, musical instruments, art supplies and books are carried here—education and amusement for children up to age fifteen. There's also some children's furniture. Another location at 155 East 23rd Street (674-4754).

Dolls and Dreams
**454 Third Ave.
(31st St.)
684-4277**
Mon. to Sat. 10:00 A.M. to 6:00 P.M.

There's not a single mass-produced toy to be found in this charming shop devoted to high-quality domestic and imported handmade toys. Stuffed animals, Sasha dolls, Käthe Kruse collectibles, T.C. Timber wooden trains and excellent art supplies (such as Caran d'Ache) are just a sampling from the wonderful assortment you can expect to find. Nothing is inexpensive, of course, but the least of these items is sure to surprise and please. The other store, at 1421 Lexington Avenue, near 93rd Street (876-2434), has a smaller but by no means less exciting selection.

Flosso-Hormann Magic Co.

304 W. 34th St.
2nd floor
279-6079
*Mon. to Sat. 10:30 A.M. to
5:00 P.M.*

This, the oldest magic shop in the United States, has been run by a series of celebrated prestidigitators since its founding in 1865. There are free demonstrations for children and tours of the Museum of Magic on Saturdays. Said to be Orson Welles's favorite store.

Go Fly a Kite

1201 Lexington Ave.
(81st–82nd sts.)
472-2623
*Mon. to Sat. 10:00 A.M. to
6:00 P.M.*

Kites from around the world in all shapes (birds, boxes, animals and planes), sizes, materials (plastic, paper, cloth) and prices ($5 and up). The Chinese kites, especially the dragons, are stupendous and inexpensive. And most of the kites can be folded up, so they're easy to transport. This gallery of flying sculptures is well known to New Yorkers, as it's been around for twenty years. Another location at Citicorp's The Market, 153 East 53rd Street (308-1666).

Johnny Jupiter

884 Madison Ave.
(72nd St.)
744-0818
*Mon. to Sat. 10:30 A.M. to
6:00 P.M.*

A delightful toy shop that is more likely to bring you back to your youth than to elevate the minds of your young ones. Gumby and Pokey are alive and well here, living amid painted tin toys, jokes, tricks, Dad's old Buick and lots more. Heartwarming memories pop out of every corner. There's also a delicious selection of kitchen things: pitchers, plates, teapots—all unusual and very fairly priced. Another location at 385 Bleecker Street, near 11th Street (675-7574).

The Laughing Giraffe

147 E. 72nd St.
570-9528
*Mon. to Fri. 10:00 A.M. to 6:00
P.M.; Sat. 10:00 A.M. to 5:00 P.M.*

The few steps down into this minuscule shop will introduce you to a world of original and creative toys, carefully chosen (space demands it) by the owner, a former elementary school teacher. Everything is amusing and intelligent, encouraging children to stretch their capabilities—and imaginations—while having a good time. There are some particularly irresistible stuffed animal puppets and an excellent choice of children's books.

Muppet Stuff

833 Lexington Ave.
(64th St.)
980-8340
*Mon. to Sat. 10:00 A.M. to
6:00 P.M.*

The Sesame Street bunch owns this fun-filled store where, in addition to the much-in-demand figures of Miss Piggy and her cohorts, you can also find clothing (including adult-size T-shirts), shoes, linen, puzzles and games, all bearing the portraits of these favorite television characters.

Penny Whistle Toys

448 Columbus Ave.

This store caters to future West Side intellectuals. In a small but airy space, you'll find a plethora of high-quality toys at every price level—from the usual Lego sets to beautiful dolls and stuffed animals. There are science kits

(82nd St.)
873-9090
Mon. to Fri. 11:00 A.M. to 9:00 P.M.; Sat. 11:00 A.M. to 7:00 P.M.; Sun. noon to 6:00 P.M.

for every sort of genius, and a lot of toys that do things, be they faux computers or manual typewriters. There's also a selection of small, inexpensive toys like we used to have in the olden days, along with puzzles, games, wooden trains and hard-paged Brimax books, which make great first readers. Unique baby toys are imported from Holland, Sweden and Greece. A smaller store for East Siders is at 1283 Madison Avenue, near 91st Street (369-3868).

Play It Again
171 E. 92nd St.
876-5888
Mon. to Sat. 11:00 A.M. to 6:00 P.M. (Wed. 3:00 P.M. to 6:00 P.M.)

This store carries lots and lots of secondhand toys in working condition, some of them practically (if not actually) new: dolls, stuffed animals, books, puzzles, bicycles, carriages, games—an enormous variety at very good prices. A place to keep in mind.

Polk's
314 Fifth Ave.
(32nd St.)
279-9034
Mon. to Sat. 9:30 A.M. to 6:00 P.M. (Thurs. to 9:00 P.M.)

The only, the unique, the incomparable shop for models, radio-controlled toys, racing sets, personal computers, science equipment and the like. This is where all serious model makers and hobbyists come to acquire the latest and greatest kits: the boats, the airplanes, the cars and the trains that enchant children of all ages, including our own.

F.A.O. Schwartz
745 Fifth Ave.
(58th St.)
644-9400
Mon. to Sat. 10:00 A.M. to 6:00 P.M. (Thurs. to 8:00 P.M.)

Is there a grown-up alive who can't remember his or her first visit to the biggest and most prestigious toy store in the country? F.A.O. Schwartz comprises three world-famous floors of toys, many exclusive items, including life-sized stuffed animals, miniature radio-controlled vehicles and toy cars that cost as much as real ones. Electric trains, dolls galore, electronic games and an excellent department for infant toys should keep every child, young or old, in his or her element. Prices are higher than elsewhere, but a visit is a must. At Christmas, the animated windows are pure fantasy come true. Note the puppet shows given Monday through Friday (only uptown) at 2:30 P.M. Another location at 5 World Trade Center, concourse level (775-1850).

Teddy's, Inc.
120 Thompson St.
(Spring St.)
226-5013
Tues. to Sat. noon to 7:00 P.M. (Fri. to 9:00 P.M.); Sun. 1:00 P.M. to 7:00 P.M.

The first exclusively teddy bear store in the city, this cozy shop has enough bears to stop Merrill Lynch, in every size, shape and form: kites, candles, catalogs, puzzles, cards, even candy. In classic cuddlies, all the best names are here: Steiff, Hermans, Gund, North American Bear, Import Toys and Eden. Naturally, the two delightful owners are teddy lovers themselves, and they understand their customers perfectly—they'll even punch holes in a shopping bag so a newly purchased teddy won't suffocate on its way home.

Toy Park

112 E. 86th St.
427-6611
Mon. 10:00 A.M. to 6:00 P.M.;
Tues. to Sat. 10:00 A.M. to 7:00
P.M. (Thurs. to 8:00 P.M.); Sun.
noon to 5:00 P.M.

The Big Apple's largest and best supermarket for toys—something common in the suburbs, but practically unheard of in Manhattan. The store is, as you'd expect, immense and very well stocked, especially with educational toys and games. You'll find a superb doll section, stuffed animals, craft items and much, much more, all at reasonable prices. Lots of happy family Sundays in store.

Youth at Play

1120 Madison Ave.
(84th St.)
737-5036
Mon. to Sat. 10:00 A.M. to
6:00 P.M.

A veritable bazaar of toys, offering a chaotic but enormous selection for children of all ages. Every available bit of space is filled with electronic games, party games, games of skill and educational games, plus sports equipment such as roller skates and skateboards, and all the more traditional toys: doll carriages, tricycles, puzzles, records, an armory of toy weapons, costumes (which you can special order if they're not in stock), an entire party goods department, school supplies and on and on. We can't list everything here, but trust us, they have it! The sales staff is helpful.

Dolls

Ludwig Beck of Munich

Trump Tower
Level D
725 Fifth Ave.
(56th St.)
308-2025
Mon. to Sat. 10:00 A.M. to
6:00 P.M.

The prettiest dolls in the city live in a quiet little corner on the top floor of Trump Tower. Created in Tuscany by Brigitte Deval, who was inspired by old Munich puppets and crib figures, these baby-size beauties are unlike any dolls you've ever seen. Each one has a name and is as expressive as an adolescent—the age she represents. All have porcelain heads and hands covered with a film of wax, hand-painted faces and moody glass eyes. Their clothing is enviable, and their shoes are made by an Italian cobbler. Each is numbered and signed under her wig. These are true works of art ... and love.

Iris Brohm Antique Store

253 E. 57th St.
593-2882
Mon. to Fri. 11:00 A.M. to 6:00
P.M.; Sat. 12:30 P.M. to 5:30 P.M.

Mrs. Brohm isn't the sort of person who will force you to buy something—she's much too attached to her wonders to part with them willingly, and you'll understand why when you see what is undoubtedly the most tempting collection of antique dolls in New York. Porcelain and biscuit dolls from Victorian times, each one prettier than the last, fill a glass case on one side of her shop. The opposite wall is devoted to doll furniture of the same era—pure marvels—and a few attractive pieces of period clothing. Nothing here dates from after the nineteenth century (except Mrs. Brohm, who, however, cares so much for her dolls that she has come to resemble them). They're expensive, but justifiably so: the smallest (about eight inches high) cost about $400 each, and the biggest (about twenty inches) are, well …. She also buys and repairs dolls.

Doll House Antics
1308 Madison Ave. (93rd St.)
876-2288
Mon. to Sat. 10:00 A.M. to 5:00 P.M.; Sun. (in Dec.) 10:00 A.M. to 5:00 P.M.

A treat for young eyes: an enchanting presentation of dollhouses with stupendously exact reproductions. From the familiar catsup bottle to the attractive bedspreads, everything is miniaturized with exquisite taste, and looks more real than the originals. The frequently changed window display is reason enough to keep coming back to this store.

Manhattan Doll Hospital/ The Doll House
176 Ninth Ave. (21st St.)
989-5220
Sun. to Fri. 10:00 A.M. to 5:00 P.M.

The old-world German owners of this shop have been in the doll business for more than 40 years, which is to say that they are true connoisseurs of dolls and dollhouses, and that they offer a very attractive array of wares in a wide range of prices. There are preassembled houses, houses you build yourself, kits to make reproductions of old homes and, in particular, an enchanting assortment of separate rooms that you can arrange to create the dollhouse of your dreams. And, the store claims, of the furniture that goes into a real home, there isn't a single item that you won't find reproduced here for your dolls, from typewriters to bathroom accessories to tea sets. It also offers a very good choice of antique dolls, including the first Madame Alexander doll ever made. What's more, Jenny and Herman repair antique porcelain, rag and rubber dolls. Experts offering expert service.

New York Doll Hospital
787 Lexington Ave. (62nd St.)
838-7527
Mon. to Sat. 10:00 A.M. to 6:00 P.M.

You don't often visit a more charming and authentic shop or meet a store owner as friendly as Irving Chais. Probably one of the only remaining craftsmen of his type in the world, he has spent 35 years reviving, repairing and reconstituting dolls of all sorts (wood, porcelain, plastic, rag) and animals of irreplaceable value to their young owners. In his doll-filled attic, he performs delicate operations on dreadfully sick porcelain bodies and unstuffed animals. It's more than a livelihood for him—dolls are a passion he shares with his parents and grandparents, who opened the New York Doll Hospital in 1900. He also possesses an extraordinary collection of antique European and American dolls, some of which date back to 1875. He has a few of the first doll automatons, as well as an exact replica of Queen Elizabeth II as a young girl (with very blue eyes, and fitted with a flowered candy-pink hat), a number of Shirley Temple dolls, complete with blond ringlets, some adorable French and German dolls from the turn of the century, W.C. Fields and Charlie McCarthy dolls (ahh, fame and immortality!) and such new old-fashioned accessories as socks, shoes, wigs and made-to-order clothing. There are also heaps of little wonders waiting to be rediscovered among big boxes full of sick patients. Prices vary considerably: accessories are inexpensive, but the older dolls average between $250 and $2,000, while repairs run from $10 to $20. A unique store undisturbed by tourists.

Tiny Doll House
231 E. 53rd St.
Mon. to Sat. 11:00 A.M. to 5:30 P.M.

An appealing shop that specializes in dollhouse furnishings, building supplies and accessories in every style—rustic, modern, art deco and so on—and of every sort—paintings, dishes, newspapers, mirrors. Absolutely bewitching and incredibly small—a triumph of craft.

Clothes

ACCESSORIES

Fogal of Switzerland
680 Madison Ave. (61st St.)
759-9782
Mon. to Sat. 10:00 A.M. to 6:00 P.M.

This little boutique is filled with fabulous legwear from Switzerland. You will find a fashionable rainbow of colors and patterns—and, miraculously, this store always seems to have your size. There is also a collection of socks, each more au courant than the next. The prices are certainly higher than Bloomingdale's house line, but we're assured that the quality at Fogal is so superb that the $15 pantyhose will last much, much longer. It's all relative, but you may find this shop absolutely essential for its great color selection and helpful sales staff.

Gindi
816 Madison Ave. (68th St.)
628-4003
Mon. to Sat. 10:00 A.M. to 6:00 P.M.

This tiny shop has the latest accessories for reasonable prices (better than at other upscale boutiques in the neighborhood). You will find a most eclectic collection of questionable costume jewelry, well-designed ivory, good-looking belts, amusing leather bags and other trendy trinkets. This is a good address for frequent visits to discover treasures among the new shipments and to chat with the young sales staff (making friends with them may be your only defense to somewhat disagreeable welcomes). Other locations at 153 East 57th Street (753-5630) and 1072 Third Avenue (935-1118).

Reminiscence
175 MacDougal (8th St.)
477-4051
Mon. to Sat. 12:15 P.M. to 8:00 P.M.

A popular and crowded shop with a terrific collection of new and used costume jewelry. The emphasis is on the young, New Wave look. There are also sunglasses, scarves, hair accessories, clothing and a huge sock bar with dozens of fun, bright socks.

Uncle Sam's Umbrella Shop
161 W. 57th St.
247-7163
Mon. to Fri. 9:00 A.M. to 5:45 P.M.; Sat. 9:00 A.M. to 5:00 P.M.

Every conceivable kind of umbrella, from Scarlett O'Hara parasols to golf umbrellas to executives' conservative black traditionals. There is also an extensive collection of walking sticks, including some exquisite antiques. Two fabulous carved pieces, safely under lock and key, once belonged to John Steinbeck. If you need a walking stick that houses a pool cue or a brandy flask, this is your place. The very friendly sales staff will help you find exactly what you're looking for. And if your favorite old umbrella is getting a big worn, Uncle Sam's will recover it with the fabric of your choice.

FURS

Alixandre
150 W. 30th St.
18th floor
736-5550
Mon. to Fri. 9:00 A.M. to 5:00 P.M.; Sat. 9:00 A.M. to noon

One of the best-known names in the fur district, and with good reason. Once you get past the speakeasy window of this bastion of beasthood (to do that, you *must* know someone who has bought a fur here, and you *must* make an appointment), you are treated as gently and as elegantly as are the furs you're shown. Alixandre's own magnificent designs satisfy young and old, forward looking and traditional, in skins from squirrel to sable. It also carries the coats of Yves Saint Laurent, Perry Ellis and Jeffrey Banks. If you can't pass muster, Alixandre furs are also sold—at almost double these discounted Seventh Avenue prices—by Bergdorf Goodman.

Robert Beaulieu
758 Madison Ave.
(65th–66th sts.)
744-6652
Mon. to Sat. 10:00 A.M. to 6:00 P.M.

Parisian-based Robert Beaulieu makes furs to play in, jet-set style: young, trendy, elegantly irreverent. He uses lots of long hairs, combining anything from rabbit to sable and working them into wild and wonderful designs, the most outstanding of which are reversible. While not unlike Fendi's designs in feeling, they sell for about half the price. The Madison Avenue store is brand new, but the sales staff (including Robert) is knowledgeable and nice, even if you only want to look.

Michael Forrest
333 Seventh Ave.
(28th–29th sts.)
19th floor
564-4726
Mon. to Fri. 9:00 A.M. to 5:00 P.M.; Sat. 9:00 A.M. to noon

Another well-known, reputable furrier with excellent skins, fair prices and a stable of designer names to his credit: Diana Vreeland (her first fur collection), Anne Klein and Viola Sylbert (who used to be with Alixandre). Again, call for an appointment.

Fred the Furrier's Fur Vault

Despite what the ads say, Fred the Furrier is not going to sell you the coat of your dreams. His styles tend to be a little on the safe side, and the skins are probably not the

(Alexander's)
731 Lexington Ave.
(58th–59th sts.)
752-0490
Mon. to Sat. 10:00 A.M. to 9:00
P.M.; Sun. noon to 5:00 P.M.

best. But the selection is incredible—especially if you're looking for mink or raccoon—and his prices are truly bargain basement.

The Fur Salon
Bergdorf Goodman
754 Fifth Ave.
(57th–58th sts.)
872-8752
Mon. to Sat. 10:00 A.M. to 6:00
P.M. (Thurs. to 8:00 P.M.)

This is what fur salons are supposed to look like: all hushed browns and beiges, lots of light and mirrors, knowledgeable salespeople catering to your whims (including an on-the-floor fitter every day until 5:00) and elegant mannequins displaying the most unusual of the furs. Bergdorf's Fur Salon sells the best quality furs, and probably has the best across-the-board selection of styles and skins of any of the retail stores. And, as if its own label weren't enough, it carries YSL, Galanos and Ralph Lauren as well, plus an entire room devoted exclusively to Fendi (the only other place that sells Fendi is Henri Bendel). If the pleasure of buying your fur could be further enhanced by buying it in the most indulgent of atmospheres, come here. Otherwise, save your money and hail a cab for Seventh Avenue.

The Fur Shop
Henri Bendel
10 W. 57th St.
2nd floor
247-1100
Mon. to Sat. 10:00 A.M. to 6:00
P.M. (Thurs. to 8:00 P.M.)

Bendel's specialty is high fashion for the small-sized woman, and the point is well made in The Fur Shop. Just because you're five foot one and a size six, don't expect to see the same old assortment of A-line minks; nothing is too chic, too big or too expensive for the savvy Bendel's customer. You'll find huge, light-as-a-feather shearling capes, patchworked minks, fitch jackets and a wonderful collection of Fendis scaled for smaller sizes (see Bergdorf's entry for the only other New York source for these amazing designs). Since many pieces are one of a kind, you'll be buying off the rack. Instant gratification of the best sort.

Goldin-Feldman
345 Seventh Ave.
(29th–30th sts.)
12th floor
594-4415
Mon. to Fri. 9:00 A.M. to 5:00
P.M.; Sat. 9:00 A.M. to noon

Friendly sales help, good service and two designer names to recommend it: Chloé and Giancarlo Ripa. It's always better with an appointment.

Ben Kahn Salon
150 W. 30th St.
279-0633
Mon. to Fri. 9:00 A.M. to 5:00 P.M.

Top-notch in quality, status and price. In addition to Ben Kahn's simply elegant designs, this salon also sells the sophisticated skins of Koos Van Den Akker. Call for an appointment.

Maximillian
20 W. 57th St.
3rd floor
247-1388
Mon. to Fri. 10:00 A.M. to 5:00
P.M.; Sat. 11:00 A.M. to 4:00 P.M.

Furs to the max. Superb, expensive and ultrachic, with everything from the sporty to the sybaritic.

Mohl Furs
345 Seventh Ave.
(29th–30th sts.)
5th floor
739-7676
Mon. to Fri. 9:00 A.M. to 5:00
P.M.; Sat. 9:00 A.M. to noon

Excellent minks, as well as all other furs. Lots of styles, and many are classic. This is the home of Bill Blass furs. Deferential treatment.

New Yorker Thrift Shop
822 Third Ave.
(50th–51st sts.)
355-5090
Mon. to Fri. 9:00 A.M. to 6:00
P.M.; Sat. 9:00 A.M. to 5:00 P.M.

A place to buy and sell. Its marked-down and almost-new furs sell from $100 on up. All are cleaned and in good condition, and many were once owned by the rich and famous.

Revillon Fur Salon
Saks Fifth Avenue
611 Fifth Ave.
(50th St.)
753-4000
Mon. to Sat. 10:00 A.M. to 6:00
P.M. (Thurs. to 9:00 P.M.)

The Revillon reputation has spread far and wide, and the label is as impressive as the pelts. These are among the finest, most fashionable and most expensive furs you can buy, in all styles, all colors and all breeds, from a floor-length sable to a sporty mink parka. Collections from Bill Blass, Oscar de la Renta, Givenchy and Joop. If you can afford it, flaunt it. Otherwise, wait for the sales in February.

The Ritz Thrift Shop
107 W. 57th St.
265-4559
Mon. to Sat. 9:00 A.M. to 5:00 P.M.

Internationally known, renowned and respected, this high-class thrift shop offers perfectly clean, glossy and adjusted (free) almost-new furs. Lots of styles and skins, including suede and leather, for men as well as for women. Good deals from about $175 on up into the thousands.

Jack/Paul Waltzer
150 W. 30th St.
2nd floor
242-6900
Mon. to Fri. 9:00 A.M. to 5:00
P.M.; Sat. 9:00 A.M. to 2:00 P.M.

Of all the furriers on Seventh Avenue, this one gets our unanimous vote for style, service and skins. Distinguished Jack Waltzer and his savvy son Paul represent the third and fourth generation of this totally professional family affair. Together with wives, sisters, cousins and staff, they make every customer feel as though the decision she is about to make is the most important one in her life—and no matter how many other neurotic women there are in the salon (Saturday mornings, count on a lot!), she is truly the star. Waltzer's variety of furs—mink, tanuki, sable, and so on—is tops, his quality undisputed and his prices fair. And unlike in most showrooms, here lots of styles are displayed in the open, so you can touch and try a wide assortment. There are no big name designers, for everything is strictly private label; yet you can count on some of the most striking furs around: never bizarre, just noticeable enough to stand out in a crowd. These people know their business. Walk-ins are welcome, but you're always better off if you call for an appointment.

JEWELRY

Costume

Ciro
711 Fifth Ave.
(55th St.)
752-0441
Mon. to Sat. 9:30 A.M. to 5:30 P.M.

The main shop of this small chain offers a varied choice of faux diamonds and gems, gold and even its own brand of watches, all at prices ranging from very low to pretty high. Among the marvels you'll find are satisfactory copies of Bulgari at a fraction of the true price and lots of real-looking pearls. While nowhere near as exciting as Jolie Gabor, it's still a nice place to know about when you're putting on the Ritz.

Detail
204 Spring St.
(Avenue of the Americas)
925-8982
Mon. to Sat. noon to 7:00 P.M.;
Sun. 1:00 P.M. to 6:00 P.M.

Funky jewelry at down-to-earth prices: earrings start at about $8, necklaces at $18. This SoHo find sells only jewelry, displayed on grids up and down the walls as well as in cases. All pieces are visibly marked with prices so you don't have to ask. Lots of plastic and faux crystals, wire sculptures, imitation Artwear, punk and, admittedly, a little junk. Still, it's worth a trip.

Jolie Gabor
699 Madison Ave.
(62nd–63rd sts.)
838-3193
Mon. to Sat. 9:30 A.M. to 5:30 P.M.

Zsa Zsa's mother owns this wonderful (though tiny) emporium of "original jewelry" fakes. Case after marvelous case is filled with large, decadent doubles of the kind of jewelry Zsa Zsa herself would adore. All the greats are here, including Van Cleef, Bulgari, even David Webb—with faux diamonds in every shape and size, strands of pearls, glittering emeralds and sapphires, golden bracelets and more. Even if you're not in the market for such baubles, this is a great store to visit. And make sure you pick up a card—it pictures the whole bedecked Gabor family (do you think their jewelry is real?).

Gindi Jewelry
153 E. 57th St.
753-5630

Fun, fabulous, funky designs: big wooden earrings, ivory bracelets, clunky necklaces and watches in every color of the rainbow. There's always something new and

Mon. to Sat. 10:00 A.M. to 7:00 P.M.

Richard Gould
545 Madison Ave.
(55th St.)
888-6012
Mon. to Fri. 10:00 A.M. to 6:00 P.M.; Sat. noon to 5:00 P.M.

Macondo
150 Spring St.
431-3224
Mon. to Sun. noon to 7:00 P.M.

Ylang-ylang
806 Madison Ave.
(67th St.)
879-7028
Mon. to Fri. 10:30 A.M. to 6:30 P.M.; Sat. 10:30 A.M. to 6:00 P.M.

wonderful to buy ... at prices that may stifle your imagination. Two other locations at 1072 3rd Avenue (935-1118) and 816 Madison Avenue (628-4003).

This is the lower end of the scale in price, but not in quality. Many pieces are inspired by Italian designers, and you can find costume Dior pieces for a few dollars, sapphire or ruby earrings for as little as $5 a pair, diamond wedding rings and eighteen-karat gold electroplated chains for mere pittances. The shop may not look like much and the reception may be mediocre, but you don't risk going broke. Another location at 20 East 58th Street (753-7696).

A SoHo clothing store that sells contemporary "gemless" jewelry at prices that can rival the rest of your outfit. But no matter, these pieces are worth every pretty penny and are often more wearable than the clothing. The best-sellers are exotic necklaces: coral and jet, twisted golden cords, sparkling crystals, even feathers. And the store's ever-changing selection is indicative of its ever-growing appeal.

This funky little shop smack in the middle of designer territory is filled with lots of high-style costume jewelry, a few semiprecious pieces and a small collection of silver designs. The accent is on ritzy and glitzy, with baubles and bangles galore, plenty of metal-looking chains, chunky necklaces and rhinestone bracelets and pins. All the pieces are striking, and almost everything is exclusive to the shop. For the area, the prices are reasonable. Another location at 324 Columbus Ave., 496-6319.

Quality

Hans Appenzeller
820 Madison Ave.
(68th St.)
570-0504
Mon. to Sat. 10:00 A.M. to 6:00 P.M. (Thurs. to 7:30 P.M)

Artwear
409 W. Broadway
(Spring St.)
431-9405
Mon. to Sat. 11:00 A.M. to 6:00

Beautiful geometrics designed in Holland. This gallerylike shop displays its contemporary collection in pedestaled cases lit with spots. Most pieces are eighteen-karat gold, silvermesh or gunmetal, rarely with any gems, and whatever style you see can be made to order in any of the other metals. Some, in fact, are only custom crafted, such as the stylized bracelets that must be made to fit your own wrist. Nothing is outrageous or pretentious—including the prices.

This stunning shop is filled with artistic treasures. More gallery than store, Artwear's jewelry looks more art than wear. In any case, you will find the most exquisite and the most daring new designs in traditional materials as well as in plastic, wood, oxidized brass, semiprecious stones

P.M.; Sun. noon to 6:00 P.M.

and metals. The prices are steep, but it makes sense when you're paying for a museum-quality piece that may be dramatic or subtle, depending on the artist's instincts. One of our favorite stops in SoHo, and apparently also a favorite of Candice Bergen, Jackie Onassis, Dyan Cannon, Shirley MacLaine and Donna Summer, who love to shop here.

Buccellati Jewelers
Trump Tower
725 Fifth Ave.
(56th–57th sts.)
308-5533
Mon. to Sat. 10:00 A.M. to 6:00 P.M.

You'd never guess it from the golden facade, but the interior of the jewelry branch of Buccellati is low-key and restrained, almost to the point of bareness. The jewelry, of course, is not. In keeping with tradition, these exclusive Italian designs are ornate, extravagant and extremely elegant. The emphasis is on workmanship, and the results are works of art. A few stories above ground, at the same Trump Tower address, there's another Buccellati shop—the "boutique." Here you'll find smaller gold items, some without stones, and silver jewelry. These are the supposedly less important pieces, which is a genteel way to say that they're more affordable.

Bulgari
Pierre Hotel
795 Fifth Ave.
(61st St.)
486-0086
Mon. to Sat. 10:30 A.M. to 5:30 P.M.

Decidedly bad manners have been mistaken for a sign of quality by many illustrious merchants. Unless you are a billionaire or a celebrity, you are paid little attention in this shop. The place, incidentally, is so small and common that you wonder for a moment if you've gone in the wrong door. But, no denying, the jewelry is both stylish and beautiful—a very Italian combination that's easy to recognize and hard to resist. The specialty is different-colored stones juxtaposed in the same ornament or mounted in brilliant gold. But take note: the stones are not first-rate—and that's public knowledge.

Byzantium
105 Thompson St.
966-5473
Wed. to Sun. noon to 7:00 P.M.

Unusual, complex pieces, mostly in eighteen- and 22-karat gold, handcrafted by a rotating group of craftsmen who excel at what they do: granulations, cloisonné, some chain making and beautiful settings for rare stones and natural crystals. The salespeople are unique, too, in that they'll tell you honestly if something doesn't look right.

Carimati Jewelers
773 Madison Ave.
(66th St.)
734-5727
Tues. to Sat. 9:30 A.M. to 6:00 P.M.

Enrico Carimati is distinguished by a penchant for beautiful stones and beautiful art. Indeed, his superbly designed Italian jewelry is displayed against art and sculpture that are often as exciting as the ornaments. Nothing, however, can really dim the sparkling elegance of these pieces. Some combine multiples of stones in heavy gold; while others show off stones of unusual colors, such as yellow sapphires. Each is unique, very wearable and very expensive.

Cartier
653 Fifth Ave.
(52nd St.)
753-0111
Mon. to Fri. 10:00 A.M. to 5:30
P.M.; Sat. to 5:00 P.M.

An entirely different atmosphere than in the Paris shop. The greeting is anonymous, and you can wander freely without attracting the slightest attention or seeming to disturb anyone at all. So even if the prices are out of reach, don't deprive yourself of the pleasure, as the variety of jewelry, objects and accessories is immense. After you've reexamined Cartier's famous Musts, make sure you look at the incredible art deco collection, located in the very next area. Pass through the main jewelry rooms, and you may think you've suddenly entered Fortunoff's—the walls become smoked mirrors, the display cases loose their patina and the jewelry actually becomes affordable. Upstairs, you'll find tableware, Limoges porcelain, silver, crystal, some objets d'art, antiques and more. It's unfortunate that the tiny Trump Tower branch of Cartier displays a fraction of the main store's merchandise with twice the snobbishness. But there's a delightful new branch in the Westbury Hotel, at the corner of Madison and 70th Street.

Aaron Faber Jewelry
666 Fifth Ave.
(53rd St.)
586-8411
Mon. to Sat. 10:30 A.M. to
6:00 P.M.

Jewelry as American art—and oh! what an art it is. Aaron Faber's constantly changing collection relies upon the talents of some 40 goldsmiths working throughout the country. Most of the pieces could loosely be called "contemporary," but, naturally, the style depends upon the artisan. Everything is handcrafted in gold, platinum or silver, and the quality of the workmanship is always high. There is also a complete custom design service. Mr. Faber imports his own pearls and opals and uses only high-grade rubies and sapphires and ideal cut diamonds. If you want to update your grandmother's brooch, he'll do that, too. Mr. Faber is also noted for his large collection of vintage and antique watches and his complete watch restoration and repair service. At any given time, he might have 500 to 600 watches in stock, from the most elegant Patek Philippe to the simplest Bulova. He also collects and sells unusual nineteenth-century pocket watches. Despite its artiness, this is truly a full-service jewelry shop. Prices can run from $100 to $25,000. Brokerage services and appraisals are also offered.

Fortunoff
681 Fifth Ave.
(54th St.)
343-8787
Mon. to Sat. 10:00 A.M. to 6:00
P.M. (Thurs. to 8:00 P.M.)

A jewelry hunter's heaven. To see the crowds around the first-floor jewelry cases, you'd think everything in them was free instead of just very reasonable. The selection is basic though good, with plenty of gold chains, bangles, rings and earrings. Upstairs are watches and clocks in similar quality and quantity, and even farther upstairs are silver, china and antiques. The service is helpful and the atmosphere always bustling. While it may not be Tiffany's, Fortunoff is a good place to know about.

Fred Joaillier
St. Regis Hotel
701–703 Fifth Ave.
(55th St.)
832-3733

Fred, of Europe, Texas and Beverly Hills fame, can now add a New York address to his roster. This newest store, at the St. Regis Hotel, carries a unique selection of gems, pearls and contemporary jewelry. For the prices he's asking, he should offer room service, too.

House of Jerry Grant
244 E. 60th St.
371-9769
Mon. to Sat. 12:30 P.M. to 6:30 P.M.

This charming little jewelry shop creates original pieces in impressive quantities and sells them at bearable prices. You can pick out one of the unusually shaped and stylish rings or bracelets, or Jerry Grant will work with you to design a personal creation, using your stones or his. And if you suffer a cruel blow of fate, you can bring Jerry your jewels: he'll either offer to sell them on commission or buy them outright. A shop that really is a bit different.

Barry Kieselstein-Cord
Henri Bendel
10 West 57th St.
2nd floor
247-1100, ext. 344
Mon. to Sat. 10:00 A.M. to 6:00 P.M. (Thurs. to 8:00 P.M.)

This closet-sized shop in Bendel's is the only New York store to sell Barry Kieselstein-Cord's gold jewelry collection. These big, gorgeous, expensive and unusually finished pieces—some worked with wonderful colored stones—are always a statement of style. His fourteen-karat gold belt buckles are also sold here, though a large assortment of his silver buckles are sold on the main floor.

Ilias Lalaounis
4 W. 57th St.
265-0600
Mon. to Sat. 10:00 A.M. to 5:15 P.M.

This internationally known Greek jeweler is based in Athens, with shops in Paris, Switzerland, Tokyo and Hong Kong. His style is easily recognized: eighteen- or 22-karat gold worked into modern adaptations of Greek art. Some designs combine stones or crystal, but the most striking pieces use such intricate metalwork methods as granulation, martelé, ciselé and filigree.

Fred Leighton
781 Madison Ave.
(66th St.)
288-1872
Mon. to Sat. 10:00 A.M. to 6:00 P.M.

Fred Leighton has one of the finest collections of estate jewelry in America. His sparkling jewelbox of a shop on Madison (and the smaller version in Trump Tower) positively glistens with elegant one-of-a-kind pieces, bought and worn by women just as elegant and unique. Fred (alias Murray) has an unerring sense of style and an uncanny knack for buying. He's amassed a major collection of art deco pieces, including works by Cartier, Van Cleef and Tiffany, and some art nouveau. There are also antique jewels, Victorian and Georgian designs and occasionally even a Renaissance piece. But don't think success has gone to his head. Nice as well as knowledgeable, this man talks to all his customers, asks about their mothers, takes Polaroids for their insurance companies and in general bustles about catering and cajoling. People come here to indulge themselves. Murray is the icing on their very rich cake.

Manfredi
737 Madison Ave.
(63rd–64th sts.)
734-8710
Mon. to Fri. 10:00 A.M. to 5:30
P.M.; Sat. 11:00 A.M. to 5:00 P.M.

A small, contemporary and stylized shop that sells jewelry of much the same ilk. Manfredi specializes in setting colored stones in pink and yellow eighteen-karat gold. All the pieces have a very special fluid, almost organic feeling. All are signed by Manfredi. The collection changes several times a year, but the point of view remains clear: less is definitely more.

Mikimoto
608 Fifth Ave.
(49th St.)
586-7153
Mon. to Sat. 10:00 A.M. to
5:30 P.M.

The originator of cultured pearls and still one of the best sources. In this quietly elegant store, you'll find beautiful cultured pearl necklaces in three lengths (choker, matinee and opera), in all sizes, colors and qualities ranging from good to superior. There are also lovely river pearl necklaces (including the rare button-sized pearls) and seed pearl chokers. Other necklaces, rings, bracelets, brooches and earrings are all simply designed to show off their pearls, though some have stones as well. A medium-size (6 mm) pearl choker can set you back $900 to $1,500. If it's black pearls you want, there are none better: that exquisite necklace by the door is a mere $300,000.

Petochi & Gorevic
635 Madison Ave.
(59th St.)
832-9000
Mon. to Sat. 10:00 A.M. to 5:45
P.M.

The Gorevic side of this Madison Avenue newcomer is antique silver; the Petochi half is fine jewelry. Although you'll find a few antique pieces mixed in, most of the collection is contemporary eighteen-karat gold designs, all made in Italy. The pieces are attractive and rich looking, with sparkling stones in heavy gold settings— very Italian and very expensive. The small watch collection is also good (and, again, expensive). The store itself is elegant and well laid out to display the antiques as well as occasional museum collections.

Poiray Joailliers
31 E. 64th St.
772-2400
By appt. only

As the neighbor of New York's new Plaza Athénée Hotel, this Parisian jeweler should have a ready-and-waiting clientele for its elegant, inimitable masterpieces.

Frank Pollak & Sons
8 West 47th St.
245-6718
Mon. to Fri. 9:30 A.M. to 5:00 P.M.

Everyone's got a jeweler on 47th Street, New York's celebrated diamond district. This fascinating block between Fifth and Sixth avenues is home to hundreds of jewelers and millions of carats. Much like an old-fashioned bazaar, each jeweler on the street does business from a booth no wider than a bedroom dresser, and while it may all seem intimidating to the novice, some of the world's best jewels, and the best buys, are to be had here. Frank Pollak, our jeweler on 47th, has been around since 1905, is still family owned and is a pleasure to deal with. Whether you want a $50 gold chain or a $50,000 antique

Tiffany bracelet, it has a large inventory to mull over. It carries mostly better-quality diamonds and gems, many of which it imports itself, and all kinds of fine jewelry, including prized estate pieces, magnificent antiques and contemporary designs. If you know exactly what you want, Pollak will special order any design for you. In addition to the standard jewelry services, Pollak offers estate appraisals and brokerage services.

Royal Copenhagen Porcelain/ Georg Jensen Silversmiths
683 Madison Ave.
(61st St.)
759-6457
Mon. to Sat. 9:30 A.M. to 5:30 P.M.

Georg Jensen deserves another mention in this book for his simple, beautiful and expensive jewelry. The epitome of understated elegance, this jewelbox of a collection includes both gold and silver pieces, some with stones, and distinctive, ultramodern watches.

F. Staal
743 Fifth Ave.
(58th St.)
758-1821
Mon. to Sat. 9:30 A.M. to 5:30 P.M.

A small, carriage-trade jeweler among the big names, and yet a store that has enjoyed a reputation for exquisite quality in stones and gold, conscientious work and impeccable service for more than a hundred years (through four generations of Staals). The jewelry here is aimed at connoisseurs, and its understated old-world elegance will satisfy the most demanding. Just about everything is one of a kind. In addition to some newer pieces, there is a very fine collection of estate jewelry. F. Staal is one of those rare dealers who proves that jewelry is a fine art.

Tiffany & Co.
727 Fifth Ave.
(57th St.)
755-8000
Mon. to Sat. 10:00 A.M. to 5:00 P.M.

The one and only. Throughout the years, this bastion of elegance has changed with the times and shunned the times, acquired a social consciousness and been the subject of books, movies and jokes, without ever losing its Tiffany touch. Recession or not, every Christmas lines of customers form around the revolving doors, waiting to buy a gift wrapped in the famous Tiffany blue box. Make this a must-see: there is always something inside you can afford. The ground floor holds the jewelry—all kinds, all prices, including some of the largest stones in the world and the exclusive collections of Elsa Peretti, Angela Cummings, Paloma Picasso and the more traditional Jean Schlumberger. Men's jewelry lines one wall, and in the back are watches, many, again, exclusively Tiffany & Co. Upstairs, check out the silver, crystal and china—there are usually table settings designed by the rich and famous. The salespeople are friendly, helpful and seemingly unaffected by the prices.

Van Cleef and Arpels
Bergdorf Goodman
744 Fifth Ave.
(57th St.)
644-9500
Salon: Mon. to Sat. 10:00 A.M. to 5:00 P.M. Boutique: Mon. to Sat. 10:00 A.M. to 5:30 P.M. (Thurs. to 7:30 P.M.)

The store bearing the mighty name Van Cleef and Arpels is conveniently located in the store bearing the name Bergdorf Goodman. Presumably, each attracts the other's customers. The Van Cleef Boutique is actually a long counter in Bergdorf's, filled with a good selection of watches (including Piaget) and, relatively speaking, the less expensive jewelry. The hallowed salon, however, actually looks much like a duty-free shop, despite the ultrathick carpeting and armed guard. And although the jewels are imported from Paris, they're mostly in quite a different style from the famous French line. All in all, considering the quality and reputation of these jewels, the initial impression is disappointing.

David Webb
7 E. 57th St.
421-3030
Mon. to Sat. 10:00 A.M. to 5:30 P.M.

David Webb believes in originality at any price, and he pulls it off. He makes jewelry of every kind, specializing in pieces that are, on the whole, very large and decorative, using lots of gold and pavé diamonds—not exactly understated elegance. The reserved welcome fits this grandiose style: two doors and a haughty receptionist before you even get a glimmer of the goods.

Harry Winston
718 Fifth Ave.
(56th St.)
245-2000
Mon. to Sat. 10:00 A.M. to 5:30 P.M.

The premier American jeweler, Winston is internationally known for his fine and costly work. The collection are superclassic, made with superb stones mounted in a conventional and slightly boring manner. Their lack of warmth and originality is reflected in this huge shop itself, but the pieces are nonetheless good investments. A luxury jeweler where you'll be treated well. An entirely new, "younger" collection by Winston is now housed in the small Trump Tower shop. Here, too, you'll be treated like royalty, and the entrance is a little less formidable.

Helen Woodhull
744 Madison Ave.
(64th St.)
472-1212
Mon. to Sat. 10:30 A.M. to 6:00 P.M.

Helen Woodhull's intricately designed jewelry combines classic, romantic and mythical elements in a truly personal style. Beautiful and unusual stones and beads—rhodolite, tourmaline, mookaite, opalite, chiastolite—are balanced by equally beautiful settings in eighteen-karat gold, silver or platinum. The collection is small and select, though the prices can be quite large. You won't want to overlook this very special place.

Watches

Gübelin
745 Fifth Ave.
(57th–58th sts.)
755-0054
Mon. to Sat. 10:00 A.M. to 5:30 P.M.

If the Patek Philippe digital outside doesn't warn you, the emerald- and diamond-encrusted Gübelin inside will: this Swiss institution carries only watches of the finest quality. In addition to its own world-renowned timepieces, it handles collections from Patek Philippe, Audemars Piguet, Ebel and Eterna, each more splendid and expensive than the next. It also has its own exclusive jewelry designs, matching the quality, craftsmanship and prices of the watches. Don't bother to walk in unless you have a few thousand dollars to play with, although once inside, you'll find no pretensions: the sales help is friendly and informative. Gübelin also has an excellent repair service for all the watches it sells. At these prices, that's the least it could do!

William Scolnik and Joseph Fanelli
1001 Second Ave.
(53rd St.)
355-1160; 755-8766
Mon. to Fri. 10:00 A.M. to 5:30 P.M.; Sat. by appt.

An incredible collection of antique clocks and watches, dating from the eighteenth to the twentieth centuries. Vintage Cartier and Tiffany pieces, turn-of-the-century wristwatches, fobs, grandfather clocks, carriage clocks and unusual collectibles—everything from Mickey Mouse to Patek Philippe. These connoisseurs will also seek out hard-to-find watches for you, as well as maintain your own collection. Repair and restoration service with free estimates, worldwide shipping and house calls for sick clocks! A top-notch establishment.

Tourneau
500 Madison Ave.
(52nd St.)
758-3265
Mon. to Sat. 10:00 A.M. to 6:00 P.M. (Thurs. to 7:30 P.M.)

Tourneau offers quite simply the best choices of watches in the easiest-to-assimilate displays in New York. All the Swiss watchmakers are represented: Audemars Piguet, Baume et Mercier, Omega, Piaget, Ebel, Jaeger-LeCoultre, Longines and so on. There are also watches by Rolex and Seiko, the Musts from Cartier, and nearly every good name you can think of, including watches by Tourneau itself, which are far from being the worst of the lot. As you can imagine with a store of this class, all styles are represented—youthful, classic, formal—and prices range from under $100 to quite a lot higher. Clocks are another specialty: small copper clocks, carriage clocks, alarm clocks and travel clocks. There are also gold quartz fobs and a few elegant accessories, such as Dupont lighters and pens. Tourneau repair service is worth mentioning, as this department can usually fix anything you can break and will revitalize older mechanical watches with new Swiss quartz movements.

Wempe
695 Fifth Ave.

An old-world atmosphere and rather snobby attitude detract from the timeless collection of only top-of-the-

(56th St.)
751-4884
Mon. to Sat. 10:00 A.M. to
6:00 P.M.

line watches and clocks: Rolex, Jaeger-LeCoultre, Ebel, Patek Philippe, Piaget, Chopard, Audemars Piguet, and its own exclusive Wempe "Fifth Avenue" watch. There's some jewelry and Dunhill and Dupont accessories too. But don't walk in with less than $1,000 in your pocket.

MENSWEAR

Antartex
903 Madison Ave.
(72nd St.)
535-9079
Mon. to Sat. 10:00 A.M. to
6:00 P.M.

L.L. Bean meets the Siberian front at Antartex. There is an extensive collection of suede and sheepskin coats, with occasional sales of up to two-thirds off. The consummate preppy can shop here for classic sweaters, simple T-shirts, mohair throws, sheepskin slippers and some of the most conservative-looking merchandise we've seen north of Brooks Brothers. Prices are reasonable, particularly during the winter-coat summer sales.

Bip
755 Madison Ave.
(66th St.)
535-0228
Mon. to Fri. 10:00 A.M. to 6:00
P.M.; Sat. 11:00 A.M. to 6:00 P.M.

Sportswear for men who like a young, casual-chic look. There's a wide choice of colors and styles, with an emphasis on cotton and on moderately classic fashions. Prices are not too high if spending $65 for a pair of prefaded pleated pants is within your weltanschauung.

Blue and White Men's Shop
50 E. 58th St.
421-8424
Mon. to Fri. 10:00 A.M. to 6:00
P.M.; Sat. 10:00 A.M. to 5:00 P.M.

Sportswear and men's accessories of a caliber we rarely see. Of the dozens and dozens of shops, however prestigious, we visited while preparing this guide, none came close to the elegance of this establishment. No other crêpe de chine shirts were as soft as these, no other loafers as supple, no other leather raincoats as fine. Antelope hide parkas, cashmere sweaters, alpaca, mohair—the quality of the clothes here, all handmade and handwoven and mostly imported from Italy, is equaled only by the sobriety of their colors and the discreet simplicity of their tailoring. And the service is on par with the merchandise: Carlo Bonini welcomes you into his tiny shop with all the charm and friendliness you'd quite naturally expect in a man with so much taste.

Brooks Brothers
346 Madison Ave.
(44th St.)
682-8800
Mon. to Sat. 9:15 A.M. to 6:00 P.M.

You can spot them on the streets: their cuffs are 1½ inches too high, their ties are subdued paislies, their shirts are blue oxford button-downs, their suits are boxy and frumpy, and their brown loafers are tasseled. These are the Brooks Brothers men. They've been shopping here since kindergarten, and these classics have gotten them through Saint Paul's, Princeton and middle-level management at Morgan Guaranty. The store is a gold mine for serious dressers to whom fashion plays second fiddle to tradition. The main floor offers a stable of shetlands, conservative ties, those shirts and handsome leather goods, plus a myriad of gifts and accessories. The upstairs menswear departments are sedate, with a sales staff that is impeccably Brooks Brothers dressed and always helpful. The Brooksgate department appeals to the boy in the Brooks Brothers man. The prices throughout are upscale—but fear not: price is irrelevant when true quality and timeless prep is the issue. There's a branch for the Wall Street crowd at One Liberty Plaza (682-8595).

Burberry's
9 E. 57th St.
371-5010
Mon. to Sat. 9:30 A.M. to 6:00 P.M.
(Thurs. to 7:00 P.M.)

The signature Burberry's plaid is found not just inside the classic trench coats (which *must* last a lifetime, on the basis of the high price tags), but on everything from ties and cummerbunds to bags, umbrellas, bathrobes and replacement liners that some enterprising people no doubt use to upgrade their lesser-made raincoats. Aside from this sea of plaid, you'll find a very well made and ultraconservative line of menswear, with an emphasis on good wools. Prices are as high as the quality.

Burton
475 Fifth Ave.
2nd floor
(41st St.)
685-3760
Mon. to Fri. 9:30 A.M. to 6:00 P.M.
(Thurs. to 7:00 P.M.); Sat. 10:00
A.M. to 6:00 P.M.

A real find for the man who likes his classics classy. These pleated pants, handsome tweed jackets, terrific all-cotton shirts, ties and suspenders are conservatively handsome without being boring. The quality is irreproachable, and the prices are lower than at such bastions of prep as Brooks Brothers. There's an adjacent women's shop selling equally classic ladies' fashions. The pleasant atmosphere and helpful salesmen make this a most enjoyable place to shop.

Charivari for Men
2339 Broadway
(85th St.)
873-7242
Mon. to Fri. 11:00 A.M. to 7:00
P.M. (Thurs. to 9:00 P.M.); Sat.
11:00 A.M. to 6:30 P.M.; Sun. 1:00
P.M. to 6:00 P.M.

The most advanced menswear (and womenswear, and uniwear) in New York. These stores—there are actually five of them between 85th Street and Broadway and 72nd Street and Columbus Avenue (each with slightly different designers), feature the newest and the best fashions from Europe, Japan and America: Armani, Matsuda, Kenzo, Ferre, Polo and Alexander Julian, just to give you an idea. If you want it first and don't mind paying, this is where to come.

Denoyer
219 E. 60th St.
838-8680
Mon. to Sat. 10:00 A.M. to
7:00 P.M.

A well-edited selection of classic high-grade clothing in this small store run by a friendly Frenchman. Everything he offers is superb: impeccable suits, very soft jacquard-weave cashmeres, attractive ties, supple leathers, functional and fashionable raincoats and stylish shoes. In the back of the store is a choice of womenswer that is just as judicious, featuring stunning silks in the winter and swimwear in the summer.

Gianpietro Boutique
207 E. 60th St.
759-2322
Mon. to Sat. 10:00 A.M. to
8:00 P.M.

A few yards along the same street as Denoyer, this Italian shop stocks sophisticated sportswear and formal wear, European-styled shoes and one of New York's dandiest collections of silk shirts. Everything looks just as expensive as it is.

Kreeger & Sons
16 W. 46th St.
575-7825
Mon. to Sat. 10:00 A.M. to 6:00
P.M. (Thurs. to 8:00 P.M.)

If you don't have time to drive up to Freeport, Maine, fear not—Kreeger & Sons will outfit you in the L.L. Bean look for slightly less. All the marvelous classics are here: ragg sweaters, practical twill trousers, flannel shirts, parkas and sports equipment. A good address no matter what your fashion addiction. Another location at 150 West 72nd Street (799-6200).

Billy Martin's Western Wear
812 Madison Ave.
(68th St.)
861-3100
Mon. to Fri. 10:00 A.M. to 6:30
P.M.; Sat. 10:00 A.M. to 6:00 P.M.

Urban cowboys come here for expensive skin boots, great-looking belts, good leather jackets and a limited selection of genre jewelry. There are some inventive leather pouches with feather trims, adorable boots for little children and a tranquil earth-tone decor that slows harried customers down. Prices are not as humble as you might wish.

J. McLaughlin
1295 Third Ave.
(75th St.)
988-6633
Mon. to Fri. 11:00 A.M. to 9:00
P.M.; Sat. 11:00 A.M. to 6:00
P.M.; Sun. 1:00 P.M. to 5:00 P.M.

Formerly known as Sea Island, this clubby East Side store has contemporary collegiate clothes in natural fabrics (of course) and gorgeous colors: flannel pants, chinos, polo shirts, striking sweaters and all-cotton sport/dress shirts, plus outstanding ties and accessories, outerwear and raincoats. Everything is well tailored, most merchandise is made especially for the store, and the prices are suitable for a young executive. It's an easy place to shop if your taste tends toward the classic, as everything coordinates beautifully. The staff is particularly helpful, and they will alter anything you buy. McLaughlin has three other East Side locations; two carry clothes for men and women, but the store on Madison between 90th and 91st Streets caters only to women.

Andre Oliver
34 E. 57th St.
758-2233
Mon. to Sat. 10:00 A.M. to
6:00 P.M.

More than 40 colors of cashmere sweaters. Classic slacks to match every one of them. The best winter mufflers. Pure silk or cotton bathrobes. Imported shirts. Distinctive ties. In an old-money townhouse, Andre Oliver sells his exclusive collection of basics to the casually elegant man. His fabrics beg to be caressed. His magnificent colors and understated styles are hard to resist, and the displays, from the outside windows to the far back walls, are simply stunning. If it weren't for the prices, we could happily live with ten of everything from this store.

Protective Fashion (Jon Jolcin)
368 W. Broadway (Broome St.)
334-9820
Daily noon to 7:00 P.M.

If you are an executive for a multinational corporation and travel a lot, you might want to send your chauffeur to defensive driving school and then down to SoHo to pick up an Excaliber protective vest. While he's there, he can also select a jacket, coat or down vest roomy enough to accommodate a ballistic panel. There are three grades of protective shields here, designed to resist anything from 9mm submachine gun fire to the more everyday hunter's 12 gauge. Prices are what you would expect to protect your life.

Stewart Ross/ Stone Free
754 Madison Ave. (65th St.)
744-3870
Mon. to Sat. 11:00 A.M. to 6:00 P.M.

You will find the sweaters here irresistible if you have an extra couple of hundred dollars on hand. The classic and retro styles and remarkable fabrics give this androgynous merchandise its distinctive look. The stars shop here for simple elegance, and you will too if you prefer the real thing with a slightly eccentric air and personal, pulled-together styling.

Patrick Sheeran
South Street Seaport
16 Fulton St. (Water St.)
344-4470
Mon. to Sat. 10:00 A.M. to 10:00 P.M.; Sun. noon to 8:00 P.M.

A bastion of all that is timeless: shetlands, cotton-knit rugby pullovers, Shaker-knit cardigans, sensible tweeds, flannel trousers, all-cotton shirting, Irish knit sweaters and Ivy League ties. It's a good address for all things conservative. Prices are commensurate with stockbrokers' and bankers' salaries.

Paul Stuart
Madison Avenue and 45th Street
682-0320
Mon. to Fri. 8:00 A.M. to 6:00 P.M.; Sat. 9:00 A.M. to 6:00 P.M.

Conservative men who like that certain Continental flair come here to stock up on beautifully made suits, sport coats, trousers and shirts. The shirt and tie selection on the main floor is extensive, the staff is helpful, the quality and styling are exceptional, and the prices are astronomical.

Saint Laurent Rive Gauche Boutique for Men
543 Madison Ave. (55th St.)
371-7912
Mon. to Sat. 10:00 A.M. to 6:00 P.M.

There's a lot to be said for this label. High style. High quality. High prices.

Verri Uomo
802 Madison Ave. (67th St.)
737-9200

Sophisticated Italian menswear at its finest, in a store straight off Via Pietro Verri. Shirts, sweaters, sportswear, suits, each more luxurious than the next, all stunningly displayed in simple alcoves. In addition to its own

Mon. to Sat. 10:30 A.M. to 6:30 P.M.

distinctive styles, all made and imported from its factory in Milan, Verri Uomo also sells clothes by Gianni Versace.

Discount

BFO and BFO Plus
**149 Fifth Ave.
(21st St.)
2nd and 6th floors
254-0059**
Daily 9:30 A.M. to 5:30 P.M.

Shirts and sweaters from Yves Saint Laurent, Cerrutti, John Henry and more for between $15 and $40 on the second floor; suits, coats and pants by the same designers for $20 to $125 on the sixth floor. You'll also find lots of clothing offered under the house label for the same prices, and fine ties with labels and price tags intact from Cardin, Ted Lapidus, Calvin Klein and Liberty of London for around $8. This shop is frequented by the best-informed New Yorkers, famous ones included. Alterations available.

Dollar Bills
**99 E. 42nd St.
867-0212**
Mon. to Wed. 8:00 A.M. to 6:30 P.M.; Thurs. and Fri. 8:00 A.M. to 7:00 P.M.; Sat. 10:00 A.M. to 6:00 P.M.

Just a few minutes from Grand Central Station you'll find one of the best discount menswear stores in New York. The choice of clothing is selective, but covers a wide range of articles. All the best designers are represented, and owner Marcel always has a friendly word for customers. Among the city's most accessible and affordable shops. It also stocks discount housewares, small appliances, beauty products and tobacco.

Merns Mart
**525 Madison Ave.
(54th St.)
371-9175**
Mon. to Fri. 9:30 A.M. to 6:30 P.M. (Thurs. to 8:00 P.M.); Sat. 9:30 A.M. to 6:00 P.M.

Up to 50 percent off well-made French, British and American suits, with shoes, jeans and sportswear as well. The store on Madison Avenue is eight times bigger than the other (in The World Trade Center, 227-5471) and is discreet and sober, relaxed and friendly—all rare qualities in discount stores. What's more, the buys are excellent, even outrageously good, depending on your taste and luck. A quick glance on the way to Brooks Brothers or Paul Stuart might save you the extra walk and quite a bit of money. Two floors of womenswear too.

Oxford Handkerchief Co.
**51 Orchard St.
(Spring St.)
226-0878**
Sun. to Thurs. 9:00 A.M. to 5:00 P.M.; Fri. to 3:00 P.M.

A real Lower East Side bargain place. Handkerchiefs, shirts and sweaters by Christian Dior, Yves Saint Laurent, Oscar de la Renta and more at 30 to 50 percent off. Worth a look.

Syms
**45 Park Pl.
(Church St.)**

Three-piece suits for $70, designer shoes for $20, flannel pants for $20 ... maybe you don't believe us? Well, head down to Syms, where an educated consumer is the best

791-1199
Mon. to Wed. 9:00 A.M. to 7:00 P.M.; Thurs. and Fri. 9:00 A.M. to 8:00 P.M.; Sat. 9:00 A.M. to 6:00 P.M.

customer. The collection of shirts (from $7 to $20) on the second floor is breathtaking. Nor are women left out: an entire floor is given over to clothes for them by big-name designers at 50 percent off. Even if you don't know labels, it's easy to verify Syms' discounts, as all articles bear their original price tags. The sales staff is friendly, and the merchandise is well organized. The store doesn't always carry the latest fashions, but you can't have everything. Note: children under the age of eighteen are not admitted without an adult.

Victory Shirt Co.
**96 Orchard St.
(Delancey St.)
677-2020**
Daily 9:00 A.M. to 5:00 P.M. (Fri. to 4:00 P.M.)

Another Lower East Side shop offering a plethora of pure cotton shirts in the purest of English styles: oxford, basket weave and broadcloth, sold under Victory's own Lord Carlton label or under department store labels, all at prices 25 percent lower than those you'll see uptown. Run by a Brit who knows his shirts like the back of his hand (or neck).

Large/Small Sizes

Imperial Wear Men's Clothing
**48 W. 48th St.
541-8220**
Mon. to Sat. 9:30 A.M. to 6:00 P.M. (Thurs. to 8:00 P.M.)

Too big or too tall to get your clothes at Barney's? In that case, go straight to Imperial, the specialists in dressing large sizes, both in height and in width (up to size 60), with some chic. Here you can obtain everything any well-dressed man wears. Prices are honest, and the choice is excellent. Brands include Pierre Cardin, Givenchy, Christian Dior, Donald Brooks, Adolfo and London Fog.

London Majesty
**1211 Avenue of the Americas
(48th St.)
221-1860**
Mon. to Sat. 9:00 A.M. to 6:00 P.M. (Thurs. to 8:00 P.M.)

English and European fashions for the biggest and the tallest can be found in this, the first New York outlet of a well-known European chain. Cashmeres and wool knits are the specialty, along with very English fabrics for the suits, jackets and sportswear, custom-made shirts and silk pajamas and shorts. English chic to the smallest (or largest) detail.

Shirts

Addison on Madison
**698 Madison Ave.
(62nd St.)
308-2660**
Mon. to Sat. 10:00 A.M. to 6:30 P.M.

This sliver of a store on Madison Avenue sells only shirts, ties and occasionally cuff links. The fresh flowers, French wine and genuine smiles are all gratis. Shirts come in four styles: button-down, regular or white collar, and French cuffed. The bodies are tailored for Americans, the elongated torsos have an extra button and the sleeves have buttoned plackets. All are pure cotton, made in France in its own factories. The colors and fine prints lean toward pastels, but they truly vary season to season. The silk ties are unusual reps. Everything is crisp, classic and contemporary. For the quality and the neighborhood, the prices—$48 to $55 a shirt—are outstanding. Addison has a second store on level C at the Trump Tower.

Bancroft Haber-dashers

363 Madison Ave.
(45th St.)
687-8650
Mon. to Fri. 8:30 A.M. to 6:00 P.M.; Sat. 9:00 A.M. to 5:00 P.M.

The largest selection of ties and men's shirts in New York, mostly in a no-iron cotton-synthetic mixture. The many branches of this store are rather dreary, but the shirts are not, and the prices are even less so. Bancroft shirts are two for $29; Arrow shirts are $18 to $21. Ties are either two for $15 or two for $29.

Custom Shop, Shirtmakers

618 Fifth Ave.
245-2499
Mon. to Sat. 9:00 A.M. to 5:50 P.M. (Thurs. to 7:50 P.M.)

This chain of stores carries an enormous choice of fabrics. The made-to-measure shirts have the same affordable prices as the ready-to-wear ones (starting at $25), but you have to order at least four—which, at these prices, should not be a problem. Four weeks' preparation time. Several locations.

Duhamell

944 Madison Ave.
(74th St.)
737-1525
Mon. to Sat. 10:00 A.M. to 6:30 P.M.

These are not just any old fabrics: Swiss net, broadcloth, Egyptian cotton, silk, Sea Island and more in more than 700 models, each more elegant than the last (minimum order of six; allow three weeks for delivery). In addition to its shirts, Duhamell offers custom-made suits, very handsome leather articles, casual wear, accessories and some jewelry.

A. Sulka

711 Fifth Ave.
(55th St.)
980-5200
Mon. to Fri. 9:00 A.M. to 6:00 P.M.; Sat. 10:00 A.M. to 5:00 P.M.

You'll have to wait four to six weeks for delivery of your made-to-measure shirt, available in a wide choice of silks and cottons (from $95). For sensitive skins there are silk pajamas (about $200) and even silk briefs ($50), custom-made. Call for an appointment. There's also a complete selection of men's ready-to-wear, furnishings and outerwear.

Tailors

Brioni

Park Avenue Plaza
55 E. 52nd St.
355-1940
Mon. to Sat. 9:30 A.M. to 6:00 P.M.

Just off Park Avenue, in the waterfalled Park Avenue Plaza, the elegant Continental man can buy his very European suits (single- or double-breasted) off the rack for $1,200 or order them custom-made in Italy for just ten percent more, on a four-week delivery schedule. Brioni also sells all types of men's furnishings, from shoes on up ... and up ... and up. And when in Rome, if you want to do as the Romans do, stop in the main Brioni shop at 79 Via Barberini.

Chipp
14 E. 44th St.
687-0850
Mon. to Sat. 9:00 A.M. to 5:30 P.M.

Ready-to-wear and classically styled made-to-measure suiting including riding clothes, in fine shetlands and flannels, and nautical wear for men, women and children. On the second floor is a collection of more contemporary clothing in some of the gaudiest colors imaginable. Chipp is known for making up specialty ties (with names, phone numbers, logos and so forth) and blazer badges in any quantity (even one). Suitable for surprising friends and relatives, but it will cost you dearly.

Dunhill Tailors
65 E. 57th St.
355-0050
Mon. to Sat. 9:30 A.M. to 6:00 P.M.

The most beautiful made-to-measure suits in all New York, and all items of men's haberdashery to complement them. Its celebrated clients happily pay $1,000 and up, with four-week delivery. For the less well heeled, there's an excellent ready-to-wear collection of comparable quality.

F.R. Tripler
300 Madison Ave.
(46th St.)
922-1090
Mon. to Fri. 9:00 A.M. to 5:45 P.M.; Sat. 9:00 A.M. to 5:00 P.M.

A long-established establishment store where you can choose from all sorts of fabrics and styles and then, six weeks later, take delivery of the exact suit you wanted, for a price that won't be much higher than what you'd pay for the reasonable off-the-rack merchandise. Custom-made shirts, too (two-month delivery). There are also excellent selections of shoes (Bally, Church and the like), ready-to-wear shirts and cashmere sweaters. The women's department on the third floor features the same quality and tradition that have earned Tripler its solid reputation for almost a century.

SHOES

Hélène Arpels
665 Madison Ave.
(61st St.)
755-1623
Mon. to Sat. 10:00 A.M. to 6:00 P.M.

Nancy Reagan shops here, which gives you an idea about the limited imagination you'll find. This is the land of elegant, conservative footwear in an elegant, conservative ambience. The wood paneling, sea-green walls, wall sconces and crystal chandeliers are a good reflection of the petite-Versailles prices. The styles are au courant in that mature sort of way, and there are some marvelous clip-on accessories to make your satin evening pumps look even more glamorous. A rather staid place with a clientele to match.

Bally
681 Madison Ave.
(62nd St.)
751-2163
Mon. to Sat. 9:30 A.M. to 6:00 P.M.

Boring, boring, boring. We cannot fault the quality, which is superb, but the styles are so sensible and so ageless that we find them oh so tedious. Nonetheless, the prices are acceptable, and the men's styles are superior to the women's. It's a good location for the classics, but the fashions are looking a little fatiguée. Several other locations.

Susan Bennis/ Warren Edwards
440 Park Ave.
(56th St.)
755-4197
Mon. to Fri. 10:00 A.M. to 6:30 P.M.; Sat. 10:00 A.M. to 6:00 P.M.

This violet and gray contemporary shop houses a fabulous collection of shoes in the latest colors, leathers and creative designs. Most of the prices hover around the $300 level (some are in the thousands), although the sales are more reasonable (but the great styles and colors are usually gone). The mixtures of leathers and skins, the au courant colors and the sense of humor reflected in these shoes make this store worth a visit. There are also some classic styles, timeless stilettos, terrific skimmers and a collection of men's shoes just as trendy and as much fun as the women's line. Popular with fashionable billionaires.

Botticelli
612 Fifth Ave.
(50th St.)
582-6313
Mon. to Sat. 10:00 A.M. to 6:30 P.M.

These women's shoes are Italian made with wit and style. The shop is fun, the leather accessories amusing and the styles terrific for trendy customers who think young. The quality is quite good, even though most of the shoes go out of season each season. That may cause some problems for more moderate fashion victims, as the prices are no bargain.

Carrano Andrea Boutique
677 Fifth Ave.
(53rd St.)
752-6111
Mon. to Sat. 10:30 A.M. to 6:15 P.M. (Thurs. to 7:45 P.M.)

Beautiful shoes, affordable prices, pleasant ambience and frequently changing stock make Carrano a shoe lover's paradise. The women's styles tend to be classic (the pumps are extremely attractive, in a wide variety of colors), but some are droll designs tossed in to keep one's sense of humor intact. A few tasteful leather accessories and a small men's department with some handsome styles round out the selection. There are several branches of Carrano, each with a tranquil environment and a helpful staff.

Church's English Shoes
428 Madison Ave.
(49th St.)
755-4313
Mon. to Fri. 9:30 A.M. to 6:00 P.M.; Sat. 9:30 A.M. to 5:30 P.M.

For the men, classic, sturdy English shoes of good reputation and quality. Fairly priced, but watch for the sales.

L'Emporio
768 Madison Ave.
(65th St.)
737-9087
Mon. to Sat. 10:00 A.M. to 6:30 P.M.

This discount women's shoe store, formerly known as Damages, offers some great finds if you have the patience to visit here often enough to catch new merchandise and the perseverance to sift through the extensive number of Italian styles. Next door to its ready-to-wear sister, the shoe shop also carries bags and a limited line of leather accessories.

Ferragamo
717 Fifth Ave.

A bastion of conservative women's shoes and elegant Italian designer clothes, Ferragamo attracts a monied,

(56th St.)
759-3822
Mon. to Sat. 10:00 A.M. to 6:00 P.M. (Thurs. to 7:00 P.M.)

Maud Frizon
49 E. 57th St.
980-1460
Mon. to Sat. 10:00 A.M. to 6:00 P.M.

Nino Gabriele
1022 Third Ave.
(60th St.)
935-9280
Mon. to Sat. 10:00 A.M. to 7:00 P.M. (Mon. and Thurs. to 9:00 P.M.)

Galo
692 Madison Ave.
(62nd St.)
688-6276
Mon. to Sat. 10:00 A.M. to 6:45 P.M.

Gucci
689 Fifth Ave.
(54th St.)
826-2600
Mon. to Sat. 9:30 A.M. to 6:00 P.M.

Charles Jourdan
Trump Tower
725 Fifth Ave.
(56th St.)
644-3830

staid crowd who is not offended by the horrifying prices. The signature scarves, accessories, sensible shoes and some dramatic fashions are all housed in this clean-line store filled with helpful and friendly salespeople.

There's enough imagination here to outfit an upscale New Wave band. The men's styles are playful and inventive, with zebra-striped inserts, woven uppers, two tones, metallics and a variety of rainbow-hued skins. The women's line has a more conservative side, to balance Frizon's penchant for detailing, unexpected touches and colors that give footwear a whole new personality. The prices are thoughtfully left off the shoes, which possibly prevents instant heart attacks among the uninitiated clientele—or at least gives everyone a fairly clear idea of the expense. There is a limited line of leather accessories.

The most avant-garde men's shoes in New York, but there are a few classic models as well. Luxurious quality leather and high prices. There's another shop just around the corner, at 169 East 60th Street (421-3250).

There is always a good selection of well-designed and wearable women's shoes. Styles tend to be fairly timeless, and the quality is reliable (prices are pretty reasonable, too). They try hard here, and the enthusiastic young salesmen will send runners to any of the other stores to find your size. The shops are tasteful, the Italian shoes elegant as well as playful, and temptation is irresistible. Other locations at 504 Madison Avenue (832-7150) and 825 Lexington Avenue (832-3922).

Part of the string in the Gucci empire. The shoes here hold no surprises: conventional ladies shop for conventional styles, many with the ever-present signature that announces to friends and neighbors the approximate price of their shoes. There are some more fashionable evening designs in pewter, gold and silver, although the standard here is reliable design, superb quality and a persistent ennui. The men's department is still immensely popular with well-dressed salesmen and the preppy set.

The new Charles Jourdan is firmly established in Trump Tower, "The World's Most Unique Shopping Complex." Well, we don't have much to say about the Tower except that it reminds us of a Houstonian interpretation of L.A.'s Rodeo Collection, but the Jourdan boutique is quite handsome. The first floor is full of those classic

Mon. to Fri. 10:00 A.M. to 7:00 P.M.; Sat. 10:00 A.M. to 6:00 P.M.

Billy Martin's Western Wear
812 Madison Ave. (68th St.)
861-3100
Mon. to Fri. 10:00 A.M. to 6:30 P.M.; Sat. 10:00 A.M. to 6:00 P.M.

McCreedy and Schrieber
213 E. 59th St.
759-9241
Mon. to Sat. 9:00 A.M. to 7:00 P.M. (Mon. and Thurs. to 9:00 P.M.); Sun. noon to 6:00 P.M.

I. Miller
Fifth Avenue and 57th Street
581-0062
Mon. to Sat. 9:30 A.M. to 6:00 P.M. (Thurs. to 7:30 P.M.)

Monique
811 Madison Ave. (68th St.)
535-9553
Mon. to Sat. 10:00 A.M. to 6:30 P.M.

Ravello
619 Second Ave. (33rd St.)
889-9236
Mon. to Fri. 10:30 A.M. to 7:00 P.M. (Thurs. to 8:00 P.M.); Sat. 11:00 A.M. to 7:00 P.M.

Vittorio Ricci
645 Madison Ave.

pumps and other Jourdan favorites, along with bags and a few accessories. Upstairs, you'll find some pretty silk blouses, sportswear and unusual sweaters. The prices are comparatively reasonable if you've spent the day checking out the couture boutiques. Friendly and helpful sales staff.

This store has the wherewithal to turn you into a cowboy from head to foot. It was originally opened by an authentic Yankee, and it offers cowboy boots from the simplest to the most exotic ($60 and up), handmade leather jackets, shirts with original Native American designs, gorgeous belts and more. Plus a line of children's wear, with fringed jackets, moccasins and the tiniest cowboy boots imaginable. Dude ranch stuff.

New York's most eclectic men's shoe store for every kind of shoe you need, be it cowboy boots (this is the only store in New York to carry Lucchese, the best brand of cowboy boots), Italian loafers or preppy Weejuns or Topsiders. Everyone should find the shoe that fits among this unbelievably large (and moderately priced) selection. Several models of women's boots, too. Other locations at 37 and 55 West 46th Street (719-1552).

This large, spacious store furnished in mauve is a supermarket of women's shoes. A quietly conservative crowd shops here for Ferragamo, Yves Saint Laurent, Casadei, Amalfi, Charles Jourdan, Bruno Magli and the house brands. Miraculously, almost everything is priced under $175, and the seasonal sales can be a gold mine for those timeless styles necessary to complete any woman's wardrobe. Nothing earth shattering here, but it's a pleasant place to find elegance, classic styling and variety.

The Italian imports here are very strappy, decorated, multicolored and European looking. You will pay prices that you would expect for imports that look like imports. Other locations at 728 Lexington Avenue (308-7710) and 47 West 8th Street (260-1830).

If you can keep the pushy salesmen off you in this small, tidy store, you'll find very attractive Bally, Bandolino, Evan Picone and Andrew Geller shoes for women at excellent prices. The sales are worthwhile.

A chic shop for fabulous men's shoes that are Continental and sophisticated. Slip-ons, alligator flapped

(60th St.)
688-9044
Mon. to Fri. 10:00 A.M. to 6:00
P.M. (Thurs. to 7:00 P.M.); Sat.
11:00 A.M. to 6:00 P.M.

and fringed loafers, suede and rubber skimmers and a host of traditional and avant-garde styles are sold at staggering prices. The women's styles are a bit less impressive, but it's easy to be tempted by the lovely Italian strapped, pieced and multitoned designs. The sales here are fabulous; shoes are practically half price. The decor is ultradeco, with subtle designs painted on the lofty blond paneling. It's a nice place to drop into from time to time to watch the handsome clients add to their leather espadrille collections. Very creative window displays brighten up the Madison Avenue neighborhood.

Roland Pierre
805 Madison Ave.
(67th St.)
570-1805
Mon. to Fri. 10:00 A.M. to 6:30
P.M.; Sat. 10:00 A.M. to 5:30 P.M.

The women's shoes in this bright, cheerful shop are perfect for a weekend in Beverly Hills. There are lots of cutouts, bows and bright colors (in season), along with several Guido Pasquali styles imported from Milan. The boots are adventuresome, and there is a limited line of leather clothing that would look appropriate in Palm Beach. Prices are manageable only if they are not an issue.

Santini e Dominici
697 Madison Ave.
(62nd St.)
838-1835
Mon. to Sat. 10:30 A.M. to
6:30 P.M.

This enjoyable store has a very stark black and white decor and an array of colorful Italian shoes for men and women that, above all, display a sense of humor. The limited collection is chic, with perfect styles for New Wavers, window designers and the eight-year-old children who shop here in tow with their Madison Avenue mothers, who prefer these fashionable alternatives to Nikes and Adidas. The prices are relatively reasonable and the trendy designs so much fun that you may easily be seduced into walking away with several of these wearable, sporty looks.

Walter Steiger
739 Madison Ave.
(64th St.)
570-1212
Mon. to Sat. 10:00 A.M. to
6:00 P.M.

The distinctive cinnamon-red doorway leads you into a haute élégante store that seems to us a bit arrogant for the classic imported ladies' shoes inside. The sales staff can be intimidating and the entire establishment takes itself entirely too seriously. Be prepared to pay $200 for a pair of shoes that are neither overly fashionable nor reliably safe.

To Boot
100 W. 72nd St.
724-8249
Mon. to Fri. noon to 7:00 P.M.; Sat.
2:00 P.M. to 6:00 P.M.

The city's classic western boot shop still has its walls of skins and hides, which are stitched up into durable boots for prices that must make Tony Lama very happy. There are also many exclusive Continental styles for the *G.Q.* readers who frequent Le Relais, along with Ralph Lauren designs that range from Maine hand-sewn loafers to English bench-made shoes. It's a comfortable place to shop, and the sales staff is quite helpful and pleasant. A new addition brings you Kiehl's Pharmacy's grooming products.

Mario Valentino
5 E. 57th St.
486-0322
Mon. to Sat. 10:00 A.M. to 6:00 P.M. (Thurs. to 7:00 P.M.)

A very classy address for this international consortium of shoe boutiques, featuring men's and women's styles from Naples. Both elegant and boringly traditional models are here alongside some more droll and daring styles. The prices are affordable, if you have an extra $150 to toss around for another pair of shoes. There is a collection of superb leather accessories and some clothing. An exclusive boutique for an exclusive clientele.

The Village Cobbler
60 W. 8th St.
673-8530
Mon. to Fri. 10:00 A.M. to 8:30 P.M.; Sat. 10:00 A.M. to 11:00 P.M.; Sun. noon to 7:00 P.M.

For women, there's the entire Bandolino line, along with Nine West, Bass and other American names. The men's shop next door carries Bass and Sperry, along with some attractive Italian shoes. Both shops are small, crowded and poorly laid out—but you won't mind when you look at the price tags, which are always low and are exceptional during the sales.

TRENDY

Antique Boutique
712 Broadway
(south of 8th St.)
460-8830
Mon. to Fri. 10:30 A.M. to 9:00 P.M.; Sat. 10:30 A.M. to 8:00 P.M.; Sun. noon to 7:00 P.M.

On a gray Lower East Side stretch of Broadway is a series of used clothing stores that cater to the local students and artists. Antique Boutique is the best by far—the largest, the best organized and, of course, the most expensive. There are two huge rooms on the street level and another downstairs, all full of classics from the '40s, '50s and '60s. There's a tailor on the premises, and all the garments are cleaned, restored and clearly marked for size. You'll find racks of beaded cashmere sweaters, pedal pushers, car coats, party dresses and button-up-the-back blouses for women; for men, there are beautiful white dinner jackets, tuxedos, madras jackets, dress shirts, bowling shirts, skinny ties and Bermuda shorts. Prices are high for such nostalgia, but the quality and selection are exceptional.

Charivari Workshop
441 Columbus Ave.
(81st St.)
496-8700
Mon. to Fri. 11:00 A.M. to 8:00 P.M.; Sat. 11:00 A.M to 7:00 P.M.; Sun. 11:00 A.M. to 6:00 P.M.

More of that triste constructivist look that is only slightly more wearable than the Parachute P.O.W. wear. Androgynous and rather nihilistic, these clothes are wildly popular with members of the avant-garde set who work in trendy shops and makes dramatic appearances in the undergound after-hours clubs. There are also some traditionals tossed in with the Yohji Yamamato womenswear. Prices are on the high side, quite an investment for this battered look.

Ciccio Bello
462 W. Broadway
(Prince St.)
475-1345

The sales staff here is forbidding, unless you're decked out like a crazed New Waver with rainbow-colored hair, a permanently disdainful look and clothes that one might mistake for a failed design experiment. The music is as

Daily noon to 8:00 P.M.

persistent as the styles, most of which look better on the rack than on the slender bodies of the models and shopgirls who outfit themselves here. But come in to take in the local color and find that perfect pair of sun-washed jeans, plastic jewelry, amusing novelties and avant-garde T-shirts.

Dianne B
**729 Madison Ave.
(64th St.)
759-0988**
*Mon. to Fri. 11:00 A.M. to 7:00
P.M.; Sat. 11:00 A.M. to 6:00 P.M.*

This cheerful medium-tech shop offers trendy clothes for women who want to look their casual-chic best. These great-looking styles have an definate sense of humor and to wear them you have to want to look "in" rather than classically shaped, particularly with Issey Miyake's oversized designs. The saleswomen are helpful, the prices to be reckoned with. These clothes make Dianne B absolutely worth a visit to update your life and enjoy this distinctive point of view. Another location at 426 W. Broadway with the same fabulous clothes in a post-modern decor, a perfect counterpart to the Dianne B look.

Filippo
**671 Madison Ave.
(61st St.)
759-6676**
*Mon. to Sat. 10:00 A.M. to
6:30 P.M.*

This all-white, slightly antiseptic shop features a window display that contains nearly all the merchandise available. The Italian styles are for contemporary thinkers with stockbrokers' bank accounts. It's hard to discover a point of view here, but you will find handsome men's shirts, some good-looking suits and jackets, assorted pieces of colorful, trendy womenswear and drawers of belts and other accessories that will give you that relaxed Filippo look. The sales staff could be more cheerful, but perhaps the frigid environment has affected their notion of customer service.

Fiorucci
**125 E. 59th St.
751-1404**
*Mon. to Sat. 10:00 A.M. to 6:00
P.M. (Mon. and Thurs. to 8:00
P.M.); Sun. noon to 5:00 P.M.*

With all the new, forward-looking boutiques that have opened, Fiorucci is beginning to look a bit tame. Nevertheless, it's still an entertaining and exciting place to shop, with a sales staff dressed in au courant Fiorucci, complete with New York New Wave hairdos. The whimsical merchandise changes frequently and the conservatively dressed clients come here for another pair of signature jeans, mini frocks, greeting cards, plastic accessories, rubber shoes, T-shirts and all the novelties that make this place so enjoyable. The space is airy, cheerful and always interesting. Diana Ross loves Fiorucci, as do Andy Warhol and Brooke Shields. Come here if only to look—but Fiorucci is seductive, so watch out!

Flip
**46 W. 8th St.
254-9810**

Leave it to the British to come up with the latest in clothing chic: tacky American classics from the '50s and early '60s. This store came to New York from London by

Mon. to Thurs. 11:00 A.M. to 9:00 P.M.; Fri. and Sat. 11:00 A.M. to 11:00 P.M.

way of Los Angeles (the Flips in those cities are tremendously popular), bringing its racks of overdyed jeans, leather pants, bold geometric shirts, vintage (but never worn) pedal pushers, party dresses and Bermuda shorts, along with all sorts of young, New Wave accessories. The prices are low and the look is slick, mass-produced and teenybopperesque.

Ron Fritts

698 Madison Ave. (62nd St.) 758-2732

Mon. to Sat. 10:00 A.M. to 6:00 P.M.

The charming owner of this individualistic shop specializes in creating one-of-a-kind fashions for customers he describes as "active women who travel a lot and need practical fabrics." The synthetic fabrics may be practical, but the styles are highly personal, and their handmade quality and artistic look belie the fact that they are not crafted from natural fibers. The lovely sweaters, feminine dresses, handwoven-look ensembles and pretty dresses are the signature here. Another location in SoHo at 351 West Broadway, near Broome Street (219-1064).

Betsey Johnson

130 Thompson St. (Houston St.) 420-0169

Mon. to Sat. noon to 7:00 P.M.; Sun. noon to 6:00 P.M.

It's very pink inside and out, and the saleswomen run around in classic Betsey, which makes the place both entertaining and decorative. This adventurous designer's knits, here in limited supply, are equally perfect for aerobics classes, for a night at Danceteria or, oddly enough, for a sedate lunch at the Carlyle; her styles are that varied. It's worth a stop to see what she's up to, and there's no pressure to leave with one of the pink lace wedding-cake dresses, a cotton-knit corset or any of the other stretchy novelty styles. Another pink but more upscale branch at 248 Columbus Avenue (362-3364).

Norma Kamali O.M.O.

6 W. 56th St. 245-6322

Mon. to Sat. 10:00 A.M. to 6:00 P.M.

The distinctive oversized, layered Kamali look is happily worn by the saleswomen, who outnumber the customers by about four to one. If you can't live without a black leather strapless dress with built-in crinoline, leotards decorated with luminous pearls, lumberjack-style layered pieces to fight winter chills, sweatshirt dressing that is beginning to look passé or long, tubelike dresses with sleeves up to two yards long, then this is your mecca. A great sense of humor and a fashionably thin body are de rigueur. Prices can be staggering, but a good eye and the regular sales will help you find pieces that are affordable, even if they are not destined to be eternally en mode.

Morgane Le Fay

151 Spring St. (W. Broadway) 925-0144

Mon. to Sun. 11:00 A.M. to 7:00 P.M.

We're not sure that even Morgane herself could spirit us into wearing these rather triste medieval styles, more appropriate for a trendy nun than for a twenty-first-century lady-in-waiting. Liliana Ordas designs these clothes, which have drama, flair and large price tags. Definitely worth a visit, to see how the sales staff assembles this layered look and to try on a few yourself. On our most recent visit, there was no evidence of Merlin in his own monastic robes.

Macondo
150 Spring St.
(W. Broadway)
431-3224
Mon. to Sun. noon to 7:00 P.M.

These fanciful creations are impractical and expensive, but they're lots of fun. Most of the clothing here are hand-painted, hand-dyed silk dresses and blouses in designs that are adventurous and sometimes outlandish—perfect for a superchic SoHo opening.

Matsuda
854 Madison Ave.
(70th St.)
988-9514
Mon. to Sat. 10:00 A.M. to 6:00 P.M.

Everything in this streamlined shop is ultra au courant in an oversized, idiosyncratic way. Accessorizing the look is integral to achieving the slightly eccentric effect, with leggings under skirts under oversized jackets over generous shirts. If you're reluctant to go overboard with this Japanese designer's look, the blouses for women and the men's shirts are terrific (if expensive), the retro jackets are in creative fabrics, and the gloves are in tasteful netting. Come here for the vision and to dress yourself for a foray to the underground or back to your gallery office.

Parachute
121 Wooster St.
(Spring St.)
925-8630
Mon. to Fri. noon to 8:00 P.M.; Sat. and Sun. 1:00 P.M. to 7:00 P.M.

This lofty space has all the joy of an East European internment camp, an impression that is heightened by the sales staff modeling the Parachute signatures with P.O.W. aplomb. The huge place is hard and cold, the New Wave music is hard and cold, and the prices are hard and cold. The monochromatics create a sea of gray, and the regulars here love to accessorize the Mugler-esque looks with T-shirts, rubber-tractor-soled shoes and heavy-metal leather belts. It's worth a visit to see how punked-out New York is dressing; who knows, you may leave with a camouflage scarf, leather bag or $500 leather jacket reminiscent of a medieval executioner's outfit. Another stark, high-tech location at 309 Columbus Avenue (799-1444).

Riding High/Carol Rollo
1147 First Ave.
(63rd St.)
832-7927
Mon. to Sat. 10:30 A.M. to 7:00 P.M.

A somewhat ominous metal door slides open onto a high-tech garage/like space, complete with a bridge spanning the two tiers. This gray place is filled with Carol Rollo designs, eccentric creations perfect for the adventurous woman. They are one-of-a-kind pieces, so you'll be sure not to run into your twin at the latest performance art event or at your after-hours club. The prices are not bargain basement, but they are affordable for the hardworking. The sales offer better prices, but by then the merchandise is pretty well picked over.

La Rue des Rêves

When visiting this odd store, it is advisable to bring your attorney with you. The people who run this fashion

139 Spring St.
(Wooster St.)
226-6736
Tues. to Sat. noon to 6:45 P.M.
(Thurs. and Fri. to 8:45 P.M.); Sun.
1:00 P.M. to 5:45 P.M.

madhouse are so insecure that if you happen to take any notes (as we have, for example) you will be cause for an all-points alarm, a lecture, harassment and an eventual parade of salespeople and security guards following you around. It almost makes us wonder if there's some sort of covert activity taking place in the back room. The shop itself is a labyrinthian circus featuring several cats, a dog, about six birds and a sales staff that looks like something out of Sheena of the Jungle. The clothes are ultratrendy: painted leathers, sequined chemises and every other fantasylike style imaginable, plus a wall of belts and accessories. The tribal decor matches the management's tribal behavior, but the place is worth checking out just to admire the expensive merchandise and have a good laugh.

Soft Machine
680 Madison Ave.
(62nd St.)
371-1417
Mon. to Sat. 10:00 A.M. to
6:00 P.M.

If São Paulo is not on your itinerary this year, stop off at this little Brazilian shop that looks and feels more like a disco, with its laser lighting and sophisticated sound board, than like a New Wavish clothing store for young-thinking women. At a given time you may find plastic shoes in the latest colors, playful clothing perfect for a trip to the Green Parrot or the Spring Street Bar, and an owner and staff who are pleasantly helpful. If you're looking to break out of the pinstripe mold or augment your wardrobe with up-to-the minute casual-chic pieces, visit the Soft Machine—you're sure to find something unique amid the clutter.

CONTEMPORARY

Agora
1550 Third Ave.
(87th St.)
860-3425
Mon. to Sat. 10:00 A.M. to 9:30
P.M.; Sun. noon to 7:00 P.M.

This charming boutique has such an eclectic collection of clothes that it lacks focus. There are conservative shirt dresses and wraparound skirts for Greenwich preppies, plus more contemporary styles for fashionable ladies of all ages. The one common thread is the astronomical pricing. If you need to take a break from looking for the perfect Victorian blouse or a golf outfit for the man in your life (there's a men's department, too), you can relax in the stunning Belle Epoque–style ice cream parlor, which transports you back to a time when shopping was something one's personal maid took care of.

Antartex
903 Madison Ave.
(72nd St.)
535-9079
Mon. to Sat. 10:00 A.M. to
6:00 P.M.

Classic dressers shop at Antartex for fabulous suede and sheepskin coats and jackets. There are also some very conservative, simple dresses, canvas safari shoulder bags, beautiful preppy sweaters and mohair throws. Prices are affordable, given the quality, and the sales can be excellent.

Laura Ashley

714 Madison Ave.
(63rd St.)
371-0606
Mon. to Sat. 10:00 A.M. to 6:00
P.M. (Thurs. to 7:00 P.M.)

This shop is as charming as all the Laura Ashley boutiques. You'll find three floors of ruffles, florals, flounces and a clientele dressed from head to toe in the signature youthful Ashley look. The home furnishings department is immensely popular; it's easy to find yourself redecorating your entire house or apartment in the lovely papers with coordinating fabrics. Prices are actually pretty reasonable if you take into account the quality and the designer heritage, which keep the overhead high. The service is personalized, and prospective brides love to visit Laura Ashley to choose from the romantic gowns that make young ladies' weddings becoming.

The Bermuda Shop

605 Madison Ave.
(59th St.)
355-0733
Mon. to Sat. 10:00 A.M. to
6:00 P.M.

Impeccable prep: handsome kilts and shetlands in the winter, and cotton-knit pullovers, rugby shirts and classic suiting in the summer. The prices are reasonable, the sales staff helpful and friendly, the styles predictable and the whole experience pleasant. Lots of J.G. Hook and plenty of house labels—this is quality, timeless ready-to-wear from reputable firms. There are some lovely, feminine sweater knits with embroidered flowers, as well as good-looking jackets and vests for the colder weather. Golf jackets, straight-line trousers, classic straight skirts and those ruffled-neck all-cotton blouses make The Bermuda Shop more attractive than Brooks Brothers; it's certainly more affordable.

Betsey Bunky Nini

746 Madison Ave.
(65th St.)
744-6716
Mon. to Fri. 10:30 A.M. to 6:00
P.M.; Sat. 11:30 A.M. to 6:00 P.M.

Youngish, hip customers come here to find the casual-chic look that the shop girls wear so well and that many women find suitably attractive. This store still carries its fabulous knits and handsome natural fiber jackets and skirts. The blond wood shop has a limited selection, but the quality is irreproachable, even if the prices are a bit too steep for impulse purchases.

Bip

755 Madison Ave.
(66th St.)
535-0228
Mon. to Fri. 10:00 A.M. to 6:00
P.M.; Sat. 11:00 A.M. to 6:00 P.M.

Bip's signature triangular metal emblem is found on the pockets of all the casual trousers and shirts here. It's a great place for well-fitting jeans, cotton pants, sweaters and shirts, all in timelessly stylish designs. Prices are on the high side of reasonable.

Brooks Brothers

346 Madison Ave.
(44th St.)
682-8800
Mon. to Sat. 9:15 A.M. to 6:00 P.M.

Fortunately, the women's clothing is a little less frumpy than the preppy menswear headquartered in this venerable institution. The shetland sweaters are superb, the silk blouses perfect for the lady executive, the suits slightly old-fashioned, the sportswear what you would expect and the shoes absolutely boring: the prices necessitate a stock market windfall. Many of the customers come here for the classic, well-made coats of a quality that will last them a lifetime (heaven knows these styles are unlikely to go out of season), and for the security of knowing that there's safety in numbers—most of their friends look exactly the same conservative way.

Burberry's
9 E. 57th St.
371-5010
Mon. to Sat. 9:30 A.M. to 6:00 P.M. (Thurs. to 7:00 P.M.)

This is the best address for conservatively stylish women who wear sensible shoes and think Issey Miyake is just a passing fancy. It is, of course, the *only* place for a classic trench coat, and the plaid that lines the coats shows up on all sorts of other things here as well. The sweaters, suits, wool skirts and cotton blouses are unerringly tame and unfailingly high priced.

Burton
475 Fifth Ave.
2nd floor
(41st St.)
685-3760
Mon. to Fri. 9:30 A.M. to 6:00 P.M. (Thurs. to 7:00 P.M.); Sat. 10:00 A.M. to 6:00 P.M.

This pleasant little shop is a must for classic dressers. The kilts, khaki golf jackets, fabulous hand-knit sweaters, timeless blouses, walking shorts and those sensible trousers Nantucket summer women love so much are all of impeccable styling and quality, at more than reasonable prices. Very helpful salespeople. There's a similar men's shop next door, stocked with equally preppy fashions.

Charivari 72
58 W. 72nd St.
787-7272
Mon. to Fri. 11:00 A.M. to 8:00 P.M. (Thurs. to 9:00 P.M.); Sat. 11:00 A.M. to 7:00 P.M.; Sun. 1:00 P.M. to 6:00 P.M.

Charivaris are cropping up on the West Side with McDonald's frequency. There's a branch for sportswear, another for menswear, a third for womenswear, yet another for the trendies and this multitiered shop for Charivari addicts. The merchandise is up-to-the-minute fashionable, with good representation from Kenzo, Issey Miyake, Perry Ellis and all the other contemporary designers that give us the structured mid-'80s look. The store is great fun to wander around in, as long as you avoid walking into any of the mirrored walls. It's exciting, it's crowded, and it's expensive, but it's also a must-visit to see how contemporary, fashion-conscious New Yorkers outfit themselves with that calculated chic look.

Chor Bazaar
801 Lexington Ave.
(62nd St.)
838-2581
Mon. to Sat. 10:00 A.M. to 7:00 P.M.; Sun. noon to 5:00 P.M.

You'll find some unusual, pretty things mixed in with the typical Chinese and Indian womenswear at Chor Bazaar, which is just down the street from Putumayo. The imported accessories and jewelry are worthwhile, and the natural fabrics (mostly cotton and silk) are perfect for surviving summers in New York. There's an in-house tailor who can custom-make dresses in the fabric of your choice.

Colony
56 Seventh Ave.
(14th St.)
924-8815
Mon. to Fri. 10:00 A.M. to 8:00

The prices are on the low side of reasonable at Colony, a very small shop crammed with sportswear for women and men. The men's selection is rather weak, but women are sure to find a cotton sweater, linen trousers, colorful dress or simple blouse they can't live without. There's

P.M.; Sat. 11:00 A.M. to 8:00 P.M.; Sun. 2:00 P.M. to 6:00 P.M.

only enough room to display one of everything, so you'll have to ask the turbaned clerks for your size. The sales can be excellent.

Pierre d'Alby
610 Fifth Ave.
(49th St.)
541-7110
Mon. to Fri. 10:30 A.M. to 6:30 P.M.; Sat. 10:00 A.M. to 6:00 P.M.

This small corner store is filled to capacity with the conservative, sporty Pierre d'Alby look. The styles are practical, wearable and slightly tame looking compared to the newer New Wavish boutiques. There are some fabulous sales here, with savings up to 60 percent. The base prices are pretty reasonable in any case, and you may find that the all-cotton shirts, handsome knits or well-fitting trousers are essential to your wardrobe.

Design Observations
282 Columbus Ave.
(73rd St.)
799-2990
Mon. to Sat. 10:30 A.M. to 9:00 P.M.; Sun. 12:30 P.M. to 7:00 P.M.

Wearable, cheerful, California-casual clothes for men and women are sold in this bright two-story shop. Lots of painted T-shirts, coveralls and minis, and some classics are tossed in as well to make shopping here a tempting pleasure. Prices are reasonable, and although the clothes are not Parachute trendy, they are fashionable in an eminently more wearable way.

Roberta di Camerino
645 Fifth Ave.
(51st St.)
355-7600
Mon. to Sat. 10:00 A.M. to 6:00 P.M.

This Italian boutique has been in residence in the Olympic Towers for some years now, offering a mixed clientele some of the more unattractive and tasteless clothes and accessories we've seen. But if you adore tapestry handbags (which look much like flocked bordello wallpaper), bright fuschia knits, gold lamé motorcycle-style jackets and the insistent gold R on everything, then you will love this store. We can only assume the Palm Beach crowd comes here to restock seasonally—it's their look.

Vera Finbert
4 W. 57th St.
333-3263
Mon. to Sat. 10:00 A.M. to 6:00 P.M.

Knits of every type and fabric, all imported from France, make this little boutique a paradise for women who love the sexy, feminine feel of angora in the winter and silk in the summer. Two-piece collections of skirts and pants are sporty as well as dressy, and the sweater dresses are always tempting. The holiday season brings particularly pretty items, with lots of beading and metallics, but the neutrals of summer are just as attractive in their casual way. Prices are within reach.

Fonda Boutique
168 Lexington Ave.
(30th St.)
685-4035
Mon. to Fri. 10:30 A.M. to 7:30 P.M. (Thurs. to 9:00 P.M.); Sat. 10:30 A.M. to 6:30 P.M.

If you don't want to be seen in the latest fashions being worn by half the women in New York, visit this personal little boutique. The selection is small but interesting: a few designer suits and dresses, leather miniskirts, beautiful antique lace blouses and dresses, silk kimonos and antique accessories and jewelry. Everything is attractive, unusual and very reasonably priced.

Le Grand Hôtel/Tales of Hoffman
471 W. Broadway
(Prince St.)
473-9718
Mon. to Fri. noon to 7:00 P.M.; Sat. noon to 6:30 P.M.; Sun. 2:00 P.M. to 6:00 P.M.

Everything here is handmade, which gives the clothes a special, couturieresque quality. The all-American designers have a sense of style as well as humor, with fabulous evening gowns as light as chiffon air, beaded blouses better than they did them in the '20s, inventive day dresses with a retro look and all the other fantasy special-occasion styles. The shop is large and sparse, and the sales staff is extremely helpful. The prices might be a bit stunning, but the workmanship is of good quality. There is a limited selection of shoes.

Grecophilia
132 W. 72nd St.
877-2566
Mon. to Sat. 10:30 A.M. to 8:30 P.M.; Sun. noon to 6:00 P.M.

This is an excellent shop for women who are on tight budgets and are fond of bright, casual cotton clothing. There are some gauzy Greek items, but most of the selections are domestic: jeans, T-shirts, mini dresses, sweaters and cotton trousers. Attractive clothing at undemanding prices.

Suzuya
130 E. 59th St.
688-8835
Mon. to Sat. 10:00 A.M. to 7:00 P.M.

Across the street from Fiorucci, this little shop is filled with similar trendy merchandise, with a few more Japanese and French designs than Italian imports. You'll find wearable, modish clothes that can go to most fashionable offices. Check in here for seasonal updates and to take advantage of the sales (prices are trendy expensive).

WOMENSWEAR

Antique · Lace

Alice Underground
380 Columbus Ave.
(78th St.)
724-6682
Daily noon to 8:00 P.M.

This basement shop is full of vintage clothes—some exquisite, others nothing more than old clothes. The honeycomb of subterranean rooms is a gold mine for customers enamored with the '50s look, wardrobe directors looking for costumes for period plays and rock-'n'-rollers searching for the perfect skirt for a night at Heartbreak. There are some Victorian beauties here, along with some of the most beautiful antique teddies we've seen in New York. The good news is that the prices are extremely reasonable.

Harriet Love
412 W. Broadway
(Spring St.)
966-2280
Tues. to Sat. noon to 7:00 P.M.; Sun. 1:00 P.M. to 6:00 P.M.

These clever people have parlayed their expertise on antique clothing into a guidebook, outlining where and how to search for the perfect antique styles. This store, which features exquisite clothing from the '20s and '30s, is a good start. If you have economic freedom, you will find this ravishing merchandise more than irresistible.

Lydia
21 E. 65th St.
861-8177
Mon. to Sat. 11:30 A.M. to
6:00 P.M.

This small shop filled with exquisite antique clothes is all overseen by the rather eccentric Lydia Gordon. The prices are fairly high and arbitrary; the quality is superb, the antique jewelry delicate and the welcome somewhat cold. A good place to find lovely Victorian blouses, authentic beaded chemises (these make '80s designs look amateurish), lovely long gowns and feminine day dresses.

Quetzal
2194 Broadway
(78th St.)
496-8340
Mon. by appt. only; Tues. to Sat. noon
to 7:00 P.M.

This extraordinary collection of antique lace is made into sensational wedding gowns, Victorian blouses, day dresses and even T-shirts. The clothes are stunning and the prices certainly reasonable (more so than the more sophisticated and established Rubicon on the East Side). There are also hand-knit sweaters touched with lace and antique trims. A good place to know about if you cherish tradition and quality workmanship.

Random Harvest
60 W. 75th St.
799-0134
Daily noon to 7:00 P.M. (Wed. to
Fri. to 9:00 P.M.)

This fresh shop with its white walls, blond wood furnishings and attractive staff has a limited selection of Victoriana, along with some exquisite '20s beaded dresses, delicate blouses and day dresses in perfect condition. The quilts, antique lace table runners, pillow shams and bedroom pretties make Random Harvest worth a stop. Prices are steep, predictable for the high quality of merchandise and the burgeoning Upper West Side.

Victoria Falls
147 Spring St.
(W. Broadway)
226-5099
Mon. to Sat. noon to 7:00 P.M.;
Sun. 1:00 P.M. to 5:30 P.M.

The lovely, feminine clothes, Victorian without being fussy, are handmade of the most superb fabrics. This pretty place is without doubt one of the most enchanting stores in New York, whether you are looking for antique blouses and dresses, hand-painted sleep shirts or beaded and bejeweled ballet shoes. There is also a house line of exquisite styles. Elegance and refinement is understated, the sales staff is cheerfully outfitted in these original styles, and the prices are rather high, although not beyond the realm of hope.

Julie Artisan's Gallery
687 Madison Ave.
(62nd St.)
688-2345
Mon. to Sat. 11:00 A.M. to
6:00 P.M.

Each item here is a handmade work of art that somehow manages to be wearable and cost less than you would expect. On a given visit you may find subtle batik jackets, exquisite silk kimonolike ensembles, clear plastic vests with purple feathers zipped into the pockets, painted leather pullovers, beautiful woven jackets, sweatshirts with long, skinny balloon fringe or any of Ivy Ross's beautifully designed titanium jewelry. The welcome can be a bit disconcerting, but persevere and you'll enjoy taking in the contents of this unique fantasyland.

Kreeger & Sons
16 W. 46th St.
575-7825
Mon. to Sat. 10:00 A.M. to 6:00 P.M. (Thurs. to 8:00 P.M.)

All the rugged, classic, unisex looks that have kept East Coast outdoorswomen looking the same for years can be found here. The Norwegian patterned pullovers, parkas, corduroy skirts and practical basics are straight off the pages of Eddie Bauer and L.L. Bean, at prices that won't hinder a shopping spree.

Lina Lee
Trump Tower
725 Fifth Ave.
(57th St.)
275-2926
Mon. to Sat. 10:00 A.M. to 6:00 P.M.

There's a touch of the gold coast in this Rodeo Collection East. All the dramatic and overpriced looks that are such a hit in L.A. are here for women who have a theatrical bent. If you've got $800 to spend on a blouse or even more for a snakeskin bag, then come here to outfit yourself from head to toe with the unique casual-chic look that has encouraged the ladies in Beverly Hills to make a career of shopping. The evening looks are around the corner under lock and key, but the crowds enjoy window shopping for this Academy Award style of dressing up.

Looking
2275 Broadway
(82nd St.)
799-6225
Mon. to Sat. 11:00 A.M. to 8:00 P.M.; Sun. noon to 6:00 P.M.

For women of all fashion persuasions. Everything from trendy minis to classic suits can be found here. The prices are extremely reasonable for the elegant silk skirts and matching jackets, fashionable frocks, dressy evening wear and more casual looks perfect for the Hamptons or for walking around Columbus Avenue on a Saturday shopping spree.

Mariko
835 Madison Ave.
(69th St.)
288-1150
Mon. to Sat. 10:00 A.M. to 6:00 P.M.

These very pretty, very feminine clothes have a theatrical flair and price tags to match. You can find plenty of silks, ruffles, flounces, glitter and puffed sleeves for a ladylike look. There are also loads of accessories to finish off your new wardrobe, which will have a slightly Palm Beach air.

Billy Martin's Western Wear
812 Madison Ave.
(68th St.)
861-3100
Mon. to Fri. 10:00 A.M. to 6:30 P.M.; Sat. 10:00 A.M. to 6:00 P.M.

City-slicker cowgirls love these Salamander (Kansas City) square dance blouses, skirts and rodeo collections that don't look ridiculous in an urban environment. The selection of boots for men, women and children is particularly handsome. The prices are for Houston oil drillers, not humble cowpokes.

McLaughlin's
1260 Madison Ave.
(90th St.)
369-4830
Mon. to Fri. 11:00 A.M. to 9:00 P.M.; Sat. 11:00 A.M. to 6:00 P.M.; Sun. 1:00 P.M. to 5:00 P.M.

For a classic, unimaginative and very proper wardrobe, McLaughlin's can't be beat. This series of handsome stores stocks everything a well-brought-up young prep needs, from corduroy shirt dresses and wool knee socks to shetland sweaters and paisley blouses. The clothes are well made, the styles timeless and the prices reasonable. Several other locations.

Ménage à Trois

760 Madison Ave.
(66th St.)
249-0500
Mon. to Fri. 11:00 A.M. to 6:00
P.M.; Sat. 11:30 A.M. to 6:00 P.M.

The most romantic clothes are designed by the stylish young ladies who own this lovely shop. Stop in to see the exquisite undershirts and panties decorated with crocheted flowers and beadwork, tea dresses in pretty florals, delicate accessories, good-looking blazers and suits or any of the other enchanting treasures Ménage à Trois has assembled for the season. The prices are a bit steep, but if you want style and such eminently feminine fashions, economy can't be an issue.

La Merceria

1456 Second Ave.
(76th St.)
628-5124
Mon. to Sat. 11:00 A.M. to
7:30 P.M.

This little boutique is filled with wonderful European hand-knit sweaters in marvelous woolens for winter and lightweight cottons and silks for summer. The patterns and designs are distinctive, the prices reasonable and the service helpful. This shop is a special find during its seasonal sales, when the pricetags are cut nearly in half!

Miso

416 W. Broadway
(Spring St.)
226-4955
Mon. to Sat. 11:30 A.M. to 6:45
P.M.; Sun. 1:00 P.M. to 6:45 P.M.

If you are looking for the perfect windup toy to treat a fashionable young lady, this shop is a must. Combining perfectly designed clothes with novelty toys is a novelty in itself, but it offers some comic relief for husbands and boyfriends in tow on a shopping spree in SoHo. As for the rest of it, this shop has beautiful, rather European clothes in fashionable, classic styles that are amazingly affordable (the prices are far below those demanded by many of the other trendy boutiques in the area and uptown). There is a good selection of legwear, plus a collection of Swiss and German cotton camisoles and panties; also some very good sales. This is one of our favorite stores in New York, and it will be one of yours, too, after a single visit.

Nicole

South Street Seaport
19 Fulton St.
(Cannon Walk)
608-1237
Mon. to Sat. 10:00 A.M. to 10:00
P.M.; Sun. noon to 8:00 P.M.

Charming Nicole Schwob runs an exceedingly engaging shop filled with handmade sweaters. They are costly but of a quality that should last forever (there's no guarantee on the designs, however, which are fashionably trendy). You'll find lovely evening styles in angora and metallics, sporty popcorn styles with embroidered detailing, Peruvian and Inca styles—even the most classic pullovers and popular preppy intarsias with little houses, dogs and happy families parading across the chests. A delightful spot full of treasures.

Paracelso

432 W. Broadway
(Spring St.)
966-4232
Mon. 2:30 P.M. to 7:00 P.M.; Tues.
to Sun. 1:00 P.M. to 6:30 P.M.

It is quite possible that only the medieval alchemist namesake of this small SoHo shop could create order amid this disarray. There are clothes everywhere: draped over partitions, piled onto any available surface, still in shipping boxes, hung six deep and covering the walls in the changing room. The serene and slightly eccentric so-called Luxor Tavella reigns over this chaos, helping customers find the perfect style and a better fit. The cottons are mostly imported, with lots of Sermoneta labels for slightly less than at its uptown address. Perseverance is the key here, and it is not difficult to walk out with a summer frock, dressier chemise or any of the other au courant styles that are quite wearable. Incognito is the big label here (which is also how Ms. Tavella may affect you, with her blue eyebrows, pink and yellow makeup and mysterious air).

Pirjo
South Street Seaport
19 Fulton St.
(Water St.)
608-5796
Mon. to Sat. 10:00 A.M. to 10:00 P.M.; Sun. noon to 6:00 P.M.

The industrious lady who owns this shop and its sister in Faneuil Hall in Boston gets her whole family into the action, knitting up lovely sweaters and hand looming pullovers. Styles are ethnic and up-to-date, with au courant prices to match. There is also a line of sweatshirt separates that provides a comfortable alternative to the woolly layered look. A very pleasant boutique with helpful service.

Putumayo
857 Lexington Ave.
(65th St.)
734-1111
Mon. to Sat. 11:00 A.M. to 7:00 P.M.

Cotton is king at Putumayo, a charming, friendly boutique featuring womenswear from such warm climes as India, Guatemala and South America. It also offers many of its own designs, simple skirts, dresses and little blouses in bright cottons. The prices are reasonable. Be sure to visit the gallery upstairs to see the changing folk art displays, which are always interesting. There's another location at 339 Columbus Avenue, near 76th Street (595-3441).

Georges Rech
711 Madison Ave.
(63rd St.)
832-3147
Mon. to Sat. 10:00 A.M. to 6:00 P.M.

Rech's French designs are joined by a host of Italians and other French imports. The prices are staggering, but the styling is Parisian chic at its best. Some absolutely lovely evening looks, unique blouses and wearable suits. The attitude of the sales staff is a bit offhand, but they are helpful when asked for information.

Yves St. Tropez
4 W. 57th St.
765-5790
Mon. to Sat. 10:00 A.M. to 6:30 P.M.

These superb silks are loved by shoppers on Rodeo Drive, who have the petro dollars to afford them. With styles ranging from the dramatic to the conservative, this store caters to women who have many different clothing needs. The evening wear is superb, although you pay for every metallic thread and every square inch of gorgeous fabric. These imports are slightly discounted at the branch at 247 East 60th Street (759-3784). It's worth a visit, even if you're just browsing.

San Francisco
975 Lexington Ave.
(70th St.)

Very unusual classics are displayed in this elegant store. In the winter, there are beautiful tweeds, cashmeres and wools; in the summer, cotton dresses, linen trousers and

472-8740
Mon. to Fri. 10:00 A.M. to 7:00 P.M.; Sat. 11:00 A.M. to 6:00 P.M.

Sermoneta
740 Madison Ave. (64th St.)
744-6551
Mon. to Fri. 10:00 A.M. to 6:00 P.M.; Sat. 11:00 A.M. to 5:00 P.M.

Sils Mara
995 Lexington Ave. (72nd St.)
988-3900
Mon. to Fri. 11:00 A.M. to 7:00 P.M.; Sat. 11:00 A.M. to 6:00 P.M.

Streets & Co.
2030 Broadway (69th St.)
787-2626
Mon. to Fri. 11:00 A.M. to 8:00 P.M.; Sat. 10:00 A.M. to 6:00 P.M.

Ann Taylor
3 E. 57th St.
832-2010
Mon. to Sat. 10:00 A.M. to 6:00 P.M. (Thurs. to 8:00 P.M.)

Therapy
799 Madison Ave. (67th St.)

cotton sweaters. The fabrics are exceptional and the styles unique and handsome—avant-garde preppy, if you will. Particularly good for men's shirts and trousers and women's skirts. Prices are shocking.

Sermoneta has the main distinction of possessing a sleepy guard dog who blocks your entry through the ornate, primitively carved wooden door. Once you're inside this little downstairs shop, you'll find loads of all-cotton dresses, blouses, nighties and skirts. Most of the items come from South America, although there is a growing stock of those Indian designs that one sees around town. The sisal bags from Kenya and Ecuador are rugged and handsome, the staff is helpful, and the prices are affordable.

The decor, atmosphere and fabrics here are much like those at neighboring San Francisco, but the styles are more straightforward preppy. The sweaters are particularly attractive, as are the lovely dresses and jackets. The men's selection is limited, but you'll find some beautiful cotton shirts. Prices are more within reason than at San Francisco, and the sales are excellent.

This airy shop is filled with fashionable classics that give new life to the tired-looking prep styles that tend to make women look less than their most feminine selves. Streets & Company has updated classic styling using impeccable fabrics: beautiful silk blouses, lovely hand-knit sweaters, superb cotton shirts and a collection of suits that makes executive dressing attractive. The accessories are tempting, the sales staff helpful and the shop bright and easy to shop in. A second branch has opened at 941 Lexington Avenue (517-9000), for Upper East Siders.

If it's wearably trendy, chic and expensive, you'll find it at Ann Taylor. The styles in any season are impeccable for those with a youthful spirit and adventurous outlook (there are also some more traditional, conservative looks, but you have to hunt for them). The fabrics are beautiful, the selection is impressive, and the sales staff is generally helpful. There is an irresistible shoe department, with Joan & David designs that may deplete your checking account but will make you popular with your fashion-conscious friends. Another location at 805 Third Avenue (308-5333) and at the South Street Seaport, 25 Fulton Street (608-5600).

What you will find here is loosely described as "an attitude" about dressing. This particular frame of mind means clothes that are fun, frivolous, one of a kind and

288-1182
*Mon. to Sat. 10:15 A.M. to
6:30 P.M.*

very expensive. Creative Ellen Lansburgh has collected an eclectic assortment of clothes that look as though they might be appropriate on Rodeo Drive or at a Beverly Hills at-home black tie dinner. In any case, you'll find wonderful fantasy pieces that are quite wearable. Holiday styles are particularly tempting: sequined skirts, kimonolike cover-ups, silk surplice tops, marvelous blouses, mini dresses and dramatic, sparkle-encrusted chiffon outfits. The staff wears the distinctive Therapy look, the positive energy level is high, the clothes are very amusing, and with little trouble you'll find yourself outfitted with a new look to rejuvenate your wardrobe and your life.

Designer

Adolfo
36 E. 57th St.
4th floor
688-4410
By appt. only

The elegant ladies who shop here regularly feel right at home in the small reception salon, where the savvy sales staff helps outfit them in the latest feminine Adolfo styles. They will make you think of Nancy Reagan's host of closest friends as they model the knit suits, beautiful evening clothes and signature Adolfo dresses that are classic and flattering to small, slender bodies. Prices are befitting this wood-paneled, chandelier-lit showroom. It is advisable to make an appointment, as all the merchandise is hidden in the back and brought to customers only on request.

Courrèges
19 E. 57th St.
755-0300
*Mon. to Sat. 10:00 A.M. to
6:00 P.M.*

All the constructed and futuristic designs of forward-thinking Courrèges are in this minimalist-decor shop. Most are branded with the trademark initials, no doubt advertising to the world what you are willing to pay for these clothes. It takes a special personality and adventurous spirit to carry off the Courrèges look.

Givenchy Boutique
954 Madison Ave.
(75th St.)
772-1040
*Mon. to Sat. 10:00 A.M. to
6:00 P.M.*

Stunning after-hours designs are frequently displayed in the windows, tempting you to enter this sacred temple to high fashion. The security guard greets you at the door, and you are welcome to peruse the beautiful clothes bearing striking price tags. Elegance for the ultrachic and ultrarich.

Kenzo Paris
824 Madison Ave.
(69th St.)
737-8640
*Mon. to Sat. 10:00 A.M. to
6:30 P.M.*

Kenzo's distinctive Japanese-French-international style (something also apparent on the cuisine scene) is featured in this petite shop filled with light wood and New York shoppers. If you love Kenzo, you'll love this store; the saleswomen wear the look, as do the customers, in varying degrees of success. Prices are to be expected, but not so overwhelming that you are prevented from submission to the marvelous skirts, handsome shirting or any of the dressier looks perfect for wearing to dinner at Café Seiyoken.

Lanvin
701 Madison Ave.
(62nd St.)
838-4330
Mon. to Sat. 10:00 A.M. to 6:00 P.M.

All the pretty and elegant Lanvin styles are in this two-tier shop, where the French staff is attractive in that dramatic Lanvin way—and they're informative as well. The prices are not all that depressing, and you may be seduced into one of the gorgeous evening gowns, pretty silk blouses to go with your Lanvin suit, or any of the other lovely items here.

Ted Lapidus
1010 Third Ave.
(60th St.)
751-7251
Mon. to Fri. 10:00 A.M. to 6:30 P.M. (Thurs. to 7:30 P.M.); Sat. 10:00 A.M. to 6:00 P.M.

This clean-line Fifth Avenue store is a tranquil shopping island filled with simple and elegant men's and women's clothes that are tasteful and fashionable, with a European flair. The prices are a bit steep, but the quality is superb. Some newer, more youthful styles are emerging, and you'll always find irresistible accessories. We've said in the past that these classic creations allow you to run from the office to a cocktail party without changing; it's still true.

Martha
475 Park Ave.
(59th St.)
753-1511
Mon. to Sat. 10:00 A.M. to 6:00 P.M.

While ladies of an indeterminate age sip coffee, the elegant couture models flounce around in the latest evening gowns and the fussy sales staff collects the perfect styles for each customer. It's old-world, luxury service; chauffeurs wait patiently outside while the security guard/doorman hails the appropriate stretch limo to retrieve its mistress, who is laden with shopping bags. The customers have been coming here for years for the couture evening wear, which varies from the invisibly conservative to the theatrically dramatic. The dressing rooms are lovely, the atmosphere is plush in that Miami sort of way, and the prices are irrelevant.

Missoni
836 Madison Ave.
(69th St.)
517-9339
Mon. to Sat. 10:00 A.M. to 6:00 P.M.

Those distinctive stripey patterns are housed in a black, clean-line, mirrored boutique in the corner of the Westbury. If Kenzo (across the street) doesn't suit your natural style, you may be delighted with a Missoni scarf, tie, pillow, cap, sweater set or any of the handsome clothing for men and women.

Sonia Rykiel Boutique
792 Madison Ave.
(67th St.)
744-0880

The black and white decor, understatedly elegant, is a perfect backdrop for Rykiel's simple knits. This shop is small and crowded with uptown customers and shelves of the distinctive stripes, sweater sets and oversize dresses. Prices are exactly what you would expect from this French diva, and for most of the customers, $300 for a

Mon. to Sat. 9:30 A.M. to 6:30 P.M. (Thurs. to 7:30 P.M.)

pullover bowed sweater is no more an affront than the $450 (and up) price tags on the dresses.

Saint Laurent Rive Gauche
855 Madison Ave. (71st St.)
988-3821
Mon. to Sat. 10:00 A.M. to 6:00 P.M.

The granddaddy of them all. This contemporary shop with aluminum ceilings and maroon walls is layered with Saint Laurent prêt-à-porter. You'll find everything from his most beautiful and wearable styles to those questionable prints and overexaggerated day looks. Some of the evening clothes are quite lovely, but the selection is less exciting than at its Parisian sister. Prices are for shoppers who never ask.

Tahari
802 Madison Ave. (67th St.)
535-1515
Mon. to Sat. 10:30 A.M. to 6:30 P.M. (Thurs. to 8:00 P.M.)

These beautifully tailored designs are offered in superb fabrics. You'll find the most impeccable blazers and gabardine suits, gorgeous silk blouses and a profusion of other handsome clothes. The looks are perfect for office to evening, and the prices are affordable considering that clothes of this quality will last you many years to come. The shop may seem snobby at first, but the sales staff eventually warms up, even if you intend only to browse.

Emmanuel Ungaro
803 Madison Ave. (68th St.)
249-4090
Mon. to Sat. 10:00 A.M. to 6:00 P.M.

This mirrored shop is full of the lovely Ungaro clothes that are simple, not fussy, and made with incredibly delicious fabrics. The young sales staff models the look, making the rather costly merchandise most appealing and accessible. Browsers are welcome, and the store has a pleasant, expensive atmosphere.

Discount

Barami
659 Lexington Ave. (55th St.)
759-1190
Mon. to Sat. 10:00 A.M. to 8:00 P.M.

This corner store is often filled with attractive merchandise, labels intact, for substantial discounts. Most of the fabrics are natural; you'll find some Carol Little and even Oscar de la Renta amid the more commonplace manufacturers. It's worth a stop now and then to check out the new shipments and take advantage of the sales. This friendly extended Iranian family also runs a sister shop, Touran, at 693 Lexington Ave. (980-9333). The helpful sales staff shuttles back and forth between stores to find the perfect size for you.

Bolton's
225 W. 57th St.
755-2527
Mon. to Sat. 10:00 A.M. to 6:45 P.M. (Mon. and Thurs. to 8:45

You have to struggle through the clutter here, but if you persevere you can find some excellent bargains in traditional, classic styles. Don't expect anything particularly fashionable, as it's strictly middle of the road, with plenty of blends and basics. Customers can outfit

P.M.); Sun. noon to 4:45 P.M.

themselves from head almost to toe—only shoes are missing from the selection. There are frequent specials on selected manufacturers, but it requires many visits to unearth anything that is especially stylish. Several other branches throughout town.

Chez Aby, Ltd.
77-79 Delancey St.
(Orchard St.)
431-6135
Mon. to Fri. 10:00 A.M to 6:00 P.M.; Sun. 9:00 A.M. to 6:00 P.M.

You'll find some very unusual European imports at nicely reduced prices. These styles are au courant in Italy and France, so you'll be sure to be the first in your neighborhood to show up in contemporary designs for half the usual price. A limited selection, but some good finds if you check in periodically.

Damages
766 Madison Ave.
(65th St.)
535-9030
Mon. to Sat. 10:00 A.M. to 6:30 P.M.

You can discover fabulous silks here amid some other, more unfortunate styles that warrant their markdown prices. The enthusiastic Russian manager makes everyone feel at home, encouraging you to make good selections and flatter yourself. It takes a little work to unearth the beautiful blouses, suits and dresses that make this place such a find. Merchandise sticks around from season to season, so don't be surprised by seeing summer frocks for sale in the dead of winter. The styles are mostly European and mostly good bargains.

Design Liquidators
2045 Broadway
(71st St.)
787-3954
Mon. to Sat. 10:00 A.M. to 8:30 P.M.; Sun. noon to 6:00 P.M.

An enormous store filled with clothes perfect for career executives and career hostesses alike. There is so much Liz Claiborne, Cathy Hardwick and Pierre Cardin that one wonders if this is a outlet for these designers. You'll see the same things at full price in other stores during the same season. It's worth checking in periodically to check out new arrivals: Dior and Harvé Benard suits, beautiful evening looks, lots of cotton and wool sweaters, skirts, trousers, silk blouses, belts—everything you need to outfit yourself and update your wardrobe, and all at discounted prices. A very good address.

Emotional Outlet
242 E. 51st St.
838-0707
Mon. to Fri. 11:00 A.M. to 7:45 P.M.; Sat. 11:00 A.M. to 6:45 P.M.; Sun. 11:00 A.M. to 5:45 P.M.

This two-story store is a great address if you have time to hunt for bargains. The labels remain in the discounted clothes, so you know exactly what you're getting. Sales here are superb (sometimes more than half off), and there are plenty of accessories that you may find you can't live without. The atmosphere is unusually pleasant; you'll be offered a cup of coffee or glass of wine, and impatient men are kept occupied at a table stocked with newspapers. The shoe/leather department is under separate management, but the discounted designer styles are quite attractive. The sales staff is very welcoming, you're free to browse at a leisurely pace, and no doubt you'll leave with one of those red plastic bags filled with treasures (there's a selection of lingerie, too). All sales are final. Another location at Seventh Avenue and 16th Street (206-7750).

Encore
1132 Madison Ave.
2nd floor
(84th St.)
879-2850
Mon. to Sat. 10:30 A.M. to 6:00 P.M.

You may pass some of the rich and famous who drop off their clothes here as you climb the stairs to this second-floor resale shop. Amid the packed racks you will see designer suits, separates, sweaters and dresses that have been worn once or twice until their owners became bored with them. Some items even have the original sales tags intact, victims, we assume, of a change of heart. Upstairs you'll find evening wear that you may have seen only yesterday in the "Eye" column of *W*. Shoppers appear to be savvy, and you may be joined by some rather dramatic-looking transvestites stocking up.

Fishkin
314 Grand St.
(Allen St.)
226-6538
Mon. to Thurs. 10:00 A.M. to 4:45 P.M.; Fri. 10:00 A.M. to 3:45 P.M.; Sun. 9:00 A.M. to 4:30 P.M.

This is the granddaddy of them all in the Orchard Street area. If you find something you love at Ann Taylor or Bloomingdale's and you call these friendly people, they'll do their best to find it for you and cut the price considerably. Loads of Harvé Benard, Crazy Horse, Williwear, Fern and Mason, Finity, Tahari—fabulous sportswear at terrific savings. The place is crowded, because smart New York shoppers know that Fishkin's prices, service and selection of merchandise can't be beat. Two other branches at 318 Grand Street (for New Wavish styles and jeans) and 63 Orchard Street (for more tailored, elegant sportswear and suits). One of the best services Fishkin offers is mail-order delivery.

Labels For Less
1116 Third Ave.
(66th St.)
628-1100
Mon. to Fri. 10:00 A.M. to 7:30 P.M.; Sat. 10:00 A.M. to 6:00 P.M.; Sun. noon to 5:00 P.M.

The labels are less, but not substantially so. Still, you'll find some very attractive things from such designers as Calvin Klein, Larry Levine and Harvé Benard at about 20 percent off normal retail. This place is particularly good for suits, casual trousers and jeans; the selection of blouses tends to the polyester. Locations throughout New York.

Peta Lewis
1120 Lexington Ave.
(78th St.)
2nd floor
744-7660
Mon. to Sat. 11:00 A.M. to 7:00 P.M. (Thurs. to 8:00 P.M.); Sun. 1:00 P.M. to 5:00 P.M.

This is a very good place for designer suits (John Anthony, Dianne B) and jackets that are appropriate for the working woman. It's a well-organized, pleasant place to shop, and while you won't find any absolute steals, the prices aren't bad—about 30 percent less than full retail.

New Store
289 Seventh Ave.
(27th St.)

In this nondescript Orchard Street store you'll find racks of bargains, from luscious silk Levante and classic Ralph Lauren to trendy Yukiko Hanai and Cathy Hardwick. The

741-1077
Mon. to Fri. 10:00 A.M. to 8:00 P.M.; Sat. and Sun. 10:00 A.M. to 6:30 P.M.

selection requires some sifting, but the discounts are good, and the styles are generally au courant and wearable. A favorite among F.I.T. students across the street and New Yorkers who resent paying uptown prices.

Large · Small

Helga Howie
733 Madison Ave.
(64th St.)
861-5155
Mon. to Sat. 10:00 A.M. to 6:00 P.M.

This San Franciscan designer has a magic touch for designs on the bias. Although the clothes may not look superb on the hangers, once you try them on you may be converted to her unique styling. Many of the styles are particularly flattering for the larger-size woman, yet there is plenty here for the smaller customer as well. The sales staff is wonderful; these friendly ladies will introduce you to Ms. Howie's designs and sell you on the finer points. Prices are Madison Avenue.

Petite Pleasures
1192 Madison Ave.
(87th St.)
369-3437
Mon. to Sat. 10:30 A.M. to 6:30 P.M.; Sun. noon to 4:00 P.M.

Pretty clothes for smaller sizes (up to size ten). You'll find sportswear, dresses and anything else you need to complete a petite wardrobe in this little shop. Salespeople are helpful, and the prices are reasonable. No haute couture, but some extremely wearable clothes.

Piaffe
841 Madison Ave.
(69th St.)
744-9911
Mon. to Sat. 10:00 A.M. to 6:00 P.M. (Tues. to Thurs. to 7:00 P.M.); Sun. noon to 5:00 P.M.

If you're tiny, come to this boutique filled with elegant, classic and amusing clothes designed for the petite woman. The saleswomen will make you feel right at home as they model the current styles, and they are sincerely helpful with hard-to-fit customers. Prices are as reasonable as one might hope for with such small delicacies.

Lingerie

Joovay
436 W. Broadway
(Prince St.)
431-6386
Daily noon to 7:00 P.M.

There are some very pretty cotton nighties, camisoles, silk panties and robes in this minuscule shop. Prices are fairly reasonable, and you may be able to find a ravishing pink and gray satin robe, a Chinese embroidered gown, some delicate, barely there panties or silken camisoles that are perfect as seductive sleepers.

La Lingerie
792 Madison Ave.
(67th St.)
772-9797

The lingerie here is so incredibly pretty that you can't imagine actually wearing it and mussing it up. The styles are strictly romantic, with beautiful satins, silks and high-quality synthetics. The all-cotton nighties and peignoir

Mon. to Sat. 10:00 A.M. to 6:30 P.M. (Thurs. to 7:00 P.M.)

Monten-apoleone
**789 Madison Ave.
(67th St.)
535-2660**
Mon. to Fri. 10:00 A.M. to 6:00 P.M.; Sat. 10:00 A.M. to 5:30 P.M.

Porthault
**57 E. 57th St.
688-1660**
Mon. to Fri. 9:30 A.M. to 5:30 P.M.; Sat. to 4:30 P.M.

Roberta
**1252 Madison Ave.
(90th St.)
860-8366**
Mon. to Sat. 10:00 A.M. to 6:00 P.M.

Wife Mistress
**1042 Lexington Ave.
(74th St.)
570-9529**
Mon. to Fri. 11:00 A.M. to 7:00 P.M.; Sat. 11:00 A.M. to 6:00 P.M.

sets are extraordinary, as the $500-plus price tags reflect. There are some very lovely all-cotton bras and panties, lacy sachets, special hangers, camisoles and nightgowns that will make you send your millionaire husband or boyfriend here at birthday, Christmas or Valentine's Day time.

This pretty boutique is without doubt one of the best addresses in New York for exquisite lingerie. The all-cotton and lace nighties are stunning (as are the prices). Even the synthetic-blend nightgowns here have a refinement that nearly belies the fabrications. Peignoir sets, dressing gowns, a limited line of underwear—each item is more beautiful than the next. You will shop alongside generous mothers on trousseau outings with their soon-to-be-married daughters. Wedding or no, it is hard to resist the seduction of these beautiful European imports. A less impressive collection of swimwear is available upstairs; the designs are classic Pucci-esque Italian styles that are good for conservative sunbathers of all ages.

The crystal chandeliers and formal atmosphere run counter to the lively floral prints, but they perfectly match the reserved welcome. It's a veritable spring bouquet of feminine fabrics, with the distinctive flower theme on everything from sheets to towels to terrycloth robes to exquisite cotton nighties. There are also plain white cotton nightgowns with embroidered detailing and perfect cotton and eyelet robes, all of which are priced within the realm of possibility. This is not haute elegance, but it's very pretty nonetheless, in that Hamptons summer porch style.

This successful boutique offers a full line of lingerie, from a great collection of knee socks and pantyhose to leotards and peignoir sets. The Ellen Stein designs are as beautiful as they are expensive, and you will find it hard to resist the all-cotton nighties or the Dior negligees of a more sophisticated allure. A welcoming staff and a friendly Bouvier de Flandres shop dog are all part of the daily routine here.

An intimate little shop where the windows seem to have all the pretty merchandise. The helpful sales staff, however, will scout out the perfect silk camisole with matching G-string, charming Lebaby French lingerie, a sweet blouson teddy, slinky gowns designed by Ellen Stein, Ora Feder, Holly Luders and Fernando Sanchez, innocent cotton nighties and some lovely bras and matching panties. A fairly good selection with good prices, although this place appears to be better for basics than for riotous impulse purchases.

Lady Madonna
816 Madison Ave.
(67th St.)
988-7173
Mon. to Sat. 10:30 A.M. to 6:00 P.M. (Thurs. to 8:00 P.M.)

This trendy store has been keeping expectant mothers in style for years. Thank heavens there is this alternative to the Sears Roebuck smock look for nine months. Customers here have a free choice of clever, fashionable, flattering styles. Prices tend to be a little steep, considering the limited period of the clothes' usefulness, but some styles can be worn after the baby is born.

Romantic/Lace

Anita Pagliaro
1030 Lexington Ave.
(73rd St.)
737-2684
Mon. to Sat. 11:00 A.M. to 6:00 P.M.

Beautiful lace blouses, wedding dresses, smocks, hats and gowns are crowded into this small shop. These are originals designed by Ms. Pagliaro herself, and many are modeled after antique Victorian patterns. Prices may seem expensive, but they are actually quite reasonable given the work and originality evident in each piece.

Rubicon
849 Madison Ave.
(70th St.)
861-3000
Mon. to Sat. 10:00 A.M. to 5:30 P.M.

The charming woman who owns this shop has a very personal approach to dressing. Recycling estate collections of lace into the most romantic gowns imaginable, she has a loyal roster of customers who come back year after year for yet another tea dress, Victorian blouse, wedding gown or even a pricey prom dress. The prices are steep, but the quality of these handmade, highly feminine clothes is beyond question. It's worth a stop here even if only to look.

Department Stores

B. Altman
Fifth Avenue and
34th Street
679-7800
Mon. to Sat. 10:00 A.M. to 6:00 P.M. (Thurs. to 8:00 P.M.)

The main floor is still elegant in a nineteenth-century way, staid and serious with its white columns, wooden fixtures and lofty ceilings. But there is no way to relieve the tedium of this store—even Krizia, Fendi and Versace get lost in the old-fashioned decor. However, the service is top-notch, the quality reliable and the merchandise occasionally exciting. The lower midtown location continues to be a liability for Altman's, as most upscale shoppers keep more uptown unless they're visiting Macy's. The monogrammed shopping bags, though, are still classics, and you can probably find what you need in a more serene environment than at the other, trendier New York stores.

Barney's
106 Seventh Ave.
(17th St.)
929-9000
Mon. to Fri. 10:00 A.M. to 9:00 P.M.; Sat. 10:00 A.M. to 8:00 P.M.

Barney's is everything they say, plus more. Its image is definitely geared toward the fashionable European, as illustrated by their Tuileries TV ad. You'll find acres of beautiful imports for men and women here. The men's departments far outnumber the ladies', and the most conservative to the most avant-garde can be found somewhere within the five-story, two-building complex. The third floor, for men, is clearly the most exciting, with the new wave of Japanese designers and contemporary menswear, all surveyed by a highly visual clientele. But superbly elegant dressers prefer the British Room and the Oak Room, where pleated trousers and finely tailored jackets are endlessly racked up. There is truly something for every man here: Armani, Klein, Lauren, Ellis, Basile, you name it.

Women have a much smaller but equally eclectic choice from the most au courant Rykiel, Rhodes, Missoni, Basile, Ellis, Kenzo and Versace in their duplex penthouse, with the classics represented by Mr. Everywhere, Ralph Lauren. Prices are serious, but these fashion statements are for women for whom price is not an issue.

Barney's also carries a small line of home furnishings and has attractive hostesses in each department, a friendly sales staff, a very interesting clientele and a sale annex across the street that New Yorkers adore. Barney's is one of a kind, and indispensable.

Henri Bendel
10 W. 57th St.
247-1100
Mon. to Sat. 10:00 A.M. to 6:00 P.M. (Thurs. to 8:00 P.M.)

This dynamic store is arguably the most innovative retail institution in New York City, even with its concession to prep, the Ralph Lauren department. The first floor is worth a visit if for no other reason than to browse through the honeycomb of upscale boutiques that seem to be perpetually filled with customers. The energy level, fashionable clientele and slightly arrogant sales staff create an environment that is both fascinating and intimidating to the newcomer. There are four floors of trend-setting, avant-garde, clever clothes, most of which manage to be eminently wearable. Geraldine Stutz has established an open forum for young, innovative designers, many of whom are blessed with the privilege of having Bendel's as a showcase for their fledgling designs. Of course, you see what can happen to some of these ingenues with the phenomenal success of Mary

McFadden: Bendel's sanction often guarantees success. Customers love to shop for Zandra Rhodes, the more conservative Jean Muir, everybody's first love, Perry Ellis, and the dozens of other designers housed in the fur department, Savvy section, Shoe Biz footwear headquarters and so on. The elegant fragrance department is civilized, Eli Zabar has a mini branch of E.A.T. on the first floor, the ultraexpensive Walter Steiger has a shoe branch. All join forces in helping you spend a great deal of money to achieve that spontaneously fashionable look trapped on the pages of *W* and *Vogue*. Christmas here is a fantasy, as are the disturbing yearlong window displays.

Bergdorf Goodman
754 Fifth Ave. (58th St.)
753-7300
Mon. to Sat. 10:00 A.M. to 6:00 P.M. (Thurs. to 8:00 P.M.)

The main floor looks slightly akin to a petit palais, with its chandeliers, ornate walls and feminine atmosphere, appropriate for its rococo personality. Fendi is here. So are Claude Montana, Krizia, Maud Frizon, Zoron and Pasta and Cheese. Elegance is Bergdorf's signature, and sophisticated ladies from all over the world shop here because they prefer to be treated like royalty instead of like unknowns, as is the case in other New York stores. The new escalators make shopping here somewhat faster than it used to be. The lingerie department is superb, and the menswear area continues to be an exercise in good taste. The place appears to be a bit drowsy and behind the times, but the fifth floor may well change your mind with its series of minishops featuring some of the best and most exciting designers working today. The BG windows still dress up Fifth Avenue and will no doubt seduce you into venturing inside for a moment of luxurious tranquility far from the Lexington Avenue maddening crowd.

Bloomingdale's
1000 Third Ave. (59th St.)
355-5900
Mon. to Sat. 10:00 A.M. to 6:30 P.M. (Mon. and Thurs. to 9:00 P.M.); Sun. noon to 5:00 P.M.

Without doubt, Bloomingdale's is the most exciting and dynamic department store in New York City (although some people think Macy's is quickly catching up, but then perhaps they work there). In any case, this institution continues to be one of the first stopping-off places for both visitors and professionals in the retail trade when they arrive in the city—for good reason, as there is always something happening here. The new Delicacies food department is Bloomingdale's effort to make this area as vital as the rest of the store. Petrossian and Guérard are here, and the store has added a new bar/café (Tasting Bar) in the basement, capitalizing on the America's renewed interest in good wines and new foods. As for the rest of the store, there is still an excellent selection of menswear, the lingerie department offers seductive (and often expensive) pretties, the contemporary department on the third floor is still exciting (although the merchandise is crammed into a limited space), the better sportswear around the corner is looking a bit conservative, but the designer areas are provocative and easy to shop in. The Main Course continues to be a winner, with a well-designed demonstration area and frequent tastings and promotions filling up Saturday afternoons. And there are still people who come to Bloomie's just to see the room displays on the fifth floor, which change four times a year. Our only reservation about this glorious establishment is the main floor, with its Biba-esque decor that makes finding things a persistent challenge. Somehow all those chic dark walls make the space theatrically forbidding, and it takes only one wrong turn to bump into one of those black walls. They spent a fortune on the renovation several years ago, so we guess the world has learned to live with it, but we feel something lighter and less dramatic would create a better welcome. When you need relief, Le Train Bleu on the sixth floor offers acceptable cuisine and a marvelous interior design complete with an urban view of East Side rooftops.

Bonwit Teller
4–10 E. 57th St.
593-3333
Mon. to Fri. 10:00 A.M. to 7:00 P.M. (Thurs. to 8:00 P.M.); Sat. 10:00 A.M. to 6:00 P.M.

Bonwit Teller is undergoing a renaissance now that it opens onto New York's most recent salute to Houston, Trump Tower. Perhaps this monument in red marble, copper and classic Texas pretension will help attract more tourists to Bonwit's, supplementing its clientele of ladies imported from Connecticut and Westchester. It's not hard to understand why the store has such a conservative following; the place looks and feels as if it would be more at home in Grosse Pointe than on 57th Street. It is a singularly suburban design that is slightly out of step in this sophisticated international city. The merchandise is to be expected—nothing particularly avant-garde, but plenty of safe styles tucked away on floors of departments that seem to us to be a bit overcrowded and stuffily designed. The best aspect of Bonwit remains the delicate violet florals on the shopping bags, a vestige of the days when this store was a venerable institution to be reckoned with, back when everyone's great-aunt came here to update her conservative seasonal wardrobe.

Gimbel's
Broadway and 33rd Street
564-3300
Mon. to Fri. 9:45 A.M. to 8:30 P.M.

Gimbel's is beginning to look a little downscale, particularly the dreary uptown branch (at 86th Street and Lexington Avenue, 348-2300), which would look more appropriate in Ohio. Even the designer womenswear is jammed alongside everything else, giving a bored, tired

(Tues. and Wed. to 6:45 P.M.); Sat. 9:45 A.M. to 6:30 P.M.; Sun. noon to 6:00 P.M.

Lord & Taylor
424 Fifth Ave.
(38th St.)
391-3344
Mon. to Sat. 10:00 A.M. to 6:00 P.M. (Thurs. to 8:00 P.M.)

Macy's
Herald Square
(W. 34th
St.-Broadway)
695-4400
Mon. to Fri. 9:45 A.M. to 8:30 P.M. (Tues. and Wed. to 6:45 P.M.) Sat. to 6:00 P.M.; Sun. noon to 6:00 P.M.

look to the floors. Clearly some merchandising effort is required to brighten things up a bit. The prices are commensurate with the low overhead, but it's so sad to shop here that the temptation to rush over to Macy's becomes more than a force of habit.

This palace of mirrors with Belle Epoque hanging lamps retains an old-world elegance but generates little excitement. It continues to be a conservative place with a clientele to match. Even the designer departments lack any noticeable drama, although all the classics are here: Donald Brooks, Gloria Sachs, both Kleins and Ralph Lauren. The Fantasia department on the third floor has some more innovative fashions, a counterbalance to the Nancy Reagan look that is so ubiquitous here. There is a very elegant ladies' shoe department on the fourth floor, the Soup Bar on the tenth floor (where you can recuperate from the nondescript menswear department) and a series of floors and departments that look like the kind of good old-fashioned retailing that is still flourishing in Cedar Rapids, Iowa. But we love Lord & Taylor because you can occasionally find great styles designed exclusively for the store, and there are excellent sales in January and July.

Macy's continues its renaissance with one department after another updated, revamped and redesigned to bring plenty more retail excitement to Herald Square. The most recent makeover is the main floor: its art deco Hollywood movie set columns and lowered ceilings create an energetic lightness. The boutiques lining the balcony offer a sophisticated mélange of gifts and clothes, with sources ranging from the Met to Santini e Domenici. The fourth floor, a veritable New Wave disco, houses junior merchandise, made all the more interesting with audiovisual shows, environmental art display fixtures and the pounding drive of New Wave music that draws the young crowds here to stock up on the latest. Macy's clearly has the key to flexibility and adaptation to the marketplace. The third floor continues to be a gold mine of designer clothes, with the Europeans alongside the Americans (the classic Lauren and romantic Ashley have their own boutiques downstairs). The basement Cellar still packs in the Saturday crowds, and the P.J. Clarke's offshoot does a land-office business. Porthault and Pratesi are on six, Gucci and Vuitton are on one. There is something for everyone in this enormous arena, and no doubt you'll love the sixth floor women's shoe department as much as the kids love their toys on the fifth floor and their parents like the acres of home furnishings on the seventh and ninth floors and the sweet temptations on two. Macy's is giving the city a run for its money, and the twenty-first-century excitement here is worth a visit. And thank God for Macy's when it comes to the holidays; how could New York survive without fireworks, Santa Claus or the Thanksgiving Day parade?

Saks Fifth Avenue
611 Fifth Ave. (50th St.)
753-4000
Mon. to Sat. 10:30 A.M. to 6:00 P.M.

This old-fashioned store has all the old-fashioned charm that made Saks everyone's grandmother's favorite store. Today, the merchandise is more exciting, although much of it you can find elsewhere for slightly less. The floors, designed around a central core like some sort of stationary lazy Susan, are a pleasure to shop on and offer irresistible merchandise. The contemporary departments are still great, and the menswear floor is filled with impeccable merchandise. The cosmetics department is one of the most popular and busiest in town, the designer floor tasteful and luxurious and the main level a honeycomb of quality (and questionable) accessories. The little freestanding boutiques on 50th Street carry superb leather accessories, stationery, gifts and more up-to-date active sportswear. The Vuitton boutique on 49th Street offers its expensive, pretentious array of vinyl. Saks is essential to New York, and it continues to bathe its clientele in an atmosphere of luxury and wealth, merely second nature to these fortunate souls.

Flowers

Bouquets à la Carte
419 E. 77th St.
2nd floor
535-3720
Mon. to Fri. 8:30 A.M. to 5:00 P.M.; Sat. 9:00 A.M. to 1:00 P.M.

Success in its 83rd Street shop has resulted in a business that is now conducted primarily by phone order. These clever people continue to make elegant or country-looking basket arrangements starting at $30. The specialty is a three-foot helium-filled balloon, to which a wicker basket brimming with flowers and candy or Champagne is attached by cascades of ribbons, streamers and paper flowers. Flowers are combined with stuffed toys and other gifts appropriate to specific occasions: magazines and candy with a floral basket for shut-ins, roses and Champagne for anniversaries. Traditional blooms are offered as well, and there are all sorts of distinctive containers: vases, baskets, teapots, bottles or cedar crates. The staff will arrange flowers for a party.

Pamela Duval
**680 Madison Ave.
(61st–62nd sts.)
751-2126**
Mon. to Sat. 9:30 A.M. to 5:30 P.M.

The window is decorated with old-fashioned needlepoint cushions embroidered with newfangled mottos, such as "Old lovers are better lovers." The shop itself is minuscule and so crammed with really very ordinary lamps, vases, knickknacks and the like that it's difficult to clear a path. But the silk flowers are magnificent, (though much less unusual than at Diane Love), and they are made into very pleasing arrangements. Nothing extraordinary or particularly original, but they're the perfect sort of thing to adorn a chest of drawers or an elegant store window.

Equipoise
**167 Seventh Avenue
South
(Perry St.)
807-7533**
*Tues. to Sat. 11:00 A.M. to
7:00 P.M.*

This unexpected art gallery–cum–floral design studio displays original airbrush artwork alongside flamboyant vases and floral arrangements. Florian Ceglarek and his staff of five are known for their eccentric and artistic arrangements, often incorporating a client's favorite object into a floral design that becomes part of the home environment. They guarantee the life of the plants they sell and service, which can be useful if you love bonsai and don't have a green thumb. Small floral arrangements begin at $30; consultation in the home runs $100 an hour.

Flowers on the Square
**1886 Broadway
(62nd–63rd sts.)
397-5882**
*Mon. to Fri. 9:00 A.M. to 7:00
P.M.; Sat. 10:00 A.M. to 6:00 P.M.*

Flowers are treated as works of art and are arranged in highly stylized displays. This place is sumptuous—the antithesis of the corner florist. The orchids are particularly stunning. Arrangements start at $35, and flowers can be bought individually.

Frangipani
**433 W. 34th St.
947-4249**
*Mon. to Fri. 11:00 A.M. to 7:00
P.M.; Sat. 9:30 A.M. to 7:00 P.M.*

The Japanese influence is at work here, where exotic flowers are used in extremely stylish arrangements starting at $25. If a Broadway actor were to send you unusual flowers, he'd probably call Frangipani. It delivers throughout the metropolitan area.

Irene Hayes Wadley & Smythe Lemoult
**1 Rockefeller Plaza
(48th Street and Fifth
Avenue)
247-0051**
*Mon. to Fri. 8:00 A.M. to 6:00
P.M.; Sat. 8:00 A.M. to 1:00 P.M.*

If any traditional New York florist enjoys particular fame, it is Irene Hayes, the first lady of flowers. She has merged with five other florists and now has a staff of 50, who continue to carry flowers and plants of high quality, even renting plants and providing party decorations. Her delivery trucks are visible throughout the city, making the rounds among the initiated. This is New York's largest retail florist, reached via FTD from around the world.

Evan G. Hughes
**522A Third Ave.
(35th St.)
683-2441**
*Mon. to Sat. 9:00 A.M. to
6:00 P.M.*

A treasure trove in an unexpected part of town, Evan Hughes has kept his clients satisfied with sensible prices for excellent-quality flowers and beautiful plants, which are displayed among the eighteenth- and nineteenth-century American country antiques for sale in his shop. He prepares fresh arrangements from $20 and excels in the country French and Flemish provincial styles. He also takes custom orders for silk flower arrangements (from $50), in your container or his. For gift givers, he prepares terrific wicker baskets filled with fruit, flowers, wine and cheese (from $45). Party and wedding services are available as well.

Japan Nursery
**135 W. 28th St.
947-6953**
*Mon. to Fri. 8:30 A.M. to 5:30
P.M.; Sat. 11:00 A.M. to 5:30 P.M.*

Lovers of Japanese gardens will like this shop, which specializes in the famous bonsai trees. The trees may be miniature, but the prices are not: you are buying living proof that a little perfection is worth more than a whole jungle. It also carries containers, nursery supplies and everything you need for Japanese gardening.

Diane Love
**851 Madison Ave.
(70th–71st sts.)
879-6997**
Mon. to Sat. 9:30 A.M. to 5:30 P.M.

Walk in and you are engulfed with an intoxicating scent of potpourri mixed from rose and jasmine—Diane Love's special concoction, which has been packaged in a complete line of room fragrance products, including candles and room spray. Her magnificent, exotic silk flowers have made her name, but they aren't the only attractions. She also sells all sorts of objects brought back from her voyages and things she herself has designed: art deco jewelry, lacquer boxes, bowls, and trays, and embroidered Chinese handbags and kimonos in old silk from the '20s and '30s are among her treasures. She has added 3,000 square feet upstairs, creating a gallery of decorative accessories and furnishings for the home, with that exclusive Diane Love decorator touch.

Mädderlake
**25 E. 73rd St.
879-8400**
Mon. to Fri. 9:00 A.M. to 5:00 P.M.

New York's affinity for the unusual floral arrangement began with Mädderlake, and the love affair is still going on in its new location. With different owners, it is also well known for garden and terrace designs and installations. When you leave town, it will service your indoor and outdoor plants. The selection of orchids, flowering plants and antique American baskets is broad and tasteful. English garden arrangements start at $50. Mädderlake makes dreams come true with choice flowers for weddings and parties.

Ronaldo Maia
**27 E. 67th St.
288-1049**

This elegant florist designs unusual containers and bud vases to house distinctive Dutch flowers and his own blend of potpourri. A simple basket of potpourri or a bud

Mon. to Fri. 9:30 A.M. to 6:00
P.M.; Sat. (Sept. to June) 11:00
A.M. to 5:00 P.M.

vase with an exquisite blossom starts at $25. The arrangements themselves (from $50 to $100) are usually presented in baskets or custom-designed vases. Customers are treated with polish, whether they come for an unusual plant or complete party services.

Manhattan Flower Works
255 W. 17th St.
620-0035
Tues. to Fri. 10:00 A.M. to 7:30 P.M.; Sat 10:00 A.M. to 6:00 P.M.; Sun. noon to 5:00 P.M.

Enter through the massive green wrought iron gates of what was once a turn-of-the-century warehouse in Chelsea, and you're greeted with spectacular artificial floral displays—10,000 square feet covered with no less than 812 varieties of flowers and 125 species of trees. Robert Currie has designed a multilevel environment for these artificial flowers, spotlighting them under green and white umbrellas, as you might see in a European market. Shop to the sounds of waterfalls, birds chirping and Handel's "Water Music," filling your own vase or one of the many containers or willow baskets. For a design fee of $10 an hour, the helpful staff arranges flowers (silk, synthetics, blends, velvet and linen, all made in China) and feathers to match your swatches. (Arrangements average $30.)

Marlo Flowers
421 E. 73rd St.
628-2246
Mon. to Fri. 11:00 A.M. to 8:00 P.M.

Marlo's world is nineteenth-century Victorian England and sixteenth- to seventeenth-century Holland. The exquisite taste of this floral designer is apparent the moment you enter the lace-curtained door of her antique-laden studio. A ceiling fan circulates the air among the potted orchids growing from two to six feet high alongside a white brick wall. Marlo's customers share her passion for old-world "flower pieces," which she wraps beautifully with antique ribbons and nosegays. Her gossamer arrangements are delicately set into old baskets, Chinese vases or early American pottery. She also designs flowery English perennial garden borders for a discerning, exclusive clientele.

Renny
27 E. 62nd St.
371-5354
Mon. to Sat. 9:30 A.M. to 6:00 P.M.

A veritable architect of bouquets, this young man brims with talent and taste and creates unusual designed arrangements, using imported flowers so beautiful that one bloom is sometimes enough. Another Renny location, at 1018 Lexington Avenue, between 72nd and 73rd streets (371-5354), offers plants and flowers in a spare but striking setting. Floral arrangements start at $35.

Salou
452A Columbus Ave.
(81st–82nd sts.)

The original owner of Mädderlake has set up his own charming shop, with a wonderful formula for pleasing his regular customers. His special gift ideas include

595-9604
Mon. to Fri. 9:00 A.M. to 7:00 P.M.; Sat. 10:00 A.M. to 5:00 P.M.

"flowers of the month" in glass vases, flowering plants (potted in terra-cotta), bouquets or mixed arrangements delivered six to twelve times a year. For sick friends, he suggests flowers with magazines, books or chicken soup, and he sends flowers with stuffed animals, candy or cake for children. Beautifully styled arrangements start at $35; a vase of roses accompanied by domestic Champagne starts at $50.

Southflower Market
55th Street and Second Avenue
335-6800
Mon. to Sat. 10:00 A.M. to 9:00 P.M.; Sun. noon to 6:00 P.M.

Southflower Market is the brainchild of a former banker who decided to bring flowers out from behind refrigerator doors and make them accessible to the public. In this bright, cheerful shop, you select from up to 80 varieties of common and uncommon flowers, purchasing by the stem from bushels of blooms. Prices range from 79 cents for freesia to $4.29 for gloriosa lilies. A stem of orchids is $2.99; gerbera (vibrantly colored African daisies) are $1.39. Helpful salespeople aid the timid in arranging bouquets, but after a few visits most get hooked on the hands-on experience. Your bouquet is wrapped European style in cellophane and ribbons. The store carries a limited choice of containers and potted plants. Its newest branch is in Macy's Cellar (695-4400), and there's another location at Columbus Avenue and 68th Street (496-7100).

Surroundings
2295 Broadway (83rd St.)
580-8982
Mon. to Sat. 10:00 A.M. to 7:00 P.M.; Sun. (Sept. to June) 11:30 A.M. to 6:00 P.M.

This large three-story shop sells standard flowers, potted plants and containers to the neighborhood trade, but it is best known for its flamboyant arrangements designed for its most devoted customers, such as the Rainbow Room, the Russian Tea Room, Martha Graham and Barbra Streisand. In addition to a variety of creative arrangements (including ikebana), starting at $30, it offers wedding floral consultation, horticultural supplies and landscaping advice. The lower-level art gallery displays and sells works by 300 different ceramists amid exotic floral arrangements and bonsai trees.

Twigs
399 Bleecker St. (11th St.)
620-8188
Mon. to Fri. 10:30 A.M. to 7:00 P.M.; Sat. noon to 7:00 P.M.

Owner Paul Bott has created a charming, old-fashioned setting in his small Greenwich Village shop. His predilection for sixteenth-century French bouquets and a love of the traditional doesn't stop him and his staff of four designers from creating unusual displays for weddings, restaurants and stores. Floral arrangements in country baskets average $30 to $40 and are beautifully wrapped for delivery all over the city. Exquisite flowers are sold individually, and a small selection of plants spills out on the sidewalk.

Food

BAKERIES

Le Bagel Château
1026 Third Ave.
(60th–61st sts.)
755-5473
Mon. to Fri. 7:00 A.M. to 10:00 P.M.; Sat. 7:00 A.M. to 11:00 P.M.; Sun. 9:00 A.M. to 8:00 P.M.

These are the best bagels in the city. Plain, salt, onion, pumpernickel, cinnamon-raisin, poppy, sesame and garlic are 30¢ apiece, and all are made fresh before your eyes—this is what New York is all about. There are good cream cheeses and fish, lots of other toppings, hearty portions, half-sour pickles and decent coffee. At breakfast and lunch, the line can be out the door. Bloomingdale's buyers eat here.

Betsy's Place
236 W. 26th St.
691-5775
Mon. to Fri. 9:00 A.M. to 6:00 P.M.

If you like bread with fruits, dates, ginger and spices of all kinds, or if you are tempted by the idea of tasting among the best chocolate-bar cookies and butterscotch brownies in town, climb up the narrow stairs to this atticlike shop swimming with colors, scents and shapes. Bright yellow shopping bags for the whimsical and beautiful gift boxes for the gourmets.

Au Bon Pain
Citicorp Center
153 E. 53rd St.
838-6996
Mon. to Fri. 7:00 A.M. to 8:30 P.M.; Sat. 9:00 A.M. to 8:00 P.M.; Sun. 10:00 A.M. to 8:00 P.M.

Bread made with authentic French flour—it's supposed to make a big difference in the taste of the rolls and loaves of French bread. The croissants and brioches are better than in many other places, but are nonetheless quite unexceptional. The Plaza Hotel serves these rolls.

Bonté
1316 Third Ave.
(75th St.)
535-2360
Mon. to Sat. 9:00 A.M. to 6:30 P.M.

Bonté is New York's best French pastry shop. Selective, with a limited choice—but oh! of what wonders! Year-round specialties (cakes with butterscotch or Grand Marnier, strawberry mousse, millefeuille, tarte tatin) and seasonal creations (the strawberry pie is perfection) have earned Maurice Bonté the best pastrycook award in France and the United States. His croissants, palm leaves and miniature madeleines would win any prize for excellence hands down. If you want to order in quantity, you'd best call in advance, as the meticulous craftsmanship that permits such results is incompatible with mass production. But Bonté resembles any other small neighborhood shop and doesn't seem likely to change its unpretentious style. We hope it doesn't.

Colette
1136 Third Ave.
(66th St.)

Colette is the progenitor of French pastry shops in New York: her antiquated shop and ageless, unsmiling salesladies testify to that. But Colette has merits: her wide

988-2605
Tues. to Sat. 8:00 A.M. to 5:30 P.M.
on the dot

variety of quiches (mushroom, tomato, spinach, onion, piperade, crabmeat and lobster, plus quiche Lorraine) are still the best, and her cakes are of high quality. We should also mention her delicious brioches, her delicate cheese straws and her very thin butter cookies topped with mocha or lemon cream, aptly called "merveilleuses." Colette offers a few traditional, simply prepared French dishes as well.

Creative Cakes
400 E. 74th St.
794-9811
Tues. to Fri. 9:00 A.M. to 5:30
P.M.; Sat. 9:00 A.M. to 11:30 A.M.

Perhaps you're feeling imaginative and would like a cake in the form of an animal, a car or a portrait of a friend. Well, look up Stephanie Crookston: with the help of her top-secret family recipes, she'll bake up a rich chocolate fudge cake with buttercream icing to match your fantasy. Prices start at $75 for a cake that feeds twenty.

Le Croissant Shop
459 Lexington Ave.
(45th St.)
697-5580
Mon. to Fri. 6:30 A.M. to 7:00
P.M.; Sat. 8:00 A.M. to 6:00 P.M.;
Sun. 8:30 A.M. to 4:30 P.M.

Two to three thousand croissants freshly baked and sold each day—that's the difficult goal set and reached by a couple of young Frenchmen, who have managed to recreate in this blue boutique the atmosphere of a Parisian corner bakery. Sit at the typical French countertables to try these airy croissants served with fresh butter, or the cinnamon, ham or cheese croissants, sausage pies, quiches, apple turnovers, almond macaroons, chocolate mousse and Alpen Zauber ice cream, washed down with a good cup of coffee or a glass of milk or juice. A tasty and inexpensive treat in the French style. There's a takeout counter for crusty breads as well. Delivery and catering service.

David's Cookies
1018 Second Ave.
(54th St.)
888-1610
Mon. to Thurs. 10:00 A.M. to 11:00
P.M.; Fri. and Sat. 10:00 A.M. to
midnight; Sun. noon to 11:00 P.M.

New York is a cookie town, and David Liederman is the cookie king. His buttery rich cookies with chunks of semisweet Lindt chocolate have set new standards in Chipwich City. All are baked before your eyes, and the best ones are still oven warm. David's French bread, reputed to be the best in New York, tastes as though it just came off the Concorde. Actually, it's baked a few blocks away and is delivered fresh to all the David's outlets daily. At only $1.25 a baguette, it's easy to become addicted. David recently added crunchy cookie ice cream to his already rich repertoire. Many other locations.

Désirs la Côte Basque
1032 Lexington Ave.
(73rd–74th sts.)
535-3311
Daily 7:30 A.M. to 7:00 P.M.

The merits of this pastry shop (with Bonté, the best in town) are unquestionable, and its considerable reputation is admirably earned. As for its sweets, the almond biscuits and petits fours are particularly tasty. The chestnut pastry boats are an unforgettable experience in their own right, and the chocolate cakes are true decadence. The savories? Côte Basque prepares its own pâtés and makes a jambon persillé and a sausage en croûte that are both remarkable. These treats can be picked out from glass cases and enjoyed on the spot in its French-style tea rooms. The shop at the Olympic Tower (653 5th Avenue, near 51st Street, 935-2220) is modern and bright, and includes a café, restaurant and bar, but it's totally devoid of the other's rustic charm.

Dumas
148 E. 57th St.
688-0905
Mon. to Sat. 8:30 A.M. to 6:30 P.M.

Everything is good, but the Saint Honorés, meringues, nut and almond rings and cookies coated with caramel are particularly outstanding. There are excellent fruit pies with flaky crusts, and a reasonable choice of cheeses, quiches, pâtés, pickles, homemade jams (including wild strawberry) and French bread—everything you need for a simple feast, as long as your palate is not too picky. Dumas is facing stiff competition from its talented neighbors on all sides. No delivery. Sometimes frosty service. Other locations at 1330 Lexington Avenue, near 88th Street (369-3900), and 1042 Madison Avenue, near 79th Street (744-4804).

Epicurean Gallery, Ltd.
443 E. 75th St.
861-0453
Mon. to Sat. 9:30 A.M. to 6:00 P.M.

A minuscule blue and white shop filled with cakes and pies, most of which have just come out of the oven: fruit shortcake, cheesecake, blackout cake, streudels and Amaretto mousse cake, as well as all sorts of pies. There's also a reasonable selection of appetizers, soups, salads and entrees. Party planning and catering, as you might expect, and cooking classes, too.

Erotic Baker
73 W. 83rd St.
362-7557
Tues. to Sat. 11:00 A.M. to 8:00 P.M.

A part of the movement that burst the straitlaces of WASP America, this shop offers chocolate, sweets and almond paste in the shapes of sexual organs, naked women and their male counterparts. Tasteless cakes (pun intended) can be special ordered in any size. It also offers sexual potholders, toothbrushes and knickknacks. Various locations.

William Greenberg, Jr., Desserts
1377 Third Ave.
(79th St.)
861-1340

Butter Cake Squares
1100 Madison Ave.
(82nd St.)
744-0304
Mon. to Fri. 8:30 A.M. to 6:00 P.M.; Sat. 8:30 A.M. to 5:00 P.M.

These excellent, typically American pastry shops have such specialties as Danish rings, almond coffee rings, cinnamon coffee loaves, cheesecakes and a spectacular (to see as well as to savor) chocolate cake. The mouth-watering brownies, rich butter cookies and sticky honey buns are reputed to be the best in the metropolis, and we couldn't disagree. The tiny Madison Avenue shop specializes in variously flavored butter cakes, schnecken, cookies and hamantaschen. No layer cakes, but everything else, which is saying a lot. Mr. Greenberg is a true New York pastry chef who knows his clientele well but who is not particularly willing to make the effort necessary to attract new customers.

J.P.'s French Bakery
54 W. 55th St.
765-7575
Mon. to Fri. 7:00 A.M. to 8:00 P.M.; Sat. 8:00 A.M. to 7:00 P.M.; Sun. 9:00 A.M. to 5:00 P.M.

This is another exquisite small French bakery where you can stock up on bread, croissants of all kinds, palm leaves and turnovers. At lunchtime, grab a good pâté, ham, rillette or cheese sandwich or stuffed croissant. Takeout and delivery.

Kramer's Pastries
1643 Second Ave.
(86th St.)
535-5955
Mon. to Sat. 8:00 A.M. to 7:00 P.M.

A neighborhood baker who deserves special attention because of the quality of his moderately priced desserts. The petits fours, palm leaves, butter and chocolate cookies and "cigarettes russes" are true delicacies; the fruit pies beg to be eaten. A nice place to know about.

Miss Grimble
305 Columbus Ave.
(74th St.)
362-5531
Tues. to Sat. 10:00 A.M. to midnight; Sun. 11:00 A.M. to midnight

The Cheesecake Queen, as she's known here. Miss Grimble's creamy filling specialty, topped off with various fruits, is well worth the calories. She's also known for her pecan and pumpkin pies, her Grimbletortes and a pretty pot de crème in a flowerpot. Cakes and pies are sold by the slice, too, and can be eaten at cozy tables.

Orwasher's
308 E. 78th St.
288-6569
Mon. to Sat. 7:00 A.M. to 7:00 P.M.

Handmade, homemade, warm-from-the-oven bread. The Orwasher family has been baking for New York since 1916. They claim to have invented raisin pumpernickel, and if they didn't, they should have. Every one of their more than 30 types of bread is delicious: sweet egg challah, seeded and plain ryes, robust corn bread, light whites, braided marble, rich banana, soda and potato breads, and intense cinnamon-raisin on Saturdays. Everything is fresh, and no preservatives are added, so your best bet is to buy for the day you need it. The salespeople act like family, giving you tastes and advice, even when you don't ask for it. Orwasher's bread is also sold at Macy's and Bloomingdale's.

Pain de Paris
72 Lexington Ave.
(61st St.)
753-4774
Mon. to Fri. 7:00 A.M. to 10:00 P.M.; Sat. and Sun. 7:00 A.M. to 8:00 P.M.

An appropriate name, even if almost everything about the bakery, from the owner to the flour used, not to mention clients and staff, is American. But the bread itself is baked daily on the spot, according to French methods and in French-style ovens, and it's authentically golden, crusty and good. There are also rolls, Vienna rolls and a modest pastry section with regular or ham and cheese croissants, brioches, light and buttery pains au chocolat, palm leaves, turnovers and fruit pies—all made with good American butter, every bit as worthy as Normandy butter, to judge by the wonderful scents drifting out to the street, the long lines of clients and the tasty results.

Guy Pascal Les Délices
939 First Ave.
(51st-52nd sts.)
371-4144
Daily 8:00 A.M. to 10:00 P.M.

It's hard to tell the difference between the Délices and the Désirs, but it still translates as outstanding French pastry. Both shops carry the same menu of excellent cookies: tuiles, langues de chat, sablés, palmiers. For a heavenly breakfast, try the apricot or almond croissants, apple turnovers or just a crusty, chewy baguette. The ganache cake is notoriously rich and chocolaty ($20), and the Délice divine ($22.50 or $20). Tarts are made in the French tradition, with a light glaze, thick crust and lots of fruit. Guy Pascal runs this shop, as well as the one in the Olympic Tower, the outlet in Zabar's and another at 1231 Madison Avenue.

Patisserie Lanciani
271-275 W. 4th St.
(Perry St.)
929-0739
Tues. to Thurs. 8:00 A.M. to 11:00 P.M.; Fri. and Sat. 8:00 A.M. to midnight; Sun. 8:00 A.M. to 7:00 P.M.

The Italian owner, formerly head pastry chef at the Plaza, and his wife, whom he met there, now make exquisite Viennese and French pastries. Decorated cakes are his specialty—towering creations of lacy chocolate art good enough to eat. On a smaller scale, his éclairs, lemon tarts and napoleons are equally delectable. His charlotte russe is made the real way, his Grand Marnier tortes are served all over the city, and the truffles—chocolate, mocha, cognac and white—are considered the best by many who know. Lanciani also does a big breakfast trade, mainly because of his flawless croissants. There are tables to indulge your fantasies at, and good coffees and cappuccino. Lanciani products are also sold at Pasta and Cheese, Third Avenue at 65th Street, and other branches.

Rigo
318 E. 78th St.
988-0052
Mon. 8:00 A.M. to 4:00 P.M.; Tues. to Sat. 8:00 A.M. to 6:00 P.M.; Sun. 9:00 A.M. to 4:00 P.M.

If you don't have a grandmother from the Old Country, Lea Josefy is the next best thing. Everything in her homey shop is baked in the back room according to Hungarian and Viennese traditions, with lots of love and butter. Berliner squares, custard tarts, rum cakes—any one is worth the visit. The house specialty is Rigo, an intense chocolate mousse cake unequaled anywhere (and sold by the slice). Flaky homemade strudels at $5.50 a pound come with apple, walnut, cheese, poppy, berry or cabbage fillings. Shiny, perfectly formed pressburger horns are filled with moist walnuts or poppy seeds. Butter-rich linzer cake also comes with several fillings. There are ten kinds of petits fours, each prettier than the next. A particularly good ungooey Danish and a cup of strong Rigo coffee start any day off right. Rigo also makes beautiful wedding cakes and tasty hors d'oeuvres.

Sarabeth's Kitchen
412 Amsterdam Ave.
(79th St.)

The charm of Sarabeth's smile is matched by that of her homey boutiques filled with tasty goodies fresh from the oven: fresh-fruit pies, individual or family size; small, golden, crusty palm leaves; brownies; rich, fat chocolate chip cookies; shortbread; white or whole wheat breads

496-6280
Wed. to Mon. 10:00 A.M. to
7:00 P.M.

and rolls; gooey cinnamon buns; and her original mouth-watering mixed-fruit jams. Everything here is made with natural products without artificial coloring, preservatives or anything else of that sort. The West Side shop has a few tables to indulge at. The new East Side branch has more, and is set up to serve brunch all day long; it's located at 1295 Madison Avenue, near 92nd Street (410-7335).

Umanoff and Parsons
467 Greenwich St.
(Watts St.)
219-2240
Mon. to Fri. 9:00 A.M. to 5:00
P.M.; Sun. 9:00 A.M. to 4:00 P.M.

Just four years ago, Jane Umanoff was baking in her own tiny kitchen. Then she met Bo Parsons. They took a few cooking courses and rented a West Side tenement, and Umanoff and Parsons was born. Now, two locations and many pies later, they have a loyal following ranging from the chic Columbus Avenue restaurants to the SoHo eating places to the East Side meeting places. They also have a loyal staff (led by manager Del) of assistant bakers to help turn out their delectable Vienna fudge cakes, butter-rich Austrian plum cakes, gorgeous lattice-topped pies, fruit tarts set in frangipane, outstanding quiches and their untraditional, unsurpassed wedding cakes—pretty enough to be pictured in *Bride's* magazine, delicious enough to order again on every anniversary. Their shop, however, is still small—and the retail business is done by phone order, with you picking up the goodies. If you call by 11:00 A.M., you can savor your sweets the same day. Call at least a day ahead for any kind of quantity, a week ahead for special items. There is also a portfolio of their wedding, birthday and other special-event cakes if you must see before you decide. Umanoff and Parsons will also completely cater any type of party—doing everything and anything except making up the guest list.

Vesuvio
160 Prince St.
(W. Broadway)
925-8248
Mon. to Sat. 7:00 A.M. to 7:00 P.M.

Anthony Dapolito's family has been baking locally for 63 years. Today, his unrivaled loaves show up on some of the best tables around town—whether they've been purchased at Dean & DeLuca or are being buttered at Raoul's. We think his hard squares or tiny twists of biting pepper biscuits are a perfectly legitimate excuse for wine and thou. Loaves of Sicilian seeded whole wheat or white and rounds of crusty toast are made for soaking up mama's sauces. Everything's fresh as the day, and the prices are ridiculously low.

Victor's Cookies
101 W. 57th St.
247-4594
Mon. to Fri. 7:30 A.M. to 9:00

Victor's is not a bakery as we've come to know them; Victor's makes only cookies. But in New York, that's enough. Within the last few years, chocolate chipperies have appeared on nearly every corner, and the competition is stiff. David's still reigns as the king, but

Victor's is the first franchise finally to give him a run for
his cookies. Victor's is the only baker of chocolate
cookies with white chocolate chunks—they are better
than anything you've ever tasted before. He also sells the
more common chocolate chip types: chocolate chocolate
chip, regular chocolate chip, nutted chip and peanut
butter chip, plus lacy oatmeal raisin cookies. His chips
are all Swiss Tobler chocolate, another novelty, and the
cookies themselves are rich and cakey, without an excess
of butter. Look out, David's—other locations are
scheduled to open around the city.

CATERERS

Jean-Pierre Briand
412 E. 55th St.
753-2872

Quality is the first and sole concern of this Frenchman—
both in the cooking, which this self-made cook prepares
himself, aided by a single assistant, and in the service
(whether for a buffet or a sit-down dinner), the table
decoration, the quality of accessories, silver serving trays
and luxurious linen. Everything is excellent. He does beef
fillets or ham en croûte, preceded by small lobsters or
seafood vol-au-vents, for a sit-down dinner (minimum of
twelve and maximum of 50); for cocktails, he will shrink
the best in French cuisine to bite size: salmon canapés,
small bits of seafood, foie gras finger rolls and mini vol-
au-vents. (For cocktails, Jean-Pierre limits his production
to 200 people, with a minimum of 40.) This is no food
assembly line, and he's quite right to believe that quantity
is rarely compatible with quality. Prices per person for a
cocktail reception vary from $12 to $16, for buffets from
$25 to $30, and for full meals from $35 to $45. Full
service is available, including all accessories, waiters and
wine, at extra cost.

The Company
242-1206

Anstice Carroll and Leslie McBride are so charming that
they'll have you eating out of the palms of their hands.
They treat beautiful, fresh food in a loving manner and
excel in its presentation—nothing stuffy or pretentious.
They decorate with flowers, fruits and vegetables, using
their private collections of American and European
baskets, antique porcelain and pottery. Their special
interests are curries, nuova cucina, sensational summer
salads and regional American cooking. When needed,
they make their own breads, muffins, preserves and
pickles. Their clients hire The Company for ten to 200
people at cocktail receptions, buffet dinners, multicourse
dinners, breakfast, lunch and brunch. Cocktail receptions
cost $12 to $25 per person; buffets run $25 to $60;

dinners, $35 to $100. Rentals, music and waiters are extra. These attractive women are fun to work with, and their appearance will be an added bonus to your good-looking guest list.

La Fête
973 Lexington Ave.
(70th–71st sts.)
535-8354

Charles Chevillot of La Petite Ferme had so many satisfied customers at his restaurant that he opened a catering business with Art Garibay. Under the supervision of chef John Skelton, La Fête designs individual menus for customers, preparing dinners for twenty to 700 or cocktail receptions for 40 to 1,000. In the summer, they'll prepare basket lunches for boat parties, with cold medaillons of lamb, foie gras en brioche, fruit, cheese and splits of Champagne (for a minimum of 50). Their French classic foods are prepared with a rustic feeling, without heavy sauces. For weddings, Bonté supplies the cakes; for theme parties, La Fête will provide costumes, decor, waiters and wine, as well as appropriate menus. A light buffet of finger food, with sliced smoked fishes, meats and poultry, is popular and ranges from $20 to $35 per person. Dinners average $30 to $50 per person.

Glorious Food
172 E. 75th St.
628-2320

In frenzied competition with its colleague and rival, Donald Bruce White, Glorious Food presents the best in American cuisine. But although the presentation is extravagantly superb, there's not much to put on your plate, and you won't risk enlarging your waistline with these sophisticated dishes. That doesn't make the menu any less mouth-watering: it's an American version of French cooking (the chef is French) and includes an original breakfast with stuffed crêpes, miniature pies and scrambled eggs. There's a sit-down dinner for twenty or more ($65 per person minimum) and cocktails for up to 4,000 ($12 to $15 per person). Nothing daunts these professionals; their genius is in organizing large-scale events. Their service staff is impeccable, and their kitchens glisten. Glorious Food will look after everything for you: linen tablecloths and napkins, dishes and even reception rooms. Truly a top caterer, whose doorway alone (a massive, handsome object in sculpted wood) indicates its class. Very much in demand, so reserve well in advance.

Good Food
355 W. 36th St.
695-2966

Laura Zarubin has brought a refreshing perspective on catering with her from San Francisco. She concentrates on freshness and original presentation to assure a happy clientele. At a party given by Moët and Chandon for 500 at the Statue of Liberty, she set up an eastern regional seaboard seafood buffet, with shrimp from Key West, crayfish from Louisiana and lobster from Maine. Her work reflects seasonal changes and stresses American foods. Her white rabbit sausage in brioche and her pear tarte tatin are very popular. Dinners for fifteen to 500 run $40 to $45 per person; cocktail parties for up to 1,500 range from $12.50 to $30 per person for food only. A young caterer on the rise, Ms. Zarubin takes pains to ensure that each event will be special.

In Service Caterers
30 Grand St.
431-5900

These talented people specialized in training butlers, waiters and bartenders for private service before launching their successful catering business in 1976. Under chef John Steeves's supervision, they turn out excellent American dishes for gala banquets given by the New York City Opera and the New York City Ballet. It's no mean feat, serving 1,000 sit-down dinners in the New York State Theater with no kitchens! Some of the superb appetizers include seafood salad on radiccio, gratin of scallops and shrimps with wild mushrooms, and salad of pâté de campagne with arugula, endive and watercress. Two special entrees are rosemary-scented saddle of veal and rack of lamb glazed with cassis. Vegetables are prepared beautifully: peeled jumbo asparagus with baby red potatoes, carrots and mini eggplants, or sautéed haricots verts with a purée of butternut squash and parsnips. Desserts are simple (Champagne ice, brandied compote of fruits) or rich (fudge pecan torte, their own chocolate truffles). They'll prepare finger food for up to 3,000 (from $8 to $20 per person) and candlelit dinners for twenty to 1,000 (from $30 to $60). The service will be faultless.

Jean Claude Caterers
726-5300

Jean Claude shares his kitchens with Jean-Pierre Briand. His cuisine is classic French with a difference: appetizers include sea scallop mousse with spinach, striped bass poached with sorrel, lobster soufflé and vol-au-vent with shellfish. Main courses are fancy and beautifully prepared: rack of lamb aux fines herbes; duckling with two melons and fresh ginger, served with sautéed watercress and accompanied by wild rice prepared with Armagnac prunes and dried apricots; and scaloppine of capon with morilles. He might follow with Bucheron cheese en croûte, and for dessert, crêpes flambés aux mirabelles, poached pears, hot raspberry soufflé or soufflé glacé Grand Marnier with chocolate sauce, decorated with spun sugar. Like Jean-Pierre Briand, he refuses to cook for large numbers; he serves a sit-down dinner for a minimum of twenty people (about $38 to $46 per person). Neither waiters nor accessories, though:

Jean Claude simply cooks. His suggested menu depends on the ovens and kitchens available.

Maison Germaine
38–09 33rd St.
Long Island City
392-7284

Mme Germaine and her husband Marcel are the best French caterers in New York, along with Jean-Pierre Briand. Highly praised by the owner of Lutèce, at whose instigation they settled in the United States twenty years ago, they are caterers of great renown, using styles and methods of cooking that represent classical cuisine at its best. Everything is perfectly prepared, without unnecessary frills. Mme Germaine will serve sixteen to 1,500 people (prices available on request). Don't be put off by the lukewarm welcome on the part of the "maison"—Mme Germaine doesn't run after business. She doesn't have to; but she will never scorn a true gourmet.

Remember Basil
11 Cadman Plaza
West
Brooklyn
858-3000

Named for Dounia Rathbone's actor-uncle Basil, this successful caterer and her partner Donald Beckwith feed society at gala parties at Radio City Music Hall, for the Metropolitan Opera and in elegant living rooms. Their beautiful and unusual appetizers include timbale of morels, paupiettes of sole with salmon mousse, smoked English trout and mussels with caviar. Stuffed Cornish hens are prepared with bacon, pecans and rosemary, and served with port-soaked figs. Noisettes of lamb or roast loin of veal are two more of their fine entrees. Their most popular dessert is an iced lemon soufflé with fresh strawberries, although the almond dacquoise with mocha praline and chocolate butter cream is a great temptation. Full-service dinners for ten to 1,000 (including accessories, rentals, waiters and gratuities) are $65 to $90 per person; cocktail parties for up to 1,000 people are $20 to $40 per person (including rentals and waiters; liquor is extra).

La Table du Roi
675 Water St.
267-6966

Launched by Cécile Arnott twelve years ago, this small catering enterprise has become one of the New York's best. It offers made-to-measure catering—Cécile will prepare the dishes you want, assisted by a team of cooks from Brittany, for the number of people you've invited, in the price range you're looking for. She learned classic French recipes from her mother and grandmother, and her inventiveness knows no bounds. The beef roulade with green peppercorns is succulent, as is her chicken in vinegar "façon Trois gros." Génoise with fruit, torte with nuts and cold soufflé with pralines are but a few of her successful desserts. And if you order a buffet, you will find all sorts of original canapés and bite-sized delights,

399

tasty and perfectly light. Everything at reasonable prices: $25 to $35 per person for a buffet, $20 for a cocktail reception and $35 to $50 for dinner. Cécile will also choose and provide wines for you and will arrange for accessories, waiters, flowers and music.

Donald Bruce White
159 E. 64th St.
988-8410

This old-school caterer was for a long time alone in a field that now has more dynamic and original competition. Donald and his American chef (who studied in France) specialize in large private and official receptions. They hold office in two superb old-fashioned brownstones. The cuisine, neither American nor French, is a sort of nouvelle cuisine composed of specialties from around the world. If, for example, you long for couscous, he'll make it for you. He'll serve 30 to 3,000 from magnificent copper dishes, which are as heavy as their contents are light.

CAVIAR

Caviarteria
29 E. 60th St.
759-7410
(800)221-1020
Mon. to Fri. 9:00 A.M. to 6:00 P.M.; Sat. 9:00 A.M. to 5:30 P.M.

Internationally known for its fresh Malossol caviar, Scotch smoked salmon and fresh and canned foie gras, this small store off Madison Avenue actually sells eight varieties of fresh caviar and six in jars: Russian, Iranian and American, as well as Kamchatka (a mixture of broken and whole eggs), are represented. And it would be a crime to deprive yourself of the real Swiss chocolate.

E.A.T.
867 Madison Ave.
(72nd St.)
879-4017
Daily 7:30 A.M. to 7:30 P.M.

Eli Zabar carries the Champagne of caviar. Be it Russian or Iranian (depending upon what's good at the time), it's always beluga, and always the best of the beluga. If he could pick each egg by hand, Eli probably would. As it is, he goes through an average of 100 tins before he finds the one to buy. He looks for big eggs, gray as stainless steel, with hardly any salt. Once he chooses his lot, he stores it in special refrigerators monitored at zero degrees. Every day he packages specially made German containers, coated to eliminate any metallic taste, and filled to the top to dispel any air. No tin sits on the shelf more than two days. He has specially made porcelain containers, too. At $30 an ounce, this is the best caviar money can buy; it's also the caviar the best money buys.

Petrossian
Bloomingdale's
Third Avenue and
59th Street
705-3176
Mon. to Sat. 10:00 A.M. to 6:30 P.M. (Mon. and Thurs. to 9:00 P.M.); Sun. noon to 5:00 P.M.

The specialist from Paris has an extremely attractive outlet on Bloomingdale's ground floor, a replica of his store on the Boulevard de la Tour-Maubourg. He has been able to offer a fairly remarkable quality of caviar: beluga, ossetra, sevruga and pressed. He also sells a quite extraordinary "extra royal" Norwegian smoked salmon, salmon roe, Périgordian truffles, goose and duck foie gras and blinis by the piece.

Poliroff/ Purepak
542 La Guardia Pl.
(Bleecker St.)
3rd floor
254-7171
Mon. to Fri. 8:00 A.M. to 4:30 P.M.

This isn't a store where you can browse, touch and smell. You can only call up and leave your order for the highest quality caviar and smoked salmon at the lowest prices. All varieties of caviar. Prices on request.

CHEESE

Cheese of All Nations
153 Chambers St.
(W. Broadway)
732-0752
Mon. to Sat. 8:00 A.M to 5:30 P.M.

An immense variety of cheese from all over. You can buy small quantities at normal prices, or wholesale by the case. Bread and hors d'oeuvres as well. The right spot to stock up for a cheese party.

Fairway Fruit and Vegetables
2127 Broadway
(75th St.)
595-1888
Mon. to Sat. 8:00 A.M. to 9:45 P.M.; Sun. 8:00 A.M. to 8:00 P.M.

Fairway literally overflows with the freshest fruits and vegetables imaginable, pasta from Raffetto's, exotic spices—and cheese. While everything is reasonably priced and of extremely high quality, the cheeses are truly outstanding. Manager Steve Jenkins runs his department with a passion; a respected member of countless cheese and gourmet societies, Steve has committed himself, and Fairway, to finding the most and the best farm cheeses in the world. His bounty is as ever-changing as his taste. He has one of the most extensive selections of New York State goat's cheese, which he sells ripened by day, week or month. He brings in fresh sheep, cow and buffalo milk cheese from here and Europe. His Italian choices are superb. And everything comes with an education. While it is often busy and hard to browse in the overexpanded corner of the store, Fairway is a cheese source that should never be overlooked.

La Fromagerie
189 E. 79th St.
772-1819
Mon. to Fri. 10:00 A.M. to 9:30 P.M.; Sat. 9:00 A.M. to 6:00 P.M.

Superb French cheeses sold by a Frenchman—this has been the case ever since Gérard du Passage, a refugee from the garment trade, opened these deliciously attractive shops. M. du Passage knows what's good and what's not, and at what point a cheese has sufficiently matured for consumption or for selling to a wholesaler. A warm, friendly sort, he lets his clients taste, advises them or chooses for them if they wish. It's a wonderful sight: creamy goat's cheese, soft Saint Nectaire, Morbier, Chaource (whole or by the slice), the majority of which are unpasteurized, thus keeping their natural flavors. There are also crusty French breads and rolls and excellent pastries—in particular, homemade coconut macaroons, fruit pies and chocolate and Grand Marnier mousses—as well as croissants and brioches from Désirs la Côte Basque, salads with tortellini, crab or tabouleh, and pâté. Two house specialties are salmon and spinach pâté and pâté panache, made with chicken, veal and ginger, wrapped in bacon. The prices, alas, are comparable to the quality. And if this description has made you hungry, ask the owner for a Parisian sandwich: a buttered roll with ham and pickle. The shop also offers Petrossian products: salmon, foie gras, caviar. Finally, there's a catering service with free delivery for all its delicacies, plus its own specially prepared dishes (such as lobster à la nage). Nothing is frozen; it's not their style. Another location at 1374 Madison Avenue, near 95th Street (534-8923).

Ideal Cheese Shop
1205 Second Ave.
(63rd–64th sts.)
688-7579
Mon. to Fri. 9:00 A.M. to 6:30 P.M.; Sat. 9:00 A.M. to 6:00 P.M.

In our opinion, supported by nearly all connoisseurs, this is the best cheese shop in the city: between 250 and 300 domestic and, above all, imported varieties—in particular, velvety goat's cheeses, triple crèmes, Pont l'Evêque, Livarot, Epoisses, Stilton and innumerable other superb sorts. There are also petits suisses, French crème fraîche (imported daily), excellent pâté and a good selection of crackers. Prices are fair, if you take into account the superlative quality of the products. A plus: the extremely knowledgeable owner, Ed Edelman, can help guide your purchases—a service that is not to be underestimated, as this is a field that requires expertise.

Joe's Italian Dairy
156 Sullivan St.
(Houston St.)
677-8780
Tues. to Sat. 7:15 A.M. to 6:30 P.M.

Ask anyone in Little Italy where to buy the best mozzarella, and they'll point you to Joe's. In the back of this tiny hole in the wall, owner Anthony turns out milky fresh mozzarella, while out in front, mama Gracie hands it over just as fast as she can. Around 2:00 P.M. a screen of smoke from the cellar announces the arrival of football-size chunks of newly smoked cheese. At $3.59 a pound (sold elsewhere for $8.50), this has to be one of the best buys in New York. On Saturdays, Anthony adds prosciutto to his bounty. The rest of the goods are of equally high quality. Only Danielle ricotta is sold and asiago is a local favorite. A small but select choice of other cheeses (predominantly Italian), sweet butter, olives and oils are also available.

Mad for Cheese
1064 First Ave.
(58th St.)
759-8615
Mon. to Fri. 10:00 A.M. to 7:00 P.M.; Sat. 10:00 A.M. to 6:30 P.M.

This shop, one among several similar, deserves notice for its charm and that of the owner, a lovely Italian woman. Her wares are honest: a large variety of cheeses, pâté from Les 3 Petits Cochons, fresh salads, quiches, prosciutto, fine groceries, coffee, a good bread section—in short, a friendly corner store. She'll also prepare cold trays for parties.

La Marca Cheese Shop
161 E. 22nd St.
673-7920
Mon. to Fri. 10:00 A.M. to 6:45 P.M.; Sat. 9:30 A.M. to 6:15 P.M.

There are 150 varieties of cheese, of which about a quarter are Italian, in this shop run by an Italian who used to be with Dean & Deluca. His specialties are custom-prepared catering trays, fresh cheese with various fruits, and a cheese pie made of alternating layers of gorgonzola and mascarpone. All the cheeses are aged on the spot by this connoisseur.

CONFECTIONS

Le Chocolatier Manon
872 Madison Ave. (71st St.)
288-8088
Mon. to Sat. 10:00 A.M. to 6:00 P.M.

This golden jewelbox on Madison Avenue treats its chocolates like gems (which they are, at $22 a pound) and its customers like royalty. Where Teuscher is whimsical, Krön fashionable and Godiva acceptable, Manon is sophisticated. The chocolates are molded works of art filled with natural wonders: orange peel in crème fraîche marzipan, pralines and memorable truffles. These are confections to be taken seriously.

Economy Candy Market
131 Essex St. (Delancey St.)
254-1531
Sun. to Fri. 9:00 A.M. to 5:30 P.M.

Candy corner. In typical Lower East Side style, this old-world candy store shows its goodies inside, outside and curb side. What a find it is! Candy like we haven't seen in twenty or 30 years. Jars and boxes of chocolate babies and bonbons, jujubes and jawbreakers. Exotic imported lentils and mints. Pistachio nuts in three sizes and three colors. Macadamias. Peanuts. Dried fruits, hefty chocolate chunks and moist halvah. Most everything is dependably fresh, the selection is unbeatable, and the prices are always right. But the shop caters more to the glutton than to the gourmet.

Elk Candy Co.
240 E. 86th St.
650-1177
Mon. to Sat. 9:00 A.M. to 6:30 P.M.

Marzipan country: a delicious homemade product that attracts a lot of hard-bitten marzipan munchers to this old-fashioned shop whose pretty window stands out in the neighborhood.

Godiva Chocolatier
701 Fifth Ave. (55th St.)
593-2845
Mon. to Sat. 10:00 A.M. to 6:00 P.M.; Sun. noon to 5:00 P.M.

These creamy (and for the most part heavy) chocolates have earned a solid reputation, despite the fact that they are made by the rather common Pepperidge Farm. Their velvety taste is well liked by many (though considered waxy by others), and the golden gift boxes make perfect offerings. Godiva chocolates are also sold in many specialty shops, gift shops and department stores. The prewrapped boxes contain a standard selection, which isn't always the best. Godiva has recently added gourmet ice cream to its inventory.

Krön Chocolatier

764 Madison Ave.
(65th St.)
2nd floor
472-1234
Mon. to Sat. 8:30 A.M. to 6:00 P.M.

Another highly ranked shop, to judge by its reputation, although not necessarily its quality. Fresh and dried fruit dipped in semisweet chocolate and fresh, intense truffles ($30 a pound) are made according to Hungarian recipes. If it's originality in presentation you're looking for, you'll appreciate the unusual sculptures and forms in bittersweet and milk chocolate: life-size female busts and legs ($60 to $75), greeting cards, telephones, records, slide rules, tennis racquets, golf balls, monograms and more. There are even chocolate chips, baking chocolate and fudge sauce. Another location at 506 Madison Avenue, near 52nd Street (486-0265).

Li-Lac Chocolates

120 Christopher St.
(Bleecker St.)
242-7374
Sun. and Mon. noon to 7:45 P.M.;
Tues. to Sat. 10:00 A.M. to
9:45 P.M.

Since 1923, this shop has been selling homemade, hand-dipped chocolates in more varieties than we care to count. But with the nouveaux chocolatiers opening up, this institution has lost some of its prestige. Its best-sellers are fudge, turtles and filled chocolates that taste and smell quite ordinary. Various locations, including Barney's and Chelsea Foods.

Perugina Chocolates

636 Lexington Ave.
(54th St.)
688-2490
Mon. to Sat. 10:00 A.M. to 6:00
P.M. (Mon., Thurs. and Fri. to
9:00 P.M.)

The classic Italian imported chocolates, including the famous "Baci" (kisses) stuffed with pralines, so delighted in by the chefs at Le Cygne and The Four Seasons. A very reasonable, if not too exotic, treat at $12.50 a pound. Admirable gift boxes and fancy filled porcelains as well.

Plumbridge

30 E. 67th St.
371-0608
Mon. to Sat. 9:30 A.M. to 6:00 P.M.

A very traditional shop, run by the same family since 1883, that caters to a distinguished American clientele, who, for the most part, have been stocking their larders here for generations. Candies are typically American: pecans coated with brown sugar and cinnamon (the house specialty, and they're homemade), mint chocolates, glazed apricots and jelly beans, from $7.50 to $18 a pound. There's also a very wide choice of gifts: paper boxes, antique Chinese porcelain plates, toys and slightly kitschy boxes filled with candy. Plumbridge does a large mail-order business, both here and abroad. For New Yorkers, the new 67th Street shop is very friendly and rarely busy.

Sweet Temptation

1070 Madison Ave.
(80th St.)
734-6082

There are several of these small, old-fashioned shops newly opened around town. Each overflows with candies in all shapes and wrappers: chocolate roller skates, gummy jogger's shoes, jawbreakers, hard candy, soft candy, spiders, hats, cowboy boots, kisses, Godiva

Mon. to Sat. 10:30 A.M. to 6:30
P.M.; Sun. 11:00 A.M. to
5:30 P.M.

chocolates, Perugina hard candy, lollipops and all-day suckers. A trip here will bring a smile to even the most blasé child's face.

Teuscher Chocolates of Switzerland

**620 Fifth Ave.
(50th St.)
246-4416**
*Mon. to Sat. 10:00 A.M. to
6:00 P.M.*

Mention Teuscher, and you're sure to start a debate: Is the delightful packaging more enticing than the Champagne truffles? Or vice versa? In any case, both are superb. The sinful chocolates are made entirely from natural ingredients and are flown in weekly from Zurich, guaranteeing their (relative) freshness. Truffles dominate the selection, in ten varieties: nougat, nut, orange, cocoa, dark or white chocolate, Kirsch (the newest) and the unrivaled Champagne. Other filled chocolates—marzipan, pralines, nuts, fruits—and solid shapes are also worth a taste … or two, or three (they're $22 a pound). The charming packaging (likewise handmade in Switzerland) changes with the season, from funny frogs to dolls to Indians, flowers, bunnies and Santas. There's another location at 25 East 61st Street (751-8482).

GOURMET MARKETS

Balducci's

**424 Avenue of the
Americas
(9th–10th sts.)
673-2600**
*Mon. to Sat. 7:00 A.M. to 8:30
P.M.; Sun. 7:00 A.M. to 6:30 P.M.*

Since 1916, this Italian family has provided Greenwich Village with excellent produce and cheese from around the world. Today it's also a mecca for prepared foods and salads, homemade pasta, fresh and smoked fish, Bell and Evans chickens, pâtés, beautiful meats, frozen game, dried fruits, breads, cakes, cookies and chocolates. The shelves are overflowing with imported jars and cans. Everything is here in huge quantity and variety, especially the well-stocked fresh produce section. The store caters clambakes, complete meals or simple cheese platters (from among 550 varieties) and has added a mail-order department.

Bloomingdale's Food Source

**1000 Third Ave.
(59th St.)
355-5900**
*Mon. to Sat. 9:45 A.M. to 6:00 P.M.
(Thurs. to 9:00 P.M.); Sun. noon to
6:00 P.M.*

The redesigned gourmet section now spreads bottled and canned temptations from around the world on two levels. There are more cheeses, butters from Normandy, Italy and Denmark, even Devon cream. Californians exult when finding a Mrs. Fields' chocolate chip cookie concession. Tired Saturday shoppers can now rest their heels at the Tasting Bar and sample Michel Guérard's pâté and salad, Marcella Hazan's pasta and Smokey's chili, plus a choice of cheeses and cakes from the takeout sections. There's still a delicious selection in the adjoining bakery, Au Chocolat, and from Petrossian caviar.

Dean & Deluca
**121 Prince St.
(Wooster St.)
254-7774**
*Mon. to Sat. 10:00 A.M. to 7:00
P.M.; Sun. 10:00 A.M. to
6:00 P.M.*

The most attractive, expensive and certainly one of the best. Patience is de rigueur while waiting to be served, but it pays off: these are the best fresh pastas in New York, and the best olives and olive oils. Also crusty breads, pâtés, about 200 cheeses (predominantly French and Italian), delicious-smelling coffees in big burlap bags and exquisite pastries. All is admirably displayed in a pleasing rustic manner by an Italian with taste and talent. At the back of the store is a small department of well - chosen kitchen utensils. Service with a smile, but huge crowds on the weekend: the lines sometimes extend to the street.

Fairway Fruits & Vegetables
**2127 Broadway
(75th St.)
595-1888**
*Mon. to Sat. 8:00 A.M. to 9:45
P.M.; Sun. 8:00 A.M. to 8:00 P.M.*

This market sells the freshest produce at incredibly low prices. In addition to the expected vegetables, you'll find white and orange peppers, Oriental eggplant, kirby, dandelion greens, Jerusalem artichokes, fresh herbs and every imaginable fruit. The shelves are stocked with popular brands of gourmet oil, vinegar, mustard and jam at very reasonable prices. The cheese selection is excellent, including French goat curd, New York State goat's cheese and crème fraîche. Coffee beans, bread and rolls, sausages, smoked salmon—just about everything a budget-conscious gourmet would want.

Fay and Allen's Food Halls
**1241 Third Ave.
(71st St.)
794-1001**
*Mon. to Thurs. 8:00 A.M. to 11:00
P.M.; Fri. and Sat. 8:00 A.M. to
12:30 A.M.; Sun. 8:00 A.M. to
10:30 P.M.*

The Grapevine section features fresh produce, a crisp salad bar (at $2.69 a pound, a positive bargain), even a fresh fruit salad bar ($3.19 a pound). This vast delicatessen has prepared dishes, foie gras, 350 kinds of cheese, assorted pâtés and meats, smoked fish and caviar. In the adjoining candy department, gift baskets can be selected or ordered. Godiva, Lindt and Perugina boxes vie with fresh Leonidas chocolates flown in once a week from Belgium. Godiva ice cream is available by the pint ($3.75). But best of all are the 150 desserts in the Konditorei. Be it babka or bread, the decision making can take forever.

Macy's The Cellar
**West 34th Street and
Broadway
695-4400**
*Mon. to Fri. 9:45 A.M. to 8:30 P.M.
(Tues. and Wed. to 6:45 P.M.); Sat.
9:45 A.M. to 6:00 P.M.; Sun. noon
to 6:00 P.M.*

The Market Place in Macy's The Cellar provides a dazzling array of packaged foods from around the world, as well as an extensive choice of fresh meats, produce, pasta and cheeses. Abundance is the key here: five varieties of smoked salmon, caviars, a garden of dried herbs in open sacks from l'Herbier de Provence, fresh breads from Vie de France, desserts from Eclair, ice cream and chocolates from Godiva and truffles from California, Neuhaus, Bruyère and Michel Guérard.

Cookie lovers may want to walk away with Amaretto di Saronno in tins up to four and a half pounds. You may wish to put together your own gift basket from Raoul Gey, Fauchon, Maxim's, the Silver Palate or Crabtree and Evelyn, or send any one of the attractive preselected assortments.

Raffetto's

144 W. Houston St.
(Sullivan St.)
777-1261
Tues. to Sat. 8:00 A.M. to 6:00 P.M.

All the best gourmet shops in the city, not to mention the best restaurants (Italian and otherwise), get their pasta fresh daily from Raffetto's. A family business since 1906, Raffetto's is still a small storefront with a big back room. And that's where the miracles happen. Gorgeous tortellini, lighter than air. Ravioli filled with spinach and cheese. Fresh egg and spinach fettuccine. Cavatelli and manicotti. Everything's rolled out and cut on large, old-fashioned machines that don't sacrifice quality for quantity. Di Nola tomatoes and sauces are sold along with freshly grated cheeses, olive oils and vinegars, arborio rice and cornmeal, if you want to roll out your own. Tortellini and cannelloni are 45¢ apiece. Fettuccine is $1.20 a pound. No wonder the lines get so long on Saturday mornings.

Todaro Bros.

555 Second Ave.
(30th St.)
532-0633
Mon. to Sat. 7:30 A.M. to 8:30 P.M.; Sun. 7:30 A.M. to 6:00 P.M.

Since it began as a salumeria in 1917, Todaro's has been serving Italian palates with salami, prosciutto, pasta and cheese. The neighbors still come in for the homemade mozzarella and the six kinds of sausage. (Oleg Cassini comes in for the honest sandwiches.) In the expanded store, the helpful staff gives tastes of the more than 200 cheeses and the pâtés and salamis. It now sells prepared Italian dishes as well, including frittatas thick with vegetables or sausage and peppers. The shelves are jammed with coffee beans, bags of flour and semolina, dried mushrooms, olives, the predictable Amaretto di Saronno and Perugina chocolates and unusual varieties of herb vinegars and nut oils. Todaro prepares gift baskets and has added a mail-order catalog.

Zabar's

2245 Broadway
(80th St.)
787-2000
Mon. to Fri. 9:00 A.M. to 7:30 P.M.; Sat. 9:00 A.M. to midnight; Sun. 9:00 A.M. to 6:00 P.M.

The biggest and the best. Now four buildings wide, with a second floor covered from floor to ceiling with housewares and small appliances. You take a number and wait your turn in each department, giving you ample time to select from an overabundance of smoked fish, fresh caviars and pâtés; 300 cheeses; roasted meats, poultry and cold cuts; salads; fresh pasta from Pasta and Cheese; coffee beans and loose tea; pickles and olives—until you're waiting in line to pay, and you spot the fresh breads. Zabar's now prepares picnic baskets ($16.75 serves two), in addition to catering. Experience this New York landmark, an institution for lovers of the good life, especially after 10:30 on Saturday night.

GOURMET TO GO

Artichoke
968 Second Ave.
(51st St.)
753-2030
Tues. to Thurs. 11:00 A.M. to 7:00 P.M.; Fri. 10:00 A.M. to 7:00 P.M.; Sat. 10:00 A.M. to 6:00 P.M.

This attractive little store prepares 30 different salads, both familiar and unusual, averaging $7 a pound. To save you a trip downtown, it also carries pâtés from Les 3 Petits Cochons, cheeses from France, Italy, England and Denmark, smoked salmon, Italian pasta, olives and oils, a selection of French, Irish, American and Italian breads, and increasingly popular croissants. A simple formula, with a classic menu that works.

As You Like It
120 Hudson St.
(N. Moore St.)
226-6654
Mon. to Fri. 10:00 A.M. to 7:30 P.M.; Sat. 10:00 A.M. to 6:00 P.M.

Owner Margaret Hess reaches beyond her TriBeCa circle with some of the city's finest desserts: chocolate génoise ($15), chocolate cake (a dense, trufflelike torte made with Belgian chocolate, $15), brownies and cookies (gingersnaps, sacristains, chocolate chips). She also carries a selective variety of French and Italian cheese, marinades and pickles, Montrachet goat's cheese, fresh strawberry preserves and excellent salads. Her chicken salads (she makes six varieties) are the most popular, although the radicchio–shiitake mushroom–spinach salad looks particularly tempting. She carries breads, meats and a good shelf stock and caters dinner parties, brunches and cocktails.

Chelsea Foods
198 Eighth Ave.
(19th St.)
691-3948
Mon. to Fri. 9:00 A.M. to 9:00 P.M.; Sat. and Sun. 9:00 A.M. to 6:00 P.M.

The tasteful owners have selected delicacies from the finest suppliers in the city and have presented them beautifully, alongside their own homemade oil, vinegar, mustard, pickles, antipasto and olives. Their love of things Italian shows in a $35 rustic pasta gift basket, a clever idea including pasta, herbs, peppers, garlic, cheese, sauce and oil. The four-egg-per-pound Fini pasta is here, alongside D&G Italian breads. Try the prosciutto bread with one of Chelsea's many Italian cheeses. Prepared salads of pasta, vegetables, meat and poultry; smoked meats and pâtés sandwiches; and homemade entrees and soups can also be enjoyed with desserts from Lanciani, Taste and other fine bakers in the twenty-seat café next door. Breakfast—with cappuccino, of course—is served until 11:30 A.M. Chelsea Foods caters spectacular buffets, dinners and parties for groups of ten or more.

Country Host
1435 Lexington Ave.
(93rd–94th sts.)
876-6525
Mon. to Sat. 9:00 A.M. to 7:00 P.M.

Rona Deme, a venerable English lady, has put together a takeout shop and catering service (722-5499) with her son and daughter-in-law that includes traditional English dishes, homemade jams, chutneys and canned fruits, tarts and tea cakes, scones and crumpets. For the holidays, she prepares mince tarts and pies, plum pudding, gingerbread and cookies. Oh, to have her cater an afternoon tea with scones, cucumber and watercress sandwiches, cream cakes and fruitcake! Remember her for Scotch eggs, Cornish pasties, steak and kidney pie, English banger sausages, treacle pie or pippins and port.

Demarchelier Charcuterie
1460 Lexington Ave.
(94th St.)
722-6600
Mon. to Sat. 10:30 A.M. to 7:30 P.M.

These stores offer a large variety of smoked meats, dry sausages, sausage in pastry and their own pâtés, as any self-respecting charcuterie must. The daily selection of prepared salads, fish, meats and poultry varies with the season. Good bread, old-fashioned homemade jams and mustards and a small choice of French desserts complete the menu. How will you ever cook again? The uptown store also caters parties and corporate accounts and prepares platters from the small but fine cheese selection. The menu can be sampled at its original restaurant at Lexington Avenue and 62nd Street, at its newest location on West 58th Street or at its branch at 954 Lexington Avenue, near 69th Street.

E.A.T.
867 Madison Ave.
(72nd St.)
879-4017
Daily 7:30 A.M. to 7:30 P.M.

E.A.T. manages to survive with inexplicably outrageous prices for a limited selection of gourmet foods. A thriving catering business for a refined and affluent clientele is what keeps Eli Zabar, the son of Broadway Zabar's, in business. The choice is limited, with prepared salads, notable smoked salmon, beluga caviar ($30 an ounce), fresh foie gras, a few excellent cakes and the famous brownies. Nowhere else have we seen fraises du bois, those deliciously sweet wild strawberries, or such enormous long-stemmed strawberries ($10 a pint). There's a café at the uptown store, at 1064 Madison Avenue (753-5171), and an E.A.T. in Henri Bendel's.

Lorenzo and Maria's Kitchen

As you walk into this very friendly, busy shop, Maria, the Uruguayan chef, can be seen preparing delicious salads and soups in the open kitchen. Husband Lorenzo, a charming Mexican, greets the neighborhood clients and

**1418 Third Ave.
(80th–81st sts.)
794-1080**
Mon. to Sat. 9:00 A.M. to 8:00 P.M.

suggests cheeses, smoked salmon, cold cuts or some of the prepared dishes for dinner. The happy customers keep coming back for the pasta salads, ratatouille, lobster bisque and the warm welcome. Shelves are crammed with Italian and French condiments.

Mangia
**54 W. 56th St.
582-3061**
*Mon. to Fri. 8:00 A.M. to 7:00
P.M.; Sat. 10:00 A.M. to 6:00 P.M.*

At lunchtime the nearby office workers crowd into this gourmet takeout shop for its excellent sandwiches, made with first-quality ingredients—often in unusual combinations—on a variety of breads. Among the salads, we find the sweet wild rice especially flavorful, a good balance to the soy roast chicken with snow peas and pecans. The baked goods are all first-rate; the blueberry muffins are moist with apples and nuts, the oatmeal ginger cookies thick and loaded with raisins. The limited selection of cheeses is predominantly French, and the helpful young staff will make platter suggestions for your office party. Delivery service weekdays from 10:15 A.M. to 3:30 P.M.

Rosemary Miller's Ltd.
**197 E. 76th St.
249-5383**
*Mon. to Sat. 10:00 A.M. to 7:00
P.M.; Sun. 11:00 A.M. to
6:00 P.M.*

Behind marble-topped counters, Ms. Miller keeps in touch with her satisfied neighborhood customers. Her own line of fresh, quality pâtés, salads and American baked goods has its confirmed devotees. No wonder she wholesales them to Bloomingdale's and other gourmet shops. At Christmas she adds authentic mincemeat pie and cranberry relish. In addition, she is known for her excellent cold cut selection, popular imported cheeses and chocolate Grand Marnier truffles. Six bakeries supply her with bread daily, and farms provide her with fresh dairy items. The shelves are lined with oils, vinegars, mustards, jams and fresh coffee beans. Ms. Miller also imparts her look of understated elegance to catered cocktail parties.

Neuman & Bogdonoff
**1385 Third Ave.
(79th St.)
861-0303**
*Mon. to Sat. 10:00 A.M. to 7:30
P.M. (open to 8:00 P.M. in summer;
closed Sat. in Aug. and on Jewish
holidays)*

Prepared foods are what bring the neighbors back to this takeout emporium with its big, open kitchen. The chicken pot pie ($7.50), is popular, the soups are excellent (try the parsnip or the chowders), and the vegetable-chicken salad (with sweet red pepper, carrots and celery) is one of the best in town ($10 a pound). Gourmets pick up beef, chicken or fish stock by the quart or pint. Of course, the store carries pâté, fresh olives, French cheeses, smoked fish, Raffetto's pasta and popular imported shelf items. During the Jewish holidays, the twelve cooks prepare a full menu of specialties, including gefilte fish, matzoh ball soup, brisket, tzimmes, matzoh and apple kugel, just like mama used to make. Its most popular catered platter is tenderloin of beef with Japanese red onion sauce.

Pasta and Cheese
1120 Third Ave.
(65th St.)
772-7595
Mon. to Sat. 10:00 A.M. to 7:30 P.M.; Sun. noon to 6:00 P.M.

There were eight green and white Pasta and Cheese shops at last count—not including its espresso bar at Bergdorf Goodman's—and its products seem to crop up in other gourmet markets all the time. This location also has a pleasing café that serves delicious Lanciani pastries on white marble-topped bistro tables until 7:15 P.M. In addition to the fresh pasta, sauces, pâtés, olives, soups, salads, cheese and breads, there are unusual fruits and vegetables in season: Cavaillon melons, Japanese cucumbers, kumquats, baby yellow tomatoes, shiitake mushrooms, radicchio, French haricots verts, even morels at $13 an ounce.

William Poll
1050 Lexington Ave.
(75th St.)
288-0501
Mon. to Sat. 9:00 A.M. to 6:00 P.M.

William Poll has been catering and offering takeout prepared foods for ages. He still can be counted on for his appetizers—miniature quiches and cheese feuilletés, both delicious, and commendable biscuits. The charcuterie section is better than the choice of cheeses, and the shelves are well stocked with the usual imported items. The smoked salmon is exquisite.

Le Porc Salut
17 E. 13th St.
355-3844
Mon. to Fri. 9:00 A.M. to 7:00 P.M.; Sat. 9:30 A.M. to 7:00 P.M.

Located in an old Greenwich Village carriage house, Les 3 Petits Cochons is an authentic French charcuterie. Of its twelve different pâtés, priced from $7.50 to $12 a pound (also found in discriminating shops throughout the city), our favorites are the pâté de campagne, pâté of duck à l'orange and wild mushroom pâté. All are made with the best ingredients, without additives. We shouldn't neglect the excellent Parisian garlic sausage, boudins and the new galantines made from turkey, duck, pheasant or chicken. For $3.50 (the price of a mediocre hamburger) you can pick up a platter of assorted hors d'oeuvres at lunch; the choice is yours. Les 3 Petits Cochons also caters hot and cold dishes, some of which are found in the store each day, along with quiches, soups, cheeses and desserts. The quality and tradition continue behind a new storefront, with a new chef from southwestern France.

Ruslan
1067 Madison Ave.
(81st St.)
371-3419
Daily 9:00 A.M. to 10:00 P.M.

Authentic Russian food is hard to come by in New York, and connoisseurs come to this café/takeout/caterer for real borscht, kulibiaka (flaky pastry stuffed with beef, salmon or whitefish), piroshki filled with meat or cabbage, pelmeni (those tender, tiny Siberian dumplings), as well as delicious salads, crêpes and desserts. After a morning or afternoon at the Metropolitan Museum of Art, it's the best place for lunch or dessert and espresso. Ruslan recently opened a second café at 435 East 86th Street (534-6561), where the menu has been expanded to include more meat and poultry specialties.

Russ and Daughters
179 E. Houston St. (Orchard St.)
475-4880
Wed. to Mon. 8:00 A.M. to 7:00 P.M.

If you can get past the racks of clothing on the sidewalk—Orchard Street is around the corner—this is the place for the best in smoked fishes, fresh Malossol caviar, dried fruits, nuts, sauerkraut, pickles, cream cheeses and imported herring. The third-generation owner, Mark Russ, prepares platters of appetizers for parties and has a thriving wholesale trade.

Donald Sacks SoHo
120 Prince St. (Wooster St.)
226-0165
Mon. to Fri. 8:00 A.M. to 6:00 P.M.; Sat. and Sun. 11:00 A.M. to 6:00 P.M.

Just across from Dean & Deluca, where Mr. Deluca himself first opened shop, this minuscule boutique, consisting of an awning, a refrigerated counter and a work table, offers a delicious range of sandwiches, fifteen attractive salads and hot and cold soups, all on the spot. Come in for breakfast at the counter, or have a brie and Westphalia ham on black bread—a favorite sandwich of Mrs. Paul Mellon—at one of the sidewalk tables. Donald Sacks caters large and small groups from breakfast through dinner and prepares sensational box lunches for city picnickers.

Self Chef
1224 Lexington Ave. (82nd St.)
288-8824
Mon. to Sat. 10:00 A.M. to 7:00 P.M.

Philippe Bernard, a Frenchman and longtime resident of New York, has been in this little shop for five years. His prepared dishes are excellent: the boeuf bourguignon, chicken basquoise, veal marengo and paupiettes of veal are quite obviously the work of no amateur. He also stocks all kinds of salads, a delicious ham brought in specially from Tennessee, his own pâtés, a good selection of cheese, bread, delicatessen items, popular brownies, a deliciously light pumpkin mousse and New York Ice sherbets—low in calories but high in flavor for the diet conscious. He'll cater parties or dinners, buffet style or as you wish.

The Silver Palate
274 Columbus Ave. (73rd St.)
799-6340
Mon. to Sat. 10:30 A.M. to 9:30 P.M.; Sun. 10:00 A.M. to 7:00 P.M.

The two women who began this shop in 1977 have parlayed their hard work into a multimillion-dollar business. It's possibly the smallest gourmet shop—only 165 square feet—in New York, but it's one of the best for salads, pastry and cookies, as well as for a great variety of homemade breads (from the usual to those made with zucchini, carrots or cranberries) and different prepared hot dishes each day. The store makes and sells its own mustards, chutneys, oils, vinegars, sweet sauces, brandied fruits and preserves. It has a thriving mail-order business, and its products are sold in stores in 48 states. The catering service and best-selling cookbook are equally successful.

SoHo Charcuterie

**195 Spring St.
(Sullivan St.)
226-3545**
Tues. to Sun. noon to 9:00 P.M.

Opened in 1975 by two enterprising young American women, this was one of the first places to combine a charcuterie with a restaurant where you can taste the dishes, an arrangement that has since become very popular. Pâtés are their specialties, but also try the salads (shrimp, noodles and tarragon chicken) at reasonable prices. The cold roast meats are beautifully prepared, and the chocolate globs (cookies made with three kinds of chocolate) have their faithful followers. They cater with dishes from the restaurant menu or selections from the retail store. If you want to try these recipes at home, pick up a copy of their new cookbook.

Washington Market

**162 Duane St.
(Hudson and W. Broadway)
233-0250**
Mon. to Sat. 7:00 A.M. to 9:00 P.M.; Sun. 9:00 A.M. to 6:00 P.M.

A spacious, very old-fashioned store with very up-to-date merchandise. The owners haven't forgotten any of the things one looks for in this kind of shop: bread, fancy sliced meats, pâtés, hard and cream cheeses, coffee, fresh pasta and sauces, condiments and sixteen different homemade salads every day. Sunday is the best day to visit; pick up the *New York Times* or *Village Voice* here, take out or have bagels and fish at the wooden tables, with fresh-ground coffee and yummy pastries. During the week financial types on their way to work grab the *Wall Street Journal* with coffee and pastry to eat at their desks, and return for the terrific sandwiches at lunchtime. There's also a busy catering business.

West Side Storey

**700 Columbus Ave.
(95th St.)
749-1900**
Daily 7:00 A.M. to 11:00 P.M.

Responding to the Upper West Side's need for a gourmet takeout establishment and restaurant, the owners set up this combination venture, which has met with great success among locals. From early morning, when the bagels, lox and salmon, coffee, croissants and breads sell best, to the evening, when the last of the day's homemade savory and sweet pies and tarts, salads, pâtés, sausages and cheeses make their way home, the place does a brisk business. The salads are not too oily or overly mayonnaised; we especially like the tuna salad with pasta, oranges and currants. The shelves are stocked with the usual mustards, oils, vinegars and teas.

Word of Mouth

**1012 Lexington Ave.
(72nd–73rd sts.)
734-9483**
Mon. to Fri. 10:00 A.M. to 7:00 P.M.; Sat. 10:00 A.M. to 6:00 P.M.; Sun. 11:30 A.M. to 5:30 P.M.

The dishes are more unusual in tone here—one could say they're a reflection of this very varied metropolis: apricot glazed ham, Szechwan sesame noodles, gazpacho salad, Tex-Mex pasta. Every season has a weekly menu of specialties. The smart, to avoid disappointment on the way home, call ahead to reserve their favorite stews and soups. Typical imported items line the shelves all the way back to the open kitchen. Get there early enough to take home some of the excellent desserts.

413

Gifts

American Country Store
969 Lexington Ave.
(70th St.)
744-6705
Mon. to Sat. 10:00 A.M. to 6:00 P.M.

An absolutely charming shop run by Mary Emmerling, a well-known expert (and author) on country Americana. Many of these rustic, colorful items for the home make excellent gifts: hand-painted pottery, antique quilts, inexpensive rag rugs, simple pioneer paintings, hand-dipped candles, rustic objets d'art and linens. There's some antique furniture as well.

Hans Appenzeller
820 Madison Ave.
(68th St.)
570-0504
Mon. to Sat. 10:00 A.M. to 6:00 P.M. (Thurs. to 7:30 P.M.)

A relative newcomer to Madison Avenue. This Dutchman has created a gallerylike environment to show off his stunning line of jewelry and gifts. If you have been looking for a mesh belt, gunmetal bar pins, modern calculators and desk accessories, black metal mesh bags, exquisitely tasteful gold earrings or other ultracontemporary designs, this shop is essential.

Asprey
Trump Tower
725 Fifth Ave.
(56th St.)
688-1811
Mon. to Sat. 10:00 A.M. to 5:30 P.M.

This venerable British institution has opened a mini branch (the parent store in London requires at least an hour of browsing to see it all) in Trump Tower. It's a specialty store filled with indispensable trifles for the upper classes: ceramic birds, leather-bound books, boudoir brush sets, $65,000 diamond necklaces, baby christening gifts, china, crystal and more. The staff, some of whom are charmingly British, welcomes browsers and does a good job of informing you about the relative merits of these beautiful gifts. Who knows—you too may find that you can't live without a gold watch, ceramic traveling sewing kit, sleek evening bag or crystal paperweight.

Cache-Cache Ltd.
758 Madison Ave.
(65th St.)
744-6886
Mon. to Fri. 10:00 A.M. to 6:00 P.M.; Sat. 11:00 A.M. to 5:00 P.M.

Come here for those sweet ceramics that look appropriate on summer porches in the Hamptons or Connecticut. It's a perfect place for wedding gifts for traditionalists who enjoy painted wicker, pretty cushions, floral vases and ceramic dishes in the shapes of asparagus, cows and ribboned boxes.

Captain Hook's
South Street Seaport
10 Fulton St.
(Water St.)

Owner Joe Hill has been established in this location for ten years, since long before the South Street extravaganza was a reality. This is without doubt one of the most entertaining and warm shopping experiences in New York. Mr. Hill is the salt of the earth, with a fondness for his marine paraphernalia, shells and

414

344-2262
Daily 10:00 A.M. to 10:00 P.M.

everyone who walks into the store. Without any problem, you will walk out of this shop—which is jammed to the hilt with brass, shells, buoys, boat fittings, and the like—with a treasure to take home.

Five Eggs
436 W. Broadway (Prince St.)
226-1606
Tues. to Sun. 12:30 P.M. to 7:00 P.M.

This little Japanese store is filled with such traditional treasures as cooking equipment, futons, handsome kimonos, bamboo soap holders, sake sets, chopsticks, books and spiraled washcloths that inflate into cats. Everything here is useful or beautiful or both, and prices are reasonable.

Foofaraw
South Street Seaport
19 Fulton St. (Water St.)
964-0478
Mon. to Sat. 10:00 A.M. to 10:00 P.M.; Sun. noon to 8:00 P.M.

Everything in this cheerful shop is painted by hand, from the tiny baby shoes to sweater dresses to little boxes to scarves to shirts to kids' clothes. You have to hunt for very stylish designs, but you will enjoy looking through the whimsical merchandise that has become so chic for upscale trend setters. Prices are reasonably reasonable.

The Gazebo
660 Madison Ave. (61st St.)
832-7077
Mon. to Sat. 9:00 A.M. to 6:30 P.M.; Sun. 1:30 P.M. to 6:00 P.M.

An enchanted forest of Americana: pastel rag rugs, quilts, painted wicker, stuffed animals, pillows, knickknacks—a whole array of country-cousin gifts. Painted plates, summer porch ceramics, a small collection of dresses and sweaters and more will keep you browsing for a while. Prices are expensive, but the quality is first-rate.

The Glass Store
1242 Madison Ave. (89th St.)
289-1970
Mon. to Sat. 10:00 A.M. to 6:00 P.M.

This airy corner shop is filled with some of the most superb and some of the most commercial glassworks we've seen. If you collect contemporary paperweights, hand-blown vases, perfume jars, swizzle sticks, glass beads, glasses, sculptures and so on, then stop in here for a look. Prices are fairly reasonable, and you will be sure to find something unique to give away or, better yet, to hold onto for yourself.

Greek Island
217 E. 60th St.
355-7547
Mon. to Sat. 11:00 A.M. to 6:00 P.M.

A great gift haven for those all-cotton rag rugs, homespun knit sweaters, understated dresses and jackets, baskets, jewelry, shoulder bags and classic black wool Greek captain's caps. Prices are reasonable, the staff is pleasant, and the shop is a nice little entree into the Islands, with Greek music and a Mediterranean ambience.

Incorporated Gallery
1200 Madison Ave. (87th St.)
831-4466
Mon. to Sat. 11:00 A.M. to 6:00 P.M. (Thurs. to 8:00 P.M.)

Loads of ceramics and a few fiber pieces make a visit here a delight for those who admire the decorative arts. Many of the pieces are functional, although the most exciting are too adventurous for everyday use. You may have to look hard, as there is so much, in varying degrees of quality, jumbled together. A good place to keep in mind for gifts for your more creative and open-minded friends.

Petit Loup American
187 Columbus Ave.
(68th St.)
873-5358
Mon. to Fri. 11:00 A.M. to 10:00
P.M.; Sat. noon to 10:00 P.M.

A bright, cheerful store filled with all sorts of soft sculptures (hanging cacti, hunting trophies for your wall), darling dolls with a handmade look, wall ornaments featuring barnyard friends, stickers, coffee mugs and a host of animal motif objects. A great place for children and their parents.

Pineapple Primitives
South Street Seaport
19 Fulton St.
(Water St.)
608-4803
Mon. to Sat. 10:00 A.M. to 10:00
P.M.; Sun. noon to 6:00 P.M.

This charming shop sells fragrant herbal wreaths, candles, scented soaps, folk-art home accessories, toys and wall decorations. Prices are reasonable.

P.S. I Love You
1242 Madison Ave.
(89th St.)
722-6272
Mon. to Sat. 10:00 A.M. to
6:00 P.M.

A tiny boutique featuring pretties of the hearts-and-flowers variety. Pastel coffee mugs, a rainbow of writing papers, greeting cards, deco-style hair accessories, hand-painted T-shirts and heart mobiles will appeal to the sentimental in you.

Saint Rémy
818 Lexington Ave.
(62nd St.)
759-8240
Mon. to Sat. 10:00 A.M. to
6:00 P.M.

The fragrance of lavender greets you as you wander into this provincial oasis. Saint Rémy carries Pierre Deux–style fabrics, loads of fresh herbs and spices, vinegars, jams, fabric-covered notebooks, and crockery—French country choices for any gift occasion.

Serendipity 3
225 E. 60th St.
838-3531
Mon. to Fri. 11:30 A.M. to
midnight; Sat. 11:30 A.M. to 2:00
A.M.; Sun. noon to midnight

A tiny store known more for its ice cream and young boy waiters than its gifts. But you can find some unusual items, such as hand-blown wine goblets, hand-painted T-shirts, coffee mugs and some unattractive, hostile-looking New Wave accessories, which seem to be a hit with the crowds of teenage girls who make Serendipity one of their favorite snack stops.

Sointu
20 E. 69th St.
570-9449
Mon. to Sat. 11:00 A.M. to 6:00
P.M. (Thurs. to 8:00 P.M.)

The Finnish word *sointu* means "harmony and balance," which is exactly what you will find in this charming shop just off Madison Avenue. It looks more like a gallery than a boutique, with enough Museum of Modern Art award winners to make any home look refined and elegant in that European way. The superb designs hail from Scandinavia as well as France, Germany, Holland, Italy and even Japan. You will find among the contemporary styles the most exquisite desk accessories, titanium jewelry, stainless steel decorative arts, black leather carryalls and those popular high-tech pens and pencils.

Prices are unbelievably reasonable, the sales staff is knowledgeable and helpful, and the location is perfect if you are staying at the Westbury. All in all, it's well worth a stop.

Tianguis Folk Art
**284 Columbus Ave.
(73rd St.)
799-7343**
Mon. to Sat. 11:00 A.M. to 8:00 P.M.; Sun. noon to 6:00 P.M.

This two-tier shop specializes in lovely treasures from Third World nations. The clothes are of the Sermoneta and Putumayo ethnic-chic style, and there are loads of colorful sashes from Guatemala, sisal bags from Kenya, gift items from Mexico and a whole host of other possibilities. The handmade sweaters are beautiful, the dresses have some impeccable workmanship, the jewelry is attractive in a folk-art way, and the sales staff is very helpful. With the reasonable prices, you'll have no trouble finding something special to take home.

The U.N. Gift Shop
**United Nations
45th Street at First
Avenue
754-7700**
Daily 9:30 A.M. to 5:30 P.M.

Forge your way through the hordes of tour groups to see the gift collections offered from member nations. Everything from Fourth World crafts to European arts are available at reasonable prices. It's a good place for holiday gifts and unusual finds.

Wax Paper
**118 Prince St.
(Greene St.)
966-4590**
Tues. to Sat. noon to 7:00 P.M.; Sun. noon to 6:00 P.M.

Everything here is handmade, from the tapered candles and wooden chopping boards to the greeting cards and lovely jewelry. It's a great place for gift shopping—especially during the holidays—if your friends like hand-blown glass, wooden boxes and hand-loomed shawls. Prices aren't bad for such pretties.

Zona
**484 Broome St.
(Wooster St.)
925-6750**
Tues. to Sat. noon to 6:00 P.M.; Sun. 1:00 P.M. to 5:00 P.M.

Zona is a new age shop with a Zen attitude about the home. If you don't have peace of mind when you enter, you will no doubt leave feeling calmer. The sparse shop is quiet, with only tranquil music playing, and the limited line of merchandise is at its bare-bones ascetic basic. You'll discover black and white Japanese river rocks, gardening tools and a marvelous collection of Soleri wind chimes here. These distinctive bells are made by workers at Arcosanti, Paolo Soleri's futuristic vision of the utopian community (lost on the desert near Scottsdale). Zona is worth a trip, and you may find yourself walking home with a bell, three pounds of glass nuggets to put in a dish or the perfect trowel for your windowsill garden.

Jenny B Goode
1194 Lexington Ave.

This charming store is filled with indispensable novelties such as Lalique ashtrays, hand-painted T-shirts, handwoven shawls, Lucite radios, herbal wreaths, fabulous evening bags, provincial crockery (including the

(81st St.)
794-2492
*Mon. to Fri. 10:00 A.M. to 7:00
P.M.; Sat. 10:00 A.M. to 6:00 P.M.*

Jorice
1057 Second Ave.
(55th St.)
752-0129
*Mon. to Fri. 10:00 A.M. to 6:30
P.M. (Thurs. to 8:00 P.M.); Sat.
10:30 A.M. to 6:00 P.M.*

Laughing Stock
South Street Seaport
19 Fulton St.
(Water St.)
964-1885
*Mon. to Sat. 10:00 A.M. to 10:00
P.M.; Sun. noon to 8:00 P.M.*

Mabel's
1046 Madison Ave.
(79th St.)
734-3263
*Mon. to Sat. 10:00 A.M. to
6:00 P.M.*

The Mad Monk
500 Sixth Ave.
(12th St.)
242-6678
*Mon. to Sat. 11:00 A.M. to 7:00
P.M.; Sun. noon to 7:00 P.M.*

The Mediter-ranean Shop
876 Madison Ave.
(71st St.)
879-3120
*Mon. to Fri. 10:00 A.M. to 5:30
P.M.; Sat. 10:00 A.M. to 5:00 P.M.*

Peter Rabbit dishware for children), deco teapots and a chorus line of stuffed animals. Definitely worth a visit.

This little treasure of a store sells handmade glass and ceramics created by talented artisans. Coowner Maurice is a charmer, with stories and background on each artist. You'll find beautiful perfume jars, vases, paperweights and a collection of sparkling objets d'art, most of which are reasonably priced. Christmas is a particularly lovely season here, with hand-blown ornaments that are almost too pretty to put away the rest of the year.

A delightful little store filled with stenciled New York motif T-shirts nicely displayed in Lucite frames, to make them look more like works of art than body wear. You'll also find New Wave accessories, cards and a very helpful sales staff. Another location at 19 Christopher Street (691-8695).

This may well be our absolutely favorite store in New York. The lovely owner has named her shop after her black and white cat, and the place is a veritable barnyard of enchanting accessories (to wear and to look at) and gifts, featuring a delightful menagerie of animals. Cat cushions, piglet belts, duck tooled leather accessories, kitty vases—everything has a naïf charm and generally affordable price. There are also some exquisite crocheted sweaters, handmade rag rugs, artisan's wallpaper and a variety of other inventive, highly personal crafts creations. We just regret that we didn't have a chance to meet Miss Mabel, who we can only presume is as enchanting as her pretty owner.

This offbeat pottery shop is filled with wonderful handmade treasures that will give your home that craftsy Rhinebeck look. There are some great finds here, from teapots and goblets to dishes and vases. Our only reservation is for the collection of baroque ceramic mirrors; they require a certain freeform visual perception to truly enjoy.

Portuguese ceramics make for very pretty planters, tea sets, trivets, vases and crockery, which fill this little shop. Fabric-covered frames and other decorative objects sport delicate print designs that are pretty without being fussy.

Metropolitan Museum of Art Shop
Fifth Avenue at 82nd Street
535-7710
Sun. 11:00 A.M. to 4:45 P.M.; Tues. 10:00 A.M. to 8:45 P.M.; Wed. to Sat. to 4:45 P.M.

If you love the objets d'art at the Met so much that you can't live without them, fear not. You can take home any of the tastefully done reproductions available in the museum's gift shop. Prints, crystal, jewelry, statuary, cards, calendars—the Met is doing a booming merchandising business with selected pieces from its collection. Prices are fairly reasonable.

The Museum Shop
Museum of Modern Art
37 W. 53rd St.
956-7544
Daily 11:00 A.M. to 5:45 P.M.

If clean-line design is your domestic trademark, you'll find all sorts of museum-endorsed home accessories that you won't be able to pass by: desk sets, pruning shears, stainless steel cream and sugar sets, children's games, crystal trifles, watches, date books, scarves and, of course, its famous cards and letters. Prices are actually reasonable for such beautifully designed works of household art. If you're a member, the prices will be even more within reach.

Mythology Unlimited
370 Columbus Ave. (78th St.)
874-0774
Mon. to Fri. 11:00 A.M. to 9:00 P.M.; Sat. and Sun. 11:00 A.M. to 6:00 P.M.

In this white tiled shop you'll find an eclectic grouping of novelties, books, trifles and objets d'art that some people simply cannot live without. But then, who can resist duck caps with bills for visors, the twenty or so amusing mini erasers, windup robot toys, books on bizarre architecture, butterfly kites, David Hockney posters, the myriad of rubber stamps, barnyard ceramic serving dishes or simulated waffles with melting butter? Definitely worth a stop if the happy crowds in this playpen aren't too forbidding.

Only Hearts
281 Columbus Ave. (73rd St.)
724-5608
Mon. to Sat. 11:00 A.M to 7:00 P.M.

This tiny slip of a store specializes in gifts and clothing touched with hearts (its motto: "If there isn't a heart on it, it's free"). Most things here are charming; some are of dubious quality but irresistible all the same if you are a romantic at heart. Salt shakers, vinyl valentine change purses, sunglasses, necklaces and bracelets, undershirts and panties all are affected with tender heartthrobs. Prices are reasonable.

Home

CHINA · CRYSTAL

Baccarat
55 E. 57th St.

Baccarat has been the crystal of kings for more than two centuries—Louis XV of France sponsored the company's

826-4100
Mon. to Sat. 9:30 A.M. to 5:30 P.M.

foundation in 1764. Its fame has since spread to the four corners of the globe, and Baccarat's premier position in table crystal is undisputed. It's a crystal with a particularly high lead content, which makes it unusually sparkling and pure. There is a wide choice of glasses, with stems and without, modern and classic, priced high but not impossibly so. In addition to its own wares, Baccarat carries Ercuis and Christofle silverware upstairs, the superb Ceralene-Raynaud china and a complete collection of Les Etains du Manoir pewter. With what's carried on the two floors of this refined shop, you could create the most elegant table in the world.

Ludwig Beck of Munich
Trump Tower
Level D
725 Fifth Ave.
(56th St.)
308-2025
Mon. to Sat. 10:00 A.M. to 6:00 P.M.

If you want to dine like a king, Ludwig Beck is the only store in America where you can see the ornate Nymphenburg porcelain collection before you buy it. Right now, a 50-piece dinner set can be had for an introductory price of $34,000. Coffee and breakfast sets and giftware are also available. Everything's strictly handmade at a castle in Germany, just as it was in the eighteenth-century. The intricate details are hand painted and gilded by artisans. Pieces are well displayed in cases—which is probably as close to them as we'll ever get.

Cardel
615 Madison Ave.
(59th St.)
753-8880
Mon. to Sat. 10:00 A.M. to 6:00 P.M.

The perfect little shop to leave a marriage list, with silverware by Christofle, porcelain by Limoges and Rosenthal and crystal by Daum, Lalique and Saint Louis, as well as vases, fruit bowls, dishes, platters and glasses. This small, crowded shop could set newlyweds up for life, in style.

Finkelstein's
95 Delancey St.
(Orchard St.)
475-1420
Sun. to Fri. 9:00 A.M. to 5:00 P.M.

Finkelstein's has been selling imported crystal at reductions of up to 50 percent for over 60 years. Unfortunately, things aren't the way they used to be, and the big names in French crystal are now unavailable. The store still carries very pretty Polish crystal, however (although that selection, too, is becoming scarce), and some Italian and Chinese porcelain.

Robin Importers
510 Madison Ave.
(53rd St.)
752-5605
Mon. to Fri. 9:00 A.M. to 6:00 P.M.; Sat. 10:00 A.M. to 5:00 P.M.

Good buys in the heart of Madison. This shop doesn't look promising from the outside, but it's the nicest surprise in the district. Everything by way of tableware can be had at discounts that range from 20 to 60 percent: tablecloths and napkins, porcelain from France, Japan, Finland and elsewhere, stoneware, cutlery, ovenproof dishes and 200 patterns of flatware, all in excellent taste, most from well-known names, some really out of the ordinary. It also carries Melior coffee makers and can replace broken glasses. A store full of attractive, practical and advantageously priced items. A best in New York.

Royal Copenhagen Porcelain/ Georg Jensen Silversmiths
683 Madison Ave.
(61st St.)
759-6457
Mon. to Sat. 9:30 A.M. to 5:30 P.M.

Opposite its Georg Jensen silver department, this tranquil and elegant store displays the entire line of Royal Copenhagen porcelains. Most of the styles are a variation of the familiar blue and white floral design, but there are several much starker styles, as well as a few more ornate. Porcelain figurines, contemporary crystal and Danish teakwood pieces are also sold. Though the prices are probably higher here than a lot of other places, it's a good shop to look in before you buy.

Steuben Glass
715 Fifth Ave.
(56th St.)
752-1441
Mon. to Sat. 9:30 A.M. to 5:00 P.M.

Steuben crystal is highest ranked in the United States, perhaps in the world. Its Fifth Avenue showroom is beautiful, and the objects displayed there are admirably simple and of extraordinary quality. Don't miss the red room in the back, where glass sculptures are on view—pieces whose prices we daren't list. But everything is skillful and inventive. Go elsewhere for wine glasses—here you'll see an ark's worth of crystal animals, vases, fruit bowls or even gifts fit for royalty, who are indeed quite often the recipients.

Carole Stupell, Ltd.
61 E. 57th St.
260-3100
Mon. to Sat. 9:30 A.M. to 6:00 P.M.

The quintessence of a certain sort of careful taste: everything in this store is of very good quality, but nothing is very contemporary. Alas, that careful taste is sometimes questionable. The mannerist ornamentation on this brand-new porcelain, crystal and silver is sometimes stuffy and dull. The most famous names are all represented here, as well as Carole Stupell's own original creations and sculptures in porcelain, sterling and bronze. Prices are exactly what you'd imagine for a store on 57th Street near Madison. A luxury boutique for cautious souls.

FABRIC

Laura Ashley
714 Madison Ave.
(63rd St.)
371-0606

Laura Ashley has enough flowery prints to make a romantic out of anyone. Her chic Madison Avenue townhouse is loaded with fabric-covered knickknacks to match her perennially blooming dresses. The top floor is

Mon. to Sat. 10:00 A.M. to 6:00
P.M. (Thurs. to 7:00 P.M.)

devoted entirely to home furnishings; rolls and rolls of
Laura Ashley line the walls in lightweight, upholstery-
weight, drawing-room-weight and quilt-backed cottons,
ranging from $11 to $25 a yard. Wallpapers (untreated,
but the staff will recommend a vinyl coater), pillows,
quilts, trimmings, lampshades and even ceramic tiles
can transform your entire house into a charming
country garden.

B&J Fabrics
263 W. 40th St.
354-8150
*Mon. to Fri. 8:00 A.M. to 5:45
P.M.; Sat. 9:00 A.M. to 4:45 P.M.*

The best spot in midtown for mid-price fabrics:
everything is of the finest quality and is designed by the
big names—Anne Klein, Calvin Klein, Perry Ellis,
Valentino, Dior. Unlike those in some stores, these
fabrics are from the latest season, rather than last
year's styles. Prices are neither particularly high nor
particularly low. The service, however, is uncommonly
cordial.

Jerry Brown Imported Fabrics
37 W. 57th St.
753-3626
Mon. to Sat. 9:00 A.M. to 6:00 P.M.

There is no polyester in this store. There are no patterns,
zippers or trims, either. What there is, however, is one of
the best and classiest selections of natural fibers to be
found, from pure silk gold lamé to pink organza, from
ivory silk to ebony linen, wool flannel to cotton lawn. If
you know exactly what you want, this clean and orderly
shop probably has it in stock. One warning: as nice as the
salespeople are, this is not a place for novices. The
clientele here ask only intelligent questions.

Fabrications
146 E. 56th St.
371-3370
*Mon. to Fri. 10:00 A.M. to 6:00
P.M.; Sat. 11:00 A.M. to 5:00 P.M.*

Although high-tech has recently invaded this
contemporary fabric store, it has, surprisingly, enhanced
the appeal rather than ruined it. The entire front portion
of this large, sunny shop is now occupied by sleek red and
black Italian furniture, mostly covered in Fabrications
black cotton duck. There are also lots of uncovered
pieces—tea carts, umbrella stands, coat racks and
gadgetry, some really quite innovative and not readily
available elsewhere. Toward the back of the store are the
more familiar Fabrications fabrics—roll after roll of pure
imported cotton, arranged like a giant rainbow, with one
group of colors leading into the next. You'll find solids,
lots of geometrics, country French and a particularly
charming collection for the nursery, covered with hearts,
animals and balloons. Most of the designs can be made
into pillows, some are for stuffed toys, and you can also
buy framed fabric panels, ready-made or in do-it-yourself
kits. Considering the quality, the fabrics are quite
reasonably priced, and the staff is helpful and patient.

Liberty of London

What could we possibly say that you don't already know
about these beautiful prints with which the best-brought-
up little girls are so prettily clothed? We will add only

229 E. 60th St.
888-1057
*Mon. to Fri. 11:00 A.M. to 7:00
P.M.; Sat. 10:00 A.M. to 6:00 P.M.*

that the shop itself is charming, full of small Liberty accessories for yourself or your home, upholstery and dress fabrics and a superb collection of glazed chintz. Cottons, 36 inches wide, are $10 to $15 a yard; 48-inch and 54-inch widths of wool and furnishings fabrics are $35 to $48 a yard.

Marimekko
7 W. 56th St.
581-9616
*Mon. to Fri. 10:00 A.M. to 6:30
P.M.; Sat. 10:00 A.M. to 6:00 P.M.*

You can feel the Nordic influence in this very quiet loft-large shop that displays its famous fabrics amid carved wooden objects, Aalto stools, rustic furniture and contemporary accessories—all for sale, and all rather expensive. The patterns themselves are beautiful, bold and bright cottons. The most popular ones are translated onto an extensive line of Dan River sheets, quilts, crib clothes and towels. Wallpaper, trims and wall hangings, as well as a line of table linens and paper products, also carry Marimekko designs. The cottons, mostly 52 inches wide, are $17 to $27 a yard, and some are vinyl coated.

Paron Fabrics
140 W. 57th St.
247-6451
*Mon. to Fri. 9:00 A.M. to 6:00
P.M.; Sat. 9:00 A.M. to 5:00 P.M.*

Where else but fashionable 57th Street could this Loehmann's-like fabric store survive and thrive? The Perry Ellis fabrics, shown a few windows down in Bendel's, and the Anne or Calvin Kleins from Bergdorf's are all here, waiting to be sewn (by you). There are rolls and rolls of quality cloth (some in limited quantities) at very reasonable prices. Miraculously, everything is labeled by content, which makes the intitial picking that much easier. The staff is about as helpful as you'd expect.

Pierre Deux
870 Madison Ave.
(71st St.)
570-9343
*Mon. to Sat. 10:00 A.M. to
5:45 P.M.*

No surprises here. Classical music, brick floors, blond wood antiques and a cheery ambience greet you in this two-story salute to Pierre Deux's provincial florals. The home furnishings department upstairs has some bright ideas to help customers bring a little color into their city lives. The saleswomen wear the ubiquitous floral print chemises and skirts, and the clients show off their quilted handbags, which still look like oversized cosmetic carryalls more appropriate for the inside of a suitcase than as an accessory to street wear. There are some adorable toys and children's clothes, so kids can grow up in style. Prices that are not unexpected for first-class florals. Another location at 381 Bleecker Street (675-4054).

Regent Fabrics
122 E. 59th St.
355-2039
*Mon. to Fri. 9:30 A.M. to 6:30
P.M.; Sat. 10:00 A.M. to 6:00 P.M.*

This is your basic, one-stop, quality East Side fabric store. On the main floor is a good (though not great) selection of cloth at decent (but not discount) prices. Most fabrics come in a large choice of colors. Occasionally what you want is on sale. Downstairs are pattern books galore, notions, knickknacks, buttons, trims and an excellent selection of yarns and knitting and crocheting paraphernalia. The staff is patient, helpful and interested. It's a nice place to do business.

FURNITURE

Bien Aimé
231 E. 51st St.
688-4643
Mon. to Fri. 10:00 A.M. to 6:00 P.M.; Thurs. 11:00 A.M. to 7:00 P.M.; Sat. noon to 5:00 P.M.

Rack systems: two sturdy poles on which you build the room of your dreams. Drafting tables, cabinets, shelves and files all connect and combine to suit your needs. Choose from aluminum, Formica or oak veneer finishes. Chairs are also available. The prices are another pleasant surprise. And while you're in the neighborhood, look around: the block on 51st Street between Second and Third avenues is, on the whole, very good for furniture.

Bon Marché
55 W. 13th St.
620-5550
Mon. to Sat. 10:30 A.M. to 6:30 P.M.

It specializes in the kind of furniture New York apartment dwellers love: wall units, bookshelves and desks, in Formica and in wood; coffee tables and affordable couches; knockoff Breuer chairs and the like. It's all very simple design, nothing extraordinary, but it is sturdy. Attractive glass items, vases, bibelots and an excellent choice of all kinds of lamps make this our favorite inexpensive furniture store. Another location at 1060 Third Avenue, near 63rd Street (620-5592).

Brancusi
938 First Ave.
(51st–52nd sts.)
688-7980
Mon. to Sat. 9:30 A.M. to 6:00 P.M. (Mon. and Thurs. to 8:00 P.M.)

If you can't find the table you want here, Brancusi will custom make it for you. An immense selection of every style, size and kind of table in every material: glass, stainless steel, chrome, brass, wrought iron and so on. Chrome mirrors, lamps and shelves, too. Acceptable but nothing more. Prices are strictly retail.

Conran's
Citicorp Center
160 E. 54th St.
371-2225
Mon. to Fri. 10:00 A.M. to 9:00 P.M.; Sat. 10:00 A.M. to 7:00 P.M.; Sun. noon to 6:00 P.M.

After London, Paris and Brussels, New York finally rated its own Conran's store, now an institution in the Citicorp Center. Here's where to find an inexhaustible supply of furniture, accessories, fabrics, linens and kitchen equipment, simple in design, easy to live with and moderately priced. Everything is appealing here, from the collection of sofas, tables, bookshelves and beds, to the imaginary dining rooms complete with tables, chairs and hanging lamps, to beds, children's desks, bunks and folding chairs. The home furnishings department, with its glasses, cutlery, dishes, vases, spices, soaps, lamps, handmade rugs, diaries, fabrics and window shades, is no less fetching. It's hard to walk out empty-handed, and at these prices, you won't want to. Another location at 2–8 Astor Place, near 8th Street (505-1515).

Knoll International
105 Wooster St.
334-1500
Tues. to Sat. 9:00 A.M. to 5:00 P.M.

Classic modern furniture at its finest. Seating, tables, cabinets and accessories by Marcel Breuer, Mies van der Rohe, Eero Saarinen, Richard Meier and the like. Luxury fabrics to order, too. This is the showroom—a huge loft space interspersed with museum-quality furniture. Prices are understandably sky-high, but all it takes is a letter from your interior designer and you can get 55 percent off list price.

Mondrian
1021 Second Ave.
(54th St.)
355-7373
Mon. to Fri. 10:00 A.M. to 6:30 P.M.; Sat. to 6:00 P.M.

The most serious spot in New York for built-to-order natural wood or lacquer furniture. It also carries a collection of modular pieces that are simple in style and fit in easily with most decors. The fourteen colors of lacquer are superb. As for the wood—oak or maple—it's constructed to your dimensions and stained according to your wishes. This is where to come for good-quality wall units, bedroom furnishings, children's furniture and magnificent color coordinates at very reasonable prices.

Maurice Villency/ Roche Bobois
200 Madison Ave.
(35th St.)
725-4840
Mon. to Sat. 10:00 A.M. to 6:00 P.M. (Thurs. to 8:00 P.M.); Sun. noon to 5:00 P.M.

Good-quality furniture whose discreet design has been earning plaudits for many years now. The ground floor has stylized pieces in beautiful materials: leather sofas and sectionals, Italian marble tables and contemporary lacquer beds, all clashing somewhat with the American and Scandinavian selections. The merchandise, however, is extremely well made. Villency is doubtless the most pleasant furniture store in New York, as its high prices attest.

Wicker Garden
1318 Madison Ave.
(93rd St.)
410-7000
Mon. to Sat. 10:00 A.M. to 6:00 P.M.

The atmosphere is very Victorian in this realm of beautifully displayed, beribboned white wickerwork. Your eye won't know where among the irresistible designs to alight first: there are beds, cradles, rocking chairs and many other objects, both old and new. At 1320 Madison Avenue there's a children's section, The Wicker Garden's Baby (348-1166). A paradise for wicker wackies.

Workbench
470 Park Ave.
(32nd St.)
481-5454
Mon. to Sat. 10:00 A.M. to 6:00 P.M. (Thurs. to 8:00 P.M.); Sun. noon to 5:00 P.M.

Contemporary, all-purpose furniture in maple, oak and teak, simplified to the point of the rudimentary, without the slightest ornamentation, at prices that are also relatively spare. Less style than Conran's, but more than many others. Nothing is in bad taste, because it's functional, well conceived and colorful (which helps compensate for its coldness). A few sofas upholstered with attractive fabrics. Various locations.

KITCHEN ·
HOUSEWARES

Bazaar de la Cuisine
1003 Second Ave.
(53rd St.)
421-8028
Mon. to Sat. 10:00 A.M. to 6:00 P.M.

Everything for the gourmet's kitchen: an absolutely remarkable array of economical imported and domestic articles displayed in every nook and cranny—including on the ceiling—of this large store. Not only is there a vast selection, but everything comes in sizes from minuscule to maximum. Espresso makers, gadgets, pots, pans, processors, an impressive collection of copperware (retinning and rentals, too). Look here first.

Bridge Kitchenware
214 E. 52nd St.
688-4220
Mon. to Fri. 9:00 A.M. to 5:30 P.M.; Sat. 10:00 A.M. to 5:00 P.M.

Professionals and amateurs alike are absolutely unanimous that this is the best-stocked store for top-quality kitchen equipment this side of the Atlantic. It's a huge showroom offering the finest in kitchenware: copper and earthenware dishes, French ovenproof porcelain, baking supplies, bowls, pots, graters, coffee makers, appliances and pastry brushes, all presented in the most functional and attractive manner possible. An entire wall is covered with the world's best knives, and there's also a fine display of copper casseroles—it's a magnificent selection of useful items at more than reasonable prices. Browsers are barely tolerated, however; this isn't Bloomingdale's, and the salespeople, though fairly pleasant, don't waste time on people who can't make up their minds.

Brookstone
South Street Seaport
18 Fulton St.
(Water St.)
344-8108
Sun. to Thurs. 10:00 A.M. to 10:00 P.M.; Fri. and Sat. 10:00 A.M. to 11:00 P.M.

Brookstone has made it to Manhattan and is nicely established in a vintage building, perfect for the homegrown nature of these household essentials. You will have no trouble picking up a clipboard and taking your own orders for an ersatz rock with a secret compartment to hide house keys, work gloves, fire starter sticks, a small whistle that "blasts with authority," beautifully designed garden tools, a mop, "the world's best" yo-yo, horseshoes, fluted Champagne glasses and a miniature beauty aid that solves the problem of "how to dry your hair in Paris." A marvelous store in which you'll find lots of fascinated shoppers and a very friendly sales staff.

La Cuisinière
867 Madison Ave.
(72nd St.)
861-4475

Alas, the window promises more than the shop itself delivers. It's true that there's a pretty assortment of French earthenware from Gien et Luneville, a little Wedgwood and Minton, some classic ceramic and iron

Mon. to Sat. 10:00 A.M. to
6:00 P.M.

cookware and a variety of other kitchen appurtenances—even some antique collectibles. The welcome is friendly, but in our opinion this is no more than a chic neighborhood store, not worthy of the fuss people make over it.

First Stop Housewares
1025 Second Ave.
(54th St.)
838-0007
Mon. to Sat. 10:00 A.M. to
6:00 P.M.

Just a few doors up from Bazaar de la Cuisine, this equally well-stocked kitchen store carries everything you need if you're not Craig Claiborne. What it lacks in selection and variety of madeleine pans and copper pots it makes up for in good, basic housewares: cookware with names you can pronounce, teapots and a wide assortment of appliances. Also: dishes, potholders, paper ware, spice racks, hooks, hangers and serving carts. In short, a very manageable place to start setting up your kitchen.

Hammacher Schlemmer
147 E. 57th St.
421-9000
Mon. to Sat. 10:00 A.M. to
6:00 P.M.

Gadget heaven: from the smallest to the biggest, the most useful to the most superfluous, the most dear to the cheapest, the most charming to the most egregious. The entire store is devoted to inventions and finds; such as remote-control car starters, barbecues, vacuum cleaners, jukeboxes, pants pressers, classic syphons, putting greens, scales and a whole new world of telecommunication aids. Hammacher Schlemmer specializes in those items that are the only ones to do what they do—or that do it better than any others. A rather mediocre welcome awaits you, unfortunately, but this store doesn't have to try harder; its reputation is unassailable. Recommended for people who appreciate original ideas.

Hoffritz for Cutlery
331 Madison Ave.
(43rd St.)
697-7344
Mon. to Sat. 9:00 A.M. to 6:00 P.M.

Scissors to cut fabric, paper, nails, hair—these are familiar enough, and you'll find them here, amid an inventory of the most exotic and ingenious varieties imaginable: scissors for cutting double-knit polyester, superspeedy scissors, silhouette scissors, scissors for cutting ribbons. You've probably never seen many of these before or realized you had need of them, but they are delightfully inventive. Hoffritz is also known for its quality knives, and it's a good source for gadgets and gifts. Various locations.

Manhattan Ad Hoc Housewares
842 Lexington Ave.
(64th St.)
752-5488
Mon. to Fri. 10:00 A.M. to 6:30
P.M. (Mon. and Thurs. to 7:00

Form always follows function in this high-tech housewares habitat, where you'll find everything that's ever been designed well, from the most useful of plastic key rings to the best of all appliances and the most elegant of Italian watches. Cookware, wire shelving, a huge quantity of high-quality pots and pans, china and stoneware, restaurant supplies (salt and pepper shakers, sugar jars, napkin dispensers), lots of chemistry-type

P.M.); Sat. 10:00 A.M. to 6:00 P.M.

flasks and more elegant glassware, plus such desk items as pens, paper clips and staplers. Everything seems so simple and stylish when it comes in red, black, white or chrome. Ad Hoc Softwares, at 410 West Broadway in SoHo, puts a soft touch on high-tech.

Pampered Kitchens
21 E. 10th St.
(University Pl.)
982-0340
Mon. to Sat. noon to 6:00 P.M.

A small, homey store of long standing that offers items combining old-world beauty and contemporary function. You'll also find a collection of antique copper instruments, pottery and baskets handmade by international craftsmen. A charming and distinctive shop.

Pottery Barn
117 E. 59th St.
741-9132
Mon. to Sat. 10:00 A.M. to 6:30 P.M. (Mon. and Thurs. to 8:30 P.M.); Sun. noon to 5:00 P.M.

These stores are the most popular for rustic and semicrystal glasses—from inexpensive barware to museum reproductions—plus stoneware, china and earthenware dishes, various accessories and the latest gadgets. The Pottery Barn is one of the most modern and best-stocked sources for a wide range of interesting, attractive and indispensable items. Watch for the major sales, when the prices are even better. Excellent remainders and seconds, especially at the warehouse, 231 Tenth Avenue (741-9120). Several locations throughout the city, including 250 West 57th Street (741-9145) and 51 Greenwich Avenue, near Sixth Avenue (741-9140).

D. F. Sanders
952 Madison Ave.
(75th St.)
879-6161
Daily 10:30 A.M. to 6:30 P.M. (Thurs. to 8:00 P.M.)

If you are looking for a perfectly designed household accessory, whether it be a simple stainless steel demitasse set, a pair of ice tongs, the ultimate vacuum cleaner, linen napkins, high-tech pens and pencils or any of the other elegant items that no proper home should be without, then rush over to D.F. Sanders and stock up on little lovelies that will give your pied à terre that Museum of Modern Art contemporary-design look.

Spice Market
265 Canal St.
(Broadway)
966-1310
Mon. to Fri. 8:00 A.M. to 6:00 P.M.; Sat. 9:00 A.M. to 6:00 P.M.; Sun. 10:00 A.M. to 5:00 P.M.

Everything to enable you to cook well—herbs and spices, packaged foods and teas, and a large selection of kitchen appliances and espresso machines—at discount prices (it goes without saying in this neighborhood). Particularly good selection of copper and aluminum utensils.

West Town House
2276 Broadway
(82nd St.)
724-5000
Mon. to Sat. 10:30 A.M. to 6:30 P.M.; Sun. noon to 5:00 P.M.

A handsome home store filled with everything from high-tech accessories and traditional wicker to good-looking linens and a limited line of furniture. Everything is well designed and merchandised in a medium-tech atmosphere that will induce you to buy a clock, desk lamp, shower curtain or any of the other contemporary temptations.

Wolfman Gold & Good Co.

**484 Broome St.
(Wooster St.)
431-1888**
*Tues. to Fri. 11:00 A.M. to 7:00
P.M.; Sat. 11:00 A.M. to 6:00 P.M.
Sun. noon to 5:00 P.M.*

This countrified city shop has made monogrammed linens SoHo chic. In a small (by loft standards) space, a profusion of china complements a wonderful collection of French sugar bowls and creamers. Restaurant goblets mix with crystal, and black and white spackled dishes look extra special on lace place mats. There's a good selection of art deco silverware, lots of unusual baskets and an assortment of pretty gadgets, candles and canisters that you won't find in every other store. There is another branch at 142 East 73rd Street (288-0404), but it is without the two charming shop cats who live in SoHo.

Zona

**484 Broome St.
(Wooster St.)
925-6750**
Tues. to Sun. noon to 5:30 P.M.

Zona is not the kind of store you'd find in Sioux City. In fact, if it were anywhere else but SoHo, it would never work. But luckily, here it is. Inside this warm, wooded space is an eclectic mixture of high-quality objects. Smith Hawken garden tools from England decoratively line one wall, while an enormous collection of Soleri wind chimes completely covers another. Soothing music fills the room. Teak garden benches and Italian terra-cotta bring the outdoors in. There are lots of other unusual objects: Japanese river rocks, a fine potpourri from Nantucket, black marbles. The mood swings with the seasons; for example, in the winter, hearth and home are the concentration. As you can imagine, everything's very textural and very experimental. The price range is as broad as is the range of merchandise.

LIGHTING

Bon Marché Lamps and Accessories

**74 Fifth Ave.
(13th St.)
620-5559**
*Mon. to Sat. 10:30 A.M. to
6:30 P.M.*

Aside from the Avenue Bazaars, you won't find any less expensive outlet for modern lamps in New York. Lamps for the office, living room, children's rooms; lamps that stand on desks, hang from the wall, stand up and clamp down—there are lamps for every use here, in every color and basic contemporary style. Another location at 1060 Third Avenue (620-5592).

Bowery Lighting

**132 Bowery
(Grand St.)
966-9855**
Daily 9:00 A.M. to 5:00 P.M.

The best source for discounted lights. Bowery Lighting could brighten up New York City and have watts to spare. The main downtown branch, in the middle of the lighting district, is a rambling barn of a store with lights standing and hanging from every available space. On the first floor an immense variety of track and recessed styles share the glow with ornate chandeliers, simple glass domes and desk and floor models. Another section has beautiful Tiffany styles. Upstairs is an entire contemporary gallery. The smaller store, at 1144 Second Avenue, near 60th

Street (832-0990), carries only contemporary lighting—the best of the downtown stock (including Kovacs, all track and recessed brands), plus some imports of its own. Both places have friendly and knowledgeable salespeople.

Just Bulbs
938 Broadway
(22nd St.)
228-7820
Mon. and Thurs. 9:00 A.M. to 6:00 P.M.; Tues., Wed. and Fri. 8:00 A.M. to 5:00 P.M.; Sat. (before Christmas) 9:00 A.M. to 6:00 P.M.

Just bulbs, and nothing else. Twenty-five thousand lights are on display in this beautifully designed warehouse of a store. And each and every one of them turns on, so you can see the light before you buy it. There are bulbs here that you can't find anyplace else: European bases with American voltage, American bases with European voltage, photography lights, color-corrected bulbs, old-fashioned bubble bulbs, fancy Christmas lights, plant lights, fluorescents that look like incandescents and vice versa ... just about any hard-to-get or hard-to-live-without bulb you want. Mother and daughter Shirley and Judi Brooks are delightful to deal with and can offer expert advice on what to buy. A complete lighting consultation for the price of one bulb.

George Kovacs Lighting
831 Madison Ave.
(69th St.)
861-9500
Mon. to Sat. 10:00 A.M. to 6:00 P.M.

George Kovacs makes lamps that talk to you, saying such things as, "See your living room for the first time." And they all have names: Big Coolie, Stubby, The Saucer. But, gimmicks aside, these are mostly well-designed contemporary lamps that come in a wide range of styles and colors. There are lots of brights, chrome and brass, as well as a large collection of Japanese paper lamps, flexible mountings and Oriental styles of the sort you see copied all over town. Most of the models are simple and pleasant, with an occasional bright spot in the bunch. The prices are never too high because nothing is really of the highest quality.

Lee's Studio Gallery
211 W. 57th St.
265-5670
Mon. to Fri. 9:30 A.M. to 6:30 P.M.; Sat. 9:30 A.M. to 6:00 P.M.

Every possible sort of small lamp is in this tiny store. You'll find anything from the most Milan high-tech to retro wall lights and floor lamps to ceiling fixtures to lights disguised as vases, sculptures, machines and flowers. A great source, since the prices are somewhat lower than standard interior designer heart-attack ones.

Let There Be Neon
451 W. Broadway
(Prince St.)
473-8630
Mon. to Fri. 9:30 A.M. to 6:00 P.M.; Sat. and Sun. noon to 5:00 P.M.

Not exactly the place to buy a good reading lamp, this cavelike store specializes in custom-designed neon: signs, furniture, even jewelry. There are lots of pieces on display, including chairs, dressing tables, mirror frames and the more common ("I love you," hearts and the Chrysler Building) signs. It's a fun place to stop, even if you aren't in the market for neon.

Light, Inc.
1162 Second Ave.

This shop is by far the most splendid modern lamp store in New York. If you like lamps that are both inventive and

(61st St.)
838-1130
Mon. to Fri. 10:00 A.M. to 6:00 P.M.; Sat. noon to 5:00 P.M.

aesthetically pleasing, unusual models, stylized forms and contemporary designs, you'll find what you're looking for here. Most of the lamps are imported from France and Italy; some are decorative, others more functional, but none banal. A full line of track lighting as well. Everything's very expensive, but a designer's discount can bring the prices back into the realm of reality.

Louis Mattia
980 Second Ave.
(52nd St.)
753-2176
Mon. to Fri. 9:00 A.M. to 5:30 P.M.

When you step through the door of this unusual shop, you will find all kinds of wall sconces and chandeliers in brass, crystal and bronze closing in on you like lush jungle foliage. It's slightly disorienting, but with Mr. Mattia acting as your guide on your lamp hunting expedition, you're sure to come out with trophies. There are two floors and thousands of items to explore, ranging from a three-color traffic signal for your rec room to a classic green-shaded Emeralite lamp for your rolltop desk, with everything imaginable in between. There is also a custom mounting and electrical conversion service that will turn anything you desire into a lamp. If you're lost and looking for the light at the end of the tunnel, this is the place to find it.

LINENS

E. Braun & Co.
717 Madison Ave.
(63rd St.)
838-0650
Mon. to Fri. 9:30 A.M. to 5:30 P.M.; Sat. 9:30 A.M. to 5:00 P.M.

Absolutely gorgeous traditional linens. Upper East Side mothers come here to stock up on exquisite monogrammed blanket covers, beautiful lace and embroidered sheets and pretty linen tablecloths with matching napkins for their young bride-to-be daughters. Sheets can be made to measure for odd-sized beds, and there are lovely sets of cocktail napkins and Swiss lace hankies to complete an elegant linen chest.

Brook Hill Linens
698 Madison Ave.
(62nd-63rd sts.)
2nd floor
688-1113
Mon. to Fri. 10:00 A.M. to 6:00 P.M.

You'll be greeted not only by a large collection of pillows covered in pastels and antique lace but also by a very friendly, helpful staff that encourages you to browse and join the mailing list so you can order these delectable bedroom pretties from home. This store carries embroidered pillows, patterns for handmade lacy coverlets and a stunning white embroidered cotton collection that is irresistible. Certainly worth a visit, particularly near the holidays, to stock up on pillows and accessories (the heart-shaped sachets are perfect) for your friends and no doubt for yourself. Prices are quite reasonable.

Descamp
723 Madison Ave.
(64th St.)

Descamp's linens are more honestly priced but somewhat less classy looking than Frette, Pratesi and Porthault, but they are of good quality, and the floral prints are

355-2522
Mon. to Sat. 10:00 A.M. to 6:00 P.M.

Frette
**787 Madison Ave.
(67th St.)
988-5221**
Mon. to Sat. 10:00 A.M. to 6:00 P.M.

Maison Henri
**617 Madison Ave.
(58th St.)
355-5463**
Mon. to Fri. 10:00 A.M. to 6:00 P.M.; Sat. 10:00 A.M. to 5:00 P.M.

Pratesi
**829 Madison Ave.
(69th St.)
288-2315**
Mon. to Fri. 9:30 A.M. to 6:00 P.M.; Sat. 10:00 A.M. to 6:00 P.M.

charming. There are accessories for babies and young children, patterns that look perfect in the Hamptons and a more tailored line for conservative boudoirs.

Only the real thing here, with a line of sensational linen, silk and cotton beauties that will turn any bedroom into a boudoir. The prices are staggering, but these pieces are of such high quality that they should last a lifetime if you're careful. A less elegant line of towels and terrycloth robes seems to be no less popular.

Thoroughly enchanting smocked dresses for little ladies and some adorable two-piece outfits for infant gentlemen supplement pretty, affordable linens for the bedroom. Owner Ginette is friendly, helpful and patient while you browse. It's hard to resist the sets of sheets with fragile lily of the valley embroidery, white-on-white appliqué and embroidery, the lovely tablecloths or any of the sweet baby pillowcases. Many items are in practical machine-washable blends. We think this little slip of a shop is absolutely charming.

There are extraordinary linen and cotton sheets here, all designed with the elegance and bearing the price tags befitting its well-heeled customers. The atmosphere is a bit formal and ceremonial, but the quality is so high and the designs are so pretty that your enthusiasm won't waver. Custom work is available if your bed won't accommodate any of the white-touched-with-color, floral, embroidered or fagoted sheets. Prices are enough to send you to bed for a week, particularly for the silk sheets and cashmere blankets. Delivery is available.

PLASTIC

Lucidity
**775 Madison Ave.
(66th St.)
861-7000**
Mon. to Fri. 10:30 A.M. to 6:30 P.M.; Sat. 11:00 A.M. to 6:00 P.M.

Perplexity
**237 E. 53rd St.
688-3571**
Mon. to Sat. 10:00 A.M. to 6:00 P.M.

Clocks, caddies, candlesticks, canes and canisters. The name says it all: this specialty shop has good-quality Lucite in every shape and form. The prices are reasonable, and a lot of the pieces are novel enough to warrant a visit. (This is *the* place for a genuine Lucite wagon.) There is a large selection of tables, chairs, desks and bath accessories, and custom-made furniture is also available.

All sorts of Lucite objects at 40 to 60 percent below retail. This might not amount to much when all you want is a pretty napkin caddy, but for a dining room table, the savings can be substantial. There are frames, kitchenware, furniture and lots of the expected accessories: recipe files, magazine racks, soap dishes, sugar holders. Perplexity also makes custom furniture.

Plastic Works!
1407 Third Ave.
(80th St.)
535-6486
Mon. to Sat. 10:00 A.M. to 7:00 P.M.; Sun. 12:30 P.M. to 5:30 P.M.

Discounted Lucite gifts, housewares and custom-made furniture. A more sophisticated assortment than Perplexity's, but not always up to the quality of Lucidity's. In addition to the Lucite, it sells everything else you can imagine in all types of plastic: desk accessories, hangers, place mats, picnic coolers, "glasses," frames, shower curtains, you name it. Most things are simply designed and reasonably priced. A good store for basics. Another location at 2107 Broadway, near 73rd Street (362-1000).

Plexicraft
514 W. 24th St.
924-3244
Mon. to Fri. 9:00 A.M. to 5:00 P.M.

Like Perplexity in midtown, this factory outlet tucked in among Chelsea warehouses and parking lots offers just about anything that can be made of Lucite or Plexiglas. Take the staff a sketch, and they'll help you design a monogrammed place mat, an étagère or a dining table. You can buy a single article or a gross, all top quality and at prices Plexicraft claims are 50 percent lower than those charged for identical items in the uptown stores.

SILVER

Buccellati
46 E. 57th St.
308-2900
Mon. to Sat. 9:30 A.M. to 5:30 P.M.

Italian silver at its best. Everything in this elegant store is designed in Milan by Mario Buccellati. He specializes in reproductions of antique Florentine silver, as expensive as they are beautiful and ornate. It's a very special style that will not appeal to those who prefer pure lines. The atmosphere is one of perfect courtesy, helpfulness and discretion. The chic Buccellati jewelry collection is also housed now in the new Trump Tower store.

Michael C. Fina
580 Fifth Ave.
(47th St.)
2nd floor
869-5050
Mon. to Fri. 9:00 A.M. to 5:30 P.M.

On the fringe of the diamond district, Michael C. Fina is not a shop like all the others. It offers a good selection of jewelry, crystal, gifts, china and clocks, but has, above all, an enormous stock of sterling at 20 to 30 percent less than most other stores. Choose from hundreds of place settings, serving pieces, bowls and trays, even a few antiques. But in order to see this fabulous selection, you have to stand patiently in line, give your name to a receptionist and wait until a salesperson is free to help you. This isn't Tiffany—but, then, neither are the prices.

Fortunoff
681 Fifth Ave.
(54th St.)

Fortunoff, "the source," has a comprehensive collection of silver to satisfy most tastes and budgets. Weave your way past the throngs around the jewelry counter and

343-8787
Mon. to Sat. 10:00 A.M. to 6:00 P.M. (Thurs. to 8:00 P.M.)

head for the third-floor antique silver department. The entire (albeit small) floor is devoted to magnificent tea services, trays, candelabras, knickknacks, flasks, one-of-a-kind pieces and special serving pieces. The turnover is great, so what you see one day may be gone the next. Some sections are constant: Old Sheffield silver plate, Victorian and Georgian silver, antique Tiffany silver. The fourth floor has more antiques, mostly from estate collections—individual pieces as well as entire services. It also offers an endless selection of most sterling, stainless and silver plate patterns on the market today, all at Fortunoff's famous discounted prices.

Jean Silversmiths
16 W. 45th St.
575-0723
Mon. to Thurs. 9:30 A.M. to 5:00 P.M.; Fri. 9:30 A.M. to 3:30 P.M.

A heavenly hodgepodge, this narrow boutique is crammed helter-skelter with piles of silver. You can buy (and sell) everything here: platters, candlesticks, tea services, coffee services, table settings—all at unbeatable prices, based fairly on the weight and quality of silver contained in the pieces. There is ridiculously priced silver plate but above all there's silver: sterling silver (98 percent pure) and pure silver (99.9 percent). The store also carries new silver, but Jean Silversmiths' specialty is the largest collection of discontinued and obsolete patterns of silver flatware in the country.

Royal Copenhagen Porcelain/ Georg Jensen Silversmiths
683 Madison Ave.
(61st St.)
759-6457
Mon. to Sat. 9:30 A.M. to 5:30 P.M.

Many of the contemporary Georg Jensen sterling and stainless patterns are sold elsewhere, but nowhere are they more beautifully displayed than in this elegant, hushed Madison Avenue store. Artfully arranged in glass-shelved cases, along with all the serving pieces, you can see the understated aesthetic and outstanding Danish craftsmanship that has made these designs so famous. Magnificent hollowware (individual pieces as well as sets), stunning candlesticks, trays and trinkets all bear the Jensen trademark. Abstract jewelry in silver and gold (some with stones) will appeal to those with modern taste … and a lot of money. The watch selection is unusual and superb.

Tiffany & Co.
727 Fifth Ave.
(57th St.)
755-8000
Mon. to Sat. 10:00 A.M. to 5:30 P.M.

Tiffany's merits yet another entry for its silver: though very classic and not all that original, the pieces are heavier than most, and the patterns are no more expensive than in other stores. In addition to the table settings, there is also a good choice of accessories in silver plate and sterling, which always make good gifts. The best American.

Image · Sound

PHOTOGRAPHY

Alkit Camera Shop
866 Third Ave.
(53rd St.)
832-2101
Mon. to Fri. 8:00 A.M. to 6:30 P.M.; Sat. 9:00 A.M. to 5:00 P.M.

A well-located, pleasant store with a very good selection of everything photographic, along with TVs, Seiko watches, binoculars, telephones and so on. The prices aren't rock-bottom, but the discount is good for a place with such an attractive atmosphere.

47th Street Photo
67 W. 47th St.
2nd floor
260-4410
Mon. to Thurs. 9:00 A.M. to 6:00 P.M.; Fri. 9:00 A.M. to 2:00 P.M.; Sun. 10:00 A.M. to 4:00 P.M.

Know what you want before venturing into this chaotic, crowded, littered store that sells cameras, film, computers, video gear, stereos, watches, typewriters, jewelry—you name it. You'll have to wait in line, and while the Hasidic Jews behind the counter are knowledgeable, they are harried and unwilling to show you much. Prices, as you can imagine, are the draw here, and they are excellent, perhaps the best in town. Look for its ads in the *New York Times* or *Wall Street Journal* to see what the selection is; if you don't like crowds, most items can be ordered over the telephone, or you can try its calmer other location at 115 West 45th Street.

Hirsch Photo
699 Third Ave.
(44th St.)
557-1150
Mon. to Fri. 8:00 A.M. to 6:00 P.M.; Sat. 10:00 A.M. to 4:00 P.M.

Hirsch is a welcome relief from the frenzied Broadway camera stores. It's well located, quiet and very well organized, with an intelligent, helpful staff. There are always good deals on used camera equipment, and while the new cameras aren't usually discounted, you will find some very good package deals.

Jems
785 Lexington Ave.
(61st St.)
838-4716
Mon. to Sat. 9:30 A.M. to 7:00 P.M.; Sun. 11:00 A.M. to 6:00 P.M.

Jems is in a good location and doesn't suffer from the intolerable crowds found at similar stores downtown. It's particularly good for camera equipment—the selection and prices are both commendable, and the service is reasonably good. In this spacious two-story shop you'll also find stereo gear, jewelry, binoculars, TVs and electronic equipment. Watch for the sales. Another location at 77 East 42nd Street (687-1333).

RECORDS ·
VIDEOTAPES

Bleecker Bob's Golden Oldies
118 W. 3rd St.
(MacDougal St.)
475-9677
Sun. to Fri. noon to 1:00 A.M. ; Sat. noon to 3:00 A.M.

Variety is not what you'll find here. It's strictly rock, and primarily vintage and current British import rock at that, along with music publications and New Wave clothing in back. There are used and rare records and a good choice of current New Wave/punk singles.

Discomat
716 Lexington Ave.
(57th–58th sts.)
759-3777
Mon. to Sat. 9:00 A.M. to 8:45 P.M.

The prices are very good in this slick, silver and red record store that sells pop and rock. Every week a "guaranteed" record is featured: you can take it home and listen to it, and if you don't love it, you'll get your money back. Aside from pop and rock, there's a decent selection of reggae and jazz. Be warned that neither checks nor credit cards are accepted. Other locations throughout the city.

Discophile
26 W. 8th St.
(MacDougal St.)
473-1902
Mon. to Thurs. 11:00 A.M. to 9:00 P.M.; Fri. and Sat. noon to 10:00 P.M.; Sun. 12:30 P.M. to 5:30 P.M.

If the crowds and noise on 8th Street get oppressive, duck into this calm oasis of music. Discophile claims to have the largest selection of classical imports in the country, and we won't dispute it. Many of the records have been owned previously, but they've been carefully checked and coded for quality. The best labels are represented, and this is *the* place to look for a hard-to-find classical favorite. There are also some jazz, folk and theater score records. Prices are excellent.

First Run
558 Third Ave.
(13th St.)
679-0049
Mon. to Sat. 11:30 A.M. to 8:30 P.M.; Sun. 2:00 P.M. to 6:00 P.M.

This small corner shop has a very good selection of current films on videotape, along with video games and accessories. You can rent or buy; the staff is helpful either way. Other locations at 1390 Third Avenue (772-3838) and 1147½ Second Avenue (935-1212).

The Golden Disc
239 Bleecker St.
(Sixth Ave.)
255-7899
Mon. to Sat. 11:30 A.M. to 8:00 P.M.; Sun. 11:30 A.M. to 9:00 P.M.

The selection is tremendous at The Golden Disc, a friendly shop carrying only used oldies. The focus is on rock and jazz and their cousins: rockabilly, blues, a cappella doo-wop and much more. The collection of rare 45s is outstanding.

Sam Goody
666 Third Ave.
(43rd St.)
986-8480
Mon. to Fri. 9:30 A.M. to 7:00 P.M.; Sat. 9:30 A.M. to 6:30 P.M.; Sun. noon to 5:00 P.M.

One of New York's best-known record stores (with branches continuing to open). The prices are good and it's an easy place to shop, but the selection is limited to the more recent releases in rock, pop, jazz and classical. A good store for a top-ten hit record, but not if you're looking for something different.

Music Masters
25 W. 43rd St.
840-1958
Mon. to Fri. 10:00 A.M. to 6:00 P.M.; Sat. 10:00 A.M. to 3:00 P.M.

A fantastic shop with more than 200,000 tapes of live opera, theater and concert performances. The tapes (which sell for $55) are arranged neatly on library shelves, along with private pressings of opera and American Musical Theater recordings. You can listen to these marvelous recordings before buying, and if you need something on which to listen to them at home, there's some top-notch stereo gear from Luxman and Tandberg. A must for opera and theater fanatics.

Orpheus Remarkable Recordings
1047 Lexington Ave.
(75th St.)
737-6043
Mon. to Sat. 10:30 A.M. to 6:30 P.M.

A small, very well organized shop with an excellent selection of high-quality pressings of classical, opera and theater score recordings. The records are rather expensive, but the quality is exceptional and the atmosphere friendly and pleasant.

Rare Bird Video
58 Wooster St.
(Broome St.)
334-8150
Daily 11:30 A.M. to 7:30 P.M.

This relatively new video shop in SoHo has a thorough selection of films on videotape, along with blank tapes and accessories. A membership costs $75 for the first year and $30 to renew; this entitles you to a 50 percent discount on rentals, a ten percent discount on sales and the opportunity to reserve the most popular, hard-to-get tapes. Local video art is sometimes shown as well.

The Record Exchange
842 Seventh Ave.
(54th St.)
247-3818
Tues. to Sat. noon to 6:00 P.M.

It's musty and messy in here, but you'll love looking through the terrific collection of rare and out-of-print records. No rock here, but there are some real gems in old jazz, classical, opera, early radio recordings and soundtracks. A collectors' shop with collectors' prices. Records are shipped anywhere.

Record Factory
17 W. 8th St.
228-4800
Mon. to Sat. 10:30 A.M. to 9:30 P.M. (Tues. and Wed. to 9:00 P.M.); Sun. 11:00 A.M. to 7:00 P.M.

This hectic store is best for rock and pop, and the selection of low-priced cutouts is noteworthy. The upstairs room has a good collection of jazz, and there's a very complete choice of cassettes for the Walkman addicts.

The Record Hunter
507 Fifth Ave.
(42nd–43rd sts.)
697-8970
Mon. to Sat. 9:00 A.M. to 6:30 P.M.

This big, chaotic, two-level store is a must for lovers of classical music and opera. The back room has a marvelous selection at good prices, with a helpful staff for the bewildered. It's also a good place to check for that hard-to-find jazz, folk, country or soundtrack record; only the selection of rock albums is thin. (But if you're looking for an old classic rock single, The Record Hunter will gladly order it for you.) There are lots of discount bins with a continually changing stock. One inconvenience: checks (even local) are not accepted.

Rock's in Your Head
157 Prince St.
(W. Broadway)
475-6729
Daily 1:00 P.M. to 8:00 P.M.

Only the latest rock (particularly New Wave and its ilk) is sold at this small shop. There's a juice bar in back to refresh weary punkers, along with a TV showing the latest videos and a good collection of rock T-shirts and buttons.

Tower Records
692 Broadway
(4th St.)
505-1500
Daily 9:00 A.M. to midnight

At last New York has the world's largest record store. If J&R isn't big enough for you, California's Tower Records puts still more under one roof. There's a very complete selection in every category, from rock and classical to children's and international folk, and the oldies singles selection is excellent. Prices are rock-bottom for discontinued classic recordings, and the open layout makes shopping a breeze. Even if Spago (L.A.'s trendy restaurant) isn't around the corner, it's worth a trip to Greenwich Village just to go through Tower's bins.

Video Buff
1221 Third Ave.
(71st St.)
744-2680
Mon. to Sat. 10:00 A.M. to 8:00 P.M.; Sun. 11:00 A.M. to 6:00 P.M.

Current films and a good selection of classics and cartoons are well displayed at Video Buff, a small, pleasant shop. Prices are competitive.

SOUND SYSTEMS · VIDEO

The Audio Exchange
28 W. 8th St.
(MacDougal St.)

This small shop a few steps down from chaotic 8th Street is crammed with the best names in stereo: Carver, ADS, Tandberg, McIntosh and so on. The service is very personal, and there's a well-equipped listening room. The Audio Exchange is particularly notable for its excellent

982-7191
*Mon. to Fri. 11:30 A.M. to 7:00
P.M.; Sat. 10:30 A.M. to 6:00 P.M.*

Crazy Eddie
212 E. 57th St.
980-5130
*Mon. to Sat. 10:00 A.M. to 10:00
P.M.; Sun. noon to 5:00 P.M.*

Harvey Electronics
2 W. 45th St.
575-5000
*Mon. to Fri. 9:30 A.M. to 6:00
P.M.; Sat. 10:00 A.M. to 6:00 P.M.*

Leonard Radio
55 W. 44th St.
840-2025
*Mon. to Fri. 9:30 A.M. to 6:00
P.M.; Sat. 9:30 A.M. to 5:00 P.M.*

Liberty Music
450 Madison Ave.
(50th St.)
753-0180
Mon. to Sat. 9:00 A.M. to 6:00 P.M.

Lyric Hi-Fi
1221 Lexington Ave.
(83rd St.)
535-5710
*Mon. to Sat. 10:00 A.M. to
6:00 P.M.*

selection of used top-of-the-line stereo gear, all of which is thoroughly checked out and carries a warranty. The prices are reasonable for the quality.

No New Yorker, visitor or resident, can escape Crazy Eddie's barrage of high-pressure advertising. True to its screaming claims, the prices are quite good, and the selection is reasonable—all the popular names. But, like the ads, the atmosphere can be frenzied, and the salespeople try too hard. A good place if you know what you want.

Harvey is one of the best stereo stores in town, whether you're looking for a $4,000 tape deck or a whole system for $250. The emphasis is on quality, top-of-the-line merchandise that is expensive (but the sales can be good). It's a big, always busy store, with a huge service department in back, excellent listening rooms, a good choice of refurbished and warrantied used stereo equipment, TVs and videotape gear, half-speed master recordings and all sorts of accessories. There's another store across the street, at 23 West 45th Street (921-5920), which carries equipment for professional musicians and recording studios.

You'll find a good choice of high-quality, high-performance stereo equipment in this large store. You can listen to any number of combinations of gear in the three rooms full of top-of-the-line components from such manufacturers as ADS and Harman Kardon. The selection of home mixing boards and equalizers is particularly good. The salesmen are low-pressure, and the prices are what you would expect for this quality; sales can be excellent. Several other locations.

Liberty features elegant stereo equipment geared toward the classical music lover. It's a spacious, two-story showroom, with comfortable listening rooms stocked with systems from Bang and Olufsen, Fisher and Nakamichi. There's a decent selection of classical records and tapes, and upstairs you'll find TVs and computers. The stereo selection is limited, but it's of good quality, and the prices aren't out of line.

High quality, low pressure, elegant surroundings and uncompromising prices. The finest names in home stereo equipment can be found here (Carver, NAD, Tandberg), and the sales staff loves music and knows how best to present it. There are also some TVs and a good choice of half-speed master records.

Tech Hi-Fi
12 W. 45th St.
869-3950
Mon. to Sat. 10:30 A.M. to 6:30 P.M.; Sun. noon to 5:00 P.M.

There are now many Tech shops around town; most are fairly small, with a limited selection but very good prices. The staff is generally friendly and helpful, and the listening rooms are well set up. A good place to check out.

Leathers

A to Z Luggage
425 Fifth Ave.
(38th St.)
686-6905
Mon. to Thurs. 9:00 A.M. to 6:30 P.M.; Fri. 9:00 A.M to 3:00 P.M.; Sun. 10:00 A.M. to 5:00 P.M.

A small shop filled to the brim with good-quality soft-side luggage, attachés, portfolios, garment bags and sets of aluminum suitcases. The prices are acceptable, the selection fairly extensive and the salespeople helpful if you ask them. Other locations throughout the city.

T. Anthony
480 Park Ave.
(58th St.)
750-9797
Mon. to Fri. 9:30 A.M. to 6:00 P.M.; Sat. 10:00 A.M. to 6:00 P.M.

This rather green, teak-paneled store is essential for anyone looking for durable, well-made, stylish luggage. Many soft-side styles update the classic leather collection, and Brooks Brothers wives in from Connecticut come here to order new sets for their college-bound children, for Aspen vacations, for business trips and for upcoming excursions to Europe. Reasonable prices. There are also traditional small leather goods, which most customers seem to enjoy having monogrammed in gold.

Artbag
735 Madison Ave.
(64th St.)
744-2720
Mon. to Thurs. 9:00 A.M. to 5:45 P.M.; Fri. 9:00 A.M. to 5:30 P.M.; Sat. 9:00 A.M. to 4:00 P.M.

This minuscule shop is tucked into Madison Avenue and has loyal customers who come here often to search for the latest stylish bag at fairly affordable prices. You, too, will find some treasures, although talent in the negotiating field may be to your advantage—the sales staff has been known to discount the prices when pushed. The sales are fabulous, making it nearly impossible to leave without one of these elegant little bags for day or evening wear. A good repair department makes this shop indispensable to many New Yorkers.

La Bagagerie
727 Madison Ave.
(64th St.)
758-6570
Mon. to Sat. 10:00 A.M. to 6:30 P.M.

Wonderful bags of all shapes, sizes and colors await you in this leather store with a slightly bored sales staff. Imports from France and Italy are fairly well priced, and there is something for everyone, from the most sophisticated ladies to punkerettes looking for balloon bags to match their Danceteria evening wardrobes. It's

440

also a good address for leather briefcases, portfolios, travel bags and a limited line of good and expensive luggage.

Bottega Veneta
635 Madison Ave. (60th St.)
371-5511
Mon. to Sat. 10:00 A.M. to 6:00 P.M.

This excessively elegant store announces that things are expensive here with its handsome carpets, beautiful display cases, tasteful seating and enough lofty space to fly kites instead of show off the luxurious bags and leather goods. All the signature woven leather bags are here at their premium prices, along with the boring shoes, the sensational luggage, the attractive accessories and the cheerful wooden horse playing the dubious role of doorman.

The Coach Store
754 Madison Ave. (65th St.)
594-1581
Mon. to Sat. 11:00 A.M. to 6:00 P.M. (closed Sat. in July and Aug.)

This classic store is oblivious to passing trends, concentrating instead on quality leather goods that have been keeping women in fashion for decades. The stylish bags in soft, natural leather have become signatures in their simplicity. The belts for men and women are of superb workmanship, in leather or preppy striped canvas and leather combinations. You'll also find small leather goods stocked in this library-style, attractive shop. Prices are to be expected for work that is of such value and for timeless styles that are a salute to conservatism.

Mark Cross
645 Fifth Ave. (51st St.)
421-3000
Mon. to Fri. 10:00 A.M. to 6:00 P.M.; Sat. 10:00 A.M. to 5:30 P.M.

This ultraelegant store, with its highly polished, tortoise-shell-look wood paneling, glass-enclosed elevator, handsome sales staff and tasteful display cases, matches the classic good taste and price tags of the merchandise it sells. It is infinitely more interesting to carry Mark Cross briefcases, luggage, wallets and handbags, with the discreet MC insignia, than to be a walking advertisement for vinylized canvas that is not only more pretentious but more expensive.

Gucci on Seven
2 E. 54th St.
7th floor
(no telephone)
Mon. to Sat. 9:30 A.M. to 6:00 P.M.

If you dig hard, you can find a few good bargains amid merchandise that looks pretty well sifted through. Seasonal losers can be found here, along with luggage, shoes, accessories and the classic carpetbag tote. Some prices are fabulous, while others are only slightly above what Gucci styles are worth in the first place. A must for people who are married to the double G.

Hunting World
16 E. 53rd St.
755-3400
Mon. to Sat. 10:00 A.M. to 6:00 P.M.

You will be greeted with the genuine fragrance of genuine leathers—curious, since the shop is filled with vinylized canvas bags with the distinctive Hunting World leather seal. Safari hunters shop here for jackets, hats and shooting bags, but there's plenty left over for fly fishermen, shoppers looking for unique gifts, women who like elephant-hair jewelry and a crowd of wealthy consumers who can afford these overpriced bags. At least the shopkeepers have a sense of humor when they explain how the vinyl-canvas treatment makes the merchandise especially durable—it ought to be, for the price. Still, if you must tote around a signature, this is a good one that has staying status.

Lancel
690 Madison Ave.
(58th St.)
753-6918
Mon. to Sat. 10:00 A.M. to
6:00 P.M.

If you enjoy walking around with the subtle signature L adorning your leather pocketbooks, vinylized canvas shoulder bags, elegant lizard-skin handbags and the other beautiful luggage and accessories found here, then Lancel is your store. The establishment is elegant, the service professional and sincere and the couture haute. A lovely import from the Place de l'Opéra in Paris.

Lederer
613 Madison Ave.
(57th St.)
355-5515
Mon. to Sat. 9:30 A.M. to 6:00 P.M.

A fabulous collection of leather goods and bags for slightly less than further uptown. There are some good knockoffs at great prices, along with a collection of leather and soft-side luggage that is as handsome as it is functional. The leather goods are equally attractive: portfolios, attachés, small leather items and must-have trifles. The handbags are European classics for the sophisticated shopper.

Mädler
450 Park Ave.
(57th St.)
688-5045
Mon. to Sat. 9:00 A.M. to 5:30 P.M.

This German leather firm offers one of the most hostile welcomes in New York. Perhaps the staff is so unfriendly because this pretentious, dark-wood-paneled shop is so often empty. Whatever the reason, it takes sheer determination to browse through the archconservative styles, to refrain from asking for the outrageous prices and to descend to the basement to examine the extensive line of attachés, portfolios and luggage.

North Beach Leather
772 Madison Ave.
(66th St.)
772-0707
Mon. to Fri. 10:00 A.M. to 7:00
P.M.; Sat. 10:00 A.M. to 6:00
P.M.; Sun. 1:00 P.M. to 6:00 P.M.

This contemporary shop is filled with some of the most adventurous, as well as classic, leathers. If you have been looking for a barely there pastel sheath, a palomino thong bikini, a traditional soft suede baseball jacket, straight-legged jeans in bright red leather, a buffalo jacket perfect for Marlboro men, a miniskirt or an Indian feathered jacket, then North Beach should be your first stop. The prices are actually within the realm of possibility, and the sales staff is attractive and very friendly.

Skin
25 E. 65th St.
2nd floor
988-0554
Mon. to Sat. 11:00 A.M. to
7:00 P.M.

Some strange-looking people run this little upstairs shop filled with dramatic leathers (an autographed promo photo from the band Kiss—customers here—should give you the picture). Everything from gold lamé leather jackets and fringed chapslike pants to tiger-striped or leopard-spotted jeans and more traditional jackets can be found here. You'll have a field day hunting through the merchandise, and the New Wave (freely translated) shopkeepers do their best to help you find what you're looking for. Prices are not too upsetting, considering the quality of these unique handcrafted designs.

Louis Vuitton
51 E. 57th St.
371-6111
Mon. to Fri. 10:00 A.M to 5:30 P.M.; Sat. 10:00 A.M. to 5:00 P.M.

A very elegant shop with a very cold atmosphere and very clichéd items sold by very snobby salespeople. If, however, you simply cannot live without a Vuitton golf bag, kitty carrier, wig box or mini sack for three-year-olds training for the Vuitton look, then you simply must hurry over for your vinyl-covered bag, without even thinking of asking the price. There's another branch at Saks Fifth Avenue, and the line is also carried at Crouch and Fitzgerald for the Grand Central commuter crowd.

Sporting Goods

The Athlete's Foot
16 W. 57th St.
586-1936
Mon. to Fri. 10:00 A.M. to 7:00 P.M. (Thurs. to 9:00 P.M.); Sat. 10:00 A.M. to 6:00 P.M.; Sun. noon to 5:00 P.M.

For fanatical runners: all models and top brands of shoes for men and women, plus a selection of clothing and accessories that is aimed at function rather than fashion. An experienced sales staff can advise you on everything from fit to form. Various other locations.

Conrad's Bike Shop
236 E. 46th St.
697-6966
Tues. to Sat. 10:30 A.M. to 5:30 P.M.

Conrad's built its reputation on quality. It has the best bikes in New York and knowledgeable salespeople to tell you about them. While the prices aren't necessarily unbeatable, the service you'll get is. Conrad's also is the best used-bicycle dealership in town, with an impressive stock comprising every brand, at half the new prices or lower. Renowned for its repair and rental service.

Dream Wheels
295 Mercer St.
(E. 8th St.)
677-0005
Tues. to Sat. noon to 8:00 P.M.

One of the rare survivors among a plethora of stores that came and went with the winds of fashion. Dream Wheels carries not only preassembled roller skates but also all the equipment, in a wide range of styles and quality, needed to make up a custom model to your liking. Some clothing, too—tights and leotards to complete the look.

Feron's Racquet and Tennis Shop

55 E. 44th St.
867-6350
*Mon. to Fri. 8:30 A.M. to 6:00
P.M.; Sat. 10:00 A.M. to 4:00 P.M.*

A shop offering lower prices than Madison Avenue for all types of racquets and a good choice of outfits for men and women. Also restringing and repairs.

The Finals

149 Mercer St.
(Houston St.)
431-1414
*Mon. and Fri. 10:00 A.M. to 5:45
P.M.; Tues. to Thurs. 10:00 A.M. to
6:45 P.M. Sun. 11:00 A.M. to
5:45 P.M.*

All the swimmers at the NYU pool sport The Finals' bathing suits. Could be because they get a ten percent discount, but it's more likely that higher education has helped them recognize good quality at better prices. Only the house brands are sold here: bathing suits in assorted competition styles, in solids or stripes, nylon or Lycra. Good swimmers' accessories, including goggles, a rainbow of swim caps, buoys, pace clocks and special Formula IV shampoo with an antichlorine agent. It also stocks some warm-ups and running clothes. Men's suits are in the $6 to $10 range; women's average $12 to $20.

Herman's

135 W. 42nd St.
730-7400
*Mon. to Fri. 9:30 A.M. to 7:00
P.M.; Sat. 9:30 A.M. to 6:00 P.M.*

The best brands of equipment, and outfits to match, for nearly every sport from the traditional to the exotic. Prices are honest, especially on the tennis and squash racquets, some of the best items to buy here. Various locations, but this shop on 42nd Street is bigger and better stocked than others.

Hunting World

16 E. 53rd St.
755-3400
*Mon. to Sat. 10:00 A.M. to
6:00 P.M.*

Everything in the way of clothing and equipment (except the guns) for a very comfortable safari. An elegant and expensive shop.

H. Kauffman and Sons Saddlery

139 E. 24th St.
684-6060
Mon. to Sat. 9:30 A.M. to 6:00 P.M.

Located where the original Bull's Head horse auctions were held, this store is filled with equipment and memorabilia. Especially noted for western saddles, but some genteel English models are sold as well. Custom-tailored clothing and accessories, too.

M.J. Knoud

716 Madison Ave.
(64th St.)
838-1434
Mon. to Sat. 9:00 A.M. to 5:00 P.M.

The rich smell of good leather welcomes you into this tiny horse emporium. Once past the equine books, calendars, cups and cards, you'll find amiable David Wright, who has been serving the elite horsey set for 57 years. All his merchandise is top quality, and he's full of advice on what to buy. He specializes in custom clothing (although there is also a large selection of stock styles), tack rooms and equipment for polo, hunting, racing, showing and pleasure. The store carries five types of traditional saddles, and all boots are made to order. David and his equally friendly daughter, Bonnie, pride themselves on knowing about 90 percent of their customers by first name. If you have any horse sense at all, you'll get to know them, too.

Miller's Harness Co.
123 E. 24th St.
673-1400
Mon. to Sat. 9:00 A.M. to 5:30 P.M.

For men, women and children: all the equipment and accessories necessary to ride a horse in the purest of western traditions. You'll find hats, clothing, boots and more, all of the highest quality. This store outfits the U.S. Olympic equestrian team.

Paragon Sporting Goods
867 Broadway (18th St.)
255-8036
Mon. to Fri. 9:30 A.M. to 6:25 P.M. (Thurs. to 7:25 P.M.); Sat. 9:00 A.M. to 6:00 P.M.

A surplus-style sports store with a very good reputation for quality and price. All the sports are covered here: skiing, tennis, hiking, baseball, football and running, for both adults and children. There are special departments for fishing, camping, golf and backpacking, plus top-of-the-line exercise equipment. A staff of young, competent sportspeople is quick to serve you.

Peck and Goodie
919 Eighth Ave. (W. 54th St.)
246-6123
Mon. to Sat. 10:30 A.M. to 6:00 P.M.

Skates for ice and asphalt, for men, women and children, made to order, all in leather—which doesn't make them particularly cheap. Children's ice skates begin at about $60; adults', $100. Blade prices start at $26. There are some ready-made styles of roller skates. A place to rely on.

The Playing Field
955 Third Ave. (57th St.)
421-0003
Mon. to Sat. 10:00 A.M. to 6:00 P.M. (Thurs. to 8:00 P.M.); Sun. noon to 5:00 P.M.

Athletic sports apparel just like your favorite team wears. This newly opened shop carries all the official brands, in sizes from infant to quarterback, of jerseys, jackets, sweats and hats. Lots of accessories, pennants and even a Billy Martin print! High quality and prices to match.

Racquet Shop
289 Madison Ave. (40th St.)
685-1954
Mon. to Fri. 9:00 A.M. to 5:30 P.M.

The store for professionals: Jimmy Connors, Ilie Nastase, John McEnroe and Harold Solomon all get strung up here. Pros and amateurs alike will find whatever it is they need—racquets in every material, every weight and size. The tennis wear department is well stocked and not too expensive.

Runner's World Sports Warehouse

275 Seventh Ave. (26th St.)
691-2565
Mon. to Fri. 10:00 A.M. to 6:00 P.M.; Sat. 10:00 A.M. to 5:00 P.M.

Hiking and running shoes and clothing. Among its staff are several expert marathoners, and all are willing and able to counsel you wisely.

Scandinavian Ski Shop

40 W. 57th St.
757-8524
Mon. to Sat. 9:00 A.M. to 6:00 P.M. (Thurs. to 7:00 P.M.)

An excellent shop for most of the popular sports: skiing, tennis, swimming, running and others. Prices aren't low, as there are neither special bargains nor discounts, but the quality of the merchandise is excellent and the quantity superb. During ski season, there's a wide range of skis and outfits, as well as equipment rental (by the day or week). Check out the shop's extremely well organized ski trips.

Sporting Woman

235 E. 57th St.
688-8228
Mon. to Sat. 10:00 A.M. to 7:00 P.M. (Thurs. to 8:00 P.M.); Sun. noon to 5:00 P.M.

For women only. This well-stocked store, opened by the owners of Athlete's Foot, carries reliable brands of clothing and equipment at honest prices for women who run, swim, sail, cycle, dance, play tennis and lift weights. In short, New York's best selection, neither too functional nor too stylish—a perfect compromise between the two, which is exactly what today's sportswomen want.

Stuyvesant Bicycle and Toy

349 W. 14th St.
254-5200
Mon. to Fri. 9:30 A.M. to 7:00 P.M.; Sat. 9:30 A.M. to 6:00 P.M.; Sun. 9:30 A.M. to 5:00 P.M.

A supermarket selection of all the best brands of American bicycles and tricycles at good prices, sold by friendly salespeople. A wide choice of sizes for adults and children, excellent service and reliable rentals.

Tennis Lady

765 Madison Ave. (65th St.)
535-8601
Mon. to Sat. 10:00 A.M. to 6:00 P.M. (Thurs. to 8:00 P.M.); Sun. noon to 5:00 P.M.

A well-chosen selection of sport clothes for women who play or want to look like they play: skirts, shorts, T-shirts, tennis panties and fabulous warm-ups. Tennis Lady offers quality brands plus its exclusive designs, which are always terribly chic and meant for fun. Good accessories.

Where to Find

AN ART ·
ANTIQUE RESTORER

Joseph Biunno
225 E. 24th St.
532-3363
Mon. to Fri. 8:00 A.M. to 4:00 P.M.

Mr. Biunno and his sons specialize in restoring valuable furniture, both antique and modern. As friendly and charming as he is, don't bother him for an old bargain sofa—he works mostly with interior designers, on pieces of the highest quality. That being the case, he'll be pleased to help you, whether you need a little piece glued back on or a complete restoration. He won't offer estimates—unless you ask.

Oxford Antique Restorers
59 E. 57th St.
355-7620
By appt. only

Another excellent spot for all repairs of antique furniture from the seventeenth, eighteenth and nineteenth centuries. All sorts of skills and crafts are available: repairing, rebuilding, gilding, lacquer work and more. Estimates in New York City are $35. Call for an appointment and ask for Connie Buckley.

Sotheby's Restoration
440 E. 91st St.
472-3463
By appt. only

This division of Sotheby Parke Bernet is surely one of the most reliable and competent places for repairs and restoration of antique furniture and works of art. Under the management of John Stair, son of the founder of Stair and Company, Sotheby's restorers will do any kind of work: cutting, carving, repair and finishing (gilding, polishing and lacquer work) on pieces in every style and from every period, whether they were bought at Sotheby's or not. They will pick up and deliver, and will estimate restoration costs on pieces before they are auctioned. For your own pieces, they will come to your house and make an estimate for $50, which is deductible from the cost of the work. Sotheby plans to expand its services to cover metal, glass and porcelain repairs.

Charles Sundquist
350 W. 31st. St.
564-9415
Mon. to Fri. 7:30 A.M. to 4:00 P.M.

A reliable repairman for all kinds of antique furniture from every period. He does conscientious work entirely by hand, offers free estimates in New York City and charges fair prices. This craftsman is recommended and used by the best antique dealers in the city.

447

A BOOK RESTORER · BINDER

Deborah Evetts
532-1538
Call Mon. to Fri. evening for an appt.

Conservator at the Pierpont Morgan Library, Mrs. Evetts also looks after restoration for private individuals—but only if the works are museum-class books printed on flat paper, and only if the client is willing to wait twelve to eighteen months before delivery and pay top prices for top work. She doesn't simply restore your book; she gives it new life. Don't bring in the old family Bible—she won't even look at it.

Ffolio 72
888 Madison Ave.
(71st–72nd sts.)
879-0675
Mon. to Fri. 10:00 A.M. to 5:30 P.M.

A very fashionable spot to buy attractive letter paper and to have business cards made, Ffolio 72 also looks after the binding of books, family albums and Bibles, movie scripts, plays or whatever you'd like to have bound in goatskin—for which it charges chic prices ($250 minimum for a simple rebinding). The service suffers from the store's popularity.

Froelich
6320 Austin St.
Rego Park
897-7000
Mon. to Fri. 9:00 A.M. to 4:30 P.M.

A specialist in leather office accessories and albums, Froelich will also do leather binding (about six weeks, $60 minimum) and decorating. He can cover your desk top in leather, for example. He also specializes in false bookshelves—why not camouflage your door with fake but attractive bindings?

Denis Gouey Book Studio
41 Union Sq.
(17th and Broadway)
929-2123
Mon. to Sat. 10:00 A.M. to 5:30 P.M.

A young and extremely likable binder from Lisieux in Normandy who has more than one string to his bow. His competence and talent allow him to do everything concerning books: modern binding, slipcases, art binding and restoration of old books and manuscripts. You can give him your rare books with total confidence—he imports from Europe the finest leathers and the best handmade acid-free paper (which won't yellow or otherwise deteriorate for about 400 years). He also copies the original binding and endpapers exactly. What's more, he doesn't charge excessive prices, given the high quality of his work. He'll show you pretty daylit studio photographs of his earlier work, as well as samples of the materials he uses and a list of prices. Denis also organizes four-week courses in bookbinding (two and a half hours a week) for $230, materials included, and offers an at-home library refurbishing service at a cost of $45 per hour.

Carolyn Price Horton
430 W. 22nd St.
989-1471
By appt. only

An expert in the art of restoring antique paper; books, maps, manuscripts and works of art have been passing through her hands for 25 years, including countless delicate repairs for museums. Count on about two months for repairs. Estimates are $45 to test the cover and report to the client; if work is completed, the estimate is absorbed in the total cost. There is a minimum of $95 per job and a size limitation of 32 by 40 inches for works of art. Carolyn Horton does all her work by hand; she loves to share information and has no secrets.

BUSINESS SERVICES

Harriet Modlin
666 Fifth Ave.
(53rd St.)
245-5175
Mon. to Fri. 10:00 A.M. to 5:00 P.M.

Ms. Modlin's many years of experience in both domestic and international travel have made her the personal travel consultant and problem solver preferred by, for example, the managing director of Reuter's News Service World Wide. No trip is too small or too far ranging for her to handle, and her rates are competitive. An extra plus is the 800 number established clients can call while traveling in case of an itinerary change. The same number can be used to consult her on weekends or after working hours.

1996 Word Processing
200 W. 79th St.
362-1996

Margaret Velard provides word processing services for the independent business that doesn't have secretarial help. She works for lawyers, engineers, playwrights—anyone who needs texts reproduced and stored, or wants one letter personalized and sent to many addresses. She'll estimate the cost of your job over the phone.

Resources
2 Tudor City Pl.
(41st–42nd sts.)
883-9119

Nancy Seifer and Barbara Peters can put order into your office or your apartment. They provide writing, editing and research services for business and professional projects and for graduate students, along with administrative support for executives working out of their homes or with small staffs. They will also pay your bills, do your errands and, if you authorize it, look after your bank account. Rates vary, depending on the services required, from $10 an hour upward.

A CHIROPRACTOR

**Jerome
Greenberg,
D.C.
Ian I.
Stromfeld,
D.C.**
35 W. 81st St.
724-0707

Two chiropractic specialists whose holistic practice offers treatment of neck and back pain and headaches caused by structural imbalances. They are members of the National Council on Nutrition and the Council on Sports Injuries. They also give lectures on nutrition and natural health care two Wednesdays a month (call for time and place).

A CLEANERS · LAUNDRY

**Mme
Blanchevoye**
75 E. 130th St.
368-7272
Mon. to Fri. 7:30 A.M. to 4:30 P.M.

Recommended by stores that sell fine linens. Sheets cost between $7 and $8.50, pillowcases, $1.25 to $1.75. Unless you're willing to venture up to 130th Street, you'll have to pay an extra 30 percent of your cleaning bill for pickup and delivery.

Danielle
1334 Lexington Ave.
(88th–89th sts.)
534-1483
*Mon. to Fri. 7:00 A.M. to 7:00
P.M.; Sat. 8:00 A.M. to 5:00 P.M.*

Another recommendation of stores that sell fine linen. Danielle does hand cleaning and dry cleaning. Prices are relatively high—a silk-covered down comforter will cost about $40—but pickup and delivery are free.

Hallak
1239 Second Ave.
(65th St.)
832-9015
*Mon. to Fri. 7:00 A.M. to 6:30
P.M.; Sat. 8:00 A.M. to 3:00 P.M.*

Joseph Hallak, a native of Marseilles who has been in business in New York for more than eighteen years, is a cleaner of the highest order. His work, even on the most delicate of fabrics, is perfect, and his prices are very reasonable. His sturdy wrappings will allow you to keep your clothes in the same condition they were in when he delivered them. One unsolicited comment from a reader of this guide: "It took me two years of living in Manhattan and many ruined silk blouses before I found Hallak, who is without a doubt one of the best in the world." Hallak will pick up and deliver between 50th and 90th streets.

**Jeeves of
Belgravia**
39 E. 65th St.
570-9130

Jeeves represents a standard of service and quality that unfortunately no longer exists anywhere else. It is the best, both in London and New York, as well as the most sophisticated, with a slight English touch. Its employees are extremely competent and use the finest equipment

Mon. to Fri. 8:00 A.M. to 6:30 P.M.; Sat. 9:00 A.M. to 4:00 P.M.

available. Your clothing will first be thoroughly inspected, and all stains will be marked. Buttons will be resewn and, if necessary, zippers will be replaced. The quality of the cleaning itself is beyond criticism. In addition to the dry cleaning service, Jeeves also looks after fine linen and does hand laundry at reasonable prices. For travelers tired of arriving at their destinations with packed clothes wrinkled, it offers a vacation wrapping service: your valise will be collected, and your things pressed and wrapped in paper. And if your closets are getting a bit cramped, Jeeves will store any temporarily unwanted items. Pickup and delivery are free for orders over $20. It's a complete clothes-care service!

Park Avenue French Hand Laundry
1305 Madison Ave.
(92nd–93rd sts.)
289-4950
Mon. to Sat. 8:00 A.M. to 6:00 P.M.

Your linen and clothing will be washed with care and attention. Delicate sheets and table linens will come back looking like new. A hand-ironed fine linen sheet will cost between $6 and $10, depending on size; tablecloths begin at $10. Free pickup and delivery for customers with charge accounts.

Perry Process Cleaners
1315 Third Ave.
(76th St.)
628-8300
Mon. to Fri. 8:00 A.M. to 6:30 P.M.; Sat. 8:00 A.M. to 2:00 P.M.

Another careful and conscientious cleaner who will take the time necessary to return your clothing to perfect condition. Most cleaners take two or three days to clean a down coat, returning it to you with the feathers still damp. Perry takes a few days longer to be sure the coat is truly dry and won't get moldy in your closet. It's built its reputation on treatment of knitwear and will repair, alter, block and hem your knits, put in new zippers or shorten the sleeves. Prices are competitive.

Ernest Winzer
1828 Cedar Ave.
The Bronx
294-2400
Mon. to Fri. 6:00 A.M. to 5:00 P.M.

This specialist in cleaning antique clothing and theater costumes will look after anyone's dry cleaning with pleasure. He usually takes two days, and the easiest or the most difficult cleaning tasks will be delivered immaculate, admirably ironed and packaged, at incredibly low prices in view of the irreproachable and reliable quality of his work.

AN ESTIMATE

Sylvia Ipsen
620 Broadway
(Bleecker and
Houston sts.)
598-9005

Sylvia Ipsen, a senior member of the American Society of Appraisers and the Appraisers Association of America, will estimate the value of your furniture, paintings, works of art and decorative objects for a fee of $100 per hour. Service includes inspection and inventory of all the items, plus a complete portfolio of beautiful color photographs of the appraised valuables in the setting of your home, whether in the city or the country. Although the fee does not include the cost of film and processing, the photographs are important in case of damage or theft. She will aid in the identification and recovery of your possessions and will help with insurance claims.

HOUSEHOLD SERVICES

Dandy Cleaning Co.
450 W. 24th St.
924-5557

Here he is. Carlos Lopez is the man you wish you had known about when your cleaning person wouldn't do windows. He'll not only do your windows at a reasonable rate (call him for an estimate) but wax your floors, clean your venetian blinds and shampoo your rug.

Maids Unlimited
767 Lexington Ave.
(60th–61st sts.)
838-6282
Mon. to Fri. 8:30 A.M to 5:00 P.M.

Whether you want a chambermaid for routine cleaning (currently $8.50 an hour) or a team of housemen for the heavy jobs ($12.50, or $17.50 with supplies and equipment), Van Lederer, who runs Maids Unlimited, has them for you. He'll also provide you with the staff for a party, along with party equipment if he's supplying personnel.

Patrick McErleam
130 Jane St.
691-5512

An energetic, if not hyperactive, man, Patrick enjoys the physical exertion of apartment cleaning. He's reliable and thorough. You may have some trouble reaching him, since he's kept busy with both residential and commercial cleaning, but if you get him, he'll be worth the wait.

Mom's Services
500 E. 83rd St.
988-8484

When you don't have the time to look for your own household help, this is the place to go. Carolyn Straker, a former teacher and a specialist in parent counseling and child development, focuses very carefully on the needs of the individual employer. The main emphasis is on full-time, sleep-out services, but occasionally she will find reliable help on a part-time or sleep-in basis.

AN INTERIOR DESIGNER

F. Anthony Benko

Interior design and renovation management. Mr. Benko knows all the painters, plasterers, wallpaper hangers and carpenters you could ever need. He'll talk with you about

15 W. 72nd St.
787-8322

what you want, and then you can leave town and come back to a newly decorated home!

Breathing Space
463 West St.
929-3258

Fay Spahn is an artist who finds inexpensive and creative solutions to apartment problems. She'll provide consultations and specific suggestions on the most efficient use of space, how to make your home reflect your unique lifestyle, how to live and work in the same place and similar concerns. And, if you want her to, she'll undertake the work necessary to carry out her suggested solutions.

Peter Piening
430 W. 24th St.
929-3688

Peter Piening is an interior designer who specializes in helping create lifestyles. He'll meet with you at your apartment in the city or your house in the country and make suggestions for an environment to suit you. He can then supervise the work that needs to be done so you don't have any of the worries.

Jeff Schlesinger
150 E. 18th St.
677-1206

Original art to order for your home or office. Jeff Schlesinger is a fine artist who has taught and exhibited his works. He will meet with you to explore your likes and needs before he begins his design. His works combine painting, drawing, photographs and printed, typed or handwritten words, and the finished piece or series of pieces will be tailored to fit your space and interests. Price will vary with the size and scope of the undertaking.

A KNIFE SHARPENER

Fred De Carlo
(201) 945-7609

One of the few wandering knife and scissors grinders left, Fred De Carlo strolls through the streets with a big bell in hand and his equipment on his back. His territory is the East Side from 52nd Street to 96th Street, between Fifth Avenue and the East River; he covers it Monday to Friday, 9:00 A.M. to 5:00 P.M. If you miss him on his rounds and your knives and scissors are desperately dull, give him a ring in the evening, and he'll arrange an appointment.

A MARBLE RESTORER

New York Marble Works

William and Louis Gleicher run a business that has been in the family for three generations. Their clients include Sotheby Parke Bernet, William Doyle, the Metropolitan

**1399 Park Ave.
(104th St.)
534-2242**
By appt. only

Museum of Art and Christies International—so you can be sure the Gleichers know what they're doing. They'll repair and restore marble or onyx statuary, fireplaces, tables, desk tops and so on, and will give you a free estimate if you bring in the object or a photo. They also do custom designs in marble from your plans or theirs. A full line of marble tile is available, as well as marble for counters or tabletops. Prices are competitive, and they'll arrange for truck transport at an additional charge.

A NEWSSTAND

Hotaling's Newsstand
**142 W. 42nd St.
840-1868**
Mon. to Fri. 7:30 A.M. to 9:30 P.M.; Sat. and Sun. to 7:30 P.M.

Hotaling's is notable for its excellent selection of out-of-town and foreign newspapers and magazines. A visit here is good therapy for temporary New Yorkers who have a bad case of homesickness.

PARTY SERVICES

Note: For the all-important edibles that mean so much to any social gathering, see Caterers, listed under Food in *The Shops* section of this guide.

James Black Event Planning
685-1498

Mr. Black wants the world to know that he does not offer catering but a personalized, distinctive and elegant service called "event planning." Tell him what kind of event you have in mind; he is capable of creating and organizing it "using original elements to move information and ideas in an entertaining way." He will plan and carry out every detail of anything from a birthday party to a sales rally.

Samantha Finch
724-2800

Calligraphy for special personal and business communications of all kinds: announcements, invitations, elegantly addressed envelopes, place cards, diplomas, certificates or mementos. And the finished work will be as simple or elaborate as you wish, with your choice of several lettering styles and many mixed-to-order ink colors. Her rate will depend on the time involved, and she will give you an estimate.

Lend-a-Hand Personnel Service

Donald Eggena has been running this company since 1971. His long list of clients includes some extremely recognizable names, such as Dustin Hoffman, Richard Dreyfuss and Shelley Winters. Mr. Eggena boasts, "Our

200 W. 72nd St.
362-8200

rates are modest, our estimates free, our services 100 percent reliable"—and we have heard that every word of his boast is true. In addition to bartenders, waiters and coat checkers he'll supply ice, mixers, glasses, napkins and just about anything else you need to make your party a success. He'll also provide office help, houseboys, kitchen help and baby-sitters. The staff members come from the world of show business, but they're all experienced or trained by Lend-a-Hand.

Quest Masters
966-0093

This unique group offers you the services of one of four experienced bards, who tells a story in which you and three to six other people become brave companions in an adventure of role-playing theater. You'll find yourself in an alien world filled with wondrous creatures and stirring events, where you may meet unicorns or kings or samurai, in castles or forests or alternate dimensions—anyplace your imagination can take you. The imaginary quest usually takes sixteen to eighteen hours spread over five fascinating evenings. Call Lionel Martinez for details on this exciting way to discover new facets of yourself.

Steve Ross
c/o Donald Smith
879-4354

Singer and pianist Steve Ross has been performing at the famed Hotel Algonquin for three years. He is available on a limited basis for private entertainment. Call his manager, Donald Smith, for rates and availability.

Paul Trueblood
246-2883

Personal pianist to Alan Jay Lerner, Josh and Nedda Logan and Betty Comden and Adolph Green, Paul Trueblood is available to entertain at private parties, either as a single or with a handpicked group of other musicians. Call him to discuss your party plans.

PERSONAL SERVICES

Let Millie Do It
Millie Emory
532-8775

If your house is in such a mess that when you look for a toothbrush the closest you can come is a hairbrush, have no fear: Millie can reestablish order throughout. She can pay your bills, help do your shopping, take your pets to the vet and organize your filing cabinet. If you can't muster the courage to face painters, plumbers or decorators, Millie will find them, direct them and put your home back just the way it was before—only neater. At Christmas she'll shop for, wrap and even deliver gifts. For $25 an hour, she'll clear both your cupboards and your conscience. She works mostly for companies but is also available for individuals.

Woman for Rent
Lisa Dorfman
475-0883

Woman for Rent takes care of personal details for very busy people who don't have the time or inclination to take care of them themselves. Lisa Dorfman will help with your relocation (either business or residence) across town or out of the country—supervising, acting as a general contractor and dealing with landlords, co-op boards and utilities. She'll take care of your boat, car or motorcycle, stand in line at the DMV and even go to traffic court if you're not contesting the ticket. She'll buy your groceries, have your luggage repaired or take unwanted merchandise back to department stores. She's honest and resourceful, and her $25-an-hour rate can buy you a lot of peace of mind.

A PERSONAL SHOPPER

Amelia Fatt
757-6300
By appt. only

The author of a brand-new book, *Conservative Chic,* has been explaining to women for more than eight years that being well dressed doesn't necessarily mean being expensively dressed. Amelia Fatt is a counselor in clothing who will come to your home for a two-hour consultation to observe and get to know you. She'll talk to you about your life, your pursuits and your tastes. Then she'll go through your wardrobe and point out the items that are particularly becoming, those that are flattering and those that don't work for you at all. You'll learn to combine different items in new ways. With your budget in mind, she'll choose clothes for you and recommend accessories. A two-hour consultation in Manhattan costs about $100. She'll travel outside the city, but traveling time will be taken into account in her fee, and eventually you'll have to come to New York to try on the clothes she has selected for you.

Inside New York
203 E. 72nd St.
861-0709

Gaile Peters and Carol Townsing have twenty years of experience in the garment center. For $150 for three hours or $250 for the entire day, they'll take you to the wholesale houses and manufacturers and show you where to find the perfect suit or handmade sweater—at discount prices. For an additional $100 they'll supply an interpreter. They can be reached by phone or mail for an appointment.

A PORCELAIN REPAIRER

Center Art Studio
149 W. 57th St.
247-3550
Mon. to Fri. 10:00 A.M. to 6:00 P.M.; Sat. and Sun. by appt.

If you have objects of great value in need of repair or restoration, bring them to this studio workshop—or let a staff member pick up and deliver anything that is too fragile for you to handle. Services cost $40 an hour, with written estimates provided when requested. The three workrooms are devoted to fine craftsmanship and care for art. The bulk of the work is in sculpture, ceramics, terra-cotta, bronzes, lacquers and stone carvings. This outfit also designs and constructs displays for artwork and documents art collections with professional photography.

Hess Repairs
200 Park Avenue South
(17th St.)
260-2255
Mon. to Fri. 10:30 A.M. to 4:00 P.M.

A shop that comes recommended by Steuben, Baccarat, Tiffany and Waterford; in other words, it's both reliable and expensive. Porcelain, glass, ivory and silver hold no secrets for Mr. Hess, who can repair the irreparable. Restoration of porcelain takes about three weeks and work on crystal about fifteen days. Excellent work done on silver, too. Minimum charge is $10, maximum runs several zeros more.

Mr. Fixit
1300 Madison Ave.
(92nd St.)
369-7775
Mon. to Fri. 10:00 A.M. to 6:00 P.M.

A not-too-exclusive craftsman. Don't hesitate to call him, even if you're not a shipping magnate and even if the item to be repaired has only personal value. Mr. Fixit repairs everything, without false snobbery. His competence is not limited to his main interest, china, but extends to crystal, ivory, jade, onyx, wood, silver, pewter, tin, porcelain, glass, gold, brass and copper. His prices are fair, neither excessive nor ridiculously low, and he'll give you an in-shop estimate for free.

Sano Studio
767 Lexington Ave.
(60th–61st sts.)
759-6131
Mon. to Fri. 9:00 A.M to 5:00 P.M.

Another absolutely reliable (and expensive) shop for all kinds of restoration of china, porcelain, ceramics and pottery. The finest interior designers in the city are all his clients, cheerfully laying out $20 to have a small chip repaired, always confident that the work will be perfect. All surfaces are pasted together and reglazed in colors that exactly match the original. Free estimates. Be prepared to wait three months for delicate work.

A PSYCHIC

Patricia Lebby Einstein
765 Greenwich St.
989-1615

A psychic with a reputation for uncanny accuracy, Patricia Lebby Einstein integrates a spiritual message with holistic technique. She conducts classes and private consultations and is available for parties, lectures, seminars and corporate consultations as well. She is also a writer on psychic and holistic subjects. Call her for an appointment in New York City or, by special arrangement, out of town.

A SEAMSTRESS

Llewellyn's Fashion Design & Custom Tailor
539 Albany Ave.
Brooklyn
774-1445

Franca Llewellyn and her associates design and construct custom clothes for men and women. They'll do a hem for $3, copy your favorite new fashion or design and make the perfect garment from the fabric you picked up on your last trip to India. They're between East New York and Maple avenues in Crown Heights, Brooklyn, but their work is worth the trip!

A SILVER RESTORER

Cliff Silver Co.
159 E. 55th St.
753-8348
Mon. to Fri. 8:00 A.M. to 4:00 P.M.

A pleasant place filled with an assortment of pewter, copper, brass and silver objects waiting to be repaired or picked up by their owners. Price is based on the time spent: $28 per hour, no matter what the piece, plus materials. This reliable shop serves Tiffany, Sotheby and William Doyle, among others. Free estimates. Appointments are recommended.

Thome Silversmith
328 E. 59th St.
758-0655
Mon. to Fri. 8:30 A.M. to 5:30 P.M.

An excellent craftsman, recommended by the best dealers for skillful refinishing, replating, polishing, cleaning and restoration of any missing piece on gold, silver, copper, bronze, pewter or brass. It may take up to three months, but according to his clients, patience is more than rewarded. Be sure not to drop in at 1:00 in the afternoon—he'll be closed for lunch.

A WATCH REPAIRER

William E. Berger Antique Clocks
29 E. 12th St.
929-1830
Mon. to Sat. noon to 6:00 P.M.
(closed Mon. and Sat. in summer)

An excellent shop for all repairs on antique or modern clocks, mechanical or electric. Free estimates in the store, or $50 at your home. Mr. Berger comes with recommendations from most of the museums and works for the best antique dealers. He also provides a winding service for antique clocks.

The Best Watch Repairs
1372 Broadway
(36th–37th sts.)
Mon. to Fri. 8:00 A.M. to 6:00 P.M.

The Schwartzes are a Rumanian couple who repair watches and jewelry, no matter how delicate. Mr. Schwartz was with Omega for 30 years, and you can entrust the finest fobs, watches and jewelry to him with total confidence. Repairs are guaranteed for one year. He also sells a selection of watches made by good manufacturers from around the world—Swiss (Longines, Movado, Zenith), American (Bulova) and Japanese (Seiko, Pulsar), at prices from $30 to $300—and he carries some attractive gold jewelry. Mr. and Mrs. Schwartz speak a number of languages, so visitors to New York can be comfortable in their friendly little store.

Fossner Time Pieces Clockshop
1059 Lexington Ave.
(56th St.)
249-2600, 980-1099
Mon. to Sat. 10:00 A.M. to
6:00 P.M.

At Fossner's, watch repair is a tradition that's been handed down from father to son for four generations. There is nobody more competent in the field than this Czechoslovakian father, sister and son. Old and new, clocks and watches, they can repair anything in about a week and will give a one-year guarantee. They also buy and sell antique watches and clocks, and their collection of fobs, carriage clocks, wristwatches and big antique pendulum clocks is fascinating. This is more than a neighborhood shop—it caters to connoisseurs.

A WIG

Raffaele Mollica
61 E. 57th St.
759-5690, 721-8228

This designer and manufacturer of fine custom wigs has clients of both genders and all ages, with both cosmetic and medical needs. He learned wigmaking in his native Italy, then worked for several famous salons before launching his own business thirteen years ago. The base for the manufacturing operation is in Italy, where he can train workers in the fine craftsmanship his designs demand, without the cost becoming prohibitive. On weekends he makes hospital calls on clients and works with children to help them become comfortable with their wigs.

ꜛʜᴇArts

Galleries

SOHO

Mary Boone/ Michael Werner Gallery
417 W. Broadway
966-2114
Tues. to Sat. 10:00 A.M. to 6:00 P.M.

Located directly across the street from Leo Castelli, Mary Boone has become renowned in the last two to three years for the work of two painters, David Salle and Julian Schnabel. Ms. Boone, a charismatic figure and society doyenne, has had the uncanny knack, intelligence and ambition to be able to (what some might say) manufacture international celebrities overnight. She and her famous "Trilby," Julian Schnabel, have been assaulted, lauded and simply talked about in the press to such a degree that their mutual achievements have become misunderstood and distorted. The resurgence of interest since 1980 in painting per se is largely due to their efforts; as a result of Mary Boone's very public approach, artists, critics, collectors and gallery goers alike have found themselves immersed in a new frenzy of activity, which has in turn had a pronounced effect upon the international art scene. In recent months Mary Boone has mounted two important historical exhibitions: the work of Richard Artschwager, the much neglected and unjustifiably overlooked American artist, and that of Francis Picabia, the Spanish surrealist whose paintings are among the most subversive in all of twentieth-century art.

Leo Castelli Gallery
420 W. Broadway
431-5160
Tues. to Sat. 10:00 A.M. to 6:00 P.M.

The most prestigious gallery for contemporary art in the world. For the past 25 years Leo Castelli has exhibited a group of primarily American artists who have become the acknowledged masters of our time. Jasper Johns, Robert Rauschenberg, Frank Stella, Andy Warhol, Roy Lichtenstein and many others had their beginnings at Castelli and remain with him to this day. The influence of this gallery on art since the end of World War II cannot be underestimated. What is shown here invariably takes hold and is generally at the forefront of modern painting and sculpture, beginning with such important movements as abstract expressionism, pop, minimalism and more recently the new wave of figurative painting. A bona fide landmark. There's another gallery location at 142 Greene Street (431-6279); Castelli Graphics is at 4 East 77th Street (288-3202).

Paula Cooper Gallery
155 Wooster St.
674-0766
Tues. to Sat. 10:00 A.M. to 6:00 P.M.

Paula Cooper is an outstanding gallery in the tradition of Leo Castelli—meaning that there exists a commitment to quality and talent and the idea that certain risks must be taken. The artists represented here include some of the most important figures in contemporary painting and sculpture: Joel Shapiro, Elizabeth Murray, Lynda Benglis, Jonathan Borofsky and Robert Mangold. There is a seriousness about the work shown here, unlike the sometimes inflated and sensational atmosphere of other galleries in the immediate neighborhood. Most of the artists are older or in their middle years, and their work reflects maturity and firmness. Paula Cooper's feeling for her artists is genuine, long-lived and entirely without fault in terms of its aesthetics.

Dia Art Foundation New York Earth Room
141 Wooster St.
473-8072

The Broken Kilometer
393 W. Broadway
473-8072

Barnett Newman
77 Wooster St.
254-1414

John Chamberlain
67 Vestry St.
925-9009
Tues. to Sat. 11:00 A.M. to 6:00 P.M.

The Dia Art Foundation, a nonprofit foundation funded by the De Menil family, maintains four permanent exhibition spaces in the greater SoHo area. Works are commissioned or owned by the foundation and are exhibited in a setting that is more akin to a museum than to a conventional, commercial gallery. The spaces are well maintained and staffed, and comprehensive printed information is offered on each work.

Most striking of the four exhibits are the two installations by Walter de Maria, the first being the New York Earth Room, fourteen tons of dark, verdant earth filling a 3,600-square-foot gallery up to knee level. The leveled dirt is balanced against a typical SoHo gallery space: white walls, ceiling columns, track lights and so on. This extraordinary sight, coupled with its pungent odor of damp earth, is a wonderful study in contrast to the ex natura quality of most art galleries.

De Maria's Broken Kilometer is composed of 500 highly polished solid brass rods arranged in five parallel rows of 100 rods each; the distance between each rod increases from the beginning of the row to the end, so that the last, barely visible rows of the rods seem to recede into nothingness. Housed in a large ground-floor gallery with high ceilings and diffuse natural light, this large piece (45 feet wide by 125 feet long) is lit by stadium lights, which activate the highly polished surface of the rods. The overall effect is one of precision, clarity and tranquillity—a beautiful, if not stunning, achievement.

The third Dia Foundation space features four paintings by the great American hard-edge painter Barnett Newman, and the fourth showcases fourteen sculptures by John Chamberlain, whose trademark is fashioning provocative forms from discarded auto body parts. It should be noted that the John Chamberlain installation is in TriBeCa, the highly industrial area southwest of SoHo. It is somewhat difficult to find and perhaps a bit intimidating to reach on foot, but is worth the effort.

Metro Pictures
150 Greene St.
925-8335
Tues. to Sat. 10:00 A.M. to 6:00 P.M.

A relative newcomer to the SoHo establishment, Metro Pictures has made its presence known with a stable of young American artists that may best be described as fashionable. All trends are spoken here, and not without some interesting results. Headliner Robert Longo's work depicts solitary, life-size black and white figures in business dress, seemingly frozen in an array of positions that suggest that they either have been shot or are merely tripping the light fantastic at some terribly chic discothèque. But some of the other work here is much less interesting. Metro Pictures is a fine example of how a gallery sets out to make a name for itself by exploiting the sensational and the merely new. Unlike at Shafrazi, there is not the slightest hint of whimsy or playfulness. This, we are constantly reminded, is serious stuff. Although Metro has been very successful and has garnered a great deal of attention (the Museum of Modern Art recently acquired a large Longo painting), it is at best art for artifice's sake.

Protetch-McNeil Gallery
214 Lafayette St.
226-8957
Hours vary

Located a bit off the beaten SoHo track in a former Con Ed power plant, Protetch-McNeil is one of the most extraordinary gallery spaces in New York. It's authentic high-tech, with 30-foot ceilings, 5,000 square feet of exhibition space and a series of underground brick catacombs that offer one of the most unique viewing experiences imaginable. Throughout the building, you are constantly aware of the industrial trappings and how the additions made by the gallery (gray carpet, polished marble, etc.) mingle with the old concrete and brick, creating a marvelous effect. The space is, for the most part, used to exhibit large-scale works by such forward-thinking sculptors as Scott Burton, Alice Aycock and Siah Armajani. Protetch-McNeil, with its older branch uptown on 57th Street, has consistently been at the vanguard of new ideas not only in sculpture but in architecture and design, exhibiting the work of such important American architects as Michael Graves and Robert Venturi. Although somewhat difficult to find, and more in the East Village than in SoHo proper, Protetch-McNeil is without question worthy of the effort.

Tony Shafrazi Gallery

A veritable hotbed of the outré, Shafrazi is the center for the new graffiti artists, kids from various ethnic backgrounds who, instead of defacing the subway

163 Mercer St.
925-8732
Tues. to Sat. 11:00 A.M. to 6:00 P.M.

system, apply their manifold talents to a more lucrative enterprise—creating "art." The gallery is a spectrum of Day-Glo excesses, culminating in an irreverence toward the "art object" that can almost be described as refreshing. Painter Kenny Scharf's canvases of Fred Flintstone and his prehistoric family in outer space and Keith Haring's cartoon characters executed in labyrinthian Magic Marker patterns, have an immediacy and a sense of humor—but their prices will leave the viewer not so much bemused as in a state of shock. The problem is that this freewheeling attitude toward the art establishment is regarded with just as much seriousness by the general public as it would be if the works were hanging in the Museum of Modern Art. Brightly lit, garish and extreme, this gallery has an image that is certainly at odds with that of its proprietor, Tony Shafrazi, a charming, articulate man who began his career selling Jasper Johns, Robert Rauschenberg, Jackson Pollock and the like.

Sonnabend Gallery
420 W. Broadway
966-6160
Tues. to Sat. 10:00 A.M. to 6:00 P.M.

Illeana Sonnabend, the former wife of Leo Castelli, has developed over the years a gallery with perhaps even more diversity than her ex-husband's. Located one floor beneath Leo Castelli, Sonnabend has an impressive group of artists that includes George Baselitz, Anselm Kiefer, A.R. Penck and Jorg Immendorff from the new school of German painting; John Baldessari, Mel Bochner and Barry LeVa from the American minimalist tradition; and Gilbert and George, English performance artists. The gallery has always had eclectic inclinations, featuring performance and conceptual art and photography as well as painting and sculpture. Not a major innovative force like Castelli, but a sound gallery with work that appeals to a broad range of tastes.

Sperone Westwater Gallery
142 Greene St.
431-3685
Tues. to Sat. 10:00 A.M. to 6:00 P.M.

Sperone Westwater is a small gallery by SoHo standards, but it has a high-powered stable of younger American and European artists. Most notably, Sperone Westwater has been the first stopping-off point for the "big three" Italian painters: Sandro Chia, Francesco Clemente and Enzo Cucchi, whose reputations and attendant publicity have, for the most part, exceeded the merits of their work. Conversely, the work of English painter Christopher Lebrun is deserving of attention, as are the often overlooked talents of American painter-sculptor Bruce Nauman, whose work since the mid-1960s has been consistently evocative and challenging. There is a sense of excitement and novelty at Sperone, and this is certainly to the gallery's credit. It seems, however, too intent upon picking up the latest names from Europe and

465

exhibiting them as contemporary masters to a sometimes all-too-gullible American art public.

Edward Thorp Gallery
103–105 Prince St.
431-6880
Tues. to Sat. 10:00 A.M. to 6:00 P.M.

Located above the SoHo post office, Thorp has developed an exciting stable of younger American artists working primarily in figurative or representational formats. Most interesting among them are Eric Fischl, a painter whose themes of adolescent sexual awakening within an environment of suburban swimming pools and country clubs emit a highly charged psychological drama; and Martin Silverman, a sculptor whose painted bronzes employ ancient mythology to address modern themes of struggle and conquest. Other artists represented included Ken Kiff, April Gornick and R.L. Kaplan.

57TH STREET

Blum/Helman Gallery
20 W. 57th St.
245-2888
Tues. to Sat. 10:00 A.M. to 6:00 P.M.

Irving Blum, a man of great erudition and charm, opened his first gallery, Ferus, in Los Angeles; it has since become legendary, exhibiting the best from both the east and west coasts. Among some of the exhibitions were Andy Warhol's first show in the United States, early exhibitions of Jasper Johns, Robert Rauschenberg and Roy Lichtenstein, and an important but overlooked exhibition of the work of the late Joseph Cornell. Moving to New York some years ago, Mr. Blum formed a partnership with Joseph Helman and opened a gallery of great influence and international repute. Concentrating on contemporary "masters" (Ellsworth Kelly, Robert Moskowitz and Richard Serra), Blum/Helman has also developed a stable of younger American artists, including Bryan Hunt, John Duff and Donald Sultan, whose work has had tremendous critical and popular success. The gallery therefore has a two-part function: promoting the new and giving added credence to the old. This serious, committed gallery always offers something of interest to gallery browser and collector alike.

Theodore B. Donson Gallery
24 W. 57th St.
Suite 302
245-7007
Tues. to Sat. 10:00 A.M. to 6:00 P.M.

This gallery shows and sells the finest prints from the fifteenth through twentieth centuries. Mr. Donson's 1984 shows include the graphic art of William Hogarth and the graphic work of a contemporary of Rembrandt, Adriaen van Ostade. The highest quality prints available on the market regularly appear on these walls. Mr. Donson is also the author of an excellent book on prints and the print market.

Fitch-Febvrel Gallery
5 E. 57th St.
12th floor
688-8522
Tues. to Sat. 11:00 A.M. to 5:30 P.M.

This small gallery, opened by Andrew Fitch and his wife, Dominique Febvrel, wasn't long in making its mark. It specializes in late-nineteenth-century master prints and drawings (mainly European, but also some American and Japanese). Here's where you'll find Redon, Bresdin, Max Klinger and Belle Epoque artists. A gallery to be watched.

Galérie St. Etienne
24 W. 57th St.
245-6734
Tues. to Sat. 11:00 A.M. to 5:00 P.M.

This small gallery resembles a university library reading room, with its glass cases filled with prints and drawings and the salon-style hanging of its exhibitions. Galérie St. Etienne specializes in Austrian and German expressionist prints and drawings by such important historical figures as Gustav Klimt, Oskar Kokoschka, Egon Schiele and Käthe Kollwitz. The atmosphere here is one of reserve and scholarship. Director Hildegard Bachert is an authority on lesser-known artists of the period. Exhibitions as such are infrequent, but when undertaken, as with the works of Käthe Kollwitz and Alfred Kubin in 1982, they are first-rate and include intelligent, well-designed catalogs.

Sidney Janis Gallery
110 W. 57th St.
586-0110
Daily 10:00 A.M. to 5:00 P.M.

Sidney Janis, one of the great deans of the New York art scene, has been in business for more than 40 years. The list of exhibitions at both his old locale (6 West 57th Street) or the gallery's new location read like a who's who in modern art: de Kooning (1953), Pollock (1952), Gorky (1953), Kline (1956), Rothko (1955), Guston (1959), Duchamp (1959), Kelly (1965), Leger (1948), Kandinsky (1948), Mondrian (1943) and Henri Rousseau (1951). Other exhibitions have displayed an originality and concern for scholarship worthy of any museum—and, indeed, many works shown at Janis over the years have ended up in museum collections, the most impressive being the Janis personal collection, now housed in the Museum of Modern Art. Janis, like Alfred Stieglitz, has sought to bring the best of European and American art together in a setting that offers a cohesive aesthetic, and his exhibitions establish or break historical precedent, no matter how unusual the concept might initially appear (as was the case with a major show of Brancusi and Mondrian in 1982, for example). Although in his early 80s, Janis remains an active dealer and member of the art community, and his gallery continues to be an inspiration and asset.

Kennedy Gallery

This gallery is entirely devoted to American art from the American Revolution up to the outbreak of World War II. The work shown, including that of the moderns, is by

THE ARTS/Galleries

40 W. 57th St.
541-9600
Mon. to Fri. 9:30 A.M. to 5:30 P.M.

nature extremely conservative. Painters such as Charles Demuth and John Marin are shown for their pictorial qualities, yet the work of tougher, more experimental artists, such as Morgan Russell, Marsden Hartley and Morton Schamberg, is not. The atmosphere is also decidedly conservative and restrained. A large gallery with rooms of hunting prints, naive oils and the like, Kennedy—although one of the leaders in the field of indigenous American painting—is rather like a glorified antique shop. Nonetheless, it does show a group of important twentieth-century American painters, including Demuth, Edward Hopper, Walt Kuhn, John Sloan and Charles Burchfield. Despite its limitations, the quiet, older, more institutionalized sensibility at Kennedy is endearing.

Marlborough Gallery

40 W. 57th St.
541-4900
Daily 10:00 A.M. to 5:30 P.M. (Sat. to 5:00 P.M.)

Marlborough, at one time a veritable institution and one of the leading international galleries, has lost some of its glory, simply from age and competition; it also suffered in no small part from its association in the improper handling of the estate of the late Mark Rothko. Aside from these concerns, Marlborough maintains a high profile, particularly in London, exhibiting the work of major American and European painters, sculptors and photographers, including Henry Moore, Francis Bacon, Kurt Schwitters, Barbara Hepworth, Oskar Kokoschka, Irving Penn, Brassai and Helmut Newton; also exhibited on occasion are works by Rodin, Degas and Renoir. Marlborough represents a group of contemporary artists such as Ron Gorchov, Red Grooms, Reuben Nakian, Arnaldo Pomodoro and Fernando Botero, whose work can best be described as inconsequential and whose reputations, let alone prices, are ludicrously inflated. The gallery itself is huge by midtown standards, yet dingy and unkempt—although it is the only gallery north of SoHo with an outdoor sculpture terrace. We have found the staff to be perfectly incompetent and uninterested when asked about particular pieces in the gallery.

Pierre Matisse Gallery

41 E. 57th St.
355-6269
Tues. to Sat. (Sept. to June) 10:00 A.M. to 5:00 P.M.

Son of the great French impressionist Henri Matisse, Pierre Matisse has been since 1932 the sole U.S. dealer for such major historical figures as Balthus, Chagall, Calder, de Chirico, Dubuffet, Giacometti, Miro and Tanguy. M. Matisse's influence cannot be overestimated. During the late 1930s, when he first exhibited the likes of Chagall, Miro and Calder, the Museum of Modern Art was a fledgling, albeit parochial, institution. It was Pierre Matisse, along with such others as Sidney Janis and the late Julien Levy, who provided a forum for current trends in European painting and sculpture to be viewed firsthand and made a case for modern European art when it was little known, let alone fashionable. Today, Matisse mounts less frequent exhibitions, yet every two years or so he puts on a true blockbuster, such as the early Chagall paintings in 1977 or the new paintings by Balthus in 1980. To have lasted more than 50 years in a business that is nothing if not capricious is a testament to this legendary art dealer's unique commitment and unswerving vision.

David McKee Gallery
41 E. 57th St.
677-1340
Daily 10:00 A.M. to 6:00 P.M.

Located in a beautiful black and gold art deco building at the corner of 57th and Madison, the David McKee Gallery merits a visit by virtue of two artists it represents, Philip Guston and Vija Celmins, whose work, although rarely shown in full-scale exhibitions, is always available for viewing. As executors of the estate of the late Guston, the gallery has access to the bulk of the last (and among the best) paintings he completed in his lifetime, powerful works that attest to the will and vision of an artist who, although dying of cancer, decided to break with his former incarnation as an abstract expressionist and create a new figurative language in paint. Celmins is an artist of consummate skill and originality whose works parody and invite comparison to the real thing: a highly detailed replica in pencil of an ocean landscape encourages microscopic investigation, and a marvelous series of rocks comprises ten real stones and ten painted papier-mâché look-alikes that are completely indistinguishable from the real. The gallery is beautifully appointed, easily accessible (unlike many other galleries on 57th Street) and very hospitably staffed.

Robert Miller Gallery
724 Fifth Ave.
246-1625
Tues. to Sat. 10:00 A.M. to 6:00 P.M.

This is far and away one of the most elegant galleries in New York, with an attention to design bordering on the compulsive. Since opening the gallery four years ago, Mr. Miller has offered a consistently exciting program of exhibitions, with a stable that includes such names as Al Held, Jean Helion, Jedd Garet, Robert Mapplethorpe, Robert Graham, Louise Bourgeois and Alice Neel. His taste is diverse but tends toward the figurative and representational. The gallery also exhibits photographs, with a splendid inventory of vintage prints from the German avant-garde and carbro-color prints of Paul Outerbridge to name but a few examples. Historical exhibitions have, in the past, included photographs and paintings by Man Ray and paintings by Marsden Hartley. Robert Miller's urbane yet open demeanor, the pleasantness of the surroundings and the competence of his staff make visiting this gallery an unalloyed pleasure.

PACE Gallery

32 E. 57th St.
421-3292
Tues. to Fri. 9:30 A.M. to 5:30 P.M.; Sat. 10:00 A.M. to 6:00 P.M.

PACE is one of the premiere galleries in the world. It encompasses such heteroclite disciplines as modern painting and sculpture, contemporary painting and sculpture, African and primitive art, fine art prints and multiples, photography and an active pubishing concern. But its vast holdings of modern and contemporary painting and sculpture have secured its reputation. Owner and director Arnold Glimscher has amassed an impressive list of major American and European artists, including Brice Marden, Chuck Close, Lucas Samaras, Robert Irwin, Agnes Martin, Isamu Noguchi, Milton Avery and the estates of Mark Rothko, Jean Arp, Ad Reinhardt and Pablo Picasso. The physical aspects of the gallery are truly state of the art, with black ceilings, white and gray walls and a host of smaller galleries situated on various floors of the building. PACE has the best of everything and exhibits it with intelligence and care.

Martin Sumers Graphics

50 W. 57th St.
541-8334
Tues. to Sat. 10:00 A.M. to 5:00 P.M.

A respectable gallery for prints by English, European and American artists from the late nineteenth and early twentieth centuries. Worth a look.

The Witkin Gallery

41 E. 57th St.
355-1461
Tues. to Fri. 11:00 A.M. to 6:00 P.M.; Sat. noon to 5:00 P.M.

A confusing hodgepodge of contemporary photographs, modern prints, books, graphics, paintings and so on, all in a gallery space seemingly furnished with props from "Bonanza." Perfectly acceptable for the casual browser and novitiate, but definitely not for the serious collector.

Daniel Wolf Gallery

30 W. 57th St.
586-8432
Mon. to Sat. 10:00 A.M. to 6:00 P.M.

Daniel Wolf is a photography gallery that, unlike Prakapas, exhibits contemporary photographers and represents their work nationally, much like a contemporary art gallery. His stable of well-known photographers includes Jan Groover, Eliot Porter, Nicholas Nixon, Arnold Newman and Andreas Feininger. A handsome gallery, it also exhibits native American baskets, pots and rugs.

MIDTOWN

Phyllis Lucas Gallery and Old Print Center

Phyllis Lucas is both a dealer in old prints and a publisher of engravings and lithographs of all sorts. She can claim credit for the distribution of the first Dali lithographs and many small illustrated books, and she sells a large collection of maps and engravings classified by subject.

981 Second Ave.
(52nd St.)
755-1516
Tues. to Sat. 9:00 A.M. to 5:30 P.M.

Neikrug Photo-graphica Gallery
224 E. 68th St.
288-7741
Wed. to Sat. 1:00 P.M. to 6:00 P.M.

The Old Print Shop
150 Lexington Ave.
(30th St.)
683-3950
Mon. to Sat. 9:00 A.M. to 5:00 P.M.

Worthwhile exhibitions are held several times annually in the store's print gallery.

Marjorie Neikrug runs one of the most important photography galleries in the city. She shows nineteenth- and twentieth-century photographs and daguerreotypes, plus rare books, stereographs and the works of contemporary photographers. Shows for 1984 include 100 Image Bank photographers, Israeli artist Gerard Allon, Ruth Gilbert, male nudes, female nudes and the Civil War.

Founded in 1898, The Old Print Shop, located on the slopes of Murray Hill, has remained one of the best places in New York for early American and nineteenth-century French and English engravings. You'll find a particularly good selection of marine scenes, landscapes, cityscapes and Currier and Ives prints, along with old American maps.

UPTOWN

Acquavella Gallery
18 E. 79th St.
734-6300
Mon. to Sat. 10:00 A.M. to 5:00 P.M.

Acquavella occupies one of New York's most distinguished French neoclassical townhouses. Built in 1908 and modeled after an eighteenth-century Bordeaux residence, the building was once owned by Duveen Brothers, the celebrated art dealers who formed the greatest collections in the United States—those belonging to J. Pierpont Morgan, Henry Clay Frick, Andrew Mellon and John D. Rockefeller, Jr. The interior is noted for its rusticated stone, black and white tiled floors and monumental stairway. Acquavella acquired the building in 1967 and exhibits nineteenth- and twentieth-century American and European painting and sculpture, with a strong emphasis on the Impressionists. Major exhibitions in the past have included Degas, Modigliani and Tanguy; all were accompanied by handsome, well-written catalogs. It is for their historical material that the gallery is noteworthy, as its recent forays into contemporary American art, with such artists as Billy Al Bengston, Sandi Stone and Catherine Warren, are uninteresting and quite at odds with the splendid eighteenth-century surroundings.

La Boetie Gallery
9 E. 82nd St.

Owned and directed by Helen Serger, La Boetie specializes in art of the early twentieth century, including Bauhaus, De Stijl, surrealism, Dada and futurism. These individual and for the most part unrelated movements

535-4865
*Tues. to Sat. 10:00 A.M. to
5:30 P.M.*

had a profound influence upon modern society, for they attempted to change the very nature of everyday life through design, ideas or the potentially revolutionary act of applying paint to canvas. La Boetie mounts one or two major exhibitions yearly: The gallery's facsimile exhibition of the Nazi's *Degenerate Art Exhibition* of 1937, for example, was of major historical importance, reproducing in great detail the works of Otto Dix, George Grosz, Max Beckmann and others condemned by the National Socialists under Adolf Hitler. Pieces shown are primarily works on paper, but a few paintings and sculptures are also on view. La Boetie offers a wealth of important historical material from one of the richest and most influential periods in the history of art.

Colnaghi Gallery
26 E. 80th St.
772-2266
*Mon. to Fri. 10:00 A.M. to 6:00
P.M.; Sat. 10:00 A.M. to 5:30 P.M.*

Occupying an entire Upper East Side townhouse, Colnaghi recently celebrated its first anniversary in New York; in London, it celebrated its (almost unbelievably) 223rd. During its renowned tenure, Colnaghi has become one of the most important galleries for and appraisers of old master English paintings and drawings; sculpture, furniture and works of art from the sixteenth to the nineteenth centuries; and European paintings and drawings from the sixteenth to the twentieth centuries. It is indeed a marvel to walk into a commercial gallery and find paintings by the likes of Tintoretto, Bronzino, Canaletto, Vermeer, Rembrandt, Van Eyck and Titian for sale—at fabulous prices, no doubt, but nevertheless available. Steeped as it is in the grand European tradition of art dealing, Colnaghi's atmosphere is decidedly reserved and intended for the serious collector. Casual viewing or browsing is of course allowed, but certainly not encouraged to any degree, although the staff is gracious. Major exhibitions, such as *Discoveries from the Cinquecento,* are accompanied by lavishly produced catalogs. Although Colnaghi focuses its attention primarily upon the works of old masters, it also exhibits and places the work of important nineteenth-century artists such as Courbet, Corot and Rousseau. A gallery experience not to be missed.

Barry Friedman Gallery
26 E. 82nd St.
794-8950
*Mon. to Fri. 9:30 A.M. to 5:30
P.M.; Sat. 10:30 A.M. to 5:30 P.M.*

This is a classically European-looking gallery replete with period furnishings, Corinthian columns, a marble fireplace and even a painted ceiling panel graced with airborne putti. The gallery's expertise lies in symbolism, Vienna Secession, art nouveau, the Pre-Raphaelites, turn-of-the-century European design and European realism of the 1920s and 1930s. The artists shown include Gustave Moreau, Fernand Khnoppf, Edward Burne-Jones, Christian Schad and the great Italian realist Cognaccio di

San Pietro. Friedman is a gallery with a clearly defined aesthetic and one that, at times, leans towards the decorative and the contrived. For the most part, however, the work exhibited is of great historical significance and (this is somewhat surprising) is invariably beautiful to look at, as if it were meant somehow to complement the furnishings of the gallery, not to stand alone as works of art. Barry Friedman also owns a furniture and design gallery called, somewhat pretentiously, "Modernism," at 984 Madison Avenue. The gallery (or shop, as some would label it) is filled with furniture and objects by some of this century's leading designers.

Xavier Fourcade Gallery
36 E. 75th St.
535-3980
Tues. to Fri. 10:00 A.M. to 5:30 P.M.; Sat. 10:00 A.M. to 5:00 P.M.

Fourcade is one of the few uptown dealers who carry exclusively American and European contemporary art. Located within a few blocks of the Whitney Museum, the gallery is known for exclusively representing the work of two important artists: Willem de Kooning, the great abstract expressionist, who at 80 years of age is still producing a remarkable body of work both on canvas and in bronze, and Malcolm Morley, a British émigré whose paintings over the years have been particularly eccentric and inspired. The work of other artists shown is generally of a high standard.

M. Knoedler and Co.
19 E. 70th St.
794-0550
Tues. to Fri. 9:30 A.M. to 5:30 P.M.; Sat. 10:00 A.M. to 5:30 P.M.

Knoedler is an internationally established and recognized gallery housed in yet another imposing Upper East Side townhouse. Owned by renowned collector and financier Armand Hammer and directed by the former senior curator of twentieth-century art at the Museum of Modern Art, Lawrence Rubin, Knoedler's credentials are impressive. Hammer's international business connections and passion for art have resulted in the exhibition of rare artworks from the Soviet Union, which without his efforts would never be seen in the West. The gallery's aesthetic emphasis rests in three major areas: Italian, Flemish and German old masters; the impressionists; and twentieth-century American painters, including Adolph Gottlieb, Alexander Calder, David Smith, Frank Stella, Richard Diebenkorn and Robert Motherwell. The old master department is open by appointment only and is in most cases reserved for those who are known to the gallery and for serious collectors. With its broad yet well-defined range of interests and its abundance of curatorial talent, Knoedler remains one of the world's leading art concerns.

Prakapas Gallery

The finest photography gallery in New York, if not the entire United States. The gallery itself is small yet well designed, with the amiably gregarious Gene Prakapas

19 E. 71st St.
737-6066
Tues. to Sat. noon to 5:00 P.M.

presiding. The photographic material is entirely vintage and historical; there are no "modern" prints made from old negatives. Mr. Prakapas, besides exhibiting the work of better-known photographers from 1900 to 1950 (Eugene Atget, Man Ray, Walker Evans), has been instrumental in bringing to light the work of many European photographers of the '20s and '30s, such as Franz Roh, Paul Citroen, Umbo, Florence Henri, Jaroslav Rossler and T. Lux Feninger. A visit here is always a profitable and enlightening experience.

Serge Sabarsky Gallery
987 Madison Ave.
(77th St.)
628-6281
Tues. to Sat. noon to 6:00 P.M.

The country's major dealer of German expressionist painting, drawing and sculpture inhabits an unassuming Madison Avenue storefront. The gallery itself is small by any standard, yet the treasures on view would be the envy of most museums. Important paintings and drawings by George Grosz, Leon Kirchner, Otto Dix, Max Beckmann, Gustav Klimt, Paul Klee and Egon Schiele line the walls. A black-velvet-curtained rear office is crammed with books, catalogs and other appurtenances of the art dealer's craft, all dominated by one of the most striking and beautiful Max Beckmann oils imaginable. Sabarsky, as well as being one of the leading dealers in work of this period, is also one of its foremost authorities and advocates, and was instrumental in placing the art of the German expressionists in its proper, lofty historical position.

David Tunick Gallery
12 E. 81st St.
570-0090
Mon. to Fri. 10:00 A.M. to 5:00 P.M.

The preeminent print dealer in the world, David Tunick exhibits only the finest material in the most elegant surroundings. Walking into the gallery may be likened to entering the house of Dior in Paris for an exclusive, private showing. Located in a beautiful townhouse just off Central Park, Tunick is filled with period furniture, dark rugs and mahogany-lined viewing rooms, all replete with a selection of old master prints and rare, limited modern prints that are second to none and include only first strikes. Among the old masters shown are Dürer, Rembrandt, Tiepolo and Piranesi. The moderns include Beckmann, Kirchner, Picasso and Toulouse-Lautrec, as well as a strong American group including Whistler, Sloan, Marsh and Stuart Davis. The inventory is extensive, as is the list of published material that accompanies exhibitions. Tunick is only for the serious collector; simple browsers are frowned upon or merely ignored. We recommend calling ahead for an appointment.

=== LONG ISLAND CITY ===

P.S. 1 (Project Studios One)
46–01 21st St.
Long Island City
784-2084
Thurs. to Sun. noon to 6:00 P.M.

P.S.1, otherwise known as the Institute for Art and Urban Resources, is a semirecycled public school that often houses adventurous exhibitions. Hailed for its prescience in mounting the German expressionist show in the fall of '83, this public space continues to sponsor challenging and engaging exhibitions. The best parts of this clumsy structure are the old classrooms, which have been converted into personalized exhibition spaces for very contemporary artists, many of whose work is underrealized. No matter; the three-story building, in a constant state of evolution, is of enough interest to warrant a visit.

Museums

America has gone art crazy. Several years ago, there was a new gold rush, this time for "The Gold of Tutankhamen." Then, in 1980, a million people—7,000 a day—jostled for place in line to see the Picassos at the incredible retrospective organized by the Museum of Modern Art. The "Treasures of the Vatican" show was no less spectacular.

These events no longer attract only aesthetes and connoisseurs. Nowadays, almost every new exhibition draws the same teeming, anonymous crowds that fill a ballpark or wait three hours to see a film. New York, like Paris, is now a city of "exhibitionists." There's something disquieting about this frenzy, whipped up by advertising, a hunger for the "not-to-be-missed" exhibition or event. But New York's appetite for art seems insatiable, and you must be ready to stand in line and elbow (and be elbowed) to attend any exhibition of the slightest importance. You should keep this in mind when planning your museum visits: don't be stingy with your time when devising your schedule.

There are more than 50 museums in New York, obviously of unequal interest. We will introduce you to the most famous ones first, and then to a few others, which are not indispensable but are by no means without interest.

MAJOR MUSEUMS

Guggenheim Museum

Fifth Avenue and 89th Street

360-3500

Tues. to Sun. 11:00 A.M. to 5:00 P.M. (Tues. to 8:00 P.M.)

It looks like a French brioche stuffed with a 400-yard spiral ramp. It has provoked myriad jokes (the museum should supply sea-sickness pills with each entrance ticket; it's the architect's revenge on the artist; etc.).

The arguments between Solomon Guggenheim and his architect, Frank Lloyd Wright, aggravated by accounts in the press and the opinions of the Urban Planning Commission, were widely discussed for a long time, and the multibillionaire patron of the arts had been dead for two years before the snail-shaped museum that bears his name finally opened its doors in 1951. After an elevator ride to the top, you begin the descent of this long reinforced concrete spiral—a brilliant creation that allows you to test your cardiovascular conditioning and the endurance of your calves, while feasting your eyes on the treasures displayed.

The museum owns, and exhibits in rotation, some 5,000 modern paintings, sculptures and drawings. The collection, which is both high in quality and intelligently planned, is dominated by the collections of Kandinsky (close to 180 canvases); Mondrian's abstract work; cubist work by Juan Gris, Georges Braque and Picasso; work by Paul Klee, Marc Chagall, Picabia, Michaux, Max Ernst and more; as well as pieces by such important contemporary American artists as Jackson Pollock and Robert Rauschenberg.

The Tannhauser collection, which became a part of the museum in 1965, is of an earlier period and includes 75 pieces (masterpieces, many of them) by Renoir, Cézanne, Van Gogh, Degas, Pissarro and Picasso (from his "Blue" period).

It would be unfair not to single out the museum's cafeteria, situated on the ground floor. The food is not only attractively presented, it is actually edible, thus affording the establishment a unique position in the otherwise lugubrious landscape of New York museum restaurants. We particularly recommend the chef's salad and the chocolate cake.

Metropolitan Museum of Art

Fifth Avenue and 82nd Street

535-7710

Tues. 10:00 A.M. to 8:45 P.M.; Wed. to Sat. 10:00 A.M. to 4:45 P.M.; Sun. 11:00 A.M. to 4:45 P.M.

The biggest art museum in the United States is one of the most dangerous in the world. Visitors risk artistic apoplexy and cultural embolism—or at least leaving with severe indigestion. Everything you might ever want to see is here—and then there's more. The visitor floats with ecstasy, but gradually dizziness sets in and soon he or she is swaying on his feet, and ends up waving the white flag, wishing dire misfortune on the authors of those guides that enjoin, "The Metropolitan—a full day or nothing."

Three hours, twelve minutes, 28 seconds—that is our absolute record. Of course, one does what one can, but if you want our opinion, anything over two and a half hours borders on the foolhardy. Above all, never enter with the intention (unless you're feeling suicidal) of roaming at random through these endless floors, halls and galleries.

A wiser course consists of first finding out what is to be seen. There's usually a temporary exhibition, and as they are generally of great beauty, they are a splendid reason for one's first trip to the museum. Then, as one exhibition will probably not have brought you to your knees, treat yourself to a stroll through the new American Wing's twenty rooms, which are, with the Astor Court (an exquisite recreation of a sixteenth-century Chinese garden courtyard), the Met's latest grand achievements. There are more stunning masterpieces to be seen in other sections, but when you're in the lap of modern America, why not discover its past as well? Displayed in a gigantic greenhouse are innumerable pieces of furniture from the eighteenth and nineteenth centuries, paintings by both naïf and professional artists, stained glass from the Belle Epoque, western bronzes, and Tiffany glass, shown in a natural setting. The message is a sound one. Until recently, America had stuffed its museums with the past of other cultures; but America, too, is a civilization with a past. So much for a first visit: and afterwards?

We must leave that up to you. A large descriptive board at the museum entrance indicates which sections are open at what times. But try not to miss the permanent gallery (the Sackler Gallery) of Assyrian art, with a spectacular display (in a different part of the museum) of the remains of the Egyptian temple at Dendur. (The Egyptian section is, after the Cairo Museum, the Louvre and the Berlin Museum, the biggest in the world.)

You should also trot off to the galleries where many impressionist masterpieces are displayed—you've seen them in reproduction, but here they shimmer before your eyes. Then lose yourself in the Lehman Collection, a series of rooms crammed with eighteenth-century paneling, important pieces of French furniture, Italian, Flemish and French painting, tapestries and magnificent classical drawings.

The latest giant addition to the Met is the Rockefeller Wing for Primitive Art. Like everything else here, it is done on a grand scale and is packed with ancient treasures.

Try to make time another day to visit the galleries of

Asian and Islamic art, the fifteen or so rooms with reconstructions of interiors of European châteaus and mansions (the exquisite Cabris mansion at Grasse, and a marvelous Louis XVI storefront from Île Saint-Louis in Paris, among others) or the overwhelming section of medieval art. Don't overlook the ground-floor boutique, either, where in addition to numerous art books there are many excellent reproductions and all sorts of attractive objects that make reasonably priced gifts.

Museum of Modern Art
11 W. 53rd St.
708-9400
Thurs. to Tues. 11:00 A.M. to 6:00 P.M. (Thurs. to 9:00 P.M.)

Here too, the Rockefeller Foundation distributed its magical manna to make the MOMA into one of the most exciting museums in the world. Created in 1929 to introduce the public to the Paris School, it later broadened its scope considerably, aiming to present not only all the most important currents in modern art, from French impressionism to American abstract expressionism (via German expressionism, dadaism and surrealism), but also to follow as well all facets of contemporary art, including architecture, photography, cinema and furniture. In addition to its permanent collection it displays a variety of temporary exhibitions, such as its incredibly successful Picasso retrospective, which proved the museum to be too small and resulted in the undertaking of a three-year expansion program. Movies are shown regularly in the afternoon, free to visitors, and art lovers can catch their breath in the cafeteria on the first floor in the new building.

Whitney Museum of American Art
945 Madison Ave. (70th St.)
570-3676
Tues. to Sat. 11:00 A.M. to 6:00 P.M.; Sun. noon to 6:00 P.M.

This granite and concrete blockhouse, the work of Marcel Breuer, looks like a truncated pyramid. It was opened in 1966 to house the excellent collection of contemporary American painting and sculpture amassed since 1930 at the instigation of Gertrude Vanderbilt Whitney, herself a sculptress. It now contains over 6,000 works, most from the twentieth century, and there are fine temporary exhibits. The Whitney's midtown branch is in the Phillip Morris headquarters on 42nd Street across from Grand Central Station.

OUTSIDE OF MANHATTAN

Brooklyn Museum
Eastern Parkway near

This massive fin-de-siècle building (since enlarged) stands at the northeast entrance of a vast botanical garden, remarkable in particular for its reconstruction of a sixteenth-century Japanese garden. It is not a cheery

Washington Avenue, Brooklyn
638-5000
Wed. to Sun. 10:00 A.M. to 5:00 P.M. (Sun. noon to 5:00 P.M.)

place, and is low on signs of life since African, Oceanic and native American cultural artifacts are seldom the stuff that works up the crowds. But if you're interested in Egyptian art, pay the place a visit. The Brooklyn Museum houses an excellent collection of sculptures, bas-reliefs, small bronzes, ceramics and jewelry dating from the predynastic period until Ptolemaic and Coptic times. There are also usually interesting temporary exhibits.

SMALLER MUSEUMS

American Craft Museum
77 W. 45th St.
391-8770
Mon. to Sat. 10:00 A.M. to 5:00 P.M.

This small, relatively new museum presents often interesting exhibitions devoted to costume and contemporary applied arts.

American Museum of Natural History
Central Park West and 79th Street
873-1300
Mon. to Sat. 10:00 A.M. to 4:45 P.M. (Wed. and Fri. to 9:00 P.M.); Sun. and hol. 11:00 A.M. to 5:00 P.M.

This immense and pompous hodgepodge is populous on Sundays with large families and Boy Scout troops. The miles of cabinets display global fauna and flora, from prehistory on, including a 90-foot-long (fiberglass) blue whale. The Gardner D. Stout rooms show off a vast ethnographical collection from Asia and the Middle East, but the museum could be more rigorous in its organization.

The museum also offers free hour-long "Highlight Tours" and two films, *To Fly* and *Living Planet. To Fly,* an excellent 30-minute film, is shown daily at the Naturemax Theatre ($3 for adults and $1.50 for children), and the two films are shown together on weekend nights.

You might also visit the Hayden Planetarium, where presentations on astronomy are given in the Guggenheim Space Theater. On the whole, though, these are less successful than those at the Reuben H. Fleet Space Theater in San Diego.

The American Numismatic Society
Broadway and 156th Street
234-3130
Tues. to Sat. 1:00 to 5:00 P.M. Note: ring bell to enter

What do Herodotus, George Washington and Caesar have in common? Their faces are all artfully engraved on various bronze, silver and gold discs, expertly displayed in the American Numismatic Society. Ring the doorbell and you will be ushered into vaulted rooms where currency spanning the period from its invention to the inflationary present can be seen. Two special exhibits trace the evolution of American currency and international medals and decorations.

The Cloisters
Fort Tryon Park
923-3700
Tues. to Sun. 10:00 A.M. to 4:45 P.M. (noon to 4:45 P.M. Sun.)

Overlooking the Hudson, beyond the Washington Bridge, lies the admirable collection of medieval art presented by the Metropolitan Museum, with the financial assistance of the Rockefeller family. Whole buildings are exhibited, and rooms from such monasteries as Saint-Guilhem-le-Désert have found sanctuary in the New World. These marvels, to which are added stained glass, tapestries and sculptures, are presented with great style. Even the gardens are works of both beauty and scholarship.

Cooper-Hewitt Museum
Fifth Avenue and 91st Street
860-6898
Sun. noon to 5:00 P.M.; Tues. 10:00 A.M. to 9:00 P.M.; Wed. to Sat. to 5:00 P.M.

The Carnegie Mansion provides a sumptuous setting for the permanent collection of European furniture, wallpapers, porcelain, glassware, antique textiles of every possible origin, bronzes, wrought iron and silverware, along with a rich selection of drawings and architectural and decorative prints. This fascinating museum also presents temporary exhibits of the highest quality. Asleep for years, the museum is presently experiencing a renaissance.

Frick Collection
1 E. 70th St.
288-0700
Sun. 1:00 P.M. to 6:00 P.M.; Tues. to Sat. 10:00 A.M. to 6:00 P.M.

On the ground floor of this Louis XV- Louis XVI-style mansion, built in 1913 for the industrialist Henry Clay Frick, awaits an exceptional collection of European painting—Bellini, Rembrandt, Holbein, Velasquez, Vermeer, Fragonard, Boucher, Claude Lorrain—shown as they were intended to be, in the living rooms and boudoirs of a (very grand) private house. A characteristic example of the (good) taste of an American tycoon in the robber baron years who grew passionate about "art," and took good advice in acquiring it.

The Hispanic Society of America
Broadway and 155th Street
690-0743
Tues. to Sat. 1:00 to 4:30 P.M.; Sun. 1:00 to 4:00 P.M.

This exhibit of Iberian (Spanish and Portuguese) painting, sculpture and decorative arts is located in the center of the Audubon Terrace. The interior courtyards and galleries contain items of art and archaeology from the earliest Spanish civilizations to the present (including colonial America), but the most interesting art pieces are paintings by such masters as El Greco, Goya and Velasquez.

International Center for Photography
Fifth Avenue and 94th Street
860-1777
Tues. 11:00 A.M. to 8:00 P.M.; Wed. to Sat. 11:00 A.M. to 5:00 P.M.

This center possesses a rich collection of works by the greatest photographers of the twentieth century. Its exhibitions are always of interest.

Jewish Museum

Fifth Ave. and 92nd Street
860-1888
Sun. 11:00 A.M. to 6:00 P.M.;
Mon. to Thurs. noon to 5:00 P.M.

This small, very active museum devoted to Jewish art and culture (manuscripts, coins, textiles, paintings, pottery and so on) often presents provocative exhibitions. A little while ago Andy Warhol's "Portrait Gallery" (the likes of Einstein, Freud, Kafka, the Marx Brothers) caused much controversy in the press.

Museum of the American Indian

Broadway and 155th Street
283-2420
Tues. to Sat. 10:00 A.M. to 5:00 P.M. Sun. 1:00 to 5:00 P.M.

Probably the most complete collection of Indian culture anywhere in North, South or Central America. A very clear presentation provides enormous amounts of information concerning the native peoples, whose self-evident artistic talents are highly valued by collectors. Located in the beautiful Audubon Terrace complex, you'll find an astonishing number of Indian treasures, from jewelry to weapons to costumes.

Museum of the City of New York

1220 Fifth Ave. (103rd St.)
534-1672
Sun. and hol. 1:00 to 5:00 P.M.; Tues. to Sat. 10:00 A.M. to 5:00 P.M.

This absolutely fascinating museum is located in a handsome neo-Georgian building, and contains remarkable models of New York's early development, and of interiors throughout the centuries. There's a delightful collection of toys and doll's houses, John D. Rockefeller's bedroom from the 1880s, puppets and an audio-visual presentation on the history of New York.

New York Historical Society

Central Park West and 77th Street
873-3400
Tues. to Fri. 11:00 A.M. to 5:00 P.M.; Sat. 10:00 A.M. to 5:00 P.M.; Sun. 1:00 P.M. to 5:00 P.M.

A visit to this museum agreeably rounds out a tour of the previous one. Here are superb collections of antique toys, New York silverware from the eighteenth and nineteenth centuries, and nineteenth-century furniture, as well as portraits, carriages and nearly all of John James Audubon's marvelous watercolor originals (433 of 435) for his *Birds of America*.

Music · Dance

The wealth of opportunity to see first-class music and dance performances in New York is mind-boggling—how do you begin to choose when you might be able to see Twyla Tharp, Placido Domingo, Leonard Bernstein, Itzhak Perlman, and Mikhail Baryshnikov? The choice of stages is superb: the grandeur and the scope of offerings at Lincoln Center, the fabulous acoustics at Carnegie Hall and the striking design of the Joyce Theater. Whether it's chamber music, modern dance or classic opera, New York is one of the finest places in the world for music and dance.

Half-price tickets to many performances are available the same day at the SEATS booth in Bryant Park, 42nd Street and Sixth Avenue (382-2323). The cash-only booth adds a modest service charge; it is open daily from noon to 7:00 P.M. And don't despair if a concert is sold out—seats are usually on sale at the last minute. Just get to the hall about 40 minutes early, and look for subscribers selling their extra tickets at the door.

LINCOLN CENTER

T his stunning complex of buildings at 64th Street and Broadway is the harmonious work of the country's greatest architects, and is the hub of musical life in New York. Something is always happening on these fourteen acres, from a Christmastime sing-along Messiah to film festivals and grand opera.

While excellent guided tours wil take you through all the halls, the best way to experience Lincoln Center is by attending its programs, which are not necessarily costly. Free events are held throughout the year in the Bruno Walter Auditorium in the Library and Museum of the Performing Arts; the Guggenheim Band's outdoor concerts in Damrosch Park are popular in the summer; and the Plaza is taken over every August by an outdoor festival with free programs all day long. Below are brief descriptions of the halls found at Lincoln Center.

Avery Fisher Hall
874-2424
874-6770
(chargeline)
Box office: Mon. to Sat. 10:00 A.M. to 6:00 P.M.; Sun. noon to 6:00 P.M.

The New York Philharmonic plays in 2,700-seat Avery Fisher Hall from mid-September to May. In summer the Kool Jazz Festival moves in, followed by the ever-popular Mostly Mozart Festival. The interior was completely demolished and rebuilt in 1976, and improved acoustics were the desired result. At intermission make sure to walk outside on the terrace to see the other audiences doing likewise.

Metropolitan Opera House
362-6000
Box office: Mon. to Sat. 10:00 A.M. to 8:00 P.M.; Sun. noon to 6:00 P.M.

The Opera House, with its two Chagall murals (uncovered at night) and magnificent Lobmeyer chandeliers from Vienna, is home to the world's finest singers from September to April, when the Met is in residence. From May to July the stage is taken over by the

American Ballet Theater, the Royal Ballet and other visiting international ballet companies.

New York State Theater
870-5570
944-9300
(chargeline)
Box office: Mon. 10:00 A.M to 8:00 P.M. ; Tues. to Sat. 10:00 A.M. to 9:00 P.M.; Sun. 11:30 A.M. to 7:30 P.M.

The State showcases Beverly Sills's New York City Opera in midsummer—at half the price of Met tickets. The New York City Ballet, with its Balanchine-trained dancers, takes over from November to February, and again from April to June. During December, the Nutcracker performances are the most sought-after tickets in town. Get your mail order in before October 15 to avoid disappointment.

Alice Tully Hall
362-1911
874-6770
(chargeline)
Box office: Mon. to Sat. 11:00 A.M. to 7:00 P.M. ; Sun. noon to 6:00 P.M.

The popularity of chamber music in New York is largely due to the outstanding resident Chamber Music Society, which performs here from October through May. The 1,096-seat auditorium is used for the New York Film Festival from September to October, and free Juilliard School concerts (Wednesdays at 1:00 P.M.). Solo recitals and ensembles keep the hall busy year round.

OTHER THEATERS

Brooklyn Academy of Music
30 Lafayette Ave.
Brooklyn
636-4100
Box office: Mon. to Fri. 10:00 A.M. to 5:00 P.M.

If you have even the slightest sense of adventure, don't hesitate to catch a cab, bus or subway to BAM, where Harvey Lichenstein continues to attract an outstanding roster of musicians and dancers. There's always something happening in one of the four halls here.

Carnegie Hall
57th Street and
Seventh Avenue
247-7459
Box office: Mon. to Sat. 11:00 A.M. to 6:00 P.M. (until 8:30 P.M. on performance evenings); Sun. noon to 6:00 P.M. (on performance days only)

Thank goodness the city bought Carnegie Hall in the 1960s, saving it from destruction. Today, an active renovation program has reproduced the original 1891 facade and improved the lobby. From October to May the hall resounds with visiting orchestras from Philadelphia, Chicago, Boston, Los Angeles and Cleveland, who appreciate its fine acoustics. The smaller Recital Hall next door is still popular for debut performances.

City Center Theater
131 W. 55 St.
246-8989
944-9300

The Moorish facade of this huge dance theater is a reminder that it was built in 1923 as a Shriner's temple. It has a beautiful new ground floor with better sight lines, and it hosts many of the country's most popular dance companies: Alvin Ailey, Joffrey Ballet, Paul Taylor, Dance Theater of Harlem and Merce Cunningham. In the

(chargeline)
Box office: daily noon to 8:00 P.M.

The Joyce Theater
175 Eighth Ave. (19th St.) 242-0800
Box office: daily noon to 6:00 P.M.

Merkin Concert Hall
(Abraham Goodman House) 129 W. 67th St. 362-8719
Box office: Mon. to Thurs. 10:00 A.M. to 6:30 P.M.; Fri. to 4:00 P.M.; Sun. noon to 4:00 P.M.

92nd Street YMHA
1395 Lexington Ave. (92nd St.) 831-8603
Box office: Mon. to Thurs. 10:00 A.M. to 9:00 P.M.; Fri. to 4:00 P.M.; Sun. noon to 6:00 P.M

The Grace Rainey Rogers Auditorium
(Metropolitan Museum of Art) 82nd Street and Fifth Avenue 570-3949
Box office: Tues. to Fri. 1:00 P.M. to 4:00 P.M.; Sat. and Sun. 11:00 A.M. to 4:00 P.M.

basement, the 299-seat Space showcases new companies and avant-garde choreography.

The former Elgin movie theater in trendy Chelsea has been gutted and brilliantly redesigned by Hardy, Holzman, Pfeiffer. It's now the city's finest hall for modern dance. This is the place to find the likes of Dan Wagoner, Erick Hawkins, Eliot Feld and Douglas Dunn. Come here just to experience the perfect interaction of design and performance.

One of the city's newest halls, the Merkin, in the shadow of Lincoln Center, seats 457. Concerts are given from September to June. This is a fine place to hear chamber music performances.

The acoustics have been vastly improved in the Y's 916-seat Kaufmann Concert Hall. In addition to shows featuring distinguished musical artists, the Lyrics and Lyricists performances are immensely popular. Ensembles and the Y Chamber Symphony perform here from October to May.

Musica Aeterna, Music from Marlboro and the Guarneri Quartet usually play here. Unlike most concert halls, credit cards are not accepted; you can get tickets through mail order or at the box office.

Theater

For an actor, Broadway is not just an address; it's synonymous with "making it" in the theater. It's the top of the pyramid for accomplished film stars, soap opera heroes, familiar situation comedy faces, television and radio announcers and thousands of struggling graduates with degrees in theater arts or visions of stardom. They all come to New York sooner or later to try to make the ultimate conquest: Elizabeth Taylor, Richard Thomas, Raquel Welsh, Farrah Fawcett, Mark Hamill, Carol Burnett and Anthony Perkins are some who have felt the lure, taken the plunge and made it big.

For the theater-goer, Broadway continues to provide the big spectacle, the splashy musical, the latest Neil Simon comedy and revivals of earlier successes. Tickets may be hard to get for the newest hit, but it's not impossible if you write in advance or call the telephone credit card services. Chargit gets $2.50–$2.75 extra per ticket. Call from outside New York State from 10:00 A.M. to 8:00 P.M. (800) 223-1814; in the city dial 944-9300. The Shubert Theaters have their own Telecharge, which gets $2.50 per ticket. Office hours are 8:00 A.M. to midnight, seven days a week (239-6200).

Many special productions, including those at Radio City Music Hall and the Jones Beach State Theater, are sold out of town or in New York through Ticketron outlets. They charge $2 extra per ticket. In New York, call 977-9020 for available shows.

Tickets at the box office window can run up to $45 for a musical or $30 for a drama. Through a commercial ticket agency, such as Golden & LeBlang (1501 Broadway, between 43rd and 44th streets, Room 1814, 944-8910), you can still get good seats when the box office says "sold out." Its commission varies from $2 plus five percent of the ticket price if purchased at the window with a credit card, to $2 plus eighteen percent of the box office price if ordered over the phone with a credit card. Hours are 8:00 A.M. to 8:00 P.M. Monday through Saturday, 9:00 A.M. to 6:00 P.M. Sundays. It pays to check there. Most hotels have a ticket office that can provide seats for even the most popular plays for a few dollars over the regular price.

The hardy and thrifty stand in line for half-price tickets on the day of performance at one of two kiosks operated by the Theatre Development Fund, a non-profit organization that helps boost theater attendance. The shortest wait is at the downtown booth, which is sheltered from the elements on the mezzanine of 2 World Trade Center (the building with the observation deck on the 107th floor). It's open Monday to Friday from 11:30 A.M. to 5:30 P.M. and Saturday from 11:00 A.M. to 3:00 P.M.; it only sells tickets for evening performances, and adds $1.25 service charge per ticket.

Longer lines form outside the kiosk at 47th Street and

Broadway daily. Tickets go on sale at noon for matinees and at 3:00 P.M. for evening performances, but get there early if you want decent seats. The same half-price plus service charge formula prevails.

Off Broadway is a catch-all term for the gamut of theaters that usually seat from 100 to 400 people, and that frequently attract Hollywood names who are interested in the playwright or director: Al Pacino and Meryl Streep have come back here after establishing themselves in Hollywood to perform in intimate theaters. Many established theaters are in Greenwich Village, including Joseph Papp's Public Theater (which also offers some half-price tickets at the box office on the day of performance). Papp's New York Shakespeare Festival moves to the Delacorte Theater in Central Park during July and August, with free outdoor performances for those willing to stand in line for the 6:00 P.M. ticket distribution.

The Village also hosts the avant-garde La Mama E.T.C. and the Performing Garage, along with the traditional Circle in the Square and the Lucille Lortel Theater, once the Theatre de Lys. The off Broadway umbrella also hangs over repertory companies with their own theaters; they are known for classic revivals and contemporary plays. Several companies perform in churches (such as the old St. Clement's or the ultramodern St. Peter's), which also offer other entertainments.

"Theater Row," a renovation of 42nd Street between Ninth and Tenth avenues, consists of a string of small theaters with a common box office (Ticket Central, open from 1:00 to 8:00 P.M. daily, 279-4200) that will accept phone reservations or credit card purchases. They are part of the off-off Broadway scene, where theaters frequently have short runs and less than 100 seats.

Since all of these theaters are not enough to employ the talents of the city's many directors, actors and playwrights, showcases are put together to display their work in unlikely theater spaces in SoHo and other parts of town. For little more than the cost of a movie ticket, these theaters offer a chance to see the actors and playwrights of tomorrow, along with more inventive and unusual theatrical experiences. The *Village Voice* usually provides the most complete listings of these off-off Broadway theaters and showcases. The Sunday *New York Times,* the *New Yorker* and *New York* magazine provide brief reviews of the current Broadway and larger off Broadway plays. The Friday *Times* lists ticket availability for the most popular plays over the weekend.

THE $\underset{\text{THE}}{}$ SIGHTS

The Sights

EXPLORING THE CITY

If you are a first-time visitor to New York, you have a certain obligation to see such well-worn sights as the Empire State Building and the Statue of Liberty. But please don't stop there. New York is rich with unusual, intriguing places, many of which are unknown to most New Yorkers. For history buffs, there are fascinating tours of Harlem, Greenwich Village and other old New York neighborhoods. For fashion mavens, there are behind-the-scenes looks into designers' studios. Theater fans can go backstage on Broadway and through Lincoln Center; the money-minded can explore the Stock Exchange and the Federal Reserve Bank. Whatever your interest, New York is interested in it, too; it is a city full of bests, biggests, oldests, firsts, strangests and wealthiests, and we are enthralled every time we visit. We've passed along some of our favorite buildings, amusements, tours and parks, and we encourage you to take off on foot—personal explorations of New York are often the most fulfilling.

Amusements

Bronx Zoo
185th Street and
Kazamiroff
Boulevard
The Bronx
220-5100
Daily 10:00 A.M. to 4:30 P.M.
Adults $1.50, children 50¢ (Tues. to
Thurs. free)

With the largest collection of animals in America—more than 3,000 animals of 1,000 species—the Bronx Zoo is among the world's most innovative wildlife sanctuaries and is worth the half-hour trip from Manhattan. Unobtrusive moats border the open domains of wild deer, moose and yak in the "African Plains." The "World of Darkness" houses nocturnal birds. The "World of Birds" aviary simulates a South African rain-forest thunderstorm daily at 2:00 P.M. Lions, monkeys, snow leopards, reptiles, great apes, penguins and elephants all roam in reasonable simulations of their natural settings. Not to be missed is the Bengali Express monorail ride through "Wild Asia," a habitat for gazelle, antelope and zebras.

Chinese Museum
8 Mott St.
(Chatham Sq.)
964-1542
Daily 10:00 A.M. to 6:00 P.M.
Admission 75¢

Don't expect the Prado or St. Peter's. These are mass tourist exhibits that cater to the quick five-minute look. The very idiosyncratic museum is located inside and above a noisy video arcade, features two well-fed chickens who dance and play tic-tac-toe (you have to see it to believe it!), and is fun and kitschy. It's an interesting lark if you want a fifteen-minute self-service learning experience about the more popular areas of Chinese life, including chopsticks, flower arranging, checkers and calligraphy. There's also an enclosed twelve-foot dragon who, for the small price of a quarter, will light up and shake its head. Ah, the inscrutable Chinese …

Coney Island
Brooklyn

Coney Island is not what it used to be (housing projects have taken over from the miles of midways and arcades)—but still, on hot summer weekends, up to a million New Yorkers migrate to the end of the subway lines to wedge themselves onto the crowded beach for a cool dip in the Atlantic. Coney Island still has Nathan's famous hot dogs (the original), the skeleton of a 250-foot parachute jump (from the 1939 World's Fair), several roller coasters (the Cyclone is still thrilling after so many years) and a two-mile boardwalk. But a visit to this once-legendary, now downtrodden amusement park is for hard-core nostalgics only.

Intrepid Sea-Air-Space Museum
Pier 86
Twelfth Avenue at
West 46th Street
245-0072
Wed. to Sun. 10:00 A.M. to
5:00 P.M.
Adults $6, children $3

Though the below-deck museum is the main attraction here, we prefer to just wander on the vast deck of the U.S.S. *Intrepid*—it's more open space than you're likely to find anywhere in Manhattan, and it gives you a feeling of escape from the throngs. The *Intrepid* was one of the key aircraft carriers in the battles against the Japanese in World War II, and its peacetime missions included recovery for NASA's manned space flights. It's an aggressive museum, full of bombs, missiles, the actual fighting planes from WWII, miniature reenactments of big battles and background sound effects that include bombs whistling through the air. The collection of airplanes dates back to the earliest ones, and is one of the best things to see here. There are planes above-board as well, and you can climb up to the various control bridges and command centers, still equipped with radar, radios, gunnery and so on.

The New York Aquarium
Surf Avenue and
West 8th Street
Brooklyn

The New York Aquarium, ensconced in Brooklyn for more than 25 years, houses hundreds of the world's marine animals, both fresh and salt water. The 35 aquariums have fish of every color and size, including some fierce looking sharks. Also of note are three seal

266-8500
Daily 10:00 A.M. to 5:00 P.M.
Adults $2.50, children $1

South Street Seaport
Water St.
(Peck Slip to
John St.)

pools and a whale pool, and the penguins continue to attract crowds of children—young and old.

If you blink your eyes, you might think you're at Quincy Market in Boston or the Wharf in Baltimore. The South Street Seaport is one in a continuing series of urban renovations that cashes in for developers and gives browsers a veritable goldmine of "interesting" shops. This Rouse development is no exception; the restored buildings are charming, housing upscale boutiques and restaurants that attract curious uptowners and tourists in addition to the staple Wall Street clientele that keeps that place busy during lunchtime.

The Seaport's maritime museum is still doing a land-office business. Tours of the exhibition vessels include a visit to the *Peking*, a 1911 square-rigger; the *Ambrose*, a 1907 lightship (floating lighthouse); and the *Lettis Howard*, an 1893 fishing schooner. The *Pioneer*, an 1885 sloop, sails for passengers in the summer months. For information, call 669-9416. (It's open 10:00 A.M. to 8:00 P.M.; tour admission is $3 for adults and $1.25 for children, with gallery tour, $3.50 for adults, $2.50 for children.)

The Seaport is a pleasant place to explore; in the summer, there's nothing better than dining al fresco while watching New York City waltz by. Although it's commercial, it provides an entertaining afternoon that both parents and their children will enjoy.

Staten Island Ferry
Battery Park

Ask many Manhattanites what they love most about New York, and they'll say "leaving it." If you want to experience the true meaning of "room to breathe" after a week of crowded sidewalks and shoulder-to-shoulder restaurants, take a ten-mile, forty-minute roundtrip ride across New York Harbor. For a little more than the price of the *New York Times* you'll get spectacular views of the stalagmite metropolis, the Statue of Liberty and Ellis Island.

Landmarks

Brooklyn Heights Promenade

Brooklyn's answer to Greenwich Village is Brooklyn Heights, an attractive enclave of brownstones and townhouses nestled in a 50-block area on a hill overlooking lower Manhattan. Its wide Promenade above

Just across the Brooklyn Bridge Brooklyn

the East River provides a spectacular view of Wall Street skyscrapers, the Brooklyn Bridge and the Statue of Liberty. At sunset, it can be the most romantic spot in the city. These tree-lined streets around Montague Street have attracted some of America's greatest writers including Walt Whitman, Herman Melville, Thomas Wolfe, W.H. Auden, Carson McCullers, Arthur Miller and Norman Mailer.

Cathedral of Saint John the Divine

Amsterdam Avenue at West 112th Street
678-6888
Daily 7:00 A.M. to 5:00 P.M.

Only an optimist would bet on when the final third of this structure will be completed. But when it is, the 1892-vintage edifice will be the world's second biggest church, inched out only by St. Peter's in Rome. As it is, you could fit Barnum's entire three-ring big top inside its 250-foot nave and still have room for a hundred elephants in the transepts.

Construction of the cathedral was halted after World War II, and only since 1979 has work resumed—on a less ambitious scale. The initial goal of the present planners is to add two imposing 294-foot Gothic towers, which will frame the majestic front facade.

Completing these will be as difficult as it would have been seven centuries ago. By choice, the planners have elected to employ authentic medieval methods and equipment to erect the towers, each of which will need 12,000 finely cut stones. In the cathedral courtyard one can view apprentice stonecutters preparing the smooth blocks from raw stone. Painstakingly, they design, cut and hew the limestone blocks with old tools, including applewood mallets and hundred-year-old chisels. Since 1979 they've been able to carve about a thousand blocks.

A ten-foot scale model of the finished cathedral is on display in the large cathedral shop. In this nonprofit gift shop one can also "donate" stones to the project: ashlars cost $100, capital stones are $5,000 each, and turrets go for $500,000 and up.

The Chrysler Building

405 Lexington Ave. (44th St.)

This celebration of art deco is a must, even if you just look at the inlaid wood elevators. Take a moment to examine the African marble and chrome lobby. The famous sunburst spire has recently received new lights that give a City of Oz look to the Manhattan skyline. The details and craftsmanship are remarkable—sadly signifying remembrances of things past.

Eastern States Buddhist Temple of America

The Buddhist Temple is found in the back room of an adjoining Chinatown souvenir shop. Residents come to kneel before Buddha (who represents compassion and mercy) and to toss joss sticks into urns to pay their respects. Followers of Taoism can also shake Tai Tai (fortune) sticks onto the floor and match the first stick

64 Mott St.
Daily 9:00 A.M. to 6:00 P.M.
Admission free

Ellis Island
**Ferry at Battery Park
and Broadway
269-5755**
*Daily, May to Oct.; call for specific
tour hours*
Adults $2, children $1

The Empire State Building
**Fifth Avenue at
34th Street
736-3100**
*Observation deck: daily 9:30 A.M. to
11:30 P.M.; Guinness Records
Exhibit Hall (947-2335): daily 9:30
A.M. to 5:30 P.M.
Adults $2.75, children $1.25*

fallen with one of the many fortunes printed on slips of paper, which look like bus transfers, on the wall.

You'll know you're in Chinatown by the pagoda-shaped phone booths and the neon dragons. All that's missing now are "Wok—Don't Wok" signs on the street corners.

Considering that Americans spend so much money restoring historical houses of no particular interest, it is a wonder that they have allowed the handsomely turreted Victorian buildings of Ellis Island to crumble like old automobiles along a desert highway; this is a critical part of the American heritage.

It is estimated that 50 percent of the American people have ancestors who passed through Ellis Island on their way to America. The first immigrants were received in 1892, and in the 68 years until its permanent closing in 1954 (immigrants now pass through Kennedy Airport) over 24 million immigrants, mostly from Europe, were processed in the halls and examining rooms of its six acres of buildings. When you step off the tour boat in front of the Great Hall, imagine the scene an immigrant faced 75 years before: the anxious crowds of fellow hopefuls, the endless questions and inspections, the fearful waiting, until, if lucky, he could leave the "Island of Hope" to begin his life in America.

It will take 50 million dollars to restore the disintegrating buildings of Ellis Island to their former state, so their future is in doubt. If Ellis Island has significance in your life—go now. This may be your last chance to visit the "gateway to America."

The Empire State Building will always command wonder. Other buildings may be higher, but this is still the big one, the "Eighth Wonder of the World," the personification of the Big City. At nearly a quarter-of-a-mile-high, for years this was the world's tallest building (now its status has slipped), the symbol of New York of no bounds, the beacon of the city of dreams. Its romance was signed, sealed and delivered in *King Kong* in 1933.

Since 1931, more than 52 million people have seen New York from the 86th- and 102nd-floor viewing platforms.

A ten-foot promenade surrounds the 86th floor, and during the day this is an excellent place to gaze at the splendor below, brushed by the breezes that can sway the building twelve inches in bad weather. We recommend the nighttime view from the 102nd floor—it's 200 feet higher and is reached by the third elevator ride of your visit.

Here, in the small, dark, circular viewing room, which

looks like a combination disco and Flash Gordon set (with twinkling lights on the ceiling, walls of polished silver and mirrors and exposed steel beams and rivets), you can gaze from twenty-odd circular windows at a glittering panorama of the world's greatest city. Go very late, or very early, as the lines for this art deco wonder are longest in midafternoon, especially in summer.

The Guinness World Record people have an attraction in the lobby, popular with youngsters: a blow-up photo, scale model and video exhibit of human achievement and excess. The exhibit contains the world's smallest book and the world's largest Raggedy Ann doll, among other abnormalities.

Grand Central Terminal
42nd Street and Lexington Avenue

Half a million people pass daily through its 300-foot, ten-story lobby, and many take the shortcut through the Pan Am Building. Under the dim but twinkling constellations in the ceiling is the world's largest color slide (it changes monthly), courtesy of Kodak.

Flatiron Building
23rd Street and Fifth Avenue

This wedge-shaped building was constructed in 1902 and named the Fuller Building. It gets its nickname from its triangular shape, designed to fit the block. For years, it was the world's tallest building.

The Fulton Fish Market
South Street (Fulton Street and Peck Slip)
Weekdays 4:00 A.M. to 7:30 A.M.

The intrepid tourist (or New Yorker) may decide to visit this early-morning wholesale fish exchange. We did. And it was worth it. Like Billingsgate Market in London, during the early morning hours, middlemen sell their suppliers' daily catch (97 percent of which is now brought in by truck from all over the country) to fish purveyors (for large restaurants), supermarket chain buyers, fish store merchants and Chinese restaurant owners, while the truckers huddle around blazing oil barrels with their coffee.

The two-block market underneath East River Drive (east of the Financial District), shuttered by day, is electric by night—aglow with stark white lights as sellers shovel and hook fish onto their large scales, calling the price and poundage into dangling microphones. Handtrucks loaded with burlap bags of oysters and clams and ice-enclosed, fish-laden cardboard boxes wheel about to fill the vans that will take the seafood to consumers throughout the New York area.

The fishmongers get their coffee and breakfast at Carmine's Bar and Grill (corner of Front and Beekman), and at 6:00 A.M. the eggs they served tasted just fine to us.

Grant's Tomb

**Riverside Drive at
122nd Street**
666-1640
*Wed. to Sun. 9:00 A.M. to
5:00 P.M.*
Admission free

A visit here answers Groucho Marx's question: "Who's buried in Grant's Tomb?" If your answer is Ulysses S. Grant, the great General of the Union Army during the Civil War and later President—you're wrong! Grant and his wife, Julia Dent, lie side by side, not buried, but *entombed* in two twelve-foot, nine-ton black marble sarcophagi, resting 130 feet beneath a beautiful domed rotunda. The open crypt was fashioned after that of Napoleon at the Hôtel des Invalides in Paris. Two rooms flanking the crypt area relate Grant's life and career through a large photographic display.

The times have taken their toll. With graffiti scrawled all over it, the exterior of the classically designed tomb now looks like a signed high school yearbook. Partly to discourage this, the local community was asked several years back to participate in designing park benches around the building. The result is a somewhat bizarre wavelike, freeform series of molded concrete benches, arches and who knows what, inlaid with thousands of small colored tile chips forming everyday objects and scenes.

We must admit, under close scrutiny it grows on you. Try to find Mickey Mouse, Donald Duck and Abraham Lincoln.

Pierpont Morgan Library

29 E. 36th St.
685-0008
*Tues. to Sat. 10:30 A.M. to 5:00
P.M.; Sun. 1:00 P.M. to 5:00 P.M.*
Suggested admission $2

A sedate and refined literary institution. In the opulent interior of this large Italian Renaissance building, you can see Morgan's private collection of rare books, art and incunabula—including one of the few Gutenberg Bibles in existence.

The New York Public Library

**Fifth Avenue and
42nd Street**
340-0849
*Mon. to Wed. 10:00 A.M. to 9:00
P.M.; Fri. and Sat. to 10:00 P.M.*

This is the second largest library in the United States, after the Library of Congress. The Beaux Arts building is guarded by the famous marble lions, Patience and Fortitude—which is what you'll need to get through the 5½ million books housed inside. Don't miss the vast third-floor reading rooms. The colorful characters who loiter out on the front steps are worth volumes in themselves. Library funding is erratic, and therefore the hours can fluctuate, so call first.

New York Stock Exchange

A sojourn to the Stock Exchange is as much a lesson in the value of instant electronics and human communications as it is a lesson in security transactions. The old tickertape machines that used to click out a

20 Broad St.
623-5167
Mon. to Fri. 10:00 A.M. to
4:00 P.M.
Admission free

never-ending chatter of market quotations, while providing confetti to shower over national heroes, are gone. In their stead, and essential to the modern workings of the exchange, are the new icons of our age—video screens and electronic scoreboards. Three thousand people work on the paper-littered 90- by 90-foot floor of the Stock Exchange. To keep them constantly informed about the up-to-the-minute trading activity, the walls of the exchange are lined with pulsating, bannerlike "electronic tickertape" screens. In addition, each of the sixteen trading booths where stocks are actually bought and sold has more than 60 monitors. Every sale is immediately recorded and transmitted via satellite to similar screens across the planet. If you've ever bought or sold stocks, you shouldn't miss seeing the human drama that goes into your transaction. If you're a neophyte, why not take in the five-minute description by a stock expert at the third-floor visitors' center before you enter the viewing area? All the hieroglyphics, symbols, codes and Wall Street "tribal behavior" will be deciphered for you.

Riverside Church
Riverside Drive and
122nd Street
222-5900
Mon. to Sat. 11:00 A.M. to 3:00
P.M.; Sun. 12:30 P.M. to 4:00 P.M.
Admission 25¢

Imagine gazing out over New York City from 400 feet up while being buffeted by the sound of 74 pealing bells. In the tower of Riverside Church you will find yourself with bells above you, bells below you, bells all around. The Riverside Church Carillon, the world's largest bell (and heaviest, with a total weight of 100 tons), is located within the Gothic tower of Riverside Church, a twenty-story elevator ride and 100 twisting steps above Riverside Drive.

Some of the bells ring hourly during the week, but we suggest you go on a weekend, when you'll be able to watch the bells being played through the windows of a small cabin centered among the labyrinthine crosswalks. Three times daily you can see the Carillon clavier (keyboard) being played by expert carillonneurs, who deftly press the 74 wooden levers (attached to the bells by wires) with their hands and feet (the six largest bells chime with the assistance of powerful motors).

Climbing a few steps further up the tower will bring you to a small, 360-degree balcony, 392 feet above Morningside Heights. Although you must peer through iron gratings and concrete buttresses, you'll get a breath-taking view.

Rockefeller Center
48th–52nd streets

Rockefeller Center is rightly praised as a model of urban planning and design. Over 250,000 people pass through its art deco buildings every day and many shop and eat in the 24 acres of underground shops that lie beneath this

**between Fifth and
Sixth avenues
489-2947**

*Observation deck Oct. to Mar.: 10:00
A.M. to 7:00 P.M.; summer: 10:00
A.M. to 9:00 P.M.
Adults $3, children $1.50
Center Tour Mon. to Sat. 10:00
A.M. to 4:45 P.M., every 45 min.
Adults $4, children $2.50*

mini-city, John D. Rockefeller, Jr., who leased the land from Columbia University in 1928 (the lease is up in 2069), had hoped it would turn out to be an international trade center; thus the Promenade, just off Fifth Avenue, is called Channel Gardens, located between the British Empire Building and La Maison Française.

Below the Promenade, framed by flags of 50 states and presided over by the eighteen-foot bronze and gold-leaf statue of Prometheus (1934), is a space where one can skate in winter or, in summer, dine serenely under the stars.

There's an open observation platform on top of the 70-story RCA building, which gives splendid and unobstructed views north to Central Park and south to the Empire State Building. You can go up alone, or as part of the Rockefeller Center Tour, which includes a quick trip through Radio City Music Hall and ends on a private garden twenty floors above Fifth Avenue with an eagle's-eye view of St. Patrick's Cathedral.

If you've always wanted to see live TV—here's your chance. NBC, also located inside the RCA building, often tapes shows in front of studio audiences. You can write ahead for tickets to NBC, 30 Rockefeller Center, N.Y., N.Y., 10020 for the "David Letterman Show" or "Saturday Night Live." Or ask at the NBC desk near the Sixth Avenue entrance to the lobby if there are any standby tickets available for shows that day (best to get there early—around 9:00 A.M.—or call 664-3055).

Also glittering at 50th is Radio City Music Hall (1932), the world's largest theater, with the world's largest chandelier and organ. It seats 6,000 and features the world-renowned Rockettes, a chorus line of 36 lithe, long-legged dancers who perform live musical spectaculars seasonally on the 144-foot stage. Backstage tours of the complex are run daily from 10:00 A.M. to 4:45 P.M. (246-4600).

Down the street, in the lower plaza of the McGraw-Hill Building (Sixth and 48th), one can find the "New York Experience" (shows Mon. to Thurs. 11:00 A.M. to 8:00 P.M., Fri. and Sat. to 9:00 P.M., Sun. noon to 9:00 P.M.; adults $4.25, children $2.50; 869-0345) a multimedia slide and sound show that will explain New York's history, peoples and culture to you in 60 minutes. It might even prepare you for the chaotic, polyphonic, New York "experience" on the street outside.

The Statue of Liberty

For almost a century the Statue of Liberty, arm outstretched, torch held high, has been a symbol of freedom and opportunity. What began as an extravagant

The American Museum of Immigration
Liberty Island,
New York Harbor
269-5755 (ferry)
732-1236 (museum)
Daily 9:00 A.M. to 4:00 P.M.
Year-round tours every hour on the hour (summer every ½ hour)
Adults $2, children $1

gift from France to the fledgling American people has become a romantic symbol for emancipation and hope. Millions of physically fit (we assume, as the climb to the crown is 168 steps and twelve stories up a narrow staircase) people see New York through the bronze lady's eyes. The vast pedestal houses The American Museum of Immigration, a fascinating place full of authentic photographs, costumes and personal artifacts. Nine slide shows weave the museum's history into a patriotic narration. We particularly love the boat ride; if you're short on time (a visit requires 1½ hours but the round-trip ride is only 45 minutes) just enjoy the fresh air, the view of the harbor and a new perspective on New York.

Trinity Church
Broadway at Wall Street
285-0872
Mon. to Fri. 7:00 A.M. to 6:00 P.M.; Sat. and Sun. 8:00 A.M. to 4:00 P.M.

Historic Trinity Church may be dwarfed by its skyscraper neighbors in the Financial District, but it has an imposing presence nonetheless and is a must for anyone even mildly interested in early America. The Gothic Revival building is actually the third Trinity Church to stand on this spot: the first, built in 1696, was destroyed by fire; the second, built in 1777, was torn down for structural weaknesses. The current building, designed by Richard Upjohn, went up in 1846 and is part of the Episcopal Church's extensive property holdings in New York.

For an excellent history lesson or a moment of tranquility amid the madness of Wall Street, wander through Trinity's colonial cemetery, founded in 1681 (predating the first church). Some of early America's greats and near-greats (Alexander Hamilton, Robert Fulton, William Bradford) are buried here.

World Trade Center
Two World Trade Center
107th floor
466-7397
Daily 9:30 A.M. to 9:30 P.M., wind and weather permitting
Adults $2.95, children $1.60
Reservations suggested

First there was the French acrobat Philippe Petit, walking a tightrope between the towers in 1974. Then there was George Willig, who scaled the South Tower in 1977 like the "human fly" he claimed to be. Then came the parachutists and hang-gliders who jumped onto and off of the decks. What next? What makes people want to risk their lives to get to the top of a tower they can reach in a scant 58-second elevator ride, just as 80,000 people do every day? Presumably it's the quarter-mile-high stage.

The views in all directions from either the 110th-floor open-air viewing platform—the world's highest—or from the enclosed high-tech viewing promenade on the 107th are spectacular.

Parks · Gardens

Bronx Park Botanical Garden

Kazamiroff Boulevard and 200th Street The Bronx 220-8700

Daily dawn to dusk; 10:00 A.M. to 4:00 P.M. for conservatory Admission free; conservatory $2.50 adults, 75¢ children

After a lengthy period in New York's asphalt jungle, we recommend a visit to the real thing. The world-famous Botanical Garden consists of 250 acres of trees and flowers from all over the world. Don't miss the orchids and exotica in the Enid A. Haupt Conservatory (closed Mondays), a national landmark. You can wander through two deserts, two jungles and a one-acre rose garden—or lose yourself in the 40-acre Hemlock Forest, through which the Bronx River meanders. Also take a look at the fern forest, palm court and rock garden, featuring plants from the world's temperate zones.

Brooklyn Botanic Garden

Eastern Parkway Brooklyn 622-4433

Tues. to Fri. 8:00 A.M. to 4:30 P.M.; Sat. and Sun. 10:00 A.M. to 6:00 P.M. Admission free

Just east of Prospect Park, the Botanic Garden is a serene, tranquil breath of fresh air. In April and May the flowers and lanes of cherry trees are magnificent. The rose garden flourishes in June, and you'll find pathways and small gardens filled with botanical jewels. The greenhouse, an exercise in elegant Victorian design (admission 25¢), overlooks a series of lotus pools. There are also such unusual features as a Japanese Garden (closed in the winter) with authentic Shinto gardens (weekends 11:00 A.M. to 1:00 P.M. and 2:00 P.M. to 4:00 P.M., admission 25¢), America's largest bonsai tree collection and a fragrant garden designed specifically for blind people, complete with Braille markers.

Central Park

59th Street to 110th Street, between Fifth Avenue and Central Park West 360-8179

Central Park is as manmade as the Empire State Building. Twenty years of loving planning and effort went into creating this natural masterpiece: sculpting the myriad lakes, planting the more than 100,000 trees, and shaping the countless sinewy paths that weave their way through this bucolic "countryside." Frederick Law Olmstead and Calvert Vaux, the *wunderkinder* of urban landscape design, planned the park in 1856. The pedestrian paths, bridle paths and sunken roadways, constantly curving to afford the visitor with new vistas at every turn, are woven into a natural tapestry so that when they cross—they don't cross. One path weaves through a tunnel, while the other arches over one of the 46 bridges (no two alike). This harmonious and seemingly effortless web is so smoothly constructed that none of the roller skaters, horseback riders, bikers or carriage riders ever has to wait at an intersection, since there are none. And we know how much New Yorkers like that!

The park is a 2½-mile, 26-ring circus, so we'll describe some of our favorite rings.

The new Wollman Ice Skating Rink reopened in winter '84; it was where Ryan O'Neal grieved for Ali MacGraw at the conclusion of *Love Story*. A little further north you'll be greeted by the 100-year-old wooden dairy, built in the Gothic Revival mode. Once a working dairy in the 1800s, it now serves as the Park Information Center (free maps, slide shows and Ranger tours—call 397-3156 for information). Nearby is a rare treat—the Victorian Carousel. Even the most sophisticated parkgoer won't be able to resist a ride on this magical antique merry-go-round (year round; 10:30 A.M.–6:00 P.M.; weekends only in winter; 879-0244 for information).

Just above the 72nd Street Fifth Avenue entrance is the elliptical Conservatory Pond. Children love to climb on the tree-sized Alice in Wonderland statue and chat with the Mad Hatter while sitting on giant toadstools. Children can enjoy the story-telling during warm months on Wednesday and Saturday at the statue of Hans Christian Andersen. With "The Ugly Duckling" toddling in front, it looks wistfully out over the pond, which is festooned on Saturday mornings in the summer with motorized regattas of remote-controlled model sailboats piloted from onshore by the citified skippers of the Model Yacht Club (Saturdays except in winter 10:00 A.M. to 4:00 P.M.; for race schedules call 397-3156).

If you amble over the hill west of here you will arrive at the bridge-spanned Central Park Lake. At the Loeb Boathouse (74th Street) along the shore you can row or paddle with the ducks, ride a bike around the lake or, if you're tired of exercise, have a hamburger at the waterside snackbar. (Boat rentals: $4 an hour with $20 refundable deposit; daily 9:00 A.M. to 6:00 P.M.; call 288-7281 for information).

Refurbished Bethesda Fountain looms on the south side of the lake. The fountain is located at the end of the elongated Central Park Mall, the Park's grand promenade, which serves as a showcase for dozens of aspiring street musicians. During the summer you may be treated to a free concert from the large bandshell at the terminus of the mall.

If you wander north of the lake through the hilly region known as the Ramble, you will notice that most of the couples feature a decided unisex look. If that look isn't to your taste, you might want to avoid this densely wooded area.

If you enter the park from the east 80s, take your picnic basket behind the Metropolitan Museum of Art to the Great Lawn. Here, on summer evenings, you can drink your wine and eat your baguette while listening to free al fresco concerts given by the New York Philharmonic and the Metropolitan Opera, surrounded by thousands of festive New Yorkers. If your taste runs to rock and roll, don't despair. In the hot summer of 1981 Simon and Garfunkel staged a reunion before 600,000 children of the '60s. Elton John, the Beach Boys, Diana Ross and other major performers have all passed through here.

Below the lawn is the modern hemispherical Delacorte Theater, home of the free Shakespeare-in-the-Park play series in summer (play info: 861-7277). Behind the theater, perched formidably on the hill arising above the small lake, stands Belvedere Castle (1869), hewn out of stone. It is the former home of the city's weather station, and it has become an environmental education center.

The upper hinterlands of the park boast Manhattan's water supply. The handsome Reservoir occupies much parkland for ten blocks in the 90s. Streaming around its 1½-mile circumference is a parade of sweatsuits; this is a mecca for uptown joggers.

If rowing, running or roller skating sound exhausting, let a dusky Appaloosa do the work for you. If you're an experienced rider and sign a release, you can rent a horse (with an English saddle) from the Claremont Riding Academy, located a block from the park on West 89th Street, and ride off into the sunset down the 4½ miles of bridle paths (Claremont: 175 West 89th Street; $18 an hour; open daily from 6:30 A.M.; reservations: 724-5100). Central Park also has tennis, croquet and lawn bowling facilities for permit holders, checkers and chess tables, a bird sanctuary, impromptu folk dancing and a children's marionette theater.

Except for summer nights when you're surrounded by the concert crowds, remember that when the sun goes down in Central Park, the things that go bump in the night come out of their lairs. Unless you relish free-fire zones, enjoy the park at night only from a comfortable window seat at one of the many bars and restaurants that surround it.

Gramercy Park

Lexington Avenue (20th–21st Streets)
Mon. to Sat. 9:00 A.M. to 4:30 P.M.

A lovely private square in the London fashion that will warm any Anglophile's heart. It is surrounded by some of the most elegant brownstones in the city. Theodore Roosevelt spent his first fifteen years at 28 East 20th Street, two blocks west of the park. You can feel his boisterous presence among the extensive memorabilia displayed in this restored Victorian townhouse.

Prospect Park
Grand Army Plaza

Central Park may be twice as large, but Prospect Park, in the center of Brooklyn, is considered by many (including its landscaper—who also created Central Park) to be the more aesthetically perfect. A large triumphal arch (honoring Civil War soldiers and sailors) stands at the entrance. Within its shaded interior lies a beautiful lake and boathouse, several eighteenth-century homesteads, a few aging but lovely pavilions and a small (rather pathetic) zoo. The park is filled in spring and summer with families, amateur ballplayers, dogs, frisbees, kites, joggers, bicyclists, roller skaters and strollers. A few local residents even tempt the fates by fishing in the lake.

Washington Square Park
Base of Fifth Avenue

This is the geographic center of the Village. Around the park's central water fountain you'll see street musicians, ventriloquists, comedians, crack frisbee throwers, skateboarding youngsters, magicians, jumproping unicyclists and disco roller skaters. The Village elders sit on the benches kibbitzing or playing speed chess in the corners. The Washington Square Arch (1892) is Stanford White's copy of a wooden arch he made three years earlier to commemorate the centennial of George Washington's inauguration.

The Tours

BY AIR

Island Heliocopter
Heliport at 34th Street and East River
895-5372
Daily 9:00 A.M. to 5:00 P.M.
$18–$100 (two-person min.)

Enjoy Superman's view of Metropolis and look the Statue of Liberty straight in the eye from a mere 75 yards distance. Five flights range in length from six to 40 minutes. We recommend the flight over Wall Street to the Statue of Liberty ($28) or the same route plus a trip up to Central Park ($40).

Pelham Airways
Seaplane Deck at 23rd Street and the East River
828-0420
April to October
$35 per 25-minute flight

A seaplane whisks you aloft from the East River for an aerial circumnavigation of Manhattan.

BY BOAT

Circle Line
**Pier 83 and West
43rd Street
(at the Hudson)
563-3200**
*Late Mar. to early Nov.: departs from
9:45 A.M. to 5:30 P.M.
Adults $10, children $5*

It's a closely guarded fact that no New Yorker has ever taken the Circle Line boat cruise around Manhattan, although it's the first thing they tell guests to do when they visit. What New Yorker has three hours to kill seeing the other sides of buildings they see every day? Let the natives fight the crowds on the streets. Experience the trip. When you return from your 35-mile, three-hour voyage, you will have a better idea of the scale of their city than do most New Yorkers. Over the loudspeakers, a guide will announce the major points of interest and fill you in on fascinating New York gossip.

And think about this as you recline gracefully in your chair sipping your private stock Campari: Diana Nyad, a young endurance swimmer, swam the same route you follow in seven hours, 57 minutes in 1975. That's one way to get around Manhattan!

Hudson River Day Line
**West 41st Street and
the Hudson River
Pier 81
279-5151**
*June to Sept.: Tues. to Sun.
Adults $10 weekdays, $12 weekends,
children half price*

A 3,000-passenger boat cruises 50 miles up the Hudson. You can picnic and swim at Bear Mountain State Park or continue on north for a three-hour visit to the military academy at West Point. The sightseeing tour of the U.S.M.A. costs an additional $2.50 for adults, $1.25 for children. This is a peaceful trip, if you don't mind being surrounded by colorful, chattering tourists.

The Petrel
**Battery Park
825-1976**
*April to Oct.: times vary
Lunch sails $6.50, others $10–$20*

Enjoy a sail (in good weather) on this 70-foot yawl, which holds 35 passengers. Lunch sails, happy hour trips and moonlit cruises with cocktails are available. This can be a mini-vacation from your vacation.

The Pioneer
**South Street Seaport
669-9400**
*May to Oct.: Mon. to Fri. 2:00 P.M.
and 6:00 P.M.; Sat. and Sun. 10:00
A.M., 2:00 P.M. and 6:00 P.M.
$15 for two*

The 102-foot schooner, the *Pioneer*, cruises New York Harbor for three-hour trips, giving passengers their chance for a floating picnic. If you want to charter the ship for three hours, just come up with $700 ($500 for two hours).

BY BUS

One of the best ways to see the sights is to roll through the city in a comfortable, up-to-date coach, complete with foreign-language services and a chatty tour guide who gives passengers an insider's view of New York. The companies listed below offer variations on the same theme: tours of lower Manhattan, uptown, all over town and a deluxe option with boat tours, the Empire State Building and other landmarks. Prices vary, so consult each individual carrier.

Campus Coach, 545 Fifth Avenue (45th Street), 682-1050.

Crossroads Sightseeing, 701 Seventh Avenue (47th Street), 581-2828.

Gray Line Sightseeing, 900 Eighth Avenue (54th Street), 397-2600.

Manhattan Sightseeing Tours, 150 West 49th Street, 869-5005.

New York Big Apple Tours, 162 West 56th Street, 582-6430.

Short Line Tours, 166 West 46th Street, 354-5122.

SPECIALTIES

Backstage on Broadway
228 W. 47th St.
575-8065
Times vary
Adults $5

Want to hear the roar of the greasepaint? A Broadway veteran will take you backstage at a major Broadway production and explain what goes on behind the scenes before the curtain goes up. Early reservations are required.

Doorway to Design
79 W. 12th St.
339-1542, 376-6161
By appt. only
$15 to $20 for a half-day program

A professional interior decorator takes you through exclusive interior design galleries, showrooms, antique dealers, artist studios and private homes. Similar services are offered for fashion fans with visits to trend-setting designers off Seventh Avenue to see where design inspiration starts.

Federal Reserve Bank
33 Liberty St.
791-6130
Mon. to Fri. 10:00 A.M., 11:00 A.M., 1:00 P.M., 2:00 P.M.
Free admission, reservations required

Reserve a week in advance if you want to set eyes on the $190 billion in the Fed's gold vault. The one-hour tour also includes the security department and cash counting. This is where the bills marked "B" come from. No free samples.

Harlem Spirituals, Inc.
95–02 65th Rd.
Rego Park
275-1408
Sun. 9:00 A.M. to 1:00 P.M.
Tours leave from Short Line tour office: 166 W. 46th St.

Friday and Saturday nights from 7:30 P.M. to midnight relive the Harlem jazz scene of the '20s, after enjoying a traditional hearty Southern soul food dinner. On Sundays from 9:00 A.M. to 1:00 P.M., friendly, multilingual guides share their love of Harlem today, with all its warts and finery, ending with gospel singing in a Baptist church. It's a tour rich in historical insights and present-day surprises.

Holidays in New York
152 W. 58th St.
765-2515
Times vary
$20–$25 per hour plus expenses

Exclusive tours of the most celebrated fashion houses, Jewish landmarks and private artist and dance studios are Holiday's specialty. Multilingual private guides will escort you via limousine or taxi.

Inside New York
203 E. 72nd St.
861-0709
Times vary

Chat with the famous designers and furriers in their studios, and cruise the Fashion Capital in private tours of Seventh Avenue, SoHo and the Lower East Side. Tour leaders are multilingual.

New York Times
229 W. 43rd St.
556-1310
Sept. to June: Fri. 12:15 P.M.
Free

Meet at the ninth floor auditorium for a tour of New York's status newspaper. It's an eye-opener.

Penny Sightseeing Company
303 W. 42nd St.
246-4220
Mar. to Nov.: Mon. and Thurs.
10:00 A.M.; Sat. 11:00 A.M.
$10 to $15

There are many interesting pockets of architecture and culture in Harlem, and if you want to see them, the best and most informative way is to take the three-hour bus tour given by the Penny Sightseeing Company. Specialists in black history, they'll point out sights associated with famous Harlemites, including Marcus Garvey, Malcolm X, Langston Hughes, Ralph Ellison and James Baldwin. You'll also see the Schomburg Center, with exhibits from its large archive of black culture; the Abyssinian Baptist Church, where the charismatic Adam Clayton Powell, Jr., once preached gospel; the 1765 Morris-Jumel mansion—a Federal-style home used by George Washington during the Revolution; and Striver's Row, Harlem's most fashionable block, containing handsome 1800s brownstones.

Schapiro's Winery
126 Rivington
(Essex St.)
674-4404
Sundays 11:00 A.M. to 4:00 P.M.
Admission free

Within the vast Essex Street Market is this enclosed village of small food and vegetable booths reminiscent of a European Sunday market. Drop by Schapiro's for a free kosher wine-making tour and tasting of the "Wine You Can Almost Cut With a Knife."

Singer's Brooklyn Tours
130 St. Edwards St.
Brooklyn
875-9084
By appt. only
$20

Call "Mr. Brooklyn," 58-year-old Lou Singer, to find out which of the many novel personalized adventures he's arranging this week: "Historic and Architectural Brooklyn," "Fantastic Flatbush," "Tiffany Fine Arts," "Ethnic Noshing" and many others. Custom tours by car or minibus.

The United Nations

First Avenue and 42nd–48th sts.
754-4440
(Foreign language tours, 754-7539)
Guided tours every 15 min. daily 9:00 A.M. to 4:45 P.M.
Adults $3, children $1.25

It is fitting that the attempt to create a world government is situated in Manhattan, chief borough in an immigrant city. Actually, we should say *on* Manhattan, as the U.N. complex (1947–1953) lies in international territory, and the postmark from the U.N. post office downstairs proves it. A visit, in effect, involves "leaving the country."

Le Corbusier, Oscar Niemeyer and Wallace Harrison (the Met) among others had a hand in selecting the designs for the familiar riverside buildings. Don't expect much from the tour that parades one million people a year through this symbol of world peace. Most of the time is spent seeing monumental gifts from member nations and walking from building to building. Escalator and air conditioning noises drown out half of the narration. Unless a council is in session, you'll see a lot of empty rooms with colored chairs. The most appropriate thing we saw was the huge neon Pepsi sign through the back window of the Security Council chamber—it has truly become an international symbol of world economic ties. Free tickets for the General Assembly (meets mid-September through December) or any other Council's meetings are available on a first-come, first-served basis half an hour before the meeting that day from the main information desk. Sessions are usually held at 10:30 A.M. and 3:30 P.M. To find out in advance what meetings will be held, look on page two or three of the *New York Times,* or call 754-1234 between 9:30 and 5:00. Earphones allow anyone to follow the debates in English, French, Spanish, Chinese or Russian—the official languages of the U.N.

The Delegates' Dining Room, overlooking the East River, is open to the public for lunch Monday to Friday 11:30 A.M. to noon and 2:00 to 2:30 P.M.—again on a first-come, first-served (literally!) basis. The delegates eat between sessions, but if they come early or late, eavesdropping can be interesting.

Souvenirs are available in the basement, tax free. And in the Assembly lobby, don't miss the Chagall Windows, the Apollo 14 moon rock, the model of Sputnik 1 or the overhead pendulum that shows that no matter what nations may do to one another, the world keeps on turning.

WALKING

Art Tours of Manhattan

A privileged way to discover new art—Ph.D.s provide lectures and tours through private art studios,

63 E. 82nd St.
772-3888
Morning or afternoon
$20 to $45

galleries, museums and major art districts. For the collector or the curious.

Friends of Cast-Iron Architecture
235 E. 87th St.
369-6004
Sun. afternoons in spring and fall
$3

Savants and cast-iron devotees lead you through the world's largest concentration of cast-iron buildings—the factories and lofts of SoHo, TriBeCa and Lower Broadway.

Greenwich Village Walking Tours
226-1426
April to Oct: daily 11:00 A.M. and 2:00 P.M.
$5

Twice a day you can make a two-hour exploration through this district, so important in the intellectual, artistic and plain eccentric history of the United States. Phone reservations necessary.

Municipal Art Society
457 Madison Ave.
935-3960
May to Oct.: Sat. and Sun. 2:00 P.M. to 5:00 P.M.
$8

This 90-year-old civic group offers a different tour each month of New York's most fascinating neighborhoods. Trained guides share their love for and expertise on architecture, history and city planning. Every Wednesday at 12:30 P.M., they offer free one-hour tours of Grand Central Station.

Museum of the City of New York
Fifth Avenue and 103rd Street
534-1672
April to Oct.: Sun.
$5

The historic, ethnic and sociological history of the different neighborhoods of New York—a new one each week—is yours with a tour led by the Museum's urban experts.

Pathfinder Walking Tour Tapes
757-1460

If you have 90 minutes to walk your way down Fifth Avenue, Wall Street, Greenwich Village, Chinatown and SoHo, and uptown Fifth Avenue, plug yourself into a Walkman and order a Pathfinder cassette for any of these five tours. The conversational narrations will educate you about New York history in an entertaining way. Order your tapes ($9.95 each plus $1 handling) from Pathfinder Productions, Box 2050, Grand Central Station, N.Y., N.Y. 10163.

THE ENVIRONS

The Environs

ESCAPE HATCH

Though New Yorkers thrive on the energy and controlled chaos that make Manhattan such an exciting city, the only way they can survive living there is by escaping to the country—as often as possible. With that in mind, we have explored the inns and restaurants in Connecticut, Long Island, New Jersey and Upstate New York, and all in all we were quite pleased with what we found. It would take an entire book to properly explore these pastoral areas, so we can only present you with a modest selection of addresses. But in the pages that follow you should have no difficulty finding several places that will made your weekend getaways memorable.

Connecticut

RESTAURANTS

11/20
Apricots
1593 Farmington Ave. (Route 4) Farmington (203)673-5405
Lunch and dinner Mon. to Sat. 11:30 A.M. to 10:00 P.M.; dinner Sun. 4:00 P.M. to 9:00 P.M. All major credit cards

American

The sons and daughters of the old-moneyed Eastern elite go to such schools as Ethel Walker's and Miss Porter's (for young ladies) and Avon Old Farms and Loomis (for young gentlemen), all of which are within easy reach of Farmington. Parents of these students (particularly those with poor grades) are constantly coming and going for consultations with the masters and mistresses, and they must have a place to eat. For many of them (and for executives from the insurance companies that dominate nearby Hartford), Apricots is the place. Here in a converted tram station they find a pub to their liking and dining areas with brick walls and enough standard bric-a-brac to give some feeling of colonial New England. When the weather is pleasant, they can linger over their drinks on a terrace overlooking the bucolic Farmington River.

Ann and Joe Howard, who somehow bring some order to the crowds on weekends, also manage to see that the food from the kitchen is just good enough to keep the crowds coming. But with 200 or more reservations, how could they do more? Some of the dishes—the straightforward ones based on earthy French recipes (escargots in garlic butter with a hint of Pernod, rack of lamb)—are exceptional, but others, particularly those that lend themselves to quantity food preparation (a mushroom and vegetable soup, for example), have no character at all. Yet ingredients are notably fresh, and the service cannot be faulted. So if you choose what must be cooked to order and avoid some of the strange concoctions (veal with sherry, lobster in a béarnaise sauce), you could enjoy a quite acceptable meal. But be sure to avoid the apricot mousse even during the fresh fruit season—great quantities are stored away far too long, and, in any event, whether the fruit is fresh or not makes very little taste difference. Count on at least $35 for three courses à la carte. You'll have a better chance of coming up with several good dishes if you opt for the five-course prix fixe meal at $28.50.

9/20
Le Chambord
1572 Post Road East
Westport
(203)255-2654
Lunch Tues. to Fri. noon to 2:00 P.M.; dinner Tues. to Fri. 6:00 P.M. to 9:30 P.M., Sat. seatings 6:00 P.M. and 9:00 P.M.
All major credit cards
French (classical)

A plaque on Le Chambord's wall announces that the readers of a local magazine chose this as the best French restaurant in Connecticut. But we believe Le Chambord might qualify as the worst French restaurant in the state and really wonder what its customers—who jam the place nightly—see in this throwback to Franco-American dining rooms of 25 years ago, except that a full, three-course meal (including a soufflé au Grand Marnier!) runs only about $18 to $22, without wine. And what do you get for that bargain rate? Prepackaged, precooked and post-heated food of a very low standard. Moules rémoulade has the texture of chicken livers, onion soup the flavor of a salt cellar, grilled swordfish with béarnaise no taste at all (it's overcooked). A nicely cooked pheasant is doused with a sauce that might have come straight from a can. Those soufflés seem to have been held up with scrambled eggs, and the crème anglaise is bitter. Even coffee comes lukewarm. We do like the chocolate roulade, however. The wine list is quite good and very reasonably priced, though a few bottles, such as a Clos Vougeot '73, are ready for retirement.

12/20
La Grange at The Homestead Inn

If we were given a million dollars to renovate a grand 1799 estate, we can't imagine doing anything differently from what these two energetic Connecticut women, Nancy Smith and Lessie Davison, did with that same amount to the Augustus Mead farm in one of the

**420 Field Point Rd.
Greenwich
(203)869-7500**
*Lunch Mon. to Fri. noon to 2:00
P.M.; dinner Sun. to Thurs. 6:00
P.M. to 8:30 P.M., Fri. and Sat.
6:00 P.M. to 9:30 P.M.
All major credit cards*
French (classical)

loveliest sections of Greenwich. The colonial motif is carried through from the front door to the dining rooms and up the stairs to the exquisite bedrooms. There is a delightful glassed-in, year-round veranda that overlooks the lawn; in winter a huge stone fireplace roars. If you wish to find the kind of old American home you see in those 1930s Katharine Hepburn movies, this is the place for you. We might also have hired chef Jacques Thiebeult, but we would have given him less to do, for the kitchen seems harried by the restaurant's success, and a little more time spent on some dishes would make a great difference. The menu is seasonal and stocked with game when appropriate; there are chilled fruit soups in summer. We have been delighted with crab Belle Haven (the section of town in which the inn sits) and with an enticing mixture of tiny green beans, foie gras, avocado and tarragon-tinged vinaigrette dressing. The billi-bi is very good and quite light, as are snails in cream. But the fish need better seasoning; poached salmon with hollandaise is dull, as is the same fish in pastry. Sweetbreads, usually served here with wild mushrooms, are a house specialty, and they are indeed the chef's forte. The veal with chestnuts is just as fine, but duck with Marsala is overcooked and dry. Watch out for surcharges on salads; at a recent meal the captain neglected to mention that the endive was $5.50 extra. Desserts are nothing more than fair, often dried out or tasting of refrigeration. The wine list is exceptionally good, but we'd like to see a few more reasonably priced vintages among the overpriced ones that dominate the list. Dinner at La Grange will cost one about $35 before wine, tax and tip.

16

Guy Savoy
**61 Lewis St.
Greenwich
(203)622-8450**
*Lunch Tues. to Fri. noon to 2:00
P.M.; dinner Mon. to Fri. 7:00 P.M.
to 9:00 P.M., Sat. seatings 6:30
P.M. and 9:15 P.M.
All major credit cards*
French (nouvelle)

Readers of our French guide know how highly we regard Guy Savoy in Paris—we have awarded his restaurant three toques and eighteen out of twenty points. So we were happily surprised to find that M. Savoy had opened another restaurant on this side of the Atlantic—not in the crush of Manhattan's streets, but on a sliver of a road in downtown Greenwich. The restaurant itself is something of a sliver, but in its design it resembles its counterpart in Paris: white walls, stuffed chairs, large plates with flowered borders, good lighting. The staff is efficient and knowledgeable, and the chef—well, except for the last Friday and Saturday nights of each month, the chef is *not* Savoy, but rather his very capable sous-chef, Yves Gonnachon. Savoy flies in each month to serve a special eight-course meal twice a night for $70. For Gonnachon's equally impressive six-course meal, the price is $45. We would eagerly dine here any night of the week, for the food is superb and light, expressing the best of what we feel about nouvelle.

Begin with écrevisse en gelée seasoned with fennel and zucchini or one of Savoy's wonderful vegetable soups with lobster. We also recommend the barely poached salmon is a perfect beurre blanc, the lovely presentation of small veal kidneys dressed with potatoes Maxim and the pink morsels of roasted pigeon or roulade d'agneau crowned with colorful vegetables julienne. For dessert there's the excellent sphinx cake, a delicate blend of chocolate and meringue, and kiwi and blood orange sorbets, which are always delicious, tart and full of flavor. The wine list is young and quite expensive for '76 Bordeaux and similar vintages. Expect to pay $100 for dinner for two, without wine; the $20 lunch menu is a remarkable bargain.

11/20
Stonehenge
Route 7
Ridgefield
(203)438-6511
Lunch Mon. and Wed. to Fri. noon to 2:00 P.M.; dinner Mon. and Wed. to Fri. 6:00 P.M. to 9:00 P.M., Sat. seatings 6:00 P.M. and 9:00 P.M.; brunch and dinner Sun. noon to 8:00 P.M.
All major credit cards
French (classical)

On ten acres of farmland (with a large, pretty duck pond) sits Stonehenge, named after England's Druid monument but amiably set in an 1832 New England house that also has many rooms to rent. Since the late 1940s it has also housed a restaurant, first owned by a flamboyant local fellow catering to theatrical types, then by legendary chef Albert Stockli and Leon Lianides, still owner of Manhattan's Coach House. Today an Englishman named Douglas Seville runs the show, keeping the place tidy both in and out of the kitchen, which is manned by Jean-Maurice Calmels. The main dining room is filled with Chippendale charm: dark woods, breakfronts and heavy draperies. The piano bar is more intimate, and while an outer greenhouse-style room seems wholly incongruous here, it's just as convivial.

Calmels's cuisine is of a fairly standard and consistent quality—good quiche, decent smoked sausage with a less than decent moutarde and superb truite au meunière, sprung from a tank right in the kitchen. The mushroom crêpe is also dependable. But stay clear of Calmels's flourishes, such as pork slices with a dreadful sweet ginger sauce. The desserts are better than average; the wine list is strong in Bordeaux, but the American bottles are the better buy. Plan to spend about $28 to $30 per person, without wine, and don't fail to take a stroll around the duck pond.

10/20
Tapestries
554 Old Post Rd., no. 3
Greenwich
(203)629-9204

Lunch Mon. to Fri. noon to 2:00 P.M.; dinner Mon. to Thurs. 6:00 P.M. to 9:00 P.M., Fri. and Sat. 6:00 P.M. to 10:00 P.M.
All major credit cards
Continental

Tapestries' decor promises so much; the kitchen delivers so little where it counts. There's no debating the pretty and stylish interiors that are housed in an old stone building just off the main street of Greenwich. The soft spotlights on vases of flowers, the aubergine-colored walls and the smart-looking bar area all coalesce with a deliberate taste that attracts younger members of Connecticut society, who seem to believe the food is as stylish as the rest of the place. But, alas, the chef is yet another of those young Culinary Institute of America graduates who believes nouvelle cuisine gives carte blanche to a cook to try anything as long as it's out of the ordinary. Thus, one gets Brie melted in stiff pastry and served with mustard and cornichons, or Szechwan chicken no Chinese would ever recognize or an oddity called "strawberry Melba." Still, you can get a good filet mignon or pasta of the day. Prices seem way out of line for this kind of food: about $30 per person, without wine.

HOTELS

•••
The Homestead Inn
420 Field Point Rd.
Greenwich
(203)869-7500
All major credit cards

If we had to find just one place to stay for a country weekend and did not wish to spend most of that weekend on the highway, we would immediately book ourselves into one of the gorgeous rooms at The Homestead Inn, a restored 1799 mansion in the Belle Haven (well named) section of Greenwich. Not too long ago, the place was a shambles, with peeling wallpaper and bad furniture. But two local women poured money into it, hiring one of New York's top designers to shore up and make livable what had been sagging and unbearable for years. The result: a striking balance of country antiques, hemstitched bedspreads, stone fireplaces, planked floors and impeccably chosen fabrics in the thirteen rooms and suites. William Inge wrote *Picnic* at this inn when it was not quite as comfortable as it is today—but we can't imagine anyone working here now, simply because this is a place for pure relaxation. The food in the restaurant downstairs is also commendable, especially the game dishes in winter.

Rooms: $65–$132.

••
Silvermine Inn

Two hundred years has done nothing but improve the Silvermine Inn, which sits by a millpond in the middle of

Perry Ave.
Norwalk
(203)847-4558
All major credit cards

a Connecticut woodlands. The Whitman family has restored and kept fresh every piece of woodwork, every banister and every pegged floorboard, while adding a remarkable collection of antique farm implements, paintings and furniture—all of which gives you a good idea of what a nostalgic family inn should look and feel like. The rooms are similarly decorated and maintained: the restaurant downstairs serves simple but hearty American standards such as scrod, chicken pie and Indian pudding.
Doubles: $55.90–$61.90.

••
Stonehenge
Route 7
Ridgefield
(203)438-6511
All major credit cards

A sprawling 1832 residence situated by a large duck pond along the Norwalk River, this splendid old house has evolved since it became an inn in 1947. In those days, the Broadway and Hollywood crowd used to come up here to get away from the mobs of fans; for years the restaurant was run by the legendary Albert Stockli, once chef of The Four Seasons. Today the place has a pleasant balance of Victorian antiques, Federalist furniture in the main dining room and overstuffed chairs from the 1940s and '50s. Two of the rooms are in the main house, and six are in cottages bordering the duck pond. This is a supremely comfortable establishment on a pastoral ten acres of farmland; not only does it have its own good restaurant, it is also less than a half hour's drive from some of the best dining rooms in the region.
Doubles: $58.50–$70.

••
The West
Lane Inn
22 Westlake Rd.
(Route 35)
Ridgefield
(203)438-7323
AE, MC, V

Route 35 is one of the most interesting old roads in upper Westchester and lower Connecticut, as it straddles some of the region's most beautiful woodlands and is dotted with grand old mansions and sturdy white farmhouses. One of these is a porched beauty called The West Lane Inn. Once associated with the fine restaurant next door (The Inn at Ridgefield), it is now independently owned and maintained in a cheery, if not particularly period, style. This is a shame, because the structure itself has a Victorian majesty, while the rooms are all modernized . Nevertheless, it's a comfortable spot in a wonderful setting, and for the price (including a Continental breakfast) the West Lane is a delightful escape.
Singles: $75; doubles: $85.

Long Island

RESTAURANTS

12/20
Gordon's
Main St.
Amagansett
(516)267-3010
Winter: lunch Tues. to Sun. noon to 2:00 P.M., dinner Tues. to Sun. 6:00 P.M. to 10:30 P.M.; summer: dinner nightly 6:00 P.M. to 10:30 P.M.
All major credit cards
Continental

The name is American, the decor is '50s Italian, the location is a 30-year tradition, the menu is Continental, and the owner-chef is Greek. This international place is a welcome relief for those of us suffering from one coulis too many, an overabundance of undercooked vegetables, too many floral arrangements on our plates and more than enough nondecor. Here you'll find a silly crystal chandelier, gilt mirrors and sconces, friendly service and a clientele made up of bow-tied plaid-pantsed Hamptons husbands with their equally attractive preppy shirt-dressed wives. It's very comfortable, and the cuisine continues to be reliable in that simple way when good products are prepared with care and affection. You can start with a perfectly ripe crenshaw melon, an avocado filled with fresh shrimp that actually taste of shrimp, slightly overcooked canelloni with a delicious meat filling or tasty clams casino. Continue with the lightly coated scampi, excellent in its sauté of garlic and olive oil, the perfectly cooked roast duckling, its skin crispy and tasty, a marvelously tender veal piccata or an equally good veal with prosciutto and provolone in a mildly oversalted sauce. Accompanying vegetables, such as creamed spinach, are perfect in that Continental restaurant style; they're predictable and reliable. The Caesar salad is excellent; the desserts are made elsewhere, except for the chocolate mousse. The wine list is limited, but there are a few good selections that will make your evening relaxed and safe. About $30 per person with wine.

14
La Côte d'Or
(Garden City Hotel)
Garden City
(516) 747-3000
Dinner Mon. to Thurs. 6:00 P.M. to 9:00 P.M., Fri. and Sat. 6:00 P.M. to 10:30 P.M.
All major credit cards
French (nouvelle)

Imagine our surprise. In the middle of this upscale but somewhat sleepy community, we encounter a hotel from the Dallas school of decor, complete with a colonial cupola (to remind us we're still in the East). The lobby is attractive in a slick sort of way, with Plexiglas chandeliers, miles of pink marble and a sophisticated-traveler ambience. There are several restaurants and bars, but work your way to the back of this palace to find La Côte d'Or. Patrick Pinon has made this his new home (he was the sous-chef at La Récolte), and he has developed a

menu not unlike his mentor's at his former establishment.
The decor is hotel elegant, the tuxedoed waiters are very
professional, and the food is a refreshing surprise.
Starters are tempting if you are tempted by cold poached
lobster with saffron sauce, salmon tartare, mussels in
Meursault and thyme, oyster broth, and poached oysters
with vermouth. The salad of duck is superb, as is the
warm salad of scallops and morels, the scallop terrine
with lemon and ginger and the sautéed quail breast with
wild mushrooms. Entrees are equally enticing: a good
salmon with broccoli and caviar sauce, sautéed
sweetbreads in feuilleté, a lovely breast of chicken with
chicken sausage, an excellent paupiette of turbot with a
mousse of pike and lobster sauce, and a gamy fillet of
venison with juniper berries. The cheese tray is uneven;
on one visit it may be first-rate and on another a shadow
of a supermarket selection, although the fresh fruit is
always perfectly ripe. Desserts are not on the same par
with dinner, but a fairly decent wine list (with prices as
astronomical as the entrees) will keep you company
through the meal. It's pricey here, at $60 per person with
a good wine—for those prices, we'd expect Lutèce in the
provinces. Pinon is on the right track; he simply needs to
settle down and bring some finesse and experience to his
cuisine to elevate it to the level of its potential.

12/20
The House on Toilsome
15 Toilsome Ln.
East Hampton
(516)324-3003
April to June: dinner Wed. to Sun.
6:00 P.M. to 10:00 P.M.; June to
Labor Day: dinner Thurs. to Tues.
6:00 P.M. to 11:00 P.M.; Labor
Day to April: dinner Thurs. to Sun.
6:00 P.M. to 10:00 P.M.
All major credit cards
Continental

What a charming name for a country restaurant, and
what a charming place it is! This is a fine old house in a
pretty section of East Hampton, far from the bustle of
the main drag in town or the main route, which seems
perpetually clogged with traffic. Why can't the
Hamptons have more modest, unassuming restaurants
like this one, instead of all those dreadful brick-faced
hovels selling the same tired seafood and overpriced
lobsters? The House on Toilsome, owned by an
ex–research psychologist and a lawyer, maintains a light
but thoroughly enjoyable menu that ranges from
perfectly cooked vegetable salads with warm duck meat,
to a good breast of chicken with fresh tomatoes and star
anise, to a hearty dish of well-seasoned and tender lamb
shanks. The excellent desserts include a classic American
brownie and a well-wrought chocolate marquise cake.
Prices at this casual but serious dining room are modest:
about $40 for two before wine, tax and tip.

13
1770 House
143 Main St.
East Hampton

If saving the Hamptons' historic houses means turning
them into inns and restaurants, then we hope
entrepreneurs will imitate the efforts of Miriam and Sid

(516)324-1770

*Winter: Sat. dinner seatings 6:30
P.M., 8:00 P.M. (in the Tavern) and
9:30 P.M.; summer: Fri. to Tues.
dinner seatings 6:30 P.M., 8:00
P.M. and 9:30 P.M.*
All major credit cards

Continental

Perle, who turned a rundown colonial house into an impeccable restoration, filled from floor to ceiling with lovely antiques. The restaurant on the premises is a sea of oak tables and brass chandeliers, while the menu—which changes every week—is a pleasant blend of cuisines, with many Oriental seasonings gentled into American provender, most of the time to good effect. These days the emphasis is more on American fare and Continental items, so you might enjoy a wonderful butternut soup or four excellent lamb chops while your companion dines on spaghetti puttanesca or filet mignon with a béarnaise. When the Long Island scallops are in season, there is no place that prepares them better than the 1770 House, and the desserts are, one after another, exceptional in the best American sense—raspberry crumble, cheesecake flavored with pumpkin, apple pie. The wine list is sensible and fairly priced. The fixed-price dinner is $26.95 per person.

10/20

Gosman's Dock

**West Lake Dr.
Montauk
(516)668-5330**
*Lunch and dinner daily noon to
10:00 P.M.*
No credit cards

Seafood

The drive to Montauk from the Hamptons is superb; the vistas are stunning, and the prospects of reaching the tip of Long Island, with its fresh air, fishing boats and provincial charm, is motivation enough. But perhaps you are hungry. There are lots of little seafood restaurants, but the big daddy of them all is Gosman's. What started as a simple family place has turned into a Disneyland-esque enterprise, housed with a collection of shops in wind-washed gray siding, offering souvenirs to the hordes of summer people. Gosman's anchors the complex, and in the summer the wait can be demanding. Off-season, the open terrace around the perimeter is closed off, but the acres of wooden tables in a rustic decor are generally filled with hearty eaters. The view here is the attraction (in our opinion), not the cuisine, which is hardly a seafood feast . You'll feast instead on the vista of the sound and the pleasure boats on summer weekends. If you are really hungry, you can settle on an acceptable broiled fresh fish, although most of the diners seem to prefer the fried scallops, fried clams, fried potatoes and all the au gratins and Newburgs. We love coming here for a drink and the view, then making a quick trip to one of the fishing boats for some fresh fish to cook at a friend's home. About $12 per person, without wine.

13 ♟

The American Hotel

If you are still looking through the 38-page wine list (offering 68 California Cabernets alone) when the waiter appears to take your order, you have every right to

Main St.
Sag Harbor
(516)725-3535
*Winter: dinner nightly 6:30 P.M. to
9:30 P.M. (Fri. to 10:00 P.M., Sat.
to 10:30 P.M.); summer: dinner
nightly 6:30 P.M. to 10:00 P.M.
(Fri. and Sat. to 10:30 P.M.)*
No credit cards
American

continue to explore this marvelously rich list, designed with a great deal of foresight and care. Eventually you will be ready to sample the fairly provincial luncheon menu that reminds us of a French country inn. The selections change according to market availability and the chef's inspiration, and you won't be disappointed with a pungent gazpacho, a gentle cream of mushroom soup, a tangy ceviche or the house terrine. Nor will you be saddened by the sprightly scallops provençale, the perfectly cooked bluefish with an interesting garlic-Roquefort topping, a hearty lamb and haricot casserole or the peasant-style sweetbreads with julienne vegetables. Desserts are made on the premises; the rum bread pudding with crème anglaise is divine, as is the Black Forest mousse. Dinner offers a similar menu: roast duckling with apricot, veal kidneys in a mustard sauce, rack of lamb with herbes de Provence and calf's liver Bercy. The clientele is a loyal host of regulars who make The American Hotel their weekend home and Hamptons residents who know a good meal when they taste it. The setting is a bit triste, with a Victorian decor that could use a little sprucing up and acoustics that make it possible to hear, in intimate detail, the gossipy conversations of your neighbors. About $25 per person for lunch with a glass of wine, slightly more at dinner.

10/20
Lobster Inn
162 Inlet Rd.
Southampton
(516)283-9828
*Lunch and dinner daily noon to 9:30
P.M. (Fri. and Sat. to 10:30 P.M.)*
AE, MC, V
Seafood

If you have two and a half hours to spend over a weekday lunch, come to the Lobster Inn, where you'll be served remarkably fresh seafood, at decent prices, by young ladies who find time to wait on tables at commercial breaks during the soap operas. Assuming that you are a patient person, you can expect (eventually) a good lobster salad, broiled fresh fish, a variety of sizes of lobster and a tired salad bar. Dinner is a bit livelier, as the TV is tuned to sports. The view is pleasant: a small inlet complete with ducks, swans and fiberglass sailboats. A favorite of local residents. Dinner for two will come to $30 with wine.

11/20
The Three
Village Inn
150 Main St.
Stony Brook
(516)751-0555
*Lunch Mon. to Fri. noon to 3:00
P.M., Sat. noon to 3:30 P.M.;
dinner Mon. to Thurs. 5:00 P.M. to
9:00 P.M., Fri. and Sat. 5:00 P.M.
to 10:00 P.M., Sun. 12:30 P.M. to*

We are quite taken with the exquisite little town of Stony Brook on Long Island's north shore, even if its antique-looking Main Street shopping area and grand post office are actually a fond re-creation by a millionaire shoe manufacturer some four decades ago. The Three Village Inn, however, does have an 1851 pedigree, and it has been a well-regarded family-style restaurant since the 1940s. It is located just off the little marina of the green-lawned town, and several of the dining rooms overlook

9:00 P.M.; tea Mon. to Fri. 3:00
P.M. to 4:00 P.M.
All major credit cards
American

the comings and goings of boats in the harbor and ducks on the grass. One might easily find almost every style of postcolonial decor at the inn, for each dining room is decorated in a different way, from the formal private room, to the homey barroom, to the white-and-blue hallway room, to the large, somewhat modernized main room. It all comes together splendidly, and every weekend the place is occupied by good husbands, wives and children taking grandmother to lunch or dinner.

The food here shows American gustatory generosity to a fare-thee-well—any dish you order will be amplified with complimentary platters of cottage cheese, rolls, crackers, Cheddar cheese, raw vegetables, homemade breads or even clam fritters. The more complicated a dish becomes, the more likely it is to be a failure, such as "colonial carpetbagger steak" stuffed with oysters. But if you stick to giant prime ribs of beef, hefty lobsters, Cheddar cheese soup or Long Island duckling, you'll have a satisfying, if not wholly pleasurable, meal. The desserts (Indian pudding, blueberry pie and chocolate icebox cake) are American classics well worth trying. Prices are moderate, with complete dinners ranging between $9.75 and $19.75; children eat for half those amounts.

HOTELS

•••
The American Hotel
Main St.
Sag Harbor
(516)725-3535
No credit cards

All seven rooms are done in an American decor with Victorian wallpaper, antiques and modern bathrooms. There is one Southwestern room with an attractive desert decor. It's a landmark building, exceedingly popular with New Yorkers, who love to make it their summer home and autumn retreat. An institution that is neither overly charming nor too bare-bones rustic.

Doubles: $65 weeknights, $85 weekends (with two-night minimum).

••
Huntting Lodge
94 Main St.
East Hampton
(516)324-0410
All major credit cards

A comfortable and definitely country inn. There are twenty rooms in this 1750s lodge that is tucked away amid the ancient elms and maples. The room decor is rustic and unassuming, most of the bathrooms are very modern, and the Palm restaurant dishes up its inimitable brand of Second Avenue steak house cuisine. It's a pleasant place, albeit lacking the landed-gentry charm of the 1770 House.

In season: singles, $50, doubles, $75–$100; off-season: singles, $35, doubles, $60–$70.

••••
1770 House
143 Main St.
East Hampton
(516)324-1770
AE, MC, V

This absolutely charming wood frame house is run by the absolutely charming Perle family. The main house is filled with antiques and clocks, more or less orchestrated to reinforce every hour. The seven rooms are cozy and attractive with four-poster beds, antiques, private baths (all up-to-date) and an early American feeling. Although the rooms in the main house are pretty, we think the best room is number twelve, which has its own entrance at the back of the house, overlooking the garden and patio. Done in blues, its four-poster bed is comfortable, the bathroom is modern, the leaded glass windows have an old-world charm, and the entire room is redolent of romance. Innkeepers Perles have restored the 1770 House to its vintage, country-elegant charm and added their own twentieth-century hospitality. You can dine here on the weekends, sampling Miriam's wide range of culinary tastes; guests are served a Continental breakfast in the morning. Very popular in the summer, and a jewel in the winter when the summer people have come and gone.
Doubles: $85–$135 (call first—rates may vary).

New Jersey

RESTAURANTS

11/20
L'Auberge de France
2310 Hamburg
Turnpike
Wayne
(201)835-9868
Lunch Mon. to Sat. noon to 2:30 P.M., Sun. 11:30 A.M. to 3:30 P.M.; dinner Mon. to Thurs. 5:30 P.M. to 10:00 P.M., Fri. and Sat. 5:30 P.M. to 11:00 P.M., Sun. 3:30 P.M. to 9:00 P.M.
CB, DC, MC, V
French (provincial)

Like thousands of French chefs before him, Jean Louis Todeschini wanted to be his own boss, so five years ago he left the kitchen at Le Cirque and took over what had been a rather somber Swiss restaurant in Wayne, an obscure community in Bergen County. He spruced up the frame building, redecorated the wraparound porch with brightly colored stained glass depicting episodes from *Les Fables de La Fontaine*, put new fixtures and furniture in the other dining areas and installed a pool for live trout. He intended to recreate in this new setting the light, innovative dishes served at Le Cirque. But to his dismay, he quickly learned that the people of Wayne, accustomed to eating at the franchises along the

519

superhighways that crisscross the area, prefer man-size portions of meat and gravy to his sort of nouvelle-style dishes.

Jean Louis compromised, and the result is not very satisfactory. Good-quality meats and fish, often well prepared, are smothered in too many sauces with too much garnishment. It is possible to eat well at L'Auberge, however, especially if you call ahead and review the menu with Jean Louis. His pâtés (duck, pheasant, pork and veal) are outstanding, the brook trout au bleu can be excellent, and a bread and butter pudding (!) with a caramel bourbon sauce is delicious. And if you are prepared to fast for a week beforehand, order the six-course "dégustation dinner" at the remarkable price of $28. The gratin of lobster (a second-course choice on the special menu) costs almost as much à la carte. There can be redeeming features to dining in New Jersey (the scenery is not one of them). We wish only that Jean Louis would duplicate the enchantment of de La Fontaine on the plates. We believe that palates, even in New Jersey, have changed for the better over the last five years. Clients are now willing to pay upward of $40 per person, without wine; what would they pay if Jean Louis turned out really refined dishes?

14 ⌂
Chez Catherine
Best Western Motel
431 North Ave.
Westfield
(201)232-1680
Lunch Tues. to Fri. noon to 2:00 P.M.; dinner Mon. to Thurs. 5:30 P.M. to 8:30 P.M., Fri. and Sat. seatings 5:30 P.M. and 9:00 P.M.
AE, MC, V
French
(provincial/nouvelle)

Westfield is a tree-lined bedroom community centered on a few blocks of shops and a 40-unit Best Western Motel, red brick pseudo-colonial structure. Yes, there is a Catherine in the building, we learn from the room clerk, and we won't need a key or a reservation to find her. She runs a restaurant, and her door is to the left. Inside, to our surprise and pleasure, we immediately feel at home in a tastefully decorated, tiny (45 seats) room, with brightly polished untensils hanging from the walls and fan-folded napkins popping up from the stemware on white linen tablecloths. We are, of course, delighted to find this little piece of provincial France in this most unlikely setting, and we expect to find a menu to match. To our amazement, Catherine prepares a number of quite elegant dishes, reflecting the influences of sophisticated nouvelle and of her own roots in the French countryside. After a hearty vegetable soup, we discover that she handles with equal skill nouvelle-style poached oysters in a nicely perfumed lobster purée, thin (and pink) slices of Muscovy duck breast with a ginger-scented red wine sauce, and exquisitely presented pears (a little overcooked) with two velvety sabayons.

To what do the residents of this otherwise

undistinguished suburban culinary wasteland owe their good fortune? Four years ago, Catherine's husband, an executive with AT&T, received orders to relocate to company headquarters at Basking Ridge, and they settled in nearby Westfield. Catherine (her French mother and Greek father ran a restaurant in Sancerre on the upper Loire) opened Chez Catherine. So the next time we're unhappy with the phone company, we'll remember the blessings it brought to New Jersey. About $35 per person, with wine.

15 ♟
Le Délice
302 Whippany Rd.
Whippany
(201)884-2727
Lunch Tues. to Fri. 11:30 A.M. to 2:00 P.M.; dinner Mon. to Sat. 6:00 P.M. to 9:30 P.M.
AE, DC

French-American (nouvelle)

New Jerseyans eat at places with such names as Fantasy Island, The Full House, Fireplace Restaurant and Bogey's—or at McDonald's, Burger King, Roy Rogers or Pizzatown, USA. A handful of these Garden State residents (executives of Warner-Lambert, AT&T) have the good sense (and the required credit cards) to visit this out-of-the-way oasis of good cooking. John Foy, the chef-owner, is largely self-taught (he abandoned a career as an accountant with Price Waterhouse), and he proves that a restaurant can survive in New Jersey even if it offers imaginative dishes (somewhere between French nouvelle and the updated American cooking). His delightful restaurant is located in an unobtrusive pink clapboard house on a quiet, tree-lined residential street, far from the garish neon signs that pollute the state's major thoroughfares. Inside you will be astonished by the sophistication and good taste: impressive floral arrangements, intimate banquettes, color-coordinated menus, stylish serving plates (from Italy), regal crystal pepper mills (from England) and a team of serious waiters and waitresses (Chilean, Greek, Scottish, Austrian) in black tie and dinner jackets.

John has composed a short, quite personal menu: a beautiful tricolored fish terrine, so fresh and light that it seems to be enveloped in a sea breeze; a more classic lobster bisque; slivers of chicken, prepared Chinese style, but with an unusual orange-scented dressing; moist and tender sweetbreads with a delicate tomato and basil sauce; and perfectly prepared (and fresh) fish with an interesting selection of garnishes, some reflecting the influence of the Orient. For our taste, John underseasons several of these creations, but he believes firmly that the salt and pepper are on the table for a purpose. In any event, these dishes stand up admirably, with or without additional seasoning.

Needless to say, we are much taken with Mr. Foy's talents, his dedication to using only the best and freshest ingredients (he has his own herb garden in the back) and his pursuit of excellence in everything he does. (The collection of wines is equal to the best lists in Manhattan, and he knows every one of them.) A three-course à la carte dinner with a modest wine can easily run to $45 or $50 per person; a seven-course fixed-price menu at $39.50 is irresistible: obviously Mr. Foy forgot some of the finance savvy he learned at Price Waterhouse. We are grateful for that.

15 Pear Tree

**42 Avenue of the
Two Rivers
Rumson
(201)842-8747**

*Dinner Sun. to Thurs. 6:00 P.M. to
9:30 P.M., Fri. and Sat. 6:00 P.M.
to 10:30 P.M.
All major credit cards*

French (nouvelle)

Blink your eyes and click your heels three times, and you might think you're back on Lexington Avenue, not on Avenue of the Two Rivers in Rumson. The beautiful botanical prints from Le Plaisir have been resurrected on the terra-cotta walls of this exceedingly handsome restaurant filled with plants, early American antiques (of the carousel-horse genre) and nature prints. Stephen Spector is at it again, this time at the beach in the former Pear Tree, which has been given a facelift and has been brightened with his distinctive, sophisticated cuisine. It is indeed a refreshing surprise to be able to dine on fish terrine, very good spinach custard with cucumber sauce, excellent chilled tomato soup with fennel, a superb seafood sausage that manages to retain the flavors of its ingredients, salmon with a mousse of sole, fillet of lamb en croûte, tender breast of quail with a perfectly poached pear (the gibier sauce is a bit too salty and thick, however), an escalope of veal with julienne leeks and truffles and halibut (a bit mealy) with a good saffron beurre blanc with peppers—instead of the expected countryside chicken pot pie, pot roast and turkey. The desserts, unhappily, are lackluster; a decent walnut tart is overloaded with whipped cream, and an almond cheesecake is, at best, unmemorable. The wine list offers plenty of depth in French reds and whites, and many have reasonable prices. The service is a bit unprofessional for such an uptown place, but it's friendly and sincere nonetheless. You will be content after a lovely dinner here amid the navy blue–blazered, prep-tied men and silk-dressed women in their pretty pumps. About $50 per person, with wine.

15 The Tarragon Tree

**225 Main St.
Chatham**

Before you plan a visit to The Tarragon Tree, we advise you to equip the car with a compass and radar and take along a good hunting dog. If you don't, you may not find the place at all, and that would be a distinct misfortune. So we will take some pains to explain that the entrance to

(201)635-7333
Dinner Mon. to Sat. 6:00 P.M. to 9:30 P.M.
MC, V
French (nouvelle)

the restaurant—identified overhead by an unlighted awning no bigger than a child's umbrella—is between the Village Hardware store and the law offices of Stickel, Frahn and Lloyd on Main Street in Chatham. Please do not be put off by the plain, unobtrusive exterior: open the door and walk in. This little room, with its beige walls, handful of tables with sparkling stemware, lovely white napery and beautiful flowers at the center of the dessert display, is an oasis of civility that will certainly surprise and delight you. What's more, you will be shown to your table with such warmth and courtesy that you will wonder whether what comes from the kitchen can possibly equal the setting and the hospitality. This doubt will be quickly dispelled. The mussel soup served in a small marmite is steaming hot and intensely flavorful, and a feuilleté of chanterelles, in a rich sauce given body with a purée of the mushrooms themselves, is exquisite. The rare Muscovy duck is tender and the peppery sauce enchanting. The veal medallions are perfect, and the accompanying feuilleté of sweetbreads and duck liver is totally satisfying. Desserts—fruit tarts and cakes baked on the premises—are acceptable enough, if not quite as extraordinary as some of the appetizers and main dishes.

The man responsible for this miracle on Main Street is Dennis Foy, chef and proprietor, who learned much of what he knows as an understudy to his brother John, who now runs Le Délice in nearby Whippany. They had a falling out, and Dennis opened this smaller, somewhat less elegant place, which serves the same type of all-but-flawless nouvelle-style dishes. We regret the fraternal rupture but hasten to note that the result is two good restaurants instead of one. About $50 per person with a good California Cabernet from the extensive and well-chosen wine list.

HOTELS

•
Molly Pitcher Inn
State Highway 35
Red Bank
(800)221-1372
N.J.:
(201)747-2500
All major credit cards

If you have wandered out to the Jersey shore looking, as we have, for yet another culinary experience in the countryside, and you don't have intimate friends in Rumson who own any of the lovely old homes overlooking the sea or otherwise, you will come to the conclusion, as we have, that the Molly Pitcher Inn is your best bet for lodging. The quasi-colonial inn with its imposing Corinthian columns and cupola overlooks the marina in the Navesink River. Ask for an end room in one of the two wings so your view is unobstructed, and you'll be able to forget the uninspired decor, which is of the

1950s motel school of design variety. There is a swimming pool, plus a coffee shop that offers an acceptable Continental breakfast served by friendly, pleasant waitresses. The inn is only a short drive to the Pear Tree, Stephen Spector's emergence from early retirement.

Singles: $40–$70; doubles: $53–$80.

Upstate New York

RESTAURANTS

14 🎩

American Bounty
Roth Hall
The Culinary Institute of America
Hyde Park
(914)452-9600
Lunch Tues. to Sat. 11:30 A.M. to 2:00 P.M.; dinner Tues. to Sat. 6:30 P.M. to 9:30 P.M.
AE

American

Curiosity about updated American cooking is not confined to SoHo and TriBeCa: you have to reserve three months in advance (on weekends) for a chance to dine at the American Bounty at The Culinary Institute of America, 75 miles up the Hudson. Here, in a wing of a huge building (built originally as a seminary) around a cloister, students devote the final three weeks of their two-year course in cooking and restaurant management to the preparation and service of imaginative dishes based on extraordinarily fresh American ingredients. If what ushers from this kitchen is an indication of what we can expect from American restaurants in the years ahead, none of us have to worry—we will eat very well indeed. Of course, much credit must be given to the chef-instructor, Tim Ryan, a youthful graduate who supervises the students in the kitchen. But this is a team effort. Two appetizers that are on the menu when local tomatoes are in season illustrate the total commitment to first-rate ingredients and honesty in preparation: a cold vegetable terrine with a tomato vinaigrette and a warm vegetable mousse with a tomato dressing. Another appetizer—tender sweetbreads with a crisp crouton and a sliver of excellent Virginia ham—is equally good. Main dishes are carefully prepared and presented: roast partridge with pecan sauce (just a hint of the pecan comes through), moist tenderloin of pork in a nicely scented cream sauce. Vegetables, served family style in au gratin serving dishes, are crisp and tasty, not the afterthought they too often seem to be elsewhere. The fruit cobbler (almost as American as apple pie) and the chocolate mousse in a barquette of pastry are as good as what comes before. Breads made by the students are interesting, if a bit sweet for our taste.

The menu changes daily and the staff rotates every three weeks, so there may be surprises. Service may lag, and the kitchen performance may not always be consistent. But anyone interested in the future of American cooking should not miss this experience.

Before undertaking their phase at the American Bounty, students play a similar role at the Escoffier Room at the other end of Roth Hall. The menu is classical French and in our judgment is less well executed. The student waiters and waitresses are not always proficient in tableside service and the use of chafing dishes. But American style does not require this type of service, and that is the future for these young men and women. About $30 per person at the American Bounty, without wine, and somewhat more for the prix fixe menu at the Escoffier Room.

15 ♟

Auberge Maxime
**Ridgefield Rd.
(Route 116)
North Salem
(914)669-5450**
*Lunch Mon. to Fri. noon to 2:30 P.M.; dinner Mon. to Sat. 6:00 P.M. to 9:00 P.M., Sun. 3:00 P.M. to 8:30 P.M.
All major credit cards*
French (classical)

Bernard Le Bris, a Breton by birth and a Tour d'Argent graduate by training, is the kind of chef we shall never tire of applauding—young, dedicated and as eager as the day in 1979 he took over Auberge Maxime from Maxime Ribera (owner of Maxime's). He has married his strong personal tastes to classical techniques, in an effort to find the proper balance for what is one of the most charming country restaurants in the region. The little restaurant's parking lot is usually jammed with Mercedes and BMWs from Westchester and Connecticut's more affluent towns, and Paul Newman is a frequent visitor. The interior is marked by a comforting wooden archway, fine napery, delicate glassware and a pretty bar. The classic menu features, as you might expect from a Tour d'Argent graduate, excellent duck dishes—pressed and with peppercorns, plums or even kumquats. Le Bris's foie de canard is wonderful, as are the ris de veau in cream and morels and the perfectly cooked roast chicken. Pastries are not quite as impressive, especially when they are wrapped around smoked salmon and sole. The wine list is far above average, and the fixed-price meal at $34 is certainly worth every penny.

14 ♟

The Box Tree
**Routes 22 and 116
Purdys
(914)277-3677**
*Dinner Sun. to Fri. 6:30 P.M. to 9:30 P.M., Sat. seatings 6:30 P.M. and 9:30 P.M.
No credit cards*
French

We have not been much impressed by Manhattan's restaurant by this name, also under Augustine Paege's ownership, but what a difference 50 miles can make in style and cuisine! The city version is stuffy and pretentious, while its country cousin is absolutely pastoral, tasteful and restrained. Set in a 1775 house of great antique interest, the restaurant has blazing fireplaces in cold weather, planked floors and polished mahogany tables. The staff is knowledgeable, the wine list is carefully culled, and the food, under Austrian-born Rudi Granser, is very good. We have no complaints with the ris de veau in a fine périqueux sauce, the sorrel soup or the côte de veau au basilic, except that they are not as stunning as the superb desserts , such as the hazelnut vacherin and the intensely flavored sorbets. If you wish—and if you've reserved long in advance—you may toddle upstairs to a François I canopied bed after dinner, to be served breakfast therein the next day. Dinner is about $80 or more for two, without wine.

13 🍳
Buffet de la Gare
155 Southside Ave.
Hastings-on-Hudson
(914)478-1671
Lunch Tues. to Sun. noon to 2:30 P.M.; dinner Tues. to Fri. 6:30 P.M. to 9:30 P.M., Sat seatings 6:30 P.M. and 9:15 P.M., Sun. 5:30 P.M. to 9:00 P.M.
All major credit cards
French (classical)

Although you can't really see the Hudson River from this Hastings-on-Hudson restaurant, you will see Westchester commuters coming off the train from the station across the street to this absolutely charming casual bistro, with an old tin ceiling, a turn-of-the-century bar, wood floors and rickety chairs. The young owners, Gwenael and Annie Goulet, are from Brittany, and their menu, though hardly à la Breton, lists hearty, robust dishes of cassoulet, duck with apples and Calvados, boeuf bourguignon and tarte tatin. This is honest bourgeois cooking, occasionally enlivened by imaginative presentations of le délice aux cinq legumes. The velouté de moules is fragrant and good, and the bombe praline glacée is a satisfying way to end a meal that will set just as well with your budget—figure on $22 per person, without wine, tax or tip.

13 🍳
René Chardain
Route 123 and West Ln.
Lewisboro
(914)533-6200
Dinner Tues. to Sat. 6:00 P.M. to 9:00 P.M.
MC, V
French (classical/provincial)

Epernay-born René Chardain moved from his respected Four Columns Inn in sylvan New Fane, Vermont, to the equally woodsy Lewisboro (just over an hour from Manhattan) two years ago. He restored a magnificent old Stanford White mansion, turning it into a fine inn/restaurant serving competently made clichés and some inspired personal specialties that work wonders with Oriental spices, such as cumin, cardamom and saffron. No longer a youngster, Chardain is still enchanted by the prospect of finding some New York State foie gras or Canadian Malpiques, and he raises his own pheasants on the property.

We can find little fault with Chardain's béarnaise- and bordelaise-sauced dishes, but we prefer his Singhalese and almond soups, his shrimp with fennel, his rillettes of pork, his terrine of scallops with peppercorns and lobster sauce, his tart sorbets, his commendable cheese selection and all of his desserts. Maître d' Frank Shaufler knows his wines and how to manage a young staff, too. Plan on about $60 for two before wine, tax and tip; there are two suites to rent upstairs.

11/20
La Crémaillère
North St.
Banksville
(914)234-9647
Lunch Tues. to Fri. noon to 2:30
P.M.; dinner Tues. to Sat. 6:00 P.M.
to 9:30 P.M., Sun. 1:00 P.M. to
8:00 P.M.
All major credit cards
French
(classical/provincial)

La Crémaillère has held onto its high reputation in the Westchester-Connecticut region for reasons that must have more to do with its idyllic setting and decor than with its rather mediocre food. The low, wood-beamed ceilings, the jolly cartoons on the walls, the pink tablecloths and the warm fireplaces in winter all add up to what many people would believe is the epitome of a French country inn. Add to this the ownership by Robert Meyzen (of the family that also owns New York's La Caravelle), and you have all the ingredients for success— but not for great cuisine. Sadly, we have had some major disappointments here, along with some qualified delights. The pink, well-seasoned sausage with lentils is hearty and good, as are the wild mushrooms in puff pastry and cream sauce. We won't quibble about the foie de canard au poivre vert or the coquelet sauté Veuve Brush (Mrs. Brush once owned this 1826 house) either. But the venison stew is heavy, the bass comes with a lackluster béarnaise, and the côte de veau with an onion confiture and wild rice is merely satisfying. Desserts can be very good, especially the chocolate dacquoise and the blueberry in pastry with a cream sauce, but what can the pastry chef have been thinking of when he made the cherry cake, fit only for a three-year-old's birthday party? La Crémaillère's wine cellar has depth in more ways than one, and you are invited to visit it. Back at your table you can sigh over the high-priced antique Bordeaux and Burgundies and settle for the more moderately priced Sancerre or Chablis noted at the top of the food menu. Dinner here will cost two close to $70 before wine, tax and tip.

12/20
Harralds
Route 52
Stormville
(914)878-6595
Dinner Wed. to Fri. 6:00 P.M. to
9:00 P.M., Sat. seatings 5:30 P.M.
and 8:30 P.M.
No credit cards
Continental

For some time we had heard of the high reputation of Harralds, in bucolic Dutchess County, so, hoping Stormville might be the home of an American Bocuse, we drove the 70 miles to find the outward signs promising: a well-restored 200-year-old barn set on eighteen acres of farmland with a fresh trout tank. Inside a stone fireplace glows, antiques adorn the walls, and Vivaldi is piped in at a discreet level. The owner, Harrald Boerger, is a grandfatherly figure who seems genuinely flattered that you've come to visit, and he reads off the day's menu offerings with the dramatic passion of an evangelist. (He is rightfully proud of his extraordinary wine list.) The food is generally very good, although not very imaginative—perfect steak au poivre, viande de boeuf with a sauce Valentine and, of course, fresh trout cooked au bleu. The linzer torte is exemplary. Harrald's wife, Ava Durrschmidt, is not a woman who takes even mild criticism mildly, but we must tell her the major fault of the kitchen: underseasoning such dishes as chicken curry, soups and duck with orange sauce. The staff, drawn mainly from students at The Culinary Institute of America, is very formal. A four-course meal without wine will cost $36 per person; expect to spend a long time eating it.

15 L'Hostellerie Bressane

**Routes 22 and 23
Hillsdale
(518)325-3412**
Dinner Mon. to Fri. 6:30 P.M. to 9:00 P.M. (sometimes closed Wed. and Thurs.), Sat. 5:30 P.M. to 9:30 P.M., Sun. 4:00 P.M. to 9:00 P.M. No credit cards

French
(provincial/nouvelle)

The Hamptons don't have a monopoly on country chic. People with money but no urge to show it off often prefer the Berkshires, with the music festival at Tanglewood, the summer playhouse at Stockbridge, the ski slopes at Great Barrington or Catamount and the easy drive from New York City. At the approaches to the wooded Berkshire hills, Jean Morel, once chef at Lafayette in the city, and his wife, Madeleine, provide these sophisticated weekenders with the ideal country restaurant and inn: classic yet up-to-date cooking in a beautiful colonial setting. The dining area consists of four small rooms, each with a fireplace and amply spaced tables. The taproom with a copper-topped bar is a good place to pause before or after dinner—again, in front of the fireplace. In winter, with snow falling outside, you'll have difficulty believing that Giovanni Boccaccio is not expected at any moment.

Despite the colonial atmosphere in the dining rooms, don't expect hot biscuits, Maryland fried chicken or apple pie. Jean Morel prepares a cuisine that reflects a familiarity with nouvelle but certainly not an infatuation with it. Fortunately he does not forget that some of the dishes he learned in his native Bresse cannot be improved upon: a marvelous country pâté, an onion soup based on his mother's recipe, duck with cabbage, sweetbreads with chestnuts, veal kidneys with a mustard cream sauce and so forth. When it's available, he also does justice to local game, including venison, pheasant and wild rabbit. But Jean knows he is living in the twentieth century: his sauces are intense and light, and he is not afraid to innovate a bit here and there, without wandering too far from the classical approach. The Calvados soufflé is an enchanting finale to what can be a perfectly balanced and enjoyable meal. Expect to pay about $40 per person, without wine. Jean operates a five-day cooking school on the premises, except in July and August.

17 Maxime's

**Old Tomahawk St.
Granite Springs
(914)248-7200**
Dinner Tues. to Sun. 6:00 P.M.

We knew we would find it sooner or later—a country restaurant that rivals the best in Manhattan and yet is close enough (about one and a quarter hours' drive) for any serious gourmet to head for the decidedly sylvan region of Granite Springs, in northern Westchester

to 10:30 P.M. (Fri. and Sat. to
11:00 P.M.)
All major credit cards
French (classical)

County. Here reside Maxime and Huguette Ribera, two dedicated restaurateurs who see to every detail, from the quality of the linen and china to the impeccable presentation of the food—and with a five-course meal at $32 (including canapés, sorbet, cheese, coffee and petits fours) they seem just as concerned about giving their customers quite a bargain. Maxime and Huguette once owned Auberge Maxime and Buffet de la Gare; they then had the bad idea of moving to Miami, but finally returned to their legions of fans in Westchester. Perhaps the sun did some good, however, for Maxime's classic cuisine is a little lighter than it used to be, though no less lavish. The cervelas de fruits de mer au saumon is superb, as is the zephir forestière au fumet de morilles, while his fish soup with saffron must rank among the most luscious renditions of this soup we can recall. Turbot in seaweed has the elements of both the sea and the saucepan in perfect harmony, while the duck confit and the galette of potatoes and truffles is classicism at its best. Just as rich and impressive is a saddle of lamb, perfectly roasted and served with tender flageolets; for those who are indecisive, an *opéra* of veal, lamb and fillet of beef noisettes in their own juices is an ideal choice. Cheeses are in perfect condition; desserts range from a pear tart in caramel to a terrine au chocolat of quite impressive richness. Even the wine list displays the owners' good sense—although it is not a great and varied list, it is a well chosen and fairly tariffed one. For those of us who enjoy the cuisine at New York's La Côte Basque or L.A.'s L'Ermitage, Maxime's is a marvelous addition to American gastronomy in the best French style. Expect to spend $85 for two, with wine.

13
Mona Trattoria
Route 22
Croton Falls
(914)277-4580
Dinner Wed. and Thurs. 6:00 P.M. to 10:00 P.M., Fri. and Sat. 6:00 P.M. to 11:00 P.M., Sun. 2:00 P.M. to 9:00 P.M.
No credit cards
Italian

Even though New York has a good number of excellent Italian restaurants, few specialize in the cuisine of a particular region, relying instead on an amalgam of southern and vaguely northern renditions of Italian dishes that are not always well known back home. At Mona Trattoria, located in the heart of some very beautiful and isolated territory on the edge of Westchester County, the menu has a decidedly Bolognese flavor, and some of the dishes approach the best we've had in the city Italians call Bologna grasso ("fat Bologna"), for the richness of its cuisine (chef Mona Martelli is a native of Bologna). The pastas are homemade and light as satin, enriched with besciamella and bolognese sauces of luxurious consistency. We love the lasagne verde bolognese, adore the gnocchi al pesto (actually a Genovese dish) and swoon over the ravioletti—tiny ravioli with a light cream and tomato sauce. In fall there are pastas with fresh white truffles for those who wish to pay the price; more everyday pastas run about $10 with appetizer portions about $6. We've often lamented how Italian chefs seem to lose heart when it comes to main courses, but at Mona Trattoria we find this to be completely untrue. The classic petto di tacchino alla bolognese is a succulent breast of turkey with thin prosciutto and fontina cheese that couldn't be better, while veal scaloppine Emiliana comes with a forcemeat of funghi procini, Parmesan cheese and a few tiny slivers of preserved white truffles that distinctly show each ingredient in perfect harmony. The scampi al curry, though hardly an orthodox Bolognese dish, is delicious too. If Italian restaurants in America fall short on their entrees, they fall down completely in their desserts, but not here: you can depend on an excellent, airy cheesecake, a rich crema di caramella and decent fruit tarts. Mona likes to give personal attention to every dish, so on weekends you'll have to linger awhile between courses. But that shouldn't be a problem in this plush, attractive 1864 mansion, especially with the attentive waiters, who will keep your wineglasses full. The wine list is not lengthy but contains some quite reasonable selections. Dinner for two, before wine, tax and tip, will be about $50, and you must pay that with cash or local check.

13
Salerno's Old Town Coach House
100 Main St.
Tuckahoe
(914)793-1557
Dinner Tues. to Sun. 5:30 P.M. to 9:00 P.M.
No credit cards
American

If you have ever wondered what a true American roadhouse restaurant looks like, a quick 35-minute drive from Manhattan will take you through the small lower Westchester towns of Bronxville and Tuckahoe to the door of an unassuming place called Salerno's, the quintessential steaks-and-chops eatery where decor and amenities are minimal but genuine atmosphere is plentiful. There are no linen tablecloths on the tables and no cloth napkins; the interior design consists of one terrible seascape, a very rustic barroom area, blackboard menus and the varnished, bright red shell of a 30-pound lobster hung over the fireplace.

You'll wait at that bar for a table, because Salerno's takes no reservations and because it is one of the region's most popular restaurants—people come here not only because it's casual, but because they get consistently excellent American cuisine. The barroom will be three deep with suburban-prep males in bright green jackets and madras trousers and women in madras jackets and bright green skirts.

Grilling and broiling are lost talents with many American cooks, but Salerno's cooks are masters of the technique, serving up abundant steaks, pork chops, calf's liver and lamb chops with consummate skill—charred or seared on the outside and pink or rare on the inside. The accompanying baked potatoes and onion rings are textbook lessons in retaining the sweet flavor of these side orders. Little did we realize that Salerno's is also capable of turning out classic French fish preparations that any toque blanche would be proud of. Sole Walewska made with lobster and a terrific hollandaise might confuse Escoffier, who intended prawns and a Mornay, but the results are glorious, as they are with other fish done in a cream and Champagne sauce or, more simply, broiled to perfect succulence and served with butter. Only Salerno's desserts fail to meet the kitchen's high standards; but the sweets are made elsewhere. The preferred potables are beer or martinis, but owners George and Al Salerno have a decent wine list at good prices. A meal for two, without wine, tax or tip, will cost about $50 in cash; no credit cards are accepted.

HOTELS

The Bird & Bottle Inn
1 Albany Post Rd.
Garrison
(914)424-3000
AE, MC, V

Anyone with a turn of mind to travel up the Hudson River to West Point Military Academy might do well to stay over and have dinner at the Bird & Bottle, which has been a waystop on the Albany Post Road since 1761 and an inn since 1940. This river country is beautiful, and the inn is bucolically situated nearby. The owners have worked hard to give the place an antique look without any of the adaptive "colonial" touches that so often ruin a country inn. You'll find Windsor chairs, old wainscoting, tin wall sconces and an excellent collection of antique bird prints in every room. There are four rooms to rent—and in the fall they are hard to come by on weekends. The price includes a fine American meal and Continental breakfast in the inn's restaurant, with its cozy wooden banquettes.

Doubles: $135; suites $155.

The Box Tree
Routes 22 and 116
Purdys
(914)277-3677
No credit cards

The Box Tree is a special place for a select few—just two rooms to let, each a gem of restoration and opulent amenities. The little white house itself dates back to 1775, and we have already praised the restaurant on the ground floor in this book. The rooms are decked out with fine antiques, Queen Anne chairs and French porcelain behind grand old cabinets. One room (a suite with sitting room and private dining room) has a more

Napoleonic provincial style, while the other is dominated by an enormous carved canopy bed from the time of François I, once owned by King Farouk. The coverlet for this bed is made of Canadian lynx, which feels just about right in the dead of winter, when Purdys (about an hour and a quarter from Manhattan) gets pretty chilly. In the morning, with a fireplace warming the inn, you are brought croissants, fresh fruit, game birds, eggs and good coffee, all of which should prepare you for a day of reading or strolling the surrounding territory à la Thoreau.

Doubles: $220.

•••
René Chardain
Route 123 and West Ln.
Lewisboro
(914)533-6200
MC, V

The Lewisboro territory in upper Westchester County is without doubt among the most beautiful rural landscapes in the region, and René Chardain, a restaurant with two rooms to rent, is one of the most remarkable mansions in this vast, rambling neighborhood of pines and maples. The house was designed by Stanford White, supposedly for Alexander Graham Bell's daughter, and to stand on the lawn and see the great expanse of stars in the New York sky is to feel something of an era when affluence meant the ability to escape—whereas now it seems the insecure rich wish to go only where their friends congregate.

There are two enormous suites at the inn—large enough to perform sufficient calisthenics to work off one of the downstairs meals—with splendid tiled bathrooms fit for a deluxe room in the Paris Ritz. For this and a Continental breakfast after a sleep in perfect silence, you will pay a mere $80 and feel completely refreshed by the experience.

Doubles: $80.

•••
L'Hostellerie Bressane
Routes 22 and 23
Hillsdale
(518)325-3412
No credit cards

Jean and Madelaine Morel have carefully refurbished the original Dutch Hearth. They have retained the eighteenth-century charm, with its exterior of handmade bricks and interior of wide-planked floors and wood paneling. You'll find all the allure of a French country inn in the six rooms with fireplace and private bath. The furnishings are tasteful, the welcome sincere and the setting absolutely beautiful. The restaurant offers wonderful provincial cuisine, making the drive here well worth your time.

Doubles: $45 with shared bath, $75 with private bath.

THE BASICS

At Your Service

SAFETY

When the Transit Authority warns women to keep their gold chains under cover, we fear the worst underground. Happily, it is still relatively safe, although subways in the dark of night are not your best transportation option. Nor is wandering around in Central Park at night or strolling on city streets that common sense tells you are not the most innocent of thoroughfares. But contrary to public image, New York is reasonably safe, and you'll find lots of people walking home in the wee hours. If you pay attention, project self-confidence, and don't take unnecessary risks, you will probably avoid any problems.

FOREIGN EXCHANGE

New York may boast of its internationalism, but its provincial side shows when it comes to providing money-exchanging facilities. Most major banks offer an exchange service, but you have to make the transaction during banking hours. If you're caught short on the weekend, try Deak-Perera at 41 East 42nd Street on Saturday between 9:00 A.M. and 5:00 P.M. Some hotels offer an exchange service, but generally only for their guests. The most comprehensive listing of exchange offices can be found in the Yellow Pages under "Foreign Money Brokers."

INFORMATION

Big Apple Report (events),
  976-2323
Listing of Dial-It Numbers
  (free), 976-1000
Police, 911
Time, 976-1616
U.S. Customs, 466-5550
U.S. Passport Office, 541-7700
Visitors' Bureau, 397-8222
Weather, 976-1212

Getting Around

AIRPORT TRANSPORTATION

Buses

Carey buses (632-0500) depart for Kennedy every twenty minutes from 5:00 A.M. to 1:00 A.M. (one hour, $6), and for La Guardia from 5:45 A.M. to midnight (45 minutes, $4.50). Departures are from the East Side Airlines Terminal at 38th Street and First Avenue and outside Grand Central Station. If you don't mind carrying your own luggage and cabbing it to the departure points, this will certainly be a better bet than the pricey taxi ride to either airport. The only less expensive airport service is the Train to the Plane subway-bus connection.

Abbey Transportation runs bus service between Newark and the major hotels from 33rd to 63rd Street on both the East and the West Side. Pickups in the city run from 7:00 A.M. to 7:00 P.M.; from Newark into Manhattan, 7:00 A.M. to midnight. For information, call (201)961-2535; the cost for the half-hour trip is about $11, plus tip and the hotel's supplemental service charge.

For the bare-bones economy minded, Transport of New Jersey has buses from the airports to the Port Authority Bus Terminal at 41st Street and Eighth Avenue for $4. The 24-hour service leaves from Platform 243 or 39. For the schedule, call 564-8484. Carey offers a free service between the Port Authority and the East Side Airlines Terminal, every half hour from 7:00 A.M. to 6:00 P.M.

Helicopter

The savvy business traveler avoids gridlock and commutes to the airport via New York Helicopter, located at 34th Street and the East River. This enterprising outfit takes credit cards for the fifteen-minute ride to Kennedy ($47.52), the six-minute trip to La Guardia ($37.80) and the ten-minute trip to Newark ($52.92). Call (800)645-3494 for additional information. Fares may be substantially reduced if you have a special airline package ticket.

Taxis

The New York Taxi Commission (869-4110) says the following rates (including tolls and tip) are "acceptable" between midtown and the three airports: La Guardia, $15; Kennedy, $25; and Newark, $35. A share-a-ride program has been successful in helping people cut costs by enabling them to share taxis to nearby destinations. If you cab it, allow about an hour to get to Kennedy and Newark and 40 minutes to reach La Guardia.

Train to the Plane

Intelligent travelers who unfortunately find themselves due at Kennedy at rush hour take no chances with the traffic and go underground. The express subway-bus connection leaves from midtown and stops on Sixth Avenue, on Wall Street and in Brooklyn; a private express bus connects the train to the planes. The 50-minute, $6 ride runs from 5:00 A.M. to midnight. For additional information call 330-1234. It's a great service if you're traveling light—financially as well as baggagewise.

═══ IMPORTANT NUMBERS ═══
Airports

Kennedy, 656-4520
La Guardia, 476-5000
Manhattan Airlines Terminal
  (tickets), 986-0888
Newark Airport,
  (201)961-2000
East Side Airlines Terminal
  (Carey Bus), 632-0500
East Side Heliport,
  (800)645-3494

Railroads

Amtrak Penn Station,
736-4545
Conrail Penn Station,
532-4900
Grand Central Terminal,
532-4900
Long Island Railroad Penn
Station, 739-4200

Subways and Buses

New York Transit Authority,
330-3000
Port Authority Bus Terminal,
564-8484

AUTO RENTAL

Only the stouthearted and the brave defy the odds and drive a private car in the city. Chauffeurs are trained more in bumper car tactics than in the genteel art of motoring. If the taxis don't get you, the lack of parking spaces will. But a car can be great asset if you want to get away from it all, and the rental companies will make it easy for you—as long as you remember to reserve in advance, particularly during the summer rush, when the entire city evacuates to the beaches. Avis: (800)331-1212; Hertz: (800)654-3131; National: (800)328-4567.

BUSES

Believe it or not, public transportation still works in New York City, and you may run into some very chic people busing around town. Buses run 24 hours a day, maps and transfers are available, routes are clearly marked, exact change (90 cents or a token) is required, and the chronically ill Grumman buses are affectionately referred to as Darth Vader transporters. There are special packages for the culture and shoppers' buses, which run along their appropriate routes. Call 330-1234 for more information, and be prepared to wait a long time for the Transit Authority to get around to helping you.

FINDING STREETS

With the exception of lower Manhattan, whose streets resemble a game of pickup sticks, New York streets are logical and simple to learn. Our best advice is to invest in a *Flashmaps* book to the city. Fifth Avenue divides the East and West Sides; to get your north-south bearings, you can chance it with the phone book's slightly obscure explanation of how to determine the cross street of an avenue address, but we think it's easier to call your destination. If you're interested in clocking your walking mileage, twenty north-south blocks equal a mile (and it takes about a minute to walk a block if you aren't window shopping); the east-west blocks are about twice as long.

LIMOUSINES

New York limos offer just about everything you could possibly want in transportation. Whether you want to go to the airport to meet your pet (who's being shipped in from Geneva), want a personal guide to the city, want to impress a date or want to practice your Jay Gatsby routine, why not book the best? Prices are competitive, and services are similar. Carey Limousine: 517-7010; Dav-El Limousines: 580-6500; Fugazy Limousines: (800)223-2455; London Towncars: 988-9700.

SUBWAYS

Although the subway system is remarkably efficient, in veiw of the demands placed on it daily, it may be hard to adjust to the sight of serious-looking adults traveling at breakneck speeds in moving comic strips. The graffiti continues to flourish like kudzu, the noise level continues to be deafening, and the crowds continue to reflect the pathos of New York humanity. But it's cheap (90 cents), it's quick, and it runs 24 hours a day. It's a bit sad compared to our beloved Métro in Paris, but it does work.

TAXIS

You can learn more about New York's immigration statistics by studying the names of the hack drivers than by visiting the immigration bureau. It seems that English is not the mother tongue to most cabbies, and you may need your own map to show them where you're traveling.

The exterior overhead lights are supposed to indicate whether the cab is free, rented, on radio call or off duty; but lately drivers are becoming somewhat arrogant, stopping for passengers more on whim than by obligation. In any case, cabs are reasonably priced, particularly for short hauls. With the subway-bus fare increase, it can be a better bargain to travel by taxi if you're with more than one person. Look for the official medallion on the hood—it authenticates a licensed cab. If you have any problems, contact the Taxi Commission at 869-4110.

Radio Taxis

If it's inclement weather, theater time or New Year's Eve, you might find it difficult to hire even a radio-dispatched taxi. However, a phone call before you depart is a more secure way than trying to flag down a cab to ensure that you'll get to the airport on time or to the opera before the curtain rises.

Goings-On

No matter what time of year, there's always some sort of worthwhile event going on in the New York area, from a major exposition to a free concert to the city's favorite pastime, a parade. We've put together a calendar of the more prominent and/or interesting events, giving dates where possible.

January

National Boat Show (mid-Jan.), N.Y. Coliseum; 757-5000.

Winter Antiques Show (mid- to late Jan.), Seventh Regiment Armory, Park Avenue at 67th Street.

Greater New York International Automobile Show (late Jan.), N.Y. Coliseum; 757-5000.

February

Chinese New Year (early Feb.), Chinatown; 397-8222, 431-3897.

Westminster Kennel Club/Westminster Dog Show (mid-Feb.), Madison Square Garden; 564-4400.

Virginia Slims Women's Tennis Championships (late Feb.), Madison Square Garden; 564-4400

Ice Capades (early Feb.), Madison Square Garden; 564-4400.

March

St. Patrick's Day Parade (March 17th), Fifth Avenue from 44th to 86th streets; 397-8222.

April

Ringling Bros. Barnum & Bailey Circus (throughout April and May), Madison Square Garden; 564-4400.

Egg Rolling Contest (Saturday before Easter), Central Park Lawn; 397-3100.

Easter Parade (Easter Sunday), Fifth Avenue from 49th to 59th streets; 397-8222.

Baseball season begins (early April): Mets, Shea Stadium, Queens; 507-8499. Yankees, Yankee Stadium, the Bronx; 293-6000.

Five-Borough Bike Tour (late April), Battery Park to Staten Island.

Cherry Blossom Festival (late April), Brooklyn Botanic Garden; 622-4433.

May

Soccer season opens (May 1): Cosmos, Giants Stadium, Meadowlands; 265-8600.

Washington Square Art Show (Memorial Day weekend and first two weekends in June), University Place; 982-6255.

Ninth Avenue International Festival (mid-May weekend), 39th to 59th streets; 397-8222.

Ukrainian Festival (third weekend), 7th Street west of Second Avenue; 674-1615, 477-0729.

L'Eggs Mini-Marathon (last weekend), Central Park West at 66th Street; 580-6880.

Rose and Orchid Show (late May), New York Botanical Garden, the Bronx; 220-8777.

City beaches open (late May).

June

Festival of Saint Anthony (first two weeks), Little Italy, Sullivan Street from West Houston to Spring streets; 777-2755.

Guggenheim Concerts (mid-June to early Aug.), Damrosch Park, Lincoln Center and Seaside Park in Brooklyn; 867-8290.

Metropolitan Opera/New York Philharmonic free concerts (all month), city parks; 755-4100.

Museum Mile (mid-June), Fifth Avenue from 82nd to 105th streets; 860-1783, 722-1313. Museums open free.

Kool Jazz Festival (late June and July), locations throughout the city; 877-1800, 787-2020.

Summerpier (weekends from Memorial Day to Labor Day), South Street Seaport; 766-9020, 397-8222. Free jazz concerts.

Belmont Stakes—Triple Crown (mid-June), Belmont Park, Queens; 641-4700.

July

Shakespeare in the Park (throughout July and into Aug.), Delacorte Court, Central Park; 535-5630, 598-7100.

Harbor Festival (July 4th), 379-8222, 466-1998, 775-8148. Parade from Bowling Green to City Hall, fireworks display; 695-4400.

American Crafts Festival (first two weekends), Lincoln Center; 677-4627.

Jazzmobile Concerts (weekdays in July and Aug.), locations throughout the city; 866-4900.

Mostly Mozart Concerts (mid-July through Aug.), Lincoln Center; 874-2424.

August

Lincoln Center Out-of-Doors Festival (throughout Aug.), Lincoln Center Plaza; 877-1800.

U.S. Open Tennis Championships (late Aug. to mid-Sept.), Flushing Meadow, Queens; 271-5100.

September

Football season opens: N.Y. Jets, (212) 421-6600; N.Y. Giants, Giants Stadium, Meadowlands; (201) 935-8222.

N.Y. Philharmonic season opens, Avery Fisher Hall, Lincoln Center; 874-2424.

Feast of San Gennaro (mid-Sept.), Little Italy, Mulberry St.; 226-9546.

Washington Square Art Show (mid-Sept.), University Place; 982-6255.

New York Is Book Country (mid-Sept.), Fifth Avenue from 47th to 57th streets; 593-3983, 661-6030.

New York Film Festival (late Sept. to mid-Oct.), Lincoln Center; 362-1911.

October

Hockey season opens: N.Y. Rangers, Madison Square Garden; 564-4400; N.Y. Islanders, Nassau Coliseum, (516) 794-9100; N.J. Devils, Brendan Byrne Arena, Meadowlands, (201) 935-6050.

New York City Marathon (last Sunday in Oct.), Staten Island to Central Park; 860-4455, 580-6880.

Ice-skating season begins, Rockefeller Center; 757-5731.

Basketball season opens: N.Y. Knicks, Madison Square Garden; 564-4400; N.J. Nets, Brendan Byrne Arena, Meadowlands, (201) 935-3900.

Thoroughbred racing season opens, Aqueduct Racetrack, Queens; 641-4700.

November

Macy's Thanksgiving Day Parade, Central Park West from 77th to 34th streets; 560-4495, 397-8222.

December

Baroque crèche and Christmas tree display (throughout Dec. and into early Jan.), Metropolitan Museum of Art; 879-5500.

Christmas tree lighting (early Dec.), Rockefeller Center; 397-8222.

Origami Christmas tree display, American Museum of Natural History; 873-4225.

W.B.A.I. Crafts Fair (the three weekends before Christmas), Ferris Booth Hall, Columbia University; 297-0707.

Messiah Sing-Along, Avery Fisher Hall and local churches; 874-2424.

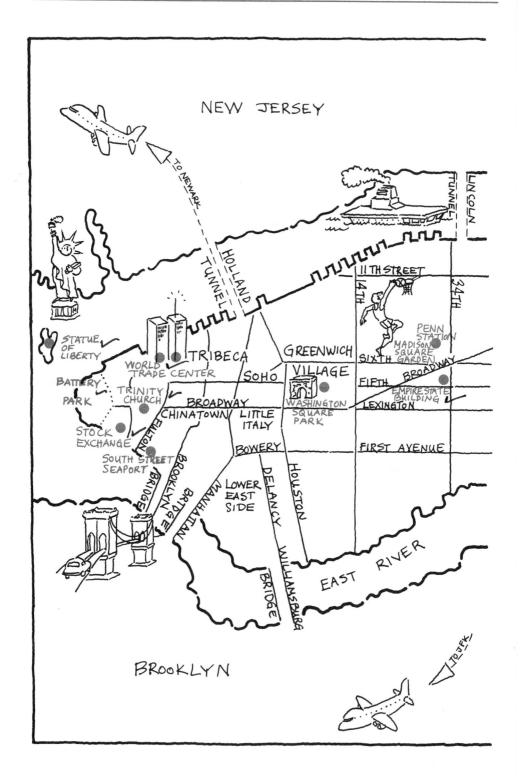

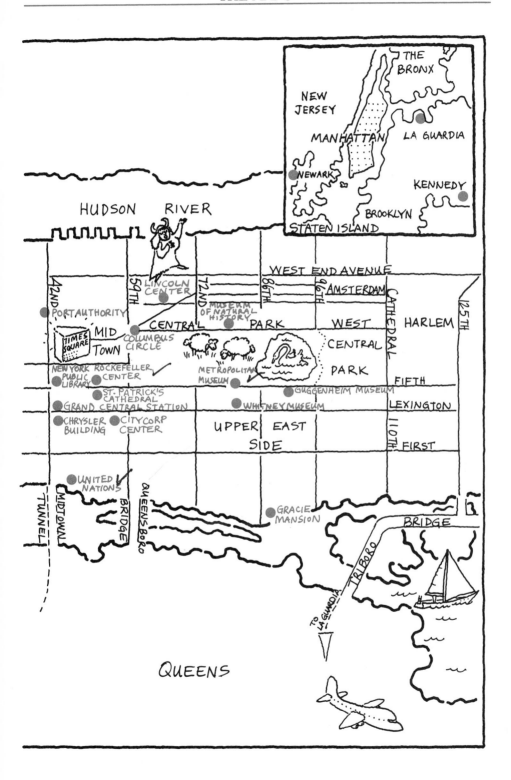

THE INDEX

C

S

T

Village –

Italian – Ennio & Michael (14) – $40 (circled)   page 37
French – La Ripaille (14) – $60   page 44
American – La Tulipe (17) – $90   page 47

West 42 – 59 th

Steak – Gallagher's (13)   60-80
* Italian – Orso (13)   60
French – René Pujol (13)   60

East 42 – 59

French – La Côte Basque (17) $80 * p. 96
am/ct. – Four Seasons (16)   — theatre dinner * p. 79
French – Lutèce (18) $120 * p. 106
Seafood – Oyster Bar (15) $60   p. 110 — fun
French – La Périgord (16)   80   * p. 111

expensive

East 59 and up

American – An American Place (17) – $80-90 – p. 131
French – Bistro Bamboche (13) – $40 very good p. 134
Italian – L'Hostaria del Bongustaio (15) – 70 – p. 148